Health Organizations
of the United States,
Canada and the World

Health Organizations of the United States, Canada and the World

A Directory of Voluntary Associations,
Professional Societies and Other Groups
Concerned with Health and Related Fields

FIFTH EDITION

Paul Wasserman
Managing Editor

Marek Kaszubski
Associate Editor

GALE RESEARCH COMPANY ● BOOK TOWER ● DETROIT, MICHIGAN 48226

Editorial Staff Manager: Effie Knight

Editorial Assistants: Jacqueline O'Brien, Linda Stemmy

Library of Congress Catalog Card Number 61-3260
ISBN 0-8103-0466-X
ISSN 0277-8653

CONTENTS

INTRODUCTION

Since the fourth edition of this work was issued in 1977, health and its related fields have undergone a continuous expansion and development. This new edition represents a complete updating and revision of content as of early 1981, and includes current and accurate details about many of the growing number of unofficial, nongovernmental, and international organizations active in the field, as well as many organizations in the newer areas of health care. Descriptive listings are provided for 1,514 organizations, societies, foundations, associations, and other nongovernmental bodies.

HEALTH ORGANIZATIONS, 5th edition, is intended to guide health and medical personnel, librarians, public officials, businesspeople, and others concerned with the health field in its broadest sense to important sources of useful information and to identify and describe those organizations which serve the health care and health related fields. Only organizations understood to be voluntary or unofficial in character are included in the volume.

A new feature of the fifth edition is a keyword index to the organizations. This supplements the subject index which continues as an important element of the book's organization.

The book is divided into three parts. The first covers national, regional, and other organizations in the United States and Canada, as well as international and regional organizations located elsewhere in the world. Descriptive listings for all these organizations have been prepared from details provided by the organizations themselves in their questionnaire responses. Even though the information concerning these groups has been secured from sources believed to be reliable, it is impossible to guarantee the accuracy of all the information given. A uniform style has been employed in drawing up the summary statements. The length of the statement required to describe any organization, however, is not an indication of the significance or importance of the work of the organization. The amount of detail has been determined in part by the degree to which the organizations cooperated in providing complete details of their own activities and characteristics. Organizations included are listed according to the names which they themselves have designated. The arrangement is alphabetical according to the sequence of letters in each word, including prepositions.

The second part of the book is a keyword index to the national, regional, and international organizations. The arrangement here is under each important term included in the name of the organization.

The third component of the book is a list of all the organizations listed arranged under each subject which relates to their activities and functions.

In order to identify the organizations contained in this work, numerous sources of information from the United States, Canada, and foreign sources were examined. Questionnaires were then dispatched to the organizations which are listed and it is through their cooperation that the details offered here have been provided. Without their valuable assistance the content of this work would have been far less useful. The responsibility for typing the manuscript in all of its meticulous detail was assumed by Jeanette Coughlin. Just as in the case of previous editions, comments, criticisms, suggestions, and advice about omissions and errors from the users of this work will be very much welcomed, and each criticism will receive careful consideration in the preparation of subsequent editions.

HEALTH ORGANIZATIONS

A

★ 1 ★
ACADEMY OF APHASIA
c/o Eran Zaidel
Department of Psychology
University of California   (213) 825-4343
Los Angeles, California 90024   Established 1962

Eran Zaidel, Ph.D., Secretary
Founded for the study of aphasia and kindred disorders.
An interdisciplinary group of neurologists, psychologists, linguists and speech therapists. Membership:
200 (active). Finances: Membership: $15.
Meetings: Annual, various locations.

★ 2 ★
ACADEMY OF DENTISTRY FOR THE HANDICAPPED
1726 Champa, Suite 422   (303) 573-0264
Denver, Colorado 80202   Established 1952

Fred Leviton, Executive Director; Jane Robinson,
     Executive Secretary
To provide continuing education opportunities to dental professionals in the dental care and treatment of
persons with handicaps. Also, to serve as an information and referral source on all aspects of dentistry
for the handicapped and to advocate for improvements
in this field of care as regards legislation and research.
Membership: 650 (dentists, hygienists, and allied professionals). Finances: Membership: $40 per year,
active; $20 for affiliate; $20 per year, foreign;
$10 for students. Meetings: Scientific, annually;
Board Meetings, semiannually. Publications: Special Care in Dentistry, bimonthly, Paul Casamassimo,
editor; ADH Newsletter, quarterly, Jane Robinson,
editor. Affiliations: National Foundation of Dentistry for the Handicapped.

★ 3 ★
ACADEMY OF DENTURE PROSTHETICS
Mayo Clinic
Department of Dentistry
Rochester, Minnesota 55901

W. R. Laney
The Academy promotes the science and art of denture
prosthetics and maintains a number of special committees concerned with tooth form, denture base materials, articulators, etc. Membership: 95.

Meetings: Annual, various locations. Publications:
Journal of Prosthetic Dentistry, monthly.

★ 4 ★
ACADEMY OF GENERAL DENTISTRY
211 East Chicago Avenue
Suite 1244   (312) 440-4300
Chicago, Illinois 60611   Established 1952

Harold E. Donnell, Jr., Executive Director
To serve and represent the interests of the general
dentist and to foster quality of continuing dental education. Activities include recording of member
continuing education records, sponsoring of continuing
education programs and related activities, representation of general dentists in legislative, dental care,
and related issues; and development of public education and public relations programs designed to increase public awareness of the need for dental care.
Membership: 22,000 (students, recent graduates, regular, associate, emeritus, and retired). Finances:
Membership: recent graduate, $15 per year; regular
and associate members: $110 per year plus one time
$15 processing fee for new members; Other Sources:
advertising sales, exhibit sales at major meetings,
sales of dental health educational materials, revenues
generated by continuing education courses. Lectureships: Albert L. Knap Memorial Lecture annually at
AGD Annual Meeting in June or July. Meetings:
Annual, in June or July, rotating throughout the
United States and Canada. Publications: General
Dentistry, bimonthly, William W. Howard, editor;
AGD Impact, 10 times per year, William W. Howard,
editor; Uppers and Lowers, periodically; Presentations, periodically.

★ 5 ★
ACADEMY OF HEALTH CARE CONSULTANTS
875 North Michigan Avenue
Suite 3342   (312) 440-0079
Chicago, Illinois 60611   Established 1958

Betty Hanna, Executive Secretary
To devise and perpetuate a code of ethics for the
practice of the profession of hospital counseling; to
organize and promote education in the form of institutes, seminars, and other professional assemblies.
Membership: 25 (M.D.'s, hospital consultants, specialists). Finances: Membership: Fellows and members, $350; associates and specialists, $200; government and quasi-government, $100. Meetings: Annual, Chicago.

★ 6 ★
ACADEMY OF ORAL DYNAMICS
2363 Philadelphia Avenue   (717) 263-2451
Chambersburg, Pennsylvania 17201 Established 1945

Freeman Frey, DDS, President; Joseph P. Skellchock,
    DDS, Corresponding Secretary-Treasurer
The Academy researches and disseminates to the dental
profession the concept of engineering principles, determined by the laws of physics, to diagnose the most
favorable force patterns of the human dentition.   All
phases of dentistry are studied and treatment implemented by Academy members.   Membership: 80 (fellowship, associate, and honorary memberships).   Finances: Fellowship: initiation fee, $150; annual
dues, $25; associate, annual dues, $15.   Meetings:
Lectures, biennially.

★ 7 ★
ACADEMY OF PHARMACEUTICAL SCIENCES
2215 Constitution Avenue, N.W.   (202) 628-4410
Washington, D.C. 20037   Established 1965

Ronald L. Williams, Executive Secretary
To serve the professions of pharmaceutical science and
the public interest; to promote scientific, technical
and academic accomplishments in all disciplines related to the discovery, testing, production and control
of drugs.   Membership: 2,500 (pharmaceutical scientists).   Awards: APS-APhA Research Achievement
Award; Research Achievement Awards, annually;
Kilmer Prize, annually; Ebert Prize, annually.
Meetings: Annual, various locations; and fall national meetings.   Publications: Academy Reporter,
bimonthly; Abstracts of Papers, semiannual; monographs, manuals, directories and book reviews.   Affiliations: A subdivision of the American Pharmaceutical Association.

★ 8 ★
ACADEMY OF PHARMACY PRACTICE
c/o American Pharmaceutical Association
2215 Constitution Avenue, N.W.   (202) 628-4410
Washington, D.C. 20037   Established 1964

Ronald L. Williams, Executive Secretary
The Academy provides a forum and mechanism whereby
pharmacists primarily engaged in rendering professional
services directly to the public may meet to discuss
and implement programs and activities which are particularly relevant and helpful to the general practitioner of pharmacy, and to provide conferences, seminars, and other meetings for the purpose of unifying
general practitioners of pharmacy.   Membership:
5,000.   Finances: APhA dues plus a $15 per year

membership dues.   Awards: Daniel B. Smith Award
for an outstanding community pharmacist.   Meetings:
Annual, with American Pharmaceutical Association.
Publications: Pharmacy Practice, monthly, Ronald
Williams, editor.

ACADEMY OF PSYCHOANALYSIS
   See: American Academy of Psychoanalysis

★ 9 ★
ACADEMY OF PSYCHOSOMATIC MEDICINE
70 West Hubbart Street, Suite 202   (312) 644-2623
Chicago, Illinois 60610   Established 1954

Thomas C. Nelson, Executive Director
To advance scientific knowledge and the practice of
medicine which relate to the interaction of mind,
body and environment through study, laboratory and
clinical research.   Membership: 900 (physicians,
dentists and allied professionals interested in somatic
disorders).   Meetings: Annual, various locations.
Publications: Psychosomatics, monthly; Directory,
annual.

★ 10 ★
ACADEMY OF SCIENTIFIC HYPNOTHERAPY
Post Office Box 12041   (714) 427-6225
San Diego, California 92112   Established 1977

T. D. Johnson, M.D., F.A.S.H., Director; W. E.
   Kemery, Ph.D., F.A.S.H., President
ASH serves as a professional organization for hypnotherapists.   Membership services include dissemination of information relating to the field, a listing in
a directory of hypnotherapists, and communication
with professional colleagues.   ASH will refer patients to the nearest qualified hypnotherapist in its
directory.   Membership: 129 (regular, charter, fellowship).   Finances: Membership: Initiation fee:
membership, $45; fellow, $100; Other Sources:
donations.   Meetings: Quarterly, Southern California.   Publications: Hypnotherapy in Review
(newsletter), quarterly, Ron Raposa, editor; bulletins.
Library: 1,200 volumes (not to be removed from
premises).   Affiliations: Kemery Institute.

★ 11 ★
ACCREDITATION ASSOCIATION FOR AMBULATORY
   HEALTH CARE, INC.
4849 Golf Road, Suite 620   (312) 676-9610
Skokie, Illinois 60077   Established 1979

Ronald S. Moen, Executive Director
Not for profit corporation to organize and operate a peer-based voluntary assessment, education, consultation and accreditation program for ambulatory health care organizations as a means of assisting them to provide the highest achievable level of care for recipients in the most efficient and sound manner. Membership: 6. Finances: Membership: $5,000 per seat on Board of Directors; Other Sources: survey fees. Meetings: Semiannual meeting of Board of Directors. Publications: Accreditation Handbook for Ambulatory Health Care, biannual, Ronald S. Moen, editor. Affiliations: American College Health Association; American Group Practice Association; Free Standing Ambulatory Surgery Association; Group Health Association of America; Medical Group Management Association; National Association of Community Health Centers. Former Name: Accreditation Council for Ambulatory Health Care.

ACCREDITATION COUNCIL FOR AMBULATORY HEALTH CARE
    See: Accreditation Association for Ambulatory Health Care, Inc.

★ 12 ★
ACCREDITING BUREAU OF HEALTH EDUCATION SCHOOLS
Oak Manor Offices
29089 U.S. 20 West   (219) 293-0124
Elkhart, Indiana 46514   Established 1965

Hugh A. Woosley, Administrator
Purposes of the Bureau are (1) to serve as a nationally recognized accrediting agency of schools for medical assistant and medical laboratory technician education programs; (2) to establish criteria and standards for the administration and operation of medical assistant and medical laboratory technician schools; (3) to enhance the profession through the improvement of schools, courses, and the quality of graduates; (4) to establish sound business and ethical standards in the field of medical assistant and medical laboratory technician education. Membership: 9 board members. Finances: Membership: Based on number of students, ranges from $250 to $1,000; Other Sources: American Medical Technologist grants. Meetings: 2 to 3 per year, various locations. Publications: Newsletter, bimonthly, Mary Reed, editor. Former Name: Accrediting Bureau of Medical Laboratory Schools.

ACCREDITING BUREAU OF MEDICAL LABORATORY SCHOOLS
    See: Accrediting Bureau of Health Education Schools

★ 13 ★
ACCREDITING COMMISSION ON EDUCATION FOR HEALTH SERVICES
1 Dupont Circle, Suite 420   (202) 659-3939
Washington, D.C. 20036   Established 1968

Gary L. Filerman, Ph.D., Executive Secretary
Accredits graduate master's degree programs in health services administration to improve the quality of professional education. Publications: Official List of Accredited Programs, annual. Former Name: Accrediting Commission on Graduate Education for Hospital Administration.

ACCREDITING COMMISSION ON GRADUATE EDUCATION FOR HOSPITAL ADMINISTRATION
    See: Accrediting Commission on Education for Health Services

★ 14 ★
ACNE HEALTH CARE CENTERS INTERNATIONAL, INC.
4651 Ponce de Leon Boulevard
Coral Gables, Florida 33146   (305) 667-7601

Dr. James E. Fulton, Jr.; Sara Fulton, Executive Director

Operates solely for the treatment of acne vulgaris. Maintains Acne Research Institute in Newport Beach where research is conducted as well as a laboratory. Publications: Farewell to Pimples, Dr. James E. Fulton, editor; Let's Talk Cosmetics, Dr. James E. Fulton, editor.

ACUPUNCTURE ASSOCIATION AND REGISTER, LTD.
    See: British Acupuncture Association and Register, Ltd.

★ 15 ★
ACUPUNCTURE FOUNDATION OF CANADA
10 St. Mary Street, Suite 503
Toronto, Ontario M4Y 1P9,   (416) 961-4131
  Canada   Established 1974

H. Adirim, D.D.S., President
The Foundation is a charitable organization of medical
doctors and dentists who are dedicated to the use of
acupuncture as a form of treatment.   It conducts formal courses in acupuncture in which Chinese philo-
sophical theory and pulse diagnosis plays a negligible
part.   The Foundation initiates research projects and
works in cooperation with other organizations and institutions having a similar purpose.   It attempts to
provide accurate information to the public and profession.   Membership: 550 (physicians, dentists, veterinarians, sustaining and sponsor members).   Finances: Membership: $100 per year; Other Sources:
donations, course tuition.   Meetings: Monthly seminars at the Acupuncture Foundation, Toronto, Ontario,
Canada.   Publications: Various monographs and articles on acupuncture.

★ 16 ★
ADDICTION RESEARCH AND TREATMENT
    CORPORATION
22 Chapel Street   (212) 834-5300
Brooklyn, New York 11201   Established 1969

Beny J. Primm, M.D., Executive Director
Operates a multi-modality drug treatment program with
six ambulatory treatment clinics and one Skills Training Center.   Treatments employed are primarily de-
toxification, methadone maintenance and drug-free
services.   Other services include individual counseling, group therapy, job development, vocational
counseling, mental health and care and recreation.
Conducts research program.   Finances: Federal government grants and medicaid reimbursement.

★ 17 ★
ADRENAL METABOLIC RESEARCH SOCIETY OF THE
    HYPOGLYCEMIA FOUNDATION, INC.
153 Pawling Avenue   (518) 272-7154
Troy, New York 12180   Established 1956

Marilyn Hamilton Light, President and Executive
    Director
The Society aims "...to further by scientific investigation, laboratory research and publication, the
knowledge of metabolic anomalies involved in hypoglycemia...thus to further the application of such
knowledge to the prevention and treatment of hypoglycemia...".   Membership: 3,500 lay and profes-

sional.   Finances: Membership: $20; Other Sources:
Subscription to newsletter, $4.   Research Fund:
John W. Tintera, M.D., Memorial Fund.   Publica-
tions: Homeostasis Quarterly, Marilyn Hamilton Light,
editor; Hypoadrenocorticism; Hypoglycemia & Me;
Safe and Dangerous; Delinquent Glands, Not De-
linquent Juveniles; The Hypoglycemia of Hypoadreno-
corticism; High Protein, Low Carbohydrate Dietary
Program; Hypoglycemia; Neurosis of Hypoglycemia;
Health Problems Among American Indians; What
Happened to Johnny?; Sugar, The Great Deceiver.
Library: Hypoglycemia Foundation Library, 4,500 vol-
umes (not for public use).

★ 18 ★
AEROSPACE MEDICAL ASSOCIATION
Washington National Airport   (703) 892-2240
Washington, D.C. 20001   Established 1929

R. R. Hessberg, M.D., Executive Vice President
The single largest, most representative professional organization composed of medical specialists, life scientists and engineers in the fields of aviation, space
and undersea medicine and astronautics - primarily
concerned with man's adaptation to the hostile environments encountered in the far reaches of space and the
depths of the oceans.   The Association seeks to advance the art and science of aerospace and undersea
medicine by stimulating investigation and the study
and dissemination of knowledge.   Membership: 3,800
(individual membership: members, fellows, associate
fellows, honorary fellows, honorary members, corporate members).   Finances: Membership: Regular,
$65; North American Nationals, $45; student, $40;
corporate, $250; Other Sources: advertising in
monthly journal, non-members subscription.   Awards:
11 annual awards for accomplishments in Aerospace
Medicine.   Meetings: Annual, alternating east,
west, central locations.   Publications: Aviation,
Space, and Environmental Medicine, monthly, John P.
Marbarger, Ph.D., editor; Volume of Preprints, an-
nually.   Affiliations: Canadian Society of Aviation
Medicine;   Civil Aviation Medical Association;
German Society of Aviation and Space Medicine;
Aerospace Medical Association of the Philippines;
Latin American Association of Aviation and Space
Medicine.

AFRICAN MEDICAL AND RESEARCH FOUNDATION
    See: International Medical and Research
          Foundation

★ 19 ★
AFRICARE, INC.
1601 Connecticut Avenue, N.W.
Suite 600   (202) 462-3614
Washington, D.C. 20009   Established 1971

C. Payne Lucas, Executive Director
Africare is a private, non-profit organization, which
works to improve the quality of life in rural Africa.
It conducts self-help programs to cultivate the land's
full potential, develop water resources, provide health
care, teach literacy, and deliver emergency assistance
to refugees. Membership: 1,385 (associate members;
sustaining members, patron, and life membership).
Finances: Membership: Associate, $5-$25 annually;
sustaining, $26-$100 annually; patron, $101-$1,000
annually; life, $1,001 or more payable at rate of
$200.20 per year for 5 years. Other Sources: pri-
vate foundations, corporations, small businesses, ch
churches, private voluntary organizations, individual
donars and U.S. Agency for International Development. Publications: Newsletter, semiannually,
Libba Conger, editor; Special Report, irregular,
Libba Conger, editor; Annual Report, yearly, Libba
Conger, editor. Library: Resource Information Center, 2,950 volumes (open to community 9-4:30; not
to be removed from premises).

★ 20 ★
AID FOR INTERNATIONAL MEDICINE, INC.
1828 Wawaset Street   (302) 655-8290
Wilmington, Delaware 19806   (302) 654-5848
                                   Established 1965

John M. Levinson, M.D., President and Founder
A.I.M. has been founded for the purpose of extending
medical help through areas where members of the
Board have personally served and documented a need,
and is registered as a cooperating agency with the
Advisory Committee on Voluntary Foreign Aid with the
U.S. Department of State, Agency for International
Development.

★ 21 ★
AIR POLLUTION CONTROL ASSOCIATION
Post Office Box 2861   (412) 621-1090
Pittsburgh, Pennsylvania 15230   Established 1907

W. G. Hamlin, Executive Vice President
A nonprofit technical and educational organization
dedicated to advancing the science and art of air pollution control. Its membership is balanced among
industrial, scientific, government, and educational
sectors. Through its Technical Council, the Association works toward international adoption of reason-

able engineering performance standards, and seeks to
establish definitions, methods, processes, procedures,
and recommended practical limits of air pollution
emissions. Membership: 8,000 (engineers, scientists,
industrial,organizations, equipment manufacturers, scientific institutions, consultants). Finances: Membership: Individual, $45; company national, $200;
company local, $100; sustaining, $500 minimum;
organizational, $200; governmental, $100. Awards:
Frank A. Chambers Award; Richard Beatty Mellon
Award; S. Smith Griswold Award. Meetings: Annual, various locations. Publications: Journal of
the Air Pollution Control Association, monthly, Harold
Englund, editor; APCA Membership Directory, annually; special reports.

★ 22 ★
ALAN GUTTMACHER INSTITUTE
360 Park Avenue South   (212) 685-5858
New York, New York 10010   Established 1969

Jeannie I. Rosoff, President; Richard Lincoln, Senior
     Vice President and Editorial Director
The Institute is devoted to systematic social research
in fertility regulation and population. Its principal
purposes are to aid in the development of sound public
policies, to promote public understanding of issues of
national and international importance, and to assist
in the creation of adequate public and private sectors
family planning programs. Meetings: Board of Directors, 3 times per year. Publications: Family
Planning Perspectives, bimonthly, Lynn C. Landman,
editor; Family Planning/Population Reporter, bimonthly, Patricia Donovan, editor; Planned Parenthood
Washington Memo, 20 issues per year; Jeannie I.
Rosoff, editor; International Family Planning Perspectives, quarterly, Lynn C. Landman, editor; various
monographs on fertility related topics, Richard Lincoln,
editor.

★ 23 ★
AL-ANON FAMILY GROUP HEADQUARTERS, INC.
115 East 23rd Street   (212) 475-6110
New York, New York 10010   Incorporated 1954

Myrna S. Hammersley, Executive Director
Al-Anon, which cooperates with Alcoholics Anonymous but is a separate entity, is a fellowship of relatives and friends of alcoholics who share their experience, strength, and hope in order to solve their
common problems and to help others do the same.
The national headquarters assists in the formation and
growth of Al-Anon/Alateen groups; refers individuals
to existing groups; assists lone members in isolated
areas; compiles an annual directory of these groups
and loners; provides information for the families of

alcoholics in hospitals and correctional institutions; compiles, publishes and distributes pamphlets, books, the monthly FORUM and periodic newsletters; handles national and international public information; furthers public education; and cooperates with outside agencies and industry. Membership: 200,000 individuals (over 16,000 groups). Finances: Membership: No fees; supported by voluntary contributions of members; Other Sources: Sale of program-oriented books and literature. Publications: FORUM, monthly; Newsletter, irregular; a large number of books, pamphlets, brochures, leaflets and other public information material.

★ 24 ★

ALCOHOL AND DRUG PROBLEMS ASSOCIATION
    OF NORTH AMERICA
1101 15th Street, N.W.   (202) 452-0990
Washington, D.C. 20005   Established 1949

Roger F. Stevenson, Executive Director
ADPA is a non-profit corporation designed to represent and be responsive to the needs of professionals in the field of alcohol and drug problems. It was founded by a group of State Alcoholism Program Directors in 1949 and today has members throughout North America at program, agency and individual levels. As both a professional and service organization, ADPA is dually oriented. It transmits concerns and concensus opinions of workers in the field to federal officials and policy makers as well as providing information and services to its broad constituency where appropriate and feasible. Membership: 2,000 individuals, 156 agencies, and 51 programs. Finances: Membership: State authorities, $300; agency, $200; individual, $25; Other Sources: Sustaining members, grants and contracts. Meetings: Annual, various locations in U.S. and Canada. Publications: Selected Papers of Annual Meeting, annual; Job Clearinghouse, monthly; ADPA Newsletters, bimonthly.

★ 25 ★

ALCOHOL EDUCATION FOR YOUTH, INC.
1500 Western Avenue   (518) 456-3800
Albany, New York 12203   Established 1905

Reverend Richard W. Dutton, Executive Director
Provides alcohol education, prevention of alcohol abuse, training of clergy/lay leaders, community consciousness-raising, family enrichment, program development and delivery, and legislative presence. Membership: 25 board members, 2,500 mailing list. (churches, church judicatories, individuals, parallel agencies). Finances: Supported exclusively by donations; Other Sources: Potentially foundation

monies. Meetings: Board, quarterly, Syracuse and Albany, New York. Publications: Action, monthly, Barbara Cullum, editor; Catalyst II; alcohol education resource workbook. Affiliations: North Conway Institute; American Council on Alcohol Problems; New York State Association of Councils on Alcoholism; New York State Council of Churches. Former Name: New York State Council on Alcohol Problems.

★ 26 ★

ALCOHOLICS ANONYMOUS, INC.
468 Park Avenue, South   (212) 686-1100
New York, New York 10016   Established 1935

Alcoholics Anonymous is a fellowship of men and women who share their experience, strength and hope with each other that they may solve their common problem and help others to recover from alcoholism. The only requirement for membership is a desire to stop drinking. There are no dues or fees for A.A. membership; self-supporting through own contributions. A.A. is not allied with any sect, denomination, politics, organization or institution; does not wish to engage in any controversy; neither endorses nor opposes any causes. The group's primary purpose is to stay sober and help other alcoholics to achieve sobriety. Membership: Over 1,000,000 individuals; 40,000 groups in 100 countries. Finances: Contributions from members. Publications: About Alcoholics Anonymous, annual.

★ 27 ★

ALCOHOLISM AND DRUG ADDICTION RESEARCH
    FOUNDATION
33 Russell Street
Toronto, Ontario M5S 2S1,   (416) 595-6000
    Canada   Established 1949

Dr. J. B. Macdonald, President
The Foundation is an agency of the province of Ontario which operates specialized research, educational, clinical, and service development programs throughout Ontario. Finances: Other Sources: Supported by the Ontario Ministry of Health through direct annual grants. Publications: The Journal, monthly, Anne MacLennan, editor; Projection, monthly; numerous books and booklets, pamphlets, reports. Library: Addiction Research Foundation Library, 10,500 volumes.

★ 28 ★
ALEXANDER GRAHAM BELL ASSOCIATION FOR
THE DEAF, INC.
3417 Volta Place, N.W.   (202) 337-5220
Washington, D.C. 20007   Established 1890

Sara E. Conlon, Ph.D., Executive Director
Organized to encourage the teaching of speech,
speechreading, and the use of residual hearing to
hearing-impaired persons, the Association welcomes to
its membership all who are interested in improving the
educational, professional, and vocational opportunities
of hearing-impaired persons. Membership: Approximately 6,500 (regular, husband/wife, student, and
life). Finances: Membership: Regular, $30; hus-
band/wife, $40; student, $15; life, $500; Other
Sources: Gift contributions, donations, book sales,
revenue from conferences, conventions, and professional meetings. Awards: Annual Alexander Graham
Bell Scholarship Competition Award; Honors of the
Association; IPO and ODAS Merit Awards (outstanding service on behalf of the hearing impaired);
AOEHI Teacher Award; Rookie Teacher Award; Program of the Year Award. Lectureships: Spring and
Fall International Lecturer Series; AGBAD Regional
Conferences. Meetings: AGBAD International Convention, biennial, various locations; AGBAD, regional meetings, quarterly, location varies; AOEHI,
IPO, ODAS, periodically, various locations. Pub-
lications: Newsounds, 10 times per year, Anne K.
Dexter, editor; The Volta Review, 7 times per year,
Richard R. Kretschmer, Jr., Ph.D., editor; books
on speech and hearing impairment, information brochures, Membership Directory. Library: Volta
Bureau Library (on-site research, contemporary and
historical; lending library--contemporary publications
on speech and deafness for Association members only).
Affiliations: International Parents' Organization;
Oral Deaf Adults Section; American Organization for
the Education of the Hearing Impaired.

★ 29 ★
ALFRED I. DUPONT INSTITUTE OF THE NEMOURS
FOUNDATION
Post Office Box 269   (302) 573-3000
Wilmington, Delaware 19899   Established 1940

G. Dean MacEwan, M.D., Medical Director;
Eugene E. Wolinsky, Administrator
For care and treatment of crippled children. Fi-
nances: The Alfred I. duPont Institute Estate; Other
Sources: Blue Cross/Blue Shield, patient fees,
"Nemours" Foundation. Library: Medical Library,
21,000 volumes.

ALLERGY FOUNDATION OF AMERICA
See: Asthma and Allergy Foundation of America

★ 30 ★
ALLERGY INFORMATION ASSOCIATION
3 Powburn Place
Weston, Ontario M9R 2C5,   (416) 244-9312
Canada   Established 1964

Susan Daglish, President
The Association was founded in order to disseminate
information for practical management of allergic disease. Membership: 3,000 (medical professionals,
dieticians, public health units, private individuals).
Finances: Membership: $10. Meetings: Annually,
in May, Toronto. Publications: Newsletter "Allergy Shot", quarterly, Susan Daglish, editor; Information Kit, Susan Daglish and Kathleen Miller, editors; Diets Unlimited for Limited Diets Cookbook,
Margaret Pollard and Wilma Verch, editors; various
information letters.

★ 31 ★
ALLIANCE FOR ENGINEERING IN MEDICINE
AND BIOLOGY
4405 East-West Highway
Suite 404   (301) 657-4142
Bethesda, Maryland 20014   Established 1969

Patricia I. Horner, Executive Director
The Alliance is a consortium of professional associations that share an active interest and participation in
the interaction between engineering and the physical
sciences and medicine and the biological sciences.
Goals are to promote the enlightened introduction and
use of advanced technology in life science research
and clinical practice through service, education, and
catalysis among its members in order to help achieve
the appropriate and relevant application of technology
to the solution of compelling human problems. Membership: 19 professional associations (full and associate membership). Finances: Membership: Full
membership--single, non-recurring assessment fee,
$1,500; annual dues, $400; associate membership--
annual dues, $400; $25 application fee; Other
Sources: Conference fees, management services, publications, grants, contracts, contributions. Meetings:
Council, semiannually; Annual Conference, various
locations; task groups and advisory committees at
various locations throughout the year. Publications:
Newsletter-Viewpoint, quarterly, Patricia I. Horner,
editor; Proceedings of the ACEMB, annually; Directory of Biomedical Engineers, biennially, Patricia
I. Horner, editor; Placement Bulletin, annually

after annual conference, Ann C. Barker, editor; Grant and Contract Reports; Summary Guidelines for Technology Procurement in Health Care Institutions; System Design of a Clinical Facility for Diagnostic Ultrasound; Biomedical Engineering Education Directory. Library: Approximately 500 volumes. Affiliations: U.S. Representative to the International Federation for Medical and Biological Engineering.

★ 32 ★
ALPHA EPSILON DELTA (THE PREMEDICAL HONOR
        SOCIETY)
University of Alabama in Huntsville
Clinical Sciences Center, #115
109 Governors Drive, S.W.
Huntsville, Alabama 35801   Established 1926

Janis Moore, Administrative Assistant
To encourage excellence in premedical scholarship; to stimulate an appreciation of the importance of premedical education in the study of medicine, to promote cooperation and contacts between medical and premedical students and educators, to bind together similarly interested students. Sponsors regional and national conferences on careers in medicine and dentistry and a biennial convention. Membership: 66,000. Maintains active chapters at accredited universities and colleges in the U.S. and Canada. The Society consists of active members, active alumni members and honorary members. Requirements for active membership are: the student shall be engaged in courses leading to the study of medicine, have completed at least 3 semesters or 5 quarters of premedical work with general scholastic standing of at least 3.0, on a 4.0 scale for "A," and also with an average of 3.0 in the sciences and rank in upper 35% of class in general scholarship. Character, general ability and personality must be considered carefully in the selection of every member. Active alumni and honorary members are members of the educational or professional fields whom the chapter deems worthy of membership. Finances: Membership: Active, $20; active alumni and honorary members, $7.50. Meetings: National, biennially, various locations. Publications: The Scalpel, semiannual; AED Newsletter, quarterly during school year, Maurice L. Moore, editor. Affiliations: Affiliated Society, American Association for the Advancement of Science; Member, Association of College Honor Societies.

★ 33 ★
ALPHA OMEGA ALPHA HONOR MEDICAL SOCIETY
525 Middlefield Road, Suite 200   (415) 329-1593
Menlo Park, California 94025   Established 1902

Robert J. Glaser, M.D., Editor
The promotion of scholarship and research in medical schools, the encouragement of high standards of character and conduct among medical students and graduates, and the recognition of high attainment in medical science, practice and related fields. Membership: 50,000 (honorary, undergraduate, alumni, and faculty). Finances: Membership: $20 induction fee, provides key, certificate of membership and subscription to official publication. All members are invited to pay $5 annual dues; Other Sources: Occasional gifts, legacies. Awards: Leaders in American Medicine Program. Meetings: Annual. Publication: The Pharos, quarterly, Robert J. Glaser, editor.

★ 34 ★
ALPHA ZETA OMEGA PHARMACEUTICAL
        FRATERNITY
c/o Robert Kirschner
80 Nottingham Court
Montvale, New Jersey 07645   Established 1919

Robert Kirschner, Director of Fraternal Affairs
Dedicated to the cultural, educational and professional advancement of pharmacy and of A.Z.O. Membership: 8,500. Finances: Membership: Established by each chapter; Other Sources: Advertising. Awards: Scholarships; Lectureship Awards; Achievement Medal for long, meritorious service to pharmacy profession. Meetings: 3 times per year, various locations. Publications: Azoan, annually, Thelma Uhler, editor.

AMBULANCE AND MEDICAL SERVICE ASSOCIATION
OF AMERICA
        See: American Ambulance Association

AMERICAN ACADEMY FOR CEREBRAL PALSY
        See: American Academy for Cerebral Palsy and
             Developmental Medicine

★ 35 ★
AMERICAN ACADEMY FOR CEREBRAL PALSY AND
        DEVELOPMENTAL MEDICINE
Post Office Box 11083   (202) 659-8251
Richmond, Virginia 23230   Established 1942

Fred P. Sage, M.D., President
To foster and stimulate interest in cerebral palsy, and correlate all aspects of the work for the welfare of

those afflicted with cerebral palsy. To encourage and stimulate special training of personnel required for the study and management of cerebral palsy. To establish and maintain the highest possible standards and qualifications for care and treatment of patients. This academy is composed of Fellows (comprising Doctors of Medicine and related fields) and Associate Members (comprising therapists and other non-doctors engaged in care of cerebral palsy and developmental disabilities) with the common interest lying in active participation in the care, treatment, diagnosis, and/or research in cerebral palsy. Membership: 900 (active, associate, foreign corresponding, honorary, emeritus). Finances: Membership: Fellow, $90 annual dues; associate, $70 annual dues. Meetings: Annual, regional courses, various locations. Publications: Journal of Developmental Medicine and Child Neurology, bi-monthly, Ronald McKeith, M.D., editor. Former Name: American Academy for Cerebral Palsy.

★ 36 ★
AMERICAN ACADEMY OF ALLERGY
611 East Wells Street   (414) 272-6071
Milwaukee, Wisconsin 53202   Established 1943

Donald L. McNeil, Executive Director
The Academy was formed for the advancement of the knowledge and practice of allergy, by discussion at meetings, by fostering the education of students and the public, by encouraging union and cooperation among those engaged in the field, and by promoting and stimulating research and study in allergy. It sponsors an annual scientific program and post-graduate course. Membership: Approximately 2,900 (physicians interested in the field of allergy). Finances: Membership: $55; fellows, $65; corresponding members, $41.25; corresponding fellows, $48.75; affiliate members, $27.50; Other Sources: Advertising in publications, annual meeting exhibits. Meetings: Annual, various locations. Publications: Journal of Allergy and Clinical Immunology, monthly, Charles E. Reed, M.D., editor; News and Notes, 3 times yearly, D. L. McNeil, editor.

★ 37 ★
AMERICAN ACADEMY OF CHILD PSYCHIATRY
1424 16th Street, N.W.,   (202) 462-3754
Suite 201A   (202) 462-3755
Washington, D.C. 20036   Established 1953

Virginia Q. Bausch, Executive Director
The Academy aims to stimulate and advance medical contributions to the knowledge and treatment of psychiatric problems of children. It has acted as the prime founder and sponsor for the National Consortium for Child Mental Health Services. Membership:

2,316 (life, fellow, active, affiliate, trainees; corresponding). Finances: Membership: $175 annually; trainees, $44; Other Sources: donations. Awards: J. Franklin Robinson Award. Meetings: Annually; scientific institutes; National Consortium for Child Mental Health Services. Publications: Journal of the American Academy of Child Psychiatry, quarterly, Melvin Lewis, M.D., editor; Newsletter, quarterly.

★ 38 ★
AMERICAN ACADEMY OF COMPENSATION
  MEDICINE
Box 336, Murray Hill Station
New York, New York 10016   Established 1947

The Academy is composed of physicians interested in working with compensation medicine. It holds symposia on medical and surgical problems in compensation medicine. Membership: 290 physicians. Finances: Membership: Fellow, $25; associate fellow, $15; member, $10. Meetings: Annual symposium, various locations. Publications: Compensation Medicine Newsletter, irregular, Samuel Peck, M.D.

★ 39 ★
AMERICAN ACADEMY OF CROWN AND BRIDGE
  PROSTHODONTICS
c/o Doctor Ronald G. Granger
30 Mill Street
Newton Center,   (617) 332-4879
  Massachusetts 02159   Established 1951

Dr. Ronald G. Granger, Secretary.
To promote the advancement of the science and art of, and research in, Crown and Bridge Prosthodontics. Membership: 302; active members, 271; honorary members, 4; associate members, 27. Finances: Membership: Initiation fee, $100; annual dues, $75; Other Sources: Sponsored guest fee, $75; student guest fee, $35. Awards: Stanley D. Tylman Student Essay Award, annually; $300 cash prize, tourist air fare to Academy Meeting in Chicago as guest of the Academy plus three days per diem. Meetings: Annual, mid-February, for 2 days, Chicago, Illinois. Publications: Journal of Prosthetic Dentistry, M.D., editor. Affiliations: Federation of Prosthodontic Organizations (FPO).

★ 40 ★

AMERICAN ACADEMY OF DENTAL ELECTRO-
    SURGERY, INC.
57 West 57th Street, Suite 1001   (212) 755-6630
New York, New York 10019   Established 1963

Maurice J. Oringer, D.D.S., Executive Secretary
The Academy's aims include encouraging the use of
electrosurgery in dentistry, improving the art and science through continuing education, development and
improvement of useful clinical techniques, and encouraging research leading to increased safety and efficiency of the electrosurgical devices and increased
efficiency and clinical effectiveness of electrosurgery
in dentistry.   Activities include conducting two scientific programs in electrosurgery annually, publication of newsletters that include reports of the scientific presentations, and cosponsoring of a research project at the Ph.D. doctoral level in the Biomedical
Engineering Program of the School of Engineering,
University of Miami.   The Academy has sponsored a
Certification Board and 2 classes of diplomats have
graduated up to now.   Membership: 400 (regular,
associate, honorary).   Finances: Membership: Regu-
lar, $35; associate, $20.   Awards: The Maurice J.
Oringer Award for excellence in dental electrosurgery;
Fellow of the Academy; Honoary Fellowships.
Meetings: Annual, various locations.   Publications:
AADE News and Reviews, quarterly, Brian F. Pollack,
D.D.S., editor.   Affiliations: American Dental
Association.

★ 41 ★

AMERICAN ACADEMY OF DENTAL GROUP
    PRACTICE
1709 Elka Lane   (608) 241-2609
Madison, Wisconsin 53704   Established 1973

Joann Junkins, Executive Secretary
The Academy's purpose is to promote group practice,
promote research, accumulate and dispense knowledge,
exchange ideas and experiences, study and develop
methods for the delivery of dental care, evaluate
conduct, performance and quality of dental practices
through an accreditation program.   Provides a voluntary accreditation program, consisting of 5 standards
which all dentist should be practicing, involving patient record, internal audit procedure, cleanliness and
infection control, protocols for patient care and acceptable performance in patient care.   A group is
two or more dentists practicing together.   Membership: 364 groups of 1,436 doctors (each group has 1
vote on all matters brought before the Academy);
active membership, other categories: individual, educational or government, and honorary membership.
Finances: Membership: $100 per group plus $10 per
doctor registered; initiation fee of $150 per group

or individual (half of yearly dues are used by regional
academies to assist with programming, administration).
Other Sources: "Friends of the Academy" meeting
revenues with exhibits.   Meetings: 5 regions have
semiannual meetings in each area and the national
meeting in conjunction with the ADA.   Publications:
AADGP Newsletter, quarterly, Joann Junkins, editor.
Library: AADGP, uncounted number of articles;
membership, $5 for 20 or more articles.   Affiliations:
Dental Group Management Association.

AMERICAN ACADEMY OF DENTAL MEDICINE
    See: American Academy of Oral Medicine

★ 42 ★

AMERICAN ACADEMY OF DENTAL PRACTICE
    ADMINISTRATION
15609 Meadow Park Drive   (602) 974-4958
Sun City, Arizona 85351   Established 1956

Virginia M. Savage, Executive Secretary
To promote the study of dental practice administration,
particularly as it applies to the dental office, among
its members and the dental professional generally.
Primary activity is an annual three-day meeting at the
Conrad Hilton Hotel in Chicago, just preceding the
Chicago midwinter meeting, consisting of an educa-
tional program in dental practice administration for
members.   Membership: 265 (98 percent private
practice, 2 percent full-time teachers).   Finances:
Membership: Initiation fee, $150; annual dues,
$150; full-time teachers and senior active members,
$60.   Fees for guests at annual meetings.   Awards:
Grants to Organization of Teachers of Dental Practice
and Dental Student Seminars Administration, annually.
Grants and funding now under direction of AADPA
Endowment and Memorial Foundation.   Meetings:
Annual, Chicago, Illinois.   Publications: Papers
from Annual Meeting, annual, Walter F. Hrin,
D.D.S., editor; The Communicator, 6 issues annual-
ly.

★ 43 ★

AMERICAN ACADEMY OF DENTAL RADIOLOGY
Medical College of Georgia
School of Dentistry   (404) 828-2935
Augusta, Georgia 30902

Dr. Charles R. Morris, President; Dr. William R.
    Wege, Executive Secretary
To promote and develop applications of the art and
science of radiology in dentistry and to promote opportunity for all professionals in dental radiology to

be able to communicate and achieve recognition of their work. Membership: 498 (active, associate, fellows, life members). Finances: Membership: $45 associate, annually; $50 active, annually. Awards: Annual Cline Fixott Senior Award. Meetings: Annual, various locations. Publications: Radiology Section of Oral Surgery, Oral Medicine, Oral Pathology, monthly, Lincoln R. Manson-Hing, editor.

★ 44 ★
AMERICAN ACADEMY OF DERMATOLOGY
820 Davis Street   (312) 869-3954
Evanston, Illinois 60201   Established 1938

Bradford W. Claxton, CAE, Executive Director
The Academy was established with the stated purpose of providing continuing education to physicians specializing in diseases of the skin. In addition, the Academy works to promote clinical practice and education and research in dermatologic medicine and surgery; promote patient care and public interest relating to dermatology; and, promote the allied health professions and health services as they related to dermatology. Membership: 5,700 (fellow, associate, non-resident fellow, affiliate, life and honorary). Awards: Gold Medal Award; Dome Lectureship; Lila Gruber Cancer Memorial Lecture Awards. Meetings: Annual National Meeting. Publications: Journal of the American Academy of Dermatology, monthly, J. Graham Smith, Jr., M.D., editor.

★ 45 ★
AMERICAN ACADEMY OF ENVIRONMENTAL
    ENGINEERS
Post Office Box 1278   (301) 762-7797
Rockville, Maryland 20850   Established 1955

Stanley Kappe, Executive Director
Primarily concerned with the certification of engineers as to their competence in the field of environmental engineering.   Also actively encourages members to contribute on engineering input to current legislation. Membership: 2,000 (professional engineers having at least 8 years experience in the field).   Awards: Edward Cleary Award; Gordon M. Fair Award. Meetings: 8 per year. Publications: The Diplomate, quarterly, Stan Kappe, editor; Membership Roster. Affiliations: Air Pollution Control Association; American Institute of Chemical Engineers; American Public Health Association; American Public Works Association of American Society for Engineering Education; American Society of Civil Engineers; American Water Works Association; Association of Environmental Engineering Professors; National Society of Professional Engineers; Water Pollution Control Federation.

★ 46 ★
AMERICAN ACADEMY OF ESTHETIC DENTISTRY
211 East Chicago Avenue, Suite 915
Chicago, Illinois 60611   Established 1975

Eric Bishop, Director of the Central Office
Founded to advance the art and science of esthetic dentistry. Membership: 55. Finances: Membership, $260. Meetings: Annual, San Francisco, California. Publications: The Journal of Prosthetic Dentistry, Judson Hickey, M.D., editor.

★ 47 ★
AMERICAN ACADEMY OF FAMILY PHYSICIANS
1740 West 92nd Street   (816) 531-0377
Kansas City, Missouri 64114   Established 1947

Roger Tusken, Executive Director
To promote and maintain high standards of family practice in medicine and surgery; to encourage and assist young men and women in preparing, qualifying and establishing themselves in family practice; to preserve the right of the family physician to engage in medical and surgical procedures for which he or she is qualified by training and experience; to assist in providing continuing education for family physicians; to advance medical science and private and public health and to preserve the patient's right to free choice of physician; and to acknowledge and assume responsible public advocacy in all health-related matters. Membership: 48,370 (active, student affiliate, resident affiliate, practicing affiliate, inactive, sustaining, life). Finances: Membership: National, $5-$75, depending on classification; state chapters, $10-$150; Other Sources: Subscription to AFP, income from advertising in AFP, sale of exhibit space at annual meetings. Awards: Journalism Awards, John G. Walsh Award, Thomas W. Johnson Award; President's Award, Certificate of Meritorious Service, Award of Merit and Certificate of Commendation. Meetings: Annual, various locations. Publications: American Family Physician, monthly, Walter H. Kemp, managing publisher, Dr. John C. Rose, medical editor; AAFP Reporter, monthly, William R. DeLay, Communications Director, Paula Jolly, Managing Editor.

★ 48 ★
AMERICAN ACADEMY OF FORENSIC SCIENCES
225 South Academy Boulevard
Suite 201   (303) 596-6006
Colorado Springs, Colorado 80910 Established 1948

Kenneth S. Field, Executive Director
The Academy aims (1) to encourage the study, improve

the practice, elevate the standards, and advance the cause of the forensic sciences; (2) to promote the standardization of scientific techniques, tests and criteria; and (3) to plan, organize, and administer meetings, reports and other projects for the stimulation and advancement of these and related purposes. Nine fields are currently included: criminalistics, jurisprudence, odontology, pathology and biology, physical anthropology; psychiatry, questioned documents, toxicology, and general. Membership: 2,300 (fellow, member, provisional member, trainee affiliate, corresponding). Meetings: Annual, in February. Publications: Journal of Forensic Sciences, quarterly, Abel M. Dominquez, Ph.D., editor; Newsletter, quarterly; Roster, annually. Affiliations: Forensic Sciences Foundation, Inc.

★ 49 ★

AMERICAN ACADEMY OF GNATHOLOGIC
    ORTHOPEDICS
4124 Farnan Street   (402) 558-5638
Omaha, Nebraska 68131   Established 1962

John M. Long, D.D.S., President
The Academy consists of dentists dealing with the prevention or correction of malocclusion and bony misformation of the jaw and face. Conducts activities in the fields of maxillofacial orthopedics/orthodontics and preventive and corrective orthodontics. Membership: 500 (certified and associate membership). Finances: Membership: $45. Awards: Wiebrecht Award - Teaching Foundation of Crozat Technique. Meetings: Semiannual, various locations. Publications: Crozat Courier, quarterly, Lauren W. Teutsch, D.D.S., editor; International Journal of Orthodontics FOA Journal of all Affiliates, quarterly, L. James Flatley, D.D.S., editor. Library: A.A.G.O., Omaha, Nebraska. Affiliations: American Academy of Gnathologic Orthopedics, American Society for the Study of Orthodontics, American Academy of Orthodontics for the General Practitioner, American Orthodontic Society; these affiliates form the Federation of Orthodontic Association who has officers chosen from members of the 4 affiliate organizations.

★ 50 ★

AMERICAN ACADEMY OF GOLD FOIL OPERATORS
c/o Dr. Ralph Boelsche
Box 57
Industry, Texas 78944   Established 1952

Dr. Ralph Boelsche, Secretary-Treasurer
The aim of operative dentistry, until the prevention of dental decay is an accomplished fact, is to retain teeth which have been damaged by decay, attrition,

erosion or accident, in a state of health and function by as conservative and permanent means as possible. To attain perfection in this aim is the objective of the American Academy of Gold Foil Operators. Further, it will encourage and support the search for the cause, prevention, and elimination of dental caries. To accomplish the immediate need, it will encourage, by practice by teaching, the management of decayed and abraded teeth in the incipency of their involvement, by the use of the most permanent and practical restorative materials available to dentistry. In this program it will use as it means of measurement - gold foil. Conducts annual meeting each fall concurrent with ADA meeting. Membership: 545 (active, associate, foreign, honorary, life). Finances: Joining fee, $25; membership: active, associate, $25; foreign, $25; Other Sources: Gold keys, available to operators at official meetings. Awards: Dental Senior Student Achievement Award. Meetings: Annual, in conjunction with American Dental Association, various locations. Publications: Journal, quarterly, Ian Hamilton, editor.

★ 51 ★

AMERICAN ACADEMY OF IMPLANT DENTISTRY
515 Washington Street   (617) 878-7990
Abington, Massachusetts 02351 Established 1952

John P. Winiewicz, Executive Director
To further the education in the field of implant dentistry. Membership: 950 (active, 350; supporting, 600). Meetings: Annual, in conjunction with ADA annual meeting, various locations. Publications: Journal of Oral Implantology, quarterly, Paul J. Mentag, M.D., editor; newsletter.

★ 52 ★

AMERICAN ACADEMY OF MAXILLOFACIAL
    PROSTHETICS
c/o Dr. R. P. Desjardins
Mayo Clinic   (507) 284-2511
Rochester, Minnesota 55901

Dr. R. P. Desjardins,   Executive Secretary-
    Treasurer
General association of professionally qualified persons engaged in the clinical practice, education, and research aspects of maxillofacial prosthetics; formed for dissemination of knowledge and establishment and maintenance of programs for research in maxillofacial prosthetics. Membership: 144 (life, active, associate, honorary, affiliate, student). Finances: Membership: $64. Awards: Ackerman Award. Meetings: Annual, various locations.

★ 53 ★

AMERICAN ACADEMY OF MEDICAL ADMINISTRA-
TORS
2590 East Devon Avenue
Suite 107   (312) 827-5890
Des Plaines, Illinois 60018   Established 1957

Ruth L. Frazier, President; Samuel White, Jr.,
   Executive Director
To encourage and foster a scientific approach to the
practice of medical administration; to provide a
means of intercommunication between health care administrators; to promote educational courses in health
care administration; to establish and improve the
standards of professional conduct in this field; to
publish scientific, educational and professional literature. Membership: 1,400 (student affiliates, nominees, members, fellows and charter members). Finances: Membership: $75 nominees; $100 members.
Meetings: Annual, various locations. Publications:
Executive Newsletter, monthly, Samuel White, Jr.,
Executive Director, editor.

★ 54 ★

AMERICAN ACADEMY OF MEDICAL DIRECTORS
5205 Leesburg Pike, Suite 207   (703) 998-0500
Falls Church, Virginia 22041   Established 1974

Roger S. Schenke, Executive Vice President;
   Saundra White, Director, Member Services
The Academy is a non-profit, voluntary membership,
educational forum exclusively for physicians in or
preparing for positions of organizational leadership.
Membership: 725 physicians (medical directors, chief
executive officers, department chairmen, presidents of
medical staff, board members, committee chairmen and
others from hospitals, industry, group practices,
HMO's, universities, government and the military).
Finances: Membership: $150 annual dues. Meet-
ings: National Conference, annual, May, various
locations; workshops and seminars. Publications:
The Medical Director, bimonthly, S. Pilato, editor;
Member Directory, annually; The Physician in Management, Roger Schenke, editor.

★ 55 ★

AMERICAN ACADEMY OF MEDICAL PREVENTICS
8383 Wilshire Boulevard, Suite 922 (213) 878-1234
Beverly Hills, California 90211   Established 1972

Bruce Halstead, M.D., President; Garry F. Gordan,
   M.D., Chairman of the Board; Lynne F. Stone,
   Executive Director
Provides referral service to patients interested in find-
ing a doctor who does chelation therapy and who is

practicing nutrition and preventive medicine. Mem-
bership: medical doctors, doctors of osteopathy,
chiropracters, nutritionists. Finances: Membership:
Fellow membership, $200; affiliate membership, $50.
Research Funds: AAMP Development Fund. Meetings:
Semiannual, May 1981, Atlanta, Georgia; November
1981, Las Vegas, Nevada. Publications: AAMP,
Newsletter, 3 times per year, Garry F. Gordon,
M.D., editor and David Steenblock, D.O., editor;
AAMP.

★ 56 ★

AMERICAN ACADEMY OF MENTAL RETARDATION
916 64th Avenue East
Tacoma, Washington 98428   Established 1960

Dr. C. Edward Meyers, President
The Academy, composed of an interdisciplinary group
of researchers in mental retardation, holds an annual
meeting for the purpose of reporting on research being
done in the field. Membership: 150. Finances:
Membership: $12. Meetings: General meeting,
annually, held jointly with the American Association
on Mental Deficiency.

★ 57 ★

AMERICAN ACADEMY OF NEUROLOGICAL
   SURGERY
c/o Phanor L. Perot, Jr., M.D.
171 Ashely Avenue   (803) 792-2421
Charleston, South Carolina 29403 Established 1938

Phanor L. Perot, Jr., M.D. Ph.D., Secretary
To promote scientific intercourse, to foster neurological surgery as a specialty, and to promote the knowledge and skill of those who devote themselves to
neurological surgery. Sponsors an annual meeting
based on scientific presentations by Academy members
and invited speakers. Membership: 165 (active,
corresponding, senior and honorary). Members are
selected only from physicians in good professional
standing who limit medical practice to neurological
surgery. Finances: Membership: $100 annually.
Awards: Annual Award, given to one individual in
neurosurgical training for original investigation.
Meetings: Annual, various locations.

★ 58 ★

AMERICAN ACADEMY OF NEUROLOGY
4015 West 65th Street, Suite 302   (612) 920-3636
Minneapolis, Minnesota 55435

Stanley A. Nelson, Executive Director

To provide an outlet for expression of professional opinions for the benefit and advancement of the neurological sciences, to stimulate the growth and development of clinical neurology by establishing an Annual Scientific Meeting at which clinical and experimental observations on neurological subjects can be presented, and establishing a neurological journal for recording clinical and clinically related experimental observations. Membership: 6,170 (junior, actives, associates, fellows). Finances: Membership: Juniors, $30; associates, actives, and fellows, $85; associate foreign and nonclinical, $50. Awards: S. Weir Mitchell Award; Essay Contest Award; Wartenberg Lecture; Cotzias Lecture. Meetings: Annual, held the last full week in April. Publications: Neurology, monthly, Lewis P. Rowland, M.D., editor.

★ 59 ★
AMERICAN ACADEMY OF OCCUPATIONAL
  MEDICINE
150 North Wacker Drive   (312) 782-2166
Chicago, Illinois 60606   Established 1946

Howard N. Schulz, Executive Director
The primary objective of the Academy is education to its members and to the medical profession in general through an Annual Scientific Meeting, short courses at universities, and co-sponsored educational courses with other associations. Membership: 700 (members, fellows, fellow emeritus, honorary, corresponding, and inactive). Finances: Membership: $60 members and fellows. Awards: Robert A. Kehoe Award for outstanding work in occupational medicine. Meetings: Annual, various locations. Publications: Journal of Occupational Medicine, monthly, Lloyd B. Tepper, M.D., editor.

★ 60 ★
AMERICAN ACADEMY OF OPHTHALMOLOGY
1833 Fillmore Street
Post Office Box 7424   (415) 921-4700
San Francisco, California 94120   Established 1896

Bruce E. Spivey, M.D., Executive Vice President;
  David J. Noonan, Deputy Executive Vice President
To promote and advance the science and art of medicine related to the eye and related structures; to support and enhance education in ophthalmology and in associated fields; to facilitate and improve the prevention, diagnosis and treatment of disorders affecting the eye and related structures. Sponsors annual scientific assembly, instruction courses and home study courses. Membership: 10,000 (active, life, honorary, associate, incactive). Finances: Mem-

bership: Active, $250; life member services, $50; Other Sources: Annual Meeting, continuing education programs and other publications. Awards: Honor Awards, Public Service Award, Edward Jackson Memorial Lecture, guest of honor at Annual Meeting. Meetings: Annual, various locations. Publications: Ophthalmology (formerly Transactions of the American Academy of Ophthalmology and Otolaryngology), monthly, Paul Henkind, M.D., Ph.D., editor; Argus, monthly, Bruce E. Spivey, M.D., editor and Maureen S. Barry, Managing Editor. Remarks: Membership categories may be expanded in the future. Former Name: American Academy of Ophthalmology and Otolaryngology.

AMERICAN ACADEMY OF OPHTHALMOLOGY AND
OTOLARYNGOLOGY
  See: American Academy of Ophthalmology

★ 61 ★
AMERICAN ACADEMY OF OPTOMETRY
117 West Broadway
Box 565   (507) 451-0009
Owatonna, Minnesota 55060   Established 1921

John N. Schoen, O.D., Secretary-Treasurer
The primary object of the American Academy of Optometry shall be to further the development of optometric science in its efforts to conserve human vision by: (1) affording an opportunity for the presentation and discussion of the results of clinical and experimental research in visual problems; (2) encouraging the scientific observation and reporting of exceptional and instructive conditions encountered in the practice of the individual fellow; (3) initiating and supporting, in suitable centers and institutions, research programs in optometric subjects. Membership: 2,700 (optometrists in private practice, and faculty people in schools and colleges and other Visual Scientists). Finances: Membership: $65 annually. Awards: The Prentice Medal awarded for outstanding research in vision; the Carel C. Koch Award for outstanding work in the field of Interprofessional Relations; Glenn Fry Award for the best paper presented at the annual meeting. Meetings: Annual, various locations. Publications: American Journal of Optometry and Physiological Optics, monthly, Wm. M. Lyle, Ph.D., editor.

★ 62 ★
AMERICAN ACADEMY OF ORAL MEDICINE
225 South Meramec Avenue   (314) 727-2420
St. Louis, Missouri 63105   Established 1945

Gunter Schmidt, D.D.S., Secretary
To promote the dissemination of knowledge of the cause, prevention, and control of diseases of the teeth, their supporting structures and adnexa, and related subjects; and to promote and foster better scientific understanding between the fields of dentistry and medicine. Membership: Active, associate, honorary, fellows, retired, life. Finances: Membership: $40, active and associate members; $20, retired. Awards: Samuel Charles Miller Memorial Lecture Award for great contribution to oral medicine and education; Certificate of Merit for Proficiency in Oral Medicine to outstanding senior dentistry student. Meetings: Annual and semiannual, locations. Publications: Journal of Oral Medicine, quarterly, Dr. Sheldon Ross, editor; Newsletter, quarterly, Dr. Harriet Goldman, editor. Former Name: American Academy of Dental Medicine.

★ 63 ★
AMERICAN ACADEMY OF ORAL PATHOLOGY
Temple University
School of Dentistry
3223 North Broad Street   (215) 221-2930
Philadelphia, Pennsylvania 19140   Established 1946

Arthur Miller, Secretary-Treasurer
To promote interchange of ideas and thoughts in the field of oral pathology. Sponsors annual meetings, symposia, seminars and publications. Membership: 750 (members, fellows). Finances: Membership: $50 per year. Meetings: Annual, various locations. Publications: Oral Surgery, Oral Medicine, Oral Pathology, monthly, Charles E. Tomich, editor. Affiliations: American Board of Oral Pathology.

★ 64 ★
AMERICAN ACADEMY OF ORTHODONTICS FOR
   THE GENERAL PRACTITIONER
3953 North 76th Street   (414) 464-7870
Milwaukee, Wisconsin 53222   Established 1959

David Watson, D.D.S., Secretary
To provide dentists in general practice with an organization in which they can augment their basic knowledge and training in orthodontics. Membership: 300 (associate, active, honorary, life, fellow). Finances: Membership: $40; Other Sources: Continuing education workshops. Awards: Fellow, Past President, Honorary Active lapel pins. Meetings: Annual, Delavon, Wisconsin; semiannual seminar, various locations. Publications: Academy Bulletin, quarterly, Dr. Eugene Gissal, editor; International Journal of Orthodontics, quarterly, Godfrey Muller, editor. Affiliations: American Society for the Study of Orthodontics; International Association for Orthodontics; Federation of Orthodontic Associations.

★ 65 ★
AMERICAN ACADEMY OF ORTHOPAEDIC
   SURGEONS
444 North Michigan Avenue   (312) 822-0970
Chicago, Illinois 60611   Established 1933

Charles V. Heck, M.D., Executive Director
To advance orthopaedic surgery through sponsorship of annual scientific meetings and the offering of courses, programs and publications. Membership: 9,271 (fellows, associate, corresponding, emeritus, honorary, reciprocal--all doctors of medicine). Finances: Membership: Fellows, $300; associate, $25; reciprocal, $10; other sources: registration fees from annual meetings, instructional and continuing education course fees, technical exhibit rentals. Awards: $6,000 for three awards annually contributed by Kappa Delta Sorority for research in orthopaedic surgery. Meetings: Annual, various locations. Publications: Bulletin, quarterly, Alexander Garcia, M.D., editor. Affiliations: Association of Orthopaedic Chairmen; Orthopaedic Research and Education Foundation; American Orthopaeduc Foot Society; Scoliosis Research Society; American Orthopaedic Society for Sports Medicine.

★ 66 ★
AMERICAN ACADEMY OF ORTHOTISTS AND
   PROSTHETISTS
1444 N Street, N.W.   (202) 234-8400
Washington, D.C. 20005   Established 1970

William L. McCulloch, Executive Director
To preserve the professional and scientific interests of the nation's certified practitioners in orthotics and prosthetics. Membership: 1,300. Finances: Membership: $75 ($15 application fee); Other Sources: Seminar income. Awards: Honorary Membership Award. Meetings: Assemblies, annually; technological seminars designed to focus attention on major developments in the disciplines, annually. Publications: Newsletter, quarterly; Annual Directory.

★ 67 ★
AMERICAN ACADEMY OF OSTEOPATHY
2630 Airport Road   (303) 632-7164
Colorado Springs, Colorado 80910 Established 1937

Martha I. Drew, Ph.D., Director

Exists in order to develop the art of osteopathic manipulative therapy and to encourage physicians to an even greater degree of proficiency in the distinctive skills of osteopathic diagnostic and therapeutic procedures. Offers graduate instruction seminars and courses, and visiting clinician program to the 14 osteopathic colleges. Membership: 1,770 (regular, first year in practice, second year in practice, student, interns, residents, associate, retired, honorary, honorary life). Finances: Membership: $100 regular; residents and interns, 1/10 regular membership; student, $5, initial; joint, 1 1/2 times regular; first year in practice, 1/3; second year in practice, 2/3's; retired, 1/3; Other Sources: Seminars, tutorials sale of publications. Awards: Andrew Taylor Still Medallion of Honor; Academy Lecturer. Meetings: Semiannual, various locations. Publications: Annual Membership Publication; Directory, annually; Newsletter, quarterly.

★ 68 ★

AMERICAN ACADEMY OF OTOLARYNGOLOGY
15 Second Street, S.W.   (507) 288-7444
Rochester, Minnesota 55901   Established 1979

Wesley H. Bradley, Executive Vice President
Professional association of medical doctors specializing in otolaryngology, plastic surgery and bronchoesophagology (diseases of the ear, nose and throat). Membership: 5,437 (physicians and surgeons). Meetings: Annual Convention, various locations. Publications: Otolaryngology and Head and Neck Surgery, bimonthly; Perceiver, bimonthly; Directory, annual; numerous manuals, brochures, monographs, abstracts and atlases.

★ 69 ★

AMERICAN ACADEMY OF PEDIATRICS
1801 Hinman Avenue   (312) 869-4255
Evanston, Illinois 60204   Established 1930

Robert G. Frazier, M.D., Executive Director;
     Gerald E. Hughes, M.D., Secretary
The objects of the Academy are to foster and stimulate interest in pediatrics and correlate all aspects of the work for the welfare of the children which properly come within the scope of pediatrics. The Academy shall endeavor to accomplish the following purposes: (1) to establish and maintain the highest possible standards for pediatric education in medical schools and hospitals, pediatric practice and research; (2) to perpetuate the history and best traditions of pediatric practice and ethics; (3) to maintain the dignity and efficiency of pediatric practice in its relationship to public welfare; (4) to promote publica-

tions and encourage contributions to medical and scientific literature pertaining to pediatrics; none of which objects is for pecuniary profit. To further these ends, the Academy has an organization at the state level in each of the 50 states, the District of Columbia, Puerto Rico and the Virgin Islands, in 8 Provinces of Canada, and in 18 Latin American countries. Liaison representation is maintained with 42 national organizations interested in the welfare of children. Membership: 18,328 (board certified pediatricians). Finances: Membership: $180 annual dues. Awards: Ratner Award; Ladd Award; Mead Johnson; Borden; Latin American Chapter Awards. Meetings: Semiannual, various locations. Publications: Pediatrics, monthly, Jerold F. Lucey, M.D., editor; News and Comments, monthly, Lucy Maloney and Edward Kittrell, editors.

★ 70 ★

AMERICAN ACADEMY OF PEDODONTICS
211 East Chicago Avenue
Suite 1235   (312) 337-2169
Chicago, Illinois 60611   Established 1948

Merle C. Hunter, Executive Director
To foster and encourage dissemination of knowledge of pedodontics through education, research and practice. Membership: 2,250 (fellows, actives, associate, life, honorary, retired, and students). Finances: Membership: Actives, fellows $185; annual membership dues, associates $92.50; life, honorary, retired and students, no dues; Other Sources: Assessment for annual meetings, according to location and activities. Awards: Graduate Pedodontic Student Thesis Award. Meetings: Annual, various locations. Publications: Newsletter, monthly, Dr. Stephen H. Wei, editor; Pediatric Dentistry-- The Journal of the American Academy of Pedodontics, quarterly, Dr. Stephen H. Wei, editor.

★ 71 ★

AMERICAN ACADEMY OF PERIODONTOLOGY
211 East Chicago Avenue
Suite 924   (312) 787-5518
Chicago, Illinois 60611   Established 1914

Marilyn C. Holmquist, Executive Secretary
To advance the art and science of peridontology and by its application, improvement and maintenance of the health of the public. Activities include annual four-day scientific session open to members and non-member dentists; public and professional education/ relations; foreign relations; student loan fund; dental health plans and public affairs; sponsorship of American Board of Periodontology. Membership:

3,900 (active, associate, affiliate, nonresident, academic). Finances: Membership: Active, $125; associate, $60; affiliate, $25; nonresident, $50; academic, $50; Other Sources: Subscriptions to Journal. Awards: Gold Medal Award $1,000; William J. Gies Award in Honor of Arthur Hastings Merritt $200; Student Award for excellence in undergraduate periodontology. Meetings: Annual, various locations. Publications: Journal of Periodontology, monthly.

★ 72 ★

AMERICAN ACADEMY OF PHYSICAL MEDICINE
    AND REHABILITATION
30 North Michigan Avenue
Suite 922   (312) 236-9512
Chicago, Illinois 60602

Creston C. Herold, Executive Director
To promote the art and science of medicine and the betterment of health through and understanding of physical medicine and rehabilitation. This organization, composed of Diplomates of the American Board of Physical Medicine and Rehabilitation, conducts continuing graduate education program in physical medicine and rehabilitation through the sponsoring of year-round courses, annual assembly and meeting, etc. Membership: 1,400 (active, associate, corresponding, senior, honorary). Finances: Membership: Active, $175; associate, $135; corresponding, $20. Awards: Frank H. Krusen Award for outstanding contribution to Physical Medicine and Rehabilitation; Walter J. Zeiter Lectureship. Meetings: Annual, various locations. Publications: Archives of Physical Medicine and Rehabilitation, monthly, G. Keith Stillwell, M.D., Ph.D., editor.

★ 73 ★

AMERICAN ACADEMY OF PHYSICIAN ASSISTANTS
2341 Jefferson Davis Highway, #700 (703) 920-5730
Arlington, Virginia 22202   Established 1973

To encourage its membership to render quality service to the health professions and the public; develop, sponsor, and evaluate continuing medical or medically related education programs for the physician assistant; assist in the role definition for physician assistants; participate in the development of criteria leading to certification of the physician assistants; develop, coordinate, and participate in studies having an impact either directly or indirectly on the physician assistant concept; serves as a public information center with respect to its members, health professions, and the public; assist with the coordination and standardization of curricula for the physician assistant; par-

ticipate in the certification of physician assistants. Membership: 6,184 (fellow, 5020; student, 1164). Finances: Membership: Renewal dues, $110 fellow; initial dues, $115; student dues, $30. Research Funds: Educational and Research Foundation, to secure federal grants and private foundation grants for research and education; will possibly secure grants from pharmaceutical companies and other sources. Meetings: Annual, various locations. Publications: AAPA News, monthly, Betsey Lyon, editor; Selected Annotated Bibliography of the Physician Assistant Profession, annual, Susan Anderson, MLS, editor; National Health Practitioner Program Profile, periodically, James Hughes, editor. Library: No restriction as to use. Affiliations: Association of Physician Assistant Programs.

★ 74 ★

AMERICAN ACADEMY OF PODIATRIC SPORTS
    MEDICINE
Post Office Box 31331   (415) 826-3200
San Francisco, California 94131   Established 1970

John L. Bennett, Executive Director
To coordinate the various disciplines of podiatry in the treatment of the modern athlete; to encourage an exchange of ideas in the area of sports medicine with allied health professions in order to provide total care of the modern athlete; to provide a consultative service for podiatrists, allied health professionals, trainers, coaches, and athletes in the management of lower extremity musculoskeletal problems of the athlete. Membership: 900 (active members until June 1983, fellow, associate). Finances: Membership: Dues, $50 annual; application fee, $50; examination fee, $150; Other Sources: Seminars. Awards: Research Grants; Research Awards. Meetings: Annual, May or June, various locations. Publications: Sports Medicine, semiannually, Robert Rinaldi and Michael Sabia, Jr., D.P.M., editors; newsletters. Affiliations: American Podiatry Association.

★ 75 ★

AMERICAN ACADEMY OF PODIATRY
    ADMINISTRATION
194 Harrison Avenue   (201) 546-1616
Garfield, New Jersey 07026   Established 1961

Rosario LaBarbera, Secretary
Doctors of podiatry (foot care) interested in practice management. Works to standardize office management procedures to create more efficient podiatry practices; conducts research on the administration and function of podiatry offices; develops formalized procedures for obtaining and training office assistants.

Membership: 200 (podiatrists). Meetings: Annual, various locations. Publications: Newsletter, quarterly; Directory of Membership, annual. Affiliations: American Podiatry Association. Former Name: American Academy of Practice Management in Podiatry.

AMERICAN ACADEMY OF PRACTICE MANAGEMENT IN PODIATRY
See: American Academy of Podiatry Administration

★ 76 ★
AMERICAN ACADEMY OF PSYCHOANALYSIS
30 East 40th Street, Suite 608   (212) 477-4250
New York, New York 10016   Established 1956

Vivian Mendelsohn, Administrative Director
To develop communication among psychoanalysts and their colleagues in other disciplines in science and in the humanities: to constitute a forum for inquiry into the phenomena of individual motivation and social behavior; to encourage and support research in psychoanalysis; to foster the acceptance of psychoanalysis and its integration in universities; and to advance the interests of psychoanalysis in all other respects. Activities include two annual meetings for scientific presentations, open to members, psychiatrists and members of the behavioral sciences including residents and interns. Membership: 879 (fellows, candidates, scientific associates). Finances: Membership: Fellows, $175; candidates, $50; scientific associates, $50. Meetings: Semiannual, various locations. Publications: Journal of the American Academy of Psychoanalysis, quarterly, Morton B. Cantor, M.D., editor; The Academy, quarterly, Ann R. Turkel, M.D., editor. Former Name: Academy of Psychoanalysis.

★ 77 ★
AMERICAN ACADEMY OF THE HISTORY OF DENTISTRY
c/o Dr. H. B. McCauley
3804 Hadley Square East
Baltimore, Maryland 21218   Established 1950

H. B. McCauley, M.D., Secretary
To stimulate interest, study and reseach in the history of dentistry; to disseminate information pertaining to dental history; to promote the teaching of dental history in the dental schools of the United States; and to cooperate with committees of dental history of other recognized organizations. Publishes a bulletin plus research papers to members; student awards in dental schools in cooperation with historical agencies

(Smithsonian Institution, Washington, D.C.); research; exhibits at meetings; etc. Membership: 350 (members are those elected persons who, through teaching, research or special interest, shall have made substanial contributions to the advancement of the knowledge of dental history). Finances: Membership: $15. Awards: M. D. K. Bremner Award; Hayden-Harris Award. Meetings: Annual, at meeting of American Dental Association. Publications: Newsletter, monthly, Malvin Ring, editor; Bulletin, quarterly, Malvin Ring, editor. Affiliations: American Association of the History of Medicine.

★ 78 ★
AMERICAN ACADEMY OF VETERINARY
  DERMATOLOGY
595 Columbian Street
South Weymouth   (617) 337-6622
  Massachusetts 02190   Established 1964

Richard K. Anderson DVM, Secretary
The Academy was founded to further scientific progress in veterinary and comparative dermatology; to coordinate research of veterinary dermatology; to provide an exclusive organization for dedicated individuals who devote a significant portion of their professional activity to research, teaching, or practice of skin diseases of animals; to further dermatological education by encouraging adequate dermatological training in veterinary colleges and by providing, by means of meeting, seminars, and courses, the opportunity for graduate veterinarians to carry on advanced studies in dermatology; to encourage and promote improved methods of diagnosis, treatment and prevention of skin diseases of animals. Membership: 100 (veterinarians who devote significant portion of their professional activities to research, teaching, or practice); associate member (veterinarians interested in veterinary dermatology but do not qualify for full membership); affiliate member (non-veterinarians interested in veterinary dermatology). Finances: Membership: Initial fee, $25; annual, $10; Other Sources: Income from presenting meetings, seminars. Research Funds: Funds are made available for research grants on an annual basis. Awards: Dermatology Achievement Award presented periodically. Meetings: Annually in conjunction with annual American Animal Hospital Association meeting. Publications: Newsletters, quarterly. Affiliations: American College of Veterinary Internal Medicine (Dermatology Specialty).

★ 79 ★
AMERICAN AGING ASSOCIATION
University of Nebraska Medical Center
42nd and Dewey Avenue   (402) 541-4416
Omaha, Nebraska 68105   Established 1970

Denham Harman, Executive Secretary
To promote biomedical aging research with the goal of increasing the healthy useful life span of man. Membership: Lay and scientific members. Finances: Membership: Regular, $10. Meetings: Annual, various locations.

★ 80 ★
AMERICAN ALLERGY ASSOCIATION
Post Office Box 7273   (415) 322-1663
Menlo Park, California 94025   Established 1978

Carol Rudoff, M.A., President; Harry Price,
    Secretary
To supply practical information to those suffering from allergies caused by foods, pollens, danders, molds; to help people cope with allergen-free diets and create allergen-free environments; to serve as an informational clearinghouse and to make referrals to other information sources. Finances: Other Sources: Donations. Publications: Living with Allergies, bimonthly, Carol Rudoff, editor; reports.

★ 81 ★
AMERICAN ALLIANCE FOR HEALTH, PHYSICAL
    EDUCATION, RECREATION, AND DANCE
1900 Association Drive   (703) 476-3400
Reston, Virginia 22091   Established 1885

Robert K. Windsor, Executive Vice President
To support, encourage, and provide guidance for personnel throughout the nation as they seek to develop and conduct school and community programs in health upon the needs, interests, and inherent capacities of the individual and of the society of which he/she is a part. Membership: 40,000 (health and safety educators, physical education educators, coaches and athletic directors, recreation leaders and students of these fields). Finances: Membership: Professional, $35-$55; student, $17.50-$37.50; Other Sources: Publication sales and advertising. Awards: The Alliance Honor Fellow Awards; William G. Anderson Award; Luther H. Gulick Award; R. Tait McKenzie Award. Meetings: Annual, various locations. Publications: Journal of Health, Physical Education and Recreation, monthly, September-May; Research Quarterly; Health Education, William M. Kane, editor; wide range of pamphlets and reference works. Affiliations: Association for the Advancement of

Health Education; National Association for Sport and Physical Education; National Association for Girls and Women in Sport; National Dance Association; American Association for Leisure and Recration; Association for Research, Administration, Professional Councils, and Societies; American School and Community Safety Association. Former Name: American Association for Health, Physical Education, and Recreation.

★ 82 ★
AMERICAN AMBULANCE ASSOCIATION
1401 21st Street, Suite 404   (916) 448-5223
Sacramento, California 95814

Robert L. Phillips, Executive Vice President
To further patient care and improve ambulance service. Membership: 150 (ambulance service providers). Finance: Membership: $250-$1,000 annually based on number of ambulances operated. Meetings: Annual, various locations; board meetings, 4-6 times per year, various locations. Publications: Newsletter, monthly, Robert L. Phillips, editor. Former Name: Ambulance and Medical Service Association of America.

★ 83 ★
AMERICAN ANIMAL HOSPITAL ASSOCIATION
3612 East Jefferson Boulevard   (219) 232-8226
South Bend, Indiana 46615   Established 1933

Robert M. Hanson, Executive Director
Basically a service organization, interested in all aspects of small animal medicine and surgery, and especially in improving and upgrading practice methods. Membership: 9,300 (hospitals, and affiliate members). Finances: Membership: Dues; Other Sources: Conventions, publications. Awards: Gaines Research Center Award; AAHA Award, Merit Awards. Meetings: Annual, various locations; regional meetings. Publications: Journal of the American Animal Hospital Association, bimonthly, William F. Jackson, D.V.N., M.S., editor; Bulletin (bimonthly newsletter); Scientific Presentations and Seminar Synopses, annual; Manual of Standards for Animal Hospitals; Manual of Clinical Cardiology; Color Atlases - Canine Skin Lesions; Variations of the Normal Retina; Diagnostic Procedures of Comparative Ophthalmology; Canine and Feline Ocular Fundus; Diseases of the Canine and Feline Conjunctiva and Cornea; Orthopedic Atlas; Ophtholmology Self-Study; Cardiology; Cytology of the Dog and Cat; Ophthalmoloby Talking, Manual I: The Retina.

★ 84 ★

AMERICAN ANOREXIA NERVOSA ASSOCIATION,
INCORPORATED

133 Cedar Lane	(201) 836-1800
Teaneck, New Jersey 07666	Established 1978

John Atchley, M.D., President
Anorexia Nervosa is a serious life-threatening disorder
of deliberate self-starvation with wide ranging physical
and psychiatric components which usually occurs during
adolescence and young adulthood and is the aftermath
of a diet. It mainly affects white females from middle and upper class families. The Association offers
the anorexic family members and professionals the opportunity to participate together in the effort to cope
with, overcome, and diminish this condition. Services offered are information, referrals, counseling,
self-help group, speakers bureau, research. Membership: 3,000 individuals (the board is comprised of
pediatricians, psychiatrists, parents, recovered
anorexics, teachers, school nurses, social workers and
layment). Finances: Membership: $10, $25, $50,
$100, $1,000. Meetings: First Saturday of every
month (self-help from group for anorexics, also for
parents, spouses and siblings). General Meetings -
5 times per year. Publications: NASW--Practice
Digest, December 1980. Affiliations: Philadelphia
chapters. Former Name: Anorexia Nervosa Aid
Society.

★ 85 ★

AMERICAN ASSOCIATION FOR ACCREDITATION
OF LABORATORY ANIMAL CARE

2317 West Jefferson Street,	
Suite 135	(815) 729-2020
Joliet, Illinois 60435	Established 1965

Lee A. Heilman, Executive Secretary
To promote a program for the accreditation of laboratory animal care facilities which will encourage, promote and facilitate scientific research that includes
the use of experimental animals. Membership: 600
(education, health and research organizations).
Meetings: Annual Board of Trustees, December,
Chicago, Illinois.

★ 86 ★

AMERICAN ASSOCIATION FOR AUTOMOTIVE
MEDICINE

Post Office Box 222	(312) 751-6581
Morton Grove, Illinois 60653	Established 1957

Health and Safety Associates, Inc., Executive
Secretariat
To promote the concept of Traffic Medicine, support

and encourage research in the effects of diseases, disabilities, and environmental factors on driver capabilities; to encourage and sponsor laws and regulations
to up-grade the standards for licensing drivers; to
support research and development programs leading to
improved bio-engineering of motor vehicles; to encourage the use of appropriate protective devices in
motor vehicles in order to increase the safety of oc-
cupants; and to encourage and promote the development and dissemination of new knowledge in the field
of traffic, vehicular, and pedestrian safety. Membership: Active, sustaining, supporting, lifetime.
Meetings: Annual, various locations. Publications:
AAAM Quarterly Journal; Proceedings of Annual
Meetings; Abbreviated Injury Scale.

★ 87 ★

AMERICAN ASSOCIATION FOR CANCER
EDUCATION

Albany Medical College	
Division of Oncology	
New Scotland Avenue	(518) 445-5037
Albany, New York 12208	Established 1967

Robert E. Madden, M.D., President; John Horton,
M. D., Secretary
Successor organization to the "Coordinators of Cancer
Teaching." The purpose of the organization is to
bring together individuals responsible for coordination
of cancer teaching and training within medical, dental, and osteopathic schools and other institutions in
which formally organized cancer teaching and training
programs are being conducted. The Organization
has acted as a sole source resource for contracts in
cancer education to the National Cancer Institute.
It has sponsored cancer teaching texts, exhibits, and
instructional packages. Membership: 750 (surgical,
medical, radiation and dental oncologists, basic science educators, nurse practitioner oncologists, professional educators, and social workers). Finances:
Membership: Annual dues, $35; Other Sources:
Registration fee for annual meetings. Lectureships:
Samuel C. Harvey Lectureship, annually. Meetings:
Annual, various locations; irregularly scheduled re-
gional meetings as appropriate. Publications: Ab-
stract Booklet, annual, Program Chairman, editor;
Cancer Newsletter (Sponsor), 4 times per year,
Charles Sherman, M.D., editor; Membership and
Constitution Bylaws (booklet), biannually, The Coun-
cil, editor. Affiliations: American Federation of
Clinical Oncology Societies.

★ 88 ★
AMERICAN ASSOCIATION FOR CANCER
    RESEARCH, INC.
1275 York Avenue   (212) 794-8189
New York, New York 10021   Established 1907

Dr. Frederick S. Philips, Secretary-Treasurer
Association of research workers for presentation and
discussion of new and significant observations and
problems in cancer; and to foster research on cancer.
Membership: 3,229 (honorary, corresponding, emeritus, active). Finances: Membership: $40 annually
for active members. Meetings: Annual, various locations. Publications: Cancer Research, monthly,
Peter N. Magee, editor; Proceedings of the American
Association for Cancer Research, annually in March.

★ 89 ★
AMERICAN ASSOCIATION FOR CLINICAL
    CHEMISTRY
1725 K Street, N.W., Suite 903   (202) 857-0717
Washington, D.C. 20006   Established 1948

William J. Campbell, Ph.D., Executive Director
The purpose for which the Association is formed is to
further the public interest by encouraging the study,
advancing the science, and improving the practice of
clinical chemistry. To achieve these objectives the
Association shall establish standards for education and
training in the field of clinical chemistry; encourage
the creation, promotion and maintenance of standards
for certification of individuals in the field of clinical
chemistry; encourage individuals in the field to
pursue advanced studies and to engage in scientific
investigations; promote scientific knowledge of clinical chemistry through meetings, seminars, discussions,
reports and publications; initiate and participate in
programs related to clinical chemistry that are in the
interest of the public; and promote programs for the
recognition of the profession of clinical chemistry.
Membership: 5,200 (member, student, emeritus).
Finances: Membership: Member, $60; student, $15;
emeritus, $15; Other Sources: Journal advertising,
national meeting. Awards: Outstanding Contributions to Clinical Chemistry; Outstanding Contributions
Through Service to Clinical Chemistry as a Profession;
Outstanding Efforts in Education and Training; Out-
standing Contributions to Clinical Chemistry in a
Selected Area; Young Investigator. Meetings: An-
nual, various locations. Publications: Clinical
Chemistry, monthly, J. Stanton King, Ph.D., editor;
Clinical Chemistry News, monthly, C. H. E.
Weathersbee, editor; Selected Methods in Clinical
Chemistry, Gerald Cooper, Ph.D., editor; Normal
Values in Pediatric Clinical Chemistry; Amiotic
Fluid; The Neonate.

★ 90 ★
AMERICAN ASSOCIATION FOR CLINICAL
    IMMUNOLOGY AND ALLERGY
104 South 39th Street
Post Office Box 912, DTS   (402) 551-0801
Omaha, Nebraska 68101   Established 1964

Howard Silber, Executive Director
The Association aims to promote allergy as a speciality, to encourage clinical allergists to continue postgraduate education and training; and to provide such
education and training. Membership: 1,200 (clinical allergists). Finances: Membership: Full fellow, $60; associate fellow, $50; Other Sources:
Grants, exhibitors' fees. Lectureships: Stanislaus H.
Jaros Memorial Lecture. Meetings: Annual, various
locations. Publications: Newsletter, bimonthly,
Howard Silber, editor; Immunology and Allergy Practice (Journal), bimonthly, Lester W. Mittelstaedt,
M.D., editor. Affiliations: American Board of
Clinical Immunology and Allergy.

★ 91 ★
AMERICAN ASSOCIATION FOR DENTAL RESEARCH
734 15th Street, N.W.
Suite 809   (202) 638-1515
Washington, D.C. 20005   Established 1920

John A. Gray, Ph.D., Executive Director
To promote advancement of dental research in the
United States and throughout the world. Membership: 3,000 (regular, student, affiliate, life).
Finances: $46 annual dues (student dues currently
being revised); Other Sources: Grants. Meetings:
Annual, in large convention cities in the United
States (meets with International Association for Dental
Research of which the AADR is a Division). Publications: Journal of Dental Research, monthly and
special issues, Dr. Barnett M. Levy, Science Editor
and Linda T. Hemphill, Managing Editor. Affiliations: International Association for Dental Research.

★ 92 ★
AMERICAN ASSOCIATION FOR HAND SURGERY
2704 Marshall Court   (608) 238-9311
Madison, Wisconsin 53705   Established 1970

Officers elected annually from active membership.
The purpose of the Association is for the advancement
of hand surgery. Hand surgery is that branch of
surgery which includes investigation, preservation,
and restoration of the function of the hand and associated structures. Membership: 406 (plastic, gen-

eral and orthopedic surgeons specializing in hand surgery). Finances: Membership: $100 annual dues. Awards: Resident's essay contest, annually. Meetings: Annual, various locations; smaller symposia and regional meetings, periodically. Publications: Hand Surgery Newsletter, quarterly, J. Joseph Danyo, M.D., editor.

AMERICAN ASSOCIATION FOR HEALTH, PHYSICAL EDUCATION, AND RECREATION
   See: American Alliance for Health, Physical
        Education, Recreation and Dance

AMERICAN ASSOCIATION FOR HEALTH PLANNING AGENCIES
   See: American Health Planning Association

★ 93 ★
AMERICAN ASSOCIATION FOR HOSPITAL
    PLANNING
2341 Jefferson Davis Highway
Century Building, Suite 830   (703) 979-6513
Arlington, Virginia 22202   Established 1950

Vaughan A. Smith
The Association's purpose is to conduct educational forums on hospital services, design and construction, capital financing, and on federal legislation and programs. It sponsors or co-sponsors sessions in conjunction with regional hospital meetings and also co-sponsors an Annual Health Planning Forum preceding the American Hospital Association each year. Membership: 500. Finances: Membership: Regular, $50; student, $10. Awards: Award of Merit to individuals who have significantly contributed to health health care planning, facilities design, and/or management and delivery of health services. Meetings: Annual, various locations.

★ 94 ★
AMERICAN ASSOCIATION FOR LABORATORY
    ANIMAL SCIENCE
210 Hannes Avenue, Suite 205   (815) 729-1161
Joliet, Illinois 60435   Established 1949

Joseph J. Garvey, Executive Secretary
Serves as a clearinghouse for the collection and exchange of information on all phases of the care and management of laboratory animals. Membership: 2,700 (individual, institutional representatives). Finances: Membership: Individual, $25; institutional,

$125; Other Sources: Annual meeting exhibit and registration fees, journal advertising, sale of manuals. Awards: Griffin Award; AALAS Research Award; AALAS Technician Scholarship Award. Meetings: Annual, various locations. Publications: Laboratory Animal Science, bimonthly, Joseph J. Garvey, editor. Affiliations: American College of Laboratory Animal Medicine; American Society for Laboratory Animal Practitioners; Association for Gnotobiotics; AALAS-Allied Trade Association.

★ 95 ★
AMERICAN ASSOCIATION FOR MATERNAL AND
    CHILD HEALTH, INC.   (415) 326-4839
Post Office Box 965   (714) 456-1301
Los Altos, California 94022   Established 1919

Harold J. Fishbein, Executive Director
The Association has been involved in maternal and child health for over half a century. It has to its credit: the establishment of obstetrical standards in hospitals; a survey which demonstrated the "pill" to be the modality of choice in acceptable family planning; sponsorship of the American Baby--the monthly publication with the largest circulation in the United States to new and expectant parents--establishing contact between the professions and the people they serve; establishment of four divisions, holding annual Congresses, with new divisions in the Pacific and South Atlantic areas in process of formation; distribution of educational material from miscellaneous sources to maternal and child health personnel and to educational institutions, and training classes; support of the Early Periodic Screening and Diagnosis (EPSDT) program. Membership: 3,500 (professionals, paramedical and schools interested in child health). Finances: Professionals, $20; paramedical, $10; Other Sources: Donations, reprint sales. Meetings: Annual, divisions: Illinois, Pacific, South Atlantic. Publications: American Baby, monthly, Judith Notte, editor.

★ 96 ★
AMERICAN ASSOCIATION FOR MUSIC THERAPY
35 West 4th Street, Suite 777   (212) 598-3494
New York, New York 10003   Established 1970

Dr. Jerrold Ross, President
To interest persons in the field of music therapy; to disseminate information to members and other professionals about the discipline; to provide job placement for certified music therapists; to approve programs of colleges and universities, and to certify qualified individuals who meet the Association's

competency standards. Membership: 500 (profession
al, student, and member organization. Finances:
Membership: $15 (student) to $20 (professional), annually. Meetings: Annual, various locations.
Publications: Quarterly Newsletter, quarterly, Carol
Merle-Fishman and Jean Okie, editors; Music Thera-
py--Journal of the American Association for Music
Therapy, annual, Barbara Hesser, editor. Affiliations: National Music Council; National Federation
of Music Clubs; National Association of Schools of
Music.

★ 97 ★

AMERICAN ASSOCIATION FOR REHABILITATION
    THERAPY, INC.
Post Office Box 93   (901) 363-7770
North Little Rock, Arkansas 72114 Established 1950

To promote the use of curative modalities within the
scope, philosophy and approved medical concepts of
rehabilitation; to advance its practices; to advance
the standards of education and training of rehabilitation therapists; to encourage and promote research;
to cooperate with other organizations in the realiza-
tion of common objectives. Membership: 300.
Meetings: Annual, various locations. Publications:
American Archives of Rehabilitation Therapy, 3 times
per year; Rehabilitation Therapy Bulletin, quarterly.

★ 98 ★

AMERICAN ASSOCIATION FOR RESPIRATORY
    THERAPY
1720 Regal Row, Suite 112   (214) 630-3540
Dallas, Texas 75235   Established 1947

To encourage, develop, and provide educational programs for those persons interested in the field of respiratory therapy; to advance the science, technology,
ethics, and art of respiratory therapy through institutes, meetings, lectures, publications, and other
means; to develop and maintain standards for the
practice of respiratory therapy; and represent respiratory therapy to health care organizations, governmental agencies, and the public. Membership: 20,000
(active, associate, student, life, and honorary).
Finances: Membership: Active and associate, $40;
student, $15. Meetings: Annual Conventions, var-
ious locations. Publications: Respiratory Care,
monthly, Phillip Kittredge, editor; AARTimes, monthly, Mary Lynn Gage, editor. Affiliations: National Board for Respiratory Therapy; The American Respiratory Therapy Foundation; The Joint Review Committee for Respiratory Therapy Education.

★ 99 ★

AMERICAN ASSOCIATION FOR SOCIAL
    PSYCHIATRY
c/o Pauline Powers, M.D.
Department of Psychiatry, Box 14
University of Southern Florida Medical School
North 30th Street
Tampa, Florida 33620   Established 1971

S. R. Dean, President; A. Friedland, President
    Elect
To promote the study of the nature, prevention, and
treatment of mental disorders; to promote the physical
and cultural well-being of mankind; to make the
knowledge and practice of social psychiatry available
to other sciences throughout the world and to the
public, including its institutions and governing bodies.
Membership: 600 (fellows, members, associates).
Finances: Membership: Fellows, $20; members,
$25; associates, $15. Meetings: Annual, various
locations. Publications: Bulletin, quarterly,
J. Carleton, editor. Affiliations: World Association for Social Psychiatry.

★ 100 ★

AMERICAN ASSOCIATION FOR THE ADVANCE-
    MENT OF TENSION CONTROL
Post Office Box 8005   (502) 588-6571
Louisville, Kentucky 40208   Established 1973

F. J. McGuigan, Ph.D., Executive Director
To disseminate scientific and technological information on tension control and to incorporate systematic
relaxation in the everyday lives of the people of the
world. Fields of application include: dentistry,
medicine, psychology, physical therapy, education,
speech pathology and human communications. Conducts research. Membership: 750. Meetings:
Annual convention, various locations. Publications:
Newsletter, quarterly; Convention Proceedings, annual.

★ 101 ★

AMERICAN ASSOCIATION FOR THE HISTORY OF
    MEDICINE, INC.
Department of the History of Medicine
Kansas University Medical Center
Rainbow at 39th Streets   (913) 588-7040
Kansas City, Kansas 66103   Established 1925

Robert P. Hudson, M.D., Secretary-Treasurer
Promotes interest, research, and writing in history of
medicine and allied sciences and professions. Membership: 950 (active members [individuals, resident in
United States or Canada], non-resident members,

constituent societies). Finances: Membership: Regular members, $18; family members, $25; constituent societies, $25; student members, $7.50. Awards: William Welch Medal; William Osler Medal; Fielding H. Garrison Lectureship. Meetings: Annual, various locations. Publications: Bulletin of the His History of Medicine, quarterly.

★ 102 ★

AMERICAN ASSOCIATION FOR THE STUDY OF
    HEADACHE
5252 North Western Avenue   (312) 878-5558
Chicago, Illinois 60625   Established 1959

The Organization is composed of doctors who are interested in research into the causes of headache, head pain, and the nature of pain itself. Membership: Approximately 500 (neurologists, psychiatrists, doctor of osteopathy, doctor of dental surgery, doctor of philosophy). Finances: Membership: Annual, $50. Awards: Harold G. Wolff, M.D., Lecture Award, Annual. Meetings: Annual, June. Publications: Headache, bimonthly, Donald J. Dalessio, M.D., editor.

★ 103 ★

AMERICAN ASSOCIATION FOR THE STUDY OF
    LIVER DISEASES
c/o Marcus A. Rothschild, M.D.
Nuclear Medicine Service VA Hospital
First Avenue at East 24th Street   (212) 686-7500
New York, New York 10010   ext. 405, 663, 458
                                 Established 1949

Marcus A. Rothschild, M.D., Secretary
To promote scientific exchange among people interested in the area of liver disease, thereby contributing to the education of physicians interested in this area and improving the quality of patient care. Membership: 750. Finances: Membership: $50 (includes price of new journal to be published); Other Sources: Pharmaceutical companies' support. Meetings: Semiannual, various locations.

★ 104 ★

AMERICAN ASSOCIATION FOR THE STUDY OF
    NEOPLASTIC DISEASES
10607 Miles Avenue   (216) 341-4335
Cleveland, Ohio 44105   Established 1929

Robert H. Jackson, M.D., President
Developed in response to a need for the study of neoplastic diseases, including basic science and clin-

ical investigation, and the relationship of etiologic carcinogens and viral tumor antigens to immuno-diagnosis and immuno-therapy. Membership: 337 (active and emeritus). Finances: Membership: $50 annually. Meetings: Annual, various locations.

★ 105 ★

AMERICAN ASSOCIATION FOR THE SURGERY
    OF TRAUMA
c/o Dr. George F. Sheldon, M.D.
San Francisco General Hospital
Department of Surgery   (415) 821-8814
San Francisco, California 94110   Established 1938

George F. Sheldon, M.D., Secretary
To cultivate and improve the science and art of the surgery of trauma and allied sciences and to elevate the medical profession and all matters as may properly come within its sphere. Membership: Professional group of surgeons specializing in the surgery of trauma. Meetings: Annual, various locations. Publications: Journal of Trauma, monthly.

★ 106 ★

AMERICAN ASSOCIATION FOR THORACIC
    SURGERY
6 Beacon Street, Suite 620   (617) 227-0760
Boston, Massachusetts 02108   Established 1917

William T. Maloney, Executive Secretary
Scientific organization composed of persons interested in the treatment of diseases of the chest, principally by surgical methods. Conducts scientific meetings for exchange of ideas. Membership: 857 (honorary, senior, active, associate). Finances: Membership: Active and associate, $75. Awards: Evarts A. Graham Traveling Fellowship - $35,000 annually. Meetings: Annual, various locations. Publications: Journal of Thoracic and Cardiovascular Surgery, monthly, Dwight C. McGoon, M.D., editor.

★ 107 ★

AMERICAN ASSOCIATION FOR VITAL RECORDS
    AND PUBLIC HEALTH STATISTICS
Bureau of Health Statistics
Post Office Box 2500   (801) 533-6186
Salt Lake City, Utah 84110   Established 1933

The Association provides the only national forum for the study, discussion and solution of the problems related to programs of vital and health statistics by state and local representatives without undue influence of Federal government officials. Membership:

220 (officials of state and local health agencies responsible for registration, tabulation and analysis of public health and other vital statistics). Meetings: Annual, various locations. Publications: Journal, bimonthly.

★ 108 ★

AMERICAN ASSOCIATION FOR WORLD HEALTH:
    U.S. COMMITTEE FOR THE WORLD HEALTH
    ORGANIZATION
2121 Virginia Avenue, N.W.   (202) 861-6922
Washington, D.C. 20037   Established 1953

Ruth W. Lubic, M.D., President; Charles L.
    Williams, Jr., M.D., Executive Vice President
To inform the American people about world health problems and programs, with special reference to the World Health Organization (WHO), and the Pan American Health Organization (PAHO). By working with public and community groups to call attention to problems and to mobilize public support for the programs of WHO and PAHO; to focus public attention on the advantages accruing to all Americans by reason of United States membership in WHO and PAHO. The Association organizes public conferences and assists national and local community groups to organize conferences and seminars on world health topics and assists such groups to find qualified speakers. Organizes an annual observance of WORLD HEALTH DAY (April 7) in cooperation with WHO. Membership: 60 organizations; 500 individuals. Finances: Membership: Individual, $15 annually; contributing members $35 annually; patrons, $100; organization, $200 to $2,500. Lectureships: Harold Diehl lectureship and luncheon, sponsored annually by the Association, at annual meeting of the American Public Health Association. Meetings: Annual, at place and time of Annual Meeting of the American Public Health Association (APHA). Frequent local meetings. Publications: American Review of World Health, annually; Newsletter, quarterly; WHO and PAHO World Health magazines, free to members; pamphlets and literature related to international health problems. Former Name: National Citizes Committee for the World Health Organization.

★ 109 ★

AMERICAN ASSOCIATION OF ANATOMISTS
Medical College of Virginia, Department of
    Anatomy
Box 101, MCV Station   (804) 786-9477
Richmond, Virginia 23298   Established 1888

William P. Jollie, Secretary-Treasurer
To advance the study of anatomical science. Mem-

bership: 2,900 (regular, sustaining associate). Finances: Membership: Regular, $25; foreign, $12; Other Sources: Contributions from sustaining associate members. Meetings: Annual, various locations. Publications: The Anatomical Record, monthly, Aaron J. Ladman, editor; The American Journal of Anatomy, monthly, John E. Pauley, editor; Anatomical News, quarterly. Affiliations: American Association for the Advancement of Science; American Institute for Biological Sciences; National Research Council; Biological Stain Commission; National Society for Medical Research; Association of American Colleges; International Committee on Anatomical Nomenclature.

★ 110 ★

AMERICAN ASSOCIATION OF AVIAN
    PATHOLOGISTS
Department of Veterinary Microbiology
Texas A & M University   (713) 845-5941
College Station, Texas 77843   Established 1957

C. F. Hall, Secretary-Treasurer
The Association promotes research and dissemination of new findings in Avian pathology, sponsors scientific meetings, and publishes scientific materials in the accomplishment of the above objectives. Membership: 540 (members, associate, honorary, life). Finances: Membership: $20; Other Sources: Subscriptions to Journal, advertising and page charges to same. Awards: P. P. Levine Award for the best paper published in each volume of Avian Diseases, $300. AAAP Service Award for contributions to Avian medicine and the AAAP, $300. Meetings: Annual, various locations. Publications: Avian Diseases, quarterly, David P. Anderson, editor; Isolation and Identification of Avian Pathogens; Avian Disease Manual.

★ 111 ★

AMERICAN ASSOCIATION OF BIOANALYSTS
818 Olive, Suite 918   (314) 241-1445
St. Louis, Missouri 63101   Established 1955

David Birenbaum, Administrator
To provide for a common meeting place of individuals teaching and applying the bioanalysis sciences; to encourage research into all phases of bioanalytical tests and testing; to diffuse analytical knowledge for the betterment of the laboratory field, and the benefit of the patient public. The Association operates a Proficiency Testing Service, and Continuing Education program; it also established the American Board of Bioanalysis, an autonomous board to certify laboratory supervisors and directors and accredit labora-

tories. Membership: 750 (directors and owners of independent medical laboratories; university faculty teaching in bioanalytical sciences). Finances: Membership: Director, $200; faculty, $60; Armed Forces, $60; supervisors, $60; Other Sources: Conventions, Proficiency Testing Services. Awards: Herbert Johnstone Memorial Fund; Michael T. Horti Memorial Fund. Meetings: Annual, various locations. Publications: AAB Bulletin, bimonthly, David Birenbaum, Publisher; Test of the Month, monthly, Victor Rodwell, editor; Annual Convention Program; Annual Proficiency Testing Programs. Library: AAB Slide Library.

★ 112 ★
AMERICAN ASSOCIATION OF BLOOD BANKS
1829 L Street, N.W., Suite 608   (202) 872-8333
Washington, D.C. 20036   Established 1948

Lois James, Executive Director
The Association runs non-profit hospital and community blood banks and transfusion services. It is composed of physicians, nurses, medical technologists, and administrators in the blood banking profession. Their goal is to make whole blood available through blood banks, to operate a clearinghouse for exchange of blood and blood credits, and encourage development of blood banks. Membership: 7,500 (institutional, associate and individual members). Meetings: Annual, various locations. Publications: News Brief, semimonthly; Transfusion, bimonthly; Review, quarterly.

★ 113 ★
AMERICAN ASSOCIATION OF BOVINE
    PRACTITIONERS
Box 2319   (317) 494-8741
West Lafayette, Indiana 47906   Established 1966

H. E. Amstutz, Executive Secretary
To endeavor to do all things necessary to promote the interests, to improve the public stature, and to increase the knowledge of veterinarians in the field of dairy and beef cattle practice. Membership: 2,800 (veterinarians interested in bovine practice). Finances: Membership: $25; Other Sources: Registration and exhibit fees at annual meetings. Meetings: Annual, various locations. Publications: Bovine Practitioner, annually, Eric Williams, editor; Annual Directory; Newsletter, monthly; Proceedings of Annual Meeting.

★ 114 ★
AMERICAN ASSOCIATION OF CERTIFIED
    ORTHOPTISTS
Duke University, Eye Center
Box 3802   (919) 684-2038
Durham, North Carolina 27706   Established 1940

Judy H. Seaber, President
Encourages the development and exchange of new ideas and techniques in orthoptics, stimulates professional growth by assisting in postgraduate instruction courses, and endeavors to advise individual orthoptists who have special or unusual problems. Membership: 450 (Orthoptists certified by American Orthoptic Council). Finances: Membership: Regular, $50 annually; Other Sources: Sale of brochures and journals, postgraduate instruction courses. Awards: Lancaster Memorial Award for meritorious contribution to orthoptics; Scobee Award for best original paper for the year; Honor Certificate; Merit Award. Meetings: Annual, with American Academy of Ophthalmology; Regional Meetings, annual. Publications: American Orthoptic Journal, annual, Eugene Helveston, M.D., editor; Prism, quarterly, Irene Leyman, editor. Affiliations: American Orthoptic Council; International Orthoptic Association; Joint Commission of Allied Health in Ophthalmology.

★ 115 ★
AMERICAN ASSOCIATION OF CLINICAL
    UROLOGISTS
2017 Walnut   (215) 569-3650
Philadelphia, Pennsylvania 19103   Established 1969

Brent H. Farber, Executive Secretary
The purpose of the American Association of Clinical Urologists is to promote the science of urology in the best interests of the public and medical profession by: the study and evaluation of socio-economic factors which affect the practice of urology; informing the membership of legislation and government actions which concern and involve the practice of urology; advancing and developing the art and science of clinical urology; continually improving the professional standards of urology and encouraging urological education; and by promoting cooperation among all disciplines interested in diseases of the genito-urinary tract, and by advising other professional groups concerning urology. Membership: 750 (practicing urologists who are members of the American Urological Association or one of its sections, and who are members of the American Medical Association). Finances: Membership: $65 annually; Other Sources: Annual meeting sponsors. Meetings: Annual, in conjunction with the American Urological Association. Publications: Monthly Newsletter.

★ 116 ★
AMERICAN ASSOCIATION OF COLLEGES OF
    OSTEOPATHIC MEDICINE
4720 Montgomery Lane, Suite 609   (301) 654-5600
Washington, D.C. 20014   Established 1970

Anthony J. McNevin, Executive Director
To promote the advancement and enrichment of education in osteopathic medicine and of the osteopathic profession. Membership: 13 accredited osteopathic colleges. Finances: Membership: $16,500; Other Sources: Grants. Meetings: Quarterly, various locations. Publications: Newsletter. Affiliations: Council of Deans; Council of Student Council Presidents; Educational Council on Osteopathic Principles; Section of Student Affairs Officers; Section of Chairman of Departments of General/Family Practice.

★ 117 ★
AMERICAN ASSOCIATION OF COLLEGES OF
    PHARMACY
4630 Montgomery Avenue
Suite 201   (301) 654-9060
Bethesda, Maryland 20014

Christopher A. Rodowskas, Jr., Ph.D., Executive
    Director
The Association was founded to promote the advancement of pharmaceutical education, research, and service in all appropriately accredited institutions that offer programs for the education of pharmacists; to stimulate the production, exchange, and dissemination of ideas and information among pharmaceutical educators, educators of other health professions, and educators in the community of higher education; to study and investigate the educational aspects concerned with providing and maintaining optimal drug usage by the public; to communicate with the public, the pharmacy profession, other health professions, and the community of higher education to improve their understanding of the importance of proper drug utilization in relation to the general health and well-being of individuals and society; to establish and maintain liaison with other health professions, governmental and other appropriate agencies, and members of the pharmaceutical industry and their associations that may further the development, support, and improvement of pharmaceutical education, research and service; to assume its advisory role for the development of policies and standards used for the accreditation of programs of pharmaceutical education; and to advise and provide consultants and consultant services regarding pharmaceutical education programs. Membership: 1,109 individuals, 72 colleges, 19 affiliate institutional. Finances: Membership: $35 individual; $5,000 institutional; Other Sources: Grants from the American Foundation for Pharmaceutical Education.

Awards: Lyman Award; Volwiler Award. Meetings: Annual meeting and Teacher Seminar, various locations. Publications: American Journal of Pharmaceutical Education, quarterly; AACP News, monthly; Roster of Teaching Personnel in Colleges of Pharmacy, annually.

★ 118 ★
AMERICAN ASSOCIATION OF COLLEGES OF
    PODIATRIC MEDICINE
20 Chevy Chase Circle   (202) 537-4950
Washington, D.C. 20015   Established 1932

Richard G. Allen, President; Richard Baerg, M.D.,
    Vice President; Robert A. Capone, Acting Executive Director
To seek improvement of podiatric education commensurate to scope of podiatric practice and health, safety and welfare of the public; to coordinate and represent the interests of podiatric education nationally; to serve as a data collection, research and information center for podiatric education; to seek and develop means of accomplishing the goals for podiatric education both in quality and quantity. Membership: 238 (colleges, hospitals, faculty, individual). Finances: Membership: $20; Other Sources: Colleges, $26,000; Individual and faculty, $20. Meetings: Annual, various locations; Executive Committee meeting, quarterly. Publications: Journal of Podiatric Medical Education, quarterly, Robert A. Capone, editor. Library: American Podiatry Association. Affiliations: American Podiatry Association Federation of Podiatry Board; National Board of Podiatry Examiners; American Board of Podiatric Surgery; Federation of Associations of Schools for the Health Professions; Coalition for Health Funding; Association Academic Health Centers.

★ 119 ★
AMERICAN ASSOCIATION OF CRITICAL-CARE
    NURSES
Post Office Box C-19528   (714) 752-8191
Irvine, California 92713   Established 1969

Sally Millar, R.N., President
Mandated by charter to provide continuing education for critical-care nurses. Membership: 37,000. Finances: Membership: $37.50. Meetings: Annual, various locations. Publications: Heart and Lung, The Journal of Critical Care, bimonthly; Focus on AACN, bimonthly.

★ 120 ★
AMERICAN ASSOCIATION OF DENTAL EDITORS
8013 Matterhorn Court, F-211
Crown Point, Indiana 46307   Established 1935

Velma Child, Executive Secretary
To engage in all those activities which will tend to promote, directly or indirectly, the advancement of all phases of dental journalism and dental literature. Membership: Approximately 325 (editors, authors and others interested in dental journalism). Finances: Membership: $20 to $55. Awards: Distinguished Service Award, annual. Meetings: Annual, various locations, in conjunction with annual session of the American Dental Association. Publications: Editors' Journal, 3 times per year.

★ 121 ★
AMERICAN ASSOCIATION OF DENTAL EXAMINERS
211 East Chicago Avenue
Suite 1846   (312) 642-2254
Chicago, Illinois 60611   Established 1883

Oscar E. Hanscom, Secretary-Treasurer
To provide for program and research to support the boards of dentistry throughout the United States. Activities include seminars, annual meetings, conferences, etc. Membership: 700 (active board members, individual active). Finances: Membership: Active and individual active, $25; member agency, $300; Other Sources: Grants from philanthropic organizations. Awards: Dentist Citizen of the Year Award; Award of Merit. Meetings: Annual, various locations. Publications: The Board Bulletin, quarterly, Dr. Edward C. Maloof, editor.

★ 122 ★
AMERICAN ASSOCIATION OF DENTAL SCHOOLS
1625 Massachusetts Avenue   (202) 667-9433
Washington, D.C. 20036   Established 1923

Harry W. Bruce, Jr., D.D.S., Executive Director
Objectives of the Association are: to stimulate the production, exchange, and dissemination of ideas and information among dental educators, educators of other health professions, and educators in the community of higher education; to study and investigate the educational aspects concerned with providing and maintaining optimal oral health care for the public; to communicate with the public, other health professions, and the community of higher education to improve their understanding of the importance of oral health care in relation to the general health and well-being of individuals and society; to establish and maintain liaison with governmental and other appropriate agencies that may further the development, support, and improvement of dental education, research, and service; to assume its major responsibility for the development of policies and standards used for the accreditation of dental education programs; to advise and provide consultants and consultation services regarding dental education programs. Membership: 3,988; institutional members, 208; individual membership, 2,841; retired members, 30; student membership, 768; honorary membership, 8. Finances: Membership: Individual, $30; student, $10; retired, $15; institutional membership assessed on a sliding dues scale; Other Sources: Grants, publications, application fees. Meetings: Annual Session, approximately 1,600 attendees; Council of Deans meeting, approximately 300 attendees. Publications: Journal of Dental Education, monthly, Harry M. Bohannan, editor; Bulletin of Dental Education, monthly, Owen R. Terry, editor.

★ 123 ★
AMERICAN ASSOCIATION OF DIABETES EDUCATORS
North Woodbury Road
Box 56   (609) 589-4831
Pitman, New Jersey 08071   Established 1974

Jeanne Panuncialman, Secretary
AADE is an independent, interdisciplinary, not-for-profit organization dedicated to providing educational opportunities for the professional growth and development of its members. AADE is dedicated to promote and aid the growth and development of quality diabetes education in the United States for the diabetic consumer. AADE works to foster communication and cooperation among individuals and organizations involved in diabetes education, nationally and internationally. Membership: 1,428 (July 1 through June 30, membership year); active (person working full- or part-time as diabetes educator); associate (person with interest in diabetes education); institutional (institution or not-for-profit organization with full- or part-time diabetes education program). Finances: Membership: Active, $30; associate, $25; institutional, $100; Other Sources: Funding from outside sources accepted to further educational needs of members. Awards: Allene Van Son Award for diabetes teaching tools, annually; Carole Sinicki Manuscript Award for articles printed in "The Diabetes Educator", annually; Ames Grant "How A Diabetic Learns" annually; Distinguished Service Award to member for loyal and outstanding service, annually. Meetings: Annual, various locations. Publications: The Diabetes Educator (journal), quarterly (April, July, October, and January), Allice Holyoke, R.N., M.S., editor; Newsletter, Bimonthly.

★ 124 ★

AMERICAN ASSOCIATION OF ELECTROMYOGRAPHY
   AND ELECTRODIAGNOSIS

732 Marquette Bank Building   (507) 288-0100
Rochester, Minnesota 55901   Established 1953

Ella M. VanLaningham, Executive Secretary
The general purpose is to increase and extend as
widely as possible the knowledge of electromyography
and electrodiagnosis and to promote the professional
association of physicians and surgeons most interested
in those fields. Membership: 1,100 (active, associate, corresponding and sustaining associate). Finances: Membership: $40 annual dues. Awards:
Student/resident award for best paper submitted for
presentation at annual meeting. Meetings: Annual,
featuring Edward H. Lambert Lecture (invited guest
speaker of international reputation). Publications:
Minimonographs and case reports, abstracts, periodically, AAEE Education Committee (editor); newsletters,
periodically, AAEE Office (editor); handouts for annual course and meeting. Affiliations: International
Federation of Societies for Electroencephalography and
Clinical Neurophysiology; National Society for Medical Research; National Committee for Research in
Neurological and Communicative Disorders.

★ 125 ★

AMERICAN ASSOCIATION OF ENDODONTISTS
ADA Building
211 East Chicago Avenue
Suite 830   (312) 266-7255
Chicago, Illinois 60611   Established 1943

Irma S. Kudo, Executive Director
To promote interchange of ideas on methods of pulp
conservation and treatment; to stimulate research
studies; to assist in establishing study clubs; to
sponsor the American Board of Endodontics and the
AAE Endowment and Memorial Foundation; to sponsor
continuing education courses for both the specialist
and the general practitioner, and to sponsor the Graduate Student Section. Membership: 2,700 (active,
student, honorary, life, associate, foreign, affiliate
and retired). Finances: Membership: Active, $150;
foreign, $150; student, $25; associate, $150.
Awards: Student Awards to outstanding dental students. Meetings: Annual, various locations. Publications: Journal of Endodontics, monthly, Irving J.
Naidorf, D.D.S., editor; Annotated Glossary of
Terms Used in Endodontics. Affiliations: American
Board of Endodontics; AAE Endowment and Memorial
Foundation.

★ 126 ★

AMERICAN ASSOCIATION OF EQUINE
   PRACTITIONERS

Route 5, 22363 Hillcrest Circle
Golden, Colorado 80401   Established 1954

Wayne O. Kester, Executive Director
To elevate the standards of practice in this branch of
the veterinary profession; to further research and
knowledge of equine diseases with the purpose of improving the quality of practice; to enlighten various
agencies on the need for better methods in horse racing and to assit in formulating them, especially as
they pertain to the profession; to improve the relationships of the veterinary profession with racing commissions, racing associations and horsemen; to promote
good fellowship among members. Membership: 3,100
active and 320 associate (limited to members from
foreign countries). Finances: Membership: $50.
Awards: Annual membership in Grayson Foundation
and Morris Animal Foundation; support of equine research projects in various colleges and universities.
Meetings: Annual, various locations. Publications:
Proceedings of Annual Meeting, Dr. Frank J. Milne,
editor; Newsletter, 3 annually, Dr. Wayne O.
Kester, editor; Membership Directory, and other
specialty publications.

★ 127 ★

AMERICAN ASSOCIATION OF FOOT SPECIALISTS
1801 Vauxhall Road   (201) 688-1616
Union, New Jersey 07083   Established 1958

Jerome J. Erman, M.D., Executive Secretary
To conduct annual education program; disseminate
information on the care and protection of the foot.
Membership: 1,005 (licensed, practicing podiatrists).
Awards: Scholarships. Meetings: Annual, various
locations. Publications: President's News Letter,
quarterly; Program Journal, annual. Affiliations:
Sponsors the American College of Foot Specialists and
the American Board of Podiatric Dermatology.

★ 128 ★

AMERICAN ASSOCIATION OF FOUNDATIONS
   FOR MEDICAL CARE

11325 Seven Locks Road   (301) 983-0404
Potomac, Maryland 20854   Established 1970

Boyd Thompson, Executive Director
To provide a better health care system for the American people; to guide and assist local medical societies in creating Foundations; to coordinate the growth
and development of Foundations. Membership:
Foundations for medical care.

★ 129 ★

AMERICAN ASSOCIATION OF FUND-RAISING
    COUNSEL, INC.
500 Fifth Avenue   (212) 524-5468
New York, New York 10036   Established 1935

John J. Schwartz, President
Organization of professional firms engaged in organizing, directing and counseling fund-raising efforts.
Activities include establishment and enforcement of
code of ethics in fund raising, research in matters related to philanthropy, dissemination of information on
fund-raising activities, counsel or organizations con-
templating fund raising, interchange of information
between members, advancement of professional practices in fund-raising, cooperation in state and federal
legislation controlling charitable solicitation. Membership: 31 (individual fund-raising companies).
Finances: Membership: By assessment of income.
Meetings: At least 3 times per year, New York City.
Publications: Giving-USA, annually; Bulletin,
monthly.

★ 130 ★

AMERICAN ASSOCIATION OF GENITOURINARY
    SURGEONS
c/o Dr. Ralph A. Straffon
9500 Euclid Avenue   (216) 444-5592
Cleveland, Ohio 44106   Established 1887

Ralph A. Straffon, M.D., Secretary-Treasurer
Professional society of physicians specializing in
genito-urinary surgery; sponsors an annual scientific
meeting. Membership: 166 (honorary members, corresponding members, fellows, active members and inactive members. Finances: Membership: Active,
$75; fellows, $35. Medals: Barringer Medal,
established 1973, presented biennially for outstanding
work in research of cancer; Keyes Medal, awarded
by Committee to person who has made notable contribution to progress of urology. Meetings: Annual,
various locations.

★ 131 ★

AMERICAN ASSOCIATION OF GYNECOLOGIC
    LAPAROSCOPISTS
11239 South Lakewood Boulevard (213) 862-8181
Downey, California 90241   Established 1972

Jordan M. Phillips, M.D., President
To teach, demonstrate, exchange ideas, distribute literature; hold meetings, seminars and conferences;
stimulate interest in gynecological laparoscopy; maintain and improve medical standards in medical schools
and hospitals regarding gynecological laparoscopy;

maintain and improve the ethics, practice and efficiency of the medical practice pertaining to obstetrics
and laparoscopy. Membership: 4,000 (obstetricians
and gynecologists). Meetings: Annual Convention,
various locations. Publications: Gynecological
Laparoscopy: Principles and Techniques; Microsurgery
in Gynecology; Endoscopy in Gynecology.

★ 132 ★

AMERICAN ASSOCIATION OF HEALTH DATA
    SYSTEMS, INC.
Post Office Box 18480   (216) 229-9744
Cleveland Heights, Ohio 44118 Established 1972

Ronald A. Morley, President; William H. Kincaid,
    Executive Director
The purpose of the Association is to aid, assist and
encourage the establishment of non-profit, regional
health data systems; to conduct scientific studies with
regard to the quality, utilization and effectiveness of
health care and health care agencies; to educate
those involved in furnishing, administering and financing health care as to the deficiencies in the quality,
utilization and effectiveness of health care and health
care agencies; and to bring to the attention of those
involved in furnishing, administering and financing
health care proposals to improve the quality, utilization and effectiveness of health care and health care
agencies. Membership: 16 active regional data
services; 6 associate organizations; 6 participating
organizations. Finances: Membership: Associate,
$150; active, $150 plus 50 cents per 1,000 dis-
charges annually; Other Sources: Attendance fees
from annual education meeting. Meetings: Annual,
various locations.

★ 133 ★

AMERICAN ASSOCIATION OF HOMES FOR THE
    AGING
1050 17th Street, N.W.   (202) 296-5960
Washington, D.C. 20036   Established 1961

The national organization representing the nonprofit,
voluntary and governmental Homes, Facilities and
Housing for the Aging, the Association provides the
united, nationwide means for identifying and solving
problems of mutual concern, thereby enabling the
Homes and Facilities to protect and advance the interests of the residents and patients served. Membership: Over 1,700 Homes and Facilities, plus a
large number of individuals and organizations. Finances: Membership dues; grants and contributions.
Awards: Awards of Honor and Distinguished Service
Awards to individuals; President's Citations to persons and organizations. Meetings: Annual, various

locations; regional and local seminars, workshops. Publications: AAHA News Scene; Washington Report; Legal News; Directory of Nonprofit Homes and Facilities.

★ 134 ★

AMERICAN ASSOCIATION OF HOSPITAL
    CONSULTANTS
2341 Jefferson Davis Highway
Suite 830   (703) 528-2700
Arlington, Virginia 22202   Established 1948

Vaughan A. Smith, President
To provide a means of education, including the exchange of information and experiences among the members; to advance the science and art of area-wide and individual hospital administration and organization and to further the efficacy of local and regional hospital, health and related programs; to establish and maintain a code of ethics for those engaged in hospital consultation and to promote the highest possible standards of hospital consultation services. Membership: 135 (nominee, associate, member, fellowship, affiliate, emeritus, honorary). Finances: Membership: $150 to $1,000 depending on membership category; Other Sources: Management fees and education programs. Awards: AAHC Award of Merit; Honorary Fellowship. Meetings: Annual Business Meeting and Continuing Education Program; Mid-Year Business Meeting and Continuing Education Program; Institutes on Hospital/Health Care Planning, 3 per year. Publications: Association News (for members only), monthly, Vaughan Smith, editor; Roster of Members, annual, Vaughan Smith, editor. Affiliations: Foundation for Health Education and Applied Research.

★ 135 ★

AMERICAN ASSOCIATION OF HOSPITAL DENTISTS
University of Minnesota
School of Dentistry, HSA 7174
515 Delaware Street, S.E.   (612) 376-4111
Minneapolis, Minnesota 55455   Established 1960

R. Pat Hylton, Jr., D.D.S., Secretary
The Association exists to promote total, comprehensive, dental health care in the hospital environment; to further the involvement of dentists in patient care, education and research in the hospital environment; to cooperate with and assist other health professions and agencies in the development of sound programs for total health care; to provide continuing education and training of the general practicing dentist and related specialist to better care for the dental needs of patients in the hospital environment; to serve as a

representative and spokesman for all dentists involved in giving care for the hospitalized patient; to provide a liaison among medicine, the hospital and the dental profession. Membership: 700 (generalists, specialists, residents in dentistry who are actively associated in full or part time hospital practice). Finances: Membership: Active, $48; associate, $48. Awards: Annual honorary award and lecture. Meetings: Annual. Publications: Journal of Hospital Dental Practice, quarterly; Newsletter, quarterly.

★ 136 ★

AMERICAN ASSOCIATION OF HOSPITAL
    PODIATRISTS, INC.
420 74th Street   (212) 836-1017
Brooklyn, New York 11209   Established 1950

Louis J. Arancia, M.D., Executive Director
To foster the elevation of the standards of podiatry practices in hospitals and health institutions; to standardize hospital podiatry procedures, charting, recording forms and methods; to promote improved harmony and understanding among personnel in podiatry and allied health professions; to assist in the educational and teaching programs of health institutions and hospitals and to foster establishment of podiatric service in health institutional affiliation and the development of podiatric internships and residencies in hospitals and institutions. Membership: 600 (podiatrists affiliated with hospitals). Meetings: Annual, with American Podiatry Association, various locations. Publications: The Hospital Podiatrist, semiannual; Membership Roster, annual. Affiliations: American Podiatry Association.

★ 137 ★

AMERICAN ASSOCIATION OF IMMUNOLOGISTS
9650 Rockville Pike   (301) 530-7178
Bethesda, Maryland 20014   Established 1913

Henry Metzger, M.D., Secretary-Treasurer
To advance knowledge of immunology and related disciplines, and to facilitate interchange of ideas and information among investigators in immunology and the various fields. Membership: 2,800 (active, emeritus, honorary). Meetings: Annually with Federation of American Societies for Experimental Biology. Publications: Journal of Immunology, monthly, Joseph D. Feldman, editor. Affiliations: A constituent society of the Federation of American Societies for Experimental Biology and the International Union of Immunological Societies.

AMERICAN ASSOCIATION OF INDUSTRIAL
NURSES, INC.
   See: American Association of Occupational
         Health Nurses, Inc.

★ 138 ★

AMERICAN ASSOCIATION OF INDUSTRIAL
         VETERINARIANS
Post Office Box 708   (317) 462-8480
Greenfield, Indiana 46140   Established 1956

Gary R. Sampson, D.V.M.
The purpose is to promote the objectives of veterinarians employed in industry. Membership: 400 veterinarians employed in industry. Finances: Membership: $10 annually. Awards: Industrial Veteri-
narian of the Year Award. Meetings: Annual,
various locations in conjunction with the American
Veterinary Medical Association.

★ 139 ★

AMERICAN ASSOCIATION OF MEDICAL
         ASSISTANTS
1 East Wacker Drive, Suite 2110   (312) 944-2722
Chicago, Illinois 60601   Established 1956

Ina L. Yenerich, RT, CMA-AC, Executive Director
Dedicated to the professional advancement of administrative and clinical personnel employed in physicians'
offices, clinics, hospitals and other medical facilities.
Activities include continuing education services, such
as approval of Continuing Education Unit programs and
guided home study courses; certification examinations
in basic and administrative and clinical specialities;
and cooperation with the Committee on Allied Health
Education and Accreditation to accredit post-secondary
medical assisting programs. Membership: 16,300
(personnel directly supervised by a physician, including nurses [RN's and LP/VN's], secretaries, recep-
tionists, laboratory technicians, bookkeepers, etc.
Finances: Membership: National dues, $25 annually;
additional local and state dues vary; Other Sources:
Examination fees; journal advertising; miscellaneous
grants. Awards: Maxine Williams Scholarship;
Dorothy and Henry Bodner Loan Fund for Education.
Meetings: Annual Convention, various locations.
Publications: The Professional Medical Assistant
(journal), bimonthly, Susan S. Croy, editor; Guided
Study Course on Anatomy, Terminology and Physiol-
ogy (workbook and cassettes); The Humanistic Medical Assistant (guided study course in human relations).
Library: American Association of Medical Assistants,
1,000 volumes (for in-office, reference use only).

★ 140 ★

AMERICAN ASSOCIATION OF MEDICO-LEGAL
         CONSULTANTS
Park Towne Place North
2200 Benjamin Franklin Parkway   (215) 561-2121
Philadelphia, Pennsylvania 19130 Established 1972

Evelyn M. Goldstein, President
The Association acts as a neutral screening mechanism
for medical malpractice cases. It is a non-profit
corporation. Membership: 90 physician-attorneys;
450 physicians. Library: AAMC, 300 volumes.

★ 141 ★

AMERICAN ASSOCIATION OF NEPHROLOGY
         NURSES AND TECHNICIANS
North Woodbury Road
Box 56   (609) 589-2187
Pitman, New Jersey 08071

Carmella Bocchino, President; Mary P. Dunlevy,
         Executive Secretary
To promote knowledge about the care of patients
with renal disease among those in the field and the
general public. Membership: 4,800 (full RN and
dialysis technicians; associate, dieticians, social
workers). Finances: Membership: Full, $35; asso-
ciate, $30; Other Sources: Solicitation from sup-
pliers, journal, meeting and seminar fees. Meetings:
Annual, various locations, regional and learning
institutes. Publications: AANNT Journal, quarterly,
Jean McMullen, editor; AANNT Newsletter, bimonthly, Nina Fieldon, editor.

★ 142 ★

AMERICAN ASSOCIATION OF NEUROLOGICAL
         SURGEONS
625 North Michigan Avenue
Suite 1519   (312) 944-4205
Chicago, Illinois 60611   Established 1931

Carl H. Hauber, Executive Director
Advancement of neurological surgery and related sciences; improvement of patient care; support of
meaningful basic and clinical research; and provision
of leadership in undergraduate, graduate and continuing education and promotion of the administrative facilities necessary to achieve these goals. Membership: 2,300 (active, foreign, associate, corresponding, candidate, lifetime, honorary). Finances:
Dues from membership; grants for study of particular
projects. Publications: Journal of Neurosurgery,
monthly, Henry G. Schwartz, M.D., editor.

★ 143 ★

AMERICAN ASSOCIATION OF NEURO-
PATHOLOGISTS
Department of Pathology
University of Iowa Hospitals and
Clinics   (319) 353-3429
Iowa City, Iowa 52242   Established 1928

Michael Noel Hart, M.D., Secretary-Treasurer
To advance the sciences of neuropathology and conduct scientific meetings in this field. Membership:
586 (active, associate, affiliate). Finances: Membership: Active, $30; associate, $25; affiliate,
$15. Awards: Two awards presented at annual
meetings for best papers. Meetings: Annual, various locations.

★ 144 ★

AMERICAN ASSOCIATION OF NEUROSURGICAL
NURSES
625 North Michigan Avenue
Suite 1519   (312) 944-4280
Chicago, Illinois 60611   Established 1968

Rita Shafer, Executive Secretary
To foster interest, education and high standards of
practice in the field of neurosurgical nursing; to encourage continuing growth in the field, and to provide a medium for communication between neurosurgical nurses in the United States and Canada. Has
developed clinical care curriculum for Neurosurgical
Nursing Practice and Certification Examination.
Membership: 1,000 (registered neurosurgical nurses;
active members, and those in allied fields such as
neurological nursing and rehabilitation, associate members). Meetings: Annual, in April, various locations. Publications: Journal of Neurosurgical Nursing, quarterly; Synapse, bimonthly.

★ 145 ★

AMERICAN ASSOCIATION OF NURSE
ANESTHETISTS
216 Higgins Road   (312) 692-7050
Park Ridge, Illinois 60068   Established 1931

The Association keeps its members informed of advances made in the science of anesthesia. It encourages continuing education following graduation
and provides its members with recognized professional
standing. Membership: Nurses who have passed the
C.R.N.A. qualifying examination. Publications:
Journal of the American Association of Nurse Anesthetists.

★ 146 ★

AMERICAN ASSOCIATION OF OBSTETRICIANS
AND GYNECOLOGISTS
c/o Edgar L. Makowski
4200 East 9th Avenue   (303) 394-7616
Denver, Colorado 80262   Established 1888

Edgar L. Makowski, M.D., Secretary
The Association's intent is to cultivate and promote
all knowledge relating to obstetrics and gynecology.
Membership: 217 (honorary fellows, life fellows,
fellows). Finances: Membership: $150. Awards:
Joseph Price Memorial Lectureship and AAOG Foundation Prize Thesis. Meetings: Annual, September,
various locations; mid-year, in Spring, various locations. Publications: Transactions of AAOG, annually, Richard F. Mattingly, M.D., editor.

★ 147 ★

AMERICAN ASSOCIATION OF OCCUPATIONAL
HEALTH NURSES, INC.
575 Lexington Avenue   (212) 355-7733
New York, New York 10022   Established 1942

Matilda A. Babbitz, R.N., M.A., COHN, Executive Director
Professional organization of nurses engaged in the
specialty field of occupational health nursing. Its
purpose is to maintain the honor and character of the
nursing profession; to improve community health by
bettering nursing service to workers; to develop and
promote standards for OHN and OHN nursing service;
to stimulate interest in and provide a forum for the
discussion of problems in the field of OHN; and to
stimulate OHN participation in all nursing activities,
local, state and national. Membership: 11,500
(registered nurses [active, associate, inactive]). Finances: Membership: $50 annually. Awards:
Annual Education Achievement Award; Annual Membership Award. Meetings: Annual, various locations, with American Occupational Medical Association and American Occupational Health Conference.
Publications: Occupational Health Nursing, monthly,
Margaret Carnine, R.N., editor; AAOHN Briefs,
bimonthly; manuals, guides, brochures, statements
on occupational health nursing. Library: Library
of the American Association of Occupational Health
Nurses. Former Name: American Association of
Industrial Nurses, Inc.

★ 148 ★

AMERICAN ASSOCIATION OF OPHTHALMOLOGY
1100 17th Street, N.W.
Suite 901
Washington, D.C. 20036   (202) 833-3447
                               Established 1956

Lawrence A. Zupan, Executive Secretary
To study and disseminate information to the medical profession and the public relating to scientific eye care; to promote conservation of vision and prevention of blindness through more effective utilization of scientific knowledge of ophthalmology and related branches of medicine. Publishes and distributes monographs, reports, pamphlets to the public and profession; provides exhibits at medical and lay meetings; provides consultative services to writers for lay publications in matters pertaining to eye care. Membership: Over 5,000 (physicians practicing ophthalmology). Finances: Membership: Professional, Free-$150; Other Sources: Sale of pamphlets and reports. Meetings: Annual, various locations. Publications: The Ophthalmologist, bimonthly; reports and monographs. Affiliations: State Ophthalmological Societies.

★ 149 ★
AMERICAN ASSOCIATION OF ORAL AND
    MAXILLOFACIAL SURGEONS
211 East Chicago Avenue
Suite 930   (312) 642-6446
Chicago, Illinois 60611   Established 1918

Bernard J. Degen, II, Executive Director
The Association's purposes are to contribute to the public welfare by advancement of the profession of dentistry and in particular the specialty of oral and maxillofacial surgery; to foster programs in education, research, standards of practice and scientific investigation in the specialty of oral and maxillofacial surgery; and to provide, among its members, opportunities for social and professional community. Membership: 3,800 (active, affiliate, life, retired and honorary). Finances: Membership: $300; Other Sources: Contributions. Awards: Research Fellowship; Research Recognition Award; Distinguished Service Award; Committeeman Award; Honorary Membership. Meetings: Annual, various locations; semiannual, Clinical Congresses, various locations. Publications: ASOS Forum, bimonthly, Dr. Daniel M. Laskin, editor; Journal of Oral Surgery, monthly, Dr. Daniel M. Laskin, editor; Membership publications, Annual Meeting Program, Clinical Congress Program. Affiliations: State Societies. Former Name: American Society of Oral Surgeons.

★ 150 ★
AMERICAN ASSOCIATION OF ORTHODONTISTS
460 North Lindberg Boulevard   (314) 993-1700
St. Louis, Missouri 63141   Established 1900

James E. Brophy, Executive Director

To promote the art and science of orthodontics. Membership: 8,000 (active). Finances: Membership: Active, $275. Awards: Milo Hellman Research Award; Albert H. Ketcham Award; Distinguished Service Scroll; Harry Sicher First Research Essay Award; Special Student Award. Meetings: Annual, various locations. Publications: American Journal of Orthodontics, monthly, Wayne G. Watson, editor; Newsletter, quarterly, James E. Brophy, editor. Library: Charles R. Baker Reference Library, 6,000 volumes. Affiliations: Great Lakes Society of Orthodontists; Northeastern Society of Orthodontists; Midwestern Society of Orthodontists; Pacific Coast Society of Orthodontists; Rocky Mountain Society of Orthodontists; Southern Society of Orthodontists; Southwestern Society of Orthodontists; Middle Atlantic Society of Orthodontists.

★ 151 ★
AMERICAN ASSOCIATION OF PASTORAL
    COUNSELORS
3000 Connecticut Avenue
Suite 300   (202) 387-0031
Washington, D.C. 20008   Established 1963

James W. Ewing, Ph.D., Executive Director
To set standards and establish criteria for the adequate training and practice of pastoral counseling; to provide certification for religious professionals engaged in counseling. Membership: 1,800 (clergy and other religious professionals of all faiths). Meetings: Annual, various locations. Publications: Journal of Pastoral Care, quarterly; Newsletter, bimonthly; directories and handbooks.

★ 152 ★
AMERICAN ASSOCIATION OF PATHOLOGISTS
9650 Rockville Pike   (301) 530-7130
Bethesda, Maryland 20014   Established 1900

Kenneth M. Endicott, M.D., Executive Officer
The advancement of the knowledge of disease. Activities include sponsorship of an annual scientific meeting. Membership: Restricted to pathologists and bacteriologists who can show evidence of creditable research in pathology or bacteriology. Finances: Membership: $70 annually; Other Sources: Sale of journal to non-members. Awards: Gold Headed Cane, Rous-Whipple Research, both awarded to acknowledge outstanding achievement in medical research. Meetings: Annual, various locations. Publications: The American Journal of Pathology, monthly, Donald B. Hackel, M.D., editor.

★ 153 ★

AMERICAN ASSOCIATION OF PHYSICIANS'
  ASSISTANTS

880 Third Avenue   (212) 688-7994
New York, New York 10022   Established 1972

Paul F. Palace, Executive Director
The purpose of AAPA is to plan, develop, and implement programs and activities which provide the physician's assistant with a progressive, active, and effective professional association operating in concordance
with established medical practitioners. Membership:
2,500 physicians' assistants in each of the currently
defined health, education, and welfare categories.
Finances: Membership; Regular, $35; student, $15.
Meetings: Annual conference, various locations. Publications: AAPA Newsletter, monthly, Paul F. Palace,
editor.

★ 154 ★

AMERICAN ASSOCIATION OF PHYSICISTS IN
  MEDICINE

500 North Michigan Avenue   (312) 661-1700
Chicago, Illinois 60611   Established 1958

Sharon Pierce, Executive Director
To promote the application of physics to medicine and
biology; to encourage interest and training in medical
physics and related fields; to prepare and disseminate
technical information in medical physics. Membership: 2,000 (junior, associate, full, corporate). Finances: Membership: Full, $45 annually; associate,
$45 annually; junior, $30 annually; corporate, $250
annually. Awards: Coolidge Award for Excellence
in Medical Physics, annual. Meetings: Annual,
various locations. Publications: Medical Physics,
bimonthly, Edward Siegel, editor.

★ 155 ★

AMERICAN ASSOCIATION OF PLASTIC SURGEONS
236 Emerson Hall
1100 West Michigan   (317) 637-4598
Indianapolis, Indiana 46223   Established 1921

The Association aims to stimulate and advance knowledge of the science and art of plastic surgery and
thereby improve and elevate the standards of practice
of this specialty. Membership: 300 (active, senior,
honorary); membership by invitation (sponsored by a
fellow). Finances: Initiation fee, $100; annual
dues, $100. Awards: Honorary Award; Honorary
Fellowship; James Barret Brown Award; Clinician of
the Year. Lectureship: Kiskadden Lecture.

★ 156 ★

AMERICAN ASSOCIATION OF POISON CONTROL
  CENTERS

c/o Anthony S. Manoguerra, Pharmacy D.
University of California Medical Center
225 Dickinson Street   (714) 294-6000
San Diego, California 92103   Established 1958

Anthony S. Manoguerra, Pharm.D., Secretary-
  Treasurer
To prevent poisonings, to assemble information on potential hazards of household products and medicines
around the home, to advise on the prevention, diagnosis and treatment of acute poisonings, to establish
standards for regional poison centers, to advice industry and government in areas of toxicology. Activities include sponsorship of an annual meeting, preparation and distribution of educational materials, development of standards for poison centers, development
and administration of a self-assessment examination for
persons working in poison centers. Membership: 500
(physicians, pharmacists, nurses, pharmacologists,
toxicologists). Finances: Membership: Individual,
$25; institutional, $100; Other Sources: Grants for
the development of educational materials on poison
prevention. Meetings: Annual, with American
Academy of Clinical Toxicology. Publications:
Meetings and Committee Reports, irregular; newsletter,
bimonthly in Veterinary and Human Toxicology, Fred
Oehme, D.V.M., editor.

★ 157 ★

AMERICAN ASSOCIATION OF PSYCHIATRIC
  ADMINISTRATORS

Saint Elizabeths Hospital
Barton Hall   (202) 574-7275
Washington, D.C. 20032

Roger Peele, M.D., President
An organization of psychiatrists intent on enhancing
the skill and status of psychiatric administrators
through professional meetings and through its own publication, a Newsletter. Professional meetings are
held about twice a year, once in conjunction with
the American Psychiatric Association's Annual Meeting,
and the other in conjunction with the Hospital and
Community Psychiatry Institute. Membership: 200.
Finances: Membership: Individual, $25 annually.
Awards: Distinguished medals or awards to those who
have provided outstanding administrative leadership in
psychiatry. Meetings: Luncheon at the American
Psychiatric Association's Annual Scientific Meeting;
1-day meeting with the APA's Hospital and Community Psychiatry Institute, various locations. Publications: Newsletter, quarterly, The President-Elect
(editor).

★ 158 ★

AMERICAN ASSOCIATION OF PSYCHIATRIC
    SERVICES FOR CHILDREN
1725 K Street, N.W.   (202) 659-9115
Washington, D.C. 20006   Established 1948

William E. Stone, M.D., Executive Director
The Association's purposes are to (1) encourage the
highest quality standards for clinical practice, training, and services; (2) offer a national focus for the
clinical point of view; (3) represent this perspective
in professional and public areas as they affect the
intellectual and social development of children and
youth; (4) provide consultation to members and others
on all aspects of service delivery including administration, accreditation, standards, financing, training,
research and continuing education; (5) foster prevention of mental and emotional disorders of the young;
(6) further the responsible development and application of clinical knowledge; (7) provide a clearinghouse of information relevant to the field; and (8)
support and/or undertake research projects dealing with
child mental health.   Membership: 400 individuals;
170 clinics and other organizations. Finances:
Membership: Individuals, $35; clinics, $500.
Awards: Freda London Award.   Meetings: Annual,
various locations; regional meetings; institutes; conferences. Publications: AAPSC Newsletter, quarterly, Erwin Janssen, M.D., editor.

★ 159 ★

AMERICAN ASSOCIATION OF PUBLIC HEALTH
    DENTISTS
University of Tennessee
College of Dentistry
875 Union Avenue   (901) 528-6252
Memphis, Tennessee 38163   Established 1937

W. Thomas Fields, Secretary-Treasurer
To promote dental public health; to provide a forum
for discussions on dental public health; to encourage
continuing education in dental public health administration and research; to promote the ideals and phi-
losophies of organized dentistry and public health.
Membership: 550 (dentists, dental hygienists, assistants, physicians, nurses and others interested in public
health).   Finances: Membership: Annual: Voting,
$25; associate, $20; student, $12.50.   Other
Sources: Publication of journal.   Meetings: Annual,
in conjunction with American Dental Association's
Annual Meeting. Publications: Journal of Public
Health Dentistry, quarterly, David F. Striffler, editor.

★ 160 ★

AMERICAN ASSOCIATION OF PUBLIC HEALTH
    PHYSICIANS
Post Office Box 522   (601) 453-4563
Greenwood, Mississippi 38930   Established 1954

Alfio Rausa, M.D., Secretary-Treasurer
To provide leadership in health matters, to discourage
fragmentation of government services and cooperate
with the private sector of medicine in the development of health policies. Membership: 500 (all
physicians, M.D., or D.O.).   Finances: Membership: $15.   Awards: Distinguished Service Award,
annual.   Meetings: Annual, various locations.
Publications: The Bulletin, bimonthly, Ben Freedman,
M.D., editor.   Affiliations: American Medical Association; American Public Health Association; National Coalition for Disease Prevention and Environmental Health.

★ 161 ★

AMERICAN ASSOCIATION OF RAILWAY SURGEONS
5657 Bellingham Road   (815) 877-5010
Rockford, Illinois 61107   Established 1888

Professional organization of physicians working with
railroad personnel. Membership: 1,200. Meetings:
Annual, September, Chicago, Illinois. Publications:
Newsletter, monthly.

★ 162 ★

AMERICAN ASSOCIATION OF RELIGIOUS
    THERAPISTS
7175 S.W. 45th Street, #303   (305) 475-8489
Fort Lauderdale, Florida 33314   Established 1958

Dale H. Ratliff, Ph.D., Executive Director;
    Pamela J. Kedrole, M.S., Membership Secretary
To promote religious perspectives in psychotherapy and
to recognize contributions to the field.   AART is a
member certifying association, requiring the masters
(Min) for membership, plus a personal interest in
religion and psychotherapy. Membership: 117
("Master" Ph.D. equivalent plus experience; Student-
Associate; "Clinical" M.Div. equivalent plus ex-
perience). Finances: Membership: $50 and up;
Other Sources: Contributions. Meetings: Semi-
annual, Fort Lauderdale, Florida. Publications:
AART Journal, annual, D. H. Ratliff, editor.

★ 163 ★
AMERICAN ASSOCIATION OF SENIOR PHYSICIANS
536 North State Street   (312) 751-6469
Chicago, Illinois 60610   Established 1975

Gerald L. Farley, Executive Director
To further the rights and benefits of senior physicians;
to assist members in planning for their future during
their coming years; and to provide information on
aspects of continuing medical education, recreation,
hobbies and other activities for senior physicians.
Membership: 3,000 (retired and non-retired physicians and their spouses who are 55 years of age or
older).

★ 164 ★
AMERICAN ASSOCIATION OF SUICIDOLOGY
2459 South Ash   (303) 692-0985
Denver, Colorado 80222

Julie Greenblatt, M.S.W., Executive Officer
The Association was established to aid the advancement of suicidology by encouraging research, education, services and training and by providing a forum
for mutual discussion of ideas and research. Membership: 450 individuals, 57 suicide prevention
centers; individual (regular, student and honorary)
and center memberships. Finances: Membership:
Regular, $40; student, $14; centers, $112. Awards:
Louis I. Dublin Award; Young Contributor's Award.
Meetings: Annual, various locations; workshops,
symposia, training programs, periodically, various locations. Publications: Suicide and Life-Threatening
Behavior, quarterly, Edwin Shneidman, Ph.D., editor;
Newslink, quarterly, Bonnie Jacob, editor.

★ 165 ★
AMERICAN ASSOCIATION OF VETERINARY
     ANATOMISTS
c/o Dr. Hermann Meyer
Department of Veterinary Anatomy
The Ohio State University
1900 Coffey Road   (614) 422-2091
Columbus, Ohio 43210   Established 1948

Professor Hermann Meyer, President
The purpose of the association is the advancement of
veterinary anatomical science, and it is organized
and operated exclusively for scientific and educational
purposes. Membership: 210 (active, emeritus, and
honorary members). Finances: Membership: $5 dues
dues. Meetings: Annual, in conjunction with American Veterinary Medical Association and with American Association of Anatomists. Publications: American Association of Veterinary Anatomists Directory;

Newsletter, Dr. Charles D. Diesem, editor; abstracts
of scientific papers presented at annual scientific
session published in Zentralblatt für Veterinär-Medizin,
Reihe C. Anatomia, Histologia, Embryologia, Paul
Parey, Publisher. Affiliations: World Association of
Veterinary Anatomists.

★ 166 ★
AMERICAN ASSOCIATION OF VETERINARY
     LABORATORY DIAGNOSTICIANS
c/o Dr. M. W. Vorhies
South Dakota State University
Brookings, South Dakota 57007   Established 1958

The purpose of the AAVLD is the dissemination of
information relating to the diagnosis of animal disease,
the coordination of the diagnostic activities of regulatory, research and service laboratories, the establishment of uniform techniques and the establishment
of accepted guides for the improvement of diagnostic
laboratory organizations as regards facilities, equipment and personnel qualifications. Membership: 550
(laboratory workers engaged in the field of disease
diagnosis in animals). Finances: Membership: $10
annually; Other Sources: Registration at the annual
meeting. Awards: E. P. Pope Memorial Award.
Meetings: Annual, various locations. Publications:
Proceedings Book of the Annual Meeting, annual,
M. W. Vorhies, editor; Newsletter, semiannual,
M. W. Vorhies, editor.

★ 167 ★
AMERICAN ASSOCIATION OF VETERINARY
     PARASITOLOGISTS
c/o Dr. T. J. Hayes
Hoffman-LaRoche, Inc.   (201) 235-2120
Nutley, New Jersey 07110   Established 1956

T. J. Hayes, V.M.D., Ph.D., Executive Director
A scientific organization of persons interested in the
advancement of veterinary parasitology. Encourages
education and research in the field; provides for exchange of information. Compiles summaries of papers
presented at annual scientific program. Membership:
160. Meetings: Annual, in July, with American
Veterinary Medical Association, various locations.
Publications: List of Members. Affiliations: American Veterinary Medical Association.

★ 168 ★

AMERICAN ASSOCIATION OF VETERINARY
    STATE BOARDS
1680 Teaneck Road   (201) 837-1814
Teaneck, New Jersey 07666   Established 1957

Robert R. Shomer, V.M.D., Secretary
To elevate educational standards by improving levels
of examination, establishing liaison between examining boards, and standardizing laws and the exchange
of information. Membership: 48 states, 2 associates,
2 Canadian, Puerto Rico, and Guam. Finances:
Membership: State, $50; associates, $5. Meetings:
Annual.

★ 169 ★

AMERICAN ASSOCIATION OF WOMEN DENTISTS
211 East Chicago Avenue
Suite 915
Chicago, Illinois 60611   Established 1922

Peter Goulding, Director of the Central Office
Organized to promote the advancement and recogni-
tion of the woman dentist. Membership: 500.
Finances: Membership: Active and associate, $40;
student, $20. Meetings: Annual, New Orleans,
Louisiana. Publications: Newsletter, Dr. Helen
Luechauer, editor.

★ 170 ★

AMERICAN ASSOCIATION OF WORKERS FOR THE
    BLIND
1511 K Street, N.W.   (202) 347-1559
Washington, D.C. 20005   Established 1895

John H. Maxson, Executive Director
Professional organization for individuals and agencies
in work with blind persons in the United States and
Canada. Membership: 3,500. Finances: Membership: Regular, $30; retired/secretary/associate,
$15; student, $10; service clubs, $35; agency,
$150-$1,000. Awards: Ambrose M. Shotwell
Medal and Scroll, and others for outstanding service
in work with blind persons. Meetings: Biennial,
odd-numbered years, various locations in the United
States and Canada. Publications: News and Views,
quarterly, T. M. DeFerrari, editor; Blindness, annual, G. Mallinson, editor; Proceeding, Biennial,
T. M. DeFerrari, editor.

★ 171 ★

AMERICAN ASSOCIATION OF ZOO VETERINARIANS
c/o Morton S. Silberman, D.V.M.
Emory University
Post Office Drawer TT   (404) 329-7423
Atlanta, Georiga 30322   Established 1967

Wilbur B. Amand, President
The Association publishes a journal of zoo animal
medicine. Membership: 600. Finances: Membership: Active and associate, $50; subscribing, $50;
student, $15. Meetings: Annual. Publications:
Journal of Animal Medicine, quarterly, Dr. Murray
Fowler, editor; Proceedings of Annual Conference,
annual.

★ 172 ★

AMERICAN ASSOCIATION ON MENTAL
    DEFICIENCY
5101 Wisconsin Avenue, N.W.   (202) 686-5400
Washington, D.C. 20016   Established 1876

The Association aims to promote the right of the
mentally retarded person to develop his potential to
the maximum to satisfy fully the needs of his personality and become, as far as possible, an independent
and useful member of the community. Membership:
11,000. Finances: Dues, active, $40; associate,
$35; affiliate, $30; student, $15; Other Sources:
Sale of publications; national conventions. Awards:
Awards are given periodically at the Annual Meeting
in such areas as education, humanitarianism, leadership, research, and service. Meetings: National
meeting, annually, various locations; regional and
state chapter meetings, annually. Publications:
Mental Retardation, bimonthly; American Journal of
Mental Deficiency, bimonthly; Adaptive Behavior
Scale, Public School and Institutional Versions; Manual on Terminology and Classification in Mental Retardation. Affiliations: World Federation for Mental
Health; International Association for the Scientific
Study of Mental Deficiency; American Academy of
Mental Retardation; Mexican Society for the Scien-
tific Study of Mental Deficiency; Bahamas Associa-
tion for the Mentally Retarded.

★ 173 ★

AMERICAN BAPTIST CHAPLAINCY AND PASTORAL
    COUNSELING SERVICES
Valley Forge,   (215) 768-2428
    Pennsylvania 19481   Established 1953

Rev. Paul W. Strickland, Director
Coordinates denominational endorsement process for

chaplains and pastoral counselors in a health care setting; recruits personnel; maintains a working relationship to all professional associations and certifying agencies for chaplains and pastoral counselors; develops policy regarding basic education and continued education for chaplaincy services. Membership: 325. Finances: Grants from Board of National Ministries, American Baptist Churches - U.S.A. Meetings: Annual, various locations. Publications: Dialogue, biennial, Paul W. Strickland, editor.

★ 174 ★

AMERICAN BAPTIST HOMES AND HOSPITALS
    ASSOCIATION

Valley Forge,   (215) 768-2442
   Pennsylvania 19481   Established 1933

Counsel and advice to institutions; recruitment of personnel; promotion of church support; regional conferences. Membership: 100 (administrators of retirement homes, nursing homes and hospitals, children's homes; special services for mentally retarded). Finances: Membership: Hospitals, $500; children's homes, $75; retirement centers and homes for aging, a minimum of $50 or $.50 per resident, whichever is larger; regional organizations, $25; nursing homes, $100. Meetings: Annual, various locations. Publications: Perspective, quarterly.

★ 175 ★

AMERICAN BLOOD COMMISSION
1901 North Fort Myer Drive
Suite 300
Arlington, Virginia 22209   (703) 522-8414
                  Established 1975

Nancy R. Holland, Administrative Director
The Commission is in the national, non-profit agency responsible for private sector implementation of the National Blood Policy, which was announced by the federal government in 1973. Goals of the Commission are: an all-voluntary blood donation system; an adequate supply of blood for the nation; highest quality, safe blood; accessibility for all those who need blood; and efficiency in the blood service system. Activities include a national blood data system; resource sharing through regionalization; uniform systems in blood bag labeling and automation; donor education, motivation and recruitment; and communication about the nation's blood system to all interested parties and to the general public. Membership: 41 (includes national non-profit organizations who are operational, professional, commercial, financial, consumer-donor; voluntary health associations). Finances: Membership: $250-$25,000; Other Sources: Sponsorship, publications and government

contracts. Meetings: Board of Directors, quarterly; Executive Committee, 3 times per year, various locations. Publications: ABC Reports, every 6 weeks, Robert C. Hubbell, editor; ABC Annual Report, annually, Robert C. Hubbell, editor; National Blood Data Center Annual Report, annually, Richard W. Switalski, editor; Regionalization Program Annual Report, annually, Suzanne G. Hayes, editor; State Legislative Initiatives, annually, Jane M. Starkey, editor; Advances in Blood Transfusion: Various Reprints and Special Reports, 1979, Robert C. Hubbell, editor. Library: American Blood Commission, approximately 300 volumes.

★ 176 ★

AMERICAN BOARD FOR CERTIFICATION IN
   ORTHOTICS AND PROSTHETICS

1444 N Street, N.W.   (202) 234-8400
Washington, D.C. 20005   Established 1948

William L. McCulloch, Executive Director
To encourage and promote high standards of workmanship and service, to encourage the maintenance of adequate facilities and the use of adequately trained personnel, and to encourage, foster and promote honest dealings and fair trade practices on the part of persons engaged in fitting prosthetic or orthopedic appliances. To promote the welfare of the physically handicapped by establishing standards for those engaged in the fitting of prosthetic or orthopedic appliances, particularly with respect to adequacy and cleanliness of facilities and proficiency and honesty in service rendered, and with the object of discouraging the practice of this profession by technically unqualified persons. To establish professional and business standards applicable to: (1) individuals engaged in the profession of fitting prosthetic or orthopedic appliances; and (2) corporations, partnerships, individuals, and any other entity operating as a firm or company engaged in the business of fitting prosthetic or orthopedic appliances. To conduct investigations, to conduct examinations and in any other way deemed necessary to ascertain whether or not such persons, corporations, partnerships, individuals, and other entities, do in fact meet the aforementioned. To collaborate with recognized educational and research organizations in order to develop constantly higher standards of service and competency. Membership: 1,600 certifees; 450 facilities (Board of Directors: 9 directors, 3 of whom are orthopedic surgeons from the American Academy of Orthopaedic of Surgeons, 3 of whom are named by the American Orthotics and Prosthetics Association, and 3 of whom are named by the American Academy of Orthotists and Prosthetists. Each director serves 3 years). Finances: Membership: Application fee: facilities, $175; annual renewal fee, $245; certifee application

fee, $75; examination fee, $300; annual renewal fee for certifees, $35. Meetings: Annual, various locations. Publications: Registry of Accredited Facilities and Certified Individuals in Orthotics and Prosthetics, annually.

★ 177 ★
AMERICAN BOARD OF ABDOMINAL SURGERY
675 Main Street   (617) 665-6101
Melrose, Massachusetts 02176   Established 1957

Blaise F. Alfano, M.D., Secretary
To improve the standards for Abdominal Surgery; to examine candidates and certify those who successfully complete the written and oral examinations. Membership: 3,000 diplomates. Finances: Membership: Application fee; examination fee Part I and Part II. Meetings: Annual examinations.

★ 178 ★
AMERICAN BOARD OF ALLERGY AND
        IMMUNOLOGY
University City Science Center
3624 Market Street   (215) 349-9466
Philadelphia, Pennsylvania 19104 Established 1972

Herbert C. Mansmann, Jr., M.D., Executive
    Secretary
The Board's purposes are to establish qualifications and examine physician candidates for certification as specialists in allergy and immunology, to establish and improve standards for the teaching and practice of allergy and immunology, and to establish standards for training programs in allergy and immunology. Membership: 2,241 certified diplomates. Finances: Registration and examination fee for certification examination.

★ 179 ★
AMERICAN BOARD OF ANESTHESIOLOGY, INC.
100 Constitution Plaza   (203) 522-9857
Hartford, Connecticut 06103   Established 1938

E. S. Siker, M.D., Secretary-Treasurer
Examines and certifies as diplomates those doctors who have completed the prescribed courses of training and satisfactorily comply with the certification requirements. Membership: 9,630 diplomates certified to date. Finances: Membership: Examination fee $400 for eligible physicians. Meetings: April and October, various locations. Member Board: American Board of Medical Specialists.

★ 180 ★
AMERICAN BOARD OF BIOANALYSIS
818 Olive, Suite 918   (314) 241-1445
St. Louis, Missouri 63101   Established 1968

David Birenbaum, Administrator
The primary functions of the American Board of Bioanalysis are: certification of individuals as Bioanalyst Laboratory Directors; certification of individuals as Laboratory Supervisors; accreditation of laboratories as Bioanalytical Laboratories; accreditation of graduate programs in Bioanalysis. Membership: 600 certified individuals. Finances: Membership: Annual fee, $25.

★ 181 ★
AMERICAN BOARD OF CLINICAL CHEMISTRY
c/o Department of Clinical Chemistry,
    Research Division
Hoffman-LaRoche   (201) 235-3853
Nutley, New Jersey 07110   Established 1950

To establish and enhance the standards of competence for the practice of clinical chemistry, including toxicological chemistry; to certify qualified specialists; to accredit predoctoral and postgraduate training programs. Conducts examinations annually for certification in clinical chemistry and clinical toxicology. Membership: 620. Meetings: Annual, various locations. Publications: Directory of Diplomates of the American Board of Clinical Chemistry. Affiliations: American Association for Clinical Chemistry; American Institute of Chemists; American Society of Biological Chemists; National Academy of Clinical Biochemistry.

★ 182 ★
AMERICAN BOARD OF CLINICAL HYPNOSIS
c/o Professor M. Erik Wright
Department of Psychology
University of Kansas   (913) 864-4131
Lawrence, Kansas 66045   Established 1956

Professor M. Erik Wright, Coordinator and
    Executive President
Examines and certifies specialized competence in the clinical application in discipline of medicine, psychology or dentistry. Membership: 500 diplomates (60% M.D.'s; 30% Ph.D.' 10% D.D.S.). Finances: Membership: Examination fee, $250; pre-exam (5 years), $100; Other Sources: Contributions,

donations.   Meetings: Executive Board, semiannual;
Examination Committees in each discipline, 1 to 2
times annually.   Publications: Directory of Diplomates, biennial with Interim Supplement.   Affiliations: American Society of Clinical Hypnosis;   International Society of Hypnosis.

★ 183 ★
AMERICAN BOARD OF COLON AND RECTAL
        SURGERY
615 Griswold, #516   (313) 961-7880
Detroit, Michigan 48226   Established 1935

Norman D. Nigro, M.D., Secretary
To promote the health of the American people through
the development and maintenance of high standards
for certification in the specialty of colon and rectal
surgery;   to conduct examinations to determine the
ability and fitness to practice the specialty of colon
and rectal surgery.   Membership: 595 diplomates.
Meetings: Certifying examinations given annually,
various locations.

★ 184 ★
AMERICAN BOARD OF DENTAL PUBLIC HEALTH
c/o Norman F. Gerrie, D.D.S.
9139 McDonald Drive   (301) 365-0352
Bethesda, Maryland 20034   Established 1950

Norman F. Gerrie, D.D.S., M.P.H., Executive
        Secretary
A non-profit corporation formed to act in the capacity of a national agency engaged in the examination
and certification of dentists as specialists in dental
public health.   Membership: 5 (dentists with additional degree of M.P.H.) Executive Committee Members; 100 corporate body members.   Finances: Membership: Annual recertification fee of diplomates of
the Board, and fee paid by each candidate for examination.   Meetings: Executive Committee of the
Board, annually, various locations; Interim Board
Meeting, annually.   Affiliations: Sponsored by
American Association of Public Health Dentists.

★ 185 ★
AMERICAN BOARD OF DERMATOLOGY, INC.
Henry Ford Hospital
2799 West Grand Boulevard   (313) 871-8739
Detroit, Michigan 48202   Established 1932

Clarence S. Livingood, M.D., Executive Director
The aims of the Board are to establish standards of
competence for physicians who seek recognition as
specialists in dermatology; set minimum requirements
of education and training in dermatology; and de-

velop facilities to provide this training.   Membership: 12; diplomates, 258 (physicians certified by
Board after training and successful examination).   Finances: Fee for voluntary examination.   Meetings:
3 times annually, various locations.   Publications:
Booklet of Information, revised yearly;   Guide for
Residency Programs in Dermatology (revised as necessary).   List of approved dermatology residence training centers in the Directory of Residency Training
Programs.   Affiliations: Member of American Board
of Medical Specialists.

★ 186 ★
AMERICAN BOARD OF HEALTH PHYSICS
5010 Nicholson Lane, Suite A   (301) 443-2850
Rockville, Maryland 20852   Established 1959

Michael S. Terpilak, Executive Secretary
Certification of Health Physicists.   Membership: 7
(5 Health Physics Society Members, 1 American Association of Physicists in Medicine Member, and 1
American Public Health Association Member).   Finances: Application fee, $125 each part (regular
examination to take Part I and II); certificate fee,
$40.   Meetings: Annual, in conjunction with Health
Physics Society Meeting.

★ 187 ★
AMERICAN BOARD OF INTERNAL MEDICINE
3624 Market Street   (215) 243-1500
Philadelphia, Pennsylvania 19104   Established 1938

John A. Benson, Jr., M.D., President
The primary purpose of the Board is to administer the
certification process through establishing requirements
of postdoctoral training related to examinations given
by the Board; obtaining substantiation by appropriate
authorities of the clinical skills of its candidates;
assessing the credentials of candidates for the examinations of the Board; and conducting examinations
for certification and recertification.   Membership:
40 individuals.   Finances: Membership: Examination fees, $300-$375.

★ 188 ★
AMERICAN BOARD OF MEDICAL SPECIALTIES
State National Bank Building
1603 Orrington Avenue
Suite 1160   (312) 491-9091
Evanston, Illinois 60201   Established 1933

Glen R. Leymaster, M.D., Executive Director
Originally established to provide a forum for exchange

of ideas, the organization presently represents all medical specialty boards in establishing, maintaining, and elevating standards for the education and for assurance of the initial and continued competence of physicians qualifying as medical specialists. Membership: 28 (regular, associate). Finances: Member boards pay dues based on new diplomates certified annually. Meetings: Annual, March and September, Chicago, Illinois. Affiliations: American Hospital Association; Federation of State Medical Boards; Association of American Medical Colleges; Council of Medical Specialty Societies; National Board of Medical Examiners.

★ 189 ★
AMERICAN BOARD OF NEUROLOGICAL SURGERY
LSU Medical Center
1542 Tulane Avenue, Suite 117   (504) 568-5969
New Orleans, Louisiana 70112   Established 1940

William F. Collins, Jr., M.D., Chairman;
    Charles E. Brackett, M.D., Vice Chairman;
    David G. Kline, M.D., Secretary/Treasurer
The primary purposes of The American Board of Neurological Surgery as stated in the by-laws are to examine the training and practice credentials as well as to conduct examinations of those candidates seeking certification by the Board and to issue certificates to those who meet the Board's requirements and satisfactorily complete its examinations. Membership: 2,643 diplomates certified by the Board. Finances: Oral examination application, $50; oral examination fee, $450; primary examination fee, $200. Meetings: Semiannual, Spring and Fall.

★ 190 ★
AMERICAN BOARD OF OBSTETRICS AND
    GYNECOLOGY, INC.
711 Stanton L. Young Boulevard   (405) 236-0130
Oklahoma City, Oklahoma 73104   Established 1927

James A. Merrill, M.D., Secretary-Treasurer
To encourage the study, improve the practice, and advance the cause of obstetrics and gynecology, subjects which should be inseparably interwoven; and to grant and to issue to physicians duly licensed by law, certificates or other equivalent recognition of special knowledge in obstetrics and gynecology. To accomplish these objectives the Board arranges and conducts examinations for candidates who, if their answers are satisfactory, are awarded the certificate or the diploma of the Board. Membership: 10 organizational members representing the nominating organizations, plus non-organizational members. Publications: Bulletin of the American Board of Obstetrics and

Gynecology, Inc., annual. Affiliations: Sponsored by the American Gynecological Society; the American Association of Obstetricians and Gynecologists; the American College of Obstetricians and Gynecologists; the Association of Professors of Gynecology-Obstetrics; and the Section on Obstetrics of the American Medical Association. The Board holds active membership in the American Board of Medical Specialties.

★ 191 ★
AMERICAN BOARD OF OPHTHALMOLOGY
8870 Towanda Street   (215) 242-1123
Philadelphia, Pennsylvania 19118 Established 1916

Robert N. Shaffer, M.D., Secretary-Treasurer
The purpose of the Board is to determine the adequacy of training, the professional prepositions, and the competence of ophthalmologists who wish to be certified; to improve the standards of graduate medical education and the facilities for special ophthalmic training; provide a comprehensive Written Qualifying Test to those ophthalmologists who meet the training requirements; to issue an appropriate certificate to those ophthalmologists who successfulyy pass the examination of the Board. The Board does not determine who may or may not practice ophthalmology, it is solely a certifying body. Membership: 13 Board Members (currently the composition of the Board with 7 consultants; approximate number of certified diplomates of the Board is 10, 732 active members). Meetings: Semiannual, Spring and Fall, time and place designated by the Board (meetings are in conjunction with oral examinations).

★ 192 ★
AMERICAN BOARD OF ORAL AND MAXILLO-
    FACIAL SURGERY
211 East Chicago Avenue   (312) 642-0070
Chicago, Illinois 60611   Established 1946

Philip J. Boyne, Secretary-Treasurer
To establish qualifications for the practice of oral and maxillofacial surgery, to conduct examinations and to certify oral surgeons whom the Board finds qualified. Membership: Regular certification. Finances: Examination fee, $500; application fee, $300. Meetings: Annual, various locations. Affiliations: American Association of Oral and Maxillofacial Surgeons; American Dental Association. Former Name: American Board of Oral Surgery.

★ 193 ★
AMERICAN BOARD OF ORAL PATHOLOGY
Tufts University
School of Dental Medicine
Department of Oral Pathology
1 Kneeland Street   (617) 956-6510
Boston, Massachusetts 02111   Established 1948

Edmund Cataldo, D.D.S., Secretary-Treasurer
To encourage the study, to elevate the standards and
to promote and improve the practice of oral pathology.
To determine the competence of those wishing to practice as oral pathologists and to arrange, conduct and
control investigations and examinations to determine
the qualifications of such individuals as may voluntarily apply for the certificate issued by the Board.
To grant and issue certificates to those who shall
voluntarily apply and be examined in oral pathology,
and to maintain a registry of holders of such certificates.   To make available to the public, the dental
and medical professions, hospitals and dental schools,
lists of oral pathologists certified by the corporation.
Membership: 206 diplomates.   Finances: Membership: $300; Other Sources: Annual registration fee,
$20.   Meetings: Semiannual, various locations.
Affiliations: American Academy of Oral Pathology.

AMERICAN BOARD OF ORAL SURGERY
    See: American Board of Oral and Maxillofacial
    Surgery

★ 194 ★
AMERICAN BOARD OF ORTHODONTICS
225 South Meramec Avenue   (314) 727-6162
St. Louis, Missouri 63105   Established 1929

Earl E. Shepard, Executive Director
To elevate the standards of the practice of orthodontics; to conduct a written examination, an oral
examination, and presentation of fifteen (15) case reports; to confer certificates upon those who meet the
Board's standards.   Membership: 1,152 (certified
orthodontists called diplomates).   Finances: Examination fee, $450; annual registration fee, $20.
Awards: The Albert H. Ketcham Memorial Award for
contribution to the science of orthodontics.   Meetings:
Annually, March.   Publications: The American
Board of Orthodontics, a directory, annual.

★ 195 ★
AMERICAN BOARD OF ORTHOPAEDIC SURGERY,
    INC.
444 North Michigan Avenue
Suite 2970   (312) 822-9572
Chicago, Illinois 60611   Established 1934

Henry H. Banks, M.D., Executive Director
To establish minimum educational standards in the
specialty, issue certificates, stimulate education, and
aid in the evaluation educational facilities in the
best interests of the public and the medical profession.   Membership: 11,004 diplomates.   Finances:
Candadate fees: certifying examination, $100 appli-
cation fee; $600 examination fee; Other Sources:
Sale of Directory of Diplomates.   Meetings: Semiannual, various locations.   Publications: Directory
of Diplomates, annually; Rules and Procedures.
Affiliations: American Academy of Orthopaedic
Surgeons; American Orthopaedic Association; American Medical Association.

★ 196 ★
AMERICAN BOARD OF OTOLARYNGOLOGY
220 Collingwood, Suite 130   (313) 761-7185
Ann Arbor, Michigan 48103   Established 1924

Walter Work, M.D., Secretary-Treasurer
To establish standards of qualification for Otolaryngologists who desire and request Board certification;
to determine which candidates fulfill these standards
of qualification; to examine such candidates and issue certificates upon satisfactory completion of requirements; to encourage development and maintenance of the highest standards in the teaching and
training of Otolaryngologists.   Membership: 25.
Finances: Application fee, $300; examination fee,
$500.   Meetings: Annual, various locations.

★ 197 ★
AMERICAN BOARD OF PATHOLOGY
112 Lincoln Center
5401 West Kennedy Boulevard
Post Office Box 24695   (813) 879-4864
Tampa, Florida 33623   Established 1936

M. R. Abell, M.D., Ph.D., Executive Director
To encourage the study of pathology, to protect the
public interest by maintaining the standards and advancing the practice of pathology as a medical specialty, to determine competency by conducting examinations for those who voluntarily apply for certification and to grant and issue certificates in pathology
to qualified applications.   The Board does not define hospital privileges, the scope of specialty

practice or who may or may not engage in the practice of pathology. Membership: 13,487 diplomates certified by the Board which 11,556 primary certificates having been issued in anatomic and/or clinical pathology and 1,931 certificates in special competence areas of pathology. Finances: Membership: Examination fee, $550. Meetings: Semiannual, various locations. Publications: Booklet of Information, annually. Affiliations: American Medical Association; American Association of Pathologists; American Society of Clinical Pathologists; College of American Pathologists; International Academy of Pathology, US-Canadian Division.

★ 198 ★
AMERICAN BOARD OF PEDIATRICS
NCNB Plaza, Suite 402
136 East Rosemary Street   (919) 929-0461
Chapel Hill, North Carolina 27514   Established 1934

Robert C. Brownlee, M.D.
To advance the science, study and practice of pediatrics; to evaluate pediatric training programs and the credentials of physicians applying for certification as pediatricians; to examine applicants and certify those qualifying as pediatricians and by otherwise attempting to advance and elevate the science, study and practice of pediatrics. Membership: 13 (20,000 certified pediatricians). Finances: Examination fee, $450. Meetings: 6 annually, various locations.

★ 199 ★
AMERICAN BOARD OF PEDODONTICS
c/o University of Nebraska
College of Dentistry   (402) 472-1375
Lincoln, Nebraska 68583   Established 1940

William S. Kramer, D.D.S., Executive Secretary
To encourage the study, improve the practice, elevate the standards and advance the science of pedodontics; and thereby to serve the cause of public health. The Board determines by examination the competence of dentists who apply for certificates in the practice of dentistry for children. Finances: Examination fee, $600; written filing fee, $100; oral, $100; case histories, $100; clinical, $300. Annual certificate renewal fee, $10. Affiliation: Sponsored by the American Academy of Pedodontics.

★ 200 ★
AMERICAN BOARD OF PERIODONTOLOGY
University of Southern California
School of Dentistry
925 West 34th Street   (213) 743-5255
Los Angeles, California 90007   Established 1939

Robert L. Reeves, Executive Secretary-Treasurer
To elevate the standards and advance the science and art of periodontology by encouraging its study and improving its practice. To conduct examinations to determine the qualifications and competence of dentists who voluntarily apply to the Board for certification as diplomates. To grant and issue diplomate certificates in the field of periodontology to qualified applicants therefor and to maintain a registry of holders of such certificates. To serve the health professions and health institutions by preparing and furnishing on requests lists of periodontists certified as diplomates of the Board. Membership: 8 (425 certified diplomates). Finances: Examination fee, $450; re-examination fee for repeating part of the exam, $200; annual registration, $35. Meetings: Semiannual, Dallas, Texas, in April or May; October meeting, various locations. Publications: Information Folder, revised as required; Roster of Diplomates, published or addenda supplied annually. Affiliation: Sponsored by the American Academy of Periodontology.

★ 201 ★
AMERICAN BOARD OF PLASTIC SURGERY
1617 John F. Kennedy Boulevard   (215) 568-4000
Philadelphia, Pennsylvania 19103   Established 1939

John E. Hoopes, M.D., Secretary-Treasurer
Certification board to investigate the qualification of, administer examinations to, and certify as diplomates medical doctors specializing in general plastic surgery. Examinations are given once a year: Part I, written, and Part II, oral. Membership: 18 directors. Meetings: Semiannual and annual, various locations.

★ 202 ★
AMERICAN BOARD OF PODIATRIC ORTHOPEDICS
Post Office Box 31331   (415) 826-3200
San Francisco, California 94131

Lawrence T. Burns, M.D., President
Certifying board in podiatric orthopedics. Examines and certifies competency of podiatrists to perform podiatric orthopedic procedures. Membership: 187 diplomates. Finances: Membership: application

fee, $50; registration fee, $300; dues, $75.
Meetings: Annual, August, in conjunction with
American Podiatry Association annual meeting, various locations. Publications: Newsletters. Affiliations: American Podiatry Association, Council on
Podiatry Education (approves the Board).

★ 203 ★
AMERICAN BOARD OF PODIATRIC SURGERY
Post Office Box 31331   (415) 826-3200
San Francisco, California   Established 1975

John L. Bennett, Executive Director
Certifies the competency of podiatrists to perform
foot surgery. Membership: 603 diplomate (Board
Certified). Finances: Membership: Dues, $25 annually; application fee, $75; registration fee (includes examination), $475. Meetings: Annual,
August, in conjunction with American Podiatry Association annual meeting, various locations. Affiliations: Approved by Council on Podiatry Education of
the American Podiatry Association.

★ 204 ★
AMERICAN BOARD OF PREVENTIVE MEDICINE,
    INC.
c/o Dr. S. R. Mohler
Wright State School of Medicine
Department of Com. Medicine
Post Office Box 927   (513) 278-6915
Dayton, Ohio 45401   Established 1948

Stanley R. Mohler, M.D., Secretary-Treasurer
To encourage the study, improve the practice, elevate the standards, and advance the cause of preventive medicine; to grant and issue to physicians
certificates of special knowledge in the various fields
of preventive medicine. The fields in which certification is granted are public health, aerospace medicine, occupational medicine, and general preventive
medicine. Membership: 3,894 (public health aerospace medicine, occupational medicine, general preventive medicine). Finances: Membership: Application fee, $100; examination fee, $500 ($250,
Part I; $250, Part II). Meetings: Semiannual,
various locations. Publications: Bulletin of the
ABPM, annually, Stanley R. Mohler, M.D., editor.

★ 205 ★
AMERICAN BOARD OF PROFESSIONAL
    PSYCHOLOGY, INC.
2025 I Street, N.W., Suite 405   (202) 833-2730
Washington, D.C. 20006   Established 1947

Margaret Ives, Executive Officer
To conduct examinations to determine the qualifications of individuals who apply for diplomas of advanced competence, and to serve the public by furnishing to persons and agencies lists of certified specialists. Membership: Approximately 2,700 certified diplomas. Awards: Distinguished Professional
Achievement Award presented to an outstanding professional psychologist. Publications: Policies and
Procedures Guide; Manual for Oral Examinations;
Newsletter: The Diplomate, semiannual, Barry
Lubetkin, editor.

★ 206 ★
AMERICAN BOARD OF PROSTHODONTICS
c/o Dr. Douglas C. Wendt
4707 Olley Lane   (703) 323-5603
Fairfax, Virginia 22032   Established 1947

Douglas C. Wendt, M.D., Secretary
The Board functions "...to examine candidates and
issue certificates to qualified specialists in the field
of prosthodontics." Membership: 600 (annual,
founder, charter, life). Finances: Membership:
$25 annual registration: $100 for each of the 4
examination phases. Meetings: Semiannual, February (Chicago) and June (variable at designated
dental schools). Publications: Journal of Prosthetic
Dentistry, monthly, Judson C. Hickey, editor. Affiliations: American Dental Association; Federation
of Prothodontic Organizations.

★ 207 ★
AMERICAN BOARD OF PSYCHIATRY AND
    NEUROLOGY, INC.
1 American Plaza, Suite 808   (312) 864-0830
Evanston, Illinois 60201   Established 1934

Lester H. Rudy, M.D., Executive Director
The chief functions of the Board are to determine the
competence of specialists in psychiatry and in neurology; to arrange, control and conduct investigations and examinations to test the qualifications of
candidates for certificates issued by the Board; to
grant and issue certificates or other recognition of
special competence in the fields of psychiatry and
neurology to successful applicants; to serve the public, physicians, hospitals, and medical schools by preparing lists of practitioners who have been certified
by the Board; to consider and advise as to any
course of study and technical training, and to disseminate any information calculated to promote and ensure the fitness of persons desirous of qualifying for a
certificate; and to contribute to the evaluation of
training programs in hospitals, clinics and medical

centers for the purpose of determining their adequacy as training centers in psychiatry and/or neurology. Membership: 16 Board members (psychiatrists and neurologists). Finances: Supported by application and examination fee. Meetings: 4-5 annual examinations.

★ 208 ★
AMERICAN BOARD OF PSYCHOLOGICAL HYPNOSIS
c/o Dr. Doris Gruenewald
5825 Dorchester Avenue
Chicago, Illinois 60637   Established 1958

Doris Gruenewald, Ph.D., President;
    Mark I. Oberlander, Ph.D., Secretary-Treasurer
The Board functions to award specialty diplomas after appropriate examinations in the fields of clinical and scientific achievement in these areas; and to protect and educate the public against the exploitive use of hypnosis. Membership: 175 diplomates in clinical hypnosis and experimental hypnosis. Finances: Membership: Application fee, $60. Awards: Annual award of the Morton Prince Prize for excellence in psychological hypnosis research. Meetings: Annual, with the Society for Clinical and Experimental Hypnosis. Affiliations: American Boards of Clinical Hypnosis; American Psychological Association; American Society of Clinical Hypnosis; Society of Clinical and Experimental Hypnosis; International Society of Hypnosis.

★ 209 ★
AMERICAN BOARD OF RADIOLOGY, INC.
Kahler East   (507) 282-7838
Rochester, Minnesota 55901   Established 1934

Kenneth L. Krabbenhoft, M.D., Secretary;
    C. Allen Good, M.D., Assistant Secretary
To improve the quality of graduate education in Radiology; to encourage the study of and to elevate the standards of training in Radiology; to determine the competence of specialists in Radiology and to arrange, control and conduct investigations and examinations to test the qualifications of voluntary candidates for certificates to be issued by the Board; to grant and issue certificates in the field of Radiology or a branch thereof to voluntary applicants who have been found qualified by the Board and to maintain a registry of holders of such certificates. Membership: 19. Finances: Examination and application fee, $750; Examinations: Annual, various locations.

★ 210 ★
AMERICAN BOARD OF SURGERY, INC.
1617 John F. Kennedy Boulevard   (215) 568-4000
Philadelphia, Pennsylvania 19103   Established 1937

J. W. Humphreys, Jr., M.D., Secretary-Treasurer
To conduct examinations of acceptable candidates who seek certification by the Board; to issue certificates of qualification to all candidates meeting the Board's requirements and satisfactorily completing its prescribed examinations; to improve and broaden the opportunities for the graduate education and training of surgeons. Membership: 22. Finances: Membership: Registration fee, $100; examination fees, written $200, oral $200. Meetings: Semiannual. Affiliations: American Surgical Association; American Medical Association; American College of Surgeons; Society of University Surgeons; Southern Surgical Association; Western Surgical Association; Pacific Coast Surgical Association; New England Surgical Society; Central Surgical Association; American Pediatric Surgical Association.

★ 211 ★
AMERICAN BOARD OF THORACIC SURGERY
14640 East Seven Mile Road   (313) 372-2632
Detroit, Michigan 48205   Established 1948

Herbert Sloan, M.D., Secretary-Treasurer
The nomination of candidates and their certification by the American Board of Thoracic Surgery. Membership: Certified to the Founders Group: 228; certified by examination, 3,650. Finances: Registration fee, $100; examination fee, $650. Meetings: Semiannual, various locations.

★ 212 ★
AMERICAN BOARD OF UROLOGY
Harborview Medical Center
325 Ninth Avenue   (206) 223-3213
Seattle, Washington 98104   Established 1935

Dr. J. Tate Mason, Executive Secretary
To render better service to the public by ascertaining and certifying the competency of any qualified physician who is specializing, or wishes to specialize in the field of urology. Membership: 12 (elected from urologic societies including American Urological Association, American Association of Genitourinary Surgeons, American College of Surgeons, American Association of Clinical Urologists, Society of University Urologists, Urologists Society of American Academy of Prediatrics). Finances: Examinations in two parts, Part I, written; Part II, oral, total fee, $800.

Meetings: 1 annually and 1 interim. Affiliations: American Urological Association; American Association of Genitourinary Surgeons; American Medical Association; Society of University Urologists; American Association of Clinical Urologists; Urology Section of the American Academy of Pediatrics. Remarks: Primary purpose is credentialing.

AMERICAN BOARD OF EXAMINERS IN SPEECH PATHOLOGY AND AUDIOLOGY
   See: Council on Professional Standards is Speech-Language Pathology and Audiology

★ 213 ★
AMERICAN BRONCHO-ESOPHAGOLOGICAL
   ASSOCIATION
200 First Street S.W.   (507) 284-3764
Rochester, Minnesota 55901   Established 1917

David R. Sanderson, M.D., Secretary
A professional association whose purpose is to study broncho-esophagology (diseases and injuries of the respiratory system and upper digestive tract). Membership: 300 otolaryngologists, chest specialists, and thoracic surgeons. Awards: Chevalier Jackson Award; Chevalier Jackson Lecture; Seymour Cohen Award. Meetings: Annual, at site of Otolaryngologic Spring Meeting. Publications: Transactions, annually; Proceedings (published in Annals of Otology, Rhinology, and Laryngology).

★ 214 ★
AMERICAN BUREAU FOR MEDICAL ADVANCEMENT
   IN CHINA
New York Academy of Medicine
2 East 103rd   (212) 860-1990
New York, New York 10029   Established 1937

John R. Watt, Ph.D., Executive Director;
   Richard Pierson, M.D., President
To support a program of medical and health training and service for the people of China. Activities include training medical and nursing personnel, sponsoring postgraduate fellowships, assisting a variety of medical and public health services (e.g., family planning and child health care); cancer education; rehabilitation of the handicapped), and providing medical and scientific equipment and supplies. Membership: 1,500. Finances: Cash gifts, grants, contributions in-kind. Meetings: Annual, New York City. Publications: Annual Report; ABMAC Bulletin, bimonthly; assorted reports, monographs and

other non-regular publications. Former Name: American Bureau for Medical Aid to China.

AMERICAN BUREAU FOR MEDICAL AID TO CHINA
   See: American Bureau for Medical Advancement
   in China

★ 215 ★
AMERICAN BURN ASSOCIATION
New York Hospital, Cornell Medical Center
525 East 68th Street, Room F758
New York, New York 10021   Established 1967

P. William Curreri, M.D., Secretary
The Association is a non-profit organization whose purposes and objectives are to stimulate and sponsor the study and research in the treatment and prevention of burns; to provide a forum for presentation of such knowledge; to foster training opportunities for individuals interested in burns; to encourage publications pertaining to the foregoing activities; and to consider such other matters as may properly come within the sphere of the Association. Membership: Approximately 1,400 active, associate, special, senior and honorary. Finances: Membership: Active, $30; associate and special, $15; initiation fee, $25. Awards: Everett Idris Evans Memorial Lecture Award; Harvey Stuart Allen Distinguished Service Award; Carl A. Moyer Resident Award; President's Continuing Education Grant; Associate Award. Meetings: Annual, various locations. Publications: Newsletter, triannually; membership directory, annually.

★ 216 ★
AMERICAN CANCER SOCIETY
777 Third Avenue   (212) 371-2900
New York, New York 10017   Established 1913

Lane W. Adams, Executive Vice President
A voluntary organization dedicated to the control and eradication of cancer. The organization is made up of 58 incorporated chartered Divisions, one in each state, the District of Columbia, Puerto Rico, and six other metropolitan areas. Through Local Units, the Division translate the Society's policies into action. Programs of research, education and service to the cancer patient are planned by a national board of 115 voting volunteer directors representing all the Divisions of the Society. Membership: 194 voting members (152 Division and Proportional Delegates and 42 Delegates-at-Large), 46 Honorary Life Members, and 11 Past Officer Directors. Finances: Annual Crusade, legacies, and bequests. Awards: Gold

Medal of the American Cancer Society, which may be presented as an individual award, a joint award, or to two or more individuals in recognition of distinguished contributions in the field of cancer control. Meetings: Annual, New York City. Publications: Cancer News, semiannually, Walter S. Ross, editor; Cancer, monthly, Jonathan E. Rhoads, M.D., editor; CA - A Cancer Journal for Clinicians, bimonthly, Arthur I. Holleb, M.D., editor. Library: 15,000 volumes; staff, 7. Affiliations: 58 Chartered Divisions within the 50 states, the District of Columbia and Puerto Rico.

★ 217 ★

AMERICAN CARDIOLOGY TECHNOLOGISTS
    ASSOCIATION
1 Bank Street, #307   (301) 258-9009
Gaithersburg, Maryland 20760   Established 1958

To promise free exchange of techniques and procedures in Cardiology technology and related fields; to provide within the scope possible educational facilities for further training and development of Cardiology Technologists; to meet from time to time to consider subjects of mutual interests in the field of Cardiology Technology; to establish a closer fraternal relationship among technologists interested in common problems; to promote efficiency and advancements in the field of scientific methods and standardization of procedures; to perform, individually and as a group, in the highest possible standards, a true service in the field of Cardiology Technology to the hospitals, physicians, and the patients concerned. Membership: 3,200 (nominees, registered, associate, honorary). Finances: Membership: Registered, $30; nominee, $20; associate, $20. Meetings: Biennially, various locations; educational seminars, irregularly, various locations.

★ 218 ★

AMERICAN CENTER FOR THE ALEXANDER
    TECHNIQUE, INC.
142 West End Avenue   (212) 799-0468
New York, New York 10023   Established 1963

Troup H. Mathews, Chairman, Board of Directors;
    Judith Leibowitz, Director (Teacher Training School)
    Ronald J. Dennis, Acting Director (School of
    Alexander Studies)
ACAT, Inc. is a non-profit educational membership corporation. Since 1963, the Teacher Training School has trained some 60 Alexander Teachers, 48 of whom comprise the present membership. A Center in San Francisco is an offshoot of this Center, and though it shares the name, has no other formal rela-

tionship. Currently run by an internally-elected Board, the Center consists of two main operations: the Teacher Training School and the School of Alexander Studies. The Teacher Training School has its own director and a curriculum committee and carries an average of 20 trainees over a 30 month course of instruction; The School of Alexander Studies has its own director and deals with research, publication, and the educational aspects of public relations. Membership: 48 (members and associate members). Finances: Membership: Members, $250 annually; associate members, $35 annually; Other Sources: Tuition, studio rental. Meetings: General Membership, annually, at the Center; Board of Directors, monthly, at the Center or alternate location. Publications (Articles): A Study in Infant Development, Alma Frank, editor; A Technique for Musicians, Frank Pierce Jones, editor; Ethology and Stress Disease, Nikolas Tinbergen, editor; Postural Management of Scoliosis, Deborah Caplan, editor; Posture, Habit and Health, Eric de Peyer, editor; The Alexander Technique, Judith Leibowitz, editor; The F. Matthias Alexander Technique, Walter Carrington, editor; Voluntary Musculature in the Human Body, Raymond Dart, editor; (Books): Body Awareness in Action, Frank Pierce Jones, editor; F. Matthias Alexander, Lulie Westfeld. Library: ACAT, Inc. Library (most materials restricted to use in Center). Affiliations: ACAT, 931 Elizabeth Street, San Francisco, California.

★ 219 ★

AMERICAN CHINESE MEDICAL SOCIETY, INC.
110 Amity Street   (212) 780-1588
Brooklyn, New York 11201   Established 1964

Dr. Dorothy C. Yang, President; Dr. Wen Hsien Wu,
    Secretary
To advance medical knowledge and scientific research; to establish scholarships and/or endowments in medical schools and hospitals of good standing and/or to donate to organizations devoted to such purposes. In the event that any fund shall be established by the members for any scholarship, endowment or any other charitable purpose, this fund shall be kept in a separate account, and such monies of said fund shall not be co-mingled with the general funds of the corporation. In the event of a dissolution of the corporation, the funds in the treasury of the corporation shall not be distributed to the members, but shall be transferred to charitable and educational organizations which shall have the same ideals, purposes and objects that this organization is organized for. Membership: 362 (physicians and scientists in the field of medicine residing on the American continent are eligible for membership). Finances: Membership: Recommended by the Board of Directors and approved by a 2/3's majority vote of the members present in

the November-December general meeting of the Society of the year prior to the next ensuing year. Awards: Scholarship Program; Annual Awards. Meetings: Annual, in May-June or November-December, time and location shall be decided by the Board of Directors. Publications: Bulletin - American Chinese Medical Society, Inc., semiannual, Dr. Thomas King, editor; American Chinese Medical Society Directory, annual.

★ 220 ★

AMERICAN CHIROPRACTIC ASSOCIATION
2200 Grand Avenue   (515) 243-1121
Des Moines, Iowa 50312   Established 1963

Louis Gearhart, D.C., Executive Director
A professional society of licensed chiropractors which provides funds for upgrading accredited chiropractic colleges, promotes legislation defining chiropractice in modern terms, sponsors Correct Posture Week (May) and Chiropractic Day (September), and conducts educational seminars and conventions. Membership: 10,750 (general, associate, courtesy, junior, foreign). Finances: Membership: $10-$280; Other Sources: Printing, seminars. Awards: Foundation for Chiropractic Education and Research; funds for education and research, fellowships, and scholarships. Meetings: Annual, various locations. Publications: Journal of American Chiropractic Association, monthly, Jerry Marsengill, editor; Healthways, 6 times annually, Tracy Mullin, editor; Directory.

★ 221 ★

AMERICAN CLEFT PALATE ASSOCIATION
331 Salk Hall
University of Pittsburgh   (412) 681-9620
Pittsburgh, Pennsylvania 15261 Established 1943

Flora P. Berk, Administrative Secretary
To encourage scientific research in the courses of cleft lip and palate; to promote the science and art of rehabilitation of persons with cleft palate and associated deformities; to encourage cooperation among, and stimulation of, those specialists interested in the rehabiliation of cleft palate persons; to stimulate public interest in, and support of, the rehabilitation of cleft palate persons. Membership: 1,500. Finances: Membership: Annual dues, $40; Other Sources: Subscription to Cleft Palate Journal ($35 per volume or calendar year). Awards: Honor Awards; service awards. Meetings: Annual, various locations. Publications: Cleft Palate Journal, quarterly, Betty Jane McWilliams, Ph.D., editor.

★ 222 ★

AMERICAN CLINICAL AND CLIMATOLOGICAL
   ASSOCIATION
Johns Hopkins School of Medicine
720 Rutland Avenue
522 Traylor Building   (301) 955-3131
Baltimore, Maryland 21205

Richard J. Johns, M.D., Secretary
Clinical study of disease. Membership: 321 (honorary, emeritus, active). Finances: Membership: Active, $50; emeritus, $20; Other Sources: Sales of the annual publication. Meetings: Annual, various locations. Publications: Transactions of the American Clinical and Climatological Association, annual.

★ 223 ★

AMERICAN COALITION OF CITIZENS WITH
   DISABILITIES
1200 15th Street, N.W.
Suite 201   (202) 785-4265
Washington, D.C. 20005   Established 1974

Dr. Frank Bowe, Director
To help disabled people obtain and protect their rights to education, employment, health care housing. Membership: 925 individuals (with physical, mental or emotional impairments), 75 organizations. Meetings: Annual Delegate Assembly, May, various locations. Publications: Action Newsletter, monthly; The Coalition, quarterly; numerous books and monographs.

★ 224 ★

AMERICAN COLLEGE HEALTH ASSOCIATION
152 Rollins Avenue, Suite 208   (301) 468-6868
Rockville, Maryland 208 52   Established 1920

James W. Dilley, Executive Director
To provide an organization in which institutions of higher education, other organizations, and interested individuals may work together to promote health in its broadest aspects for students and all members of the college community. Membership: 364 institutions, 1,040 individuals (institutions of higher education, health professionals engaged in the delivery of health services at colleges and universities, students, and others with an interest in the health of academic communities). Finances: Institutional membership dues depend on enrollment; 4-year institutions, $175-$1,300; 2-year institutions, $125-$220; international institutions, $100-$325. Individual membership dues are based on a sliding scale, according to annual earned income; Other Sources: Annual meeting

registration fees, consultation fees, sales of publications, revenue from commercial advertising in journal. Awards: Edward Hitchcock Award; Ruth E. Boynton Award; Lewis Barbato Award for Student Leadership. Meetings: Annual meeting, Board meetings, meetings of 15 regional and state affiliate association. Publications: Journal of the American College Health Association, bimonthly, James B. McClenahan, M.D., editor; Action, 10 times annually, Linda DeRoo, editor.

★ 225 ★
AMERICAN COLLEGE OF ALLERGISTS, INC.
2141 14th Street   (303) 447-8111
Boulder, Colorado 80302   Established 1942

Shirley Schoenberger, Executive Secretary
To promote and advance the study, laboratory and clinical knowledge of allergy; to advance and maintain the highest possible standards among those engaged in the practices of allergy... Membership: 1,867 (physicians specializing in the practice of allergy). Finances: Membership: Active fellows, $50; foreign fellows, $20; associate fellows, $40; foreign, $10; Other Sources: Exhibits at annual meetings, grants for education and research, sale of journal. Awards: Scientific and Education Council with funds for postgraduate education and scientific research. Meetings: Annual, various locations, postgraduate courses. Publications: Annals of Allergy, monthly, M. Coleman Harris, M.D., editor.

★ 226 ★
AMERICAN COLLEGE OF ANESTHESIOLOGISTS
515 Busse Highway   (312) 825-5586
Park Ridge, Illinois 60068   Established 1947

John W. Andes, Executive Secretary
To aid in coordinating the educational activities of the American Society of Anesthesiologists; establish and maintain a continuing education program, including a self-evaluation program; certify qualifying physicians as Fellows of the American College of Anesthesiologists, denoting educational achievement in the medical specialty of anesthesiology; maintain a registry of Fellows... Membership: 8,172 (fellows).

★ 227 ★
AMERICAN COLLEGE OF APOTHECARIES
874 Union Avenue   (901) 527-6807
Memphis, Tennessee 38163   Established 1940

D. C. Huffman, Jr., Executive Vice President
To disseminate information, make studies of and advance, public health information through pharmacists to the public. Membership: 900 (full fellow, associate, hospital, faculty, administrative and service). Finances: Membership: Full, $125; all other categories, $35. Meetings: Semiannual, various locations. Publications: A.C.A. Newsletter, monthly; The Voice of the Pharmacist, biweekly; The Physician's Newsletter, monthly; The Patrons' Newsletter, monthly, Kenneth B. Roberts, editor.

★ 228 ★
AMERICAN COLLEGE OF CARDIOLOGY
9111 Old Georgetown Road   (301) 897-5400
Bethesda, Maryland 20014   Established 1949

William D. Nelligan, CAE, Executive Director
The mission of the American College of Cardiology is to ensure optimal care for persons with cardiovascular disease or the potential for developing cardiovascular disease and, ultimately, through appropriate educational and socio-economic activities to contribute significantly to the prevention of cardiovascular diseases. Membership: 10,243 (cardiologists, pediatric cardiologists, thoracic surgeons, internists devoting a large percentage of their practice to cardiovascular disease, recognized scientists in the field of cardiology). Finances: Membership: Full fellows, $110; associate fellows over age of 36, $110; associate fellows under age 36, $80; affiliate members over age of 36, $110; affiliate members under age 36, $50; affiliates in training, $25. Awards: Distinguished Fellow; Honorary Fellow; Convocation Medalist; Gifted Teacher Award; Distinguished Service Award. Meetings: Annual Scientific Session, various large cities in different sections of the country; 30-35 continuing education programs at the College; 35 continuing education courses through the year in various parts of the country. Publications: American Journal of Cardiology, monthly, Simon Dack, M.D., FACC, editor; Cardiology (newsletter), quarterly, Patricia A. Ulander, Managing editor. Library: Griffith Resource Library, 950 monographs, 85 AV titles, 80 journals, newsletters, (restricted to cardiovascular health professionals). Griffith Resource provides library support for learning center programs and membership.

★ 229 ★
AMERICAN COLLEGE OF CHEST PHYSICIANS
911 Busse Highway   (312) 698-2200
Park Ridge, Illinois 60068   Established 1935

Alfred Soffer, M.D., Executive Director
 To further undergraduate and postgraduate medical education and research in diseases of the chest (heart and lung) throughout the world; to promote the highest standards of scientific endeavor in the speciality of chest diseases in all countries. Membership: 10,500 (fellow, associate, affiliate, honorary, fellow emeritus). Finances: Membership: $110, below age 35 -$85; fellowship fee, $100; Other Sources: Educational grants, exhibits, advertisements, and registration fees. Awards: Cecile Lehman Mayer Research Award; Alfred A. Richman Essay Contest College Medal; International College Medal. Meetings: Annual, various locations; Regional Congress, biennial, various locations; International Congress, quadrennial, various locations. Publications: Chest, monthly, Alfred Soffer, editor; Bulletin, quarterly. Affiliations: Associated Member of the Council for International Organizations.

★ 230 ★
AMERICAN COLLEGE OF CLINICAL
     PHARMACOLOGY
19 South 22nd Street   (215) 563-9560
Philadelphia, Pennsylvania 19103   Established 1969

Elliot Vessel, M.D., President
To promote the science of clinical pharmacology and to maintain and encourage a commitment of excellence in the investigational and clinical testings of drugs. Seeks to apply sound principles in human drug therapy. Membership: 556 (individuals who have earned the degree of Doctor of Medicine or a doctorate in any one of the biomedical sciences; individuals who have had at least 3 years of training or the equivalent in basic science, internal medicine or an allied field). Awards: McKeen Cattell Award for excellence in clinical pharmacology. Meetings: Annual, various locations. Publications: Journal of Clinical Pharmacology, 8 annually; Directory, biennial.

★ 231 ★
AMERICAN COLLEGE OF DENTISTS
7315 Wisconsin Avenue,
Suite 352N
Bethesda, Maryland 20014   (301) 986-0555
                                  Established 1920

Robert J. Nelsen, D.D.S., Executive Director
To urge the extension and improvement of measures for the control and prevention of oral disorders; to encourage qualified persons to consider a career in dentistry so that dental health services will be available to all and to urge broad preparation for such a career at all educational levels; to encourage grad-

uate studies and continuing educational efforts by dentists and auxiliaries; to encourage, stimulate and promote research; through sound public health education, to improve the public understanding and appreciation of oral health service and its importance to the optimum health of the patient; to encourage the free exchange of ideas and experiences in the interest of better service to the patient; to cooperate with other groups for the advancement of interprofessional relationships in the interest of the public; and to make visible to the professional man the extent of his responsibilities to the community as well as to the field of health service and to urge his acceptance of them; in order to give encouragement to individuals to further these objectives, and to recognize meritorious achievements and potentials for contributions in dental science, art, education, literature, human relations and other areas that contribute to the human welfare and the promotion of these objectives--by conferring Fellowship in the Colleges on such persons properly selected to receive such honor. Membership: 4,670 (active, honorary, life members). Finances: Membership: Membership fee $325; annual dues, $50. Meetings: Annual, various locations. Publications: Journal of the American College of Dentists, quarterly, Dr. Robert I. Kaplan, editor; News and Views (newsletter) quarterly, Dr. Robert J. Nelsen, editor.

★ 232 ★
AMERICAN COLLEGE OF EMERGENCY PHYSICIANS
Post Office Box 61911   (214) 659-0911
Dallas, Texas 75261   Established 1968

Arthur E. Auer, Executive Director
Provides a means by which physicians engaged in the practice of emergency medicine might pool their knowledge, seek solutions to common problems, and work together to set standards and develop methods for the professional practice of emergency medicine. Membership: 10,000. Finances: $250. Meetings: Annual Scientific Assembly; annual symposium; winter workshop; clinical conferences; seminars, all held at various locations. Publications: Annals of Emergency Medicine, monthly, Ronald L. Krome, M.D., editor; ACEP Hotline; Emergency Medicine Residency Newsletter; Emergency Department Organization and Management, A. L. Jenkins, M.D., editor. Library: Emergency Medical Services Information Center, 2,000 books, 182 journals (service for members and Emergency Medicine Service related organizations). Affiliations: Emergency Medical Foundation; University Association for Emergency Medicine; Society for Teachers of Emergency Medicine, Emergency Residents' Association, Liaison Residency Endorsement Committee.

★ 233 ★
AMERICAN COLLEGE OF FOOT ORTHOPEDISTS
Post Office Box 31331   (415) 826-3200
San Francisco, California 94131   Established 1950

Dr. David M. Davidson, President
To advance the standards of practice and quality of
services of podiatrists who devote a major portion of
their professional efforts to podiatric orthopedic management of foot problems.   Membership: 340 (fellows).   Finances: Membership: Dues, $50; appli-
cation fee, $50; examination fee, $200; seminar
fees vary.   Awards: Research awards; awards to
support development of podiatric orthopedic residency
programs in hospitals/colleges/clinics.   Meetings:
Annual, August, in conjunction with American Podiatry Association, various locations.   Affiliations:
American Podiatry Association.

★ 234 ★
AMERICAN COLLEGE OF FOOT SPECIALISTS
Post Office Box 54   (201) 688-1616
Union, New Jersey 07083   Established 1962

Dr. Jerome J. Erman, President
To promote continuing education in the field of Podiatric Medicine.   Membership: Open to the profession (all licensed foot specialists and students of
podiatric medicine).   Finances: Other Sources:
Registration fees for seminars.   Meetings: 4 to 6
times annually.

★ 235 ★
AMERICAN COLLEGE OF FOOT SURGEONS
Post Office Box 31331   (415) 826-3200
San Francisco, California 94131   Established 1950

John L. Bennett, Executive Director
To promote the art and science of foot surgery; to
disseminate among its members and the podiatry profession in general knowledge of foot surgery; to encourage and maintain the highest professional standards
among its members.   Membership: 750 (fellow, associate).   Finances: Membership: Application fee,
$150; examination fee, $150; dues, $100; Other
Sources: Seminar; journal publication.   Meetings:
Annual, various locations.   Publications: Journal of
Foot Surgery, quarterly, Richard P. Reinherz, D.P.M.,
editor; newsletters; pamphlets on foot surgery.
Affiliations: American Podiatry Association.

★ 236 ★
AMERICAN COLLEGE OF GASTROENTEROLOGY
299 Broadway   (212) 227-7590
New York, New York 10007   Established 1932

Daniel Weiss, Executive Director
A society of surgeons and physicians who specialize
in disorders of the stomach and digestive system.
Membership: 1,500.   Finances: Membership: Fel-
lows, associate fellows, members, $100;   Other
Sources: Contributions, subscriptions and advertising.
Meetings: Annual, various locations.   Publications:
American Journal of Gastroenterology, monthly,
Archer E. Lindner, M.D., editor.

★ 237 ★
AMERICAN COLLEGE OF GENERAL PRACTITIONERS
   IN OSTEOPATHIC MEDICINE AND SURGERY
2500 East Devon   (800) 323-5919
Des Plaines,   (312) 298-2565
   Illinois 60018   Established 1950

To advance the standards of general practice in the
field of Medicine and Surgery by encouraging and
improving the educational opportunities for the training
of general practitioners; to aid in establishing a Department of General Practice in hospitals; and to
promote a general understanding of the scope of the
services rendered by the General Practitioner.   The
College conducts educational seminars and holds annual educational conventions. Membership: Over 3,000
(osteopathic physicians and surgeons).   Finances:
Membership: $100.   Meetings: Annual, various
locations.   Publications: Monthly Official Publication, Ronald Goldberg, D.O., editor.   Affiliations:
American Osteopathic Association.

★ 238 ★
AMERICAN COLLEGE OF HOSPITAL
   ADMINISTRATORS
840 North Lake Shore Drive   (312) 943-0544
Chicago, Illinois 60611   Established 1933

Stuart A. Wesbury, Jr., Ph.D., President
To elevate the standard of hospital administration; to
establish a standard of competence for hospital administration; to develop and promote standards of education and training for hospital administrators; to educate hospital trustees and the public to understand
that the practice of hospital administration calls for
special training and experience; to provide a method
for conferring Fellowships in hospital administration on
those who have done or are doing noteworthy service
in the field of hospital administration.   Membership:
15,000, including 3,000 student associates (nominees,

members, fellows, student associates). Awards:
James A. Hamilton Hospital Administrators' Book
Award, $500 cash and medallion to author of excep-
tional book on the administrative process; Dean Con-
ley Award, best article published in the hospital literature; Edgar C. Hayhow Award, best article published in the society's quarterly Journal, Hospital &
Health Services Administration; Hudgens' Memorial
Award, to an outstanding Young Hospital Administrator
of the Year; Gold Medal Award for Excellence in
Hospital Administration, to exceptional affiliate who
is a practicing administrator; Silver Medal Award, to
an exceptional administrator in a non-hospital position (with association, in education, consulting, agency, etc.); Honorary Fellowships (3) to outstanding
contributors to administration in some health service
capacity. Meetings: Annual, various locations.
Publications: Hospital & Health Services Administration, quarterly, Lynn C. Wimmer, editor; ACHA
News, monthly; Directory, biennially.

★ 239 ★
AMERICAN COLLEGE OF INTERNATIONAL
    PHYSICIANS, INC.
3030 Lake Avenue, Suite 12   (219) 424-7414
Fort Wayne, Indiana 46805   Established 1975

Antonio B. Donesa, M.D., Executive Director
A cooperative endeavor by physicians from many
countries and nations practicing in the United States
and Canada to solve common concerns for the future
of medicine in the United States and abroad.   The
College seeks to provide its input into national policies which deal with international health activities,
international medical education, ethics, research and
international exchange.   It hopes to be the international arm of organized American medicine, and plays
an activist role in international health activities.
The College is open to all physicians educated in the
United States, Canada and abroad; its major objective is to foster and promote the betterment of the
health of all peoples and to advance the art and science of medicine. Membership: 600 (regular fellows, M.D.'s licensed to practice in U.S. and Canada; associate fellows, M.D.'s without license in
U.S. and Canada [residing in U.S.]; affiliate fellows, M.D.'s without license in U.S. and Canada
[residing outside North America]; teachers in allied
professions; student fellows, honorary fellows).
Finances: Membership: Annual dues regular, $50;
associate and affiliate, $25; student, $10; Other
Sources: Convention fees. Awards: Distinguished
Fellowship Award (none yet awarded); Service
Awards (physicians who distinguish themselves in their
service to the College). Meetings: Annual Convocation of Fellows and Scientific Assembly; seminars,
symposia, forums, various locations (irregular). Pub-

lications: ACIP Bulletin, quarterly, A.B. Donesa,
M.D., editor; Proceedings of Convention, annually,
Publications Committee (editors); Convention Book,
annually, Publications Committee (editors). Library:
ACIP Library, restricted to researchers.

★ 240 ★
AMERICAN COLLEGE OF LABORATORY ANIMAL
    MEDICINE
c/o Dr. William S. Webster
University of Massachusetts Medical Center
Department of Animal Medicine
55 Lake Avenue North   (617) 856-3151
Worcester, Massachusetts 01605 Established 1957

Dr. Alan L. Kraus, President; Dr. Norman H.
    Altman, President-Elect; Dr. William S. Webster,
    Secretary-Treasurer
To encourage education, training and standards of
training and experience for veterinarians professionally
concerned with the care and health of laboratory
animals; and to recognize qualified persons in laboratory animal medicine by certification examination
and other means.   Activities include sponsorship of
scientific programs on comparative medicine topics,
continuing education programs for its members, publication of texts and the presentation of symposia on
various facets of experimental animal medicine to the
scientific community. Membership: 302 diplomates
(veterinary specialists in laboratory animal medicine);
active diplomates; retired or emeritus diplomates and
honorary diplomates. Finances: Membership: $30
annually; Other Sources: Annual dues, certification
examination fees; royalty income from texts; banquet
fees; forum fees. Meetings: Biennial, in conjunction with the American Veterinary Medical Association. Publications: Biology of the Laboratory Rab-
bit, Academic Press, 1974; Biology of the Guinea
Pig, Academic Press, 1976; The Laboratory Rat,
Academic Press, 1979; Spontaneous Animal Models
of Human Diseases, Academic Press, 1979. Affiliations: American Veterinary Medical Association.

★ 241 ★
AMERICAN COLLEGE OF LEGAL MEDICINE
875 North Michigan Avenue
Suite 3342   (312) 440-0080
Chicago, Illinois 60611   Established 1960

Betty Hanna, Executive Secretary
To elevate standards of legal medicine; to do all
things necessary and proper to disseminate knowledge
in the field of legal medicine by whatever means appropriate, including lectures, seminars, discussions
and publication; to form branches and chapters where

permitted by law and when authorized by the Board of Governors. Membership: 625 (fellows, associate in medicine, associate in law, associate in science, affiliate, emeritus, honorary, corresponding fellows and associates). Finances: Membership: Fellows, $150 annually; associates, $90 annually; affiliates, $75 annually; Other Sources: Educational Conference. Awards: Student Award for outstanding papers on a medical-legal subject by medical and law students. Meetings: Annual, 3 1/2 days, various locations; 1 day mid-year meeting, late fall, various locations; additional meetings co-sponsored with other organizations, various locations. Publications: Legal Aspects of Medical Practice, annually, Cyril H. Wecht, M.D., J.D., F.C.L.M., editor; Journal of Legal Medicine, (law review type publication), quarterly, Lee S. Goldsmith, M.D., J.D., F.C.L.M., editor; Newsletter, quarterly.

★242★
AMERICAN COLLEGE OF MEDICAL GROUP
   ADMINISTRATORS
4101 East Louisiana Avenue   (303) 753-1111
Denver, Colorado 80222   Established 1956

Fred E. Graham II, Ph.D.
The purposes of the College are to encourage medical group practice administrators to improve and maintain their proficiency and to provide appropriate recognition of their achievement; to establish a program which sets uniform standards of admission, advancement, and certification in order to achieve the highest possible standards through education in the profession of medical group practice administration; to participate in the development of educational and research programs for the advancement of the profession; to inform the medical profession and the general public of the value of trained and experienced men and women in the management of the administrative affairs of all forms of group practice; and to instill in its membership a constant awareness of the high ideals and traditions of the medical profession and medical group administration so that its members will conduct themselves in such a manner as to augment those ideals and traditions. Membership: 700 (nominee, member, fellow). Finances: Membership: $50 annually. Awards: Harry J. Harwick Award for Excellence. Meetings: Annual, various locations. Publications: ACMGA Newsletter, semiannual, Fred E. Graham, II, Ph.D.; various brochures. Affiliations: Medical Group Management Association; Center for Research in Ambulatory Health Care Administration.

★243★
AMERICAN COLLEGE OF MEDICAL IMAGING
Post Office Box 27188   (213) 275-1393
Los Angeles, California 90027   Established 1976

R. L. Wilson, M.D., President
Provides continuing medical education for radiologists and others in health care field. Membership: Physicians. Finances: Membership: $100 annually. Meetings: General Meeting, annual (first one planned for 1984), various locations; regular meetings, quarterly, various locations. Publications: ACMI News, quarterly.

★244★
AMERICAN COLLEGE OF NEUROPSYCHIATRISTS
Academy Office
405 Grand Avenue   (513) 222-4213
Dayton, Ohio 45405   Established 1937

G. Joseph Stricker, C.A.E., Executive Director
Promotes study and research in neurology and psychiatry in the osteopathic profession. Membership: 250 (psychiatrists, neurologists, physicians in training persons in interrelated professions). Meetings: Annual, with American Osteopathic Association, various locations. Publications: Bulletin, quarterly; Directory, semiannual. Affiliations: American Osteopathic Association.

★245★
AMERICAN COLLEGE OF NEUROPSYCHO-
          PHARMACOLOGY
134 Wesley Hall
Vanderbilt University   (615) 322-2869
Nashville, Tennessee 37240   Established 1961

Ray Oakley, Ph.D., Secretary
To promote and encourage the scientific study and application of neuropsychopharmacology. Membership: 400. Awards: Paul A. Hoch Award for outstanding research in the field. Meetings: Annual, various locations. Publications: Bulletin, semiannual; Roster, annual.

★246★
AMERICAN COLLEGE OF NUCLEAR PHYSICIANS
1101 Connecticut Avenue, N.W.
Suite 700   (202) 857-1135
Washington, D.C. 20036   Established 1974

James A. McBain, Jr., Executive Director
To foster the highest standards of nuclear medicine

service and consultation to the public, hospitals and referring physicians; to advance the science of nuclear medicine; to promote the continuing competence of practitioners of nuclear medicine. Membership: 1,000 (physicians and scientists). Meetings: Annual, various locations. Publications: Update, monthly; Newsletter, quarterly.

★ 247 ★
AMERICAN COLLEGE OF NURSE-MIDWIVES
1012 14th Street, N.W., #801   (202) 347-5445
Washington, D.C. 20005   Established 1955

Fay Lebowitz, Administrative Director
The College's objectives are to study, develop and evaluate standards for nurse-midwifery care of women and infants; to study, develop and evaluate standards for nurse-midwifery education; to support and assist in the development of nurse-midwifery services and educational programs, in association with allied professional groups; to evaluate and approve nurse-midwifery services and educational programs; to determine the eligibility of individuals to practice as Certified Nurse-Midwives, and to assume responsibility for National Nurse-Midwifery Certification; to facilitate and coordinate the efforts of nurse-midwives who in the public interest provide quality services to individuals and childbearing families; to establish channels for communication and cooperation with other professional and non-professional groups on a regional, national and international basis; and to promote research and the development of literature in the field of nurse-midwifery. Membership: 1,700 (active, 1,022; life, 142; associate, 178; student, 294). Finances: Membership: Active, $150; life, $2,250; associate, $60; student, $60. Meetings: Annual Convention. Publications: Journal of Nurse-Midwifery, bimonthly, Elsevier North-Holland, Inc., editors; Quickening, bimonthly, ACNM Headquarters, editors.

★ 248 ★
AMERICAN COLLEGE OF NURSING HOME
    ADMINISTRATORS
4650 East-West Highway   (301) 652-8384
Washington, D.C. 20014   Established 1963

J. Albin Yokie, Executive Vice President
The College's purposes are to elevate the standard of nursing home administration; to establish the standard of competence for nursing home administration; to develop and promote standards of education and training for nursing home administrators; and to advance the quality of patient care in long term care institutions to the highest possible level. Membership:

6,000 (members, fellows, associates, student affiliates). Finances: Membership: Active, $140; associate, $85; student affiliate, $25; inactive, $25. Awards: Administrator of the Year Award; Journalist of the Year Award; Educator of the Year Award. Meetings: Annual, various locations. Publications: Long-Term Care Administrator, monthly, Richard Healy, editor; Journal of Long-Term Care Administration, quarterly, J. Albin Yokie, editor.

★ 249 ★
AMERICAN COLLEGE OF OBSTETRICIANS AND
    GYNECOLOGISTS
1 East Wacker Drive, Suite 2700   (312) 222-1600
Chicago, Illinois 60601   Established 1951

Warren H. Pearse, M.D., Executive Director
The College aims to establish and maintain the highest possible standards for obstetric and gynecologic education, practice and research; and to perpetuate the history and best traditions of obstetrics and gynecologic practice and ethics. Membership: 23,000 (fellows, honorary fellows, associate fellows, life fellows, affiliate fellows, junior fellows). Finances: Membership: Dues. Awards: Mead Johnson Award for Graduate Training. Meetings: Annual, various locations. Publications: Obstetrics and Gynecology, monthly, Richard Mattingly, editor; ACOG Newsletter, monthly, Robert R. Mander, editor; numerous patient and professional brochures; catalogue.

★ 250 ★
AMERICAN COLLEGE OF OSTEOPATHIC HOSPITAL
    ADMINISTRATORS
930 Busse Highway   (312) 692-2351
Park Ridge, Illinois 60068   Established 1953

Michael F. Doody, President
A voluntary professional society dedicated to the development of osteopathic hospital administration. It aims to establish criteria of competency and set standards to ensure that such administrators continue to progress and develop further skills through participation in professional development programs and to contribute to the advancement of efficient hospital administration. Membership: 150 hospital administrators and assistants. Finances: Membership: Fellow, $125; member, $125; nominee, life fellow, honorary fellow, life member, $80. Meetings: Annual, various locations; Conference and Convocation. Publications: News Brief, quarterly, Lin Fish, editor; Annual Directory, annually, Lin Fish editor.

★ 251 ★

AMERICAN COLLEGE OF OSTEOPATHIC
   OBSTETRICIANS & GYNECOLOGISTS
900 Auburn Road, Suite 103   (313) 332-6360
Pontiac, Michigan 48057

Jerry Polsinelli, D.O., Executive Director;
   Anita H. Atkins, D.O., President
To establish and maintain the highest possible standards
for osteopathic obstetrics and gynecology; to foster
osteopathic obstetric and gynecologic practice and
research; to maintain the dignity and efficiency of
osteopathic obstetric and gynecologic practice in its
relation to public welfare; to recommend and promote
osteopathic obstetric and gynecologic education in
osteopathic medical schools and hospitals; to maintain standards for membership and grant recognition
and titles to its membership; to nominate the members of the American Osteopathic Board of Obstetrics
and Gynecology; and to assist the American Osteopathic Association, allied societies and the general
public in furthering the philosophy of the osteopathic
concept. Membership: 237 (candidate membership
[residents in training]; regular membership [board
eligible]; senior membership [board certified]; affiliate membership [related specialty]; life membership
[no dues]). Finances: Membership: $175 regular
and senior   Other Sources: Dues and Convention
Registration are the main source of income. Awards:
Distinguished Service Award. Meetings: Annual
Convention, various locations; Annual Postgraduate
Course, various locations. Publications: Newsletter,
2-3 times annually, E. A. Slotnick, D.O., editor.

★ 252 ★

AMERICAN COLLEGE OF OSTEOPATHIC SURGEONS
3132 Ponce de Leon Boulevard   (305) 444-2267
Coral Gables, Florida 33134   Established 1926

Robert C. Erwin, D.O., Executive Director;
   Wanda L. Highsmith, Assistant Executive Director/
   Convention Manager
To encourage the study of the science of surgery, surgical diagnosis, pathology, and the application of
principles, practice, and treatment thereof. Activities include programs of continuing surgical and medical education at the Annual Clinical Assembly of
Osteopathic Specialists, the planning and conduct of
several annual courses and seminars at the graduate
and postgraduate levels, plus courses in surgical anatomy and clinical teaching conducted in cooperation
with colleges of osteopathic medicine and with osteopathic hospitals; improvement in postinternship training in fellowship, preceptorship and residency in surgery and in many surgical specialties; maintenance
of high ethical standards and compliance with them
by Members and osteopathic physicians registered as

Candidates for Membership. Membership: 703 (members; candidates, fellows, associate and honorary
members). Finances: Membership: Membership application fee, $150; annual dues, $250; candidate
application fee, $25; annual validation fee, $25;
associate membership fee, $25; annual dues, $15
Other Sources: Registration and exhibit fees during
annual assembly; advertising fees. Awards: Distinguished Osteopathic Surgeon Award; Fellow in the
American College of Osteopathic Surgeons; Orel
F. Martin Award. Meetings: Clinical Assembly of
Osteopathic Specialists, annually; Postgraduate
Course in Surgery, annually; Inquisition Surgical
Forum, annually; Review Courses. Publications:
ACOS News, monthly, Charles Gnaegy, editor;
Membership Directory and Bylaws, annually. Affilia-
tions: A.C.O.S. Urological Section; A.C.O.S.
Thoracic-Cardiovascular Section; A.C.O.S. Neuro-
logical Surgeons Section.

★ 253 ★

AMERICAN COLLEGE OF PODIATRIC
   RADIOLOGISTS
c/o Dr. Irving H. Block
1 Lincoln Road Building, #308   (305) 531-9866
Miami Beach, Florida 33139   Established 1942

Irving H. Block, Secretary
The College's purposes include the encouragement of
interest in podiatric roentgenology, the study and use
of the x-ray, the study of x-ray films and their preparation for evaluation, the dissemination of knowledge
of podiatric roentgenology and of the design and
manipulation of the instruments pertaining thereunto,
and the reading and interpretation of radiographs for
diagnostic purposes. It provides postgraduate courses
in roentgenology, conducts research, disseminates advances in podiatric roentgenology, sponsors study
groups, contributes papers and releases to the Journal
of the American Podiatry Association, and provides
lectures for regional and national scientific meetings.
Membership: 100 (full fellows, associate fellows,
applicants in process). Finances: Examination fee,
$100; annual fee, $45. Awards: Student awards
for research papers to members of graduating classes
of podiatry colleges. Meetings: Annual with American Podiatry Association, various locations; Regional meetings, New York, New Jersey, mid-west,
west coast. Affiliations: American Podiatry Association.

★ 254 ★

AMERICAN COLLEGE OF PODOPEDIATRICS
10515 Carnegie Avenue   (216) 231-3300
Cleveland, Ohio 44106   Established 1978

Dr. Robert Gosselin, President; Dr. Herman Tax,
   Secretary-Treasurer
To educate the community in Podopediatrics; to acquaint the community in the needs and demands of
the child as a patient; to coordinate the various disciplines of Podiatric Medicine, Medicine, Biomechan-
ics, Surgery, and Physical Therapy in the treatment
of children; to stimulate research in the area of
musculoskeletal pathomechanics, gait analysis, orthotic
control and surgery as applied to the child; to encourage an exchange of ideas with members of allied
health professions in order to provide total care for
children; to sponsor a podopediatrics seminar on a
yearly basis to disseminate current knowledge to the
profession and allied professions; to be active in the
advancement of the American College of Podopediatrics. Membership: Approximately 150 (members,
honorary members, fellows). Finances: Membership:
$25 annually; Other Sources: Seminars. Meetings:
Biennial, various locations. Affiliations: American
Podiatry Association.

★ 255 ★
AMERICAN COLLEGE OF PREVENTIVE MEDICINE
1015 15th Street, N.W.   (202) 789-0003
Washington, D.C. 20005   Established 1954

Kent W. Peterson, M.D., Executive Vice President
A professional society for physicians engaged in
practice, teaching, or research in preventive medicine. Membership: 2,000 (fellows, 1,600; members, 350; affiliate members, 40; international members, 20). Finances: Membership: Fellowship, $95
annually; members, $65 annually; affiliates/inter-
national, $25 annually; Other Sources: Endowed
lectureship. Lectureships: Katharine Boucot Sturgis
Lectureship, presented at annual fall meeting.
Meetings: Semiannual, various locations. Publications: Preventive Medicine Newsletter, quarterly,
D.V. Helm, editor; Spectrum, quarterly; Katharine
Boucot Sturgis Lectureship, annually.

★ 256 ★
AMERICAN COLLEGE OF PROSTHODONTISTS
6800 Park Ten Boulevard
Suite 145 East   (512) 732-6403
San Antonio, Texas 78213   Established 1970

Linda Wallenborn, Central Office Director
To foster interest in the specialty of prosthodontics
with the objective of improving the quality of treatment of the prosthodontic patient through educational
activities designed to bring new ideas, techniques
and research into clinical practice and to enhance
the prosthodontic services received by the public.

Membership: Approximately 1,100 (Fellows: diplomates of the American Board of Prosthodontics; associates: persons who have completed formal training
in an approved course in prosthodontics; affiliates:
persons enrolled in approved graduate or residency
programs; life members). Research: Annual Prosthodontic Research Competition. Meetings: Annual,
week preceding the Annual Session of the American
Dental Association, various locations. Publications:
ACP Newsletter, quarterly, Dr. Robert Elliot, editor;
Classic Prosthodontic Articles, volumes I, II, III.

★ 257 ★
AMERICAN COLLEGE OF PSYCHIATRISTS
1700 18th Street, N.W.   (202) 797-4858
Washington, D.C. 20009   (202) 797-4855
                                    Established 1963

Shervert H. Frazier, M.D., President
To promote continuing education of its members.
Membership: 500 (members, fellows). Finances:
New members: $50 initiation fee plus $100 annual
dues; fellows: $100 initiation fee plus $100 annual
dues; to change status from member to fellow: $50.
Awards: Dean Award; Bowis Award. Meetings:
Annual, various locations. Publications: Papers
from annual meetings.

★ 258 ★
AMERICAN COLLEGE OF PSYCHOANALYSTS
137 East 66th Street   (212) 734-0220
New York, New York 10021   Established 1969

Robert S. Murford, M.D., Secretary General
An honorary and scientific professional organization,
seeks to contribute to the constructive development of
psychoanalysis; to provide professional leadership and
support high standards in the practice of psychoanalysis;
to provide a scientific forum for various theoretical
points of view; to encourage the understanding, acceptance and constructive utilization of sound analytic
concepts by an informed public. Membership: 200
(physicians psychoanalysts). Meetings: Annual Col-
loquium and Scientific Meetings, April or May, various locations; also holds annual meetings in February.
Publications: Bulletin, 3 annually; ACPn Archives.

★ 259 ★
AMERICAN COLLEGE OF RADIOLOGY
20 North Wacker Drive   (312) 236-4963
Chicago, Illinois 60606   Established 1923

William C. Stronach, Executive Director

To advance the science of radiology and improve radiologic service to the sick by means of the study of the economic aspects of the practice of radiology, and the encouragement of improved education facilities for radiologists. Membership: 14,000 (radiologists, certified by the American Board of Radiology, and radiologic physicists). Finances: Membership and fellowship, $175. Awards: Gold Medal presented to radiologists for outstanding service in the field of radiology. Meetings: Annual, various locations. Publications: ACR Bulletin, monthly, Charles Honaker, editor.

★ 260 ★

AMERICAN COLLEGE OF SPORTS MEDICINE
1440 Monroe Street   (608) 262-3632
Madison, Wisconsin 53706   Established 1955

To promote and advance medical and other scientific studies dealing with the effect of sports and other physical activities on the health of human beings at various stages of life; to cooperate with other organizations, physicians, scientists and educators concerned with the same or related specialties; to arrange for mutual meetings of physicians, educators and allied scientists; to make available postgraduate education in fields related to these sciences; to initiate, promote and correlate research in these fields; to edit and publish a journal, articles and pamphlets pertaining to various aspects of sports, other physical activities and medicine; and to establish and maintain a sports medicine library. Membership: 8,000 (fellows, graduate students, honorary fellows, fellows emeritus, members emeritus, and associate members). Finances: Membership: Members and fellows, $35; graduate students and student affiliates, $15; associate members, $7; Other Sources: Funds from annual meetings. Awards: Citations and Honor Awards; New Investigator Award; Traveling Scholar Award. Meetings: Annual, various locations. Publications: Medicine and Science in Sports and Exercise, 5 times annually; Sports Medicine Bulletin, quarterly, Carol Christison, editor. Affiliations: Federation Internationale de Medecine Sportive.

★ 261 ★

AMERICAN COLLEGE OF SURGEONS
55 East Erie Street   (312) 664-4050
Chicago, Illinois 60611   Established 1913

C. Rollins Hanlon, M.D., Director
To maintain an association of surgeons, not for pecuniary profit, but for the benefit of humanity by advancing the science of surgery and the ethical and competent practice of its art. Activities include

continuing education surgical meetings, primarily in North America; approval of hospital and residency programs in general surgery and the surgical specialties; approval of cancer follow-up programs in hospitals and workshops on administration of cancer registries; professional and public education seminars for physicians, nurses and lay personnel to improve all phases of care of the injured; research scholarships for graduate training in surgery; joint operation with National Institutes of Health of Organ Transplant Registry; motion picture programs; administration of program of self-evaluation and assessment; study on surgical services in the United States in collaboration with the American Surgical Association; collaboration with 82 local chapters of the College; encouragement of surgical research. Membership: 43,000 (specialists in general surgery and in the surgical specialties). Finances: Membership: $190 for North Americans, $70 for international fellows; Other Sources: Contributions and grants. Meetings: Annual Clinical Congress, various locations; Annual Spring Meeting, various locations. Publications: Surgery, Gynecology and Obstetrics, monthly, Dr. Loyal Davis, editor; Bulletin, monthly, Dennis Connaughton, editor.

★ 262 ★

AMERICAN COLLEGE OF UTILIZATION REVIEW
      PHYSICIANS, INC.
1108 North Second Street   (717) 697-4428
Harrisburg, Pennsylvania 17102 Established 1973

Betty J. Hamman, Executive Director
Organized to educate physicians and related health personnel, research, set standards of practice and measure competence in the field of Utilization Review and Quality Assurance. Membership: 1,000 (fellow, affiliate, institutional, hospital). Finances: Membership: $50-$225; Other Sources: Registration fees for Seminars, Newsletter subscriptions, Study Guide orders, grants from Pharmaceutical Companies. Meetings: National Seminar, annual, major cities throughout the United States; Regional Seminars, annual, major cities in areas of Regional Chapters. Publications: ACURP Newsletter, monthly, Thomas W. Murphy, M.D., editor; Study Guide in Quality Assurance and Utilization Review. Affiliations: American Board of Quality Assurance and Utilization Review Physicians.

★ 263 ★

AMERICAN COLLEGE OF VETERINARY
    MICROBIOLOGISTS
Veterinary Medical Research Institute
Iowa State University   (515) 294-7644
Ames, Iowa 50011   Established 1966

Richard F. Ross, Secretary-Treasurer
To further educational and scientific progress in veterinary microbiology; to strengthen pre- and post-
doctoral instruction in the discipline; to promote high
professional standing; to establish standards for training and to issue certificates of competence in veter-
inay microbiology.   Activities include annual certification examinations for persons seeking to receive
certificates of competence, and continuing education
programs for diplomates and other interested in veterinary microbiology. Membership: 180 (diplomates,
affiliates). Finances: Membership: Examination fee
and $10 membership, annually. Meetings: Annual,
July, in conjunction with American Veterinary Medical Association, various locations; Annual, November,
in conjunction with Conference of Research Workers
in Animal Diseases, various locations. Affiliations:
American Veterinary Medical Association.

★ 264 ★

AMERICAN COLLEGE OF VETERINARY
    OPHTHALMOLOGISTS
University of Florida
J. Hillis Miller Health Center
Box J-115   (904) 392-4744
Gainesville, Florida 32610   Established 1970

Dr. R. M. Gwin, Secretary-Treasurer
To advance ophthalmology in all phases of veterinary
medicine; to encourage education, training and research in veterinary ophthalmology; to establish
standards of training and experience in this field and
to recognize individuals who have fulfilled such
standards. Membership: 64 (private ophthalmology
practice, institutional [research-teaching]). Meetings: Annually, Fall, in conjunction with the American Academy of Ophthalmologists (A.A.O).

★ 265 ★

AMERICAN COLLEGE OF VETERINARY
    PATHOLOGISTS
Post Office Box 2108   (301) 468-6348
Rockville, Maryland 20852

Paul K. Hildebrandt, D.V.M., Secretary-Treasurer
To further scientific progress in the specialty of veterinary pathology; to establish standards of training
and experience for qualification of specialists in vet-

erinary pathology; and, to further the recognition of
such qualified specialists by suitable certification and
other means.   Conducts annual seminars and scientific programs designed for continuing education of
veterinary pathologists. Membership: 514. Finances: Membership: $60. Meetings: Semiannual,
various locations. Publications: Veterinary Pathology, bimonthly, John Shadduck, editor.

★ 266 ★

AMERICAN COLLEGE OF VETERINARY RADIOLOGY
c/o S. K. Kneller
157 Veterinary Medical University
    of Illinois   (217) 333-2000
Urbana, Illinois 61801   Established 1966

S. K. Kneller, Secretary
To advance the art and science of veterinary radiology; to protect the public from incompetence by
examining and certifying voluntary candidates as
diplomates; to encourage evaluating training programs in the field; to pursue continuing education
programs. Membership: 86 (diplomates, 75; charter
diplomates, 5; emeritus diplomates, 2; associate
members, 4). Finances: Membership: $50 annually
to diplomates; Other Sources: Examination fee,
$100. Meetings: Annual, in conjunction with
Radiology Society of North America, 1980 Dallas,
1981 and 1982 Chicago. Publications: Veterinary
Radiology, bimonthly, W. H. Rhodes, editor.

★ 267 ★

AMERICAN CONFERENCE OF GOVERNMENTAL
    INDUSTRIAL HYGIENISTS
Post Office Box 1937   (513) 661-7881
Cincinnati, Ohio 45201   Established 1938

William D. Kelley, Executive Secretary
This professional society, composed of employees of
official governmental units responsible for fulltime
programs of industrial hygiene, educators, and researchers in industrial hygiene, is denoted to the development of administrative and technical aspects of
worker health protection.   The society functions
mainly as a medium for the exchange of ideas and
the promotion of standards and techniques in industrial
health. Membership: 2,000 (full, associate, technical, and student members). Finances: Membership: $15 annually; Other Sources: Sale of publi-
cations. Awards: Annual awards are presented to
members or group of members for outstanding contributions to the field. Meetings: Annual, various
locations. Publications: Transactions of Annual
Meetings, annually; Threshold Limit Values, annually; professional monographs.

★ 268 ★
AMERICAN CONFERENCE OF THERAPEUTIC
    SELFHELP/SELFHEALTH SOCIAL ACTION CLUBS
B 1104 Ross Towers
710 Lodi Street   (315) 471-4644
Syracuse, New York 13203   Established 1960

Shirley Burghard, R.N.
The Conference's intent is to provide self-help for
those suffering from mental diseases through poetry
therapy, relaxation techniques, natural food diets,
and other means, as well as to campaign actively for
the rights of the mentally ill.   The organization's
scope has recently been expanded to include services
to the physically handicapped, the aged, and those
in prisons. Membership: 500. Finances: Membership: $6 annually; Other Sources: Periodical ad-
vertising, grants. Awards: Mention in International
Who's Who of Poetry. Meetings: Annual, various
locations. Publications: Constructive Action for
Good Health Magazine, monthly, Shirley Burghard,
editor; Selfhelp Poetry Anthology, periodically.
Affiliations: North American Conference on Human
Rights and Psychiatric Oppression. Former Name:
American Conference of Therapeutic Selfhelf/Self-
health Social Clubs.

AMERICAN CONFERENCE OF THERAPEUTIC
SELFHELP/SELFHEALTH SOCIAL CLUBS
    See: American Conference of Therapeutic
        Selfhelp/Selfhealth Social Action Clubs

★ 269 ★
AMERICAN CONGRESS OF REHABILITATION
    MEDICINE
30 North Michigan Avenue   (312) 236-9512
Chicago, Illinois 60602   Established 1921

Creston C. Herold, Executive Director
To promote and advance the art and science of rehabilitation medicine; to provide a scientific forum
for communication among the rehabilitation disciplines;
to provide national leadership in the development of
an improved and expanded delivery system for rehabilitation services; to enhance individual professional
development through continuing education in scientific
assemblies, seminars, and postgraduate courses; to
recognize and honor contributors to scientific research,
education and practice in rehabilitation medicine; to
assist in the recruitment of personnel for careers in
the many disciplines of rehabilitation medicine.
Membership: 2,465 (active, associate, corresponding,
student, honorary). Finances: Membership: Active
graduated from $75 to $50; associate, $45; corre-
sponding, $35; student, $15. Awards: Gold Key

Award for extraordinary service to the cause of rehabilitation medicine; Bernard M. Baruch Essay
Award - cash awards to medical students; ACRM
Essay Contest - cash awards to interns, resident and
graduate students. Meetings: Annual, various locations. Publications: Archives of Physical Medicine
and Rehabilitation, monthly, Alfred J. Szumski,
Ph.D., editor; Newsletter.

★ 270 ★
AMERICAN COUNCIL OF INDEPENDENT
    LABORATORIES, INC.
1725 K Street, N.W.   (202) 659-3766
Washington, D.C. 20006   Established 1937

To promote the profession of laboratory science, management and service among commercial, independent,
taxpaying laboratories for their clients in industry,
government and the public. Membership: 240 (laboratory firms in the fields of testing, research, development, surveying and inspection in science, engineering and related disciplines). Finances: Membership: $300 to $1,520. Awards: Annual award
for greatest contribution to the laboratory industry.
Meetings: Annual, various locations. Publications:
Newsletter, monthly; Labvoice, 3 or 4 times annually; Directory, biennially.

★ 271 ★
AMERICAN COUNCIL OF OTOLARYNGOLOGY
1100 17th Street, N.W.
Suite 602   (202) 659-4591
Washington, D.C. 20036   Established 1968

Harry W. McCurdy, M.D., F.A.C.S., Executive
    Director
A non-profit organization whose membership represents
the majority of United States otolaryngologists; the
only national group serving otolaryngology in legislative, regulatory and socio-economic areas. Membership: 4,000 (active, resident, military/government,
retired). Finances: Membership: Active, $95;
resident, $20; military/government, $60; retired,
$15; Other Sources: Contributions, mailing list and
publication sales. Meetings: Coordinator: Combined Otolaryngological Spring Meetings, annually,
various locations. Publications: The American
Council of Otolaryngology Newsletter, 8 annually,
Moira DeWilde, editor; Courses, Meetings and Workshops for Otolaryngologists, quarterly, M. J. Wares,
editor; Job Information Exchange Service, quarterly,
M. J. Wares, editor; Catalog of Otolaryngologic
Audio-Visual Training Aids, 5 Manuals for Medial
Assistants in Otolaryngology; Otologic Referral Criteria for Occupational Hearing Conservation; patient-

education leaflets.   Affiliations: Approximately 100 national, regional, state and urban otolaryngologic societies.

★ 272 ★
AMERICAN COUNCIL OF THE BLIND
1211 Connecticut Avenue, N.W.
Suite 506   (202) 833-1251
Washington, D.C. 20036   Established 1961

Oral O. Miller, President; Durward K. McDaniel,
    National Representative
The ACB is a national membership organization primarily composed of blind people striving through advocacy and legislative activities to improve the lives of blind people in the United States.   The Council also offers services in the following areas: information and referral on all aspects of blindness, legal consultation, leadership training, speakers referral service, chapter and program development assistance, representation on boards and advisory committees both governmental and private.   Membership: 13,000 (state membership; national professional or special interest organization membership; ACT-at-large; sustaining; nonvoting individual membership; sustaining, nonvoting organizational membership). Awards: Service Awards.   Meetings: Annual Convention, July, various locations.   Publications: Braille Forum, monthly, Mary T. Ballard, editor (in large print, braille, disc and cassette).   Affiliations: 47 state affiliates and 14 special and professional interest groups; ACB is officially associated with: Affiliated Leadership League of and for the Blind of America; American Coalition of Citizens with Disabilities; Braille Authority of North America; Leadership Conference on Civil Rights; National Accreditation Council for Agencies Serving the Blind and Visually Handicapped; National Voluntary Organizations for Independent Living for the Aging; Save Our Security Coalition; Washington Health Security Action Coalition; World Council for the Welfare of the Blind.

★ 273 ★
AMERICAN COUNCIL ON PHARMACEUTICAL
    EDUCATION
1 East Wacker Drive   (312) 467-6222
Chicago, Illinois 60601   Established 1932

Daniel A. Nona, Executive Director
Accreditation of colleges of pharmacy.   Develops standards of accreditation for colleges, enforces the standards and consults on pharmaceutical educational activities.   Membership: 10 (3 delegates each from National Association of Boards of Pharmacy, American

Association of Colleges of Pharmacy, American Pharmaceutical Association; 1 delegate from American Council on Education).   Meetings: Semiannual, usually Chicago.   Publications: List of Accredited Colleges of Pharmacy, annually or more frequently; List of Approved Providers of Continuing Education; Accreditation Manual.

★ 274 ★
AMERICAN DANCE THERAPY ASSOCIATION
2000 Century Plaza, Suite 230   (301) 997-4040
Columbia, Maryland 21044   Established 1966

Pat Latteri, Executive Secretary
The Association works to establish and maintain high standards of professional education and competence in the field.   ADTA stimulates communication among dance therapists and members of allied professions through publication of a national newsletter, printing of current and relevant papers, monographs, bibliographies and annual conference proceedings.   ADTA holds an annual conference and supports formation of regional groups, conferences, seminars, workshops and meetings throughout the year.   Membership: 1,000 (regular, associate and student).   Finances: Membership: Regular, $50; associate, $40; student, $25. Meetings: Board Meetings, triannually; Annual Business Meeting, various locations.   Publications: American Journal of Dance Therapy, biennial, Rachel Harris, editor; Newsletter, bimonthly; Conference Proceedings, monographs, and bibliographies.

★ 275 ★
AMERICAN DEAFNESS AND REHABILITATION
    ASSOCIATION
814 Thayer Avenue   (301) 589-0880
Silver Spring, Maryland 20910   Established 1966

Sharon H. Carter, Executive Director
To promote the development and expansion of professional rehabilitation services for deaf people; to provide a forum and a common meeting ground so that the organization may be instrumental in bringing about a better understanding of deaf people as a whole by encouraging students, professional persons, and laymen to develop more than a superficial understanding of the needs and problems of this group; to promote and encourage scientific research of the needs and problems engendered by deafness which inhibit in important ways the successful overall functioning of a deaf person; to promote and develop recruitment and training of professional workers with the deaf; to cooperate with other organizations concerned with deafness and the deaf and with rehabilitation and allied services in promoting and encouraging legislation

pertinent to the development of professional services and facilities for the deaf people. Membership: 630 (professionals, teachers, parents, students, retired persons, counselors, audiologists, religious workers, social workers, anyone interested in the field of deafness). Finances: Membership: Regular, $30; student, retired, associate, $15; family members, $30 for first member, $12 for each additional member; Other Sources: Subscriptions to Journal of Rehabilitation of the Deaf; grant activity; monograph sales. Meetings: Biennial, various locations. Publications: Journal of Rehabilitation of the Deaf, quarterly, Glenn Lloyd, Ed.D., editor; ADARA Newsletter, monthly; Independent Living Skills for Severely Handicapped Deaf People (monograph 5), Sue Ouellette, Glenn Lloyd, editors; Deafness Annuals II, III, IV; New Vistas for Competitive Employment of Deaf Persons (monograph 2), W. Craig, J. Collins, editors; Model State Plan for Vocational Rehabilitation of Deaf Clients (monograph 3), Jerome Schein, editor. Affiliations: Local chapters and special interest sections (SCD, Deaf-Blind, Counseling). Former Name: Professional Rehabiliation Workers with the Adult Deaf.

★ 276 ★
AMERICAN DENTAL ASSISTANTS ASSOCIATION
666 North Lake Shore Drive   (312) 664-3327
Chicago, Illinois 60611   Established 1925

Lois A. Klinger, CDA, Executive Director
To share in the responsibility for quality dental health care delivery to all; to advance the practice of dental assisting toward the highest standards of performance obtainable by supporting and encouraging formal education and in providing quality continuing education; to endorse a recognized national and/or state credential for the dental assisting profession; and to communicate effectively with all members of health related professions. Membership: Approximately 22,000 (active, student, life, and honorary). Finances: Membership: Active, $50; student, $10. Meetings: Annual Session and ADAA District Workshops, various locations. Publications: The Dental Assistant, bimonthly, Shirlee Tabas, editor; Legislative Update, Bimonthly, Shirlee Tabas, editor.

★ 277 ★
AMERICAN DENTAL HYGIENISTS' ASSOCIATION
444 North Michigan Avenue   (312) 440-8900
Chicago, Illinois 60611   Established 1923

Rodney S. Brutlag, Executive Director
To cultivate, promote and sustain the art and science of dental hygiene, to represent and safeguard the common interest of the members of the dental hygiene profession, and to contribute toward the improvement of the health of the public. Membership: 25,000 active, over 10,000 students. Finances: Membership: Active, $62.50; student, $10. Meetings: Annual, various locations. Publications: Dentaly Hygiene, Journal of the American Dental Hygienists' Association, monthly, Wilma Motley, R.D.H., editor; Education Directions for Dental Auxiliaries, quarterly, Wilma Motley, R.D.H., editor; Horizons Newsletter, bimonthly. Affiliations: American Dental Hygienists' Association Foundation; Dental Hygiene Commission for Assurance of Competency; HY-PAC (Political Action Committee).

★ 278 ★
AMERICAN DENTAL SOCIETY OF
    ANESTHESIOLOGY
211 East Chicago Avenue
Suite 915   (312) 664-8270
Chicago, Illinois 60611   Established 1953

Peter C. Goulding, Executive Director
To develop and further the field of anesthesiology in dentistry; to disseminate information and publish material of interest concerning anesthesiology in dentistry; and to foster higher standards of education as regards to teaching of anesthesia in dental schools. Activies include annual meetings, workshops and conferences on pain control, liaison activities with other health organizations, scientific programs on both component and national levels. Membership: 3,200 (active, associate, foreign, resident, intern, affiliate). Finances: Membership: Active, associate, foreign, $50; affiliate, resident, $15; student, $10; Other Sources: Journal advertising, contributions. Awards: Heidbrink Award to dentists who have contributed to the advancement of anesthesiology within the field of dentistry; Special Service Award to members who have contributed greatly to the society. Meetings: Annual, various locations. Publications: Anesthesia Progress, bimonthly, Norman Trieger, M.D., editor; Newsletter, bimonthly, Dr. Herbert Berquist, editor.

★ 279 ★
AMERICAN DENTAL SOCIETY OF EUROPE
57 Portland Place
London H1N 3AH, England,   (01) 580-7146
    United Kingdom   Established 1873

Brian J. Parkins, Honorary Secretary
To assist in maintaining contact between graduates of North American Dental Schools who now reside and practice in Europe. The main activity is in the Annual Meeting. Membership: 145 (active, honorary, and retired from active practice). Finances: Membership: $50 annually. Awards: Scholarships for

graduates of European Dental Schools to study in North America. Meetings: Annual, various locations in Europe. Publications: Programme for the Annual Meeting, annually; The American Dental Society of Europe, A History: 1873-1973.

★ 280 ★
AMERICAN DENTAL TRADE ASSOCIATION
1140 Connecticut Avenue, N.W.
Suite 810   (202) 659-1630
Washington, D.C. 20036   Established 1882

Nikolaj M. Petrovic, CAE, President
To promote and encourage the development, production and distribution of equipment and materials for the dental profession, dental schools and dental laboratories so as to enable its members to perform the highest degree of useful service for the public health and welfare; to conduct studies, programs and projects to further the welfare of the industry; to collect, assemble and disseminate statistical and management information. Membership: 150 (distributor, manufacturer, associate, honorary). Finances: Membership: Manufacturers and distributors (the annual dues rate is computed on the basis of total dollar volume of domestic and Canadian sales as defined in the ADTA By-laws including sales of branches, divisions and subsidiaries for 2 years prior to the year in which application is submitted, lowest membership fee $250); associate (manufacturers representative: individual, $500; company, $500 initial and $50 per person thereafter; foreign company: individual, $500; company, $500; dental practice administration consultant: individual, $500; company, $500 initial and $50 per person thereafter; consumer dental products companies: individual, $1,500; company, $1,500; distribution cooperatives: individual, $500; company, $500); honorary life membership is exempt from registration fees, dues, or assessments; Other Sources: Investments. Research Funds: American Fund for Dental Health. Meetings: Annual, various locations; ADTA also sponsors Educational Seminars throughout the year, various locations. Publications: UPDATE - ADTA's Newsletter, bimonthly, Nikolaj M. Petrovic and Margie Challoner, editors; Annual Report, annual, Niolaj M. Petrovic and Margie Challoner, editors; Exhibit Chairman--May We Help?, Nikolaj M. Petrovic and Margie Challoner, editors; Manufacturers Sales Report, Nikolaj M. Petrovic and Margie Challoner, editors; Guidance Manual for Conformance with Radiation Control for Health and Safety Act of 1968; Good Manufacturing Practice Manual. Affiliations: American Dental Association; American Surgical Trade Association; American Fund for Dental Health; American Student Dental Association; Chicago Dental Society; National Association of Dental Laboratories; American

Dental Hygienists Association.

★ 281 ★
AMERICAN DENTISTS FOR FOREIGN SERVICE
619 Church Avenue   (212) 436-8686
Brooklyn, New York 11218   Established 1967

Herman Ivanhoe, D.D.S., President
The agency's aim is to assist indigent countries throughout the world. AOFS has shipped over 1,200 dental operations to Chile, Colombia, Peru, Equador, Honduras, Egypt, Israel, Nigeria, Botswana, South Pacific Islands, South Korea, South Vietnam, etc. Activities also include establishing a Tropical Flouride Program for children in the West Indies, donating equipment for the development of dental schools and obtaining admission for foreign graduate and postgraduate students in the United States. Membership: 100 (executive board officers, honorary, regular). Finances: Annual dues, $10; Other Sources: Donations from non-members. Meetings: 8 times annually at 619 Church Avenue in Brooklyn. Publications: Newsletter, once or twice annually, Stetta Kalka, editor.

★ 282 ★
AMERICAN DERMATOLOGIC SOCIETY FOR
    ALLERGY AND IMMUNOLOGY
Mayo Clinic
Department of Dermatology   (507) 284-2536
Rochester, Minnesota 55901

Roy S. Rogers, III, M.D.; Larry E. Millikan, M.D.
Originally founded to promote education and discourse in advances in allergy and immunology within the specialty. Major efforts are in education. Future efforts in funding, training grants are expected. Membership: 150. Finances: Membership: $25 annually; Other Sources: Support for the annual meeting and the Merriam Sulsberger prize, Ortho Pharmaceuticals, Ortho Dermatologics, and Ortho Diagnostics, other pharmaceutical support from Barnes-Hind of major nature. Awards: Annual Merriam B. Selzberger prize in Dermatologic allergy and immunology. Meetings: Annual, late September. Publications: Papers periodically appear primarily in the International Journal of Dermatology and the Journal of American Academy of Dermatology.

★ 283 ★

AMERICAN DIETETIC ASSOCIATION
430 North Michigan Avenue   (312) 280-5000
Chicago, Illinois 60611   Established 1917

John C. Thiel, Acting Executive Director
Aims include improvement of the nutrition of human
beings; the advancement of the science of dietetics
and nutrition; and the promotion of education in
these and allied areas. Membership: 39,500 (active, life, honorary, inactive, associate, dietetic
technician, retired). Finances: Membership: $60
annually; Other Sources: Journal subscriptions, exhibits, advertising. Meetings: Annual meeting,
various locations; workshops, institutes. Publications: Journal of the American Dietetic Association,
monthly, Dorothea Turner, editor; Courier, bimonthly.
Library: Lulu C. Graves Library. Affiliations: Dietetic Associations in all states, the District of Columbia, and Puerto Rico.

★ 284 ★

AMERICAN DIGESTIVE DISEASE SOCIETY
420 Lexington Avenue, Suite 1644   (212) 687-3088
New York, New York 10017   Established 1973

Martin I. Hassner, Executive Director
The organization was formed to call public attention
to the health difficulties caused by "common" digestive diseases; to assist those patients with an understanding of treatment modalities and expectations; to
work for additional government funding of digestive
disease research; to involve those who are as yet un-
damaged in health regimens that might work for them
with educational materials on such areas as vitamins,
fasting, bran, cholesterol, health foods, junk foods
and so forth, seeking changes in medical education to
prepare the physician for more successful care in gastrointestinal medicine with an emphasis on preparing
the general practitioner and internist. Membership:
Individual, family, professional. Finances: Membership: $25 lay membership up to $100 status; $25
professional membership. Meetings: Annual; quarterly, board; monthly, executive committee. Publications: Living Healthy, monthly, Dr. Nicholas
Hightower and Martin Hassner, editors; Dialogue,
periodically, Martin Hassner, editor; Health Advisor,
periodically, Martin Hassner, editor. Affiliations:
American College of Gastroenterology; American
Gastroenterological Association; American Society
for the Study of Liver Disease; American Society of
Gastrointestinal Endoscopy.

★ 285 ★

AMERICAN DIOPTER AND DECIBEL SOCIETY
522 Walnut Street   (412) 672-7486
McKeesport, Pennsylvania 15132   Established 1958

E. A. Rittenhouse
To provide a forum for the exchange of knowledge
and experience among accredited ophthalmologists
and otolaryngologists and other physicians and scientists interested in such medical problems; to spread
scientific knowledge of these problems among physicians of America and other countries; to engage in
and to encourage and promote medical research and
experimental work of all kinds and to help in every
way in bringing such work to the notice of the medical profession and the general public if warranted;
and to devote any available income in excess of cost
of operation, and any other available resources to research and educational projects. The Society has
provided medical instruments to needy hospitals in the
Carribean area and has made donations to other medically depressed areas. Membership: 200. Finances: Membership: $25 annually; Other Sources:
Advertising in seminar programs.

★ 286 ★

AMERICAN ELECTROENCEPHALOGRAPHIC SOCIETY
2163 North Lake Parkway
Suite 105   (404) 934-1620
Tucker, Georgia 30084   Established 1946

Fay S. Tyner, Executive Secretary
To promote contacts between investigators in Electroencephalography and in related fields of interest, and
between this Society and other similar societies
throughout the world; to further understanding and
knowledge of electroencephalography and related
studies; to arrange for the exchange of public data
in these fields, and to review manuscripts for any interested publication; to assist in the formation of international committees for the establishment of uniform
standards, techniques, and procedure throughout the
world; to assist in setting up standards for training,
examination, and qualification of clinical electroencephalographers and technicians, and to draw up
minimum specifications for apparatus used, in order
that high standards of clinical electroencephalography
may be established and maintained. Membership:
1,184 (physicians, Ph.D.'s, engineers, technologists
engaged in clinical and/or research electroencephalography. Finances: Membership: $35; initiation
fee, $25; Other Sources: Exhibits at meetings.
Awards: Hans Berger Award, for original study in
this field. Meetings: Annual, various locations.
Affiliations: Internationatl Federation of Societies for
Electroencephalography and Clinical Neurophysiology.

★ 287 ★
AMERICAN ELECTROLYSIS ASSOCIATION
Post Office Box 204   (312) 623-6100
Evanston, Illinois 60204   Established 1958

The Association's purpose is to activate state organizations, nurture and educate electrologists, and help
with legislation to regulate the practice of electrolysis. Membership: State affiliated associations, comprised of 1,000 individuals. Finances: Membership:
Associate membership, $40; affiliate membership, $25,
annually. Meetings: Conventions; seminars. Publications: AEA News, quarterly, Elizabeth Albanese,
editor.

★ 288 ★
AMERICAN ENDODONTIC SOCIETY
1400 North Harbor Boulevard, #104 (714) 870-5590
Fullerton, California 92635   Established 1969

Ramon Werts, D.D.S., Executive Director
To promote and provide educational and scientific information on the Sargenti Method of endodontics for
the general practitioner.   Conducts workshops and
seminars presenting the latest endodontic developments,
studies and research, and sponsors a Fellowship degree
program to honor members for their accomplishments in
endodontic practice. Membership: 10,000 (general
membership with fellowship degree offered after 3 or
more years of membership). Finances: Membership:
$45 annually. Meetings: Annual, in conjunction
with the American Dental Association Annual Session,
various locations. Publications: Newsletter, quarterly, Julian Jackson Agency (editor); Hotline, occasionally, Julian Jackson Agency (editor);   Saving
Teeth (patient education flier in English and Spanish).

★ 289 ★
AMERICAN EPIDEMIOLOGICAL SOCIETY
c/o Theodore C. Eickhoff, M.D.
4200 East 9th Avenue   (303) 394-7233
Denver, Colorado 80262   Established 1924

Theodore C. Eickhoff, M.D., Secretary-Treasurer
The Association's intent is to promote the study and
discussion of epidemiological problems. Membership:
Active, 16; emeritus, 75 (membership is multidisciplinary and by invitation only). Meetings: Annual,
various locations.

★ 290 ★
AMERICAN EPILEPSY SOCIETY
179 Allyn Street, Suite 304   (203) 246-6566
Hartford, Connecticut 06103   Established 1946

The purposes of this Society are the acquisition, dissemination and application of knowledge concerning
epilepsy in all its phases: biologic, clinical and
social; the promotion of better care and treatment
for persons subject to seizures; promotion of personal
contacts between medical investigators in epilepsy and
investigators in related fields of interests; the promotion of contacts between this Society and other similar socities throughout the world. Membership:
1,000 (active, 948; senior, 52). Finances: Membership: $65 annually; Other Sources: Annual
Meeting/Exhibitors. Awards: Lennox Lecture (given
at annual meeting by distinguished worker in the field
of epilepsy; Lennox Award (monetary award to an
individual who has made outstanding contributions in
the field of epilepsy; Lennox Fellowship (support of
a 2 year fellowship for a junior investigator in the
field of epilepsy). Meetings: Annual Meeting held
every other year in New York City or in a West
Coast city. Publications: Epilepsia, bimonthly,
Arthur A. Ward, Jr., editor. Affiliations: International League Against Epilepsy.

★ 291 ★
AMERICAN EQUILIBRATION SOCIETY
211 East Chicago Avenue
Suite 915
Chicago, Illinois 60611   Established 1955

Eric Bishop, Director of the Central Office
Organized for the study of lesions in the temporo-
mandibular joint and related structures. Membership:
705 (active, associate, life, honorary). Finances:
Membership: $45. Awards: Research funds avail-
able for T.M.J. studies. Meetings: Annual,
Chicago, Illinois. Publications: Compendium, annual, Dr. Richard E. Coy, editor; The Journal of
Prosthetic Dentistry, Dr. Judson Hickey, editor.

★ 292 ★
AMERICAN FEDERATION FOR CLINICAL RESEARCH
6900 Grove Road   (609) 848-1000
Thorofare, New Jersey 08086   Established 1940

Charles B. Slack, Executive Secretary
To promote and encourage original research in clinical
and laboratory medicine; to welcome as members and
provide an accessible forum for young persons engaged
in such research. Membership: 10,500 (regular -
persons under 41 years of age; senior - persons who

actively stimulate younger persons to pursue research in clinical and laboratory medicine; corporate). Finances: Membership: $25, including annual subscription to Journals; Other Sources: Corporate dues. Meetings: Annual, rotating in New Jersey. Publications: Clinical Research, 5 times annually, Elizabeth M. Short, M.D., editor.

★ 293 ★

AMERICAN FERTILITY SOCIETY
1608 13th Avenue, South
Suite 101   (205) 933-7222
Birmingham, Alabama 35256   Established 1944

Herbert H. Thomas, M.D., Medical Director
To extend knowledge of all aspects of fertility and problems of infertility and mammalian reproduction; to provide, through its meetings, a rostrum for the presentation of scientific studies dealing with all phases of these subjects, and an opportunity for formal and informal discussions among investigators in this field. Membership: 7,000 (active, associate, life, honorary). Finances: Membership: $75. Meetings: Annual, various locations. Publications: Fertility and Sterility, monthly, Roger D. Kempers, M.D., editor; Newsletter.

AMERICAN FOUNDATION FOR OVERSEAS BLIND
   See: Helen Keller International, Inc.

★ 294 ★

AMERICAN FOUNDATION FOR PHARMACEUTICAL
   EDUCATION
Radburn Plaza Building
14-25 Plaza Road   (201) 791-5192
Fair Lawn, New Jersey 07410   Established 1942

Albert B. Fisher, Jr., Ph.D., President
Supports pharmaceutical education and awards educational grants. It is committed to uphold and improve pharmaceutical education, colleges of pharmacy and pharmacy students (United States citizens only), in conformity with its purposes. It is organized to accept and administer gifts, legacies, bequests and funds and to make disbursements for the promotion of pharmaceutical education. Membership: American Association of Colleges of Pharmacy, American Pharmaceutical Association, American Society of Hospital Pharmacists, Drug Wholesalers Association, Incorporated, National Association of Boards of Pharmacy, National Association of Chain Drug Stores, National Association of Retail Druggists, National Wholesale Druggists' Association, Pharmaceutical Manufacturers

Association, The Proprietary Association. Finances: The Foundation derives its income from individuals and voluntary contributions of the drug and allied manufacturing industries. Meetings: Board of Directors, annual, New York City; Board of Grants, annual, Washington, D.C.

★ 295 ★

AMERICAN FOUNDATION FOR THE BLIND, INC.
15 West 16th Street   (212) 924-0420
New York, New York 10011   Established 1921

Alfred P. Lisi, Acting Executive Director
To promote higher standards of service on behalf of blind and deaf-blind persons. The program of services includes: research; consultation and field service; professional development; technical operations; publications; and library service. Awards: Migel Medal for outstanding service to blind people, research funds. Publications: Journal of Visual Impairment and Blindness (general professional journal in inkprint, braille, and recorded editions); AFB Newsletter, quarterly (describing services and programs of the Foundation); Washington Report, 6 times annually (reporting on governmental activities effecting blind persons); Directory of Agencies Serving the Visually Handicapped (published in odd-numbered years, listing local and state agencies for the blind); monographs; pamphlets; manuals. Library: Migel Memorial Library, 35,000 volumes.

★ 296 ★

AMERICAN FRACTURE ASSOCIATION
Post Office Box 668   (309) 662-4491
Bloomington, Illinois 61701   Established 1938

Barbara Dehority, Executive Secretary
The advancement of medical science through the study, investigation and development of the various accepted types of treatment of fractures of bone. Activities include annual meetings in the fall and occasional clinical meetings during the year. Finances: Membership: Dues, $50-$35. Meetings: Annual, various locations. Publications: American Fracture Association, annually; presentations given at annual meetings.

★ 297 ★

AMERICAN FUND FOR DENTAL HEALTH
211 East Chicago Avenue
Post Office Box 7740-A   (312) 787-6270
Chicago, Illinois 60680   Established 1955

Robert J. Desmond, Executive Vice President and Secretary

Originally founded in 1955 as a national fund-raising organization for dental education, the American Fund for Dental Health expanded horizons in 1974 to include support of research projects and programs to enhance dental service delivery in addition to its traditional support of dental education. The Fund designs and administers programs sponsored by other foundations, allocates grants, administers its own programs and raises funds in support of dentistry. It is the only national, independent dental fund-raising agency in the country. Membership: Not a membership organization. Meetings: 3 times annually, various locations. Publications: Annual Report, annually; Fund Reporter, periodically; brochures and booklets. Affiliations: Sponsoring organizations: American Dental Association; American Dental Trade Association; American Association of Dental Schools.

★ 298 ★
AMERICAN GASTROENTEROLOGICAL ASSOCIATION
6900 Grove Road   (609) 848-1000
Thorofare, New Jersey 08086   Established 1897

Charles B. Slack, Executive Secretary
The Association has been established for the general purposes of studying the normal and abnormal conditions of the digestive organs and the problems connected with their metabolism, and of conducting scientific research and investigation related to or connected with the digestive organs and the problems connected with the metabolism thereof. The organization's primary activity involves holding scientific sessions. Various subcommittees function to improve caliber of teaching of this sub-specialty and to encourage financial support for training and research in this field. Membership: 3,100 (80 percent physicians of internal medicine certified in gastroenterology; 15 percent composed of radiologists, pathologists, surgeons and physiologists with a special interest and competency in gastroenterology). Awards: Friedenwald Medal, annually, to distinguished senior member for contributions to the field. Meetings: Annual, various locations. Publications: Gastroenterology, monthly, John S. Fordtran, editor.

★ 299 ★
AMERICAN GENETIC ASSOCIATION
818 18th Street, N.W.   (202) 659-2096
Washington, D.C. 20006   Established 1903

To encourage the study of the laws of heredity, and to promote their application in the improvement of plants, animals and human racial stocks. Membership: 1,600 (regular, life). Finances: Membership: Regular, $20 (foreign, $2 extra); life, $175; Other Sources: Subscriptions, $35 annually. Awards: Meyer Medal awarded for outstanding contributions in plant exploration; Wilhelmine E. Key invitational lecture in human genetics, annually. Meetings: Annual, Washington, D.C. Publications: Journal of Heredity, bimonthly, B. C. Kuhn, editor. Affiliations: AAAS; Agricultural Research Institute; International Genetics Federation.

★ 300 ★
AMERICAN GERIATRICS SOCIETY
10 Columbus Circle   (212) 582-1333
New York, New York 10019   Established 1942

Kathryn S. Henderson, Executive Director
The Society aims to encourage, promote and sponsor research in the broad field of geriatrics and gerontology; acquire, organize and disseminate, among physicians, medical students, nurses, social service workers, sociologists, biologists and other interested groups, information about aging and diseases of the aging and aged through publication of a monthly Journal, sponsorship of an annual scientific meeting and interim symposia and seminars; initiate and participate in ways and means of improving the health care and treatment of aging and aged individuals; stimulate and foster the development of affiliate regional organizations with professional and/or lay members dedicated to the broad general, as well as more specific, purposes of the parent national body; and establish and maintain liaison with other groups concerned with aging and its problems, including medical schools, hospitals, research foundations, industry, labor, voluntary health organizations, governmental agencies, women's auxiliaries and clubs and senior citizen groups, and serve in an advisory capacity to such groups when that shall be in the interests of and compatible with the expressed purposes of the Society. Membership: 8,000 (physicians and interested paramedical personnel). Finances: Membership: $35 annually; Other Sources: Advertising in Journal. Awards: Edward Henderson Lecture Award; Willard O. Thompson Award; Edward B. Allen Award; Malford W. Thewlis Award; Edward Henderson Memorial Fund Award. Meetings: Annual scientific meeting. Publications: Journal of the American Geriatrics Society, monthly, Charles E. Lyght, M.D., editor; Newsletter of the American Geriatrics Society, monthly, Kathryn S. Henderson, editor.

★ 301 ★

AMERICAN GROUP PRACTICE ASSOCIATION
20 South Quaker Lane   (703) 751-1000
Alexandria, Virginia 22314   Established 1949

Donald W. Fisher, Ph.D.
To serve and represent the organizational, policy and
proprietary interest of group practice physicians and
dentists. Activities include accreditation, research,
education, insurance programs, physician placement,
consultation, governmental relations, and publications.
Membership: 400 group practice organizations with
about 14,000 physicians and dentists (multi and single
specialty groups including fee-for-service, prepaid,
profit and not-for-profit). Finances: Membership:
$65 each professional staff member, minimum $200,
maximum $6,000; Other Sources: Educational pro-
grams, publication sales, grants and contracts. Research Funds: Funded from general funds, grants and
contracts. Awards: Russel V. Lee Annual Award
Lectureship awarded annually to outstanding group
practice leaders; Wallace M. Yater Medal awarded
periodically for outstanding service to the American
Group Practice Association. Meetings: Annual, national and regional meetings; seminars and institutes.
Publications: Group Practice Journal, monthly,
Elizabeth M. Goodfellow, editor; Membership Directory, biennial, Elizabeth M. Goodfellow, editor;
books, pamphlets and monographs relating to organizational and health delivery matters. Library:
AGPA Library. Affiliations: American Group Practice Foundation; Group Practice Political Action
Committee; Accreditation Association for Ambulatory
Health Care, Inc.

★ 302 ★

AMERICAN GROUP PSYCHOTHERAPY ASSOCIATION
1995 Broadway, 14th Floor   (212) 787-2618
New York, New York 10023   Established 1943

Marsha S. Block, Chief Executive Officer
To publish and to make publications available on all
subjects relating to group psychotherapy, to encourage
the training of and to establish and maintain high
standards in the qualifications of group psychotherapists
and in their practice, to encourage and promote research in group psychotherapy. Activities include
sponsorship of an Annual Training Institute and Scientific Conference and of an AMA accreditation program. Membership: 3,000 (psychologists, psychiatrists, psychiatric social workers, psychiatric nurses,
and others); 22 affiliate societies; 7 foreign affiliate associations. Finances: Membership: Associate,
$45; full, $55; foreign, $20; fellows, $70; Other
Sources: Funds from the annual institute and conference. Meetings: Membership, annually; Board,
semiannually; institute and conference, annually;

various locations. Publications: International Jour-
nal of Group Psychotherapy, quarterly, Zanvel A.
Liff, Ph.D., editor; Membership and Geographical
Directory; Guidelines for the Training of Group Psy-
chotherapists; Consumer's Guide and Group Therapy;
A Brief History of the AGPA; Information About
AGPA; Newsletter; Annotated Bibliography of Films
on Group and Family Psychotherapy.

★ 303 ★

AMERICAN HEALTH CARE ASSOCIATION
1200 15th Street, N.W.   (202) 833-2050
Washington, D.C. 20005   Established 1949

Thomas G. Bell, Executive Vice President
To show how the nursing home profession contributes
to the public good by providing individualized rehabilitative, social and spiritual services as well as
physical care; to emphasize the role of AHCA in
providing quality care through the setting of standards,
peer review, and professional recognition; to build
public support for legislation designed to enhance the
nursing home profession's ability to serve the public;
to acquaint Congress and the executive branch with
the existence of this public support. Activities include maintaining channels of communication with the
nation's news media and the general public to assure
an effective flow of information through these channels; conducting conferences, workshops, and seminars for the education of the membership; maintaining
government and allied field liaison and conducting an
annual convention. Membership: 7,500 (full membership made up of individual nursing homes, associated professional members, and associated business
members). Finances: Yearly operating budget is
established and individual dues are levied at the national convention held in the fall of each year.
Awards: National Better Life Awards, given in the
categories of Media, Patient Care, Government,
Humanitarian Services Award, and Education; the
Volunteer of the Year Award, and the Teen Volunteer
of the Year Award. Meetings: Annual, various locations; Governing Council, quarterly. Publications: AHCA Weekly Notes, weekly; The American
Health Care Association Journal, bimonthly. Affiliations: 48 state associations.

★ 304 ★

AMERICAN HEALTH FOUNDATION
320 East 43rd Street   (212) 953-1900
New York, New York 10017   Established 1969

Ernst L. Wynder, M.D., President and Medical
    Director; John D. Twiname, Managing Director
The American Health Foundation is a non-profit

institution dedicated to the enhancement of health and longevity, the prevention of disease, and the reduction of medical care costs through research, education and health promotion services. Awards: Eleanor Naylor Dana Award for Preventive Medicine, annual, $5,000, for significant contributions to the field of preventive medicine; Lifeline Award, annual, to individuals who have made major contributions to the prevention of disease. Publications: Preventive Medicine, bimonthly, Ernst L. Wynder, M.D., editor. Affiliations: Naylor Dana Institute for Disease Prevention.

★ 305 ★

AMERICAN HEALTH PLANNING ASSOCIATION
1601 Connecticut Avenue
Suite 700   (202) 232-6390
Washington, D.C. 20009

Harry P. Cain, Executive Director
Conducts research; disseminates information; serves as clearinghouse for health planning concepts; conducts programs of technical assistance; provides continuing education; maintains placement service and speakers bureau. Membership: 1,400 individuals; 200 health planning agencies; 45 others. Finances: Membership. Awards: Annual Schlesinger Award. Meetings: Annual, various locations. Publications: Today in Health Planning, weekly; publishes legislative bulletins, position statements and technical documents on plan developments and project review. Former Name: American Association for Health Planning Agencies.

★ 306 ★

AMERICAN HEARING RESEARCH FOUNDATION
55 East Washington Street
Suite 2105   (312) 726-9670
Chicago, Illinois 60602

Eugene L. Derlacki, M.D., President;
   William L. Lederer, Executive Director
The American Hearing Research Foundation is a non-profit organization that has three fundamental purposes: to provide financial assistance for medical research into the causes, prevention and cure of deafness, impaired hearing and balance disorders; to encourage the collaboration of clinical laboratory research; to broaden teaching of the medical aspects in hearing problems and disseminate the latest and most reliable scientific knowledge to physicians and the public. Finances: Public support and revenues.

★ 307 ★

AMERICAN HEART ASSOCIATION
7320 Greenville Avenue   (214) 750-5300
Dallas, Texas 75231   Established 1924

Dudley Hafner, Executive Vice President
To support research, education and community service programs with the objective of reducing death and disability from heart and blood vessel diseases; to coordinate the efforts of physicians, nurses, social workers and others engaged in the fight against heart and circulatory disease. Membership: 120,000 (general and voting memberships; separate membership in Scientific Councils). Finances: Membership: Local autonomy (local affiliate and/or chapter decide on the membership fee); Other Sources: Contributions, special events, bequests. Research Funds: Combined National and Affiliate Research Budget is $22 million. Meetings: Annual Scientific Session, November. (1981 schedule: November 16-19, Dallas, Texas; 1982 schedule: November 15-18, Dallas, Texas; 1983 schedule: November 14-17, Anaheim, California; 1984 schedule: November 12-15, Washington, D.C.). Publications: Circulation, monthly, Elliot Rapaport, M.D., editor; Circulation Research, monthly, Brian F. Hoffman, M.D., editor; Modern Concepts of Cardiovascular Disease, monthly, J. O'Neal Humphries, M.D., editor; Cardiovascular Nursing, bimonthly, Louise Mansfield, R.N., editor; Current Concepts of Cerebrovascular Disease--Stroke, bimonthly, Oscar M. Reinmuth, M.D., editor; Hypertension, bimonthly, Harriet P. Dustan, M.D., editor; Stroke--A Journal of Cerebral Circulation, bimonthly, Fletcher McDowell, M.D., editor; Arteriosclerosis: A Journal of Vascular Biology and Disease, bimonthly, Edwin L. Bierman, M.D., editor. Library: American Heart Association--National Center, 4,000 volumes; (lends monographs to AHA staff and other libraries, not to individuals). Affiliations: Mended Hearts.

★ 308 ★

AMERICAN HOLISTIC MEDICAL ASSOCIATION
6932 Little River Turnpike   (703) 642-5880
Annandale, Virginia 22003   Established 1978

Jean Ann Caywood, Administrator
Organization of health care professionals interested in furthering the practice of holistic health care, a concept that stresses the integration of physical, mental, emotional and spiritual concerns with environmental harmony. As an organization accredited by the Liaison Committee on Continuing Medical Education (LCCME), to provide continuing medical education, the American Holistic Medical Association certifies that various continuing medical education offerings meet stated criteria, provided they are used

and completed as designed. Membership: 500 (licensed physicians [M.D.'s and D.O.'s], medical or osteopathic students). Finances: Membership: $250, practicing physicians; $60, retired/disabled; $60, interns/residents; $35, students; Other Sources: Newsletter and Journal subscriptions and advertising. Meetings: Annual, in conjunction with the educational programs of the American Holistic Medical Institute, usually late May or early June, LaCrosse, Wisconsin. Publications: Holistic Medicine (newsletter), monthly, Kelly Benson, M.D., editor; Journal of Holistic Medicine, semiannual, Elmer M. Cranton, M.D., editor. Affiliations: American Holistic Medical Institute (educational and research foundation of the Association).

★ 309 ★
AMERICAN HOLISTIC MEDICAL INSTITUTE
6932 Little River Turnpike   (703) 642-5880
Annandale, Virginia 22003   Established 1976

Jean Ann Caywood, Administrator
Education and research in the various aspects of holistic medicine and holistic health; name changed from Biogenic Institutes of America to American Holistic Medical Institute in 1980, when the first educational program was held. Membership: 30 general members (lay public); professional members (clergy, nurses, physical therapists, physician assistance, etc.); industrial members (company suppliers); organizational members (holistic organizations). General and professional are individual memberships. Finances: Membership : General members, $50; professional members, $75; industrial members, $300; organizational members, $150; Other Sources: Educational programs; development fund. Meetings: Annual, in conjunction with the Annual Meeting of the American Holistic Medical Association, generally late May or early June, LaCrosse, Wisconsin; occasional co-sponsorships with other organizations. Affiliations: American Holistic Medical Association (the related physician's organization). Former Name: Biogenic Institutes of America.

★ 310 ★
AMERICAN HOME ECONOMICS ASSOCIATION
2010 Massachusetts Avenue, N.W.   (202) 862-8300
Washington, D.C. 20036   Established 1909

Dr. Kinsey B. Green, Executive Director
To provide opportunities for members to cooperate in the attainment of the well-being of individuals and of families, the improvement of homes, and the preservation of values significant in home life. Activities include publication of two professional journals and

other publications; conduct of an annual meeting; committee activities; programs for professional and subject-matter sections; direction of an international family-planning program; sponsorship of a Center for the Family; cooperation with many other private and public organizations and with the International Federation of Home Economists. Membership: 40,000 (home economists in business, homemaking, research, college groups, etc.). Finances: Membership: Active, $55; reserve, $35; student, $15. Awards: Annual scholarships and fellowships. Meetings: Annual. Publications: Journal of Home Economics, 5 times annually; Home Economics Research Journal, quarterly, Joan Gordon, editor. Library: AHEA Library, 1,000 volumes.

★ 311 ★
AMERICAN HOSPITAL ASSOCIATION
840 North Lake Shore Drive   (312) 280-6000
Chicago, Illinois 60611   Established 1898

John Alexander McMahon, President
The Association's purpose is to promote the welfare of the public through its leadership and through its assistance to members in the provision of better health care for all people. It serves its members through education, research, dissemination of information, legislation, consultation, and assistance with local public relations efforts. Membership: 6,400 institutional members; 31,100 personal members. Finances: Membership: Students, $12.50; personal members, $25-$120; institutional members, no minimum, $21,982 maximum. Awards: The Trustees' Award; Citation for Meritorious Service; Honorary Membership; Justin Ford Kimball Award; Distinguished Service Award. Meetings: Annual Convention, various locations; Annual Meeting, Washington, D.C. Publications: The Hospital Medical Staff, monthly, Daniel S. Schechter, editor and publisher; Hospitals, semimonthly, Daniel S. Schechter, editor and publisher; Trustee, monthly, Daniel S. Schechter, editor and publisher; The Voluntary Leader, quarterly, Daniel S. Schechter, editor and publisher; Hospital Week, weekly, Daniel S. Schechter, editor and publisher; 30-35 books yearly; American Hospital Association Guide to the Health Care Field, annually; Hospital Statistics, annually; Hospital Literature Index. Library: Asa S. Bacon Memorial Library, 30,000 volumes. Affiliations: American Society Central Service Personnel; American Society for Hospital Food Services Administration; American Society for Hospital Risk Managers; American Society for Nursing Services Administration; American Society for Patient Representatives; American Society Hospital Engineering; American Society Hospital Public Relations; American Society Hospital Purchasing and Materials Management; American Society Hospital

Social Work Directors; American Society for Directors of Volunteer Services; American Society Health Manpower Education and Training; American Society for Hospital Personnel Administration; American Society for Hospital Planning; American Society of Hospital Attorneys.

★ 312 ★

AMERICAN HYPNOTISTS' ASSOCIATION, INC.
Glanworth Building, Suite 6
1159 Green Street   (415) 775-6130
San Francisco, California 94109   Established 1959

Rafael M. Bertuccelli, M.D., Ph.D., President
To promote, encourage and engage in scientific research within the field of Ethical Hypnosis and related sociology and to announce the results of such research to the different branches of the medical and psychological professions using ethical hypnosis, in their respective fields; to discover new uses of ethical hypnosis; to compile and keep records on all known types or methods in induction used; to co-operate with all professional associations and societies concerned; to do any and all things necessary and proper for the advancement of ethical hypnosis, and to do any and all things which may be deemed necessary to effectuate any or all of the foregoing purposes and as are authorized by the laws governing each sovereign state; to conduct training programs. Membership: 382 (only those members holding doctorates in any of the allied healing arts and duly licensed by their respective boards will be considered prospective membership in the American Hypnotists' Association, Inc.). Meetings: Annual, various locations in the United States, Canada, or Mexico. Publications: Monthly Newsletter, monthly, Dr. R. M. Bertucce, editor (restricted only to members). Library: Hypnosis Technical Center, 3,200 volumes (members only). Affiliations: International Association of Hypnotists (London, England).

★ 313 ★

AMERICAN INDUSTRIAL HYGIENE ASSOCIATION
475 Wolf Ledges Parkway   (216) 762-7294
Akron, Ohio 44311   Established 1939

William E. McCormick, Managing Director
To increase the knowledge of industrial hygiene through interchange and dissemination of information; to promote the study and control of environmental factors affecting the health and well-being of industrial workers. Membership: 4,900 (individual members and industrial associate members). Finances: Membership: Individual, $25; industries, $150.

Meetings: Annual, various locations. Publications: AIHA Journal, monthly, Robert S. Lee, editor; Hygienic Guides; Industrial Noise Manual; Air Pollution Manual; Analytical Abstracts; Heating and Cooling for Man in Industry; Basic Industrial Hygiene.

★ 314 ★

AMERICAN INSTITUTE OF FAMILY RELATIONS
5287 Sunset Boulevard   (213) 465-5131
Los Angeles, California 90027   Established 1930

Edward C. Peacock, Executive Director
The Institute is a pioneering and progressive organization committed to strengthening family life and promoting individual development.   It boasts a diversity of counseling (individual, group, couple or family), educational, and research programs which reach out to a variety of people with a variety of needs. Membership: Open to all interested persons. Finances: Membership: Fees for counseling, classes, sale of publications, grants, contributions, all fees on sliding scale of annual income. Meetings: Board of Directors Meeting, bimonthly, Los Angeles, California. Publications: Family Life, bimonthly, E. C. Peacock and J. Larson, editors. Library: Roswell-Johnson, 5,000 volumes.

★ 315 ★

AMERICAN INSTITUTE OF MEDICAL CLIMATOLOGY
1023 Welsh Road   (215) 673-8368
Philadelphia, Pennsylvania 19115   Established 1958

Harold W. Schaefer, President; Margaret Kornblueh,
        Secretary-Treasurer
The Institute has been formed to promote the sciences of bioclimatology and biometeorology by organizing, conducting, and correlating pertinent studies on the relationship between weather and climate and life in all its phases.   The scope of the investigations includes all measurable, observable or otherwise determinable meteorotropic, psychotropic and physiological effects of the atmosphere. Membership: 100 (M.D.'s, engineers, physiologists, physicists, businessmen). Finances: Membership: U.S.A., $11; foreign, $14; Other Sources: Sales of scientific materials. Meetings: Board of Directors, annually, Philadelphia, Pennsylvania; Scientific Meetings, irregularly. Publications: Newsletter to membership, quarterly. Affiliations: International Society of Biometeorology.

★ 316 ★

AMERICAN INSTITUTE OF NUTRITION
9650 Rockville Pike   (301) 530-7050
Bethesda, Maryland 20014   Established 1928

Max Milner, Ph.D., Executive Officer
Organized to further the extension of the knowledge
of nutrition and to facilitate personal contact between
investigators in nutrition and closely related fields of
interest.   The Institute sponsors and organizes the
Annual Meeting with the Federation of American Societies for Experimental Biology; maintains liaison
with other scientific societies, federal and United
Nations agencies; supplies information on the field
of nutrition, educational requirements and the field
opportunities.   Membership: 2,000 (active, associate,
honorary, emeritus; United States, Canada, and
foreign).   Finances: Membership: Journal subscriptions, $30 annual; member dues, $29 annual; Other
Sources: Donations from industry and foundations.
Awards: Borden Award, $1,000; Osborne and Mendel
Award, $1,000; Conrad A. Elvehjem Award, $1,500;
Mead Johnson Award, $1,000; Lederle Award,
$1,500; Bio-Serv, $1,000; Annual Graduate Student Awards, 5 at $500; Annual Graduate Research
Scholarships, 4 at $5,000.   Meetings: Annual, var-
ious locations, April.   Publications: Journal of Nutrition, monthly, James S. Dinning, editor; Nutrition Notes (newsletter), quarterly, Samuel G. Kahn,
editor.   Library: Federation of American Societies
for Experimental Biology.   Affiliations: Federation
of American Societies for Experimental Biology;
American Society for Clinical Nutrition; National
Nutrition Consortium.

★ 317 ★

AMERICAN INSTITUTE OR ORAL BIOLOGY
Post Office Box 481   (714) 499-1286
South Laguna, California 92677   Established 1943

Dr. Philip J. Boyne, President
This organization is based upon the desire of practicing dentists to participate in the unique educational
experience, learning from outstanding presentations of
foremost authorities in various disciplines and fields of
health care and biologic research and at the same
time enjoying an environment of good fellowship and
scientific rapport, through which they can establish a
basis for the enhancement of dental care delivery and
for the improvement of the quality of professional life
in general.   Membership: Approximately 150 annually (M.D.'s and D.D.S.'s).   Finances: Annual Seminar, tuition fee per participant $225.   Meetings: An-
nual, Spa Hotel, Palm Springs, California.   Publications: Proceedings Manual - 1980, annual,
A.I.O.B., editor.

★ 318 ★

AMERICAN INSTITUTE OF THE HISTORY OF
  PHARMACY
University of Wisconsin
Pharmacy Building, Office of Director
Madison, Wisconsin 53706   Established 1941

John Parascandola, Director
To equip the pharmacist for citizenship in the world
of intellectual and moral responsibility by making him
familiar with the non-technical aspects and humanistic ramifications of the profession, and to do pharmacy's share in the cooperative endeavor for making the
historical record of world civilization as complete as
possible.   Membership: 1,335 (active and supporting).   Finances: Membership: Active, $20; sup-
porting, $25.   Awards: Kremers Award (national),
Urdang Medal (international), both for distinguished
writing of pharmaceutical history.   Meetings: Annual, various locations.   Publications: Pharmacy in
History, quarterly, George Bender, editor; A.I.H.P.
Notes, irregularly, John Parascandola, editor.

★ 319 ★

AMERICAN INSTITUTE OF ULTRASOUND IN
  MEDICINE
4405 East-West Highway, Suite 504   (301) 656-6117
Washington, D.C. 20014   Established 1955

Stephen J. Jerrick, Ph.D., Executive Director;
   Barry B. Goldberg, M.D., President (1981-1982);
   Marvin C. Ziskin, M.D., President (1983-1984)
Founded to advance the art and science of ultrasonics
in medicine and research.   Its activities are educational, literary and scientific.   To further this purpose, the AIUM has established committees to direct
its various activities.   Currently these committees
are: Administrative, Archives, Biological Effects,
Central Program, Education, Ethics, Public Relations,
Publications, Standards, Regional Groups, Constitution,
Finance, Professional Standards, Project Development
and Reflections.   Membership: 4,500 (physicians,
engineers, physicists, technical specialists, manufacturers and medical students).   Finances: Membership:
Fellows and members, $60 annual; associate, $50
annual; affiliate, $40 annual.   Meetings: Spring
Education Meeting, annual, various locations; Annual Convention, various locations.   Publications:
Reflections (newsmagazine), quarterly, Marvin Ziskin,
M.D., editor; Sonic Exchange (buyers' guide), annually, Michael Meinerz, editor; numerous pamphlets,
brochures and books.   Affiliations: Society of Diagnostic Medical Sonography; American Registry of
Diagnostic Medical Sonographers.

★ 320 ★

AMERICAN JOURNAL OF NURSING COMPANY
10 Columbus Circle   (212) 582-8820
New York, New York 10019   Established 1900

Philip E. Day, President and Publisher
To advance the public knowledge of, and to foster
and publish research on problems related to the science and art of professional nursing; to uphold the
highest standards and promote the improvement of professional nursing and nursing theory to students, the
profession and the general public by printed publications and audio-visuals. Publications: American
Journal of Nursing, monthly, Thelma M. Schorr, editor; Nursing Outlook, monthly, Penny A. McCarthy,
editor; Nursing Research, bimonthly, Florence Downs,
editor; MCN, The American Journal of Maternal
Child Nursing, bimonthly, Barbara E. Bishop, editor;
Geriatric Nursing: American Journal of Care for the
Aging, Cynthia Kelly, editor; International Nursing
Index, quarterly, Jacqueline L. Picciano, editor.
Library: Sophia F. Palmer Library, over 9,000 vol-
umes. Affiliations: American Nurses' Association.

★ 321 ★

AMERICAN LARYNGOLOGICAL ASSOCIATION
1234 19th Street, N.W.   (202) 223-2676
Washington, D.C. 20036   Established 1879

William M. Trible, M.D., Executive Secretary
Organized originally in New York State for the study
of laryngology and rhinology and the publication of
papers relating thereto.   An annual meeting has been
held every year and The Transactions published.
Membership: Limited to 100 active members, currently 92 (active, emeritus, corresponding). Finances: Membership: Only active members pay dues
which vary annually; Other Sources: Some trust
funds exist. Awards: DeRoaldes Medal; Cassel-
berry Award for research; Daniel C. Baker Lectureship; Research Fund. Meetings: Annual, in the
Spring. Publications: Transactions of the American
Laryngological Association, annual, Dr. Gabriel
Tucker, editor.

★ 322 ★

AMERICAN LARYNGOLOGICAL, RHINOLOGICAL
    AND OTOLOGICAL SOCIETY, INC.
c/o Ann R. Holm
2954 Dorman Road   (215) 356-8348
Broomall, Pennsylvania 19008   Established 1895

William M. Trible, M.D., Executive Secretary;
   Ann R. Holm, Administrative Assistant
The Society for the presentation and discussion of

scientific papers and procedures as they apply to the
practice of otolaryngology; the promotion and diffusion of medical knowledge; the issuance of periodic publications concerned with progress, study, and
research in the specialty of otolaryngology; and the
advancement of high professional and ethical standards.
Membership: 708 (active, senior, emeritus, honorary,
associate). Awards: The Mosher Award; The
Fowler Award. Meetings: Annual, various locations.
Publications: Transactions, 6 times annually, Joseph
H. Ogura, M.D., editor.

★ 323 ★

AMERICAN LEBANESE SYRIAN ASSOCIATED
    CHARITIES, INC.
539 Lane Avenue
Memphis, Tennessee 38105   Established 1957

Danny Thomas, President; Baddia J. Rashid,
    National Executive Director
The organization's purpose is to raise funds for the
support of St. Jude Children's Research Hospital in
the treatment, research, and cure of childhood catastrophic diseases.   A.L.S.A.C.'s activities include
residential drives, radiothons, and other special events.
Membership: 2,500 (annual, family and life membership). Finances: Other Sources: Individual donation. Research Funds: All research funds given to
St. Jude Hospital. Meetings: Annual, various locations. Publications: A.L.S.A.C. News, quarterly, Paul B. Parham, editor; Newsletter, semiannual, St. Jude Children's Research Hospital.

★ 324 ★

AMERICAN LEPROSY MISSIONS, INC.
1262 Broad Street   (201) 338-9197
Bloomfield, New Jersey 07003   Established 1906

Roger K. Ackley, President
The agency seeks the conquest of leprosy through research, public education, specialized training, and
the best possible medical treatment and rehabilitation.
It provides these services for victims in Asia, Africa
and South America.   It also gives scholarship grants
to selected medical personnel for specialized training;
arranges for teaching seminars in this country and
abroad; makes surveys of leprosy needs in developing
countries at the request of governments; and conducts a public education program to help erase the
historical stigma of the disease which has long ham-
pered treatment and research. Membership: 50,000
(individual, group contributors). Finances: Other
Sources: Corporate gifts, government grants. Lectureships: Kellersberger Lectures, Addis, Ababa,
Ethopia. Meetings: Annual meetings of the

Corporation; biennial meeting of the Board at headquarters in Bloomfield, New Jersey. Publications: ALM Bulletin, semiannual, Wendy Littman, editor; Physical Therapy in Leprosy for Paramedicals, Ellen Davis Kelly, Ph.D., editor. Library: Limited volumes and use by arrangement. Remarks: Member of International Leprosy Association (London, England).

★ 325 ★
AMERICAN LUNG ASSOCIATION
1740 Broadway   (212) 245-8000
New York, New York 10019   Established 1904

James A. Swomley, Managing Director
The Association aims to help Americans prevent lung disease, obtain effective treatment, and learn to live with disabled breathing; to develop knowledgeable medical care teams equipped to provide comprehensive and continuing care for all lung disease patients. To carry out these aims, the association conducts scientific meetings, seminars, and courses; publishes professional and technical publications; conducts programs in breathing training for lung disease victims, non-smokers rights programs, and air conservation programs. Membership: 8,000. Finances: Other Sources: Contributions; Christmas Seal Campaign; gifts; bequests; memorials. Awards: Edward Livingston Trudeau Medal, annually; Will Ross Medal, annually; Amberson Lecture at Annual American Lung Association/American Thoracic Society Meeting; research grants; fellowships; medical education awards. Meetings: Annual, various locations. Publications: Bulletin, monthly, Lucille Fisher, editor; American Review of Respiratory Disease, monthly, Gareth M. Green, M.D., editor; Clinical Notes on Respiratory Disease, Donald C. Kent, M.D., editor; Basics of RD, Robert Loudon, M.D., editor; newsletters, leaflets; posters; booklets.

★ 326 ★
AMERICAN MASSAGE AND THERAPY ASSOCIATION
Post Office Box 1270   (615) 245-8071
Kingsport, Tennessee 37662   Established 1943

James C. Bowling, National Executive Secretary
To advance the science of massage therapy and related techniques; to raise the standards of these professionals so as to merit the respect and confidence of all; to foster a spirit of cooperation and exchange of ideas and techniques among its members. Conducts meetings, workshops, demonstrations, educational lectures and seminars. Membership: Approximately 2,000 (active, associate, student, honorary). Finances: Membership: Active, $65; associate and student, $20. Awards: Annual Meritorious Service

Award, scholarship fund. Meetings: Annual, various locations; Regional conferences. Publications: Massage Journal, quarterly; Registry and Yearbook, annually, Marilyn Frender, editor.

★ 327 ★
AMERICAN MEDICAL ASSOCIATION
535 North Dearborn Street   (312) 751-6000
Chicago, Illinois 60610   Established 1847

James H. Sammons, M.D., Executive Vice President
The AMA was founded to promote the science and art of medicine and the betterment of the public health. The AMA is concerned with cultivating and advancing medical knowledge; fostering high quality medical care for all, along with broadening availability; decelerating health-care costs; elevating the standards of medical education; facilitating and encouraging constructive dialogue among medical professionals and the community; and examining current medical care delivery systems with the purpose of developing new methods that will be more responsive to the total health needs of the public. Membership: 231,162 (physicians [2 or more years in practice or voluntary commissioned officers], $250 annually; first year in practice, $125 annually; interns, residents and obligated officers, $35 annually; medical students, $15 annually). Finances: Other Sources: Various publications, video clinics for continuing medical education. Meetings: Annual meeting, June or July, Chicago; Interim meeting, first week of December, various locations; Winter Scientifc meeting, January, various locations. Publications: Journal of the American Medical Association (JAMA) weekly, William R. Barclay, M.D., editor; American Medical News, weekly, Larry Boston, editor; 9 Specialty Journals, monthly, various editors under the direction of William R. Barclay, M.D.; numerous directories, books and pamphlets. Library: AMA Division of Library and Archival Services, 110,000 volumes (used by members, staff; used by public after requesting in writing). Affiliations: Participants in Lockheed Dialog; Medline; Midwest Health Science Library Network; New York Times Information Bank; OCLC, Inc.

★ 328 ★
AMERICAN MEDICAL ASSOCIATION AUXILIARY, INC.
535 North Dearborn Street   (312) 751-6166
Chicago, Illinois 60610   Established 1922

Hazel J. Lewis, Executive Director
To assist physicians in protecting and improving public health; provide volunteer health services to

communities. Membership: 81,000 (physicians' spouses). Finances: Membership: $11 annual dues. Meetings: Annual Convention, June, Chicago, Illinois; Annual Leadership Confluence, October, Chicago, Illinois. Publications: Facets, five annually, Kathleen T. Jordan, editor; Direct Line Newsletter, bimonthly, Cynthia L. Ryskamp, editor; National News, bimonthly, Kathleen T. Jordan, editor; Package Programs on 10 health topics; Community Planning Brochure; Legislative Action Workbook; Marketing Membership Manual.

★ 329 ★

AMERICAN MEDICAL ASSOCIATION EDUCATION AND RESEARCH FOUNDATION

535 North Dearborn Street   (312) 751-6000
Chicago, Illinois 60610   Established 1962

James H. Sammons, M.D., Executive Vice President
Receives and distributes funds to United States medical schools; administers loan guarantee programs for medical students, interns and residents through guarantee funds consisting of contributions from physicians, medical societies and auxiliaries, foundations, private industry and the general public. Not a membership organization, managed by the Board of Trustees of the American Medical Association (see American Medical Association entry).

★ 330 ★

AMERICAN MEDICAL ELECTROENCEPHALOGRAPHIC ASSOCIATION

850 Elm Grove Road   (414) 784-3646
Elm Grove, Wisconsin 53122   Established 1964

Henry A. Brandt, M.D., President;
   Robert H. Herzog, Executive Secretary
Founded for the advancement of clinical electroencephalography with the scientific programs prepared with primary emphasis on clinical electroencephalography; to promote the development of training programs for clinical electroencephalographers and EEG technicians. Membership: 550 (physicians). Finances: Membership: $75 annually (includes subscription to clinical EEG Journal). Awards: Ralph Rosen, M.D., Memorial Lecture. Meetings: Annual, various locations. Publications: Clinical EEG Journal, quarterly, Frederick A. Gibbs, M.D., editor.

★ 331 ★

AMERICAN MEDICAL FLY FISHING ASSOCIATION

Box 1008   (606) 679-5775
Somerset, Kentucky 42501   Established 1969

Veryl F. Frye, M.D.
Organized to combine physicians' professional interests with that of fly fishing mainly for trout. Membership: 100 (general). Finances: Membership: $20 annually; Other Sources: Patches, hat (lapel) pins. Meetings: Annual, August, West Yellowstone, Montana.

★ 332 ★

AMERICAN MEDICAL PUBLISHERS ASSOCIATION

c/o G. J. Gallagher
428 East Preston Street   (301) 528-4211
Baltimore, Maryland 21201   Established 1961

G. James Gallagher, President; Jerry Newman, President Elect; Mercedes Bierman, Secretary-Treasurer
To promote the distribution of medical books and periodicals; to exchange information on common industry problems; to improve communications with medical faculties and with educational organizations in medicine; to establish and maintain good relations with bookstores, libraries, and other book outlets. Activities include committees on copyright, exhibits, distribution totals and professional relations; market surveys; and periodic seminars on industry problems. Membership: 35 (medical publishers). Finances: Membership: $100 annually. Meetings: Semiannual, Key Medical Conventions.

★ 333 ★

AMERICAN MEDICAL RECORD ASSOCIATION

875 North Michigan Avenue
Suite 1850, John Hancock Center (312) 787-2672
Chicago, Illinois 60611   Established 1928

Carolyn B. Cave, Ph.D., RRA
To promote the art and science of medical record administration and to improve the quality of comprehensive health information services for the welfare of the public. Activities include regional institutes and workshops, annual meeting, professional assistance to members, establishes and maintains standards for schools and develops and updates curricula, provides for examination of candidates for accreditation and registration and maintains a registry of qualified medical record practitioners, administers the "Independent Study Program in Medical Record Technology", acts in an advisory capacity to governmental agencies and other institutions on health care records, publishes books and pamphlets on medical record practice, conducts research projects on the medical record field, maintains liaison with 52 component state organizations and the International Federation of Health Record Organizations, conducts study tours in foreign

countries, recruits students to the profession. Membership: Over 23,000 (active, associate, student, inactive, honorary). Finances: Membership: Active registered record administrator, $80; active accredited record technician, $60; associate, $30; inactive, $15; student, $10; Other Sources: Institutes and workshops, journal subscriptions, advertising and publications, sale of exhibit space at annual meeting and contracts and grants. Meetings: Annual, various locations. Publications: Journal of the American Medical Record, bimonthly, Carolyn B. Cave, Ph.D., RRA, editor; Association; Counterpoint, bimonthly, Carolyn B. Cave, Ph.D., RRA, editor. Library: Foundation of Record Education of AMRA Library, 2,500 volumes. Affiliations: 52 component state associations.

★ 334 ★
AMERICAN MEDICAL SOCIETY ON ALCOHOLISM
733 Third Avenue   (212) 986-4433
New York, New York 10017   Established 1954

Sheila B. Blume, M.D., President
This organization is a component of the National Council on Alcoholism, Inc. (see separate entry). The Society's purpose is to serve as a forum for such physicians as are interested in the problems of alcoholism and other addictive disorders, to extend knowledge in these fields, to promote dissemination of that knowledge and to enlighten and direct public opinion in regard to these problems. Activities include publication and distribution of a journal, provision of the faculty for a number of courses for physicians at Schools of Alcohol Studies, and the introduction of intrinsic education on alcoholism into medical school. Membership: 890 (physicians). Finances: Membership: $50. Awards: AMSA Medal. Scholarships: 3 annually to the Rutgers Summer School of Alcohol Studies. Publications: Alcoholism: Clinical and Experimental Research.

★ 335 ★
AMERICAN MEDICAL STUDENT ASSOCIATION
14650 Lee Road
Post Office Box 131   (703) 968-7920
Chantilly, Virginia 22021

Paul R. Wright, Executive Director
Committed to the improvement of health care and health care delivery to all people; to provide the active improvement of medical education; to involve its members in the social, moral and ethical obligations of the profession of medicine; to assist in the improvement and understanding of world health problems; to contribute to the welfare of medical stu-

dents, interns, residents and post-MD trainees; and to advance the profession of medicine. Membership: 24,000 (active [medical students], 22,500; affiliate [pre-meds, residents, practicing physicians], 1,000; sustaining [residents, practicing physicians, health-related organizations and corporations], 500). Finances: Membership: Active, $20 (one-time fee for 4-year medical school career); affiliates, $15 annually; sustaining, $25-$500; Other Sources: Contributions, grants. Meetings: National Annual Meeting, various locations; Regional Fall Workshops, various locations. Publications: The New Physician, monthly, Todd Dankmyer, editor; Infusion, monthly, Phyllis Gapen, editor.

★ 336 ★
AMERICAN MEDICAL TECHNOLOGISTS
710 Higgins Road   (312) 823-5160
Park Ridge, Illinois 60068   Established 1939

Chester B. Dziekonski, Executive Director
To elevate standards in the fields of medical technology and to maintain constant education of technologists in their field by scientific seminars and conventions. Membership: 13,500 (medical technologists, medical laboratory technicians, medical assistants, laboratory supervisors, associate members in the biological sciences related to medicine). Finances: Membership: $80 original application; renewal $70; Other Sources: Journal subscription, $7. Awards: Medical Technology Awards for: (1) an original paper on a new concept in medical laboratory science; (2) an original idea regarding clinical laboratory instruments; (3) a new laboratory procedure or technique. Meetings: Annual, various locations. Publications: Official Journal of the American Medical Technologists, bimonthly, Chester B. Dziekonski, editor.

★ 337 ★
AMERICAN MEDICAL WOMEN'S ASSOCIATION, INC.
465 Grand Street   (212) 586-8683
New York, New York 10002   Established 1915

Lorraine Loesel, Executive Director
A professional membership organization for women physicians. The Association aims for progress in medical science, humanism in the act and service of practicing medicine, education at all levels, and cooperation with medical and health organizations in allied health fields. Membership: 6,000 (active, associate, student). Awards: Glasgow Awards for women at the top of their graduating classes; Carroll Birch Manuscript Award; Scholarship Loan Fund. Meetings: Annual, various locations. Publications:

Journal of the American Medical Women's Association, monthly, M. Irene Ferrer, M.D., editor; What's Happening in AMWA?, quarterly, Lorraine Loesel, editor. Affiliation: Medical Women's International Association.

★ 338 ★
AMERICAN MEDICAL WRITERS ASSOCIATION
5272 River Road, Suite 370   (301) 986-9119
Bethesda, Maryland 20016   Established 1940

Lillian Sablack, Executive Secretary
To advance standards of communication in medicine and allied sciences; to elevate professional status and increase national recognition of medical communications. Membership: Approximately 2,000 (physicians and others engaged or interested in medical writing or other aspects of medical communication). Finances: Membership: $35 annually; Other Sources: Corporate dues. Awards: Harold Swanberg Distinguished Award for members; Medical Book and Medical Film Awards. Meetings: Annual, various locations. Publications: AMWA Newsletter, bimonthly, Mark C. Christmeyer, editor; Medical Communications, published quarterly, Edith Schwager, editor; AMWA Freelance Directory, annual. Affiliation: A.A.A.S.

★ 339 ★
AMERICAN MENTAL HEALTH FOUNDATION, INC.
2 East 86th Street   (212) 737-9027
New York, New York 10028   Established 1924

Dr. Valentine W. Zetlin, President;
   Ralph A. Suris, Administrative Director
The American Mental Health Foundation, Inc., a national research organization for the advancement of mental health as well as its associate organization, the International Institute for Mental Health Research of Zurich and Geneva, are dedicated to extensive and and intensive research in the theories and techniques of psychotherapy and to the implementation of needed reforms. A great number of the leading professionals in the field of psychiatry and psychotherapy from many different countries participate in the ongoing projects of this unique international research network whose efforts cover the most important areas and urgent issues of the mental health field. The Foundation's and the Institute's efforts have resulted in the development of better and less expensive treatment methods highly acclaimed here and abroad. Publications: Joint research endeavors of the American Mental Health Foundation and the International Institute for Mental Health Research are published in English, French and German; occasionally published in other languages. Affiliations: The International Institute

for Mental Health Research, Zurich and Geneva; the French-American Institute for Mental Health, Paris; The World Federation for Mental Health.

★ 340 ★
AMERICAN NAPRAPATHIC ASSOCIATION
3330 North Milwaukee Avenue   (312) 282-2686
Chicago, Illinois 60641   Established 1909

Chester C. Smith, Corresponding Secretary
To advance and protect the interests and welfare of the members, and the profession of Naprapathy in general, in any manner and by whatever means that lie within the power of the Association, with the object in view of raising the dignity, prestige and standing of the profession in the fullest possible degree so that every legal recognition and protection may be enjoyed by the members wherever located. Membership: 125. Finances: Membership: Application fee, $10; annual dues, $10; monthly dues, $11. Awards: $4 of the monthly dues are turned over to the Naprapathic Education and Research Foundation for education and research. Meetings: Semiannual, annual, various locations. Publications: Voice of Naprapathy, 2 or 3 times annually, Raymond M. Webster, editor; Journal of Naprapathy, monthly, Maryann Harris, editor. Affiliations: Illinois Naprapathic Association; Naprapathic Education and Research Foundation; Chicago National College of Naprapathy.

★ 341 ★
AMERICAN NATIONAL STANDARDS INSTITUTE
1430 Broadway   (212) 354-3300
New York, New York 10018   Established 1918

Donald Peyton, Executive Vice President
Ensure competent, efficient, and timely development of standards; minimize duplication and overlap; provide the procedures to ensure voluntary consensus among parties affected by a standard; provide a neutral forum where standards needs are identified and met. Membership: 860 companies, 170 national organizations. Finances: Membership: Organizations, $1,000; company membership dues rate based on sales or assets; Other Sources: Sale of standards. Publications: Annual Catalog; Progress Report; biweekly periodicals, ANSI Reporter and Standards Action.

★ 342 ★
AMERICAN NATURAL HYGIENE SOCIETY, INC.
698 Brooklawn Avenue   (203) 366-6229
Bridgeport, Connecticut 06604   Established 1946

Jo Willard, Executive Director
Natural Hygiene is the system which helps people to
live in harmony with the physiological needs of the
human organism, thereby maximizing health.   By
supplying the body with the basic requirements of
nature--natural vegetarian diet, unpolluted air, exercise, rest, sleep, mental and emotional poise, wholesome environment, and productive activity--health is
assured, the natural immunity against illness is most
fully manifested, and the self-healing powers resident
within the body are given full reign.   Membership:
Approximately 5,000 (cross section of population).
Finances: Membership: $15 annually; Other Sources:
Contributions.   Meetings: Chapters in many states
and countries (on request).   Publications: Health
Science, bimonthly, Jack Dunn Trop, editor; numerous books.

★ 343 ★
AMERICAN NEUROLOGICAL ASSOCIATION
c/o James Toole
Bowman Gray School of Medicine
Winston-Salem, North Carolina   (919) 727-4598
   North Carolina 27103   Established 1875

James Toole, M.D., Secretary-Treasurer
The advancement of neurological science.   Membership: 700 (senior, active, associate, honorary, corresponding).   Finances: Membership: Initiation fee,
$100; active, $75; associate, $25.   Meetings:
Annual, various locations.   Publications: Transac-
tion of ANA, annual, Roger Duvoisin, M.D., editor.

★ 344 ★
AMERICAN NURSES' ASSOCIATION, INC.
2420 Pershing Road   (816) 474-5720
Kansas City, Missouri 64108   Established 1896

Myrtle K. Aydelotte, Ph.D., R.N., F.A.A.N.,
   Executive Director; William L. Kuehn, Ph.D.,
   Director, Department of Communications
To foster high standards of nursing practice; to promote the professional and educational advancement of
nurses, and the general welfare of nurses, to the end
that all people may have better nursing care.   Membership: 180,000 registered nurses.   Finances: Membership: $55; Other Sources: Grants and contracts.
Meetings: Biennial, various locations.   Publications:
The American Nurse, 10 issues annually, Patricia
McCarty, editor; American Journal of Nursing,
monthly, Thelma Schorr, editor; numerous reports,
etc.

★ 345 ★
AMERICAN NURSES' FOUNDATION, INC.
2420 Pershing Road   (816) 421-5770
Kansas City, Missouri 64108   Established 1955

Myrtle K. Aydelotte, Ph.D., R.N., F.A.A.N.,
   Executive Director
The primary goal of the American Nurses' Foundation
is to encourage individuals, groups, and institutions to
improve health care in the United States by maximizing the impact of nursing.   In working toward
this goal, ANF concentrates its activities in three
areas: analysis of public health policy issues of priority to nursing; support for the career development
of nurses pursuing investigative studies; and assistance to the educational and research activities of the
American Nurses' Association.   The bases of its interest in policy analysis are educational preparation
of nurses, nursing manpower, and cost containment.
Membership: ANF is not a membership organization.
Finances: Other Sources: Public and private grants
and contributions.   Awards: Small grants (2,100)
for nurse-directed research projects; Awards are made
annually.   Guidelines are announced annually in
March.   Affiliations: American Nurses' Association.

★ 346 ★
AMERICAN OCCUPATIONAL MEDICAL
   ASSOCIATION
150 North Wacker Drive   (312) 782-2166
Chicago, Illinois 60606   Established 1915

Howard Schulz, Executive Director
To foster the study of the problems peculiar to the
practice of occupational medicine and surgery, and to
unite into one organization members of the medical
profession whose interest lies in the field.   The Association encourages the development of methods
adapted to the conservation and improvement of health
among workers and promotes a more general understanding of the purposes and results of the medical
care of these workers.   Membership: 3,608 (active,
fellows, life, associate, honorary, inactive).   Finances: Membership: Associate, $20; active, fel-
lows, $100 plus component society dues.   Awards:
Knudsen Award; Health Achievement in Industry
Award; Meritorious Service Award; Adolph G.
Kammer Merit in Authorship Award.   Meetings: Annual, various locations.   Publications: Journal of
Occupational Medicine, monthly, Lloyd B. Tepper,
M.D., editor; committee reports, reprints.   Affiliations: 29 component societies.

★ 347 ★

AMERICAN OCCUPATIONAL THERAPY ASSOCIATION, INC.

1383 Piccard Drive (301) 948-9626
Rockville, Maryland 20852 Established 1917

James J. Garibaldi, Executive Director
The intentions of the Association are to (1) improve and advance the practice of occupational therapy to insure that the breadth and quality of services adequately meet the health care needs of the society it serves; (2) improve and advance education and qualification in occupational therapy; (3) establish standards of performance; (4) foster research and study of occupational therapy; and (5) engage in other activities to further the dissemination of knowledge of the practice of occupational therapy. Membership: Over 29,000. Finances: Membership: Fees; Other Sources: Grant funds. Awards: Award of Merit and Eleanor Clarke Slagel Lectureship, annual; Certificate of Appreciation. Meetings: Annual, various locations. Publications: American Journal of Occupational Therapy, 12 times annually, Elaine J. Viseltear, editor; Newsletter, monthly; Yearbook (registry). Affiliations: 51 state and regional associations including District of Columbia and Puerto Rico.

★ 348 ★

AMERICAN OPHTHALMOLOGICAL SOCIETY

200 First Street S.W. (507) 284-3726
Rochester, Minnesota 55901 Established 1864

Thomas P. Kearns, M.D., Secretary-Treasurer
Professional society of physicians specializing in the diseases of the eye. Activities include annual scientific meeting. Membership: 225 (associate, active, emeritus). Finances: Membership: $10 plus assessments. Awards: Howe Medal for Advancement in the Scientific Aspects of this Field, annually. Meetings: Annual, usually in Hot Springs, Virginia. Publications: Transactions of the American Ophthalmological Society, annual, Stanley M. Truhlsen, M.D., editor.

★ 349 ★

AMERICAN OPTOMETRIC ASSOCIATION

243 North Lindbergh Boulevard (314) 991-4100
St. Louis, Missouri 63141 Established 1898

Richard Averill, Executive Director
To advance, improve and enhance the vision care of the public; to unite optometrists; to encourage and assist in the improvement of the art and science of optometry; to elevate unceasingly the standards and ethics of the profession of optometry; to protect and defend the inalienable right of every person to freedom of choice of practitioner and to restrict the practice of optometry and any part of it to those who have been trained, qualified and licensed to practice the profession. Membership: 20,000 optometrists. Finances: Membership: $300. Awards: Apollo, Optometrist of the Year Award; Distinguished Service Award. Meetings: Annual Congress; state and regional meetings, various locations. Publications: Journal, monthly, Dr. Milton Eger, editor; AOA News, semimonthly, Suzy Farren, editor. Library: 9,000 volumes. Affiliations: 50 state associations.

★ 350 ★

AMERICAN OPTOMETRIC FOUNDATION

4715 Cordell Avenue
Washington, D.C. 20014 Established 1947

Dr. John R. Kennedy, President
The Foundation was organized in response to a need for the provision of fellowships, scholarships, research grants, and special awards for worthy student of optometry. Membership: 3,000 optometrists, optical wholesalers and manufacturers. Finances: Membership: Average, $25 (no set amount). Awards: William C. Ezell, Fellowship; Spurgeon Eure Award; Irvin Borish Award; J. Harold Bailey Award; Kohn Award; Vincent Salierno Scholarship; American Optical Scholarship; Corning Scholarship. Meetings: Educational Seminars, various locations throughout the United States. Publications: Update, quarterly, Edward J. Renauer, editor. Affiliations: American Optometric Association; Association of Schools and Colleges of Optometry.

★ 351 ★

AMERICAN ORGANIZATION FOR THE EDUCATION OF THE HEARING IMPAIRED

1537 35th Street, N.W. (202) 337-5220
Washington, D.C. 20007 Established 1967

Sara E. Conlon, Executive Director;
Sandy North, Secretary
To promote excellence in the education of hearing-impaired children and adults. To this end this Organization's efforts shall be dedicated to: teaching of oral communication and the development of quality oral programs; encouragement of scientific study of the educational and verbal communicative processes; exchange of information among educators through publication dissemination of research finds, professional meetings and seminars. Membership: Teachers of the hearing impaired may be active members; student members are non-voting members; these are students

in a professional preparation program. Finances: Membership: Alexander Graham Bell Association, $25 with AOEHI membership, $7.50. You must hold membership in the Alexander Graham Bell Association for the Deaf in order to be a member in AOEHI; Other Sources: Gifts and conference fees. Awards: Teacher of the Year Award, annual, given to a "master" teacher nominated by professionals in the field; Program of the Year Award, annual, given to a "master" teacher nominated by professionals in the field; Rookie Teacher of the Year Award, annual, given to a "master" teacher nominated by professionals in the field. Meetings: Biennial, in conjunction with the Alexander Graham Bell Association for the Deaf Convention, various locations. Publications: AOEHI Newsletter, quarterly, Sandy North, editor; articles written by members of the organization appear in the Volta Review. Affiliations: Alexander Graham Bell Association for the Deaf (parent organization); International Parents Organization; Oral Deaf Adults Section.

★ 352 ★
AMERICAN ORTHOPAEDIC ASSOCIATION
444 North Michigan Avenue
Chicago, Illinois 60611   Established 1887

To foster the exchange of ideas in the prevention and treatment of diseases of the musculo-skeletal system and associated structures and in the alleviation and treatment of the results of trauma. To stimulate teaching and research related to the cause, care, and prevention of trauma and these disease processes. To afford recognition to those persons who make outstanding contributions to this field. Membership: 400 (active, honorary, corresponding, emeritus); by invitation only. Finances: Membership: Active, $250. Meetings: Annual, various locations.

★ 353 ★
AMERICAN ORTHOPAEDIC SOCIETY FOR SPORTS
     MEDICINE
70 West Hubbard, Suite 202   (312) 644-2623
Chicago, Illinois 60610   Established 1972

Thomas Nelson, Executive Director; Robert Larson, M.D., President; John Feagin, Jr., M.D., Secretary
The Society promotes, supports and develops investigative knowledge of Sports Medicine; promotes and supports education of physicians and non-physicians in the prevention, recognition and treatment of sports injuries. Membership: 600 (active, associate, affiliate, honorary, emeritus). Finances: Membership: Physicians, $145; non-physicians, $50; Other

Sources: Scientific Meetings, Journal Subscriptions. Awards: O'Donoghue Award. Meetings: National meetings, semiannual, various locations. Publications: The American Journal of Sports Medicine, bimonthly, Jack Hughston, M.D., editor.

★ 354 ★
AMERICAN ORTHOPEDIC FOOT SOCIETY
5495 Fernhof Road   (415) 483-2500
Oakland, California 94619   Established 1970

Dr. Richard Kiene, President
This Society is an organization for orthopedic surgeons who are specifically interested in foot problems. Membership: 225 (full membership and associate membership). Finances: Membership: $75 annual. Meetings: Preceding the meeting of the American Academy of Orthopedic Surgeons. Publications: Journal of the Foot and Ankle, 6 times annually, Melvin Jahss, M.D., editor.

★ 355 ★
AMERICAN ORTHOPSYCHIATRIC ASSOCIATION,
     INC.
1775 Broadway   (212) 586-5690
New York, New York 10019   Established 1924

Marion F. Langer, Ph.D., Executive Director
The twofold purpose of the Association is (1) to unite and provide a common meeting ground for those engaged in the study and treatment of problems of human behavior and (2) to foster research and spread information concerning scientific work in the field of human behavior, including all forms of abnormal behavior. Membership: Approximately 8,000 (psychiatrists, psychologists, psychiatric social workers, educators, anthropologists, pediatricians, public health personnel, sociologists, nurses). Finances: Membership: Members, $35; fellows, $45. Meetings: Annual, various locations. Publications: American Journal of Orthopsychiatry, quarterly, Edmund W. Gordon, Ed.D., editor; Orthopsychiatry and the School, Morris Krugman, Ph.D., editor; The Bender Visual Motor Gestalt Test: Test Cards and Manual of Instruction, Lauretta Bender, M.D., editor; A Visual Motor Gestalt Test and Its Clinical Ues, L. Bender, M.D., editor; Case Studies in Childhood Emotional Disabilities, George Gardner, Ph.D., M.D., editor; The Six Schizophrenias, S. J. Beck, Ph.D., editor; Reprint No. 4 - Further Explorations of the Six Schizophrenias: Type S-3, H.B. Molish and S. J. Beck, editors.

★ 356 ★
AMERICAN ORTHOPTIC COUNCIL
University of Iowa
Department of Ophthalmology
Iowa City, Iowa 52242

W. E. Scott, M.D.
To provide training for orthoptist students; to examine and certify orthoptist candidates; to encourage continuing postgraduate study of orthoptics; to set standards of ethical and professional conduct for orthoptists. Sponsored and supported by American Medical Association, American Ophthalmological Society, American Academy of Ophthalmology and Otolaryngology. Membership: 12 council members--ophthalmologists, 4 council members--orthoptists. Meetings: Annual, various locations. Publications: The American Orthoptic Journal, annual, Eugene Helveston, editor.

★ 357 ★
AMERICAN ORTHOTIC AND PROSTHETIC
    ASSOCIATION
1444 N Street, N.W.   (202) 234-8400
Washington, D.C. 20005   Established 1917

William L. McCulloch, Executive Director;
    Sonja I. McCamley, Assistant Executive Director
AOPA was formed after World War I as part of the concerted effort to assure better rehabilitative care of amputee veterans. Later, this expanded to a general concern for all orthopeadically handicapped patients. As a consequence, AOPA now cooperates with a number of agencies (Veterans Administration, Health, Education, and Welfare, Crippled Childrens Bureau, etc.) to identify qualified practitioners and facilities, as well as to promote new research and technology in orthotics and prosthetics. Membership: 750 business entities (independent health care outlets which provide orthotic and prosthetic services as well as educational and research institutions). Finances: Membership: $320 annual; Other Sources: Convention, publications, etc. Awards: American Orthotic and Prosthetic Educational Fund. Meetings: Annual convention. Publications: Orthotics and Prosthetics.

★ 358 ★
AMERICAN OSTEOPATHIC ACADEMY OF
    ORTHOPEDICS
1444 East 8th Street   (816) 471-6744
Kansas City, Missouri 64106   Established 1941

William J. Monaghan, D.O., Secretary-Treasurer
To foster an maintain the highest possible standards in the specialty of orthopedic surgery. Membership: 260 (active, associate, honorary and candidates).

Finances: Membership: Active, $200; associate, $125. Awards: Scientific paper writing award for residents. Meetings: Mid-year each May; annual, each October, in conjunction with the Annual Clinical Assembly of Osteopathic Specialists. Publications: The Orthopod, semiannual. Affiliations: American Osteopathic Association.

★ 359 ★
AMERICAN OSTEOPATHIC ASSOCIATION
212 East Ohio Street   (312) 280-5800
Chicago, Illinois 60611   Established 1897

Edward P. Crowell, D.O., Executive Director
To promote the public health, to encourage scientific research, and to maintain and improve high standards of medical education in osteopathic colleges. Publishes periodicals and provides other membership service, accredits and approves osteopathic colleges and hospitals, supports research, promotes public health and information service. Membership: 14,460 (regular - members are osteopathic physicians and surgeons, graduates of approved colleges of osteopathic medicine; associate - members are teaching, research, administrative or executive employees of approved colleges, hospitals, divisional societies or affiliated organizations; interns, residents). Finances: Membership: Regular, $275 ($100 for regular members serving obligated service in uninformed services); interns, $5; residents, $20; Other Sources: Advertising fees from monthly publications. Funds: Research Fund of American Osteopathic Association; A. T. Still Osteopathic Foundation and Research Institute; Distinguished Service Certificates for Outstanding Accomplishments by Members. Meetings: Annual, various locations. Publications: Journal of the A.O.A., monthly, George W. Northup, D.O., editor; The D. O., A Publication for Osteopathic Physicians and Surgeons, monthly, George W. Northup, D.O., editor; Yearbook and Directory of Osteopathic Physicians, annual. Library: American Osteopathic Association, 6,000 volumes. Affiliations: National Osteopathic Foundation, colleges of specialty practice and other organizations.

★ 360 ★
AMERICAN OSTEOPATHIC COLLEGE OF
    DERMATOLOGY
c/o 5565 Memorial Drive, Suite K (404) 296-5704
Stone Mountain, Georiga 30083   Established 1958

James D. Bernard, D.O., F.A.O.C.D.,
    Secretary-Treasurer
To improve the standards of the practice of dermatology, to stimulate study and extend knowledge in the

field of dermatology, and to promote a more general understanding of the nature and scope of the services rendered to the other divisions of practice, hospitals, clinics, and the public by osteopathic dermatologists. Membership: 86 (active: D.O.'s certified in dermatology, whose practice is devoted 75 percent or more to the specialty; candidate: graduate of a recognized college of osteopathy and licensed to practice within the state from which he applies, who has expressed a major interest in dermatology; associate: persons directly affiliated with the practice of dermatology who possess an appropriate degree in science, psychology, sociology or related field, or qualifications acceptable to the executive board; also an honorary membership). Finances: Membership: Member, $25 annually; resident, $5 annually; Other Sources: Donations from drug companies. Meetings: Annual, in conjunction with American Osteopathic Association, various locations.

★ 361 ★

AMERICAN OSTEOPATHIC COLLEGE OF
    PATHOLOGISTS
2160 Idlewood Road   (404) 491-8473
Tucker, Georgia 30084   Established 1954

Morris Osattin, D.O., President; Robert Fogel, D.O., President Elect; Michael R. Wulf, D.O., Secretary-Treasurer
To improve the practice of pathology; to develop the application of osteopathic concepts in the field of pathology; to study and promote such arts and sciences as may directly or indirectly improve the practice of pathology; to provide instruction in the practice of pathology for such osteopathic physicians as are considered qualified; to maintain and promote the highest moral and ethical standards in the practice of pathology. Activities include residency training program and educational seminars. Membership: 180 (active, candidate and associate). Finances: Membership: Active, $150; candidate and associate, $10. Meetings: Semiannual, various locations.

★ 362 ★

AMERICAN OSTEOPATHIC COLLEGE OF
    PROCTOLOGY
840 East Mount Hope
Lansing, Michigan 48910   Established 1953

Coburn Bland, D.O., Secretary-Treasurer
To achieve and promote better methods in the treatment of proctology. Membership: 160 (associate, senior, honorary, life). Finances: Membership: $60 annual dues; Other Sources: Exhibitors at conventions. Awards: Julius Sobel Essay Award for

Interns; Horace Emery Essay Award for Residents. Meetings: Mid-year and annual, various locations. Publications: Proctoscoup, quarterly, Harold Kirsch, editor. Affiliations: East-Central States Society of Proctology.

★ 363 ★

AMERICAN OSTEOPATHIC COLLEGE OF
    REHABILITATION MEDICINE
1720 East McPherson Street   (816) 665-8679
Kirksville, Missouri 63501   Established 1954

W. Hadley Hoyt, D.O., Secretary-Treasurer
The organization carries on activities to improve the practice of rehabilitation medicine, stimulate study and extend knowledge in this field, and to promote a general understanding of the service rendered by psychiatrists. Programs are carried out by the functions of committees and officers. Membership: 100 (active, candidate, associate, and honorary). Finances: Membership: Dues, active, $150; candidate and associate, $25; Other Sources: Contributions, conventions and meetings. Awards: Special Service Awards; Fellow in A.O.C.R.M.; Thomas D. Webber, D.O. Memorial Lecture Award; Annual Literary Award, Pre and Post Doctoral Categories. Meetings: Annual, in conjunction with American Osteopathic Association convention; semiannual scientific seminars, various locations. Publications: A.O.C.R.M., quarterly, Marvin B. Zwerin, D.O., editor; Rehabilitation Medicine Review. Affiliations: American Osteopathic Association.

★ 364 ★

AMERICAN OSTEOPATHIC HOSPITAL ASSOCIATION
930 Busse Highway   (312) 692-2351
Park Ridge, Illinois 60068   Established 1934

Michael F. Doody, President
This voluntary, non-profit corporation representing osteopathic hospitals throughout the nation provides a mechanism through which and by which member hospitals may act collectively in their common interest by carrying out a variety of programs aimed at improving the representation of member hospitals and by providing them with management services and programs to aid in the delivery of quality osteopathic health care. Membership: 162 active institutional members; 87 personal members; 12 organizational members. Finances: Sliding-scale formula based on a hospital's expenses annually. Awards: Annual Award of Merit. Meetings: Annual, various locations. Publications: Osteopathic Hospitals, 10 times annually; AOHA Annual Directory; Directory of Intern Training Hospitals, annually; AOHA

Newsletter, biweekly; Capital Report, monthly; Focus, monthly; all publications are edited by Lin Fish. Library: Membership Lending Library, 500 volumes. Affiliations: American College of Osteopathic Hospital Administrators.

★ 365 ★

AMERICAN OTOLOGICAL SOCIETY, INC.
1000 East High Street
Charlottesville, Virginia 22901   Established 1868

Cary N. Moon, Jr., M.D., Secretary-Treasurery
To advance the science of otology. Election to membership in this Society is made by the active membership, with proposal for membership being made by members and election based upon significant contributions to otology. Membership: 186 (active, senior, emeritus, associate, honorary). Finances: Assessments are made annually to the active members to finance the cost. Awards: The Society has research funds controlled by the Board of Trustees of the Research Fund from which grants are made annually. An Award of Merit is made on occasions for notable contributions to otology. Meetings: Annual, various locations. Publications: Transactions, Richard Gacek, M.D., editor.

★ 366 ★

AMERICAN PANCREATIC ASSOCIATION
Mayo Clinic
Gastroenterology Unit
Rochester, Minnesota 55901   Established 1971

V.L.W. Go, M.D., Executive Secretary
The specific purpose of the Association is to sponsor an annual meeting at which unpublished research can be presented and discussed. The annual meeting covers the entire spectrum of research interests related to the pancreas. Membership: 250 (M.D.'s, both clinical and research). Finances: Membership: Dues, $15 annually. Meetings: Annual, various locations. Former Name: American Pancreatic Study Group.

AMERICAN PANCREATIC STUDY GROUP
  See: American Pancreatic Association

★ 367 ★

AMERICAN PARENTS COMMITTEE DIVISION,
  CHILD WELFARE LEAGUE OF AMERICA
1346 Connecticut Avenue, N.W.   (202) 833-2850
Washington, D.C. 20036   Established 1946

Jay Well, Chairman
To work for federal legislation on behalf of children. Activities include working for appropriations for child health, welfare and social service programs and working to pass legislation of benefit to children and familites. Membership: The American Parents Committee works on public policy of concern to the 400 CWLA agencies. Meetings: Semiannual. Publications: Voting Scorecard, annual, Nancy F. McConnell, editor.

★ 368 ★

AMERICAN PARKINSON DISEASE ASSOCIATION
116 John Street, Room 417   (212) 732-9550
New York, New York 10301

Louis DeLuca, Executive Director
A non-profit agency that provides funds for research in Parkinson's disease, patient evaluation and treatment centers, dissemination of literature, counseling for patients and families, and educational seminars. Membership: Contributors number over 80,000. Finances: Other Sources: All private contributions, also sponsors fund-raising events such as dinners, etc. Awards: Seed-money grants for research projects available, duration 18 months, $15-$20,000 usually awarded; Cotzias Award, carries a stipend of $50,000 a year for 3 years, awarded to one senior medical researcher. Meetings: Executive Board, 6-7 times annually; Medical Board, quarterly; Patient Support Group, monthly. Publications: A Manual for Patients with P.D., Dr. Fletcher McDowell, editor; Aids and Equipment, Marilyn Robinson, editor; Exercises for the P.D. Patient, Jean LaVigne, editor; Speech Problems, Dr. Florence Weiner, editor; biennial newsletter.

★ 369 ★

AMERICAN PEDIATRIC SOCIETY
c/o David Goldring, M.D.
500 South Kings Highway   (314) 367-6880
St. Louis, Missouri 63110   Established 1888

David Goldring, M.D., Secretary-Treasurer
To bring together men and women for the advancement of the study of children and their diseases, for the prevention of illness and for the protection of health in childhood, for the promotion of pediatric education and research, and to honor those who by their

contributions have aided in its advancement. Membership: 985 (active, emeritus, and honorary). Finances: Membership: $25 annually for active members. Awards: The Howland Medal and Howard Award ($3,000), awarded annually. Meetings: Annual, various locations. Publications: Pediatric Research, monthly, Joseph Bellanti, M.D., editor.

★ 370 ★
AMERICAN PHARMACEUTICAL ASSOCIATION
2215 Constitution Avenue, N.W.   (202) 628-4410
Washington, D.C. 20037   Established 1852

William S. Apple, President
The improvement and promotion of the public health, fostering inter-professional relations, publishing scientific and practical information to pharmacists, supporting pharmacy education and licensure and registration, and formulation and enforcement of a professional code of ethics. Membership: 39,000 active and associate members; 13,000 student members. Finances: Membership: Active, $65; associate, $30; student, $10. Awards: Research Achievement Awards; Ebert Prize; Kilmer Prize; Daniel B. Smith Award; Hugo H. Schaefer Medal; Award for Advancement of Industrial Pharmacy (sponsored by the Industrial Pharmaceutical Technology Section of the APhA Academy of Pharmaceutical Sciences); Literary Award (sponsored by the APhA Section on Federal Pharmacy); and National Science Fair - International Pharmacy Award. Meetings: Annual, various locations. Publications: American Pharmacy, monthly, William E. Small, editor; Journal of Pharmaceutical Sciences, monthly, Mary H. Ferguson, Ph.D., editor; APhA Weekly, David R. Bohardt, editor; Contemporary Pharmacy Practice, quarterly, Peter P. Lomy, editor. Library: 20,000 volumes. Affiliations: Academy of Pharmacy Practice; Academy of Pharmaceutical Sciences; Student APhA; Section on Federal Pharmacy; American College of Apothecaries; and 19 affiliated state pharmaceutical associations.

★ 371 ★
AMERICAN PHARMACEUTICAL ASSOCIATION
  ACADEMY OF PHARMACEUTICAL SCIENCES
2215 Constitution Avenue, N.W.   (202) 628-4410
Washington, D.C. 20037   Established 1965

Ronald L. Williams, Executive Secretary
The Association's primary aim is to elevate and promote scientific, technical and academic accomplishment in all the disciplines related to the discovery, testing production, control and socioeconomics of drugs in the interest of public welfare. Membership: 2,500 pharmaceutical scientists in academic, govern-

ment, industry, and other fields. Finances: Membership: $10 annually in addition to American Pharmaceutical Association dues. Awards: APhA Foundation - Academy of Pharmaceutical Sciences Research Achievements Awards; APhA - Academy of Pharmaceutical Sciences Research Achievement Award for the Stimulation of Research; The Ebert Prize; The Koltoff Gold Medal Award in Analytical Chemistry; The Kilmer Prize; Advancement of Industrial Pharmacy Award. Meetings: Semiannual, various locations; regional meetings. Publications: Academy Reporter (newsletter), bimonthly, Ronald L. Williams, editor. Affiliations: American Pharmaceutical Association.

★ 372 ★
AMERICAN PHYSICAL FITNESS RESEARCH INSTITUTE
824 Moraga Drive   (213) 476-6241
Los Angeles, California 90049   Established 1958

Max Ruderian, Chairman
The Institute is a non-profit, charitable, educational foundation. Its main purpose is to research, produce, and distribute information on all aspects of health and fitness in order to help raise the overall quality of life. All programs are free, as a public service. Finances: Private donations. Publications: Health's-A-Poppin Bulletin, semiannual, Marion Wells, editor; Health's-A-Poppin--An Anthology on Total Wellness, Grusha D. Paterson, M.A., editor; Pyramid. Library: Total Wellness Research Library, 500 volumes.

★ 373 ★
AMERICAN PHYSICAL THERAPY ASSOCIATION
1156 15th Street, N.W.   (202) 466-2070
Washington, D.C. 20005   Established 1921

Royce P. Noland, Executive Director
The object of the Association is to meet the physical therapy needs of the people through the development and improvement of physical therapy education, practice and research and to meet the needs of its members through the following functions: (1) promote legislation to protect the interest of the public and the rights of the members; (2) represent physical therapy before governmental, professional, and voluntary groups and agencies; (3) promote and protect the professional status and the economic and general welfare of members; and (4) provide for the dissemination and exchange of information relating to physical therapy. Membership: 32,161 (active, inactive, life, student, affiliate, honorary). Finances: Membership: Active, inactive, and affiliate, $75; student, $15. Awards: Lucy Blain Service Award;

Mary McMillan Lectureship Award; Golden Pen Award; Marian Williams Award for Research in Physical Therapy; Dorothy Briggs Memorial Scientific Inquiry Award. Meetings: Annual conference, various locations. Publications: Physical Therapy, monthly, Marilyn Lister, editor; Progress Report (membership newsletter), 10 issues annually, Tommye Pfefferkorn, editor.

★ 374 ★
AMERICAN PHYSICIANS FELLOWSHIP FOR
      MEDICINE IN ISRAEL
2001 Beacon Street   (617) 232-5382
Brookline, Massachusetts 02146   Established 1950

Manuel M. Glazier, M.D., National Secretary
The American Physicians Fellowship is a charitable organization of physicians and other medical personnel, it is the largest organization of its kind in the history of Judaism. The APF influences the mechanics by which the level of medicine in Israel is raised through fellowships; sending various specialists to Israel on "Teaching Tours"; sending money, requested text books and desirable drugs. The APF has been selected by the Israeli authorities as the sole organization to secure and coordinate volunteer surgical, medical and paramedical personnel from the United States and Canada to serve Israeli civilians during an emergency. It has recruited and organized skilled volunteers who are prepared to leave when they are needed. The Israeli Government has awarded the Yom Kippur War Scroll of Honor to the APF for its aid during that crisis. Membership: 8,500 (most are physicians who live in 49 states of the Union, 8 provinces of Canada, Mexico, Belgium, Brazil, Curacao, Italy, Panama and Scotland). Publications: APF News, semiannual, M. M. Glazier, M.D., editor. Former Name: American Physicians Fellowship for the Israel Medical Association.

AMERICAN PHYSICIANS FELLOWSHIP FOR THE
ISRAEL MEDICAL ASSOCIATION
      See: American Physicians Fellowship for Medicine
            in Israel

★ 375 ★
AMERICAN PHYSICIANS POETRY ASSOCIATION
230 Toll Drive   (215) 364-2990
Southampton, Pennsylvania 18966   Established 1976

Richard A. Lippin, M.D.
Founded as a forum of communication among doctors who enjoy reading, writing and sharing poetry.

Membership: 90 (M.D.'s, and D.O.'s, whose common interest is a love of poetry). Finances: Membership: Dues, $10 annually. Meetings: Occasional poetry readings. Publications: Newsletter, semiannual, R. A. Lippin, M.D., editor. Library: Now in the process of forming.

★ 376 ★
AMERICAN PHYSIOLOGICAL SOCIETY
9650 Rockville Pike   (301) 530-7164
Bethesda, Maryland 20014   Established 1887

To promote the increase of physiological knowledge and its utilization. Important activities of the Society include the organization of meetings at which the results of researchers are presented and discussed, and the primary publication of the research contributions in physiology. Other activities include the publication of various handbooks and the development of audiovisual materials for the teaching of physiological subjects to undergraduate and graduate level students. Membership: 5,800 (regular, associate, corresponding, emeritus, honorary, and sustaining associate). Finances: Membership: Regular, $75; corresponding, $75; associate, $50; student, $10. Awards: John F. Perkins, Jr. Memorial Award; Porter Physiology Development Program; Bowditch Lecturer; Ray G. Daggs Awards; Harwood S. Belding Award in Environmental Physiology; Renal Section Award for Excellence in Renal Research; Hoffman La Roche Prize in Gastrointestinal Physiology. Meetings: Annual, Spring and Fall. Publications: American Journal of Physiology: Cell Physiology, bimonthly, P. Horowicz, editor; American Journal of Physiology: Endocrinology and Metabolism, monthly, E. Knobil, editor; American Journal of Physiology: Gastrointestinal and Liver Physiology, monthly, L. R. Johnson, editor; American Journal of Physiology: Heart and Circulatory Physiology, monthly, E. Page, editor; American Journal of Physiology: Regulatory, Integrative and Comparative Physiology, bimonthly, F. E. Yates, editor; American Journal of Physiology: Renal, Fluid and Electrolyte Physiology, monthly, T. E. Andreoli, editor; American Journal of Physiology (Consolidated), monthly; Journal of Applied Physiology: Respiratory, Environmental and Exercise Physiology, monthly, L. E. Farhi, editor; Journal of Neurophysiology, monthly, W. D. Willis, editor; Physiological Reviews, quarterly, S. G. Schultz, editor; The Physiologist, bimonthly, O. E. Reynolds, editor; Handbooks of Physiology; Clinical Physiology series; slide/tape programs in physiology. Affiliations: Federation of American Societies for Experimental Biology; American Institute of Biological Sciences; International Union of Physiological Societies.

★ 377 ★
AMERICAN PODIATRY ASSOCIATION
20 Chevy Chase Circle, N.W.   (202) 537-4900
Washington, D.C. 20015   Established 1912

Norman Klombers, Acting Executive Director
To federate and bring into one organization the qualified practitioners of podiatry in the United States, its
territories and possessions, as well as those in foreign
countries; to elevate the standards of education of
those practicing podiatry; to further in interests of
the public through the support of appropriate legislation bearing on the subject and practice of podiatry;
to promote a feeling of fellowship among practitioners
and to guard and foster the interests of its members;
to disseminate information among related professions
and the general public concerning foot health and foot
care; and to promote and participate in scientific
research programs designed to improve the foot health
of the nation and the quality of administered foot
care. Membership: 7,700 (active, associate, resident, life, affiliate, honorary, senior). Finances:
Membership: Active, $300; others, $55-$225.
Awards: William J. Stickel Memorial Awards for
Podiatric Research; Armour Award for Podiatric Liter-
ature; Cole Award for Podiatric Research; Annual
Meeting Exhibit Awards. Meetings: Annual, various
locations. Publications: Journal of the American
Podiatry Association, monthly, E. Dalton McGlamry,
D.P.M., editor; Desk Reference, annual. Library:
William J. Stickel Memorial Library, 1,000 volumes.
Affiliations: American Academy of Podiatry Adminis-
tration; American Association of Hospital Podiatrists;
American College of Foot Orthopedists; American
College of Foot Radiologists; American College of
Foot Surgeons; American Podiatry Student Association;
American Podiatry Women's Association; American
Society of Podiatric Medicine; American Podiatry
Association Auxiliary.

★ 378 ★
AMERICAN PODIATRY ASSOCIATION AUXILIARY
3970 Oakland Avenue, North
Suite 402   (414) 332-6138
Shorewood, Wisconsin 53211   Established 1938

Mrs. William N. Gearhard, Executive Secretary
The purpose of this auxiliary is to be of assistance
to the American Podiatry Association and its affiliated
state auxiliaries and to promote and interest others in
the matters pertaining to the profession of podiatry.
Membership: 1,500 (spouses and relatives of members
of the American Podiatry Association are eligible,
either through membership in a state auxiliary or
where no auxiliary exists, by the payment of dues to
the national auxiliary treasurer). Finances: Membership: National dues, $8 plus $1 assessment (for

executive secretary), annually; Other Sources: The
organization is exclusively for philanthropic and educational purposes. Donations can be received but
are channeled through a philanthropic fund. Meetings: Annual Meeting, coincides with the American
Podiatry Association Meeting, which is held in a different city each year. Publications: Bulletin,
quarterly, Mrs. William N. Gearhard, editor; Membership Directory, semiannual, Mrs. William N.
Gearhard, editor. Affiliations: 27 state auxiliaries.

★ 379 ★
AMERICAN PRINTING HOUSE FOR THE BLIND, INC.
1839 Frankfort Avenue
Post Office Box 6085   (502) 895-2405
Louisville, Kentucky 40206   Established 1858

Carson Y. Nolan, Vice President and General
   Manager
Publication of literature for the blind, in all media;
manufacture of tangible aids for use by the blind.
Activities include manufacture of braille books,
braille music, braille magazines, talking books and
magazines, large type textbooks, educational recorded
tapes, tangible aids. Finances: Federal appropriations under "Act to Promote the Education of the
Blind" for school books and educational aids; payment for materials produced; donations from general
public.

★ 380 ★
AMERICAN PROFESSIONAL PRACTICE ASSOCIATION
292 Madison Avenue   (212) 949-5950
New York, New York 10017   Established 1963

George J. Arden, Executive Director
   Bernadette Surak, Executive Secretary
The Association offers established medical and dental
practitioners, osteopaths, and students of these professions unique programs in areas of low cost group
insurance, loan programs, practice management advisory services, major merchandise discounts, and educational and travel benefits, including practice and
money management seminars. Membership: 46,000.
Finances: Membership: Dues, $15 annually. Meet-
ings: 4 annually, New York City. Publications:
The APPA Digest (newsletter), bimonthly; Professional
Corporation/Pension Update (newsletter), quarterly.

★ 381 ★
AMERICAN PROSTHODONTIC SOCIETY
919 North Michigan Avenue
Suite 2108
Chicago, Illinois 60611   Established 1928

Robert B. Underwood, D.D.S., Executive Director
The advancement of the science of prosthetic dentistry in all its various phases; to assist those who are seeking improvement and education in such type of oral reconstruction; to encourage research work among its members; to be alert to and aid in the development of scientific artificial denture procedures with a view to improving the health and comfort of dental patients; to promote a high standard of ethics in professional relations between its members as well as between its members and their patients. Membership: 1,300 (active, life, honorary). Finances: Membership: $75 annual dues; $100 initiation fee for active members. Meetings: Semiannual, Chicago; annual held at time and place of annual American Dental Association meeting. Publications: Journal of Prosthetic Dentistry, monthly, Judson G. Hickey, editor. Affiliations: American Dental Association.

★ 382 ★
AMERICAN PROTESTANT HOSPITAL ASSOCIATION
1701 East Woodfield Road   (312) 843-2701
Schaumburg, Illinois 60195   Established 1924

Charles D. Phillips, Ed.D., President
To associate all Protestant hospitals having affiliations with one or more Protestant churches and those non-profit hospitals which associate themselves with Christian activities, for purposes of fostering improvement, promoting efficiency, seeking cooperation, and securing adequate covering of the field of hospital endeavor. Membership: 250 institutional hospitals; 1,500 personal members made up of administrators, chaplains, etc. Finances: Membership: Personal, $55; institutional, $99-$1,155; sustaining, $250; Other Sources: Advertising, annual program and record book. Meetings: Annual, various locations. Publications: Bulletin, quarterly, Charles D. Phillips, editor; Newsletter; Establishing Protestant Chaplaincy in Protestant Hospitals. Affiliations: Protestant Health and Welfare Assembly.

★ 383 ★
AMERICAN PSYCHIATRIC ASSOCIATION
1700 18th Street, N.W.   (202) 797-4900
Washington, D.C. 20009   Established 1844

Melvin Sabshin, M.D., Medical Director
To improve the treatment, rehabilitation, and care of the mentally ill, the mentally retarded, and the emotionally disturbed; to promote research, professional education in psychiatry and allied fields, and the prevention of psychiatric disabilities; to advance the standards of all psychiatric services and facilities; to foster the cooperation of all who are concerned with the medical, psychological, social, and legal aspects of mental health and illness; and to make psychiatric knowledge available to other practitioners of medicine, to other scientists, and to the public. Membership: 26,000 (general members, fellows, associate members, members-in-training, distinguished fellows, honorary fellows, corresponding fellows, corresponding members). Finances: Membership: $30-$205; Other Sources: Grants and awards. Awards: Hofheimer Award; Isaac Ray Lectureship Award; McGavin Award; Morse Award; Distinguished Service Award; Blanche F. Ittleson Prize; Founders Award; Foundations' Fund Prize for Research in Psychiatry; Agnes Purcell McGavin Award; Hospital and Community Psychiatry Service Achievement Awards; Guttmacher Award; Vestermark Award. Meetings: Annual, Hospital and Community Psychiatry Institute, various locations. Publications: American Journal of Psychiatry, monthly, John Nemiah, M.D., editor; Hospital and Community Psychiatry, monthly, John Talbot, M.D., editor; Psychiatric News, biweekly, Herbert Gant, editor; and other monographs and books. Library: American Psychiatric Museum Association, Inc., 12,000 volumes. Affiliations: 76 district branches.

★ 384 ★
AMERICAN PSYCHOANALYTIC ASSOCIATION
1 East 57th Street   (212) 752-0450
New York, New York 10022   Established 1911

Helen Fischer, Administrative Director
To study and advance psychoanalysis; to advocate and maintain standards for the training of psychoanalysts and for the practice of psychoanalysis; to foster the integration of psychoanalysis with other branches of medicine and to encourage research in all fields having to do with the scientific knowledge and welfare of man. Membership: 2,650 (active, associate, affiliate). Finances: Membership: Active, $200; associate, $105; affiliate, $65. Meetings: Semi-annual, various locations. Affiliations: 36 Affiliated Societies and Study Group; 26 Accredited Training Institutes.

★ 385 ★
AMERICAN PSYCHOLOGICAL ASSOCIATION
1200 17th Street, N.W.   (202) 833-7600
Washington, D.C. 20036   Established 1892

Michael S. Pallak, Executive Director
To advance psychology as a science and as a profession, and as a means of promoting human welfare. It attempts to further these objectives by holding annual meetings, promoting research in psychology, publishing psychological journals, and working toward improved standards for psychological training and services. Membership: 50,000 (associates, members, and fellows). Finances: Membership: Members and fellows, $69; associates, $54. Awards: Distinguished Scientific Contribution Award; Distinguished Professional Contribution Award; Distinguished Teacher Contribution Award; National Media Awards. Meetings: Annual, various locations. Publications: APA Monitor, 10 issues annually (includes 12 issues of Section 2: APA Monitor Classified Advertising & Employment Bulletin); American Psychologist, monthly; Contemporary Psychology, monthly; Abnormal Psychology, bimonthly; Applied Psychology, bimonthly; Comparative and Physiological Psychology, bimonthly; Consulting and Clinical Psychology, bimonthly; Educational Psychology, bimonthly; Psychological Bulletin, bimonthly; Counseling Psychology, bimonthly; Psychological Review, bimonthly; Personality and Social Psychology, monthly; Developmental Psychology, bimonthly; Professional Psychology, bimonthly; Experimental Psychology: General, quarterly; Experimental Psychology: Human Learning, bimonthly; Experimental Psychology: Human Perception, quarterly; Experimental Psychology: Animal Behavior, quarterly; Journal Supplement Abstract Service (JSAS), quarterly; Psychological Abstracts (Issues plus Index), monthly; PsycSCAN: Applied, quarterly; PsycSCAN: Clinical, quarterly; PsycSCAN: Developmental, quarterly. Affiliations: Psi Chi Honor Society; 7 regional associations; 53 state associations; 34 divisions.

★ 386 ★
AMERICAN PSYCHOLOGY - LAW SOCIETY
University of Maryland School of Law
500 West Baltimore Street   (301) 528-5619
Baltimore, Maryland 21201

To promote exchanges between the disciplines of psychology and law; to promote research relevant to legal problems using psychological knowledge and to promote psychological research using the legal setting and related legal research techniques; to promote education of lawyers and psychologists with respect to each other's professional field; to promote legislation and social policies consistent with current states of psychological knowledge; to promote effective use of psychologists in processes and settings of the law. Membership: 525 (psychologists and lawyers). Finances: Membership: $20 annually. Meetings: Annual, Business Meeting; Biennial, National Con-

vention. Publications: Journal of Law and Human Behavior, quarterly, Bruce Sales and Harvey Perlman, editors; AP-LS Newsletter, quarterly, Richard Izzett, editor.

★ 387 ★
AMERICAN PSYCHOPATHOLOGICAL
    ASSOCIATION
New York University School of Medicine
Department of Psychiatry
HN 323   (212) 340-5716
New York, New York 10016   Established 1910

Dr. Murray Alpert, Secretary
To promote scientific study of problems of abnormal psychology. Membership: 250 (psychiatrists and psychologists conducting independent research in psychopathology). Finances: Membership: $50 annually, registration at meeting. Awards: Morton Prince Award; Paul Hoch Award. Meetings: Annual. Publications: Proceedings of Annual Meeting, annual, Program Chairman, editor.

★ 388 ★
AMERICAN PSYCHOSOMATIC SOCIETY
265 Nassau Road   (516) 379-0191
Roosevelt, New York 11575   Established 1944

Joan K. Erpf, Executive Assistant
The American Psychosomatic Society, through its principles and activities, represents the point of view that psychosomatic medicine is a way of approaching problems of health and disease. It is an approach which attempts to apply the best and most modern psychodynamic understanding of human personality function in all phases of medical practice--diagnosis, therapy, and research. The Society functions for the purpose of providing scientific and clinical forums where serious workers from all health disciplines may communicate, pool knowledge, consider problems of conceptual relationships, and develop ideas that will stimulate further research and the development of sound principles that may be applied in clinical practice and medical education. The membership includes social scientists and psychologists, as well as specialists from all medical disciplines. Because of the intrinsic medical and psychological nature of the field, the largest representations have been from internal medicine and psychiatry. Membership: 800 (regular, associate, emeritus, corresponding, honorary). Finances: Membership: Regular, $50; associate, $25. Meetings: Annual, various locations. Publications: Psychosomatic Medicine, bimonthly, Herbert Weiner, editor.

★ 389 ★
AMERICAN PSYCHOTHERAPY ASSOCIATION, INC.
Post Office Box 2436
West Palm Beach, Florida 33402   Established 1970

Ronald L. Bair, Th.D., President;   Sandra A. Simonds,
    Secretary
The Association was founded to promote psychotherapy
as a science; improve qualifications of professionalism
of all psychotherapies through a code of ethics; offer training programs in psychotherapy; work to prevent psychotherapy from becoming monopolized by any
one profession; combat various economic, sexual,
class, and racial exploitations; compile statistics;
sponsor competitions; and bestow recognition awards
to associations and individuals making outstanding contributions to the profession.   To further these aims,
the Association maintains a board of examiners in psychotherapy.   Membership: 150 (clergymen, drug and
alcohol counselors, psychotherapists, physicians,
psychologists, and family, marriage, and personal
counselors).   Finances: Membership: Full, fellow,
$50; diplomats, $150; Other Sources: Training program fees.   Awards: Certificate of Awards (for outstanding contributions to psychotherapy).   Meetings:
Convention, annual, various locations.   Publications:
APA Observer, bimonthly, Ronald Bair, editor;
Journal, annual, Sandra A. Simonds, editor; Bulletin, periodically.   Library: American Psychotherapy
Association Library.   Affiliations: National Psychological Association.

★ 390 ★
AMERICAN PUBLIC HEALTH ASSOCIATION
1015 15th Street, N.W.   (202) 789-5600
Washington, D.C. 20005   Established 1872

William H. McBeath, M.D., M.P.H., Executive
    Director
Founded in 1872, APHA's purpose is to protect and
promote personal, environmental, and mental health;
to exercise leadership with health professionals and
the general public in health policy development and
action, with particular focus on the interrelationship
between health and the quality of life and on developing a national policy for health care and services,
as well as solving technical problems related to
health.   APHA is the parent organization for its 53
state and local public health associations.   The expertise of APHA's individual members encompass more
than 45 disciplines in the health field, representing
all areas of interest in the broad spectrum of the
health professions.   Activities of the Association include publication of technical books and reports,
guidelines, standardization and surveys, disease control, and other health topics.   Membership: 30,000
individuals and 53 affiliated associations (individual

and organizational).   Finances: Membership: Individual dues $40 annually; agency dues based on in-
dividual agency's size and number of employees.
Awards: Sedgwick Memorial Medal (for distinguished
service in public health); Jay S. Drotman Award (to
a young health professional who has challenged traditional public health policy or practice in a creative
and positive manner); Presidential Citation (for persons
not professionally engaged in public health practice
who have made outstanding contributions to the advancement of public health or the profession); Martha
May Eliot Award (for achievements in maternal and
child health); John Snow Award (epidemiology);
Helen R. Stacey Awards (food and nutrition); Richard
H. Schlesinger Award (community health planning);
Difco Award (laboratory); Kimble Methodology Award
(laboratory); Spiegelman Award (statistics); Rema
Lapousse Award (epidemiology and statistics); Carl S.
Shultz Memorial Award (population); Public Health
Nursing Awards (distinguished career; creative
achievement); and Public Health Education Awards.
Meetings: Annual, various locations; Leadership
Conference, Washington, D.C.   Publications:
American Journal of Public Health, monthly, Dr. Al-
fred Yankauer, editor; The Nation's Health, monthly, Kathryn Foxhall, editor; Washington News
Letter, monthly, Robert Barclay, editor; Control of
Communicable Diseases in Man (13th edition), 5-year
update, Abraham Benenson, editor; Standard Method
for the Examination of Water and Wastewater (15th
edition, published jointly with AWWA and WPCF),
5-year update, David Jenkins, Arnold Greenberg,
Joseph J. Connors, editors; publishes other books on
bacterial and viral diagnostic procedures; examination of dairy products; St. Louis Encephalitis; nutrition assessment; ambulatory and medical care, health
care in correctional institutions; examination of foods;
viruses in water.   Affiliations: 53 state and local
public health associations.

★ 391 ★
AMERICAN RADIUM SOCIETY, INC.
Office of the Secretariat
Radiation Oncology Study Center
925 Chestnut Street   (215) 574-3181
Philadelphia, Pennsylvania 19107   Established 1916

Norah duV. Tapley, M.D., President;
    Morton Kligerman, M.D., Secretary
The American Radium Society, Inc., was founded in
the year 1916 by a pioneer group of active physicians
who were scientifically interested in radiation therapy.
The objectives of the Society shall be to promote the
study of cancer in all its aspects; to encourage liaison among the various medical specialists concerned
with the treatment of cancer; to continue the scientific study of all modalities effective in the

management of cancer and allied diseases and to enhance the quality of life of the cancer patient.
Membership: 750 (active membership may be held by
physicians and allied scientists). Finances: Membership: $100 annual dues; $125 initiation fee. Lectureship: Sponsors a lecture at each annual meeting
in memory of Henry Harrington Janeway's pioneer work
in the field of radium therapy. Lecturers are selected because of their outstanding scientific contributions and each is presented with the Janeway Medal.
Meetings: Annual, various locations; March 4-8,
1981, Phoenix, Arizona; March 14-18, 1982, San
Antonio, Texas. Publications: Cancer, bimonthly,
Jonathan Rhoads, editor; International Journal of
Radiation Oncology, monthly, Philip Rubin; Biology
Physics; American Journal of Roentgenology, monthly,
Melvin Figley, editor.

★ 392 ★
AMERICAN RED CROSS
17th and D Streets, N.W.   (202) 737-8300
Washington, D.C. 20006   Established 1881

George M. Elsey, President
Operating under congressional charter, the American
Red Cross performs such duties as may devolve upon a
national Red Cross Society in carrying out the purposes of the Geneva Conventions, serves armed forces,
veterans, and their families, aids disaster victims in
this country and assists other Red Cross societies in
time of emergency, and carries on other activities
concerned with the health and well-being of the
American people. Activities include services to
armed forces and their families, disaster services,
blood services (provides donations, fractionation of
blood, blood and blood products for research), nursing
services, first aid services, water safety services, community services, international services, and youth services. Finances: Membership: Members are contributors of $1 or more in the annual campaigns for
members and funds. Most chapter campaigns are in
partnership with United Way. Youth members enroll
in the schools on a classroom or group basis; Other
Sources: Special contributions for disaster relief, interest earned on general fund securities, income from
endowment and other invested funds, contributions for
Youth Services and grants. Awards: The Harriman
Award for outstanding volunteer service in the Red
Cross, the Ann Magnussen Award for outstanding nursing service, and a Certificate of Merit for persons
with Red Cross training who have performed a first
aid or lifesaving act adjudged as meritorious while
saving or attempting to save a life, and Health and
Safety Service Awards for youth. Meetings: Annual,
various locations. Publications: The Good Neighbor, bimonthly; Annual Report; program materials;
home nursing, first aid, small craft, and water safety

textbooks. Library: 13,000 volumes. Affiliations:
International Committee of the Red Cross; League of
Red Cross Societies. Its affiliates are divisions at
the regional level and chapters at the local level.

★ 393 ★
AMERICAN REGISTRY OF CLINICAL RADIOGRAPHY
    TECHNOLOGISTS
2501 North Stiles, Suite 400   (405) 525-6767
Oklahoma City, Oklahoma 73105   Established 1955

Rosalee Bridge, Executive Secretary
In 1955, the American Registry of Clinical Radiography Technologists was formed by a small group of
working technologists, properly certified by the only
certifying registry then in existence, who objected to
the domination imposed upon them professionally.
Policies were determined by working technologists,
and all leadership positions held by them with the belief that the organization should be composed of,
governed by and for the benefit of technologists.
Registry purpose is to maintain high standards of education and training; to promote public health and
safety; to promote approved continuing education
and conduct educational seminars; to recommend
methods of continued competency to the membership
after initial certification; to evaluate, examine and
certify the competency of technologists applying for
registration. Membership: Under 5,000 (radiography
technologists; associate). Finances: Membership:
$45 annual renewal fee; Other Sources: Examination
fees. Awards: Distinguished Service Awards, annual; Citation Awards, annual; Order of the Gold-
en Ray for the Outstanding Member of the Year, annual. Meetings: National conference, annual,
various locations; State Society Meetings, 2-4 times
annually, various locations. Publications: Journal
of The American Registry of Clinical Radiography
Technologists, quarterly, Rosalee Bridge, editor;
R. T. Certification Process Brochure; RCCE Process
Brochure; Examination Instructions; Policy Manual.

★ 394 ★
AMERICAN REGISTRY OF MEDICAL ASSISTANTS
569 Terry Parkway   (504) 366-6948
Gretna, Louisiana 70053   Established 1950

Dr. C. H. Truehart, Founder and President
Qualifies and registers all medical office help, both
in clinical and secretarial duties; issues certificates
of qualification; seeks to establish standards of training. Membership: 7,051 (assistants to physicians in
office practice, clinic and laboratories). Awards:
Outstanding Medical Assistant Award. Meetings:
Annual, various locations.

★ 395 ★
AMERICAN REGISTRY OF RADIOLOGIC
     TECHNOLOGISTS
2600 Wayzata Boulevard   (612) 377-8416
Minneapolis, Minnesota 55405   Established 1922

Roland C. McGowan, Executive Director
Examination and certification of x-ray technologists,
nuclear medicine technologists and radiation therapy
technologists. Membership: Approximately 120,000.
Finances: Membership: Application fee, $35; re-
newal fee, $6; Other Sources: Re-examination fees,
sale of official emblems. Meetings: Board of Trustees, semiannual. Publications: Directory of Registered Technologists, each January. Affiliations:
Cosponsored by: American College of Radiology and
American Society of Radiologic Technologists.

★ 396 ★
AMERICAN RHINOLOGIC SOCIETY
2929 Baltimore, Suite 105   (816) 561-4423
Kansas City, Missouri 64108   Established 1954

Pat A. Barelli, M.D., Secretary-Treasurer
Provides forum for the exchange of knowledge and
experience among accredited rhinologists and other
physicians and scientists interested in rhinologic problems; and to spread scientific knowledge of these
problems among the rhinologists and other physicians
of America and other countries. Membership: 250
(regular, associate, charter, honorary, life fellows,
junior). Finances: Membership: $100; annual
dues, $150; Other Sources: Contributions. Awards:
Doctor Maurice H. Cottle Honor Award; Golden
Head Mirror Honor Award. Meetings: Annual Scientific Meeting; 2 to 3 courses annually. Publications: Newsletter, American Rhinologic Society,
Pat A. Barelli, M.D., editor; seminar workshop
books.

★ 397 ★
AMERICAN ROENTGEN RAY SOCIETY
c/o Raymond A. Gagliardi, M.D.   (313) 338-0491
880 Woodward Avenue   (313) 858-3040
Pontiac, Michigan 48053   Established 1900

Raymond A. Gagliardi, M.D., Secretary
Dedicated to the advancement of medicine through
the science of radiology. Membership: 1,463 (radiologists and allied scientists). Finances: Membership: Active, $75; corresponding, $75; Other
Sources: Commercial exhibits at annual meeting.
Awards: Gold, silver, bronze medals and certificates
of merit for scientific exhibits at annual meeting;
The Caldwell Medal, annual; The President's Award,

annual, to a resident radiologist for a scientific preparation. Meetings: Annual, various locations, in
the United States and Canada. Publications: American Journal of Roentgenology, monthly, Melvin M.
Figley, M.D., editor; The American Journal of
Neuroradiology, bimonthly, Juan M. Traveras, M.D.,
editor. Affiliations: The Society for Photo-Optical
Instrumentation and Engineering.

★ 398 ★
AMERICAN SCHIZOPHRENIA ASSOCIATION
Huxley Institute
1114 First Avenue   (212) 759-9554
New York, New York 10021   Established 1964

Mary Ellen Roddy, Executive Director
The aims of the Association are to stimulate and support genetic and biochemical research; to disseminate
research findings to medical professionals and the general public; to educate the afflicted regarding the
nature of their illnesses and the availability of treatment resources; and to shorten the gap between discovery and application by encouraging the development of effective and economical systems of health
care. To further these aims, the Association supports
the belief that we are now on the brink of a biological revolution that can be hastened by the development of orthomolecular medicine, which has been defined as the preservation of good health and treatment
of disease by varying the concentrations in the human
body of substances normally present in the body and
required for health. Membership: 1,056. Finances: Membership: Contributing, $20; participating,
$40; sustaining, $100; life, $1,000; Other Sources:
Private contributions. Awards: The Dixie Annette
Award ($10,000 for the cure of schizophrenia).
Meetings: Semiannual, New York City. Publications: Huxley Institute (Canadian Schizophrenia
Foundation Newsletter, quarterly, Fannie Kahan, editor; The Journal of Orthomolecular Psychiatry, quarterly, Fannie Kahan, editor. Library: The Louis
and Charlotte J. Moran Library, 215 volumes. Affiliations: The Canadian Schizophrenia Foundation.

★ 399 ★
AMERICAN SCHOOL HEALTH ASSOCIATION
1521 South Water Street
Post Office Box 708   (216) 678-1601
Kent, Ohio 44240   Established 1927

Charles J. Baer, Executive Director
To promote comprehensive and constructive school
health programs--health services, health instruction,
and a healthful school environment; to establish
guidelines for standards of excellence and competency

for the professionals who make up the school health team; to serve as a professional liaison among the disciplines in the field of school health and cooperate with local, state and national organizations in behalf o of all school health personnel. Membership: 10,000 (school physicians, nurses, dentists, dental hygienists and health educators). Finances: Membership: Regular, fellow, $30; student, $15; life, $350; Other Sources: Sale of publications. Awards: William A. Howe Award; Distinguished Service Award; Honorary Fellowship Award; Appreciation Award. Meetings: Annual, various locations. Publications: Journal of School Health, monthly, Gay E. Groomes, editor; various information booklets. Affiliations: State School Health Associations; State School Health Affiliates.

★ 400 ★

AMERICAN SOCIAL HEALTH ASSOCIATION
260 Sheridan Avenue, Suite 307   (415) 321-5134
Palo Alto, California 94306   Established 1912

Samuel Knox, Contact Person
American Social Health Association is the only national voluntary agency dedicated to assisting the millions of victims avoid serious consequences resulting from Herpes Symplex II and other venereal diseases through information, clinic referrals and vaccine research.   The Association provides direct local service to communities through the VD National Hotline, an information and referral service.   The Hotline was inaugurated in early October 1979.   Another direct service of the Association is provided through HELP program. Publications: Hotliner, quarterly; How to Cope with Herpes; Q.A. About Herpes; Q.A. About VD; NGU; CMV' Body Pollution; Women and VD; Sexually Active VD; Hotline Poster; Hotline Flyer; Hotline Pamphlet.

★ 401 ★

AMERICAN SOCIETY FOR ADOLESCENT
   PSYCHIATRY   (215) 566-1054
24 Green Valley Road   (215) 566-2772
Wallingford, Pennsylvania 19086   Established 1967

Mary D. Staples, Executive Secretary
The Society provides a national forum, international affiliations, sponsors regional conferences, and is an advocate for the mental health needs of adolescents. It publishes an annual volume Adolescent Psychiatry, a Newsletter and a Membership Directory. Membership: 1,700 (19 local chapters and members-at-large; almost all members are psychiatrists trained and interested in adolescence; some chapters allow for membership by other MH disciplines). Finances: Mem-

bership: $30 annually for American Society for Adolescent Psychiatry and local Society dues (about $20). Awards: William Schonfeld Award, annual (to an outstanding contributor to Adolescent Psychiatry); Distinguished Service Award, from time to time, (to some member who has rendered unusual service to the Society). Meetings: Annual, in the same city as, and just preceding, the American Psychiatric Association. Publications: Annals of Adolescent Psychiatry, annual, Sherman C. Feinstein, M.D., editor; Newsletter, 3 times annually, Allan Z. Schwartzberg, M.D., editor; Membership Directory, biennially, Mrs. Mary Staples, editor. Affiliations: Adolescent Psychiatry Societies in Europe, Israel, Canada, South America; liaison with many psychiatric organizations.

★ 402 ★

AMERICAN SOCIETY FOR AESTHETIC PLASTIC
   SURGERY
3956 Atlantic Avenue   (213) 427-8898
Long Beach, California 90807   Established 1967

Jerome R. Klingbeil, M.D., Executive Officer
ASAPS is a specialty medical organization which provides continuing education to members in the area of aesthetic plastic surgery, mainly through presentation of papers, study sessions and scientific sessions; keeps members abreast of latest techniques, instruments, etc. Membership: 450 (board-certified plastic surgeons). Meetings: Annual, April or May, various locations. Publications: Plastic and Reconstructive Surgery, monthly; Membership Directory, biennial.

★ 403 ★

AMERICAN SOCIETY FOR ARTIFICIAL INTERNAL
   ORGANS
Post Office Box 777   (305) 391-8589
Boca Raton, Florida 33432   Established 1955

Karen K. Burke, Executive Director
To promote the increase of knowledge about artificial internal organs and of their utilization. Membership: 1,400 (active, associate, corporate). Finances: Membership: $70. Meetings: Annual, in April, various locations. Publications: Journal ASAIO, quarterly, Pierre M. Galletti, editor.

★ 404 ★

AMERICAN SOCIETY FOR CELL BIOLOGY
4326 Montgomery Avenue
Post Office Box 30371   (301) 652-4041
Bethesda, Maryland 20014   Established 1961

Emma Shelton, Ph.D., Secretary and Executive
   Officer
To promote and develop the field of cell biology.
Annual meetings include symposia, workshops, lectures,
etc. Membership: 4,000. Finances: Membership:
Regular, $20; student, $10; subscribing, $80; Other
Sources: Annual meetings. Meetings: Annual, various
locations. Publications: Journal of Cell Biology,
monthly, Dr. Raymond B. Griffiths, editor.

★ 405 ★
AMERICAN SOCIETY OF CHILDBIRTH EDUCATORS,
   INC.
7113 Lynnwood Drive
Post Office Box 16159   (813) 988-2976
Tampa, Florida 33687   Established 1971

Jeannette L. Sasmor, R.N., Ed.D., President
This Society aims to provide a medium for the exchange and dissemination of information relating to
prepared childbirth as a shared family experience; to
provide information to qualified professionals regarding
standards, techniques, and skills relevant to the concept of prepared birth; to conduct courses for prospective parents in connection with prepared childbirth; to enlist and maintain participation by professionals as members of the association to further the
purposes of the corporation; and to publish scientific
journals and textbooks in the field of prepared childbirth. Membership: Registered nurses and medical
doctors.

★ 406 ★
AMERICAN SOCIETY FOR CLINICAL
   INVESTIGATION
c/o Michael Frank, M.D.
NIAID, National Institute of Health
Building 10, Room 11N232   (301) 496-5270
Bethesda, Maryland 20205   Established 1909

Michael M. Frank, M.D., Secretary-Treasurer
Advancement of medical science; the cultivation of
clinical research by the methods of the natural sciences; the correlation of science with the art of
medical practice; the encouragement of scientific investigation by the medical practitioner; the diffusion
of a scientific spirit among its members; and the publication for national and international distribution of
papers on the methods and results of clinical research.
Membership: 1,571 (active, emeritus). Meetings:
Annual, second week in May, various locations.
Publications: Journal for Clinical Investigation,
monthly, Philip Majerus, M.D., editor.

★ 407 ★
AMERICAN SOCIETY FOR CLINICAL NUTRITION
9650 Rockville Pike   (301) 530-7110
Bethesda, Maryland 20014   Established 1960

G. M. Knight, Executive Officer
To promote teaching and research in the field of human nutrition. Membership: 525 (active, retired).
Finances: Journal subscription, $45. Awards:
McCollum Award, $1,000. Meetings: Annual,
various locations. Publications: American Journal
of Clinical Nutrition, monthly, T. B. Van Itallie,
editor. Affiliations: American Institute of Nutrition;
Federation of American Societies for Experimental Biology.

★ 408 ★
AMERICAN SOCIETY FOR CLINICAL
   PHARMACOLOGY AND THERAPEUTICS
1718 Gallagher Road   (215) 825-3838
Norristown, Pennsylvania 19401   Established 1900

Elaine Galasso, Executive Secretary
To promote and advance the science of human pharmacology and therapeutics, and in so doing to maintain the highest standards of research, education, and
exchange of scientific information. Membership:
1,258 (active, associate, emeritus, fellow, life).
Finances: Membership: Active, $60; associate,
$45/$25. Awards: Oscar B. Hunter Memorial
Award in Therapeutics. Meetings: Annual, various
locations. Publications: Journal of Clinical Pharmacology and Therapeutics, monthly, Walter Modell, editor.

★ 409 ★
AMERICAN SOCIETY FOR GASTROINTESTINAL
   ENDOSCOPY
Post Office Box 1565
Manchester-by-the-Sea,   (617) 227-0760
   Massachusetts 01944   Established 1941

William T. Maloney, Executive Secretary;
   Melvin Schapiro, M.D., Secretary
To further knowledge of gastrointestinal diseases
through the use of endoscopic techniques in clinical
practice and research. Membership: 2,400 (senior,
active, honorary, trainee, corresponding). Finances:
Membership: $75. Awards: Rudolph Schindler
Award. Meetings: Annual, various locations.
Publications: Gastrointestinal Endoscopy, quarterly,
Bernard M. Schuman, M.D., editor. Affiliations:
Council of Regional Endoscopic Societies.

★ 410 ★
AMERICAN SOCIETY FOR GERIATRIC DENTISTRY
1121 West Michigan Street   (312) 291-8669
Indianapolis, Indiana 46202

Dr. Saul Kamen, D.D.S., President (Jewish Institute
for Geriatric Care, 271-11 76th Avenue, New
Hyde Park, New York 11040); Sheila Wool
Mordarski, R.D.H., M.S., Secretary
More than 15 years ago under the leadership of the
late Dr. Arthur Elfenbaum the Society has grown to
spread knowledge and clinical skills of the dental profession for the elderly. To promote delivery of dental care to the elderly; to work with the dental
curriculum in an effort to better train dental students.
Membership: 250 (dental professionals, students, hygienists). Finances: Membership: Journal subscription, $12; students, $15; membership and subscription to journal, $40. Meetings: Annual, February,
Chicago, Illinois; Annual Scientific Sessions, in conjunction with the Chicago Dental Society. Publications: Journal of the American Society for Geriatric
Dentistry, biennial; Special Care in Dentistry, bimonthly, Dr. Sidney Epstein, editor; Oral Health
for Long Term Care Patient, booklet.

★ 411 ★
AMERICAN SOCIETY FOR HEAD AND NECK
    SURGERY
Division of Otolaryngology
Albany Medical College   (518) 445-5575
Albany, New York 12208   Established 1959

Jerome C. Goldstein, M.D., Secretary
Established to promote training and disseminate advances in head and neck surgery, both reconstructive
and rehabilitative. Membership: 385 (active, associate, corresponding, junior, senior, honorary). Finances: Membership: Active, $75. Meetings: An-
nual, various locations.

★ 412 ★
AMERICAN SOCIETY FOR HEALTH MANPOWER
    EDUCATION AND TRAINING OF THE AMERICAN
    HOSPITAL ASSOCIATION
840 North Lake Shore Drive   (312) 280-6111
Chicago, Illinois 60611   Established 1970

V. Brandon Melton, Director
The ASHME&T is the professional society for persons
who are responsible for the education function in
health care settings. ASHM&T members manage, design, conduct, and evaluate education programs for
healthcare professionals and support personnel, physicians, volunteers, patients, and the community-at-

large. Membership: 1,850 (human resources development specialists, patient and community health educators, inservice trainers, media specialists). Finances: Membership: Regular, $40; student, $20;
associate, $70; Other Sources: Conferences, sale of
publications, audiotapes. Awards: Charter Recognition Award; Distinguished Service Award; Distinguished Achievement Award. Meetings: Annual,
various locations across the country. Publications:
Hospitals Magazine, biweekly, Dan Schechter, editor;
Cross Reference on Human Resources Management,
bimonthly, Kathi Esqueda, editor; For Members Only,
bimonthly, V. Brandon Melton, editor; Summary of
JCAH Standards; Monograph Series on Healthcare
Education; Bibliographies on Human Resources Development, Patient and Community Health Education.
Library: Asa A. Brown Memorial. Affiliations: 33
affiliated chapters nationwide.

★ 413 ★
AMERICAN SOCIETY FOR HOSPITAL CENTRAL
    SERVICE PERSONNEL
840 North Lake Shore Drive   (312) 280-6160
Chicago, Illinois 60611   Established 1966

Clarence Daly, Director
The Society is devoted to the education, development,
and expansion of skills and standards of hospital central service personnel. Activities and services include long-term professional growth opportunities,
meetings, institutes, and film loan privileges. Membership: 650 (supervisors, technicians, aides). Finances: $42.50 annually. Meetings: Convention,
annually with the American Hospital Association,
various locations; institutes; educational meetings.
Publications: Hospital Central Service Newsletter,
bimonthly. Library: American Hospital Association
Library, 27,500 volumes. Affiliations: Affiliated
chapters in 15 states.

★ 414 ★
AMERICAN SOCIETY FOR HOSPITAL ENGINEERING
840 North Lake Shore Drive   (312) 280-6144
Chicago, Illinois 60611   Established 1962

To advance the development of effective hospital engineering in the health care institution. ASHE is
the only professional society devoted exclusively to
the education, development and expansion of skills
and standards of the engineering profession as performed in hospitals, related patient care institutions,
government, and voluntary health organizations. Membership: 2,600. Finances: Membership: $42.50. Meet-
ings: Convention, annual; various institutes. Publications: American Society for Hospital Engineering.

Newsletter; Engineering Handbook.   Affiliations: American Hospital Association.

★ 415 ★
AMERICAN SOCIETY FOR HOSPITAL FOOD
    SERVICE ADMINISTRATORS
840 North Lake Shore Drive   (312) 280-6416
Chicago, Illinois 60611   Established 1967

Mary R. DeMarco, R.D., Secretary
To promote continual improvement of the administrative functions of food service departments of health care institutions through interchange of information, educational programs and activities to foster continuing education and development of management skills of society members.   The Society serves in an advisory capacity in the field of food service to hospital administration and promotes cooperation with health care institutions and allied associations in further development of improved administrative systems and procedures.   Membership: 2,000 (active, associate). Finances: Membership: $35.   Awards: Dietary Products Scholarship Award; Dorothy Killian Scholarship.   Meetings: Annual, various locations.   Publications: Hospital Food Service, quarterly, Hildegard A. Klemm, staff editor; educational material.   Affiliations: American Hospital Association.

AMERICAN SOCIETY FOR HOSPITAL NURSING
SERVICE ADMINISTRATORS
    See: American Society for Nursing Administrators

★ 416 ★
AMERICAN SOCIETY FOR HOSPITAL PERSONNEL
    ADMINISTRATION
840 North Lake Shore Drive   (312) 280-6428
Chicago, Illinois 60611   Established 1964

Janine Faklis, Director
The Society was founded in order to enhance the growth, development and education of hospital personnel management professional.   Membership: 1,800 (personnel directors and other individuals having management responsibility for personnel administration). Finances: Membership: $42.50.   Awards: Literature Award.

★ 417 ★
AMERICAN SOCIETY FOR HOSPITAL PUBLIC
    RELATIONS
c/o American Hospital Association
Division of Public Affairs
840 North Lake Shore Drive   (312) 280-6359
Chicago, Illinois 60611

Catherine Pekie, Society Director
The Society's objectives are to continuously raise hospital public relations standards; to serve at a national medium for the exchange of ideas; and to encourage expansion of public relations activities in the hospital field.   Membership: 1,200 (hospital public relations practitioners).   Finances: Membership: $40.   Meetings: Annually, in conjunction with the American Hospital Association; semiannual board meetings. Publications: Hospital Public Relations, monthly, Kathi Esqueda, editor.   Affiliations: American Hospital Association.

AMERICAN SOCIETY FOR HOSPITAL PURCHASING
AGENTS
    See: American Society for Hospital Purchasing
        and Materials Management

★ 418 ★
AMERICAN SOCIETY FOR HOSPITAL PURCHASING
    AND MATERIALS MANAGEMENT
840 North Lake Shore Drive   (312) 280-6000
Chicago, Illinois 60611

To bring about close cooperation among hospital purchasing agents and materials managers in order to promote efficiency in hospital purchasing; to cooperate with hospitals and allied associations in matters pertaining to purchasing, standardization, and simplification; to encourage and assist members to develop their knowledge and increase their effectiveness in hospital purchasing and materials management; to provide a medium for the interchange of ideas and dissemination of material relative to same.   Membership: 1,127 (material managers and purchasing agents for medical material).   Finances: Membership: $37.50 and $67.50 for AHA non-member institutions. Awards: George R. Gossett Award.   Publications: Newsletter: Hospital Purchasing, bimonthly, Debra A. Reinold, staff editor.   Library: Asa Bacon Memorial, 27,500 volumes.   Former Name: American Society for Hospital Purchasing Agents.

★ 419 ★
AMERICAN SOCIETY FOR HOSPITAL RISK
   MANAGEMENT
840 North Lake Shore Drive   (312) 280-6425
Chicago, Illinois 60611   Established 1980

Marsha Ladenburger, R.N., M.H.A., Director
To promote and enhance the professional practice of
risk management in hospitals and related institutions.
The Society provides an important forum for the sharing of ideas and experiences and assists individuals
involved in hospital risk management to deal effectively with the growing and continually changing demands
of the field. Membership: Approximately 700 (active membership, Type C: those employed by a hospital or other health care provider, that is an institutional member of the AHA, or employed by an allied
hospital association; Type D: those employed by a
hospital or other health care provider, that is not an
institutional member of the AHA; associate member:
those actively involved in the risk management function of an AHA member institution but who are not
employees of that institution [a person from that institution who is an active member of the society must
validate]). Finances: Membership: Annual dues:
active member, Type C, $50; Type D, $80; associate member, $100. Meetings: Annual, workshops
on national, regional and local level throughout the
whole year. Publications: Newsletter of the Society for Hospital Risk Management. Affiliations:
American Hospital Association.

★ 420 ★
AMERICAN SOCIETY FOR MEDICAL TECHNOLOGY
330 Meadowfern Drive   (713) 893-7072
Houston, Texas 77067   Established 1932

Paul Hubbard, Executive Vice President
To promote and maintain high standards in clinical
laboratory methods and research and to advance the
standards of education and training in this field.
Membership: 26,000 (active, associate, inactive,
student, corresponding). Finances: Membership:
Active, $48; associate, $36; inactive, $10; stu-
dent, $10; corresponding, $20; Other Sources: Advertising, grants, sales, donations. Awards: 12 annual scholarships awarded to undergraduates and graduate students and for research. Meetings: Annual,
various locations. Publications: American Journal
of Medical Technology, monthly, Ina Lea Roe, editor;
ASMT News, 11 times annually, Lynda Cooper, editor;
Selected manuals and educational publications.

★ 421 ★
AMERICAN SOCIETY FOR MICROBIOLOGY
1913 I Street, N.W.   (202) 833-9680
Washington, D.C. 20006   Established 1899

R. F. Acker, Executive Director
Promotion and dissemination of scientific knowledge
in microbiology and related subjects to stimulate scientific investigations and their applications, to plan,
organize, and administer projects for the advancement
of knowledge in this field, and to improve education
in the science, to promote programs of professional
recognition, and to foster the highest professional and
ethical standing of microbiologists. Activities include scientific journals and book publications, scientific meetings, technical film library, and career
promotion. Membership: 31,050 (26,600 regular;
100 sustaining; 3,900 student). Finances: Membership: Dues; sale of journals, books and reprints;
grants. Awards: Eli Lilly and Company Award in
Microbiology and Immunology; Fisher Award for Applied and Environmental Microbiology; Carski Foundation Distinguished Teaching Award; Becton-Dick-
inson Award in Clinical Microbiology; Foundation
for Microbiology Lectureships; ASM Lectureships;
New Brunswick Scientific Company Lectureship;
President's Fellowships. Meetings: Annual, various
locations; Interscience Conference on Antimicrobial
Agents and Chemotherapy, annual; ASM Conferences.
Publications: Journal of Bacteriology, monthly,
Dr. Simon Silver, editor; Journal of Clinical Micro-
biology, monthly, Dr. Henry Isenberg, editor; Jour-
nal of Virology, monthly, Dr. Robert Wagner, editor;
Microbiological Reviews, quarterly, Professor H. V.
Richenberg, editor; Antimicrobial Agents and Chemo-
therapy, monthly, Dr. Leon H. Schmidt, editor;
Applied and Environmental Microbiology, monthly,
Dr. James M. Tiedje, editor; Infection and Immunity,
monthly, Dr. Joseph W. Shands, editor; International
Journal of Systematic Bacteriology, quarterly, Dr.
Erwin F. Lessel, editor; ASM News, monthly, Dr.
Robert F. Acker, editor. Affiliations: 36 local
branches, American Academy of Microbiology; Na-
tional Registry of Microbiologists; American Board of
Medical Microbiology; American Board of Immunol-
ogy.

★ 422 ★
AMERICAN SOCIETY FOR NURSING SERVICE
   ADMINISTRATORS
840 North Lake Shore Drive   (312) 280-6410
Chicago, Illinois 60611   Established 1967

Mary E. Fuller, R.N., President
To advance the development of effective administration in nursing service in health care institutions/
agencies by providing a medium for the interchange

of ideas and dissemination of information and materials relative to nursing service administration, provide a platform within the hospital field from which nursing service administrators speak, and to promote educational program and activities to strengthen nursing service administration. Membership: 2,500. Finances: Membership: $50-$80. Meetings: Board meetings, quarterly, Chicago, Illinois; annual meeting, various locations; semiannual program meetings, various locations. Publications: Nursing Service Administration, quarterly, Louise L. Henry, editor. Affiliations: Birmingham Regional Hospital Council of Birmingham (Alabama); Alabama Society for Nursing Service Administrators; Hospital Council of National Capital Area, Inc.; Florida Society for Hospital Nursing Service Administrators; Directors of Nursing Conference--Connecticut Hospital Association; Massachusetts Society for Nursing Service Administrators; The New Jersey Society for Nursing Service Administrators; Hospital Nursing Service Administrators of Southern New Jersey; Pennsylvania Society for Hospital Nursing Service Administrators; North Carolina Foothills Society for Nursing Service Administrators; West Virginia Society for Hospital Nursing Service Administrators; Maryland Society for Nursing Service Administrators; Virginia Chapter for Hospital Nursing Service Administrators; Kentucky Society for Hospital Nursing Service Administrators; Tennessee Society for Nursing Service Administrators; Illinois Society for Nurse Administrators; Iowa Chapter for Nursing Service Administrators; Ohio Society for Hospital Nursing Service Administrators; South Carolina Society for Nursing Service Administrators; Indiana Society for Hospital Nursing Service Administrators; Michigan-Greater Detroit Area Association of Nursing Service Administrators; Wisconsin Society for Nursing Service Administrators; Kansas Society for Nursing Service Administrators; Twin City Area Society for Hospital Nursing Service Administrators; Area D Society for Nursing Service Administrators (Minnesota); South Dakota Chapter of Nursing Service Administrators; Louisiana Society of Nursing Service Administrators; Texas Society for Hospital Nursing Service Administrators; Oklahoma Society for Nursing Service Administrators; Arizona Society for Nursing Service Administrators; New Mexico Society for Nursing Service Administrators; Oregon Society for Nursing Service Administrators; Association of Washington State Directors of Nursing Administration; Montana Society for Nursing Service Administrators; Idaho Society of Nursing Service Administrators (Conference A); California Society for Nursing Service Administrators. Former Name: American Society for Hospital Nursing Service Administrators.

★ 423 ★
AMERICAN SOCIETY FOR PARENTERAL AND
    ENTERAL NUTRITION, INC.
1025 Vermont Avenue, N.W.
Suite 810   (202) 638-5881
Washington, D.C. 20005   Established 1975

Karen Kight McMullen, Executive Director
Physicians, nurses, dietitians, pharmacists, nutritionists, etc. dedicated to the fostering of good nutritional support of patients during hospitalization and rehabilitation. By promoting the team approach and by educating health care professionals at all levels, A.S.P.E.N. encourages the development of improved nutritional support procedures and improved patient care. A.S.P.E.N. also undertakes the development and validation of guidelines for the nutritional assessment and support of individuals in both disease and health. Membership: 3,000 (physicians, nutritionists [Ph.D.], members of industry, dietitians, nurses, pharmacists, students/residents, and administrators). Finances: Membership: Physicians and nutritionists, $100; dietitians, nurses, pharmacists, administrators, $50; students, $35; (members of industry fee determined by degree); Other Sources: Contributions from various pharmaceutical companies. Meetings: Annual Clinical Congress, various locations. Publications: A.S.P.E.N. Update Newsletter, bimonthly, Timothy Sykes, Ph.D., editor; Journal of Parenteral and Enteral Nutrition, bimonthly, Michael Caldwell, M.D., Ph.D., editor; monographs related to the field, annual. Affiliations: European Society for Parenteral and Enteral Nutrition (E.S.P.E.N.); International Society for Parenteral and Enteral Nutrition (I.S.P.E.N.).

★ 424 ★
AMERICAN SOCIETY FOR PHARMACOLOGY AND
    EXPERIMENTAL THERAPEUTICS
9650 Rockville Pike   (301) 530-7060
Bethesda, Maryland 20014   Established 1908

Dr. Houston Baker, Executive Officer
To promote pharmacological knowledge and its use among scientists and to issue publications for this purpose. Membership: 3,000 (regular, affiliate, student/fellow, honorary, retired; composition: academic and industrial researchers). Finances: Membership: Regular, $50; affiliate, $40; student/fellow, $25; annual. Awards: John J. Abel Award in Pharmacology; ASPET Award for Experimental Therapeutics; Bernard B. Brodie Award in Drug Metabolism; Harry Gold Award; Epilepsy Research Award for Outstanding Contributions to the Pharmacology of Anitepileptic Drugs; Theodore Weiker Memorial Award; Torald Sollman Award in Pharmacology; Goodman and Gilman Award. Meetings:

Semiannual, various locations. Publications: Journal of Pharmacology and Experimental Therapeutics, monthly, Eva K. Killam, editor; Pharmacological Reviews, quarterly, Paul L. Munson, editor; Molecular Pharmacology, bimonthly, Norman Kirshner, editor; The Pharmacologist, quarterly, Houston Baker, editor; Rational Drug Therapy, monthly, Walter Modell, editor; Drug Metabolism News Letter, quarterly, Floie Vane, editor; Drug Metabolism and Disposition, bimonthly, Kenneth Leibman, editor; Clinical Pharmacology and Therapeutics, monthly, Walter Modell, editor. Affiliations: Member of Federation of American Societies for Experimental Biology.

★ 425 ★
AMERICAN SOCIETY FOR PHARMACY LAW
Department of Pharmacy
Washington State University   (509) 335-4750
Pullman, Washington 99163   Established 1974

Joseph G. Valentino, Chairman
Founded for the purposes of furthering legal knowledge, communicating accurate legal information to practicing lawyers and pharmacists; fostering knowledge and education pertaining to the rights and duties of pharmacists; distributing information of interest to the membership via a newsletter; and providing a forum for exchange of information pertaining to pharmacy law. Membership: 250 (pharmacist-attorneys; pharmacists; attorneys; student members). Finances: Pharmacists-attorneys, $15; pharmacists, attorneys, $10; student members, $5. Awards: James H. Beal Award. Meetings: Annual, various locations. Publications: Rx IPSA LOQUITUR, monthly, Dr. Larry M. Simonsmier, editor.

★ 426 ★
AMERICAN SOCIETY FOR PSYCHOPROPHYLAXIS
   IN OBSTETRICS, INC.
1411 K Street, N.W., Suite 200   (202) 783-7050
Washington, D.C. 20005   Established 1960

Melba A. Gandy, Executive Director
To contribute to the well-being of the family unit and its members through the child-rearing years, nationally and internationally, by advancing education in the psychoprophylactic (Lamaze) method of childbirth preparation; and education in parenting through the conduct of educational seminars, lectures, panels, studies, and other forms of educational communication; and to create a productive environment for childbirth educators, other maternal/child health professionals, and persons and groups interested in childbirth education, child development, parenting and the well-being of the family. Membership: 7,000 (physicians

[licensed physicians whose practices are associated with the childbearing years or the welfare of children]; parents; professionals [certified childbirth educators and other maternal/child health professionals]). Finances: Membership: Dues vary dependent upon existence of local chapter in geographical area; members who do not reside in chapter areas joint national only, and dues are: physicians, $45; professionals, $30; parents, $10; Other Sources: Teacher training fees; sales of educational materials; contributions. Awards: Research award given annually; no funds for sponsorship of research. Meetings: 20 continuing education conferences annually. Publications: Genesis, bimonthly; books, booklets, reprints, program guides, brochures, etc.

★ 427 ★
AMERICAN SOCIETY FOR PUBLIC ADMINISTRATION
   (ASPA)
1225 Connecticut Avenue, N.W.
Suite 300   (202) 785-3255
Washington, D.C. 20036   Established 1930

Keith F. Mulrooney, Executive Director
   Charlotte D. Gillespie, Director of Communications
A national organization for those interested in improving the public service at all levels of government. Varied programs involve the exchange, development, and dissemination of information about public administration. The Society has a newspaper, Public Administration Times, which lists job openings in the field of public administration worldwide. Membership: 25,000 (regular, student, contributing, life). Finances: Membership: Based on present salary: under $10,000 annually, $20; $10,000-$14,000 - $30; $15,000-$19,999 - $35; $20,000-$24,999 - $40; $25,000-$44,999 - $45; over $45,000 - $50; foreign membership, $45; life membership, $1,000; Other Sources: Sale of books, subscription sales of publications, national conference, display advertising in publications. Awards: Several awards granted. Meetings: Annual conferences, various locations. Publications: Public Administration Review, 6 times annually, Lou Gawthrop, editor (subscription costs: U.S., $35 annually, foreign, $40 annually); Public Administration Times, semimonthly, Keith F. Mulrooney, editor (subscription costs: $25 annually); all subscriptions must be pre-paid in U.S. dollars; Perspectives on Budgeting, series (1 volume of), Allen Schick, editor; Professional Public Administrators, series (1 volume of), Chester Newland, editor; Public Administration Review Cumulative Index, 40-year index, Lou Gawthrop, editor. Affiliations: National Association of Schools of Public Affairs and Administration.

★ 428 ★

AMERICAN SOCIETY FOR SURGERY OF THE HAND
2600 South Parker Road, Suite 132   (303) 755-4588
Aurora, Colorado 80014   Established 1945

Gail M. Gorman, Administrative Director;
   Charles R. Ashworth, M.D., Secretary
To furnish leadership and to foster advances in Surgery
of the Hand; to affort a forum for the exchange of
knowledge pertaining to the practice of Surgery of the
Hand; to stimulate research, investigation and teaching in the method of preventing, correcting and treating diseases of the hand arising from congenital, developmental, nutritional, traumatic or other causes;
to enhance the study and practice of Surgery of the
Hand by establishing lectureships, scholarships, foundations, and appropriate evaluation procedures; to
afford recognition to those who have contributed to
Surgery of the Hand by extending to them membership
in the Society. Membership: 504 (active, associate,
corresponding, honorary, inactive). Finances: Membership: $100 annually. Research Funds: Bunnell
Traveling Fellowship; Research Seed Grants; Founders
Lecture. Meetings: 1 Annual Meeting per year;
1 Mid-Year Members Meeting per year, 8-12 continuing education courses annually. Publications: The
Journal of Hand Surgery, bimonthly, Adrian E. Flatt,
M.D., editor; The Bibliography of Surgery of the
Hand, annual, John P. Adams, M.D., editor; The
Hand--Examination and Diagnosis, 1 time, Society
publication; videotapes on selected topics in Surgery
of the Hand.

★ 429 ★

AMERICAN SOCIETY FOR THE ADVANCEMENT
   OF ANESTHESIA IN DENTISTRY
475 White Plains Road   (914) 961-8136
Eastchester, New York 10707   Established 1929

Antonio Reyes-Guerra, Jr., Executive Secretary
An organization of dentists and physicians to study
and advance the science of anesthesiology. Activities include research, papers and clinics. Membership: 400 (physicians, dentists, etc.). Finances:
Membership: Initiation, $25; annual dues, $25.
Meetings: March, October, New York City. Publications: Transcripts, semiannual, Dr. Antonio
Reyes-Guerra, editor; Newsletter; Proceedings of
the Society, biennial.

★ 430 ★

AMERICAN SOCIETY OF ABDOMINAL SURGEONS
675 Main Street   (617) 665-6102
Melrose, Massachusetts 02176   Established 1959

Blaise F. Alfano, M.D., Executive Secretary
Provides continuing surgical education for those who
operate within the abdomen. Membership: 13,000
(fellows, junior fellows). Finances: Membership:
$100; Other Sources: Grants from pharmaceutical
firms. Awards: Distinguished Service Award; Journalism Award. Meetings: Annual, various locations.
Publications: Journal of Abdominal Surgery, bimonthly, John M. Langone, M.D., editor; Surgeon;
Monthly Bulletin; selected monographs. Library:
Donald Collins, M.D., Memorial Library, 600 volumes.

AMERICAN SOCIETY OF ADLERIAN PSYCHOLOGY
   See: North American Society of Adlerian
         Psychology

★ 431 ★

AMERICAN SOCIETY OF ALLIED HEALTH
   PROFESSIONS (ASAHP)
1 Dupont Circle, N.W., Suite 300   (202) 293-3422
Washington, D.C. 20036

Richard J. Dowling, J.D., Executive Director
Provides a forum for communications and action-
program development and implementation for schools of
allied health (both two- and four-year), national professional associations, clinical-service programs and
individual practitioners. Serves as Washington liaison members. Membership: 125 schools; 25 associations; more than 2,500 individuals. Finances:
Membership: Annual dues: institutions and organizations, $800; individuals, $35; Other Sources: Government and foundation grants and contracts.
Awards: Distinguished Service Award; President's
Award; Distinguished Author Award. Lectureship:
Mary Switzer Memorial Lecture. Meetings: Annual,
November, (1980 - Memphis, Tennessee; 1981 - Reno,
Nevada; 1982 - Chicago, Illinois; 1983 - Philadel-
phia, Pennsylvania); Institutional, Spring, Washing-
ton, D.C.; regional, various locations, 15 annually.
Publications: Allied Health Trends, monthly, R. J.
Dowling, editor; Journal of Allied Health, quarterly,
J. E. Burke, editor; Proceedings of the National
Forum on Allied Health Accreditation; Glossary of
Allied Health Titles.

★ 432 ★

AMERICAN SOCIETY OF ANESTHESIOLOGISTS
515 Busse Highway   (312) 825-5586
Park Ridge, Illinois 60068   Established 1905

John W. Andes, Executive Secretary

To associate and affiliate into one organization all of the reputable physicians in the United States, its territories and possessions, who are engaged in the practice of or are otherwise especially interested in anesthesiology; to encourage specialization in this field, to raise the standards of the specialty by fostering and encouraging education, research and scientific progress in anesthesiology, and by recommending standards of postgraduate education for qualifications as a specialist in anesthesiology and furthermore by recommending standards for approval of postgraduate training centers; to disseminate information in regard to anesthesiology; to protect the public against irresponsible and unqualified practitioners of anesthesiology; to edit and publish literature in the field of anesthesiology and related fields; to safeguard the professional interests of its members, and in all ways to develop and further the specialty of anesthesiology for the general elevation of the standards of medical practice. Activities include an annual scientific meeting, refresher courses, a publication program and scientific and educational activities through committees. Membership: 16,771 (active, resident, life, honorary, retired, affiliate). Finances: Membership: Active, $125; resident, $15; affiliate, $62.50 $62.50. Meetings: Annual, various locations. Publications: Newsletter, monthly, Henri S. Havdala, M.D., editor; Anesthesiology, monthly, John D. Mickenfelder, M.D., editor. Affiliations: American College of Anesthesiologists.

★ 433 ★
AMERICAN SOCIETY OF BARIATRIC PHYSICIANS
5200 South Quebec Street, #300   (303) 779-4833
Englewood, Colorado 80111   Established 1950

Randall B. Lee, Executive Director; W. L. Asher, M.D., Director of Professional Affairs
To advance and improve the standards of practice and quality of professional service in the field of bariatrics; to improve the educational opportunities for the training of bariatricians; to stimulate original research, study and investigation by collecting and disseminating the results of each work for the education and improvement of the profession's knowledge in the prevention, diagnosis and treatment of disease; to establish and maintain a specialty Board of Bariatrics; to provide for examination of candidates who wish certification in bariatrics, such certified specialists to be designated as Diplomates of the American Board of Bariatric Medicine; and to increase among members of the profession and of the laity the understanding of the nature of the service rendered by the bariatrician in relation to other divisions of practice. Membership: 530 (physicians). Finances: Membership: Dues, $175 annually; Other Sources: Contributions, continuing education programs. Research

Funds: Research fund established by members' contributions; lectureships. Meetings: Annual and semiannual, Las Vegas, Nevada; regional meetings, various locations. Publications: Obesity and Bariatric Medicine, bimonthly, W. L. Asher, M.D., editor; Newsletter, monthly.

★ 434 ★
AMERICAN SOCIETY OF BIOLOGICAL CHEMISTS
9650 Rockville Pike   (301) 530-7145
Bethesda, Maryland 20014   Established 1906

Charles C. Hancock, Executive Officer
To further the extension of biochemical knowledge and to facilitate personal intercourse between American investigators in biological chemistry. Activities include an annual scientific meeting, publication of the Journal of Biological Chemistry, sponsorship and support of a lectureship program in conjunction with the annual meeting, and engagement in other activities aimed at the fulfillment of the purposes of the organization. Membership: 5,194 (active, 4,769; emeritus, 350; honorary, 75). Finances: Membership: $35 annually; Other Sources: Journal operations, investments, grants, meetings, contracts for special projects. Awards: Travel fund for younger biochemists to ensure participation in meetings of the International Union of Biochemistry (triennial congresses). Meetings: Annual, various locations. Publications: Journal of Biological Chemistry, semimonthly, Herbert Tabor, editor. Affiliations: National Research Council; AAAS; Council of Academic Societies; AAMC; FASEB; PAABS.

★ 435 ★
AMERICAN SOCIETY OF CLINICAL HYPNOSIS
2400 East Devon Avenue
Suite 218   (312) 297-3317
Des Plaines, Illinois 60018   Established 1957

William F. Hoffman, Jr., Executive Director
To bring together professional people in the medical, dental, and psychological fields using hypnosis, and to set up standards for training. It shall cooperate with all scientific disciplines in professional and public relationships in regard to the use of hypnosis and it shall stimulate research and publication in the field. Membership: 4,000 (A.M.A.; A.P.A.; A.D.A.). Finances: Membership: $55 annually, doctor in active practice; student affiliate, $20 annually. Meetings: Local, monthly workshops; annual, various locations. Research Funds: Education and Research Grants by ASCH-ERF. Publications: Newsletter, 8 times annually; American Journal of Clinical Hypnosis, quarterly, Sheldon B. Cohen, M.D.,

editor; Directory, annually. Affiliations: British Society of Medical and Dental Hypnosis, London, England; Nihon Saimin Kenkyukai, Tokyo, Japan; Grupa de Estudio Sobre Hipnosis Clinica y Experimental, Mexico, D.F., Mexico; Sociedad Argentina de Hipnosis Medica e Hipnoanalisis, Buenos Aires, Argentina; Sociedad Uruguaya de Hipnosis Clinica, Montevideo, Uruguay; Sociedade Paulista de Hipnotismo, Sao Paulo, Brazil; Sociedad Chilena de Hipnosis Clinica y Experimental, Santiago, Chile; American Association for the Advancement of Science; member of World Federation of Mental Health; supports the Council of Societies in Dental Hypnosis.

★ 436 ★

AMERICAN SOCIETY OF CLINICAL ONCOLOGY
435 North Michigan Avenue
Suite 1717   (312) 644-0828
Chicago, Illinois 60611   Established 1964

Alfred Van Horn, III, Executive Director
To promote and foster the exchange and diffusion of information and ideas relating to neoplastic diseases, with particular emphasis on human biology, diagnosis and treatment; to further the training of all persons in clinical research and in the total care of patients with neoplastic disease; to encourage optimal communication between the various specialties concerned with neoplastic diseases. Membership: 2,735 (internists, surgeons, pediatricians, pathologists, radiologists). Finances: Membership: $20. Meetings: Annual, various locations.

★ 437 ★

AMERICAN SOCIETY OF CLINICAL PATHOLOGISTS
2100 West Harrison Street   (312) 738-1336
Chicago, Illinois 60612   Established 1922

Meryl H. Haber, M.D., Executive Vice President
To promote the public health and safety by a wider application of pathology to the diagnosis and treatment of disease; to stimulate research in all branches of pathology; to establish standards for performance of various laboratory procedures; to conduct seminars and other educational programs; to prepare, publish, and disseminate educational materials designed to acquaint pathologists, medical technologists, and other laboratory personnel with scientific developments in the field of clinical laboratory medicine; to establish (or participate in the establishment of) voluntary standards and curricula for the training of medical technologists and other paramedical laboratory personnel; to establish and maintain a voluntary program for the examination and certification of medical technologists and other paramedical laboratory personnel,

including the maintenance of a registry wherein paramedical laboratory personnel who voluntarily seek to be registered may, upon meeting (and continuing to meet) the standards established by the Society be registered. Membership: 26,000 (fellows, associates, juniors, foreign, affiliates). Finances: Membership: $10-$200. Awards: Ward Burdick Award - gold medal to Fellow for outstanding contributions in the field of Pathology; Sheard-Sanford prizes to students and interns in pathology; Annual Exhibit Award for exhibits dealing with education and original investigation. Meetings: Semiannual, various locations. Publications: American Journal of Clinical Pathology, monthly, Myrton F. Beeler, M.D., editor; Laboratory Medicine, monthly, Elmer W. Koneman, M.D., editor; ASCP Newsletter, monthly, Deanna Duby, editor. Library: Resource Center, 3,730 volumes.

★ 438 ★

AMERICAN SOCIETY OF COLON AND RECTAL
  SURGEONS
615 Griswold, #516   (313) 961-7880
Detroit, Michigan 48226   Established 1899

Harriette Gibson, Administrative Secretary
To facilitate the dissemination and investigation of knowledge relating to the colon, rectum and anus, and particularly the publication of this knowledge and investigation of medical and surgical treatment pertaining thereto. Membership: 1,100. Meetings: Annual convention, various locations throughout the United States. Publications: Diseases of the Colon and Rectum, 8 times annually, John R. Hill, M.D., editor.

★ 439 ★

AMERICAN SOCIETY OF CONSULTANT
  PHARMACISTS
2300 9th Street, South
Suite 515
Arlington, Virginia 22204   (703) 920-8492
                              Established 1969

R. Tim Webster, Executive Director
A national professional society of pharmacists who specialize in providing pharmaceutical services to long-term care facilities, the membership serves over 700,000 of the nation's 1.3 million nursing home beds. Membership: 1,500 (active, associate, student, allied). Finances: Membership: Active, $110; associate, $45; student, $25; allied, $500. Awards: George F. Archambault Award; Richard S. Berman Service Award. Meetings: Annual and Mid-Year Conferences, various locations. Publications: ASCP UPDATE, monthly, R. Jim Webster, editor.

★ 440 ★

AMERICAN SOCIETY OF CONTEMPORARY
    MEDICINE AND SURGERY
6 North Michigan Avenue   (312) 236-4673
Chicago, Illinois 60602   Established 1965

John G. Bellows, M.D., Ph.D., Director;
    Michael E. DeBakey, M.D., President
The Society is dedicated to continuing medical education in all new modalities in medicine, surgery, and ophthalmology. Membership: Approximately 6,000 (all fields of medicine and surgery). Finances: Membership: $60; Other Sources: Journal subscriptions. Awards: Achievement Awards elected by the Board of Directors. Meetings: Annual, February-March, usually in resort areas. Publications: Comprehensive Therapy, monthly, John G. Bellows, M.D., Ph.D., editor; books, brochures, and audio-visual materials for general distributions. Affiliations: AVMS/Audiovisuals in Medicine and Surgery; Mediphone; Medical VideoCom.

★ 441 ★

AMERICAN SOCIETY OF CYTOLOGY
130 South 9th Street
Suite 810   (215) 922-3880
Philadelphia, Pennsylvania 19107   Established 1951

Warren R. Lang, M.D.,
To promote research on the clinical application of exfoliative cytology for the purpose of early cancer detection. A forum is held for those interested in the assessment of hormonal, premalignant, and malignant changes detected by cellular evaluation. Membership: 3,900 (medical-physicians; non-medical professional - doctors of science and philosophy, dentists; associate - cytotechnologists; honorary and life - physicians). Finances: Membership: Medical, $65; non-medical professional, $25; associate, $25; Other Sources: Grants. Awards: Annual award (medal, certificate, $500, and travel expenses to annual meeting) to person or group demonstrating meritorious achievement in the field of cytology. Meetings: Annual, various locations. Publications: The Cytotechnologists's Bulletin, bimonthly.

★ 442 ★

AMERICAN SOCIETY OF DENTISTRY FOR CHILDREN
211 East Chicago Avenue
Suite 920   (312) 943-1244
Chicago, Illinois 60611   Established 1927

Dorothy J. McCord, CAE, Executive Director
To advance and disseminate to the dental profession and the public knowledge of all phases of dentistry for children, including service programs and programs of recognition of outstanding achievement in the field of dentistry for children or of general health care for children in the field of teaching or practice, or both. Membership: 12,000 (dentists, students). Finances: Membership: $50. Awards: Award of Recognition; Award of Excellence; Distinguished Service Award. Meetings: Annual, various locations. Publications: Journal of Dentistry for Children, bimonthly, George Teuscher, editor.

★ 443 ★

AMERICAN SOCIETY OF ELECTROENCEPHALO-
    GRAPHIC (EEG) TECHNOLOGISTS, INC.
32500 Grand River Avenue, #103   (313) 476-6899
Farmington, Michigan 48024   Established 1959

Janet Brotherhood, R. EEG T., Executive Secretary
ASET is a national organization of and for EEG technicians and technologists whether in training; employed in clinical, research, or educational aspects of EEG; or engaged in related electrophysiological pursuits. The Society encourages the development and maintenance of high technical and ethical standards of EEG technologists. Its further purpose is to foster and facilitate proper methods of study and means of meeting and exchanging ideas concerning technical progress in EEG. Membership: 2,100 (active only). Finances: Membership: $25 annually. Awards: Maureen Berkeley Memorial Award, given annually for best paper by a technologist published in the American Journal of EEG Technology. Scholarships: 5, $200 to attend Annual Scientific Meeting and/or courses sponsored by ASET. Meetings: Annual, various locations. Publications: American Journal of EEG Technology, quarterly, Sharon Franklin, R. EEG T., editor; ASET Newsletter, quarterly, Janet Brotherhood, R. EEG T., editor. Affiliations: The American Electroencephalographic Society; The American Society of Allied Health Professions; The American Board of Registration of EEG Technologists; The International Organization of Societies for Electrophysiological Technology; Epilepsy Foundation of AM; Joint Review Committee on Education in EEG Technology (AMA).

★ 444 ★

AMERICAN SOCIETY OF EXTRA CORPOREAL
    TECHNOLOGY
Reston International Center
Suite 322
11800 Sunrise Valley Drive   (703) 860-1858
Reston, Virginia 22091   Established 1964

George M. Cate, Executive Director;
    Linda J. Lawton, Deputy Executive Director
To develop programs to improve the practice of extra
corporeal technology through education and services
to members; encourage research and continuing education for the field, enhance the professionalism of
the individual member.   Membership: 1,100 (active,
associate, student).   Finances: Membership: $50
active and associate; $15 student; $10 initial fee;
Other Sources: Convention registration, exhibits,
corporate sponsorships, advertising in Journal and
Newsletter, course registration fees.   Awards:
William Harvey Research Award; John Gibbon Medallion; Polystan Education Award; Fellowship Award;
Sci-Med Award; Perfusionist of the Year; T.M.P.
Award of Excellence.   Meetings: Annual, East,
West and Midwest in southern locations.   Publications: Journal of Extra Corporeal Technology, 6 times
annually, Emily Taylor, editor; AmSECT News,
monthly, Scutter Newton, editor.

★ 445 ★

AMERICAN SOCIETY OF GROUP PSYCHOTHERAY
    AND PSYCHODRAMA
39 East 20th Street   (212) 260-3860
New York, New York 10003   Established 1942

Stephen F. Wilson, A.C.S.W., Executive Director
The Society is dedicated to the development of the
fields of group psychotherapy, psychodrama and sociometry.   The aims are to establish standards for specialists in group psychotherapy, psychodrama and allied methods, and to aid and support the exploration
of new areas of research, practice, teaching and
training.   Membership: 1,000 (psychiatrists, psychologists, sociologists, social workers, educators,
group workers, mental health workers, and other professional persons).   Finances: Membership: $35
regular members; $25 student members; $35 plus $3
mailing costs for foreign members.   Meetings: Annual Meeting, held in April, New York City.
Publications: Group Psychotherapy, Psychodrama &
Sociometry Journal, annual; Newsletter, annual.

★ 446 ★

AMERICAN SOCIETY OF HEMATOLOGY
Hospital of the University of Pennsylvania
Hematology Section
3400 Spruce Street   (215) 662-3929
Philadelphia, Pennsylvania 19104   Established 1959

Alvin Mauer, President; Ernst Jaffe, Vice President;
    Eugene Frenkel, Treasurer; Sanford J. Shattil,
    Secretary
The Society aims to engage exclusively in charitable,

scientific and education activities and endeavors, including specifically but not limited to promoting and
fostering, among the many scientific and clinical disciplines, the exchange and diffusion of information
and ideas relating to blood and blood forming tissues
and encouraging investigations of hematologic matters.
Membership: 3,000 (active, emeritus, honorary).
Finances: Membership: $60, new members; $55,
old members.   Awards: Dameshek Prize. Lectureships:
Stratton Lectureship.   Meetings: Annual, various
locations.   Publications: Blood, monthly, Paul
Marks, M.D., editor.

★ 447 ★

AMERICAN SOCIETY OF HOSPITAL ATTORNEYS
840 North Lake Shore Drive   (312) 645-8217
Chicago, Illinois 60611   Established 1968

Shirley A. Worthy, Director
To disseminate information on health care, law and
legislation.   Membership: Attorneys who represent
or are employees of hospitals or other health organizations.   Meetings: Annual, various locations.
Publications: Society Newsletter, monthly; Membership Roster, annual; also provides to members publications for AHA.

★ 448 ★

AMERICAN SOCIETY OF HOSPITAL PHARMACISTS
4630 Montgomery Avenue   (301) 657-3000
Washington, D.C. 20014   Established 1942

Joseph A. Oddis, Executive Vice President
To provide the benefits and protection of qualified
hospital pharmacists to patients, institutions, and other
health workers; to assist in providing an adequate
supply of qualified hospital pharmacists; to assure a
high quality of professional practice; to promote research in hospital pharmacy practices and the pharmaceutical sciences in general; to disseminate pharmaceutical knowledge.   Accredits pharmacy residency
training programs, conducts continuing education programs, publishes drug information and other pharmacy
literature, reviews and comments on applicable legislation and government regulations, promotes research
activities.   Membership: 19,000 (active, associate).
Finances: Membership: Regular, $55; student, $10;
4-year pledge scale, $10-$55; 3-year postgraduate
student scale, $15-$55; Other Sources: Publication
sales; grants.   Awards: Harvey A. K. Whitney
Lecture Award; Donald E. Francke Medal.   Meetings: Annual, various locations; midyear clinical
meeting, annual, various locations; International
Clinical Study Tour, annual, various locations; Summer Seminar, annual, various locations; National

Institutes, annual, various locations. Publications: American Journal of Hospital Pharmacy, monthly, William A. Zellmer, editor; A.S.H.P. Newsletter, monthly, William A. Zellmer, editor; American Hospital Formulary Service, 6 times annually, Judith Kepler, editor; International Pharmaceutical Abstracts, semimonthly, Dwight Tousignaut, editor.

★ 449 ★

AMERICAN SOCIETY OF HUMAN GENETICS
Medical College of Virginia
Box 33   (804) 786-9632
Richmond, Virginia 23298   Established 1948

Judith A. Brown, Ph.D., Secretary
Professional organization of human geneticists; holds annual meetings for presentation of research reports, publishes research and summary papers in human genetics, news exchange for members; improvement of professional standards in human genetics. Membership: Approximately 1,800 (active - those with professional interest in human genetics or hereditary diseases; associate - interns, graduate students, research assistants; corresponding - otherwise qualified but residents outside of North America; emeritus - retired active members). Finances: Membership: Active, $25; corresponding, $25; associate, $20 or $4 without journal subscription. Awards: William Allan Award. Meetings: Annual, various locations. Publications: American Journal of Human Genetics, quarterly, William Mellman, editor. Affiliations: A.A.A.S.; N.R.C.

★ 450 ★

AMERICAN SOCIETY OF INTERNAL MEDICINE
2550 M Street, N.W., Suite 620   (202) 659-0330
Washington, D.C. 20037   Established 1956

William R. Ramsey, Executive Director
The primary goal of ASIM, the fifth largest national medical specialty organization, is to achieve the continued improvement of patient care. A related goal is to promote the growth and enhancement of the specialty of internal medicine and its subspecialties. ASIM objectives include: to be an advocate of the patient, to increase the effectiveness and efficiency of the internist; to improve the practice environment of the internist. Membership: 17,000 (specialists in internal medicine in the United States and its possessions; 51 state component societies). Finances: Membership: National $125, plus state component dues. Meetings: Semiannual, various locations. Publications: The Internist, monthly, William Campbell Felch, M.D., editor; The Internist's Intercom, monthly; Component Societies Officers Bulletin,

monthly; manuals, brochures, forms for internists' offices. Affiliations: 51 state component societies.

★ 451 ★

AMERICAN SOCIETY OF LABORATORY ANIMAL
      PRACTITIONERS
c/o Dr. Harry Rozmiarek
USAMRIID, Fort Detrick   (301) 663-7221
Frederick, Maryland 21701   Established 1966

Harry Rozmiarek, D.V.M., Ph.D., Secretary-
      Treasurer
To promote the dissemination of ideas, experiences, and knowledge among veterinarians engaged in laboratory animal practice, and to encourage postgraduate education of veterinarians entering or presently engaged in this field; to provide training and encourage research in basic and clinical problems relating to laboratory animal practice; to act as spokesman for its members before the veterinary profession and before other medical organizations and groups; and to actively encourage the training of veterinarians in laboratory animal practice, at both the pre- and post-doctoral levels, and assist those carrying on such training programs. Membership: 300 plus (veterinarians interested in Laboratory Animal Medicine). Finances: Membership: $10 annually. Meetings: Biennial, with the A.V.M.A. meetings. Publications: Synapse, quarterly, Christine S. F. Williams, D.V.M., editor. Affiliations: AVMA; AALAS.

★ 452 ★

AMERICAN SOCIETY OF LAW AND MEDICINE, INC.
520 Commonwealth Avenue
Suite 212   (617) 262-4990
Boston, Massachusetts 02215   Established 1971

Elliot L. Sagall, M.D., President; A. Edward
      Doudera, J.D., Executive Director
The Society's purpose is to continue medicolegal education on a multidisciplined basis. Its holds seminars and symposia on topics and subjects of medicolegal interest, publishes 3 journals, and acts as a clearinghouse for medicolegal information. Membership: Over 2,100 (physicians, attorneys, nurses, hospital administrators, insurance company personnel, etc.). Finances: Membership: $60. Awards: John P. Rattigan, M.D., Student Essay Contest Award. Meetings: Seminars and symposia, various locations and times. Publications: Medicolegal News, 6 annually, George Annas, J.D., MPH, editor; American Journal of Law and Medicine, biennial, John A. Norris, J.D., MBA, editor; Nursing Law and Ethics, (monthly newsletter). Library: American Society of Law and Medicine, 2,000 volumes; 700 journals.

★ 453 ★

AMERICAN SOCIETY OF MASTER DENTAL
    TECHNOLOGISTS, INC.
Post Office Box 248
Oakland Gardens,   (212) 428-0075
    New York 11364

Charles Cottone, C.D.T., T.F., President;
    Sue Heppenheimer, Executive Secretary
To provide educational resources such as text materials, instructors and guidance for technicians interested in becoming Master Dental Technologists.
Membership: Approximately 90 (dental lab technicians; associate members after written and practical
examinations--Master Dental Technologists). Finances: Membership: $40 annually. Meetings: 1 Ma-
jor Presentation annually; in addition, representation
at 4-6 Dental Laboratory State Meetings annually.

★ 454 ★

AMERICAN SOCIETY OF MAXILLOFACIAL
    SURGEONS
120 Oakbrook Center Mall
Oak Brook, Illinois 60521   Established 1947

C. A. Janda, M.D., Administrative Officer
To stimulate and advance knowledge of the science
and art of maxillofacial surgery, and therby to improve and elevate the standard of practice. Membership: 150 (doctors of medicine and doctors of dental surgery who have at least 5 years of recognized
graduate training and experience in the practice of
maxillofacial surgery). Meetings: Annual, various
locations.

★ 455 ★

AMERICAN SOCIETY OF NEPHROLOGY
6900 Grove Road   (609) 848-1000
Thorofare, New Jersey 08086   Established 1966

Charles B. Slack, Inc.
To advance the knowledge of nephrology and to foster
the dissemination of this knowledge through national
scientific meetings, cooperation with other national
societies of nephrology and by other means approved
by the members on recommendation by the Council.
Membership: 3,100 (M.D. and Ph.D. accepted--
member category only; must reside in Central or
North America). Finances: Membership: $20 an-
nually; Other Sources: Meeting registration income.
Meetings: Annual, late November and early December. Publications: Program of the American
Society of Nephrology, annual.

★ 456 ★

AMERICAN SOCIETY OF NEURORADIOLOGY
c/o Michael S. Huckman, M.D.
Rush Presbyterian St. Luke's Medical
    Center
Department of Diagnostic Radiology (312) 942-5781
Chicago, Illinois 60612   Established 1962

George Wortzman, M.D., President; Michael S.
    Huckman, M.D., Secretary
To promote neuroradiology. Membership: 640
(senior, junior, corresponding, honorary, inactive,
emeritus). Finances: Membership: Junior, $75;
senior, $90. Awards: Cornelius Dyke Award, an-
nual, for the outstanding paper submitted by a trainee
or junior faculty person in the field of Neuroradiology. Meetings: Annual, various locations. Publications: American Journal of Neuroradiology, bimonthly, Juan M. Taveras, M.D., editor.

★ 457 ★

AMERICAN SOCIETY OF OPHTHALMOLOGIC AND
    OTOLARYNGOLOGIC ALLERGY
c/o William P. King, M.D.
1415 3rd Street, Suite 507
Corpus Christi, Texas 78404   Established 1941

William P. King, M.D., Secretary-Treasurer
Study and treatment of allergy in the fields of oph-
thalmology and otolaryngology. Membership: 600.
Finances: Membership and annual dues. Meetings:
Annual, various locations. Publications: Transac-
tions, annual, James T. Spencer, M.D., editor.

AMERICAN SOCIETY OF ORAL SURGEONS
    See: American Association of Oral and
        Maxillofacial Surgeons

★ 458 ★

AMERICAN SOCIETY OF PARASITOLOGISTS
Tulane University
Department of Biology   (504) 865-6226
New Orleans, Louisiana 70118   Established 1924

The Society fosters association of persons interested in
parasitology and related sciences to improve teaching,
promote investigation, and advance knowledge of the
sciences. Membership: 1,600 (active, student,
emeritus, honorary and senior inactive); 1,900 subscribers. Finances: Membership: Active, $35;
student, $20; Other Sources: Journal subscriptions,
$40. Awards: Henry Baldwin Ward Medal, awarded
yearly to outstanding investigator under the age of 40.

Meetings: Annual, various locations. Publications: Journal of Parasitology, bimonthly, Justus Mueller, editor. Affiliations: Southern California Parasitologists; Helminthological Society of Washington; Annual Midwestern Conference of Parasitologists; Southwestern Association of Parasitologists; Southeastern Society of Parasitologists; Northern California Parasitologists; Rocky Mountain Conference of Parasitologists; New Jersey Society of Parasitologists.

★ 459 ★

AMERICAN SOCIETY OF PHARMACOGNOSY
College of Pharmacy
The Ohio State University
500 West 12th Avenue   (614) 422-1423
Columbus, Ohio 43210   Established 1959

Larry W. Robertson, Secretary
To promote the growth and development of pharmacognosy (a study of drugs of a natural origin); to provide the opportunity for associations among workers of the field; to provide opportunities for presentation of research achievements; to promote the publications of meritorious research in natural products. Membership: 425 (United States, foreign, associate). Finances: Membership: United States, $25; foreign, $35; associate, $2. Meetings: Annual, various locations. Publications: The Journal of Natural Products (Lloydia), 6 issues annually, Jack L. Beal, editor; ASP Newsletter, 3 times annually, Ralph N. Blomster, editor.

★ 460 ★

AMERICAN SOCIETY OF PLASTIC AND RECON-
     STRUCTIVE SURGEONS
29 East Madison Street
Suite 800   (312) 641-0593
Chicago, Illinois 60602   Established 1931

Dallas F. Whaley, Executive Vice President
The Society's objectives are (1) to promote and further medical and surgical training and research pertaining to the study and treatment of congenital and acquired deformities; (2) to disseminate information regarding clinical and scientific progress in plastic and reconstructive surgery; (3) to provide opportunity for the exchange of experiences and opinion through discussion, study and publications; (4) to promote the art and science of plastic surgery and to communicate to the members and the general public the advancement and improvements made in the field of plastic surgery; (5) to develop and encourage the practice of high standards of personal and professional conduct among physicians; (6) to conduct and cooperate in courses of study for the benefit of persons desiring to fit

themselves for the specialty of plastic surgery and related fields; to hold meetings and conferences for the mutual improvement and education of members; (7) to acquire, preserve, and disseminate data and valuable information relative to the functions and accomplishments of plastic surgeons; (8) to cooperate with local or regional groups of plastic surgeons in the common endeavor to advance the specialty; and (9) to promote the purpose and effectiveness of plastic surgeons by any and all means consistent with the public interest. Membership: 1,707 (candidate, active, honorary, life, associate, senior corresponding, junior corresponding, retired associate). Finances: Membership: Active, $350; associate, $200; candidate, $275; Other Sources: Voluntary contributions; Educational Foundation activities; exhibits at annual meeting. Meetings: Annual, various locations. Publications: Plastic and Reconstructive Surgery, monthly, Robert Goldwyn, M.D., editor; newsletter, monthly. Affiliations: Educational Foundation of the American Society of Plastic and Reconstructive Surgeons.

★ 461 ★

AMERICAN SOCIETY OF PSYCHOPATHOLOGY
     OF EXPRESSION
c/o Dr. Irene Jakab
University of Pittsburgh
3811 O'Hara Street   (412) 624-2132
Pittsburgh, Pennsylvania 15261   Established 1964

Irene Jakab, M.D., Ph.D., President
To assure collaboration of the various specialists in the United States connected with psychiatric research, research in sociology, psychology, and other fields, who are interested in the problems of expression and in the artistic activities. Membership: Approximately 100 (psychiatrists, psychologists, art critics, artists, art therapists, etc.). Finances: Membership: $40 (includes Confinia Psychiatrica); Other Sources: Donations. Meetings: Biennial, various locations. Publications: Psychiatry and Art, Proceedings of Conventions, Irene Jakab, editor; Newsletter, irregular. Affiliations: International Society of Psychopathology of Expression.

★ 462 ★

AMERICAN SOCIETY OF PSYCHOSOMATIC
     DENTISTRY AND MEDICINE
2802 Mermaid Avenue   (212) 372-4569
Brooklyn, New York 11224   Established 1948

Leo Wollman, M.D., Executive Director
To inculcate in the practices of those professional practitioners of hypnosis, a strong desire to advance

in both thinking and practice for the ultimate benefit of their patients; to provide scientific training and experience by means of sectional meetings, annual meetings, seminars and instruction groups for individual and group training in the principles and practice of scientific hypnosis. Membership: 700 (active, honorary, associate, foreign). Finances: Membership: $25; Other Sources: Journal subscription, $30. Awards: Annual awards to deserving individuals. Meetings: Annual, various locations. Publications: Journal of the American Society of Psychosomatic Dentistry and Medicine, quarterly, Leo Wollman, editor.

★ 463 ★

AMERICAN SOCIETY OF RADIOLOGIC
    TECHNOLOGISTS
55 East Jackson Boulevard
Suite 1820   (312) 922-3962
Chicago, Illinois 60604   Established 1920

Marilyn Holland, President
To advance the science of Radiologic Technology; to establish and maintain high standards of education and training; to elevate the quality of patient care and to improve the welfare and socioeconomics of radiologic technologists. Membership: Over 20,000 (active, inactive, associate, student, life, emeritus, honorary, fellow). Finances: Membership: Active, associate, $30; inactive, $10; student, $7; fellow, $20; Other Sources: Sale of publications. Meetings: Annual, various locations. Publications: Radiologic Technology, bimonthly, Ward M. Keller, R.T., editor; ASRT Scanner, bimonthly, Michael Almada, editor. Affiliations: 50 state affiliated societies, D.C. and 3 other city affiliated societies.

★ 464 ★

AMERICAN SOCIETY OF SAFETY ENGINEERS
850 Busse Highway   (312) 692-4121
Park Ridge, Illinois 60068   Established 1911

Judy T. Neel, Executive Director
To promote the advancement of the profession and contribute to the well-being and professional development of its members. Membership: 16,000 (professional, affiliate, student). Finances: Membership: $45 membership; $25 application fee. Awards: Professional Paper Awards for outstanding articles published in "Professional Society". Meetings: Annual, various locations; technical sessions in conjunction with National Safety Congress, annually, Chicago. Publications: Professional Safety, monthly, Ellen Zielinski, editor; technical monographs.

★ 465 ★

AMERICAN SOCIETY OF SANITARY ENGINEERING
Post Office Box 9712   (216) 835-3040
Bay Village, Ohio 44140   Established 1906

Gael H. Dunn, Executive Secretary
Founded primarily for the purpose of promoting the welfare, health and safety of the public through better sanitary engineering principles. It has sought to encourage standardization and practical and scientific plumbing installations. Membership: 2,800 (plumbing contractors, public health officials, plumbers, plumbing wholesalers, manufacturers' representatives, doctors). Meetings: Annual, various locations. Publications: Newsletter, monthly; A.S.S.E. Yearbook, annual, Gael H. Dunn, editor.

★ 466 ★

AMERICAN SOCIETY OF THERAPEUTIC
    RADIOLOGISTS
20 North Wacker Drive   (312) 236-4963
Chicago, Illinois 60606

Mrs. Sheila A. Aubin, Executive Secretary
The Society aims to benefit the patient by promoting the highest possible standards of therapeutic radiology, by improving the training of therapeutic radiologists and by providing clinical and laboratory researchers into the frontiers of knowledge of the specialty. The Society operates a placement service designed to aid therapeutic radiologists, residents in therapeutic radiology, medical clinics, and hospital medical staffs. Membership: 1,555 (active, associate, corresponding, retired, emeritus, honorary, junior). Finances: Membership: Active, $50; associate and corresponding, $25; active application fee, $20; associate and corresponding application fee, $10. Meetings: Annual. Publications: Cancer, monthly, Jonathan Rhoads, M.D., editor; International Journal of Radiation Oncology Biology Physics, bimonthly, Philip Rubin, M.D., editor.

★ 467 ★

AMERICAN SOCIETY OF TRANSPLANT SURGEONS
c/o G. Melvine Williams, M.D.
Johns Hopkins Hospital
Baltimore, Maryland 21205   Established 1974

The Society was founded in response to a need felt by the majority of active transplant surgeons in the United States and Canada to organize as a group in order to exchange scientific information, sponsor collaborative projects, promote the education of transplant surgeons, and insure that there was some formal constituted body which other organizations and/or agencies could go to for information and a consultation in transplantation. Membership: 276 (active members are those who pay dues and reside in the Un United States and Canada; honorary members are surgeons residing in other countries or distinguished individuals in the field of transplantation but who are not surgeons). Finances: Membership: Dues, active members, $55 annually. Awards: Contributions received from greatful patients and from the membership and from industrial firms enable us to invite a distinguished speaker each year and provide him with an honorarium. Meetings: Annual, Chicago, Illinois. Publications: Transplantation (best scientific papers published in one issue of this journal), annual. Remarks: There are no permanent officers, they are elected annually.

★ 468 ★

AMERICAN SOCIETY OF TROPICAL MEDICINE
      AND HYGIENE
Post Office Box 46502
Parkdale Branch
Cincinnati, Ohio 45246   Established 1952

The advancement of Tropical Medicine and Hygiene, including medicine, nursing, engineering, entomology, parasitology, and allied specialties in this field. Membership: 1,855 (active, life, honorary, emeritus). Finances: Membership: Active, $30; student, $15. Awards: Walter Reed Medal; Bailey K. Ashford Medal; Joseph A. LePrince Medal. Meetings: Annual, various locations. Publications: American Journal of Tropical Medicine and Hygiene, bimonthly, Paul C. Beaver, editor; Tropical Medicine and Hygiene News, bimonthly, Colvin Gibson, editor.

★ 469 ★

AMERICAN SOCIETY OF VETERINARY
      OPHTHALMOLOGY
Office of Secretary-Treasurer
1820 August   (405) 377-2134
Stillwater, Oklahoma 74074   Established 1957

A. J. Quinn, D.V.M., Secretary-Treasurer
The objectives of the Society are to further scientific progress in veterinary ophthalmology and to promote improved methods of diagnosis, treatment and prevention of disease in animals. It provides an opportunity for veterinarians to carry on advanced studies by the dissemination of new information in ophthalmology and encourages additional ophthalmological training in veterinary colleges. Membership is open to veterinarians who are actively engaged in any branch of veterinary science. Membership: 175 (member, charter member, associate, honorary). Finances:

Membership: Active, $25. Meetings: Business meetings, annual, in conjunction with the American Animal Hospital Association's annual convention, various locations; scientific programs are presented annually by ASVO members at the AAHA and AVMA Conventions. Publications: Newsletter (members only), irregular. Affiliations: American Veterinary Medical Association.

AMERICAN SPEECH AND HEARING ASSOCIATION
      See: American Speech-Language-Hearing
            Association

★ 470 ★

AMERICAN SPEECH-LANGUAGE-HEARING
      ASSOCIATION   (800) 638-6868
10801 Rockville Pike   (301) 897-5700
Rockville, Maryland 20852   Established 1925

Frederick T. Spahr, Ph.D., Executive Secretary
To encourage basic scientific study of the processes of individual human communication, with special reference to speech, hearing, and language; to promote investigation of disorders of human communication and foster improvement of clinical procedures with such disorders; to stimulate exchange of information among persons and organizations thus engaged; and to disseminate such information. Membership: 35,000 plus (regular, graduate student, spouse, life). Finances: Membership: $34; membership with certification, $95; graduate student, $25; spouse, $60; Other Sources: Journal subscriptions, conventions, certification fees, miscellaneous. Awards: Federal grant funds received for research and training projects. Meetings: Annual Convention, Regional Conferences, workshops, various locations. Publications: Journal of Speech and Hearing Disorders, quarterly; Journal of Speech and Hearing Research, quarterly; Asha Monthly Journal; Language, Speech and Hearing Services in Schools, quarterly; selected monographs; reports. Affiliations: American Council of Applied Linguistics; Child Development Associate Consortium; Coalition for Health Funding; Coalition of Independent Health Professions; Council on Postsecondary Education; Council of Specialized Accrediting Agencies; Interagency Committee for Handicapped Children; International Association of Logopedics and Phoniatrics; National Academy of Television Arts and Sciences; National Association of Home Health Agencies; Rehabilitation International U.S.A. Former Name: American Speech and Hearing Association.

★ 471 ★
AMERICAN SPINAL INJURY ASSOCIATION
250 East Superior Street
Room 619   (312) 649-3425
Chicago, Illinois 60611   Established 1975

G. Heiner Sell, M.D., President;
  Marianne G. Kaplan, Executive Secretary
To foster, promote, augment, develop and encourage
knowledge and investigation of the causes, cure, prevention of spinal injury and related trauma; the pursuance of excellence in spinal injury patient care; to
coordinate development of regional spinal injury care
systems throughout the nation; to promote and exchange ideas between professionals in the field of
spinal injury management; to standardize medical
terminology in spinal injury; to foster, support, promote, augment, develop, coordinate and encourage
basic research in the field of the management of spinal injury and related trauma; to develop and encourage teaching and educational material and provide
specialized training for physicians and allied health
professional personnel in the management of spinal injury from inception through early care, comprehensive
rehabilitation, vocational or avocational pursuits,
housing, and ultimately follow on to demise; to
foster, promote, support, augment, develop and encourage education of the medical profession and laity
in the prevention and the proper management of spinal
injury including the necessity for specialized regional
spinal injury centers, provision for educational and
vocational training, removal of architectural barriers
and promotion of a society more conducive to the
physically inconvenienced individual including adequate housing and transportation and to establish criteria for centers and/or systems of total spinal injury
management, and to provide optimal care of the spinal
injured person; and to promote other suitable and
proper activities directed toward the accomplishment
of the foregoing purposes. Membership: 245 (specialty board certified Doctors of Medicine and Doctors
of Osteopathy actively engaged in the treatment of
spinal paralytic patients or otherwise having made a
significant contribution to the advancement of the
basic sciences or one of the clinical fields of practice as are applicable to treatment of spinal injury
and who reside permanently in North America). Finances: Annual dues, $80; initiation fee: $70;
Other Sources: Revenues from annual clinical meetings. Awards: American Spinal Injury Association
Foundation. Meetings: Annual Clinical (Scientific)
Meetings, various locations. Affiliations: American
Spinal Injury Association Foundation.

★ 472 ★
AMERICAN STUDENT DENTAL ASSOCIATION
211 East Chicago Avenue   (312) 440-2795
Chicago, Illinois 60611   Established 1971

The Association's aims are to educate and involve its
members in the social, moral and ethical obligations
of the profession of dentistry; to be involved and
committed to the improvement of the health care and
health care delivery to all people; to promote the
active improvement of dental education; to promote
the improvement and understanding fo world health
problems; to contribute to the welfare of dental students; to contribute to the development of interprofessional activities; and to advance the profession of
dentistry. Membership: 17,000 (dental students).
Finances: Membership: $15; Other Sources: Grants.
Awards: ASDA Preventive Dentistry Award. Meetings: Annual, Chicago, Illinois. Publications: The
New Dentist, 9 times annually.

★ 473 ★
AMERICAN SURGICAL ASSOCIATION
c/o W. Gerald Austen, M.D.
Massachusetts General Hospital
Department of Surgery
32 Fruit Street   (617) 726-2050
Boston, Massachusetts 02114   Established 1880

W. Gerald Austen, M.D.
To advance surgery and to provide the fellows with
an annual meeting and a forum for presentation and
discussion of scientific surgical papers. Membership:
350 active members. Meetings: Annual, various
locations. Publications: Transactions of the American Surgical Association, annually.

★ 474 ★
AMERICAN SURGICAL TRADE ASSOCIATION
111 East Adams Street   (312) 272-5420
Chicago, Illinois 60603   Established 1977

Louis H. Markle
Founded in 1961 for free distribution of surgical supplies and equipment to needy institutions throughout
the world. Distribution is channeled through existing
secular and religious organizations in the United
States. Membership: Autonomous body with Board
of Directors; originally founded under sponsorship of
American Surgical Trade Foundation presently number-
ing 600. Finances: Other Sources: Contributions
from dealers and manufacturers of health supplies, and
from the American Surgical Trade Association. Meetings: Semiannual, various locations. Former Name:
Surgical Trade Foundation.

★ 475 ★
AMERICAN THERMOGRAPHIC SOCIETY
Post Office Box 98   (617) 896-6440
Brewster, Massachusetts 02631   Established 1969

Norma M. Oldfield, Executive Director
To study infra-red emanation in health and disease,
as well as its application to clinical medicine and
scientific research; to educate those interested in the
advancement of the technique and instrumentation.
Membership: 250 (including physicians, physicists,
technologists, biomedical engineers, veterinarians,
nurses). Finances: Voting member, $35; non-voting
member, $20; corporate, $200; Other Sources:
Sponsorship from industry. Meetings: Symposia, annually; mini-seminars. Publications: The Thermographic Quarterly, quarterly, David Winsor, M.D.,
editor.

★ 476 ★
AMERICAN THORACIC SOCIETY
1740 Broadway   (212) 245-8000
New York, New York 10019   Established 1905

S. R. Iannotta, Executive Director
To serve as the medical section of the American Lung
Association and to promote research, education and
clinical practice in all aspects of lung disease.
Membership: 8,000 (active, associate, senior, hon-
orary). Finances: Membership: Active, $42; as-
sociate, $20; Other Sources: Support from American
Lung Association. Awards: Honorary membership.
Meetings: Annual, various locations. Publications:
American Review of Respiratory Disease, monthly,
Gareth M. Green, M.D., editor; ATS News, quar-
terly, Mary Thornton, editor. Affiliations: 42
State Thoracic Societies; 7 scientific assemblies.

★ 477 ★
AMERICAN THYROID ASSOCIATION
University of Massachusetts Medical Center
55 Lake Avenue, North   (617) 865-3115
Worcester, Massachusetts 01605   Established 1923

A. B. Hayles, M.D., Secretary
Acquisition and spread of knowledge of the thyroid
gland and its diseases. Membership: 525 (active,
senior, corresponding, honorary). Finances: Membership: Initiation fee, $25; annual dues, $20.
Awards: Van Meter-Armour Award. Meetings: Annual, various locations.

★ 478 ★
AMERICAN TRAUMA SOCIETY
875 North Michigan Avenue   (312) 649-1810
Chicago, Illinois 60611   Established 1968

Susan L. Weed, Executive Director
The ATS mission is to reduce needless killings and
cripplings by mobilizing public and professional support for improved systems of pre-hospital and in-
hospital care and by promoting programs in research,
education and the prevention of injury. Membership:
4,400 (3,300 medical doctors and 1,100 laymen).
Meetings: Annual, various locations; also holds annual symposia. Publications: Traumagram, quarterly;
Media Resource Catalog.

★ 479 ★
AMERICAN TYPE CULTURE COLLECTION
12301 Parklawn Drive   (301) 881-2600
Rockville, Maryland 20852   Established 1925

Robert E. Stevenson, Ph.D., Director
Founded to promote research, service, and education,
the organization maintains over 20,000 authentic
strains of bacteria, fungi, protozoa, algae, viruses,
and cells; distributes cultures to the scientific community; acts as a depository for cultures involved in
patent applications and for confidential safe-keeping
of proprietary cultures; carries out freeze-drying of
proprietary cultures; conducts taxonomic identification processes and packages biohazardous materials;
publishes manuals providing essential information on
ATCC cultures and their uses; promotes molecular
approaches to taxonomy employing DNA studies and
biochemical and morphological characterization of
microorganisms; develops computer assisted bacteria
identification systems; characterizes and systemitizes
fungi; isolates and characterizes cell lines from human biopsy materials; and conducts studies on the
long term stability and freeze-drying technology of
viruses. Finances: Other Sources: Service charges
from distribution of cultures; research grants and contracts. Meetings: Annual, ATCC Headquarters.
Publications: Catalogue of Strains I, biennially,
Harold D. Hatt, editor; Catalogue of Strains II, biennially, Harold D. Hatt, editor. Affiliations:
American Association of Immunologists; American Institute of Biological Sciences; American Phytopath-
ological Society; American Society of Biological
Chemists; American Society for Microbiology; American Society of Parasitologists; American Society of
Zoologists; American Society of Tropical Medicine
and Hygiene; Genetics Society of America; Infectious Diseases Society of America; Mycological Society of America; National Research Council-National
Academy of Sciences; Society of Protozoologists;
Tissue Culture Association.

★ 480 ★

AMERICAN UROLOGICAL ASSOCIATION
1120 North Charles Street   (301) 727-1100
Baltimore, Maryland 21201   Established 1902

Richard J. Hannigan, Executive Secretary
To encourage the study of and to maintain the highest
possible standards for urological education, practice
and research; to establish, support or aid any scientific association, institution, or research organization
which is calculated to improve and elevate the standards of urology; to perpetuate the history and best
traditions of urological practice and ethics; and to
promote the publication of scientific literature pertaining to urology. Membership: 4,900 (active,
senior, inactive, honorary, associate, corresponding).
Finances: Membership: $180. Awards: Annual es-
say competition, funds available for research upon application to Research Committee. Meetings: Annual,
various locations. Publications: Journal of Urology,
monthly, William W. Scott, editor. Affiliations:
Association divided into 8 geographical sections:
Mid-Atlantic, New England, New York, North Central, Northeastern, South Central, Southeastern and
Western. Each has its own officers and holds meetings.

★ 481 ★

AMERICAN VENEREAL DISEASE ASSOCIATION
Post Office Box 22349   (714) 233-2215
San Diego, California 92122   Established 1924

W. O. Harrison, M.D., Secretary-Treasurer
The Association aims for the control and ultimate
eradication of venereal diseases, and works to support
research in all aspects of the venereal diseases including medical, epidemiologic, laboratory, social,
and behavioral studies; to recognize outstanding contributions in venereal disease control; and to disseminate authoritative information concerning venereal
disease. Membership: 700. Finances: Membership: $22 annually United States, Canada, Mexico;
$25 annually foreign. Awards: Thomas Parran
Award; AVDA Achievement Award. Meetings: Annual, various locations. Publications: Sexually
Transmitted Diseases, quarterly, W. M. McCormack,
editor.

★ 482 ★

AMERICAN VETERINARY MEDICAL ASSOCIATION
930 North Meacham Road   (312) 885-8070
Schaumburg, Illinois 60196   Established 1863

D. A. Price, Executive Vice President
To advance the science and art of veterinary medicine and to fulfill the basic professional needs of the
nation's veterinarians, providing them with effective
group action and representation beyond the scope of
the individual. Membership: 31,000 (active, associate, affiliate, honorary, student). Finances:
Membership: $100; Other Sources: Advertising in
journals; registration and exhibitor fees at annual
meeting. Awards: AVMA Foundation; AVMA
Award; Public Service Award; 12th International
Veterinary Congress Prize; Practitioner Research
Award. Meetings: Annual, various locations. Publications: Journal of the American Veterinary Medical
Association, semimonthly, Arthur Freeman, editor;
American Journal of Veterinary Research, monthly,
Arthur Freeman, editor; career and owner information
pamphlets.

★ 483 ★

AMERICAN WOMEN"S HOSPITALS SERVICE
225 West 34th Street   (212) 947-1721
New York, New York 10001   Established 1917

Alma Dea Morani, M.D., President
To support medical and hospital services for the care
of the indigent sick and prevention of disease in various parts of the world, particularly through the work
of women doctors. Medical relief service through
support of clinics and other facilities in India, Korea,
Philippines, Taiwan, Thailand, Bolivia, Haiti and the
Southern Highlands, and Arizona, U.S.A.; grants
are made to certain medical institutions in the United
States and emergency grants are sometimes made (as
in the Alaskan earthquake). Finances: Public subscriptions. Meetings: Quarterly, New York City.
Publications: Quarterly leaflets. Affiliations:
American Medical Women's Association; Medical
Women's International Association; Pan-American
Medical Women's Alliance.

★ 484 ★

AMPUTEE SHOE AND GLOVE EXCHANGE
1635 Warwickshire Drive
Houston, Texas 77077   Established 1956

Dr. R. E. Wainerdi
This is a free shoe and glove exchange for amputees.
The Exchange lists sizes, style preference, and ad-
dresses--they do not handle or mail shoes or gloves.
They put amputees in touch with each other through
a central listing service. There is no fee; all costs
are privately covered. All listings are confidential
and for amputees only. Membership: Approximately
150 amputees of all ages. Finances: No fee.

★ 485 ★
ANIMAL MEDICAL CENTER
510 East 62nd Street   (212) 838-8100
New York, New York 10023   Established 1910

William J. Kay, D.V.M., Chief of Staff
The Center is dedicated to excellence in medical and
surgical care for animals, the performance of high-
quality clinical research of benefit to animals as well
as to humans, and the furtherance of education for
veterinarians and parmedics.   Objectives include
internships and residencies in veterinary internal medicine, veterinary surgery and veterinary pathology.
Board Certification in veterinary specialties is available after successful completion of training programs,
and the Center has become a referral center for pet
animals from a wide sector of the Northeast and other
parts of the United States. Membership: 4,000 (associate, substaining, patron, sponsor, professional,
club, company, foundation). Finances: Membership:
$10 to $1,000; Other Sources: Patient fees; bequests; legacies; contributions; research funds from
pharmaceutical, governmental, and foundation grants.
Meetings: Seminars and lectures, weekly; board
meeting, monthly, New York City.   Publications:
Annual report; scientific publications.   Library:
1,500 volumes, over 100 journals.

★ 486 ★
ANIMAL NUTRITION RESEARCH COUNCIL
c/o Dr. Roger L. Garrett
Diversified Laboratories, Inc.
3251 Old Lee Highway
Fairfax, Virginia 22030   Established 1940

Roger L. Garrett, Secretary-Treasurer
To stimulate interest in research in animal nutrition;
to promote collaborative studies of assay methods for
nutritional factors; to provide a medium for the discussion of assay technics and results; to plan and administer projects for the advancement and application
of knowledge in animal nutrition and for the betterment of assay technics; and to cooperate with control
officials and associations to help accomplish these objectives. Membership: 425 (those profesionally
trained and interested in animal nutrition). Finances:
Membership: $3; Other Sources: Donations, monies
received for scientific and statistical studies.   Meetings: Annual, Washington, D.C.

★ 487 ★
ANNA FULLER FUND
333 Cedar Street   (203) 436-0533
New Haven, Connecticut 06510 Established 1932

Union Trust Company, Administrative Trustee;
    R. E. Handschumacher, Scientific Advisor
To alleviate suffering from disease, primarily cancer,
by research as to cause, treatment, and care; by
education of the public of prevention and treatment.
Grants are made only to charitable institutions for the
above purposes. Finances: Trust established by
Egbert C. Fuller. Research: Research grants (generally less than $10,000 annually to young investi-
gators); postdoctoral fellowships. Meetings: 2 or 3
annually, New Haven, Connecticut. Publications:
Annual report.

ANOREXIA NERVOSA AID SOCIETY
    See: American Anorexia Nervosa Association,
    Inc.

ANOREXIA NERVOSA AND ASSOCIATED
DISORDERS, INC.
    See: National Association of Anorexia Nervosa
        and Associated Disorders, Inc.

★ 488 ★
ARTHRITIS FOUNDATION
3400 Peachtree Road   (404) 266-0795
Atlanta, Georgia 30326   Established 1948

Clifford M. Clarke, CAE, President
Founded to develop a nationwide research program designed to discover the causes of, and to improve the
methods of treating, curing and preventing arthritis
and related rheumatic diseses.   Has established fellowships and other study programs designed to increase the number of individuals qualified to conduct
research with respect to, and to specialize in the
treatment, cure and prevention of such diseases. Has
fostered the development of centers devoted to research
and education in arthritis.   Conducts programs of
medical education to increase the appreciation of the
medical profession as to what can be done to bring
effective treatment to arthritis patients and conducts
a program of general public and patient education.
Raises funds to support the above programs. Membership: Members are the governing House of Delegates, 201. Finances: Other Sources: Public support given the 71 chapters of the Foundation, some
direct contributions and grants are received by the
National organization. Awards: Medical Fellowships; Grants to arthritis centers; Cecil Awards for
excellence in writing on the subject of arthritis in
print or electronic media. Meetings: Annual,
House of Delegates; Annual, scientific session for
medical profession, various locations. Publications:

Arthritis and Rheumatism Journal, monthly, Jeri Jordan, editor; Bulletin on Rheumatic Diseases, 8 times annually, Jeri Jordan, editor; National Arthritis News, quarterly, Lindsay Wyatt, editor; numerous leaflets and pamphlets on the diseases of arthritis and the treatment thereof.

★ 489 ★

ASIA PACIFIC ACADEMY OF OPHTHALMOLOGY
3885 Round Top Drive   (808) 946-2042
Honolulu, Hawaii 96822   Established 1957

W. J. Holmes, President
To foster the study and dissemination of knowledge and further the study of diseases of the eye; to promote scientific exchange and help establish closer personal and professional contacts among those interested and working in ophthalmology; to organize and hold regional congresses which promote and support research and programs for the prevention of blindness. Membership: 10,000 ophthalmic surgeons. Finances: Conference registration fees; donations. Awards: Jose Rizel Medal for excellence in ophthalmology. Meetings: Triennially, various Asian countries or Australia and New Zealand. Publications: Transactions of the Asian Pacific Academy of Ophthalmology, quadrennially. Affiliations: Ophthalmologic societies in Asia and Oceania.

★ 490 ★

ASSEMBLY OF EPISCOPAL HOSPITALS AND
   CHAPLAINS
1015 N.W. 22 Avenue   (503) 229-7057
Portland, Oregon 97210

Rev. C. K. Trewhella, Treasurer
The Assembly encourages the chaplaincy programs be developed on the soundest professional level using clergy trained in pastoral ministry skills. AEHC promotes the development of paid or volunteer chaplaincy programs in all hospitals. The Assembly reinforces the spiritual foundations on which all Episcopal hospitals and institutions were organized. Membership: 400 to 500. Finances: Membership: Institutional, $50; personal, $25; associate, $10; student or retired, $5. Meetings: 4-day meetings are held in early March each year in conjunction with the Protestant Health and Welfare Assembly and the College of Chaplains. Publications: Chaplair, quarterly, Jane L. Hoskovec, editor. Affiliations: Protestant Health and Welfare Assembly.

★ 491 ★

ASSEMBLY OF HOSPITAL SCHOOLS OF NURSING
840 North Lake Shore Drive   (312) 280-6407
Chicago, Illinois 60611   Established 1968

Suzanne F. Whitehead, R.N., Secretary
To promote and encourage recognition, support, and improvement of hospital schools of nursing. Membership: 250 Hospital Schools of Nursing (institutional membership). Finances: Membership: $300 annually; Other Sources: American Hospital Association. Meetings: Annual, Chicago, Illinois. Publications: Hospital Schools of Nursing; Newsletter of the Assembly of Hospital Schools of Nursing; American Hospital Association, monthly, Carole Bolster, editor. Affiliations: American Hospital Association.

ASSOCIATION FOR ACADEMIC HEALTH CENTERS
   See: Association of Academic Health Centers

★ 492 ★

ASSOCIATION FOR ACADEMIC SURGERY
c/o Dr. Brian D. Lowery
410 West 10th Avenue   (614) 421-8553
Columbus, Ohio 43210   Established 1966

Dr. Brian D. Lowery, Secretary-Treasurer
The Association was established to stimulate young surgeons to pursue careers in academic surgery and support them in establishing themselves as investigators and educators; to provide a forum for members to present papers on subjects of clinical and laboratory investigations; to promote interchange of ideas between senior surgical residents, junior faculty, and established academic surgeons; and to facilitate communication among academic surgeons in all fields. Membership: 1,600. Finances: Membership: $50. Award: Resident Research Presentation Award. Meetings: Annual, various locations. Publication: Journal of Surgical Research, monthly.

★ 493 ★

ASSOCIATION FOR ADVANCEMENT OF BEHAVIOR
   THERAPY
420 Lexington Avenue   (212) 682-0065
New York, New York 10170   Established 1966

Mary Jane Eimer, Executive Director
To provide an open forum for persons interested in the problems and in the general advancement of the theories and techniques underlying the various facets of behavior therapy. Membership: 3,000 (full, associate and student--M.D., Ph.D., DSW, Ed. S.,

R.N., MSW, MA, MS). Finances: Membership: Annual dues; Other Sources: Membership dues, royalties, convention registration, publications. Awards: President's New Researcher Award, annually; (each year, the President of AABT will target an area and invite papers that are in press or have been published during the last 2 years by an author who is 5 years or less post-training, post Ph.D., post residency, etc.). Meetings: Annual, various locations. Publications: Behavior Therapy, 5 times annually, Alan Kazdin, Ph.D., editor; Behavioral Assessment, quarterly, Rosemary Nelson, Ph.D., editor; The Behavior Therapist, bimonthly, John Lutzker, Ph.D., editor; Audio-Visual Directory; Directory of Graduate Study in Behavior Therapy; AABT Membership Directory; Guidelines for Choosing a Behavior Therapist; Ethical Issues for Human Services/Professional Consultation and Peer Review Services.

★ 494 ★
ASSOCIATION FOR APPLIED PSYCHOANALYSIS
85 Medford Road   (212) 727-3611
Staten Island, New York 10304   Established 1952

Dr. William D. Katz, Executive Director
To facilitate and promote training and research in the field of applied psychoanalysis; to advance the application of psychoanalytic theories in industry, education, social sciences, art, philosophy, and human relations; to promote interdisciplinary cooperation among the various fields to which applied psychoanalysis can make a significant contribution; to establish professional standards in the application of psychoanalytic principles. Membership: 270 (professional psychoanalysts, fellows, associates, affiliates). Finances: Membership: Professional, $35; associate, $30; affiliate, $25; Other Sources: Subscriptions to IMAGO. Meetings: Annually, usually New York City. Publications: IMAGO, quarterly, Harry Slochower, Ph.D., editor; Directory, biennially; Newsletter, quarterly. Affiliations: Council of Psychoanalytic Psychotherapists.

ASSOCIATION FOR CHILDBIRTH AT HOME
    See: Association for Childbirth at Home,
         International

★ 495 ★
ASSOCIATION FOR CHILDBIRTH AT HOME,
    INTERNATIONAL (ACHI)
Post Office Box 39498   (213) 668-1132
Los Angeles, California 90039   Established 1972

Tonya Brooks, President; Linda Bennett, Executive Director
An independent international organization supporting home birth. ACHI works toward improvement of the quality of life in the world by improving maternity care through identification and implementation of correct obstetrical and pediatric technology. This would mean the eradication of birth injuries and brain damage from obstetrical procedures as well as the reduction of preventable birth defects. ACHI also supports the pioneering research on "cures" for genetic or inherited birth defects. The Association offers childbirth classes that focus on teaching essential and accurate technical obstetrics to parents. This enables parents to make knowledgeable and responsible decisions as to where, how, and with whom they will give birth. This is accomplished through data presentations, experience sharing discussions and media presentations by trained certified ACHI leaders presenting a series based on 10 years of research. The ACHI home birth series is offered throughout the United States and Canada and in increasing areas around the world. Membership: Over 10,000 (membership increases weekly - parents, childbirth, educators, professional and lay peoples internationally). Finances: Membership: $10 parents trained through ACHI; $20 all others; Other Sources: Training programs, fundraising. Awards: Outstanding Teacher Award (presented annually to 1 or more of ACHI Certified Teachers); Great Humanitarian Award (presented annually to individuals in the childbirth arena who have contributed greatly to the well-being of mothers and babies). Meetings: Teacher Training Seminars, approximately monthly (national); Advanced Training Seminars, approximately quarterly (national); 5-Day Intensive Midwifery Seminars, approximately quarterly (national); Special Topics Seminars (for professionals); periodic 6-8 week series, Parent Series—offered continually at International Office, and Internationally by all ACHI certified teachers (6-week series). Publications: Giving Birth At Home, standard text, Linda Bennett and Tonya Brooks, editors; Birth Notes (professional journal), quarterly, Linda Bennett and Tonya Brooks, editors; Giving Birth, A Layman's Guide to Perinatology, Linda Bennett and Tonya Brooks, editors. Library: ACHI Library, approximately 100 volumes, for reference use only. Former Name: Association for Childbirth at Home (ACAH).

★ 496 ★
ASSOCIATION FOR CHILDREN AND ADULTS WITH
    LEARNING DISABILITIES
4156 Library Road   (412) 341-1515
Pittsburgh, Pennsylvania 15234   Established 1964

Jean S. Petersen, Executive Director

ACLD's major goals are to encourage research, stimulate development of early detection programs and educational techniques, create a climate of public awareness and acceptance, disseminate information, and provide advocacy for the learning disabled. <u>Membership:</u> 60,000 parents and professionals. <u>Finances:</u> Membership: $10 annually; Other Sources: Publication sales, grants, and donations. <u>Meetings:</u> Annual, various locations. <u>Publications:</u> ACLD Newsbriefs, bimonthly, Betty Lou Kratoville, editor. <u>Former Name:</u> Association for Children with Learning Disabilities.

ASSOCIATION FOR CHILDREN WITH LEARNING DISABILITIES
   See: Association for Children and Adults with Learning Disabilities

★ 497 ★
ASSOCIATION FOR CHILDREN WITH RETARDED MENTAL DEVELOPMENT, INC.
817 Broadway   (212) 470-7200
New York, New York 10003   Established 1951

Ida Rappaport, Executive Director
Offers professionally supervised programs for mentally retarded young adults and children including rehabilitation centers, sheltered workshops, social centers, activities for daily living, and day treatment programs. Operates group homes and Intermediate Care Facilities in the State of New York. <u>Membership:</u> 5,000 (professionals, parents). <u>Awards:</u> Man or Woman of the Year Award, annually, for his or her contributions toward improvements in the lives of the mentally retarded. <u>Meetings:</u> Annual, New York City; quarterly borough division meetings. <u>Publications:</u> A/CRMD on the Record, monthly; Children's Mandate, quarterly; Directory, annual.

★ 498 ★
ASSOCIATION FOR CLINICAL PASTORAL EDUCATION
475 Riverside Drive, Suite 450   (212) 870-2558
New York, New York 10115   Established 1967

Charles E. Hall, Executive Director
The Association aims to foster clinical pastoral education as a part of theological education and of continuing education for ministry, and to encourage clinically trained ministry in churches and in health care institutions. It defines standards for clinical pastoral education, certifies CPE supervisors and accredits CPE centers. <u>Membership:</u> CPE Supervisors, theo-

logical schools, accredited CPE centers and individuals. <u>Meetings:</u> Annual, various locations; regional conferences. <u>Publications:</u> Journal of Pastoral Care, quarterly, John Patton, editor.

★ 499 ★
ASSOCIATION FOR EDUCATION OF THE VISUALLY HANDICAPPED
919 Walnut Street, 7th Floor   (215) 923-9555
Philadelphia, Pennsylvania 19107   Established 1853

Mary K. Bauman, Executive Secretary
To improve material and methods of teaching the visually handicapped, and to expand the opportunities for the visually handicapped to take a contributory place in society. <u>Membership:</u> 2,350 (teachers, supervisors, administrators, ancillary staff serving visually handicapped children and youth, chiefly in day or residential schools). <u>Finances:</u> Membership: Income; Other Sources: Gifts. <u>Meetings:</u> Biennial, various locations. <u>Publications:</u> Education of the Visually Handicapped, quarterly; Fountainhead, quarterly, Mary Bauman, editor; selected papers.

★ 500 ★
ASSOCIATION FOR GNOTOBIOTICS
Roswell Park Memorial Institute
Department of Dermatology
666 Elm Street   (716) 845-3105
Buffalo, New York 14263   Established 1961

Dr. Patricia M. Bealmear, Executive Secretary
To stimulate research in the field of basic and applied gnotobiotics; to expedite the dissemination of information relative to gnotobiotics and gnotobiotic technology; to stimulate the production, maintenance, distribution and use of gnotobiotes; to establish standards for the microbiological testing and husbandry practice with gnotobiotes, and to establish a certification program; to establish an acceptable nomenclature in the field of gnotobiotics. <u>Membership:</u> 415 (professional, industrial). <u>Finances:</u> Membership: Individual, $5; student, $2; industrial, $100. <u>Meetings:</u> Annual, various locations. <u>Publications:</u> Annual meeting publications. <u>Affiliations:</u> American Association for Laboratory Animal Science; American Association for Accreditation of Laboratory Animal Care.

★ 501 ★

ASSOCIATION FOR HEALTHCARE QUALITY (AHQ)
CWRU School of Medicine
2119 Abington Road   (216) 229-9744
Cleveland, Ohio 44106   Established 1969

William H. Kincaid, Executive Director
AHQ members believe in a multidisciplinary approach
by health care professionals and others in encouraging
and supporting quality assurance activities in the
health care field, and in a free interchange of ideas
as the best way to promote improvement in systems,
in health records, and ultimately in the quality of
care. Membership: Approximately 400 (personal and
institutional). Finances: $30 personal membership;
$65 institutional membership; Other Sources: Con-
ferences and subscriptions. Meetings: Annual Multidisciplinary Conference on Healthcare Quality,
usually June, various locations. Publications: AHQ
Review of Quality Assurance in Patient Care, bimonthly (February-December), W. H. Kincaid, editor.
Former Name: Association for Health Records (AHR).

ASSOCIATION FOR HEALTH RECORDS
    See: Association for Healthcare Quality

★ 502 ★

ASSOCIATION FOR HOSPITAL MEDICAL
        EDUCATION
1911 Jefferson Davis Highway
Suite 905   (703) 521-1133
Arlington, Virginia 22202   Established 1956

Gloria M. Coleman, Executive Director
The mission of AHME is to support and enhance the
professional activities of persons involved in medical
education in community hospitals through educational
activities, dissemination of information and by presenting the viewpoints of its members in the development of national policies. Membership: 734 (324
individual members; 400 hospital members - directors
of medical education; directors of medical affairs;
directors of continuing medical education; residency
program directors). Finances: Membership: Individual membership, $135; institutional membership (hos-
pital), $400; (latter category allows up to 4 repre-
sentatives under the single $400 cost). Awards:
John C. Leonard Award (for exemplary contributions
in the area of continuing, graduate, and undergraduate medical education in the community hospital).
Meetings: 4 annually, various locations. Publications: AHME Annual Report, annual, Gloria M.
Coleman, editor; AHME News, monthly, Gloria M.
Coleman, editor; resource materials for members.
Affiliations: AHME Regional Councils I, II, III, IV,

V, and VI; member of LCCME; LCGME; NRMP;
ECFMG.

★ 503 ★

ASSOCIATION FOR HUMANISTIC PSYCHOLOGY
325 9th Street   (415) 625-2375
San Francisco, California 94103   Established 1962

Elizabeth Campbell, Executive Officer
The Association for Humanistic Psychology is a world
wide network for the development of the human sciences in ways which recognize their distinctively human qualities, and which work toward fulfilling their
innate capacities as individuals and as members of
society. AHP exists to link, for support and stimulation, people who have a humanistic vision of the
person; to encourage others to share this view; and
to show how this vision can be realized in the life
and work of all. Membership in AHP is open to
anyone who shares these values and wishes to support
their efforts. Membership: 6,600 (educators, psychologists, social workers, clergy, physicians, psychiatrists, lay persons). Finances: Membership:
Comprehensive, $40; general, $20; organizational,
$100-$500; sponsoring (life), $600-$1,000; Other
Sources: Annual meetings, regional meetings, publication sales. Meetings: 1 Annual Meeting; 2 Regional Meetings annually; Annual Meeting, various
locations; regional meetings, eastern and midwestern.
Publications: AHP Newsletter, monthly, Carol Guion,
editor; Journal of Humanistic Psychology, quarterly,
Thomas Greening, editor; AHP Resource Directory,
annually (with updates). Affiliations: Humanistic
Psychology Institute.

★ 504 ★

ASSOCIATION FOR POETRY THERAPY
Bussolati Institute   (212) 473-0392
1029 Henhawk Road   (516) 546-2295
Baldwin, New York 11510   Established 1969

Jack J. Leedy, M.D., Executive Director
To apply the principles and techniques of poetry therapy as an added dimension in psychiatry, medicine,
education, and rehabilitation of the physically and
emotionally handicapped. Membership: 120 (certified, regular, student). Finances: Membership:
Certified, $15; regular, $10; student, $5. Meet-
ings: Annual conference, New School for Social Research, New York, New York. Publications: APT
News, annually, Jack J. Leedy, M.D., editor.

★ 505 ★

ASSOCIATION FOR RESEARCH IN GROWTH
    RELATIONSHIPS
University of Rhode Island
Department of Education
Kingston, Rhode Island 02881   Established 1956

Thomas P. Nally, Executive Secretary
The Association provides a means for cooperation in
the achievement of understanding of the dynamics of
life, for promoting research in growth relationships
and for making available results of efforts and findings.
Membership: 85 (research workers). Finances:
Membership: $1 annually. Meetings: Annual with
American Educational Research Association. Publi-
cations: ARGR Journal, November and April, Richard
Clark and Jerry Wohlfred, co-editors.

★ 506 ★

ASSOCIATION FOR RESEARCH IN NERVOUS AND
    MENTAL DISEASE, INC.
Mount Sinai School of Medicine
1 Gustave Levy Place   (212) 348-8133
New York, New York 10029   Established 1920

Dr. Bernard Cohen, Secretary-Treasurer
To encourage, promote, foster and assist investigations and research in nervous and mental disease by
having an annual symposium on related subjects and
publications of these proceedings. Membership:
1,000 (neurologists, psychiatrists, and research-related
professionals). Finances: Membership: $30 annually.
Awards: Annual Award (to oustanding doctor in field
of neurology or psychiatry). Meetings: Annual,
New York, New York. Publications: Proceedings
of the Association for Research in Nervous and Mental
Disease.

★ 507 ★

ASSOCIATION FOR RESEARCH IN VISION AND
    OPHTHALMOLOGY, INC.
c/o Dr. Paul Henkind
Post Office Box C-1002
Wykagyl Station   (914) 635-2154
New Rochelle, New York 10804   Established 1928

Paul Henkind, M.D., Secretary-Treasurer
Encouragement of ophthalmic research for the prevention of blinding eye diseases, improved diagnosis and
therapy, and open discussion and dissemination of this
information. Membership: 2,400 (regular, educational, contributing, life, honorary). Finances:
Membership: Regular, $50; educational, United
States residency only, $35; contributing, $75; life,
$1,000. Awards: Proctor Medal for long continued

research of blinding eye diseases; Friedenwald Award
for research of blinding eye diseases. Meetings:
Annual, various locations. Publications: Investigative Ophthalmology, monthly, Alan Laties, editor.

★ 508 ★

ASSOCIATION FOR RETARDED CITIZENS OF THE
    UNITED STATES
2501 Avenue J   (817) 640-0204
Arlington, Texas 76011   Established 1950

Philip Roos, Executive Director
The promotion of the welfare of mentally retarded
persons of all ages. Seeks to foster the advancement
of research, treatment, services and facilities and to
develop broad understanding of the problems of mental
retardation. Through its national staffs, provides
state and local units and communities with consultation and guidance to improve service service and programs for mentally retarded persons. Activities include the promotion of education for retarded persons,
adequate residential care, recreation and religious
education programs, legal advocacy services and research. Membership: Over 300,000 in 1,900 state
and local units (including parents of retarded children,
professional persons and community leaders). Finances: Member units each pay a proportionate share
based on wealth and population factors. Awards:
Research grants awarded by Research Advisory Committee to individual researchers in membership-estab-
lished priority areas including preventive, behavioral
and biomedical research, analyses of residential alternatives and parent training methods. Meetings:
Annual, various locations. Publications: The Arc,
6 issues annually, Liz Cogburn, editor; Arc Action,
quarterly. Former Name: National Association for
Retarded Citizens.

★ 509 ★

ASSOCIATION FOR THE ADVANCEMENT OF
    BLIND AND RETARDED, INC.
164-09 Hillside Avenue   (212) 523-2222
Jamaica, New York 11432   Established 1956

Martha Rosen, Max Posner, Executive Directors
A non-profit membership association which conducts
day treatment programs, day school for children,
group residences for young adults, and intermediate
care facilities. Finances: Contributions; funds
from New York State Department of Education and
Board of Education. Publications: Journal, annually.

★ 510 ★
ASSOCIATION FOR THE ADVANCEMENT OF
    MEDICAL INSTRUMENTATION
1901 North Fort Myer Drive
Suite 602   (703) 525-4890
Arlington, Virginia 22209   Established 1965

Michael J. Miller, Executive Director
A nonprofit, international organization established
with the objective of improving patient care by furthering advances in medical instruments, devices, and
systems and their use. Membership: 4,500 (individual, associate, institutional, corporate). Finances:
Membership: Individual, $55; institutional, $150;
associate, $25; corporate, based on amount of sales.
Meetings: Annual, various locations. Publications:
Medical Instrumentation, bimonthly, Dwight Harken,
editor; AAMI News, bimonthly, Michael Miller,
editor.

★ 511 ★
ASSOCIATION FOR THE ADVANCEMENT OF
    PSYCHOANALYSIS OF THE KAREN HORNEY
    PSYCHOANALYTIC INSTITUTE AND CENTER
329 East 62nd Street   (212) 752-5267
New York, New York 10021   Established 1941

Mario Rendon, M.D., President;
    Jeffrey Rubin, M.D., Secretary
To foster psychoanalytic training, to encourage re-
search; to further discussion of psychoanalytic sub-
jects; to disseminate information to the field. Mem-
bership: 73. Finances: Membership: $150; Other
Sources: Subscription series. Meetings: Monthly,
New York City; Annual Karen Horney Lecture.
Publications: The American Journal of Psychoanalysis,
quarterly, Helen DeRosis, editor. Library: Muriel
Ivimey Library, 3,500 volumes. Affiliations: Amer-
ican Institute for Psychoanalysis of the Karen Horney
Psychoanalytic Institute and Center.

★ 512 ★
ASSOCIATION FOR THE ADVANCEMENT OF
    PSYCHOTHERAPY
114 East 78th Street   (212) 288-4466
New York, New York 10021   Established 1939

Stanley Lesse, M.D., President
An eclectic psychotherapeutic organization which
serves as a forum for all schools of though. The
Association sponsors future research in the health sciences. Membership: 405 psychiatrists interested in
psychotherapy. Finances: Membership: $50 an-
nually; Other Sources: Journal. Meetings: Annual, various locations. Publications: American

Journal of Psychotherapy.

ASSOCIATION FOR THE CARE OF CHILDREN IN
HOSPITALS
    See: Association for the Care of Children's
    Health

★ 513 ★
ASSOCIATION FOR THE CARE OF CHILDREN'S
    HEALTH
3615 Wisconsin Avenue, N.W.   (202) 244-1801
Washington, D.C. 20016   Established 1965

Beverley Johnson, Executive Director
ACCH seeks to foster and promote the health and
well being of children and families in health care
settings by education, interdisciplinary interaction
and planning and research. Membership: 3,000
(full, student, supporting, lifetime; members include
a variety of disciplines: medicine, nursing, child
life, social work, psychology, recreation, parents).
Finances: Membership (United States): $30; student,
$15; supporting, $50; lifetime, $350; Other
Sources: Conference income, grants. Meetings:
Annual, 4-day educational conference. Publications:
Children's Health Care (Journal), quarterly, Mary
Cerreto, editor; ACCH News (Newsletter), bimonthly, Barbara Steele, editor; Preparing Children and
Families for Health Care Encounters; Child Life Activities: An Overview; Directory of Child Life Pro-
grams in America. Affiliations: 32 regional affiliates (in the United States and Canada) of ACCH mem-
bers. Former Name: Association for the Care of
Children in Hospitals.

★ 514 ★
ASSOCIATION FOR THE PSYCHOPHYSIOLOGICAL
    STUDY OF SLEEP
Henry Ford Hospital
Sleep Disorders and Research Center
2799 West Grand Boulevard
Detroit, Michigan 48202   Established 1964

Thomas Roth, Ph.D., Executive Secretary-Treasurer
To exchange information on research in sleep.
Membership: 500 (psychiatrists, neurologists, psychologists, and physicians interested in the study of sleep
and related fields). Finances: $15; Other Sources:
Publication fee, $68. Meetings: Annual, various
locations.

★ 515 ★

ASSOCIATION FOR VOLUNTARY STERILIZATION
708 Third Avenue   (212) 986-3880
New York, New York 10017   Established 1943

Ira Lubell, M.D., Executive Director
To promote male and female voluntary sterilization on
a national and worldwide basis as an effective means
of contraception, and to make the option of sterilization available to all.   To prevent unwanted concep-
tions and the problems they cause, and to facilitate
stabilization of human population on a level the environment can support.   Membership: 8,000 general,
supporting, sustaining, patron.   Finances: Membership: $15-$500; Other Sources: Private foundation
grants, U.S. Department of State Grant for funding
the AVS International Project.   Research: Grants
for voluntary sterilization services.   Meetings: Annual, spring, New York.   Publications: AVS News,
quarterly, Miriam Ruben, editor; Report Pamphlet,
annual, Betty Gonzales, R.N., editor; IPAVS Newsletter, semiannual, Marilyn Schima, Ed.D., MPH,
editor.   Library: AVS-IPAVS, volumes: 500 and
2,500 reprints.   Affiliations: World Federation of
Associations for Voluntary Sterilization.

★ 516 ★

ASSOCIATION FOR WOMEN VETERINARIANS
c/o Dr. Judith H. Spurling, D.V.M.
2731 West Belleview
Littletown, Colorado 80123   Established 1947

Judith H. Spurling, D.V.M., Secretary
To make women an integral part of veterinary medicine, to make professional women more aware of
themselves as well as others aware of them; to aid
students.   Membership: 500 women veterinarians and
students.   Finances: Membership: Full (veterinarians
only), $25; student (veterinarian students only), $5;
associate (non-veterinarians), $10; Other Sources:
Subscription to Bulletin, $10.   Awards: Grants-in-
aid; Outstanding Woman Veterinary Award.   Meetings: Annual, with the American Veterinary Medical
Association.   Publications: AFWV Bulletin, quarterly, Dr. Ann-si Li, editor.   Former Name: Women's
Veterinary Medical Association.

★ 517 ★

ASSOCIATION OF ACADEMIC HEALTH CENTERS
11 Dupont Circle, Suite 210   (202) 265-9600
Washington, D.C. 20036   Established 1968

John R. Hogness, M.D., President
National health manpower education association with
a primary interest in all aspects of post-secondary
health manpower education and the related research
and service functions.   The Association is both interdisciplinary and multi-professional in its focus.
Membership: 100 (regular membership - available to
academic health centers and statewide university systems in the United States; associate membership -
available to academic health centers outside the
United States; Canadian institutions are eligible for
either category of membership).   Finances: $3,750.
Meetings: Semiannual.   Former Name: Association
for Academic Health Centers.

★ 518 ★

ASSOCIATION OF ACADEMIC PSYCHIATRISTS
9001 West Watertown Plank Road   (414) 259-1414
Milwaukee, Wisconsin 53226   Established 1967

John L. Melvin, M.D., Secretary
To promote the advancement of teaching and research
in physical medicine and rehabilitation within the
area of academic medicine; to act as a sounding
board and forum for the exchange of ideas and information; to promote the dissemination of information
to future physicians who will be practicing this art
and science; to become involved in the exchange of
information from other areas of the field of medicine
both in basic sciences and in the clinical areas of
teaching and research.   Conducts research programs.
Membership: 220 (full-time academic physicians
practicing in the specialty of physical medicine and
rehabilitation and certified by the American Board of
Physical Medicine at the rank of Assistant Professor
or higher).   Publications: Directory, annually;
Newsletter, quarterly.

★ 519 ★

ASSOCIATION OF ALLERGISTS FOR MYCOLOGICAL
      INVESTIGATIONS
444 Hermann Professional Building   (713) 526-8931
Houston, Texas 77030   Established 1938

Warren J. Raymer, President
Air analysis studies to determine distribution and con-
centration of mold-fungi; study of extraction techniques with mold-fungi; clinical evaluation of mold
fungi, in respect to the allergens prepared, and in
relation to air-borne concentrations; additional
phases of research.   Membership: 39 (physicians
practicing 2,250 individuals).   Finances: Membership dues, outside support.   Meetings: Annual, various locations.   Publications: Journal of Medical
Education, monthly; AAMC Directory of American
Medical Education, annual; President's Weekly Activities Report; AAMC Education News, 5 times

annually; Medical School Admission Requirements, annual.

★ 520 ★
ASSOCIATION OF AMERICAN INDIAN PHYSICIANS
6801 South Western, Suite 206   (405) 321-1122
Oklahoma City, Oklahoma 73139   Established 1971

William Wilson, Executive Director
The Association is a professional organization of American Indian and Alaskan Native Physicians. It was founded as a charitable, educational and scientific corporation to provide a forum for the exchange of information between American Indian physicians; recruit American Indian students into the health professions; and provide consultation to governmental and other agencies about American Indian health matters. Membership: 50 licensed allopathic and osteopathic physicians who identify themselves as American Indians and Alaskan Natives. Finances: Membership: General, $25; student, $12.50. Meetings: Annual and bimonthly. Publications: AAIP Newsletter, every 2 to 3 months; Health Careers Handbook, Don Jennings, editor; Brochures and Title IV Film Brochure Billy.

★ 521 ★
ASSOCIATION OF AMERICAN MEDICAL COLLEGES
1 DuPont Circle, N.W., Suite 200
Suite 200   (202) 828-0400
Washington, D.C. 20036   Established 1876

John A. D. Cooper, M.D., President
The Association has as its purpose the advancement of medical education and the nation's health, in pursuit of works with many national and international organizations, institutions, and individuals interested in strengthening the quality of medical education at all levels, the search for biomedical knowledge, and the application of these tools to providing effective health care. As an educational association representative of members having similar purposes, the primary role of the AAMC is to assist those members by providing services at the national level which will facilitate the accomplishment of their mission. Such activities include collecting data and conducting studies on issues of major concern, evaluating the quality of educational programs through the accreditation process, providing consultation and technical assistance to institutions as needs are identified, synthesizing the opinions of an informed membership for consideration at the national level, and improving communication among those concerned with medical education and the nation's health. Membership: 126 medical schools; 408 teaching hospitals; 70 academic socie-

ties; 1,496 individuals. Finances: Membership dues, outside support. Meetings: Annual, various locations. Publications: Journal of Medical Education, monthly; AAMC Directory of American Medical Education, annual; President's Weekly Activities Report, quarterly; Medical School Admission Requirements, annual; AAMC Curriculum Directory, annual; New MCAT Student Manual.

★ 522 ★
ASSOCIATION OF AMERICAN PHYSICIANS
c/o Dr. Charles C. J. Carpenter
University Hospital of Cleveland
2065 Adelbert Road   (216) 444-3245
Cleveland, Ohio 44106   Established 1886

Charles C. J. Carpenter, Secretary
A small society of persons who have distinguished themselves in medical research and education, primarily in the field of internal medicine, the Association holds one meeting a year at which time research is presented. Membership: 820. Finances: Membership: $60 (dues). Awards: Kober Medal; Kober Lectureship. Meetings: Annual, various locations. Publications: Transactions of the Association of American Physicians, annually. Library: 93 volumes.

★ 523 ★
ASSOCIATION OF AMERICAN PHYSICIANS AND
 SURGEONS
8991 Cotswold Drive   (703) 425-6300
Burke, Virginia 22015   Established 1943

Frank K. Woolley, Executive Director
United for the purpose of analyzing our problems and formulating action to improve medical care for all Americans, preserving freedom of choice for patient and doctor, protecting the practice of private medicine, educating physicians and the public to recognize and resist programs that would weaken or destroy our free choice system of medical care. Membership: Doctors of Medicine. Meetings: Annual, various locations. Publications: Newsletter--The Voice for Private Doctors, monthly, F. K. Woolley, editor. Affiliations: Our United Republic Political Action Committee (OURPAC); Physicians and Surgeons Legal Defense Fund; Americans Against Socialized Medicine.

★ 524 ★
ASSOCIATION OF AMERICAN VOLUNTEER
   PHYSICIANS
Post Office Box 107   (313) 329-2257
Marysville, Michigan 48040   Established 1974

Dennis J. Gates, M.D., President
The purpose of this organization is to promote National and International Health through the collective activities of Health Professionals, who have previously served in a voluntary health program in the United States or a foreign country. Membership: 375 annual, life, and associate. Finances: Membership: Annual, $10; life: below age 45, $100; to age 55, $60; to age 65, $40; over age 65, $25. Meetings: Annual, with AMA Convention.

★ 525 ★
ASSOCIATION OF CANADIAN FACULTIES OF
   DENTISTRY
5059 Dentistry Pharmacy Building
Edmonton, Alberta T6G 2H7,   (403) 432-5762
   Canada   Established 1968

Dr. G. W. Myers, Executive Director
The Association acts as the Canadian national voice of dental education. Membership: 10 Canadian faculties of dentistry. Meetings: House of Delegates, annual, various locations; Executive Council, semiannual, various locations; Biennial Conference, various locations.

★ 526 ★
ASSOCIATION OF CANADIAN MEDICAL COLLEGES
151 Slater Street
Ottawa, Ontario K1P 5N1,   (613) 237-0070
   Canada   Established 1943

D. O. W. Waugh, M.D., Ph.D., Executive Director
To advance Canadian medical education; to provide information to prospective medical students and faculty members; to cooperate in the conduct of accreditation programs. Membership: 16. Finances: Membership: Based on school enrollment; Other Sources: Grants. Meetings: Annual, various locations. Publications: Forum, bimonthly, D. O. W. Waugh, M.D., editor. Affiliations: Association of Universities and Colleges of Canada.

★ 527 ★
ASSOCIATION OF CANADIAN MEDICAL COLLEGES:
   SPECIAL RESOURCE COMMITTEE ON INSTRUC-
   TIONAL MEDIA
1-157 Clinical Sciences Building
University of Alberta
Edmonton, Alberta T6G 2G3,   (403) 432-6561
   Canada

Dr. Charles M. Bidwell, Chairman
The Association's purpose is to act as a source of information and to advise and make recommendations to ACMC on matters related to media support for medical education in Canada. It holds information exchange sessions for all interested in the use and management of audiovisual media production and program use in health science teaching. Membership: Representatives and Delegates from the 16 medical colleges in Canada. Finances: Cost of attendance at annual meeting borne by each Dean of Medicine who sends a representative or by other faculty or agency that sends an observer. Meetings: Annually, various locations. Publications: Newsletter, D. A. Gibson, editor, Dalhousie University, Halifax, Nova Scotia, Canada.

★ 528 ★
ASSOCIATION OF CLINICAL SCIENTISTS
University of Connecticut School of Medicine
Department of Laboratory Medicine
263 Farmington Avenue   (203) 674-2328
Farmington, Connecticut 06032   Established 1949

F. William Sunderman, Jr., M.D., Secretary-
   Treasurer; F. William Sunderman, M.D., Ph.D.,
   Director of Education
To promote education and research in clinical science by practical methods; to maintain and improve the accuracy of measurements in clinical laboratories and to promote uniformity in clinical laboratory procedures; to encourage cooperation between physicians and non-physicians groups concerned with the application of scientific methods to medical practice; to support the principles and ethics of the practice of medicine and all of its constituent basic sciences. Membership: 735 (active fellows, emeritus fellows, honorary fellows, corresponding fellows, associate members, and junior members). Finances: Membership: $63; enrollment fee, $15. Awards: Clinical Scientist Award for outstanding contribution to clinical laboratory science. Lectureships: Abraham J. Gitlitz Memorial Lectureship; Claude P. Brown Memorial Lectureship. Meetings: Fall and Spring, various locations. Publications: Annals of Clinical and Laboratory Science, bimonthly, F. William Sunderman, M.D., Ph.D., editor.

★ 529 ★

ASSOCIATION OF CYTOGENETIC TECHNOLOGISTS
University of California
Department of Pediatrics, 677-S   (415) 666-1017
San Francisco, California 94143   Established 1975

Judith Carol Canham
To promote the development of all phases of cytogenetics; to foster the exchange of information among
those interested in cytogenetics; to encourage cooperation among persons actively engaged in cytogenetics; to stimulate an interest in cytogenetics as a
career. Membership: 600 (open to all persons with
an interest in cytogentics); active members (those
residing in the United States, Canada, or Mexico who
are currently employed in cytogenetics); associate
members (those not currently employed in the field);
corresponding members (those residing outside the
United States, Canada, or Mexico); sustaining members (those institutions and individuals having an interest in cytogenetics and wishing to give financial
support to the organization). Finances: Membership:
$20, active and associate members; $25, corresponding members; $250, sustaining members, payable in
United States currency on July first, the beginning of
the fiscal year. Meetings: Annual, first weeking
in June, various locations in the United States;
occasional local meetings. Publications: Karyogram,
6 issues annually, Barbara Kaplan, editor; Act Laboratory Directory, annual, Barbara Kaplan, editor;
Technical Manual: Cytogenetics, new publication
1980, Marilyn Hack, Helen Lawce and Denise
Sihvonen, editors.

★ 530 ★

ASSOCIATION OF FACULTIES OF PHARMACY OF
        CANADA
c/o Dr. J. A. Wood
College of Pharmacy
University of Saskatchewan
Saskatoon, Saskatchewan S7N 0W0,   (306) 343-4779
    Canada   Established 1944

J. A. Wood, Executive Director
The intent of the Association is to promote pharmaceutical education and research; to provide opportunity for interchange of ideas and discussion of curricula
and teaching methods with a view to their continual
improvement; to encourage high and uniform educational standards in pharmacy throughout Canada; and
to make recommendations to the Canadian Pharmaceutical Association or other appropriate bodies regarding
educational policies and the advancement of the science and practice of pharmacy. Membership: 8
(Faculties of Pharmacy; individual membership, 114).
Finances: Membership: Constituent, $1,200; indi-
vidual, $10; affiliate, $25; Other Sources: Cana-

dian Pharmaceutical Association; Canadian Foundation for the Advancement of Pharmacy; The Pharmaceutical Industry. Meetings: Annual with Canadian
Pharmaceutical Association, various locations. Publications: Proceedings of the Association of Faculties
of Pharmacy of Canada, annually. Affiliations:
Canadian Pharmaceutical Association.

★ 531 ★

ASSOCIATION OF FOOD AND DRUG OFFICIALS,
    INC.
Box 3   (401) 277-2833
Barrington, Rhode Island 02806   Established 1896

Promote and offer uniformity of laws affecting foods,
drugs, cosmetics, devices and product safety; encourage and promote enforcement of said laws; encourage and support programs which will contribute to
consumer protection consistent with the broad purposes
of said laws; assist members in their technical work
and development; cooperate with other professional
groups in advancing consumer protection under such
laws; disseminate information concerning food and
drug law enforcement and administration through its
official publications; encourage and promote cooperative enforcement programs between states and related
federal agencies. Membership: 600. Finances:
Membership: Regulatory, $25; associate (industry),
$100 and $200; corresponding, $25. Awards:
Harvey W. Wiley Award. Meetings: Annual, on
rotation basis through 7 regional sections. Publications: Quarterly Bulletin, quarterly, Orlen J.
Weimann, editor; Proceedings Issue, annually, Orlen
J. Weimann, editor; Reprints of Bulletin Articles;
News & Views, bimonthly newsletter; Uniform Laws
and Regulations.

ASSOCIATION OF FRENCH SPEAKING DIABETES
AND METABOLISM SPECIALISTS
    See: French Language Association for Research
        on Diabetes and Metabolic Diseases

★ 532 ★

ASSOCIATION OF LIFE INSURANCE MEDICAL
        DIRECTORS OF AMERICA
4601 Market Street
Post Office Box 7378   (215) 472-5000
Philadelphia, Pennsylvania 19101   Established 1889

Frank T. Mansure, M.D., Secretary
The objective of this association shall be to advance
the science of medicine as applied to insurance.
Membership: 750 (active, emeritus). Finances:

Membership: $55 annually; $25 admission fee.
Meetings: Annually, various locations (President's
Home Office). Publications: The Journal of Insurance Medicine, quarterly, Theodore Plucinski, M.D.,
editor; Transactions, annually, John C. Robinson,
M.D., editor.

★ 533 ★
ASSOCIATION OF MEDICAL ILLUSTRATORS
5820 Wilshire Boulevard, #500   (213) 937-5514
Los Angeles, California 90036   Established 1945

Jean Replogle, Executive Director
A non-profit organization with international membership. The professional objectives of the A.M.I.
are to further the study of medical illustration; to
encourage the advancement of this and other allied
fields of visual education; to advance medical education; and to promote understanding and cooperation
with the medical and related professions. Membership: 525 (active, associate, distinguished, student,
overseas active, overseas associate, honorary, sustaining members). Finances: Membership: Active, $75;
associate, $60; student, $20; overseas, $25; Other
Sources: Contributions. Awards: Special Awards,
at annual meeting for Art Salon Exhibits; Brodell
Memorial Lecture, annual meeting. Meetings: Annual, first week in October, various locations. Publications: Medical Illustration (general information
brochure); Journal of Biocommunication, quarterly;
AMI Newsletter, bimonthly.

★ 534 ★
ASSOCIATION OF MEDICAL REHABILITATION
    DIRECTORS AND COORDINATORS
3830 Linklea Drive   (713) 665-4253
Houston, Texas 77025   Established 1953

Paul Heft, Executive Director
To promote and advance the professional growth of
directors of rehabilitation centers; to improve the
treatment of patients, and to advance the status of
its members. Membership: Approximately 554 (certified, active, elected, honorary). Finances: Membership: Certified, $30; active, $30; elected, $15.
Awards: A.B.C. Knudson Rehabilitation Award to a
public figure who has advanced rehabilitation work;
Academic, Professional Achievement Awards; life
membership. Meetings: Annual, various locations.
Publications: Bulletin, quarterly, Frank Deyoe, editor; Annual Membership Directory; Annual Report.
Affiliations: National Rehabilitation Association;
American Congress of Rehabilitation Medicine; International Association of Rehabilitation Facilities;
American Association for Rehabilitation Therapy.

★ 535 ★
ASSOCIATION OF MEDICAL SCHOOL PEDIATRIC
    DEPARTMENT CHAIRMEN
c/o Jean A. Cortner, M.D.
Children's Hospital of Philadelphia
34th and Civic Center Boulevard   (215) 596-9186
Philadelphia, Pennsylvania 19104   Established 1960

Jean A. Cortner, M.D., Secretary-Treasurer
To organize department chairmen to improve communications for better child health care; for purposes of
postgraduate education among pediatricians; for better
relations for the recruitment of house staff. Membership: 142 (pediatric department chairmen). Finances: Membership: $100 annually. Meetings:
Annual, various locations.

★ 536 ★
ASSOCIATION OF MENTAL HEALTH
    ADMINISTRATORS
425 13th Street, N.W.
Suite 1230   (202) 638-6662
Washington, D.C. 20004   Established 1959

John P. Sullivan, President
The AMHA is a group organized to promote peer relationships and to achieve the highest level of professional management skill through the attainment of
proficiency in the promotion and advancement of the
latest technology in principles, guidelines and standards for the practice of modern management. Membership: 1,100 individual members; 100 agency members. Finances: Membership: Active, fellow, $75;
associate, $30; student, $20; agency, $100-$450
based on budget of agency or number of individual
memberships covered. Meetings: Annual Meeting,
various locations annually; regional meetings, 5-7
annually, various locations. Publications: Journal
of Mental Health Administration, semiannual; AMHA
Newsletter, monthly, Priscilla A. Smith, editor.
Affiliations: Liaison relationships with the National
Associations in the Health Care field, particularly
those dealing with MH/MR/DD Alcohol and Substance
abuse.

★ 537 ★
ASSOCIATION OF MENTAL HEALTH CLERGY, INC.
1700 18th Street, N.W.   (202) 797-4900
Washington, D.C. 20009   Established 1948

Chaplain George E. Doebler, Executive Director
The Association of Mental Health Clergy was founded
as an organization of pastors, priests and rabbis "who
minister to the religious needs of mental patients."
Membership: Approximately 600 (in United States and

Canada; associate, member, certified, retired).
Finances: Membership: Associate, $25; member,
$45; certified, $75; retired, $15; Other Sources:
Initial certification fees. Awards: Anton T. Boisen
Award. Meetings: Annual Meetings, held concur-
rently with the Annual Meetings of the American Psychiatric Association. Publications: AMHC Newsletter, quarterly, George E. Doebler, editor; AMHC
Forum, triannual. Affiliations: Council on Ministry
in Specialized Settings; Joint Council on Research
in Pastoral Care and Counseling.

★ 538 ★

ASSOCIATION OF MILITARY SURGEONS OF THE
        UNITED STATES
Post Office Box 104
10605 Concord Street, Suite 306   (301) 933-2801
Kensington, Maryland 20795   Established 1891

Walter Welham, RADM, MC USN Ret.
Devoted to the advancement of all phases of federal
medicine and medicine in general, including allied
sciences related to the federal service.   Sponsors insurance plans for members including term life and ac-
cidental death and dismemberment. Membership:
10,000 (composed of those who are or who ever have
been commissioned officers--regular, reserve, National
Guard, AUS--of the constituent services; those duly
appointed full-time members of the professional medical staffs of the Army, Navy, Air Force, USPHS and
the VA; officers of the medical services of other
countries; those who are, or who ever have been,
consultants to the Chiefs of the Federal Medical Services.   The Association has sections that include
physicians, dentists, veterinarians, pharmacists, nurses,
physical therapists, occupational therapists, dieticians,
optometrists, podiatrists, and administrators of the constituent services). Finances: Membership: Annual
dues, $20. Awards: John Shaw Billings Award;
Joel T. Boone Award; Ray E. Brown Award; Andrew
Craigie Award; Richard A. Kern Lecture Award;
Federal Nursing Service Award; Founders Medal;
Gorgas Medal; Philip Hench Award; William C.
Porter Lecture; Major Louis Livingston Seaman Prize;
Edward R. Stitt Lecture Award; Sustaining Member-
ship Lecture Award; Sir Henry Wellcome Medal and
Prize; Paul Dudley White Award. Meetings: An-
nual, various locations. Publications: Military
Medicine, monthly, Col. Ernest A. Brav, USA, Ret.,
editor.

★ 539 ★

ASSOCIATION OF NATIONAL, EUROPEAN AND
      MEDITERRANEAN SOCIETIES OF GASTRO-
      ENTEROLOGY
c/o Dr. L. O. Standaert
222 Lange Lozanastraat
B 2000 Antwerp, Belgium   Established 1947

Dr. L. O. Standaert, Secretary-General
To promote the knowledge of the basic sciences and
clinical medicine in the field of gastroenterology.
Membership: 31 (European and Mediterranean Societies of Gastro-Enterology). Finances: Membership:
$100 for a 4 year period. Awards: George Brohee
Award, $1,000, biennially. Meetings: Congress,
every 4 years, European or Mediterranean countries.
Publications: Proceedings of the meeting published
by the secretary of the Congress. Affiliations:
European and Mediterranean Societies of Gastroenterology.

★ 540 ★

ASSOCIATION OF OFFICIAL ANALYTICAL
      CHEMISTS
1111 North 19th Street   (703) 522-3032
Arlington, Virginia 22209   Established 1884

David B. MacLean, Executive Director
The AOAC obtains, develops, tests and adopts uniform precise and accurate methods for the analysis of
foods, feeds, drugs, agricultural products, pesticides,
cosmetics, fertilizers, air, water, and other products
affecting public health and safety. Meetings: Annual Convention, October, Washington, D.C. Publications: Journal, bimonthly; Official Methods of
Analysis of the AOAC and other reference works.

★ 541 ★

ASSOCIATION OF OPERATING ROOM NURSES
10170 East Mississippi Avenue   (303) 755-6300
Denver, Colorado 80231   Established 1949

Jerry G. Peers, R.N., Executive Director
To improve standards of operating room nursing care.
Membership: 30,000 (active and associate composed
of registered professional operating room nurses).
Finances: Membership: $35; Other Sources: Annual
conference registration fees, sale of exhibit space at
Congress, advertising in official journal. Meetings:
Annual National Congress, various locations; local
chapter meetings, monthly seminars and institutes.
Publications: AORN Journal, monthly, Elinor
Schrader, editor. Affiliations: 296 local AORN
chapters, other professional and health care societies.

ASSOCIATION OF OPERATING ROOM
TECHNICIANS
See: Association of Surgical Technologists, Inc.

★ 542 ★
ASSOCIATION OF ORTHOPAEDIC CHAIRMEN
University of California Medical Center
San Francisco, California 94143   Established 1971

Dr. Donald Kettelkamp, President
To provide a forum for discussion of problems related
to undergraduate and graduate orthopaedics in medical schools; to provide a mechanism of coordination
and planning activities requiring cooperation between
orthopaedic departments and/or orthopaedic residencies; to serve as an active liaison unit between the
specialty of orthopaedics and those organizations interested in medical education. Membership: Chairmen
of Departments of Orthopaedics and/or Directors of
AMA approved orthopaedic residency programs. Finances: Membership: $100. Meetings: Annual in
conjunction with Association of American Medical
Colleges.

★ 543 ★
ASSOCIATION OF PATHOLOGY CHAIRMEN, INC.
University of Vermont College of Medicine
Department of Pathology   (802) 656-2210
Burlington, Vermont 05405   Established 1967

John E. Criaghead, M.D., Secretary-Treasurer
Organized for chairmen of medical school departments
of pathology to better communicate and interact for
the benefit of improved education, administration,
research, and funding. Membership: 135 (chairmen
of accredited United States medical school departments
of pathology). Finances: Membership: $200 per
department. Meetings: Spring and fall, in association with other major medical meetings; subject to
change. Publications: APC Newsletter, quarterly,
Secretary-Treasurer. Remarks: The Secretary-
Treasurer of the APC is elected for a 3-year term;
his office functions as the office of the organization;
other officers serve for 1-year terms.

★ 544 ★
ASSOCIATION OF PEDIATRIC ONCOLOGY NURSES
    (APON)
c/o Andi Wood, R.N.
St. Jude's Children's Research Hospital
Post Office Box 318   (901) 525-8381
Memphis, Tennessee 38101   Established 1974

Mrs. Ann Pryor, President; Mary Jo Cleaveland,
    Vice President; Debra S. Gaddy, Corresponding
    Secretary; Andi Wood, Treasurer
The group recognized and responded to the need for
an organization that would address the issues and
problems associated with caring for children with cancer. The purpose is to improve the care of children
with cancer and this is carried out by means of public
discussion groups, forums, panels, lectures, publications
and similar programs. Membership: 250 (nurses
working with pediatric oncology patients or interested
in their care; this includes staff nurses, clinical
specialists, educators, and administrators). Finances:
Membership: Full membership, $25 annually; Other
Sources: Newsletter subscription, $15 annually.
Meetings: Annual, September or October, various
locations; an intermediate educational meeting is
held each spring, various locations. Publications:
APON Newsletter, quarterly, Dianne Fochtman, editor; Cancer Chemotherapy Concepts: Theoretical
Concepts and Nursing Implications (handbook); Stand-
ards of Pediatric Oncology Practice (pamphlet); A
Pediatric Oncology Nursing Textbook (in preparation).

★ 545 ★
ASSOCIATION OF PHYSICIAN ASSISTANT
    PROGRAMS
2341 Jefferson Davis Highway
Suite 700   (703) 920-5730
Arlington, Virginia 22202   Established 1972

Donald W. Fisher, Ph.D., Executive Director
To serve as a forum for physician assistant training
program personnel; to provide a vehicle to represent
physician assistant programs in relating to other professional organizations, federal and state governments,
and the public. Membership: 49 programs training
the assistant to the Primary Care Physician. Finances: Membership: $500. Meetings: Annual and
Midyear Meetings. Publications: National Health
Practitioner Program Profile, annual, James Hughes,
editor; Annotated Bibliography, Susan Anderson, editor. Affiliations: American Academy of Physicians'
Assistants; National Commission on Certification of
Physician Assistants.

★ 546 ★
ASSOCIATION OF PODIATRISTS IN FEDERAL
    SERVICE
c/o LTC D. W. Hunt Qtrs 2382   (206) 964-5020
Fort Lewis, Washington 98433 Established 1961

D. W. Hunt DPM LTC MSC, Executive Secretary
Licensed podiatrists on active duty with the United
States Armed Forces or serving as United States

government employees in the Public Health Service or the Veterans Administration. Encourages research and study in an effort to advance the practice of podiatry and the field of public health in general. Membership: 170 (Army, 56; Navy 14; Air Force, 35; Veterans Administration, 48; Public Health Service, 16). Finances: Membership: Component dues, $25 annually. Meetings: Annual, in conjunction with the Annual meeting of the American Podiatry Association. Publications: Newsletter, 4-5 annually; Dr. Robert Blake, editor.

★ 547 ★
ASSOCIATION OF PROFESSIONAL BASEBALL
    PHYSICIANS
c/o Dr. Paul Jacobs
1218 West Kilbourn   (414) 276-6000
Milwaukee, Wisconsin 53233

Dr. Paul A. Jacobs, President;
    Dr. Stan London, President Elect
Care and prevention of professional baseball players. Interested in all aspects of health and safety of these athletes. Primarily directed to major league baseball. Membership: 30-40. Finances: Membership: Assessment.

★ 548 ★
ASSOCIATION OF PROFESSORS OF MEDICINE
1 DuPont Circle N.W., #250   (202) 828-0482
Washington, D.C. 20036   Established 1954

To meet at least once a year to keep members current with problems that are common to Departments of Medicine. Membership: 124 (department chairmen). Finances: Membership: $420. Awards: Annual to Department Chairman for unusual contribution in the administration of education research and patient care. Meetings: Semiannual, rotating.

ASSOCIATION OF REHABILITATION FACILITIES
    See: National Association of Rehabilitation
        Facilities

★ 549 ★
ASSOCIATION OF REHABILITATION NURSES
2506 Gross Point Road   (312) 475-7530
Evanston, Illinois 60201   Established 1974

Dagny N. Engle, R.N., Executive Vice President
To advance the quality of rehabilitation nursing service throughout the community by offering educational opportunities, to promote an awareness and interest in rehabilitation nursing and improve the expertise of personnel on all levels and by facilitating the exchange of ideas in rehabilitation programs. Membership: 1,700 (regular membership in ARN is open to registered nurses concerned with or engaged in the active practice of rehabilitation nursing). Finances: Membership: $40 annually; Other Sources: Annual Meeting and Regional Seminars; Rehabilitation Nursing Journal; sale of bibliography and standards. Meetings: Annual Meeting, late fall, various locations; 7 regional seminars, biennially. Publications: Rehabilitation Nursing, bimonthly, Barbara A. McHugh, editor; Standards of Rehabilitation Nursing Practice; Rehabilitation Nursing and Related Readings: A Bibliography; Core Curriculum of Rehabilitation Nursing (in progress). Affiliations: Member of the Federation of Specialty Nursing Organizations; ANA.

★ 550 ★
ASSOCIATION OF SCHOOLS AND COLLEGES OF
    OPTOMETRY
1730 M Street, N.W., Suite 210   (202) 833-3374
Washington, D.C. 20036   Established 1946

Lee W. Smith, M.P.H., Executive Director
The Association represents the professional programs of optometric education in the United States and Canada to the public and the health community. In addition, it maintains cognizance over policies and programs affecting optometric education and provides counsel and comment to the legislative and executive branches of government. The Association maintains three standing councils in the areas of Academic Affairs, Institutional Affairs and Student Affairs which play a major role in the development of new schools of optometry and the establishment of curriculum and clinical program models. Membership: 18 institutions (13 active institutions; 2 provisional; 3 affiliate). Finances: Membership: Active, $6,500; provisional, $3,000; affiliate, $500; individual, $20; sectional, $100; Other Sources: Federal and private contracts and grants. Awards: 1979 "Best Issue Runner Up", Journal of Optometric Education, Optometric Editors Association; 1980 "Best National Optometric Journal", Journal of Optometric Education, Optometric Editors Association. Meetings: Annual, Washington, D.C., and various locations. Publications: Journal of Optometric Education, quarterly, Harriet E. Long, editor; Information for Applicants to Schools and Colleges of Optometry, annual; Optometry College Admission Test Announcement, annual. Remarks: Students interested in pursuing the doctor of optometry (O.D.) degree are directed to request the booklet, "Information for Applicants to Schools and Colleges of Optometry,"

available free of charge.

★ 551 ★
ASSOCIATION OF SCHOOLS OF PUBLIC HEALTH
1500 Wilson Boulevard, Suite 807 (703) 525-0334
Arlington, Virginia 22209 Established 1941

Michael K. Gemmell, Executive Director
To promote and improve education of professional
public health personnel. Activities include examination of criteria for degrees in public health; examination in depth of specific areas of public health
training; data collection among the schools of public
health profiling applicants, students, graduate; information channeling service to federal and private
agencies, potential students and among the schools
themselves. Support and facilitate the advancement
of public health education as a part of a major effort
to assist in meeting national goals in disease prevention and health promotion and maintenance. Membership: 21 members plus 1 affiliate non United States
member; (active members are limited to those schools
which are accredited by the appropriate national accrediting agency; associate members are those schools
which have the necessary resources and are working
toward becoming accredited; affiliates have special
interests in common with ASPH). Finances: Membership: ASPH receives its revenues from membership
dues from the institutional members as well as from
several contracts and projects. Meetings: Semiannual, various locations.

★ 552 ★
ASSOCIATION OF STATE AND TERRITORIAL
DENTAL DIRECTORS
c/o Charles E. Zumbrunnen
Bureau of Dental Health
New Hampshire Department of P. H. Services,
Health and Welfare Building
Hazen Drive
Concord, New Hampshire 03301

Naseeb L. Shory, President;
Charles E. Zumbrunnen, Secretary-Treasurer
To consider policies or recommendations of agencies,
public or private, pertaining to dental health which
may affect the administration of the dental health
programs of the department of health of states, territories, or possessions of the United States, especially
in its interstate or federal relationships, and to adopt
policies of the Association for guidance of its members. Membership: 56 (chief public health dental
official in each state and territorial health department, or equivalent). Finances: Membership: $10.
Meetings: Annual, various locations. Affiliations:

Association of State and Territorial Health Officials;
American Dental Association.

★ 553 ★
ASSOCIATION OF STATE AND TERRITORIAL
HEALTH OFFICIALS
1015 15th Street, N.W.
Suite 404 (202) 789-1044
Washington, D.C. 20005

George K. Degnon, CAE, Executive Director
The purpose of this Association is to consider any
policy of any agency, public or private, pertaining
to human health which may affect the administration
of the department of health of any State, Territory
or possession of the United States, especially in its
interstate of Federal relationships, and to adopt policies of the Association for the guidance of its members. Membership: 57 (health official of all states
and territories).

★ 554 ★
ASSOCIATION OF STATE AND TERRITORIAL
MATERNAL AND CHILD HEALTH AND CRIPPLED
CHILDREN'S DIRECTORS
301 Centennial Mall South
Post Office Box 95007 (402) 471-2907
Lincoln, Nebraska 68509 Established 1944

Robert S. Grant, M.D., Secretary-Treasurer
To provide for an association of persons directly responsible for the administration of State and Territorial
Maternal and Child Health and Crippled Children's
programs directed towards the improvement of maternal
health and health of children including crippled children. Membership: Approximately 140 (full members,
associate, honorary); MCH and CC Directors. Finances: Membership: Annual, full membership, $20;
associate, $10. Meetings: Annual, various loca-
tions. Affiliations: Association of State and Territorial Health Officers.

★ 555 ★
ASSOCIATION OF STATE AND TERRITORIAL PUBLIC
HEALTH NUTRITION DIRECTORS
c/o H. Lee Fleshood, Ph.D.
R. S. Gass State Building
Ben Allen Road (615) 741-7218
Nashville, Tennessee 37216 Established 1940

The Association's purpose is to serve as a channel
through which directors of public health nutrition programs of states, territories, commonwealths, districts,

and possessions of the United States may exchange and share methods, techniques, and information for the enrichment and improvement of public health nutrition programs. Membership: 52 (directors of public health nutrition programs in states, districts, and territories). Finances: Membership: $20 annually. Meetings: Annual. Publications: Newsletter of the Association of Public Health Nutrition Directors, 3 to 4 times annually, Joyce Kline, Ph.D., editor. Affiliations: Association of State and Territorial Health Officials.

★ 556 ★

ASSOCIATION OF SURGICAL TECHNOLOGISTS, INC.
Caller No. E   (303) 987-9010
Littleton, Colorado 80120   Established 1969

Mark C. Liebig, Ph.D., Executive Director
To improve through certification, accreditation, and continuing education, the preparation of surgical technologists so that high professional standards are met and encouraged by those involved in total patient care. Membership: Approximately 13,000 (students, surgical technologists, certified surgical technologists). Finances: Membership: Dues, $35; local chapter dues, $3-$15. Meetings: Annual conference, various locations. Publications: The Surgical Technologist, bimonthly, William Teutsch, editor; AST News, bimonthly, William Teutsch, editor; The Administrator, bimonthly, William Teutsch, editor. Affiliations: American Medical Association; American College of Surgeons; American Hospital Association; Committee on Allied Health, Education and Accreditation (CAHEA). Former Name: Association of Operating Room Technicians.

★ 557 ★

ASSOCIATION OF TEACHERS OF MATERNAL AND CHILD HEALTH
c/o Albert Chang, M.D., M.P.H.
School of Public Health
Room 36070   (213) 825-9481
Los Angeles, California 90024

C. Arden Miller, M.D., President;
    Roy Smith, M.D., M.P.H., Vice President;
    Albert Chang, M.D., M.P.H., Secretary-Treasurer
To promote educational and research activities in the field of maternal and child health. Membership: 50 (individual). Finances: Membership: $20 annually. Meetings: Semiannual; Fall, with the American Public Health Association; Spring, with Directors of Maternal and Child Health and Crippled Children's Services, various locations.

★ 558 ★

ASSOCIATION OF TEACHERS OF PREVENTIVE MEDICINE
c/o Peter L. Andrus, M.D.
Baylor College of Medicine
Texas Medical Center   (713) 790-4906
Houston, Texas 77030   Established 1954

Peter L. Andrus, M.D., M.B.A., Secretary-Treasurer
The intent of the Association is to promote the development of instructional and scientific skills and knowledge in the field of preventive and community medicine. Membership: 600. Finances: Membership: Regular, $35; sustaining, $50; institutional, $200; associate, $10. Meetings: Annual, with the American Public Health Association. Publications: Journal of Community Health, quarterly, R. L. Kane, M.D., editor; ATPM Newsletter, quarterly, William H. Barker, M.D., editor; monographs.

★ 559 ★

ASSOCIATION OF UNIVERSITY ANESTHETISTS
c/o Milton H. Alper, M.D.,
Children's Hospital Medical Center
Department of Anesthesiology
300 Longwood Avenue   (617) 734-4440
Boston, Massachusetts 02115   Established 1953

Milton H. Alper, M.D., Secretary
To advance the art and science of anesthesia; to encourage members to pursue original investigations in the clinic and in the laboratory; to develop methods of teaching anesthesia; to encourage interchange of ideas among the members. Membership: 250 (full time faculty in university-affiliated anesthesia departments). Meetings: Annual, various locations.

★ 560 ★

ASSOCIATION OF UNIVERSITY PROGRAMS IN HEALTH ADMINISTRATION (AUPHA)
1 DuPont Circle, Suite 420   (202) 659-4354
Washington, D.C. 20036   Established 1948

Gary L. Filerman, Ph.D., President
An international consortium of university-based programs offering graduate and undergraduate education in health services administration and hospital administration. It undertakes research projects and educational programs to improve the quality of health services administration education. Membership: Institutional, 148; personal, 300 (full member-graduate, associate member-graduate, full member-undergraduate, associate member-undergraduate, affiliate graduate, affiliate undergraduate, international affiliate).

Finances: Membership: $40-$660, annually; Other Sources: Foundation grants and federal grants and contracts. Awards: Significant Contribution Award. Meetings: Annual, various locations. Publications: Program Notes, 8 times annually, Gary L. Filerman, Ph.D., editor; Staff Report, monthly, Barbara Sheppard, editor; International Directory of Graduate and Undergraduate Programs and Centers for Advanced Study in Health Administration, annual; Health Services Administration Education, biennial; Health Services Administration (flyer), annual; AUPHA Publications List, annual. Library: Resource Center for Health Services Administration Education, 2,000 volumes (visitors must make appointment with coordinator, lending via interlibrary loan, charge for photocopying).

★ 561 ★
ASSOCIATION OF UNIVERSITY RADIOLOGISTS
20 North Wacker Drive, Suite 2920 (312) 236-4963
Chicago, Illinois 60606   Established 1952

Sheila A. Aubin, Executive Secretary
To encourage academic careers, excellence in teaching and research, and to represent academic radiologists on a national level. Membership: 850 (active and emeritus). Finances: Membership: $55 annually. Awards: Memorial Medal and $1,000 for best scientific paper by a resident in radiology. Meetings: Annual, various locations. Publications: Investigative Radiology, monthly, Richard H. Greenspan, M.D., editor.

★ 562 ★
ASSOCIATION OF VISUAL SCIENCE LIBRARIANS
c/o Nancy Gatlin
Southern College of Optometry
1245 Madison Avenue   (901) 725-0180
Memphis, Tennessee 38104 Established 1968

Nancy Gatlin, Librarian
Foster development of the individual libraries of members and cooperation among them; develop mechanisms of controlling and making available vision information; develop services for individuals having frequent vision information needs; secure financial assistance for accomplishing goals; develop standards for optometry school library services; recruit, train, and help young visual science librarians. Membership: 40 (librarians associated with visual science libraries). Meetings: Annual with American Academy of Optometry, various locations.

★ 563 ★
ASSOCIATION OF WESTERN HOSPITALS
830 Market Street   (415) 421-8810
San Francisco, California 94102 Established 1927

Kathryn E. Johnson, Executive Vice President
The Association of Western Hospitals is a non-profit educational organization dedicated to the improvement of health care delivery in the 13 western states. AWH provides a broad program of continuing education for a wide range of health care professionals. Membership: 2,000 (institutional and personal members). Finances: Membership: Personal dues, $20; institutional dues, $75-$375, based on hospital bed size; Other Sources: Membership, convention, educational programs. Awards: The organization has as a separate entity the Association of Western Hospitals Educational and Research Foundation which gives grants to hospital consortia for educational purposes. Meetings: Meeting, annual, with rotation between Anaheim and San Francisco, California. Publications: Hospital Forum, 7 times annually, Susan Anthony, editor; Monthly Report, monthly, Gladys Horiuchi, editor; Foundation News, 3 times annually, Robert Stein, editor.

★ 564 ★
ASSOCIATION TO ADVANCE ETHICAL HYPNOSIS
60 Vose Avenue   (201) 762-3132
South Orange, New Jersey 07079 Established 1956

Harry Arons, Consultant
The objectives of this organization are to promote a better understanding of hypnosis among the public; to promote scientific research in hypnosis and the interchange of knowledge among those practicing it; to establish a Code of Ethics in the practice of hypnosis; and to expose and discourage malpractice in hypnosis. Membership: 1,500. Finances: Membership: Certified, $40; regular, $30. Meetings: Annual convention, various locations. Publications: Suggestion Bulletin, bimonthly, Martin M. Segall, editor.

★ 565 ★
ASTHMA AND ALLERGY FOUNDATION OF
    AMERICA
19 West 44th Street   (212) 921-9100
New York, New York 10036

Rita Kasky, Executive Director;
    Sheldon C. Siegel, M.D., President
The Asthma and Allergy Foundation of America is a non-profit membership organization which mission is to bring together people concerned about asthma and

allergy, mothers and fathers, doctors and other health professionals, and the 38,000,000 allergy sufferers themselves, so they may better deal with the problems of allergic diseases; to bridge the information gap that causes harmful misunderstanding between those who suffer from asthma and allergies and those with whom they come in contact, family members, friends, teachers, fellow workers, employers, public officials and the general public; to provide fellowships to encourage more young doctors to become allergists; to encourage increased research into methods of treatment, prevention and cure of allergic diseases. Membership: 1,500 (individuals). Finances: Membership: $10 minimum; Other Sources: Donations from corporations, foundations, individuals. Awards: Fellowships and Fellowship Support Grants. Publications: Hay Fever; Handbook for the Asthmatic; Allergy in Children; Skin Allergy; Insect Stings; Mold Allergy; Food Allergy; Drug Allergy; Tips for Teachers; Questions and Answers About Asthma and Allergic Diseases; In Touch (newsletter), quarterly; Membership Brochure. Affiliations: 14 chapters in the United States. Former Name: Allergy Foundation of America.

★ 566 ★
ATLANTIC CEREBRAL PALSY ASSOCIATION, INC.
24 Bristol Street
Fredericton, New Brunswick   (506) 454-2804
 E3B 4W3, Canada   Established 1972

Harold J. Pollock, President
The Association is made up of voted members from the five local associations in the Atlantic Provinces, Prince Edward Island, New Brunswick, and Nova Scotia. The purpose is to have a strong voice with government or agencies. Finances: Membership: Member, $2; association, $25; Other Sources: Fund raising letters and sundry means of raising funds on the local level. Meetings: Quarterly, various locations. Affiliations: Canadian Cerebral Palsy Association.

★ 567 ★
AUSTRALIAN FREEDOM FROM HUNGER CAMPAIGN
Post Office Box 395
Camberra City, A.C.T.,   (062) 480555
 Australia   Established 1961

W. J. Hobbin, National Director;
 G. Hogan, National President
The agency was established as a response to the world wide "campaign" against hunger promoted by the United Nations Food and Agriculture organization. Its aims are (1) to raise awareness of the Australian

public to the problems of hunger, malnutrition, and poverty, and to develop an understanding of the more complex issues and underlying causes behind these problems; and (2) to raise funds and otherwise support activities to meet these problems in the Third World and, if necessary, at home. Publications: Action for Development; brochures and educational booklets. Library: Ideas Centre, several thousand pamphlets and journals.

★ 568 ★
AUXILIARY TO THE AMERICAN PHARMACEUTICAL
 ASSOCIATION, INC.
520 Truett Drive   (904) 385-4425
Tallahassee, Florida 32303   Established 1936

Hinton F. Bevis (Betty), President
The Auxiliary has been established (1) to promote sociability and create good will among its members; (2) to assist the American Pharmaceutical Association in its endeavors; and (3) to maintain a Student Loan Fund for needy and deserving junior and senior pharmacy students and to spouses of paid members of nationally affiliated Pharmacy Student Auxiliary Clubs during their last two years of professional pharmacy training. Membership: 200 excluding student members (life, 120; regular (active), 80; student (unknown at this date)). Finances: Membership: Life, $100 annually; active membership, $10 annually; student, $1 annually; Other Sources: Donations to Student Loan Fund, usually through memorials. Research Funds: Student Loan Fund (The Irene Parks Student Loan Fund); Achievement certificates to local and state auxiliaries. Meetings: Annually, in conjunction with the American Pharmaceutical Association. Publications: Auxiliary Newsletter, semiannual, Hinton F. Bevis, editor. Affiliations: A non-profit organization, a separate entity but gets membership from American Pharmaceutical Association rolls (active).

B

★ 569 ★
BALKAN MEDICAL UNION
Strada Gabriel Peri 1   16.78.46
R-70148 Bucharest, Romania   Established 1932

M. Popescu Buzeu, Secretary-General
To study problems of morbidity and prophylactic and curative methods; to promote reciprocal understanding among the doctors of the region. Membership: National sections in 7 countries; individual doctors in

area. Finances: Dues, grants. Meetings: Congress, biennially, various locations. Publications: Archives de l'Union Medicale Balkanique, bimonthly; Bulletin, bimonthly; Annual Report.

★ 570 ★
BARREN FOUNDATION
6 East Monroe Street   (312) 346-4038
Chicago, Illinois 60603   Established 1959

Rosella Shapiro, Chairman
Philanthropic organization supporting education and some research in the field of reproductive endocrinology. Sponsors lay and medical seminars in the field, a postgraduate course for physicians, and Childless Couples Public Information Center. Finances: Membership: $10-$100; Other Sources: Contributions, events. Awards: Barren Medal for outstanding research; Dr. M. Edward Davis Fund. Lectures: The State of Art Lecture by Barren Medal recipient. Meetings: Bimonthly, Chicago, Illinois; Annual Symposia. Publications: Brochures.

★ 571 ★
BAY AREA PHYSICIANS FOR HUMAN RIGHTS
Post Office Box 14546   (415) 673-3189
San Francisco, California 94114   Established 1977

Dale McGhee, M.D., President;
   Robert Bolan, M.D., Secretary
Physicians and medical students, both men and women, in all specialties of medicine. Objectives are to improve the quality of medical care for gay men and lesbians; to educate physicians, both gay and non-gay, in the special problems of gay patients; to educate the public about health care needs of homosexuals; to maintain liaison with public officials about gay health concerns; to offer the gay physician support through social functions and consciousness-raising groups. Sponsors research into medical problems of special interest to homosexual patients; provides speakers bureau, physician referral service, and educational programs at monthly meetings; compiles statistics. BAPHR is serving as the national coordinating organization for other regional associations of gay physicians until a national umbrella group is formed. Membership: 300. Finances: Membership: Voting member, physician: $50; non-voting patron: $50; intern, resident (voting member): $20; medical student (voting member): $5; retired physician (voting member): $5; Other Sources: Fund-raising events. Meetings: Monthly general meeting either in private home or San Francisco Medical Society Building; monthly executive board meeting, private homes. Publications: BAPHRON, monthly, Dennis McShane,

M.D., editor.

★ 572 ★
BEHAVIOR GENETICS ASSOCIATION
University of Iowa
Department of Zoology   (319) 353-4462
Iowa City, Iowa 52242   Established 1970

J. P. Hegmann, Secretary
The Association aims to promote the scientific study of the interrelationship of genetic mechanisms and human and animal behavior through sponsorship of scientific meetings, publications, and communications among and by members of the association; to encourage and aid the education and training of research workers in the field of behavior genetics; and to aid in dissemination and interpretation to the general public, of knowledge concerning the interrelationship of genetics and behavior, and its implications for health, human development, and educations. Membership: 300 (regular and student members). Finances: Membership: Regular, $18; student, $10. Publications: Behavior Genetics, quarterly, Jan Bruell, executive editor.

★ 573 ★
BEHAVIOR THERAPY AND RESEARCH SOCIETY
c/o Journal of Behavior Therapy and Experimental
     Psychiatry
Temple University Medical School
Eastern Pennsylvania Psychiatric Institute
Henry Avenue   (215) 849-0607
Philadelphia, Pennsylvania 19129 Established 1970

Pearl Epstein, Administrative Secretary
Clinical and clinical research fellows united to promote basic research which is relevant to the theory and practice of behavior therapy, to stimulate the exchange of information concerning such research, to encourage the application and teaching of the results of such research to the treatment of emotional and other behavioral problems. Advises professionals and agencies seeking behavioral therapy service. Membership: 200-250 clinical and clinical research fellows. Finances: Membership: $15 annually; enrollment fee, $10. Meetings: Annual symposium in conjunction with the American Psychiatric Association, various locations. Publications: Journal of Behavior Therapy and Experimental Psychiatry, quarterly, Joseph Wolpe, M.D., editor; Roster of Clinical Fellows, Behavior Therapy and Research Society.

BELL (ALEXANDER GRAHAM) ASSOCIATION FOR
THE DEAF, INC.
    See: Alexander Graham Bell Association for the
       Deaf, Inc.

★ 574 ★
BETA SIGMA KAPPA
35 Wisconsin Circle, Suite 414
Washington, D.C. 20015   Established 1928

Tony Mahlman, Administrative Director
To stimulate scientific attainment and profound ethical
practice by holding forth the prize of membership in
the fraternity; to facilitate, by material means,
worthy research work in ocular science; to acquite
and publish scientific books and publications in the
field of ocular science. Membership: 1,500 (active,
life, honorary, student). Finances: Membership:
$15 membership fee; $15 annual dues. Awards: 1
Silver Medal per school of optometry, awarded to student with highest grade point, annually; a maxium of
2 Gold Medals annually, to members for outstanding
service to the field; research grants on approval of
Board of Regents. Meetings: Annual, in conjunction
with American Optometric Association convention.
Publications: The Ocularum, 3 times annually,
Dr. Jerry Friedman, editor.

★ 575 ★
BETTER HEARING INSTITUTE
1430 K Street, N.W., Suite 600   (202) 638-7577
Washington, D.C. 20005   Established 1973

Joseph J. Rizzo, Executive Director
Better Hearing Institute is a nonprofit, nonmembership
educational organization whose primary goal is the
alerting of Americans to hearing loss and available
hearing help. Finances: Other Sources: Contributions from foundations, government, corporations and
individuals. Publications: We Overcame Hearing
Loss, Better Hearing Institute (author); Nerve Deafness and You, G. Gardner, M.D., editor; Tinnitus
or Head Noises, N. L. Barr, Jr., M.D., editor;
Sounds or Silence; The Communicator (newsletter),
quarterly.

★ 576 ★
BETTER VISION INSTITUTE, INC.
230 Park Avenue   (212) 682-1731
New York, New York 10017   Established 1929

Lawrence O. Aasen, Executive Secretary
To educate the public to the need for regular complete professional vision care. Sponsors programs
through all available media. Membership: 3,115
(ophthalmic manufacturers, wholesalers and dispensers;
optometrists; ophthalmologists). Finances: Membership: Dues based on number of people engaged or on
volume of business. Meetings: Business meetings
only, major cities, USA. Publications: Information
leaflets, folders, booklets, brochures.

BICKELL (J. P.) FOUNDATION
    See: J. P. Bickell Foundation

★ 577 ★
BIG BROTHERS/BIG SISTERS OF AMERICA
117 South 17th Street, Suite 1200   (215) 567-2748
Philadelphia, Pennsylvania 19103   Established 1977

William G. Mashaw, National President;
    David W. Bahlmann, Executive Vice President
The program provides a unique child welfare service
that combines the friendship of a mature, stable volunteer (man or woman) with the skill of a social worker to help children, primarily from single-parent families, grow into responsible and happy adult members
of society and their communities. The primary needs
of the young person are met through mutual goal setting among the volunteer, parent, child and worker;
the personal friendship that develops between one
adult and one child; the knowledge on the part of
the girl or boy that somebody cares for her/him as an
individual human being. A corollary is to provide
the opportunity for socially concerned men and women
to make a highly personal investment of themselves
and their time in children in their communities.
Membership: 390 affiliated agencies (5 levels of affiliations [associate, applicant, provisional, agency-
in-formation, full]). Finances: Membership: Full
member agencies pay a graduate percentage of prior
year's expenditures (minimum $750; maximum $8,000);
all others pay a flat fee determined by level of affiliation; Other Sources: Contributions from individuals, corporations, foundations and organized federations. Awards: United Way's Gold Award of Excellence. Meetings: 3 National Board of Directors
Meetings; 12 Regional Meetings; 1 Annual Meeting
(held in June); various national locations. Publications: The Correspondent (newsletter), monthly,
Diane M. Stratton, editor; Annual Report, annually;
Citizen Board Development Program Manual; Fund
Raising Review; National Agency Directory; Standard
Operations Manual; Recommended Service Delivery
Procedures Manual; Agency-in-Formation Manual.
Affiliations: Member of American Humanics; Nation-
al Assembly; National Collaboration for Youth;
American Society of Association Executives. Former

Name: Big Brothers of America and Big Sisters International, Inc.

BIG BROTHERS OF AMERICA
See: Big Brothers/Big Sisters of America

BIG SISTERS INTERNATIONAL INC.
See: Big Brothers/Big Sisters of America

BIOFEEDBACK RESEARCH SOCIETY
See: Biofeedback Society of America

★ 578 ★
BIOFEEDBACK SOCIETY OF AMERICA
4301 Owens Street   (303) 420-2889
Wheat Ridge, Colorado 80033   Established 1969

Francine Butler, Ph.D., Executive Director
An open forum for the exchange of ideas, methods and results of biofeedback and related studies. Its emphasis is primarily on scientific investigations of human behavior and human potential, both in basic and clinical settings. Membership: 2,000 (member, affiliate, student). Finances: Membership: Member, $30; student, $15. Meetings: Annual, various locations. Publications: Proceedings, annual. Former Name: Biofeedback Research Society.

BIOGENIC INSTITUTES OF AMERICA
See: American Holistic Medical Institute

★ 579 ★
BIOLOGICAL PHOTOGRAPHIC ASSOCIATION
Box 2603 West Durham Station   (919) 493-4854
Durham, North Carolina 27705   Established 1931

Sam A. Agnello, Executive Director
Seeks to advance the techniques of biophotography and illustration in the various fields of the life sciences. The BPA Board of Registry conducts a certification program in this field. A Jobs Hotline provides members with latest information on openings in the field. Workshops in biophotography and in management are conducted several times annually. Membership: Approximately 1,400 (active [professionals in the field]; affiliate [interested persons]; student [enrolled persons studying biophotography]). Finances: Membership:

Active, $50; affiliate, $47.50; student, $25; Other Sources: Gifts and bequests; Journal subscriptions; annual meetings. Awards: Louis Schmidt Award; H. Lou Gibson Presidential Award; Fellowship in BPA. Meetings: Annual meetings, various locations. Publications: Journal of Biophotography, quarterly, Thomas P. Hurtgen, editor; BPA News, 8 times annually, Richard H. Ray, editor; Biophotography, Thomas P. Hurtgen, editor.

★ 580 ★
BIOLOGICAL STAIN COMMISSION
University of Rochester Medical Center
Box 607   (716) 275-2751
Rochester, New York 14642   Established 1922

Eric A. Schenk, Secretary
To promote the standardization of specifications for the identification, purity and performance of the more important biological stains, in order that they may be relied upon as standard tools in biological research. In cooperation with manufacturers and distributors of biological stains the Commission carries on a program of stain certification, under which dyes meeting the Commission's specifications can be marketed as "Certified Biological Stains". This program is centered in a research and assay laboratory maintained at the above address. The Commission conducts and promotes research into the nature and applications of biological stains. Membership: 80 (membership is by invitation, consists of professional scientists in the fields of biology and medicine and allied areas). Finances: Membership: $9.50; Other Sources: Fees from companies participating in the Commission's program of stain certification. Awards: A limited number of small research grants are made in the interests of progress toward the Commission's objectives. Meetings: Annual, various locations. Publications: Stain technology, bimonthly, J. B. Longley, editor; Conn's Biological Stains, R. D. Lillie, editor; Staining Procedures, G. Clark, editor.

★ 581 ★
BIOMEDICAL ENGINEERING SOCIETY
Post Office Box 2399   (213) 789-3811
Culver City, California 90230   Established 1968

Fred J. Weibell, Ph.D., Secretary-Treasurer
The purpose of the Biomedical Engineering Society is to promote the increase of biomedical engineering knowledge and its utilization. The Society was incorporated as a nonprofit organization in response to a need to give equal status representation to both biomedical and engineering interests. Membership: Approximately 750 (senior membership, membership,

student membership, sustaining membership and emeritus membership). Awards: ALZA Distinguished Lecturer. Meetings: Annual, various locations. Publications: Annals of Biomedical Engineering, quarterly, Peter H. Abbrecht, editor; Biomedical Engineering Society Bulletin, quarterly, Daniel J. Schneck, editor.

★ 582 ★
BIOPHYSICAL SOCIETY
Office of the Secretary
National Biomedical Research Foundation
Georgetown University Medical Center
3900 Reservoir Road, N.W.   (202) 625-2121
Washington, D.C. 20007   Established 1957

Dr. Winona C. Barker, Secretary
To encourage development and dissemination of knowledge in biophysics. Membership: 3,400 (regular, student). Finances: Membership: Regular, $17.50; student, $5. Meetings: Annual, various locations. Publications: Biophysical Journal, monthly, Dr. John Gergely, editor

★ 583 ★
BLIND SERVICE ASSOCIATION
127 North Dearborn Street   (312) 332-6767
Chicago, Illinois 60602   Established 1924

Beatrice Fredman, Executive Director
The Association was founded as a voluntary organization by Mrs. Gottfried Bemstein to counteract idleness of blind children by reading to them in volunteers' homes. Its current purpose is reading and recording and some individualized service, primarily to blind and visually handicapped college students and employed persons with visual disability; referral service, consumer information to blind homemakers. Its philanthropies include scholarship grants, eye clinics, school for retarded (blind), blind children's recreation program, and children in braille classrooms, deaf-blind club. Activities include a Christmas party for consumers and periodic cultural events (theater, concerts). Service limited to Chicago metropolitan area. Membership: Approximately 200 members; same number of non-member volunteers. Finances: Membership: $10-$100 up; Other Sources: Contributions via direct mail solicitation; legacies, memorial and "happy day" contributions, etc. Meetings: Monthly and annual, Chicago.

★ 584 ★
BLINDED VETERANS ASSOCIATION
1735 DeSales Street, N.W.   (202) 347-4010
Washington, D.C. 20036   Established 1945

Sumner A. Vale, Acting Executive Director
To assist the blinded veterans to re-integrate themselves into a sighted community. This is done through the Field Service Program, which attempts to make maximum utilization of community resources on behalf of individual blinded veterans; by maintaining close liaison with federal, state, and local agencies, both public and private, serving blind persons; by undertaking public education which seeks to portray blindness in realistic but unemotional terms; and through the Outreach Employment Program which assists blinded veterans in gaining employment. Membership: 1,800 regular members (those whose blindness resulted directly from their service in the armed forces); 1,200 associate members (veterans whose blindness is unconnected with their service in the armed forces). Finances: Membership: Regular, $8; associate, $4; Other Sources: Private grants, direct mail solicitation, federal contracts. Awards: Achievement Award (annually to outstanding blinded veterans); Diener Award (annually to blinded veteran having contributed to his local organization). Meetings: Annual, various locations. Publications: BVA Bulletin, 6 times annually, Sumner A. Vale, editor.

★ 585 ★
BLUE CARD, INC.
2121 Broadway   (212) 873-7400
New York, New York 10023   Established 1940

Helen Kober, Executive Director
Financial support to Jewish immigrants who were victims of Nazi persecution and to their children. Financial assistance for the aged, sick, unemployed; for education, rehabilitation, retraining, medical care, and psychiatric aid for adults and children; for special schooling, recreation and vacations. Finances: Fund raising. Meetings: Annual, New York City.

★ 586 ★
BLUE CROSS ASSOCIATION
676 St. Clair   (312) 440-6000
Chicago, Illinois 60611   Established 1948

Walter J. McNerney, President
To promote the efficiency and effectiveness of Member Plans in their efforts to provide the American population with a voluntary, not-for-profit, community-

based financing mechanism for obtaining high quality health care services in an efficient manner, as well as in their efforts to effectively and efficiently administer government programs; to promote commonality of objectives among Member Plans; and to provide leadership where collective action is required. Membership: 78 (69 United States plans, 8 Canadian, 1 Jamaica, and 9 associate plans). Finances: Membership: Membership dues. Meetings: Annual meeting of members; bimonthly meeting of Board of Governors and Executive Committee, various locations. Publications: Blue Print for Health, annual; Inquiry, quarterly. Library: 25,000 volumes.

★ 587 ★
BLUE SHIELD ASSOCIATION
676 St. Clair (312) 440-6000
Chicago, Illinois 60611 Established 1946

Walter J. McNerney, President;
  William E. Ryan, Senior Executive Vice President
To promote the efficiency and effectiveness of Member Plans in their efforts to provide the American population with a voluntary, not-for-profit, community-based financing mechanism for obtaining high quality health care services in an efficient manner, as well as in their efforts to effectively and efficiently administer government programs; to promote commonality of objectives among Member Plans; and to provide leadership where collective action is required. Membership: 74 (68 United States plans; 6 affiliate plans; 5 Canadian; 1 Great Britain). Finances: Membership: Membership dues. Meetings: Annual Meeting of members; bimonthly meeting of Board of Directors and Executive Committee. Publications: Blue Print for Health, annual; Inquiry, quarterly. Former Name: National Association of Blue Shield Plans.

★ 588 ★
BMDP STATISTICAL SOFTWARE
University of California (213) 825-5547
Los Angeles, California 90024 Established 1959

Wilfrid J. Dixon, Director
To further biomedical research through the development of the mathematical and statistical methods and the data handling facilities required to enhance such research. The project is an investigation of the utilization of computing equipment and techniques in biomedical research. Finances: Grant from Division of Research Resources. Publications: Numerous articles on results of research; Annual Report. Former Name: Health Sciences Computing Facility.

★ 589 ★
BOCKUS INTERNATIONAL SOCIETY OF
  GASTROENTEROLOGY
c/o Franz Goldstein, M.D.
Lankenau Hospital (215) 896-7360
Philadelphia, Pennsylvania 19151 Established 1958

Franz Goldstein, M.D., Secretary-General
To promote the discipline of gastroenterology with particular reference to international cooperation and goodwill. Membership: 350. Finances: Membership: $20; Other Sources: Educational, research grants from private and public agencies. Awards: Research funds awarded on merit of application by research committee and the Board of Trustees. Meetings: Annual, various locations. Publications: Proceedings, biennial.

BODY INVERSION ORGANIZATION
  See: Gravity Awareness Centers

★ 590 ★
BRAILLE INSTITUTE
741 North Vermont Avenue (213) 663-1111
Los Angeles, California 90029 Established 1919

Russell W. Kirbey, Executive Director
J. Robert Atkinson, who was blind, established the Universal Braille Press in 1919 to provide reading materials for the blind. The Universal Braille Press was the forerunner of the present day Braille Institute which has become Southern California's unique center for services to the blind. Its programs are directed toward helping the blind lead independent lives in a sighted world. It offers taining, counseling, and recreational opportunities for blind men, women and children. It operates the largest braille press in the western United States and the Braille Institute Library--one of the largest of its kind. Finances: Other Sources: Contributions, bequests and foundation grants. Publications: Braille Mirror, monthly, Betty Kalagian, editor; Inter-View, monthly, Frances Cannon, editor; Outlook, monthly, Susan Cluck, editor; Scene (newsletter to donors and public), 3 times annually, Margi Stapleton, editor; The Librarian, 3 times annually, Margi Stapleton, editor; Expectations, annual, Betty Kalagian, editor; Light (annual report), annual, Margi Stapleton, editor. Library: Braille Institute Library, 254,702 volumes (for the blind, legally blind and physically handicapped). Remarks: Braille Institute has community centers for the blind in Palm Springs, Anaheim (serving Orange County) and Santa Barbara. Volunteer community centers are located in Santa Ana and Long Beach. These centers enable Braille Institute to

serve many of the blind of Southern California.

BRAILLE (LOUIS) FOUNDATION FOR BLIND
MUSICIANS, INC.
    See: Louis Braille Foundation for Blind Musicians,
    Inc.

★ 591 ★
BRAIN INFORMATION SERVICE
Center for the Health Sciences
University of California
Los Angeles, California 90024   (213) 825-6011

Michael H. Chase, Director
To provide information in the brain sciences to researchers and clinicians interested in the fields of
neurochemistry, neuroendocrinology, neuropharmacology, neuroanatomy, neurophysiology and central nervous system correlates of behavior. Publications:
Neurochemical Transmitters and Modulators, semimonthly; Neuroendocrine Control Mechanism, Hypothlamic
Pituitary-Gonadal System, semimonthly; Development
Neurobiology, monthly; Index to Current Literature
of the Journal, Electroencephalography and Clinical
Neurophysiology, monthly; Memo of Current Books in
the Brain Sciences, monthly; Memory and Learning-
Research in the Nervous System, monthly; Sleep Bulletin, monthly; Cerebral Evoked Potentials, quarterly;
Endorphins and Opiate Receptors, quarterly; Neuro-
immunology, quarterly; Proteins in the Nervous System, quarterly.

★ 592 ★
BRAIN RESEARCH FOUNDATION, INC.
(Affiliate of the University of Chicago)
134 South LaSalle Street   (312) 782-4311
Chicago, Illinois 60603   Established 1953

William E. Fay, Jr., Chairman, Board of Trustees;
    Clinton E. Frank, Vice Chairman, Board of Trustees
To promote research on the brain; to further professional and scientific education, public education,
clinical and related care; and to establish one or
more brain research institutes. Membership: 238
(life, regular, trustee). Finances: Gifts and donations. Research Funds: Brain Research Institute,
Univeristy of Chicago. Meetings: Annual, various
locations; reguar quarterly Board meetings. Affiliations: Women's Council-Brain Research Foundation,
Illinois Federation of Women's Clubs; Professional
Women for Brain Research

★ 593 ★
BREAST CANCER ADVISORY CENTER
Post Office Box 224
Kensington, Maryland 20795   Established 1975

Rose Kushner, President and Executive Director
Medical service organization dedicated to helping
anyone with any aspect of breast problems, especially cancer. The Center has provided pre- and post-
surgical aid regarding referrals, information about
treatment options (primary and advanced) and psychological support to more than 10,000 women and their
families since its founding. In addition, the BCAC
helped create NURSUPPORT, a similar program conducted by oncological nurses at the George Washington University Hospital in Washington, D.C. Finances: Other Sources: Contributions. Publications:
Numerous brochures, booklets and articles. Library:
Private, with a collection devoted to cancer.

★ 594 ★
BRETHREN'S HOME
750 Chestnut Street   (513) 548-4117
Greenville, Ohio 45331   Established 1974

Wilbur E. Mullen, President
An association of retirement and nursing homes and
hospitals owned by or affiliated with the Church of
the Brethren to care for the needs of their members
and neighbors who are in need of their services.
Membership: 25 retirement homes, nursing homes and
hospitals. Finances: $50 annually. Meetings:
Annual, in conjunction with the Protestant Health and
Welfare Assembly. Former Name: Church of the
Brethren Homes and Hospital Association.

★ 595 ★
BRITISH ACUPUNCTURE ASSOCIATION AND
    REGISTER, LTD.
34 Alderney Street   (01) 834-1012
London SW1V 4EV, England, United Kingdom

Sidney Rose-Neil, Dr. Ac., F. Ac. C., Executive
    Council Chairman
The Association aims to promote and encourage the
study and knowledge of acupuncture, which is a
branch of medicine founded upon the principle that
health is dependent upon a proper balance of vital
energy forces within the body; to establish the status,
regulate the conduct, and protect the interests of
practitioners of acupuncture so as to promote and
maintain in the public interest proper standards for
the practice of acupuncture; to establish, maintain
and publish a register of qualified acupuncturists, and
to promote honorable practice; to exclude malpractice

and to decide all questions of professional conduct and etiquette among practicing acupuncturists; to promote scientific investigation and research into the philosophy, technique or practice of acupuncture and to do all such things likely to lead to the integration of knowledge of acupuncture and to the growth, dissemination or improvement of the philosophy, technique or practice of acupuncture and the improvement thereby of public and personal health and hygiene; to establish colleges and schools for education and training in the principles and practice of acupuncture; to form or otherwise acquire and to maintain, extend and improve libraries, clinics, sanatoria and the like, and all services ancillary thereto in pursuance of scientific research and education in acupuncture and the combat of ill-health thereby; to consider all questions affecting acupuncture and acupuncturists and where desirable to promote deputations; to petition Parliament, and to take any other steps to press for and secure changes in the law affecting acupuncture and acupuncturists in furtherance of the objects of the Association; to conduct appeals; to solicit, advertise for, or otherwise request, and to receive, hold and make use of donations or contributions in specie or property of any kind for the purpose of the Association and in furtherance of its objects. Membership: Life, fellows, honorary fellows, ordinary members. Finances: Membership: Full, $70; overseas $20. Meetings: Congress, annually. Publications: Journal of Acupuncture, Sidney Rose-Neil, editor; journal articles, monographs. Affiliations: International Society of Acupuncture. Former Name: Acupuncture Association and Register, Ltd.

★ 596 ★
BRITISH DIABETIC ASSOCIATION
10 Queen Anne Street
London W1M 0BD, England   (01) 323-1531
    United Kingdom   Established 1934

Robert L. Allard, Secretary-General
To protect interests of the diabetic community of the United Kingdom, to give financial support to research into the cause and possible cure and prevention of diabetes mellitus. Membership: 70,000. Finances: Membership: Full £2.50; pensioners 50 p; Other Sources: Donations; investment income. Awards: Annual grants of £320,000. Meetings: Semiannual, various locations. Publications: Balance, bimonthly. Affiliations: 230 branches.

★ 597 ★
BRITISH MEDICAL
British Medical Association House
Tavistock Square
London WC1H 9JP, England   (01) 387-4499
    United Kingdom   Established 1832

To promote the medical and allied sciences, and to maintain the honor and interests of the medical profession. Membership: 64,896. Publications: British Medical Journal, weekly, S. Lock, editor; Specialist Journals; reports and monographs. Library: Nuffield Library, 85,000 volumes plus periodicals. Affiliations: World Medical Association; Commonwealth Medical Association.

★ 598 ★
BROTHER'S BROTHER FOUNDATION
824 Grandview Avenue   (412) 431-1600
Pittsburgh, Pennsylvania 15211 Established 1958

Robert A. Hingson, M.D., Medical Director;
    Luke L. Hingson, Executive Director
Since its establishment, the Foundation has worked in 70 countries including the United States and Canada, to provide life-saving vaccines to 13 million people; to demonstrate improved medical techniques; and to donate medical supplies, equipment, vegetable seeds, food insecticides, water purification chemicals, hospital equipment, farm tools, school books and eyeglasses. This help has been provided directly to those in need, as well as to organizations and local governmental agencies who in turn service the destitute. Recently the Foundation has supplied emergency medical and rehabilitation services for disaster in Peru and Nicaragua (earthquakes in 1970, 1972 and 1976); Niger (drought in 1974); Honduras, Dominican Republic, Dominica and St. Lucia (hurricanes in 1974, 1979, 1980); and St. Vincent (volcanic eruption in 1979). Membership: Volunteer doctors, dentists, nurses, other health professionals, and laymen from all fields. Finances: Other Sources: Contributions, gifts. Meetings: Annual, Pittsburgh, Pennsylvania Headquarters; monthly, Executive Committee Meetings, Pittsburgh, Pennsylvania Headquarters. Publications: Report to Contributors, semiannual, Luke L. Hingson, editor; Contributions to Medical and Disaster Periodicals, irregular, Robert A. Hingson, M.D., and Luke L. Hingson, editors.

BUREAU FOR ANIMAL HEALTH AND PRODUCTION
    See: Interafrican Bureau for Animal Resources
        of the OAU

C

★ 599 ★

C. G. JUNG FOUNDATION FOR ANALYTICAL
    PSYCHOLOGY, INC.
28 East 39th Street   (212) 697-6430
New York, New York 10016   Established 1962

A. J. Sherman, Executive Director
To sponsor public lectures, film showings, seminars,
workshops, and symposia on analytical psychology;
to maintain the Archive for Research in Archetypal
Symbolism (ARAS); to disseminate the work and
thought of Carl Gustav Jung and develop understanding of the range and applicability of analytical psychology; to foster the preparation and training of new
Jungian analysts. Membership: 1,300 (professional
analytical psychologists, active members who have had
Jungian analysis, and the general public). Finances:
Membership: $30-$2,500; Other Sources: Books
sales; lectures, seminars, film showings, workshops,
and symposia; contributions resulting from fund raising efforts. Publications: Quadrant, semiannually,
Joan Carson, Ph.D., editor.

★ 600 ★

C. S. MOTT CENTER FOR HUMAN GROWTH AND
    DEVELOPMENT
275 East Hancock   (313) 577-1115
Detroit, Michigan 48201   Established 1973

T. N. Evans, M.D., Director
Its purpose is to bridge the gap between science and
service; to provide more rapid application of basic
research to clinical medicine; to educate people to
carry on this important work and to disseminate information to the public to enable every child to be
wanted and well born. Specialists such as geneticists,
endocrinologists, biochemists, surgeons, psychiatrists
and embryologists are gathered at the Mott Center to
provide a major thrust in research and clinical medicine to improve perinatal services to the end of reducing fetal and neonatal mortality and morbidity.
Diagnosis and treatment for problems of infertility-
fertility and specific problems of family planning; endocrinology; gynecological defects amenable to surgical corrections; genetic counseling and prenatal
diagnosis are among the services offered to patients
referred to the Mott Center. Research is the primary
function of this center. This encompasses clinical as
well as basic research. Studies in reproductive physiology and in biochemistry of sperm and cervical

mucus will lead to new and better contraceptives, and
healthier pregnancies and births. Finances: Other
Sources: Most of the research is supported by grants
from governmental agencies and private foundations;
gifts and bequests from individuals for support of medical programs, research and equipment are appreciated.
Meetings: Harold C. Mack Symposium, biennially,
Detroit, Michigan. Publications: Annual Report,
annually, T. N. Evans, M.D., editor.

★ 601 ★

CAJAL CLUB
University of Kansas
College of Health Sciences
    and Hospital   (913) 588-7002
Kansas City, Kansas 66103   Established 1947

Howard A. Matzke, Secretary-Treasurer
To contribute to the welfare of neuroanatomy and
neuroscientists; to provide an opportunity for congenial scientists with a special interest in the nervous
system to confraternize annually. Membership: 450
(neuroscientists). Finances: Membership: $5 an-
nually. Meetings: Annual.

★ 602 ★

CANADIAN ASSOCIATION FOR HEALTH, PHYSICAL
    EDUCATION, AND RECREATION
333 River Road
Vanier City, Ontario K1L 8B9,   (613) 746-5909
    Canada   Established 1933

Dr. Thomas Bedecki, Executive Director
A nationwide, voluntary, nonprofit, nonpolitical professional association dedicated to raise Canadian
health, recreation and physical education, standards.
The Association seeks to promote the professional
growth and technical competence of its members, to
foster the exchange of ideas, to make fact-finding
studies, and to cooperate with various cultural and
athletic organizations whose objectives are to enhance
the lives of Canadians physically, recreationally and
aesthetically. Membership: 3,000 (teachers,
coaches, recreationalists, government employees).
Finances: Membership: Professional, $40; associate,
$40; Other Sources: Sale of publications. Awards:
Contract grants. Meetings: Annual, various locations, all committees. Publications: CAHPER Journal, bimonthly, Mrs. Pat Rutt, editor; various monographs and pamphlets.

CANADIAN ASSOCIATION FOR MEDICAL RECORD
LIBRARIAN
   See: Canadian Health Record Association

★ 603 ★
CANADIAN ASSOCIATION FOR THE MENTALLY
   RETARDED
Kinsmen NIMR Building
4700 Keele Street   (416) 661-9611
Downsview, Ontario, Canada   Established 1958

G. Allan Roeher, Ph.D., Executive Secretary
To promote the welfare of the mentally retarded and
to generate and administer funds on their behalf; to
strengthen or improve existing facilities and help the
mentally retarded achieve their rightful place in
today's society. Membership: Parents, volunteers,
professionals, local and provincial associations. Finances: Voluntary contributions; government funds.
Awards: Scottish Rite Bursary Awards. Meetings:
Annual conference; Executive and Board meetings,
various locations. Publications: Deficience Mental/
Mental Retardation, quarterly, Mrs. Leslie Howsam,
editor; Transcan Newsletter. Library: John Orr
Foster Memorial Library. Affiliations: National Institute on Mental Retardation; 10 Provincial Associa-
tions for the Mentally Retarded; Committee of 25 for
Handicapped Children; Yellow Knife Association for
Retarded Children; Bahamas Association for Retarded
Children; Yukon Association for Retarded Children;
Jamaica Association for Mentally Handicapped Chil-
dren.

CANADIAN ASSOCIATION FOR THE PSYCHIATRIC
TREATMENT OF OFFENDERS
   See: Canadian Association for Treatment of
        Offenders

★ 604 ★
CANADIAN ASSOCIATION FOR THE WELFARE
   OF PSYCHIATRIC PATIENTS
Post Office Box 39, Station "J"
Toronto, Ontario M4J 4X8,   (416) 691-3499
   Canada   Established 1969

G. Tori Salter, Director
To encourage scientific research and study into the
cause, effective treatment and prevention of mental
illness; to engage actively in promoting a better understanding of the problems of mental illness on the
part of the general public; to serve as ombudsmen for
the mentally handicapped; and to engage in a continual program of recruitment for volunteer visitors for

the mentally ill in the hope that no patient--no matter how long disabled--will lack a helping hand to
assist in his remotivation and rehabilitation. Membership: 106 men and women from both professional
and non-professional backgrounds. Finances: Membership: Active, $10; associate, $3; Other Sources:
Donations, gifts from charitable foundations. Meetings: Monthly, various locations. Publications:
Newsletter, quarterly. Former Name: Psychiatric
Hospital Patients' Welfare Association.

★ 605 ★
CANADIAN ASSOCIATION FOR TREATMENT OF
   OFFENDERS
2282 Clarke Drive
Abbotsford, British Columbia   (604) 853-9081
   V2S 3V3, Canada   Established 1975

Florence L. Nichols, M.D., President
The Association was founded in response to a need for
establishing offender psychotherapy and clinical criminology as scientific specialties in Canada. It promotes cooperation with allied disciplines and furthers
international exchange of information. Membership:
Psychiatrists and other doctors; socail worker; nurses
and lawyers working in forensic institutions. Finances: Membership: $25. Meetings: Annual, various
locations. Publications: International Journal of
Offender Therapy and Comparative Criminology, 3
times annually, Dr. Melitta Schmideberg, editor.
Affiliation: Association for the Psychiatric Treatment
of Offenders. Former Name: Canadian Association
for the Psychiatric Treatment of Offenders.

★ 606 ★
CANADIAN ASSOCIATION OF ANATOMISTS
Department of Anatomy
University of British Columbia
Vancouver, British Columbia   (604) 228-2680
   V6T 1W5, Canada   Established 1956

The Association's purpose is to advance the knowledge
of anatomy and to represent anatomical sciences in
Canada. Membership: 300 (elected, honorary,
emerits, charter, associate). Finances: Membership:
$8 annually (elected), plus C.F.B.S. Levy, $20
annually; others $4 annually. Awards: J.C.B.
Grant Senior Scientist Award; Murray L. Barr Junior
Scientist Award; Arthur W. Ham Graduate Student
Award. Meetings: Annual, various Canadian Universities. Publications: Canadian Association of
Anatomists, annual, Dr. B. H. Bressler (1980-1983),
editor; Newsletter.

★ 607 ★

CANADIAN ASSOCIATION OF ELECTROENCE-
    PHALOGRAPH TECHNOLOGISTS, INC.
c/o W. C. Tinkess
R.R. #2
Lindsay, Ontario K9V 4R2,   (705) 324-2999
    Canada   Established 1951

W. C. Tinkess, UE., RET., RCT., CMET., President
The upgrading, continuing education of EEG Technologists and the standards of Electroencephalographic
care, clinical approach, for the Dominion of Canada.
Membership: 400 (registered technologists and associa-
ates). Finances: Membership: $27. Awards: 2
papers for Electroencephalography, subsequently published. Meetings: Annual. Publications: Spike
and Wave; Newsletter (for members/associates).

★ 608 ★

CANADIAN ASSOCIATION OF GASTRO-
    ENTEROLOGY
c/o Dr. D. L. DaCosta
Hotel Dieu Hospital
Division of Gastroenterology   (613) 544-3310
Kingston, Ontario K7L 3H6,   ext. 364
    Canada   Established 1962

Dr. D. L. DaCosta, Secretary
An organization of individuals, mainly medical doctors, interested in all aspects of gastroenterology.
Membership: 254 (gastroenterologists, gastrointestinal
surgeons, radiologists and pathologists). Finances:
Membership: $35 annually. Awards: R. D.
McKenna Memorial Lecture, annually; Annual
C.A.G. Medal for Research. Meetings: Annual,
in conjunction with the Royal College of Physicians
and Surgeons of Canada. Publications: NIL, irregular, Dr. D. J. Buchan, editor.

★ 609 ★

CANADIAN ASSOCIATION OF MEDICAL
    RADIATION TECHNOLOGISTS
280 Metcalfe Street, Suite 410
Ottawa, Ontario K2P 1R7,   (613) 234-0012
    Canada   Established 1943

A. A. Mattila, Executive Director
To promote and encourage the science and art of radiological technique and to consider and discuss all
subjects affecting it; to promote the formation of, to
assist, to guide, to encourage and to form a central
association for local associations of radiological technicians throughout Canada; to facilitate the exchange of information and ideas on matters affecting
the science and practice of radiological technique

and allied subjects. Membership: 8,200. Awards:
Gevaert Essay Award; George Reason Cup; Phillips
Rose Bowl; Petrie Award; Welch Memorial Lecture;
Dr. M. Mallett Award; Mallinckrodt Award. Meet-
ings: Annual, various locations. Publication: The
Canadian Journal of Radiography, Radiotherapy and
Nuclear Medicine, bimonthly, A. A. Mattila, man-
aging editor. Former Name: Canadian Society of
Radiological Technicians.

★ 610 ★

CANADIAN ASSOCIATION OF OPTOMETRISTS
210 Gladstone Avenue, Suite 2001
Ottawa, Ontario K2P 0Y6,   (613) 238-2006
    Canada   Established 1941

D. N. Scheafer, Executive Director
Founded in 1941 to meet an expressed need to represent and unite all optometrists in Canada. The Association has worked since then to establish and maintain optometry's position as the primary care practice
in the field of vision and eye care. Membership:
2,000 optometrists. Finances: Varies per province.
Award: C.A.O. President's Award. Meetings:
General Congress held biennially, various locations;
Council meets biennially, or more frequently as required. Publication: Canadian Journal of Optometry, quarterly, G. M. Belanger, editor.

★ 611 ★

CANADIAN ASSOCIATION OF PATHOLOGISTS
Mount Sinai Hospital
Department of Laboratories
600 University Avenue
Toronto, Ontario M5G 1X5,   (416) 596-4453
    Canada   Established 1949

Dr. K. P. H. Pritzker, Secretary-Treasurer
The advancement of pathology and its allied sciences
in all aspects. The promotion of the interests of
pathologists and allied scientists in Canada. The
maintenance of a high standard of proficiency among
the pathologists and allied scientists of Canada. Activities include Continuing Medical Education, the
maintenance of laboratory standards and the training
of technicians. Membership: 644 (ordinary, 453;
associate, 40; corresponding, 37; junior, 74; honorary, 17; emeritus, 23). Finances: Membership:
$15-$70. Meetings: Annual, various locations.

★ 612 ★

CANADIAN ASSOCIATION OF RADIOLOGISTS
1440 St. Catherine Street West
Suite 806
Montreal, Quebec H3G 1R8,   (514) 866-2035
  Canada   Established 1937

Alva Ekstrand Pentecost, Executive Secretary
To advance the art and science of radiology and to
promote its interest in relation to medicine, with particular reference to the clinical, research, educational, ethical and economic aspects thereof. Activities
include an annual meeting at which scientific papers,
exhibits and commercial exhibits are presented; 20
committees and 15 district councilors who arrange
local meetings and then report to the Association
twice a year; and committees covering fields of economics, ethics, public relations, training of radiologists, technicians, etc. Membership: 1,600 (full -
physicians qualified in the speciality of radiology;
members elect - radiologists in training; retired;
associate - physicists, etc.; life; honorary). Finances: Membership: Initiation fee, $10; full mem-
ber, $95; associate member, $30; resident-in-train-
ing, no charge; Other Sources: Commercial exhibits
at annual meeting; medical journal. Meetings:
Semiannual, annual, various locations. Publications:
Journal of the Canadian Association of Radiologists,
quarterly, C. S. Houston, M.D., editor; Illuminator,
newsletter, every 6 weeks.

★ 613 ★

CANADIAN ASSOCIATION OF SOCIAL WORKERS
55 Parkdale Avenue, 4th Floor
Ottawa, Ontario K1Y 1E5,   (613) 728-1865
  Canada   Established 1928

Gweneth J. Gowanlock, Executive Director
To promote, develop and sponsor activities appropriate
to the strengthening and unification of the social work
profession; to encourage and assist in the development of high professional standards amongst its members; to promote the well-being and development of
its members as professional people; to provide a
means through which its members may take action on
issues of social welfare; to edit and publish books,
papers, journals and other forms of literature respecting social work in order to disseminate information to
members as well as to members of the public; and to
encourage specialized studies in social work among its
members and to provide assistance and facilities for
special studies and research. Membership: Approximately 6,000 (active, non-practicing and student,
professional social workers--includes both English and
French-speaking). Meetings: Annual, various locations. Publications: The Social Worker, quarterly.
Affiliations: Provincial Associations.

★ 614 ★

CANADIAN BIOCHEMICAL SOCIETY
c/o Dr. Barry D. McLennan
University of Saskatchewan
Department of Biochemistry
Saskatoon, Saskatchewan 07N 0W0 (306) 343-2226
  Canada   Established 1957

Dr. Barry D. McLennan, Secretary
The Society has been established "in order to foster
the development of Biochemistry in Canada." Its
activities include sponsorship and organization of scientific meetings and symposia, provision of scientific
advice to government policy developers. Membership: 766 (regular, student, and emeritus members).
Finances: Membership: Regular, $48; student, $22.
Awards: Ayerst Award (in recognition of meritorious
biochemical research by an individual under 40 years
of age); CBS Visiting Lectureship. Meetings: Annually in June, various locations. Publications:
CBS Bulletin, semiannually, D. B. Smith, editor.
Affiliation: Canadian Federation of Biological Societies.

★ 615 ★

CANADIAN BOARD OF REGISTRATION OF
  ELECTROENCEPHALOGRAPH TECHNOLOGISTS
E.E.G. Department, University Hospital
339 Windermere Road
London, Ontario N6A 5A5,   (519) 673-3698
  Canada   Established 1974

Dr. Warren Blume, Chairman
The Board is the examining body for the Canadian
Association of Electroencephalograph Technologists.
All arrangements for exams are processed by the
Secretary-Registrar, exams are compiled by the Board.
Accreditation of teaching hospitals will be in effect
as of September 1982. Membership: Over 400 reg-
istered electroencephalograph technologists (full and
associate). Finances: Membership: $100 (registra-
tion fee and 2 exam fees). Meetings: Annual Board
Meetings; telephone conference calls. Affiliations:
Canadian Association of Registered Electroencephalograph Technologists.

★ 616 ★

CANADIAN CARDIOVASCULAR SOCIETY
1455 Peel Street, Room M-31
Montreal, Quebec H3A 1T5,   (514) 288-8141
  Canada   Established 1949

Dr. R. E. Rossall, President
The purpose of the Society is to promote the gathering
and dissemination of knowledge of the Heart and

Circulation for the benefit of the public. Its only activity is an Annual Meeting. Membership: 665 (life members, honorary members, regular members; physicians, surgeons or scientists whose primary interest in practice of cardiology, cardiovascular surgery, or in research in these or related fields). Finances: Membership: $50 annually per member (not including honorary and life members). Awards: Annual C.C.S. Research Award. Lectureship: Annual C.C.S. Lectureship; John Keith Lectureship; Canadian Heart Foundation Guest Lectureship. Meetings: Annual, various major cities in Canada. Publications: Program of Annual Meeting (includes abstracts of papers being presented).

★ 617 ★
CANADIAN CHIROPRACTIC EXAMINING BOARD
423 Colborne Street
London, Ontario N6B 2T2,   (519) 434-4493
    Canada   Established 1963

J. A. Langford, Chairman
The Board was founded in order to establish and maintain a high standard of competence at a uniform level for anyone seeking to practice chiropractic in Canada. Membership: Entrance to practice qualification only; not involved in continuing membership. Finances: Other Sources: $200 to take exam in Canada; $250 to take exam outside of Canada. Affiliation: Canadian Chiropractic Association.

★ 618 ★
CANADIAN COORDINATING COUNCIL ON
    DEAFNESS
55 Parkdale Avenue   Voice (613) 728-0936
Ottawa, Ontario K1Y 1E5,   TTY (613) 728-0954
    Canada   Established 1975

K. George Wolf, Executive Director
The Council is a national co-ordinating agency charged with promoting the rights and interests of hearing impaired Canadians. Its objective is to assume an advocacy role on behalf of the hearing impaired by co-ordinating the efforts of all member groups in dealing with issues at the national level. Our work is carried out with the help of ten provincial councils who in turn represent local organizations active in the field of hearing impairment. Membership: May be individual or associate (agency application); there are 24 board members, half of these board members are hearing impaired. Finances: Membership: Individual, $5; associate, $25. Meetings: Semiannual, in Ottawa. Publications: Communication, 6 issues annually, Gwenyth Andrews, editor; The Law and the Deaf, Vol. I, II, published

1980; Deafness, the Invisible Handicap, published 1977; Directory of Provincial Councils, published 1979; The Wallace Report, Study of the Hearing Impaired in Canada, Information Resource Centre on Hearing Impairment, published 1973. Affiliations: Alberta Government Telephones, Edmonton, Alberta; Centre d'accueil Manoir Cartierville, Montreal, Quebec; The Corporation of the City of Mississauga, Mississauga, Ontario; Deaf Television Resource Centre, Toronto, Ontario; The Elks Purple Cross, Regina, Saskatchewan; Institution des Sourd de Montreal, Montreal, Quebec; Mississauga Hearing Aid Centre, Mississauga, Ontario; Winnipeg Community Centre for the Deaf; Ottawa Silent Athletic Club, Ottawa, Ontario.

★ 619 ★
CANADIAN COUNCIL FOR EXCEPTIONAL
    CHILDREN
c/o Donald Warren
6450 Thorold Stone Road
Niagara Falls, Ontario L2J 1B3,   (416) 354-1951
    Canada   Established 1958

Donald Warren, Executive Secretary-Treasurer
An offshoot of the American Council, Canadian CEC is examining the condition of exceptional children in Canada and is planning programs geared to Canadian needs. The local chapters have the responsibility of insuring that all exceptional children in their locations have adequate educational opportunity and community services. CEC also prepares materials and conducts workshops to help special educators and others develop the skills needed to influence governmental action. Membership: Over 4,200 members engaged in professional work relating to the education of exceptional children, fulltime college or university students, and persons interested in exceptional children and their education; 58 local and student chapters; and 5 provincial federations. Awards: CEC In Canada Award; Joan Kershaw Publication Award; John McIntosh Chapter Award; Sam Robinovitch Research and Evaluation Award; Special Education Policies Award. Meetings: Biennial, various locations. Publications: Exceptional Children, 8 times annually; Teaching Exceptional Children, quarterly; Update, bimonthly; Special Education in Canada, quarterly; numerous other publications. Affiliation: Council for Exceptional Children. Former Name: Council for Exceptional Children in Canada.

★ 620 ★
CANADIAN COUNCIL OF THE BLIND
96 Ridout Street S
London, Ontario N6C 3X4,   (519) 434-4339
   Canada   Established 1944

Paul J. Chovancek, Executive Director
Rehabilitation of the blind through social and recreational activities. <u>Membership</u>: 92 affiliated clubs
composed of blind persons. <u>Finances</u>: Membership:
Token membership fee of $2 per year per club; Other
Sources: Financed by The Canadian National Institute
for the Blind. <u>Awards</u>: Award of Merit gold medal
and citation for persons giving outstanding service to
the blind. Book of Fame, in which are inscribed
the names of blind persons who have been outstanding
in their chosen fields. <u>Meetings</u>: National and Divisional: annual, various locations. <u>Publications</u>:
The CCB Outlook, quarterly, Mary G. Patterson,
editor.

★ 621 ★
CANADIAN COUNCIL ON HEALTH EDUCATION
605-71 Sparks Street
Ottawa, Ontario K1P 5N2,   (613) 232-4063
   Canada   Established 1978

Michael E. Palko, Executive Secretary
To promote the development of an informed public
opinion on matters related to healthful living and environment by: building increased public awareness in
health matters, mobilizing community groups in support
of health education, providing expert testimony to
legislative and other policy-making bodies; to publish and disseminate health information and literature;
to provide an opportunity for public participation in
health education programs through national conferences
and regional seminars; to provide effective tools for
educating the public on health matters; to assist in
the co-ordination of health education programs by improving communication between various organizations;
to foster co-operation between existing private, public
and voluntary health education efforts; to serve as a
clearinghouse for interchange of information among
individuals and organizations across Canada so as to
encourage multidisciplinary approaches to issues in
health education and health promotion; to inform the
public of training facilities in health education as
well as other Canadian sources of health information.
<u>Membership</u>: Present 120; anticipated 1,800 (physi-
cians, nurses, consumers, teachers, health educators,
etc.). <u>Finances</u>: Membership: Individual, $15;
corporate/association, $75; Other Sources: Grants
and sale of publications. <u>Meetings</u>: Annual, in
conjunction with the Council's sponsored national conferences, Ottawa, Canada. <u>Publications</u>: Membership Newsletter, quarterly, M. E. Palko, editor;

Special reports on health promotion and health education.

★ 622 ★
CANADIAN COUNCIL ON HOSPITAL
   ACCREDITATION
1815 Alta Vista Drive, Suite 206
Ottawa, Ontario K1G 3Y6,   (603) 523-9154
   Canada   Established 1958

A. L. Swanson, M.D., F.A.C.H.A., Executive
   Director; James H. Murray, M.D., F.A.C.P.M.,
   Associate Executive Director
To establish standards for hospital operation and assist
hospitals to attain these standards; to conduct a survey and accreditation program for Canadian Hospitals,
Long Term Care Centres, and Mental Health Services;
to recognize compliance with standards by the issuance of certificates; to publish accreditation literature, correspond with health care institutions to promote a high quality of health care in all its aspects,
improve utilization and clinical appraisal; and to
survey eligible institutions and issue certificates of
accreditation. <u>Membership</u>: 5 national associations
(Canadian Hospital Association, Canadian Medical
Association, Royal College of Physicians and Surgeons
of Canada, L'Association des medecine de langue
française du Canada, Canadian Nurses Association).
<u>Finances</u>: Membership: $7,500 per seat on the Coun-
cil's Board of Directors; Other Sources: Survey fees
charged to health care institutions ($730 per surveyor
day in 1981). <u>Meetings</u>: 5 times annually, Ottawa,
Ontario, Canada. <u>Publications</u>: Guide to Hospital
Accreditation, 1977; Guide to Accreditation of Long
Term Care Centres, 1978; Guide to Accreditation of
Canadian Mental Health Services, 1975; General
Guidelines - Survey of Ambulatory Health Care Cen-
tres; Voluntary Hospital Accreditation - What's It All
About?, 1980; Voluntary Accreditation for Long Term
Care Centres - What's It All About?, 1980; Aims
and Objectives, 1980. <u>Library</u>: 800 volumes, in-
cluding technical manuals and guides.

★ 623 ★
CANADIAN COUNCIL ON SOCIAL DEVELOPMENT
Post Office Box 3505, Station C
55 Parkdale Avenue
Ottawa, Ontario K1Y 4G1,   (613) 728-1865
   Canada   Established 1920

The Council develops and promotes social policies
based on research and the consensus of informed and
concerned citizens. Reports, periodicals, and briefs
in the broad fields of income security, housing, personal social services, health, social planning, citizen

involvement, and law and social development are published, and conferences and seminars are held. Membership: 1,688 individuals, 652 agencies. Finances: Membership: Participating, 25; agency, $30-$300; library, $35; Other Sources: Government grants, corporation and special grants, contributions. Publications: Perception, bimonthly, Jean-Guy Carrier, editor in chief; Social Development, irregular, CCSD, editor; Canadian Fact Book on Poverty, 1979; Canadian Fact Book on Income Distribution, 1980; Foster Care and Adoption in Canada, 1980.

★ 624 ★
CANADIAN CYSTIC FIBROSIS FOUNDATION
161 Eglington Avenue East, Suite 503
Toronto, Ontario M4P 1J5,   (416) 485-9149
    Canada   Established 1960

Amy M. Downs, Executive Director
To conduct research into the basic causes and treatment of cystic fibrosis; to aid those afflicted with cystic fibrosis; to raise funds and allocate the same for the above purposes. Membership: 38 chapters. Finances: Funds raised by chapters; donations from Kinsmen Clubs; student fund raising. Research Funds: Grants to Cystic Fibrosis treatment and research clinics, to recognized research investigators; Scholarships, Fellowships and summer studentship.

★ 625 ★
CANADIAN DENTAL ASSOCIATION
1815 Alta Vista Drive
Ottawa, Ontario K1G 3Y6,   (613) 523-1770
    Canada   Established 1902

Hubert Drouin, Executive Director
To promote the art and science of dentistry and its collateral branches and the advancement of the dental profession. Membership: 8,000. Finances: Membership: Annual grants from provincial associations and individual membership fees. Meetings: Annual, various locations. Publications: Journal of the Canadian Dental Association, monthly, Elizabeth McKee, editor. Library: Sidney Wood Bradley Memorial Library, 6,400 volumes. Affiliations: Canadian Academy of Periodontology; Canadian Society of Oral Surgeons; Canadian Association of Orthodontists; Canadian Academy of Endodontics; Canadian Academy of Pedodontics; Canadian Academy of Prosthodontics; Canadian Society of Public Health Dentists; Canadian Academy of Restorative Dentistry; Canadian Academy of Oral Pathology; Canadian Academy of Oral Radiology; Association of Prosthodontists of Canada.

★ 626 ★
CANADIAN DENTAL RESEARCH FOUNDATION
1815 Alta Vista Drive
Ottawa, Ontario K1G 3Y6,   (613) 523-1770
    Canada   Established 1920

The Foundation works to encourage Canadian dental research. It is operated through the Canadian Dental Association. Finances: Interest from trust fund.

★ 627 ★
CANADIAN DERMATOLOGICAL ASSOCIATION
11, Cote du Palais
Quebec, Quebec G1R 2J6,
    Canada   Established 1925

Raymond Lessard, M.D., Secretary
To promote the knowledge, teaching, and status of dermatology. Membership: 269. Finances: Membership: $40. Awards: Barney Usher Research Award. Meetings: Annual, various locations.

★ 628 ★
CANADIAN DIABETES ASSOCIATION
123 Edward Street, Suite 601
Toronto, Ontario M5G 1E2,   (416) 593-4311
    Canada   Established 1953

The Canadian Diabetes Association is a national volunteer association. The main efforts of the Association are concentrated in medical research, education and discovery in the field of diabetes mellitus. The CDA represents the views, interests and concerns of diabetic Canadians to all levels of government, the corporate sector, and employers. It also operates summer camps for the up to 10,000 Canadian children with diabetes. Membership: 24,000 (individuals). Finances: Membership: Family, $7; senior citizen, $3; Other Sources: Donations from individuals and corporate contributions, bequests. Research Funds: Medical research conducted through the Charles H. Best Fund. Meetings: Annual, various locations in Canada. Publications: Diabetes Dialogue, quarterly. Affiliations: Branches in more than 100 communities across Canada. Former Name: Canadian Diabetic Association.

CANADIAN DIABETIC ASSOCIATION
    See: Canadian Diabetes Association

★ 629 ★

CANADIAN DIETETIC ASSOCIATION
7 Pleasant Boulevard, Suite 214
Toronto, Ontario M4T 1K2,   (416) 925-2225
  Canada   Established 1935

Eleanor Sortome, Executive Director
To promote optimum nutritional care for Canadians,
the advancement of nutrition and dietetics, and improvement of the status of dietitians; to promote education of the public; to establish and maintain
standards of dietary work; to publish informative articles about dietetics and nutrition. Membership:
3,425 (active 3,119; retired 151; life 155). Finances: Membership: Active, $55; retired, $20;
life, $550; Other Sources: Conferences, investments,
workshops, sale of Journals. Awards: CDA Memorial Award; W. D. College Award; Bernard Award;
Exhibitors' Awards (2); McCain Foods Award; Economics Laboratory Award; CDA Undergraduate Awards
(5); Goodhost Outstanding Achievement Award; Annual Memorial Lecture of the Violet Ryley-Kathleen
Jeffs Foundation. Meetings: Annual Conference,
various locations. Publications: Journal of the
Canadian Dietetic Association, quarterly, Diane
Charter, editor; Communiqué, quarterly, Linda
Dietrich, editor. Affiliations: Canadian Pediatric
Society; Canadian Hunger Foundation; Canadian
Hospital Association; Canadian Diabetes Association;
Canadian Council on Children and Youth; Caribbean
Association of Nutritionists and Dietitians; Interna-
tional Committee on Dietetic Associations.

★ 630 ★

CANADIAN FEDERATION OF BIOLOGICAL
    SOCIETIES
c/o Dr. G. R. F. Davis
Post Office Box 498, Sub 6
Saskatoon, Saskatchewan S7N 0W0,   (306) 343-7384
  Canada   Established 1958

Dr. G. R. F. Davis, Honorary Secretary/Treasurer
To bring together persons who are interested in the
biological sciences; to disseminate information on the
results of biological research through scientific meetings and publications; to encourage exchanges between constituent societies; and to act for the member societies when concerted action is desirable.
Membership: 3,500 (full members of societies are also
members of the Federation; other society members are
not). Meetings: Annual, various university campuses.
Publications: Canadian Federation News, annual;
Proceedings of Annual Meetings of Federation, annual,
J. R. Trevithick, editor; Programme of Annual Scientific Meetings. Affiliations: Canadian Physiological Society; Pharmacological Society of Canada;
Canadian Association of Anatomists; Canadian Bio-

chemical Society; Nutrition Society of Canada;
Canadian Society of Canada; Canadian Society for
Cell Biology; Canadian Society for Immunology; So-
ciety of Toxicology of Canada.

★ 631 ★

CANADIAN FEDERATION OF VOLUNTARY HEALTH
    PLANS
c/o 150 Ferrand Drive
Don Mills, Ontario M3C 1H6,   (416) 429-2661
  Canada   Established 1972

To assist individuals and employed groups of individuals in obtaining health services not available under
existing government programs, and for this purpose to
promote the development and study of voluntary non-
profit health services throughout Canada. Membership: 8 Canadian organizations. Meetings: Annual,
various locations.

★ 632 ★

CANADIAN FOUNDATION FOR ILEITIS AND
    COLITIS
294 Spadina Avenue
Toronto, Ontario M5T 2E7,   (416) 366-2776
  Canada   Established 1974

Gordon Priest, National President;
    Julian M. Sorsby, Executive Director
The Foundation is a national voluntary research organization devoted to investigating the etiology and
treatment of Crohn's disease and Ulcerative Colitis.
In addition to an extensive education program aimed
at the public and the medical profession, it is involved in funding research, fellowships, career awards
and student awards. Membership: 2,500 family
members (general membership and life membership).
Finances: Membership: General membership, $15
annually; life membership, $100; Other Sources:
Special event fund raising, chapter fund raising and
other fund raising programs. Awards: Grants in aid
of research for 2 years and renewal; research training fellowships (2 and 3 years); summer student
scholarships, student research awards, medical school
book prizes. Meetings: Quarterly, in every medical school host city. Publications: The Journal,
quarterly, National Education Committee (editor);
various brochures on Crohn's Disease and Ulcerative
Colitis. Affiliations: Chapters throughout Canada.

★ 633 ★
CANADIAN HEALTH RECORD ASSOCIATION
187 King Street East
Oshawa, Ontario L1H 1C3,   (416) 728-9743
Canada   Established 1949

Janet Milner, Executive Director
The intent of the Association is to maintain standards
governing the collection, utilization and retrieval of
medical data. Membership: 2,800 health record ad-
ministrators and technicians. Meetings: Annually,
various Canadian locations. Publications: Guide for
Medical Record Departments in Canadian Hospitals;
Code of Practice for Safeguarding Health Information;
Guidelines to the Code of Practice. Former Name:
Canadian Association of Medical Record Librarians.

★ 634 ★
CANADIAN HEARING SOCIETY
60 Bedford Road   Voice (416) 964-9595
Toronto, Ontario M5R 2K2,   TTY (416) 964-2066
Canada   Established 1940

Denis Morrice, Executive Director
The Society works with the deaf and hard of hearing
to provide better channels of communication with the
community. Services include audiological testing;
hearing aid program; rehabilitation and social services, including job placement, counseling and interpreting; TTY (telephone for the deaf) and technical
devices; and information services. There are 10
regional offices throughout Ontario, in addition to the
Head Office in Toronto. Membership: 15,000 (the
deaf and hard of hearing, their families, and interested professionals). Finances: Membership: $2 an-
nually; Other Sources: Private and corporate donations; government grants; United Way; productive
income. Publications: Vibrations, quarterly, Brian
Hunter, editor; miscellaneous pamphlets. Library:
Canadian Hearing Society Library, 300 volumes.

★ 635 ★
CANADIAN HEART FOUNDATION
1 Nicholas Street, Suite 1200
Ottawa, Ontario K1N 7B7,   (613) 237-4361
Canada   Established 1956

E. McDonald, Executive Director
To co-ordinate and facilitate the efforts or organizations and individuals interested in heart disease with a
view to reducing the morbidity and mortality therefrom in Canada. A federation of Provincial Heart
Foundations. Supports research in the cardiovascular
and cerebrovascular fields, and passes on information
through a program of professional and lay education.

Membership: Over 75,000 volunteers. Finances:
Public appeals; gifts; donations. Meetings: Annual, various locations. Publications: Pamphlets on
cardiovascular disease. Affiliations: Provincial
Heart Foundations with offices in major Canadian
cities; Canadian Cardiovascular Society; Canadian
Council of Cardiovascular Nurses; Canadian State
Society; International Society and Federation of Cardiology.

★ 636 ★
CANADIAN HOSPITAL ASSOCIATION
410 Laurier Avenue West, Suite 800
Ottawa, Ontario K1R 7T6,   (613) 238-8005
Canada   Established 1931

Jean-Claude Martin, President
The Association consists of a federation of provincial
hospital associations, the Catholic Health Association
of Canada, the Canadian Medical Association, and
the American Hospital Association, in cooperation with
the federal and provincial governments and voluntary
non-profit organizations in the health field. Membership: 14 (11 provincial and regional hospital/
health associations, the Catholic Health Association
of Canada, the Canadian Medical Association, and
the American Hospital Association). Finances: Membership: Pro-rated between hospital associations with
a nominal fee for the Catholic Health Association of
Canada and the American Hospital Association; Other
Sources: Sale of publications; educational courses.
Awards: George Findlay Stephens Memorial Award,
annually, to an outstanding Canadian for noteworthy
service in the hospital and health field. Meetings:
Annual, various locations. Publications: Dimensions
in Health Service, monthly, Jean-Claude Martin, ed-
itor; Canadian Hospital Directory, annually, Jean-
Claude Martin, editor; Hospital Trustee, bimonthly,
Jean-Claude Martin, editor; Canadian Hospital Law
2nd Edition; Directory of Long-Term Care Centres in
Canada. Library: Canadian Hospital Association
Library. Affiliations: All national hospital and
health related organizations and associations; the
International Hospital Federation.

★ 637 ★
CANADIAN INSTITUTE OF PUBLIC HEALTH
     INSPECTORS
121-1330 15 Avenue, S.W., Suite 121
Calgary, Alberta T2T 0X7,   (403) 245-0680
Canada

Lil Lahara, Executive Secretary-Treasurer
To promote the advancement of sanitary sciences; to
raise the status, standards and rewards of the Public

Health Inspector. Membership: 1,000 (student, regular, life, honorary). Finances: Membership: $30-$50 per member; Other Sources: Sustaining members, magazine, convention revenue. Meetings: Membership Meeting, annual; Executive meetings, quarterly. Publications: Environmental Health Review, quarterly, Reg Cyr, editor; career brochure, Public Health Inspector.

★ 638 ★
CANADIAN LUNG ASSOCIATION
75 Albert Street, Suite 908
Ottawa, Ontario K1P 5E7   (613) 237-1208
    Canada   Established 1900

Dr. Earl Hershfield, Executive Director
To enlist the cooperation of individuals and organized bodies with the medical profession with a view to reducing the morbidity and mortality in Canada of tuberculosis and respiratory diseases by prevention and treatment thereof; to encourage and promote scientific studies into basic mechanisms of lung disorders and their application to the diagnosis, treatment and prevention of respiratory diseases. Membership: 1,000. Finances: Membership: $10-$15; Other Sources: Government grants, assessment of provincial/lung associations, Christmas Seal Campaign, bequests and memorial donations. Awards: 6 percent of total Christmas Seal Campaign returns for research grants, national. Publications: Canadian Lung Association Bulletin, quarterly, Doris Goodwin, editor; Annual Report; various information pamphlets, brochures, etc. Affiliations: Provincial and local lung associations. Former Name: Canadian Tuberculosis and Respiratory Disease Association.

★ 639 ★
CANADIAN MEDIC ALERT FOUNDATION, INC.
176 St. George Street
Toronto, Ontario M5R 2N1,   (416) 923-2451
    Canada   Established 1961

Maxine P. Sinclair, Executive Director
The Foundation exists to identify individuals with medical problems, register them by serial number, issue warning bracelets, update information regularly and have that information available by telephone toll free around the clock to hospitals and doctors in case of emergency. Membership: 280,000 individuals in Canada. Finances: Membership: $12 for life; Other Sources: Volunteer donations. Meetings: Annual directors meetings. Affiliations: Medic Alert International.

★ 640 ★
CANADIAN MEDICAL ASSOCIATION
1867 Alta Vista Drive
Post Office Box 8650
Ottawa, Ontario K1G 0G8,   (616) 731-9331
    Canada   Established 1867

Robert G. Wilson, M.D., C.M., Secretary General
To promote the medical and related arts and sciences and to maintain the honor and the interests of the medical profession. Membership: 33,000 (medical doctors). Finances: Membership: $70 annually. Awards: Medal of Service and F.N.G. Starr Award; Blackader, Tisdall Memorial Lecture; Osler Oration. Meetings: Annual meetings, various locations. Publications: Canadian Medical Association Journal, 26 issues annually, Dr. Andrew Sherrington, editor; Canadian Journal of Surgery, 6 annually, Dr. L. D. MacLean and Dr. C. B. Mueller, editors. Affiliations: 35 organizations.

★ 641 ★
CANADIAN MENTAL HEALTH ASSOCIATION
2160 Yonge Street
Toronto, Ontario M4S 2Z3,   (416) 484-7750
    Canada   Established 1918

George Rohn, General Director
To improve attitudes toward mental illness and the mentally ill, to improve the treatment and caring services for the mentally ill, to work for prevention of mental illness and for the promotion of mental health. Membership: 30,000. Finances: Membership: $5; Other Sources: Community funds, government grants, campaigns, donations. Awards: Marjorie Hiscott Keyes Medal for psychiatric nursing; Association's National Award for distinguished service. Publications: Education books, reports, pamphlets. Library: 20,000 items.

★ 642 ★
CANADIAN NURSES' ASSOCIATION
50 The Driveway
Ottawa, Ontario K2P 1E2,   (613) 237-2133
    Canada   Established 1908

Helen K. Mussallem, Executive Director
To seek conditions conducive to the best possible patient care, and the prevention of illness. To achieve these purposes, the profession directs continuous attention to the quality and quantity of nurses available for the health team; the standards of preparation and performance of these nurses; the social and economic well-being of members of the profession; and the advancement of science, knowledge, techniques and

competence within the profession. Membership: 127,746. Finances: Fees determined by provincial associations. Meetings: Annual, various locations. Publications: The Canadian Nurse, monthly, M. Anne Besharah, editor; L'Infirmiere canadienne, monthly, Claire Bigué, editor. Library: 10,000 books, 450 periodicals. Affiliations: International Council of Nurses.

★ 643 ★
CANADIAN OPHTHALMOLOGICAL SOCIETY
Post Office Box 8844
Ottawa, Ontario K1G 3G2,   (613) 731-6493
   Canada   Established 1937

J. Paul Le Bel, Executive Director
To promote the development and advancement of Ophthalmology in all its aspects; in instruction, in research and in patient care for the public welfare. Membership: 637 (active, senior, life, honorary, non-resident, junior, and associate A and B). Finances: Membership: Senior 20% of active; non-resident 20% of active; junior 10% of active; associate A 100% of active; associate B 20% of active; life and honorary, no fee). Meetings: Annual, various locations. Publications: Canadian Journal of Ophthalmology, quarterly, Dr. Donald Mills, editor.

★ 644 ★
CANADIAN ORTHOPTIC COUNCIL
555 University Avenue   (416) 597-1500
Toronto, Ontario M5G 1X8,   ext. 2438
   Canada   Established 1966

To maintain and improve orthoptic standards and promote knowledge related to orthoptics. To maintain the honor and integrity of orthoptics as an auxiliary branch of ophthalmology in the Medical Profession. To foster a national interest in orthoptics. Composed of representatives from the Canadian Ophthalmological Society, Canadian Medical Association, Canadian Orthoptic Society, and a representative from each province. Membership: 135. Finances: Membership: $10 annual fee; Other Sources: Training Centres; Canadian Ophthalmological Society. Meetings: Annual, in conjunction with the Canadian Ophthalmological Society, various locations. Affiliations: Canadian Ophthalmological Society; Canadian Medical Association; Canadian Orthoptic Society.

★ 645 ★
CANADIAN ORTHOPTIC SOCIETY
c/o Mrs. Pamela Fairchild
4694 De La Peltrie
Montreal, Quebec H3W 1K3,   (514) 737-3538
   Canada   Established 1966

Frances Williams, Executive President;
   Pamela Fairchild, Secretary-Treasurer
To maintain and improve orthoptic standards and promote knowledge related to Orthoptics; to maintain and honor the integrity of Orthoptics as an auxiliary branch of ophthalmology in the Medical Profession; to foster a national interest in Orthoptics activities; organizes an annual meeting held in various cities across Canada in conjunction with the Canadian Ophthalmological Society. At the meeting there is a scientific session devoted to Orthoptics, a business meeting, and planned social gathering to promote personal contact between Canadian Orthoptist. Membership: 110 (active, 95; inactive, 11; honorary, 4). Finances: Membership: $40 annually (active); $12.50 annually (inactive); Other Sources: Annual convention registration. Meetings: Annual convention, various locations. Publications: Newsletter, 3 times annually. Affiliations: Quebec Orthoptic Association; International Orthoptic Association; Canadian Orthoptic Council.

★ 646 ★
CANADIAN OSTEOPATHIC AID SOCIETY
575 Waterloo Street
London, Ontario N6B 2R2,   (519) 439-5521
   Canada   Established 1960

M. Torney, Executive Secretary
The Society was founded to aid and support the development of osteopathic health care in Canada. It is working to have the laws changed to permit full practice rights for Doctors of Osteopathy to practice as qualified physicians. Membership: 622 (Class A and Class B members, supporters). Finances: Membership: $5 annually; Other Sources: Supporters who make donations, bequests. Meetings: Annually, at Society headquarters. Affiliations: Affiliated Chapters in Regina, Montreal, and several in Ontario.

★ 647 ★
CANADIAN OSTEOPATHIC ASSOCIATION
575 Waterloo Street
London, Ontario N6B 2R2,   (519) 439-5521
   Canada   Established 1926

Margaret Torney, Administrative Secretary
The Association's objectives are to promote the

advancement of osteopathic medicine; to stimulate, conduct and publish research; to elevate educational standards; and to help with the progress of osteopathic medicine in Canada. Membership: 32 (regular, associate, affiliate, life and honorary life). Finances: Revenue received from provincial or divisional osteopathic organizations. Meetings: Annual, in conjunction with scientific seminars.

★ 648 ★
CANADIAN OTOLARYNGOLOGICAL SOCIETY
c/o Dr. Wm. Crysdale
Hospital for Sick Children
ENT Department
555 University Avenue
Toronto, Ontario M5G 1X8,   (416) 597-0218
   Canada   Established 1946

Dr. Wm. Crysdale, Secretary
To study otolaryngological problems in relation to public health and welfare; to establish friendly relations between its members; to facilitate for its members the means of acquiring fuller knowledge of their profession by meetings and publications relative to the science, practice and teaching of otolaryngology; to foster and maintain the closest harmony and cooperation with other members of the medical profession; to advice the Canadian Medical Association in regard to the medico-political and economic matters of the Society; to encourage through bursaries or other form of grant support original work of research in otolaryngology. Membership: 528 (active, associate, emeritus, affiliate, honorary). Finances: Membership: Active, $170; associate, $45; emeritus, no charge. Awards: Hodge Memorial Award. Meetings: Annual, various Canadian cities. Publications: Journal of Otolaryngology, 6 times annually, P. Alberti, editor. Affiliations: American Council of Otolaryngology; Centurion Club.

★ 649 ★
CANADIAN PAEDIATRIC SOCIETY
Centre Hospitalier Universitaire
   de Sherbrooke
Sherbrooke, Quebec J1H 5N4,   (819) 563-9844
   Canada   Established 1923

Victor Marchessault, M.D., Executive Vice President
Aims of the Society are (1) promote by the efforts of its members, the role of Child Advocacy, as an important function of the Society in its relations with the public, government and other health professional groups; (2) promote the advancement of knowledge of the sciences pertaining to infancy, childhood and adolescence; (3) establish friendly relations among its

members; (4) establish the interests of paediatricians as specialists; (5) facilitate, for its members, the means of acquiring fuller knowledge of their profession by professional meetings and by the publication of articles and papers relating to the science, practice and teaching of the diseases of infancy, childhood and adolescence. Membership: 945 (associate, emeritus, fellow, honorary, life, provisional, sustaining members). Finances: Members: Fellows, $125; associate and sustaining, $30; Other Sources: Grants to finance special projects. Awards: The Ross Annual Award; Mead Johnson Education Grant; Mead Johnson Visiting Professorship; Heinz Symposium. Meetings: Annual Meeting, in June, various locations; regional meeting, 1 or 2 annually; Committee meetings, approximately 10 annually. Publications: Monthly Newsbulletin, Donald Delahaye, M.D., editor.

★ 650 ★
CANADIAN PARAPLEGIC ASSOCIATION
520 Sutherland Drive
Toronto, Ontario M4G 3V9,   (416) 422-5640
   Canada   Established 1945

A. C. Clarke, Managing Director
To promote the treatment, rehabilitation and re-establishment in the community of persons who have suffered spinal cord injury with residual paralysis; to promote the general welfare of these people; to provide re-establishment counsellor services. Membership: Approximately 4,500. Finances: Membership: $5; Other Sources: Government grants, private and corporate donations. Meetings: Annual, various locations. Publications: Caliper, quarterly, Michael E. Ryan, editor.

★ 651 ★
CANADIAN PARKS/RECREATION ASSOCIATION
333 River Road
Tower B - 11th Floor
Ottawa, Ontario K1L 8B9,   (613) 746-7740
   Canada   Established 1945

Denny Neider, Executive Director
National independent, voluntary, not-for-profit, service, research and education organization actively engaged to enhance the quality of life of all Canadians through "the stimulation and advancement of National, Provincial, Regional and Municipal Parks, Recreation and Leisure Services, facilities and programs in Canada." The Association offers services to develop and support the administrative and technical abilities of members, citizens, communities and agencies; to improve the quality of programs and

facilities, and to keep members informed of events which affect the profession and the quality of park and recreation services; and works towards achieving its goals through a Board of Directors represented by professional and public interest, and many Action Committees, comprised of interested members. Membership: 2,300 members (individual, practitioners, associate, student); corporate. Finances: Membership: Individual, $35 practitioner; $35 associate; $18 student; corporate from $35 to $415. Meetings: 2 Board of Directors and 2 Executive Committee annually, plus various Committee meetings, held in cities across Canada. Annual General Meeting and Annual Conference, in August annually, various Canadian cities. Publications: Recreation Canada, 5 times annually, Denny Neider, editor; Parks/ Recreation roster, annually; RecreAction newsletter.

★ 652 ★

CANADIAN PHARMACEUTICAL ASSOCIATION
1815 Alta Vista Drive
Ottawa, Ontario K1G 3Y6,   (613) 523-7877
   Canada

Leroy Fevang, Executive Director
To advance the science and practice of pharmacy. Membership: Approximately 9,500 (registered pharmacists). Finances: Membership: $30; Other Sources: Publication of text and other books. Awards: Annual award to student in each School of Pharmacy (selected by faculty) for proficiency. Meetings: Annual, various locations. Publications: Canadian Pharmaceutical Journal, monthly, D. L. Thompson, editor; Compendium of Pharmaceuticals and Specialties (French and English editors), annual, D. L. Thompson, editor; Canadian Journal of Pharmaceutical Sciences, quarterly; Canadian Self-Medication (1st edition), triennial; Supplemental Information on Medications (SIMS).

★ 653 ★

CANADIAN PHYSIOLOGICAL SOCIETY
c/o Dr. R. S. Smith
Department of Surgery
University of Alberta
Edmonton, Alberta T6G 2G3,
   Canada   Established 1935

Dr. R. S. Smith, Secretary
The Society's purpose is to support the advancement of physiology and its related branches of science, as well as to promote a friendly spirit among those Canadians who are engaged in these fields. Membership: 526 (emeritus, honorary, ordinary, associate). Finances: Membership: Annual membership dues.

Awards: Distinguished Lecturer Award. Meetings: Annually, in January, various locations; annually in June with the Canadian Federation of Biological Societies, various locations. Publications: Physiology Canada, 3 issues annually, Dr. M. A. Bisby, editor.

★ 654 ★

CANADIAN PHYSIOTHERAPY ASSOCIATION
25 Imperial Street
Toronto, Ontario M5P 1B9,   (416) 485-1139
   Canada   Established 1920

Nancy P. Christie, Executive Director
Concerned with the registration of qualified physiotherapists; with the promotion of physiotherapy as an integral part in the program of rehabilitation; with standards of training and professional practice; and with the participation in national and international affairs concerned with physiotherapy. Membership: 4,728. Finances: Membership: Active, $100; inactive, $30; active part-time, $60. Awards: Constance Beattie Memorial Fund. Publications: Journal, 6 times annually, Joan Cleather, editor. Affiliations: World Confederation for Physical Therapy.

★ 655 ★

CANADIAN PSYCHIATRIC ASSOCIATION
225 Lisgar Street, Suite 103   (613) 234-2815
Ottawa, Ontario K2P 0C6,   (613) 234-6644
   Canada   Established 1951

Lea C. Metivier, Chief Administrative Officer
The Association operates for (1) the mutual benefit of psychiatrists of Canada; (2) the exchange of scientific information; (3) the representation of the members in their relationships with the Canadian Government, universities, medical associations; and (4) the encouragement of psychiatric education in universities and hospitals for the improvement and extension of treatment of the mentally ill. Membership: 2,200 (active, member-in-training, associate, corresponding, affiliate, honorary, life, and inactive). Finances: Membership: Active, $125; member-in-training, associate, corresponding, $30; affiliate, $25. Meetings: Annual, various locations. Publications: Canadian Journal of Psychiatry, 8 times annually, Dr. E. Kingstone, editor; Canadian Psychiatric Association Bulletin, 6 times annually, Dr. Colin M. Smith, editor. Affiliations: Provincial psychiatric associations, and the Canadian Medical Association.

★ 656 ★

CANADIAN RED CROSS SOCIETY
95 Wellesley Street East
Toronto, Ontario M4Y 1H6,   (416) 923-6692
    Canada   Established 1896

H. Tellier, National Commissioner;
    Muriel E. Craig, Secretary
To furnish aid to the sick and wounded of the armed
forces in time of war and to all war victims, both
civilian and military, in accordance with the spirit
and conditions of the Geneva Conventions for the Protection of War Victims, dated August 12, 1949, which
Canada has ratified; to bring to the knowledge of the
people of Canada the beneficent provisions of such
Conventions; in time of peace or war to carry on
and assist in work for the improvement of health, the
prevention of disease and the mitigation of suffering
throughout the world. Activities include blood transfusion service, veterans' services, international relief,
emergency services, first aid health and community
services, water safety service, small craft safety,
tracing and reunion bureau, outpost hospitals, nursing
stations, Red Cross youth, Red Cross corps. Membership: 1,500,000. Finances: Public appeals;
government grants; United Way Fund raising campaigns. Meetings: Annual, various locations.
Publications: Service, quarterly, Ross Fyfe, editor.
Affiliation: League of Red Cross Societies.

★ 657 ★

CANADIAN RHEUMATISM ASSOCIATION
Rheumatology Service
Centre hospitalier universitaire
Sherbrooke, Quebec J1H 5N4,   (819) 565-2050
    Canada   Established 1935

André Lussier, M.D., F.R.C.P.(C), Secretary-
    Treasurer
The Association aims to disseminate knowledge and
promote research in the field of arthritis and related
diseases. Membership: 200 (rheumatologists, specialist physicians and research workers). Finances:
Membership: $45. Lectureships: Dunlop-Dottridge
Lecture. Meetings: Annual, in conjunction with
the Royal College of Physicians of Canada, various
locations. Affiliations: Royal College of Physicians
of Canada.

★ 658 ★

CANADIAN SAVE THE CHILDREN FUND
720 Spadina Avenue
Toronto, Ontario M5S 2W3,   (416) 960-3190
    Canada   Established 1921

Gordon S. Ramsay, National Directory
An international development agency which is the
Canadian member of the Save the Children Alliance.
Its policy is based on the Declaration of the Rights of
the Child, and on-going programs are geared to improve the lives of children and their families and
communities through integrated development activities
promoting self-help. Publications: Promises, quarterly. Affiliations: Save the Children in Norway,
Denmark, United States, Britain.

★ 659 ★

CANADIAN SCHIZOPHRENIA FOUNDATION
2229 Broad Street
Regina, Saskatchewan S4P 1Y7,   (306) 527-7969
    Canada   Established 1969

I. J. Kahan, General Director
Formed to raise the levels of treatment and preventive
work for schizophrenia and other diseases. The
Foundation provides information about a variety of
illnesses, their treatment and prevention. Information
and assistance is given to enable the patient to receive effective medical help. They have established
a large publication department for the provision of
information. Membership: About 2,000 individuals.
Finances: Membership: $10, $20, and $40; Other
Sources: Donations, sale of literature. Meetings:
Annual international conventions; numerous local
meetings. Publications: Journal of Orthmolecular
Psychiatry, quarterly, I. J. Kahan, editor; Huxley-
C.S.F. Newsletter, quarterly, I. J. Kahan, editor;
and many other publications. Affiliations: Huxley
Institute; overseas foundations.

★ 660 ★

CANADIAN SOCIETY FOR CELL BIOLOGY
c/o Dr. I. B. Heath
York University
Biology Department
4700 Keele Street
Downsview, Ontario M3J 1P3,   (416) 667-3748
    Canada   Established 1965

Dr. I. B. Heath, Secretary
The Society's purpose is to further all aspects of research, teaching, and communication in the field of
cell biology. Membership: 300, mainly university
personnel. Finances: Membership: Annual dues--
full member, $12; student, $8.50. Meetings:
Semiannual. Publications: Canadian Society for
Cell Biology Bulletin, quarterly, Dr. Vern Seligez,
editor; CSCB Bulletin, Dr. Robert Tongvoy, editor.

★ 661 ★

CANADIAN SOCIETY OF CLINICAL CHEMISTS
151 Slater Street, Suite 906   (613) 233-5623
Ottawa, Ontario K1P 5H3,   Established 1956
  Canada   Incorporated 1965

N. Lorraine Chellingworth, Executive Secretary
Aims are to raise the standard of practice of clinical
chemistry and to elevate the professional status of
clinical chemists.   The Society has contributed significantly to the professional development of clinical
chemists in Canada.   The efforts of the Committee
on Certification have resulted in a program by means
of which fully qualified clinical chemists may now be
recognized by the awarding of certificates.   Full
members of the Society are eligible to apply for Certification. Membership: 533 (full, associate, student, honorary, emeritus). Finances: Membership:
Full, $60; associate, $55; student, $15; certified
member pays an extra $10. Awards: General Diag-
nostics (Canada) Lectureship; Ames Award; MED-
CHEM Award; Cybermedix Award. Lectureship:
MDS Lectureship. Meetings: Annual, various locations. Publications: Clinical Biochemistry, D. B.
Tonks, editor; CSCC News, bimonthly, Arlene
Crowe, editor.

★ 662 ★

CANADIAN SOCIETY OF CYTOLOGY
c/o Dr. G. H. Anderson
Cancer Control Agency of British Columbia
2656 Heather Street
Vancouver, British Columbia
  V5Z 3J3, Canada   Established 1961

Dr. G. H. Anderson, Secretary/Treasurer
The Society aims to coordinate the activities of pathologists who practice cytopathology in Canada.
Membership: 320 full (pathologists and other medically qualified practitioners) and affiliate (cytotechnologists) members. Finances: Membership: Full, $10
annually; affiliate, $5 annually. Lectureships:
Ortho Guest Lectureship. Meetings: Annually,
various locations. Publications: Acta Cytologica,
bimonthly, Dr. G. Wied, editor.

★ 663 ★

CANADIAN SOCIETY OF DENTISTRY FOR
  CHILDREN
2953 Bathurst Street
Toronto, Ontario M6B 3B2,   (416) 783-0419
  Canada   Established 1950

Dr. Donald L. Rife, Executive Secretary-Treasurer
The purpose of the Society is the advancement of

knowledge of all phases of dentistry for children and
the dissemination of this knowledge to the profession
and the public. Membership: Variable number of
general practitioners and specialists in paedodontics.
Finances: Membership: $50. Meetings: Annual,
various locations.

★ 664 ★

CANADIAN SOCIETY OF ELECTROENCEPHA-
  LOGRAPHERS, ELECTROMYOGRAPHERS AND
  CLINICAL NEUROPHYSIOLOGISTS
Dr. Andrew Eisen
Department of Diagnostic Neurophysiology
Vancouver General Hospital
855 West 12th Avenue
Vancover, British Columbia
  V5Z 1M9, Canada

This is a professional and scientific society, with its
main function being to provide a forum for the scientific development of the disciplines of electroencephalography, electromyography and clinical neurophysiology. Membership: 200 (full, associate,
honorary). Finances: $20. Awards: Annual Es-
say Award. Meetings: Annually, various locations.
Affiliations: Canadian Congress of Neurological Sciences; International Federation of Societies of EEG
and Clinical Neurophysiology.

★ 665 ★

CANADIAN SOCIETY OF HOSPITAL PHARMACISTS
175 College Street
Toronto, Ontario M5T 1P8,   (416) 979-2049
  Canada

Donna M. Shaw, Executive Director
A voluntary organization of hospital pharmacists
formed to enhance the standards of practice in hospitals and the role which pharmacists play in the
general organization pattern of hospitals.   Its objectives are as follows: to improve and extend the
usefulness of hospital pharmacists to the institution
which they serve and the profession of pharmacy in
general; to provide a means by which pharmaceutical
information can be conveyed to hospital pharmacists,
to endeavor to make pharmacy an important part of
the program of health services in Canada; to take
such action as may be within its power to obtain a
higher standard of proficiency among hospital pharmacists in Canada. Membership: 1,400 (active, associate, supporting, student, honorary, honorary life).
Finances: Membership: Active, associate, supporting, $45; student, $10 (plus provincial branch fees
of varying amounts); Other Sources: Grants and
major education program, the Professional Practice

Conference held annually. Awards: The Awards Program, 8 grants; 11 awards available to individuals (or groups) for significant innovations, developments, and research in various aspects of hospital pharmacy. Meetings: Annual Meeting, various locations. Publications: Canadian Journal of Hospital Pharmacy, bimonthly, Professor J. L. Summers, editor; Pharmascope, 4 to 6 times annually, Donna M. Shaw, editor; Employment Opportunities Bulletin, monthly, Donna M. Shaw, editor.

★ 666 ★

CANADIAN SOCIETY OF LABORATORY
   TECHNOLOGISTS
Post Office Box 830
Hamilton, Ontario L8N 3N8,   (416) 528-8642
   Canada   Established 1936

E. Valerie Booth, Executive Director
To promote and maintain a nationally-accepted standard of medical laboratory technology by which other health professionals and the public are assured of effective and economical laboratory services. To promote, maintain and protect the professional identity and interests of the medical laboratory technologists. The Society is a membership organization and the standards and certifying body for medical laboratory technologists in Canada. Membership: 19,581 (active, inactive, trainee, associate, laboratory assistant). Finances: Membership: Active, $45; associate, $35; inactive and laboratory assistant, $27; trainee, $20; Other Sources: Examination fee, publications. Awards: Gold Medal Award; 5 scientific paper awards; 4 lectureships; 1 scholarship award; Founders' Fund grants. Meetings: Annual, various locations. Publications: Canadian Journal of Medical Technology, bimonthly, Leslie D. Mellor, editor; Bulletin, monthly, L. Seibel, editor. Library: Continuing education loan library, 360 volumes (members only). Affiliations: British Columbia Society of Medical Technologists; Ontario Society of Medical Technologists.

★ 667 ★

CANADIAN SOCIETY OF MICROBIOLOGISTS
Secretariat,
85 rue Albert Street, Suite 500
Ottawa, Ontario K1P 6A4,   (613) 238-5678
   Canada   Established 1951

Dr. D. J. Kushner, President;
   Dr. I. J. McDonald, Secretary-Treasurer
To promote the advancement of microbiology in all its aspects and to facilitate the interchange of ideas between microbiologists. The membership includes scientists and students from all biological disciplines who are interested in the study and application of microbiology and related subjects. Membership: Approximately 800 (ordinary, student, honorary, emeritus). Finances: Membership: Ordinary, $27; student and emeritus, $13.50; Other Sources: Advertising revenue from CSM Newsletter and annual programme and abstracts. Awards: Canadian Society of Microbiologists Award; Hotpack Lecture; Canadian Society of Microbiologists Graduate Student Presentation Award. Meetings: Annual, various locations across Canada. Publications: CSM Newsletter/Bulletin de Nouvelles SCM, 3 times annually, Dr. R. M. Stevenson, editor; CSM Annual Programme and Abstracts, annual. Affiliations: Canadian Federation of Biological Societies; Association of Scientific, Engineering and Technological Community of Canada; International Association of Microbiological Societies.

CANADIAN SOCIETY OF RADIOLOGICAL
TECHNICIANS
   See: Canadian Association of Medical
        Radiation Technologists

★ 668 ★

CANADIAN SOCIETY OF RESPIRATORY
   TECHNOLOGISTS
395 Waterloo Street
Winnipeg, Manitoba R3N 0S7,   (204) 452-1207
   Canada   Established 1964

To encourage and develop training programs for Respiratory Technologists; to advance the skill and art of respiratory technology through institutes, lectures; to facilitate cooperation between this and other paramedical professions. Membership: 1,050 (registered, student, associate). Finances: Membership: Registered, $50; student, $120; associate, $40; inactive, $10. Awards: Gold Medal; G. Trudell Award. Meetings: Annual, various locations. Publications: Canadian Respiratory Technology, quarterly, T. Yachemetz, editor.

★ 669 ★

CANADIAN SPEECH AND HEARING ASSOCIATION
c/o Department of Speech Pathology
Room 308, Corbett Hall
University of Alberta
Edmonton, Alberta T6G 2G4,
   Canada   Established 1964

Margaret Roberts, President; Judy Branch, President Elect; Frederick Greenberg, Past President; Louise Coderre, Secretary; Einer Boberg, Treasurer To contribute to the advancement of the scientific study of the processes of individual human communication in speech and hearing; to encourage research and investigation into human speech and hearing disorders; to disseminate information by discussion, and by meetings, and such media as may lawfully be available to the Association, to the public in general, and in particular those persons or classes of persons involved with or having care of individuals in whom speech and hearing disorders may be diagnosed and treated; and to regulate the standard of proficiency of the membership and to promote and improve the performance of the highest ethical standards of practice in the profession of the diagnosing and treatment of speech and hearing disorders. Membership: 700 (speech-language pathologists, audiologists, students in training). Finances: Membership: Regular, $60; students, $20; associates, $30. Awards: Honors (of the Association); Distinguished Service Award; Medal for Outstanding Professional Achievement. Publications: Human Communication, 3 times annually, Dr. Frank Wilson, editor; Newsletter (Hear Here), every 6 weeks, Elaine Heaton, editor.

CANADIAN TUBERCULOSIS AND RESPIRATORY DISEASE ASSOCIATION
See: Canadian Lung Association

★ 670 ★
CANADIAN VETERINARY MEDICAL ASSOCIATION
360 Bronson Avenue
Ottawa, Ontario K1R 6J3,   (613) 236-1162
   Canada   Established 1948

S. Burns, Executive Secretary
To cultivate and advance the art and science of veterinary medicine and surgery and to maintain the honor and interest of the veterinary profession; to conduct, direct, encourage, support or provide for exhaustive surgical and medical veterinary research; to elevate and sustain and improve the professional character and education of veterinarians in Canada. Membership: 3,566 (full, associate). Finances: Membership: Full, $75; associate, $37.50. Awards: CVMA Veterinary Research Trust Fund; CVMA Medal; CVMA Award. Meetings: Annual, various locations. Publications: Canadian Veterinary Journal, monthly, Dr. L. P. Phaneof, editor; Canadian Journal of Comparative Medicine, quarterly, Dr. R. G. Thomson, editor. Affiliations: World Veterinary Association; Commonwealth Veterinary Association; 10 Provincial Veterinary Medical Association.

★ 671 ★
CANCER CARE, INC. AND THE NATIONAL CANCER FOUNDATION, INC.
1 Park Avenue   (212) 679-5700
New York, New York 10016   Established 1947

Irene G. Buckley, Executive Director
A voluntary social service agency, Cancer Care, Inc., and its parent organization, The National Cancer Foundation, Inc. (see also separate entry), provide professional counseling and planning to advanced cancer patients and their families. Plans for care-at-home may include provisions for nursing care, homemaker and home health aides, housekeepers, and other services. When appropriate, supplementary financial assistance is available to self-maintaining families to help them extend their resources in meeting these needed services. Collaborates with medical, health and welfare agencies in community planning for the catastrophically ill. The agency conducts programs of professional consultation and education, social research, public affairs and public education on a national and worldwide basis. Membership: 15,000 volunteers. Finances: Voluntary contributions, United Way of Tri-State, mail appeals, benefits, gifts and bequests, etc. Awards: Volunteer recognition, media, community service. Meetings: Board, 7 times annually, agency office; annual, June, agency office. Publications: Proceedings of the 4th National Symposium; 1973 study, The Impact, Costs and Consequences of Catastrophic Illness on Patients and Families; 1977 study, Listen to the Children--a study of the impact on the mental health of children of a parent's catastrophic illness; Annual Report; Report to Contributors, semiannual; The Lamp, semiannual, for volunteers; The Communicator, monthly, for staff; monographs, research and professional reports; article reprints; testimonies; speeches; training films. Library: Professional research library.

★ 672 ★
CANDLELIGHTERS
123 C Street, S.E.   (202) 544-1696
Washington, D.C. 20003   Established 1969

Grace Powers Monaco, Chairperson
Aim is to help parents of cancer afflicted children and their families to cope with emotional and other stresses produced by the disease through encouraging the formation of parents peer-support groups, through providing educational information to assist parents in understanding the disease, and in developing ways of structuring their lives to cope with it. The group is also active in making legislative analyses of the needs of cancer afflicted parents/children and testifying before congress on the needs of children and their

families with respect to cancer research and support services. Membership: Approximately 125 groups in 47 states, Canada and England; made up of parents who have had or do have a child with cancer and their family members. Finances: Other Sources: Donations. Meetings: Usually monthly. Publications: Candlelighters National Newsletter, every 2 1/2 months, Grace Powers Monaco, Esquire, editor; Handbook for Parents; individual group newsletters; parents' publications, Teen Newsletter.

★ 673 ★
CANSURMOUNT
American Cancer Society
777 Third Avenue   (212) 371-2900
New York, New York 10017   Established 1973

To help people better understand and cope with cancer. It is a volunteer program which serves cancer patients, their families, and those involved with the care and treatment of cancer patients. Because most CanSurmount volunteers have cancer themselves, they are in a position to add a unique dimension to the traditional health care team. The model program has developed over a 2-year period at Presbyterian Medical Center in Denver. Founder, Dr. Paul K. Hamilton, Jr., oncologist, invited four of his cancer patients to discuss the idea of special need of the cancer patients. These four volunteers began to visit a few hospitalized cancer patients in order to share with them insights and concerns, hopes and frustrations. In 1978 CanSurmount was adopted by the American Cancer Society as a national program. Membership: Cancer patients. Finances: Small staff support from the A.C.S., but entirely volunteer works. Affiliations: Hospital based chapters in 18 states, Canada and Australia.

★ 674 ★
CARIBBEAN FOOD AND NUTRITION INSTITUTE
Post Office Box 140   927-8338
Kingston 7, Jamaica, West Indies

To investigate all factors related to food and nutrition in the Caribbean area; to act as a catalyst among persons and organizations concerned with the field of food and nutrition; to develop community nutrition-education programs; to promote the teaching of nutrition in schools, teachers' colleges, technical institutions and universities; and to encourage and assist the governments of member territories in the formulation and implementation of national food and nutrition policies. Membership: 17 countries of the Caribbean. Finances: PAHO/WHO regular budget; grants from UNICEF, US/AID; Commonwealth Caribbean Govern-

ments and the Ford Foundation. Publications: Cajanus, quarterly; Food Balance Sheets for the Caribbean; Food Composition Tables for Use in the English-Speaking Caribbean; Guidelines to Food and Dietary Services in the Contemporary Caribbean; Guidelines to Young Child Feeding in the Contemporary Caribbean; Institutional Food Service: A Guide for Supervisors; Malnutrition and Gastroenteritis in Children: A Manual for Hospital Treatment and Management; Meal Planning for Diabetics; The National Food and Nutrition Survey of Barbados; The National Food and Nutrition Survey of Guyana; The National Food and Nutrition Survey of St. Lucia; Nutrient-Cost Tables, quarterly; Nutrient-Cost Reference Tables for Use in the Caribbean; Nyam News (nutrition news packets monthly); Protein Foods for the Caribbean; Recommended Dietary Allowances for the Caribbean; Strategy and Plan of Action to Combat Gastroenteritis and Malnutrition in Children Under Two Years of Age; Understanding Diabetes.

★ 675 ★
CARROLL CENTER FOR THE BLIND
770 Centre Street   (617) 969-6200
Newton, Massachusetts 02158 Established 1936

Rachel Ethier Rosenbaum, Executive Director
A non-profit organization which offers rehabilitation services to legally blind adults (ages 16 and up); community rehabilitation services for all ages; volunteer services; public education; and professional training. The central work is the residential rehabilitation program for newly blinded adults. Clients stay for approximately three months. Their curriculum consists of classes in mobility; communication skills such as: braille handwriting, tape-recording, typing, spoken communication, etc.; personal management, which consists of techniques of daily living, grooming, dressing, eating skills, housekeeping skills and general self-care. Finances: Other Sources: MCB fees paid through state rehabilitation funds; through support from foundations, grants and contributions from the public. Meetings: Board of Directors, quarterly. Publications: Aids and Appliances Review, quarterly, Robert McGillivray, editor. Library: Brendon Library, approximately 650 volumes. Former Name: Catholic Guild for All the Blind.

★ 676 ★
CASUALTY ACTUARIAL SOCIETY
1 Penn Plaza
250 West 34th Street, 51st Floor (212) 560-1018
New York, New York 10001   Established 1914

David P. Flynn, Secretary
To advance the knowledge of actuarial science as

applied to the problems of insurance, other than life insurance, and to promote and maintain high standards of conduct and competence within the actuarial profession. Membership: 900 (fellows, associates). Finances: Membership: Fellows, $80; associate, first 5 years, $60, then $80. Awards: Woodward-Fondiller Prize for outstanding research paper; Dorweiler Prize for original research paper. Meetings: Semiannual, various locations. Publications: Yearbook, annually; Proceedings of CAS, annually, D.C. Forker, editor; various books and pamphlets.

CATHOLIC GUILD FOR ALL THE BLIND
    See: Carroll Center for the Blind

★ 677 ★
CATHOLIC HEALTH ASSOCIATION OF CANADA
312 Daly Avenue
Ottawa, Ontario   (613) 238-8471
    Canada   Established 1939

Reverend Everett MacNeil, Executive Director
A national Catholic organization comprised of people involved in the health field, professionally or voluntarily, out of a Christian motivation. To promote respect for the inherent dignity of each person and to reverence that unique experience of life, of sickness, and of death; to promote and to stimulate concern for health as a total process, including the maintenance, restoration and extension of health as a part of the full development of the human person and of our society; to help develop structures which foster holistic health, respect, and reverence for those who are sick, aged, disabled and dying; to mediate or build bridges between the different groups in our society that are involved in, responsible for and have an effect on health as a total process; to assist in preparing the contemporary Canadian community for the critical health problems of the future; to probe the ethical issues in the life sciences, and in collaboration with the magisterium of the Church, to provide guidelines for action; to collaborate at all levels in assuring that competent and compassionate pastoral care is available in the health apostolate; as an ecclesial community, to be aware and supportive of current social justice concerns particularly those with health care implications; to intensify the humanizing of health care in cooperation with other groups in society; to stimulate and support research on the fundamental root diseases and crippling illnesses of our society, as well as on methods of health care and its delivery. Membership: Institutional, 146; affiliate, 3; associate, 250; personal, 600; (institutional: hospital and homes; affiliate: organizations, institutions, companies; associate: reli-

gious congregations, bishops, Catholic Women's Leagues; personal: individuals interested in all aspects of health care). Finances: Membership: Institutional: hospitals, 035% of operational budget; homes, $150; affiliate, $300; associate, $100; personal, $15; Other Sources: Government grants, donations, fund-raising. Meetings: Board meetings, quarterly; 2 major educational events/conventions. Publications: C.H.A.C. Review/Revue A.C.C.S., bimonthly, Rev. Everett MacNeil, editor; Quidnunc, occasional newsletter, Rev. Everett MacNeil, editor; Special Issues (i.e., Pastoral care, euthanasia, aging, etc.), Rev. Everett MacNeil, editor; Biannual Directory, biennial, Rev. Everett MacNeil, editor. Library: CHAC, 1,200 volumes. Former Name: Catholic Hospital Association of Canada.

★ 678 ★
CATHOLIC HEALTH ASSOCIATION OF THE
    UNITED STATES
1438 South Grand Boulevard   (314) 773-0646
St. Louis, Missouri 63104   Established 1915

John E. Curley, Jr., President
The Association is an ecclesial community dedicated to and faithful to the healing mission of the Church, promoting the health of those who are sick or infirmed by age or disability; by respecting human dignity in the experience of sickness and death. The purpose of the Association is also to promote and implement the Mission of the Association by assisting Catholic Church-related health care organizations, to provide optimal health care services and programs, which contribute to the physical, emotional, spiritual and social well-being of the people and communities served. Membership: 1,503 (hospitals, 633; long term care facilities, 239; associate, 103; personal, 528) Finances: Other Sources: Advertising; publications; institutes; workshops. Meetings: Annual Assembly, various locations. Publications: Hospital Progress, monthly, Carol S. Boyer, editor; News-Briefs, monthly; The CHA in Washington, monthly; books, brochures and pamphlets. Library: 10,000 volumes, staff, 3. Former Name: Catholic Hospital Association.

CATHOLIC HOSPITAL ASSOCIATION
    See: Catholic Health Association of the
        United States

CATHOLIC HOSPITAL ASSOCIATION OF CANADA
    See: Catholic Health Association of Canada

★ 679 ★

CATHOLIC MEDICAL MISSION BOARD
10 West 17th Street   (212) 242-7757
New York, New York 10011   Established 1928

Joseph J. Walter, Director and President
To improve with medical supplies and volunteer lay
personnel the quality of medical care given charitably
to the sick in underdeveloped areas overseas, regardless of religious affiliation.   Activities include ship-
ment of bulk quantities of pharmaceuticals, medical
instruments and equipment to medical installations
(hospitals, dispensaries, clinics), overseas, all costs
paid; recruitment of lay medical personnel to volunteer their professional services to medical installations
overseas for periods of 6 months or more; fund raising
to support these operations.   Finances: Fund raising
campaigns in United States and Canada.   Publications: Medical Mission News, bimonthly, Raymond
Ganly, editor; Professional Placement Newsletter,
bimonthly, Vincent Hogan, editor.

★ 680 ★

CENTER FOR HEALTH ADMINISTRATION STUDIES
University of Chicago
5720 South Woodlawn Avenue   (312) 753-4191
Chicago, Illinois 60637   Established 1950

Ronald Anderson, Director
To contribute through social and economic research
and through education toward the continual improvement of health services in the United States; to train
research personnel and practitioners such as hospital
administrators, executives and policy formulators, and
provide them with the tools necessary for the exploration of new alternatives to the present organization of
medicine.   Membership: A component of the Graduate School of Business, University of Chicago.   Finances: University funds; contributions; grants.
Publications: Annual Symposium; numerous research
monographs and reports.

★ 681 ★

CENTER FOR OCCUPATIONAL HAZARDS, INC.
5 Beekman Street   (212) 227-6220
New York, New York 10038   Established 1977

Michael McCann, Ph.D., President and Executive
     Director; Monona Rossol, Director of Art Hazards
     Information Center
Clearinghouse for research and education on health
hazards in the arts and crafts, theater, and museum
conservation.   Includes (1) Information Center -
answers written and telephone inquiries, has extensive
list of publications; (2) publishes Art Hazards News-

letter; (3) lecture/workshop program; (4) consultation
program.   Finances: Other Sources: New York
State Council on Arts, National Endowment for Arts,
tax-exempt contributions, earned income.   Publications: Art Hazards Newsletter, 10 issues annually,
Michael McCann, editor; numerous books and pamphlets.   Library: The Information Center Library
(by appointment, available to artists, physicians, scientists and others interested in the health hazards of
art materials).

★ 682 ★

CENTER FOR THE STUDY OF AGING AND
     HUMAN DEVELOPMENT
Box 3003
Duke University Medical Center   (919) 684-2248
Durham, North Carolina 27710   Established 1955

George L. Maddox, Ph.D., Director
The Center's programs are organized in three Divisions:
Research, Training, and Evaluated Services.   The
Duke Center's published objectives in gerontology include (1) multidisciplinary research; (2) career and
short-term training; (3) information evaluation, storage and retrieval; (4) consultation; (5) cooperative
development of gerontological activities with units
inside and outside the University; and (6) the development, evaluation and dissemination of model
service programs.   Membership: 62 (senior fellows
representing a wide variety of disciplines of the University).   Finances: No membership fees; Other
Sources: NIA, AoA, NIMH.   Meetings: Conferences, workshops and seminars held throughout each
year.   Publications: Center Report, periodically;
Center Reports on Advances in Research, periodically;
over 35 monographs and over 650 articles published
by Center Senior Fellows.

★ 683 ★

CENTER FOR ULCER RESEARCH AND EDUCATION
     (CURE)
VA Wadsworth Hospital Center
Building 115, Room 217   (213) 825-5091
Los Angeles, California 90073   Established 1974

Morton I. Grossman, M.D., Ph.D., Director
To gain new knowledge about peptic ulcer and dis-
seminate this knowledge to doctors, patients and the
general public.   Membership: 15 key investigators,
12 investigators, 14 affiliated investigators, 7 associ-
ates; these investigators work at 8 different hospitals:
UCLA, UC San Diego, VA Wadsworth, VA Sepulveda,
VA La Jolla, Kaiser-Permanente, VA Dallas, Harbor-
UCLA.   Finances: Other Sources: Supported by
National Institutes of Arthritis, Metabolism and

Digestive Diseases (NIAMDD) and the CURE Foundation which exists solely for the support of the Center. Fellowships: National Institutes of Health Fellowships. Meetings: Semiannual, all day research; semimonthly seminars at VA Wadsworth Hospital (Building 115 or 114). Publications: A CURE News, 3 times annually; CURE Foundation brochure; Patient brochure.

★ 684 ★
CENTRAL ASSOCIATION OF ELECTROENCEPHA-
　　LOGRAPHERS
c/o Phiroze L. Hansotia, M.D.
Marshfield Clinic, Neurology - 4D
1000 North Oak Avenue　　　　(715) 387-5351
Marshfield, Wisconsin 54449　　Established 1947

Phiroze L. Hansotia, M.D., Secretary-Treasurer
To further interest in electroencephalography; to discuss matters and present papers pertaining thereto. Membership: 325 (electroencephalographers, EEG technicians, neurologists, psychologists, psychiatrists, electronics engineers, neurosurgeons, neurophysiologists, interested persons in various fields). Finances: Membership: $5. Meetings: Annual or semiannual, various locations. Affiliations: American Electroencephalographic Society.

★ 685 ★
CENTRAL ASSOCIATION OF OBSTETRICIANS AND
　　GYNECOLOGISTS
Mayo Clinic
200 1st Street, S.W.　　　　　(507) 284-4100
Rochester, Minnesota 55901　　Established 1929

George D. Malkasian, Jr., M.D., Secretary-
　　Treasurer
The objective of this Association is the encouragement and promotion of the study and practice of obstetrics and gynecology. Membership: Active membership limited to 515; 450 (life, honorary, non-resident). Finances: Membership: $75. Awards: Prize Award of $1,000 and Certificate of Merit of $500 for the best and second best investigative or clinical works in the specialty by an accredited physician, research worker or medical student within the geographic confines of the Association. Central Association Award of $250 for best paper presented on the Program, exclusive of the above awards. Meetings: Annual, various locations.

★ 686 ★
CENTRAL SOCIETY FOR CLINICAL RESEARCH
Christ Institute of Medical Research
2141 Auburn Avenue　　　　　(513) 369-2560
Cincinnati, Ohio 45219　　　　Established 1929

Gilbert M. Schiff, M.D., Secretary-Treasurer
Established for the cultivation of clinical research. Membership: 1,300 (active and emeritus). Finances: Membership: Active, $70. Meetings: Annual, Chicago, Illinois. Publications: Journal of Laboratory and Clinical Medicine, monthly, Charles Mengel, M.D., editor.

★ 687 ★
CHEAR (INTERNATIONAL FOUNDATION FOR
　　CHILDREN'S HEARING EDUCATION AND
　　RESEARCH)
871 McLean Avenue　　　　　(914) 237-2676
Yonkers, New York 10704　　　Established 1969

David Pravda, President; Sara Kessler, Secretary
To raise monies for research for cure of nerve deafness; on a national scale, to do for deafness what is being done for other diseases and handicaps; to help parents and the public understand deafness and do something about it; to improve education and educational facilities for the deaf and hearing-impaired. Membership: 2,000 plus. Finances: Other Sources: Donations. Research Funds: Grants for Deafness Research; Scholarships for Schools (both public and private) that have educational programs for the hearing impaired and are interested in mainstreaming education of the deaf or who specifically service hearing impaired children. Meetings: Quarterly, CHEAR office. Publications: Hearing Research Development, quarterly, D. A. Pravda, editor.

★ 688 ★
CHILD HEALTH ASSOCIATE PROGRAM
University of Colorado Medical Center C219
4200 East 9th Avenue　　　　(303) 394-7963
Denver, Colorado 80262　　　Established 1969

Virginia Moore, M.D., Co-Director;
　　Richard D. Krugman, M.D., Co-Director
Project of the University of Colorado Medical Center to train highly competent non-physician primary health care providers for children in ambulatory setting. Finances: State funds and grants from numerous sources.

★ 689 ★
CHILD WELFARE LEAGUE OF AMERICA
67 Irving Place   (212) 254-7410
New York, New York 10003   Established 1920

Joseph H. Reid, Executive Director
Organized to improve care and services for deprived,
dependent, neglected children, youth, and their families; the League provides consultation, conducts research, develops standards for services, sponsors annual
regional conferences, maintains a reference library and
information service, conducts agency or community
surveys, administers special projects, and publishes a
journal, other professional literature, and an annual
directory of affiliate agencies.   The League merged
with the Florence Crittenton Association in 1976.
Membership: 400 agencies.   Finances: Dues from
agencies, public and private grants, bequests, contributions.   Meetings: Board meetings, semiannually.
Publications: Child Welfare, 10 times annually, Carl
Schoenberg, editor; Annual Directory; books and
monographs.   Library: 3,000 volumes.

★ 690 ★
CHILDBIRTH WITHOUT PAIN EDUCATION
    ASSOCIATION
20134 Snowden   (313) 341-3816
Detroit, Michigan 48235   Established 1959

Flora Hommel, Executive Director
To set up and maintain an educational institution for
the instruction in and promulgation of the Psychoprophylactic Method of Painless Childbirth for expectant
parents, medical and teaching personnel, interested
lay groups, and supervised school groups; to educate
and train teachers, monitrices, and the public-at-
large; to engage in research activities that may be
carried out in cooperation with physicians, registered
nurses, and others for the purpose of discovering improved techniques and methods in the Psychoprophylactic Method of Painless Childbirth and related areas of
family-centered maternity care; to encourage the establishment in other communities of groups and/or
chapters having the same or similar purposes; and to
give aid and support to already existing groups.   The
Association, a member group of the International
Childbirth Education Association is a certified ICEA
Teacher Training Center, which conducts teacher and
monitrice training.   Membership: Approximately
3,000 (former and current students, physicians, nurses,
interested individuals).   Finances: Membership:
Couple, $2; single, $1; life, $35; professional,
$10; contributing, $5; sustaining, $10; supporting,
$25; sponsoring, $100; Other Sources: Contributions, class fees.   Membership: Biennial Conference,
various locations.   Publications: CWPEA Newsletter,
bimonthly; Memo, bimonthly (alternating with News-

letter); Conference Proceedings, biennial.   Library:
100 volumes.   Also Known As: Lamaze Birth Without Pain Education Association.

★ 691 ★
CHILDREN'S BLOOD FOUNDATION, INC.
342 Madison Avenue   (212) 687-1564
New York, New York 10017   Established 1952

Mrs. Michael Katz, Executive Director
Seeks to combat diseases of the blood in children such
as leukemia, hemophilia, hemorrhagia of the newborn,
thalassemia (Cooley's anemia), sickle cell anemia and
other anemias.   Operates center in The New York
Hospital complex which includes diagnostic and treatment clinics, progressive research laboratories and intensive training of physicians in the specialty of
pediatric hematology/oncology.

★ 692 ★
CHILDREN'S EYE CARE FOUNDATION
1015 15th Street, N.W.   (202) 789-0880
Washington, D.C. 20005   Established 1971

George K. Degnon, CAE, Executive Director
To expand and support centers for training pediatric
ophthalmologists; to conduct research in the special
problems of children's eye care; to promote public
education and service in the field.   Membership:
500.   Publications: Newsletter, irregular.

★ 693 ★
CHILDREN'S LIVER FOUNDATION, INC.
28 Highland Avenue   (201) 761-1111
Maplewood, New Jersey 07040   Established 1975

Maxine Turon, President; Gail Rempell, Vice
    President; Jeff Rempell, D.M.D., Treasurer
To support system for parents; to support research,
education of medical world as well as lay public.   Produces public service announcements.   Membership:
1,000 (general).   Finances: Membership: $15 an-
nually per family; Other Sources: Fund Raising Activities (raffles, dinner, dances, auctions, etc.);
memorials; corporations and foundations; fund raising
letter.   Awards: Research Awards.   Meetings:
Annual meeting, each June, Chicago, Illinois.
Publications: CLF Newsletter, quarterly, G. Rempell,
editor.   Affiliations: The Michael McGough Research Fund, London, England.   Remarks: The CLF
Inc. has chapters across the country and is presently
setting up a national registry and a national liver
transplant program.

★ 694 ★

CHILDREN'S MEDICAL RESEARCH FOUNDATION
Royal Alexandra Hospital for Children
Post Office Box 61
Camperdown, N.S.W.,   (02) 519-8761
    Australia 2050   Established 1958

D.S.I. Burrows, C.B.E., President
To ensure that all children born are able to grow, to
play, to learn, to communicate, to work, to marry,
to reproduce and in their turn to grow old gracefully,
with a quality of life unhampered by defects or disabilities stemming from ancestral genetic faults or from
environmental hazards before or after birth.   The
Foundation believes that prevention is better than cure,
but that where prevention is not yet possible a satisfactory form of treatment must be found.   Further,
the Foundation believes that research is the first link
in a chain of communication and care which leads to
these objectives.   Membership: Approximately 45
staff (research and administration).   Finances: Membership: Members of fund raising committees throughout the state vary pay nominal membership fee;
Other Sources: Donations, invested funds, grants and
legacies.   Awards: Grants and grants-in-aid for research within the Royal Alexandra Hospital for Children are awarded each year.   Meetings: Management
Committee, monthly.   Publications: Annual Report,
annual; reports in various journals for C.M.R.F.
Affiliations: Royal Alexandra Hospital for Children;
Institute of Child Health.

CHILDS (JANE COFFIN) MEMORIAL FUND FOR
MEDICAL RESEARCH
    See: Jane Coffin Childs Memorial Fund for
          Medical Research

★ 695 ★

CHINA MEDICAL BOARD OF NEW YORK, INC.
622 Third Avenue, 34th Floor   (212) 682-8000
New York, New York   10017   Established 1928

Patrick A. Ongley, M.D., President
Established to extend financial aid to the Peking
Union Medical College and/or like institutions in the
United States of America.   Activities are to assist
local Asian medical institutions to improve the health
levels and services in Asian societies; to assist local
institutions in Asia to improve the quality and increase
the numbers of appropriate health practitioners in
those societies.   The purpose is to help Asians solve
Asian medical education problems.   The countries
and territories in which the Board has programs are
China (People's Republic), Hong Kong, Indonesia,
Korea, Malaysia, Philippines, Singapore, Taiwan,

and Thailand.   No grants are made to individuals.
Membership: 12 members and trustees.   Meetings:
Biennially.   Publications: Annual Report.

CHLORELLA INTERNATIONAL UNION
    See: Microalgae International Union

★ 696 ★

CHRISTIAN ASSOCIATION FOR PSYCHOLOGICAL
    STUDIES
26705 Farmington Road   (313) 477-1350
Farmington Hills, Michigan 48024   Established 1955

J. Harold Ellens, Ph.D., Executive Secretary
The Association aims to help the various professional
persons in the fields of psychology, psychiatry, and
related professions to explore these areas for a clearer
understanding of their work and to articulare and promote the hardship of Christ in these scientific disciplines.   Membership: 800-1,000.   Finances: Regular, $35; student, $20; agency, $50.   Research:
Research funds are available.   Meetings: Annual.
Publication: The Bulletin, quarterly, J. Harold
Ellens, editor.   Affiliation: 8 regional organizations.

★ 697 ★

CHRISTIAN DENTAL SOCIETY
5235 Sky Trail   (303) 794-2290
Littleton, Colorado   80123   Established 1962

Dr. Everett C. Claus, Executive Secretary
Organized to undergird Christian Mission Dental Clinics in schools, mission compounds and hospitals.   To
encourage and aid American Dentists to serve short
tours of duty, being Ambassadors for American Dentistry, teaching, consulting, demonstrating the latest
and newest techniques nationally and worldwide.
Membership: 300-400 dentists.   Finances: Membership: $50 annually; Other Sources: Gifts.
Meetings: Annual, with American Dental Association,
various locations.   Publications: Christian Dental
Society News, quarterly, Dorothy Claus, editor.

★ 698 ★

CHRISTIAN MEDICAL COMMISSION
World Council of Churches
150 route de Ferney
CH-1211 Geneva 20,   (022) 33-34-00
    Switzerland   Established 1968

Dr. Stuart J. Kingma, Director

Serves as an enabling organization to sponsor the complete coordination of all church related medical facilities within a country and the promotion of joint planning activities with government departments of health; promotes the development of community health programs to redress the present imbalance in services, is currently engaged in studies on the Christian understanding of health, healing and wholeness and on the financing of primary health care. Membership: 20 (elected Commissioners). Finances: Other Sources: Funds from national churches and development agencies. Meetings: Annual Commission Meeting. Publications: Contact, 6 times annually, in English, French, Portuguese and Spanish; Contact special series anthologies and selected readings; Report on the CMC Annual Meeting, annually; Report on the Activities and Concerns of the Christian Medical Commission, annually.

★ 699 ★
CHRISTIAN MEDICAL SOCIETY
1616 Gateway Boulevard
Post Office Box 689   (214) 783-8384
Richardson, Texas 75080   Established 1946

Joseph Bayly, General Director;
   Donald F. Westra, Executive Director
To provide spiritual ministry to the medical and dental professions, medical missions to Central America and foreign mission health programs. Membership: 5,000 (physicians, dentists, medical and dental students and others in recognized medicine and dental professions); regular membership; academic membership; associate membership; House Staff membership, in training; missionaries; students and Friends of the Society. Finances: Membership: Up to $140 annually; Other Sources: Gifts. Meetings: House of Delegates, annually; Board of Trustees, quarterly; family and regional conferences held annually around the country. Publications: News and Reports, bimonthly, Susan Pantle, editor; Journal, quarterly, Joseph Bayly, editor.

★ 700 ★
CHRISTIAN RECORD BRAILLE FOUNDATION, INC.
4444 South 52nd Street   (402) 488-0981
Lincoln, Nebraska 68506   Established 1899

B. E. Jacobs, Manager-Secretary
The Foundation's purpose is to make personal contact with blind people, offering them the assistance of the free services of the Foundation and helping them contact agencies which might best suit their particular needs. The free services consist of a lending library, monthly and bimonthly magazines in braille, large print materials, records, cassette tapes, and a summer

camping program known as National Camps for Blind Children for children ages 9 to 19. Area representatives also contact business and professional persons, acquainting them with the program and thus giving them the opportunity of helping to support the free services to blind people. Membership: 150 (100 field representatives, 40 head office personnel, 10 division directors). Finances: Other Sources: Donations, wills, trusts. Awards: Small scholarships are granted to worthy blind students wishing to continue their education. Publications: Life and Health (braille, record), monthly; Christian Record (braille), monthly; Children's Friend (braille), monthly; Young and Alive (braille and large print), monthly; Student (braille and recorded), monthly; Talking Magazine (recorded), bimonthly; Encounter (recorded), monthly; Richard Kaiser, editor of all. Library: Christian Record Braille Foundation Library, 8,100 volumes.

★ 701 ★
CHRISTOPHER D. SMITHERS FOUNDATION, INC.
Oyster Bay Road   (516) 676-0067
Mill Neck, New York 11765   Established 1952

R. Brinkley Smithers, President
Currently supports organizations performing educational service, treatment and research in the field of alcoholism; initiates its own projects in this field, primarily by writing and publishing booklets for industry, educational organizations and the general public. Meetings: Annual, New York State. Publications: Various monographs on alcoholism.

CHURCH OF THE BRETHREN HOMES AND
HOSPITAL ASSOCIATION
   See: Brethren's Home

CITIZENS FOR BETTER CARE IN NURSING HOMES,
HOMES FOR THE AGED AND OTHER AFTER CARE
FACILITIES, INC.
   See: Citizens for Better Care, Inc.

★ 702 ★
CITIZENS FOR BETTER CARE, INC.
163 Madison Avenue   (313) 962-5968
Detroit, Michigan 48226   Established 1969

Susan A. Rourke, Executive Director
Consumer advocacy agency formed to improve the quality of care for the residents of nursing homes, homes for the aged and other long term care facilities

and services through individual advocacy, legislation and judicial change. Membership: 1,500 (individuals and organizations; 8 chapters chartered to carry out programs in Michigan). Finances: Membership: $2 seniors and low income; $10 regular; $20 organizational; $25 patron; $50 supporting; $100 life; Other Sources: Federal grants, 70%; Torch Drive/Community Chest, 20%; Contracts and donations, 10%. Meetings: Governor Board meets 2nd Saturday; chapters establish own meeting dates. Publications: How to Choose a Nursing Home; Residents Rights in Michigan Nursing Homes; CBC Newsletter. Former Name: Citizens for Better Care in Nursing Homes, Homes for the Aged and Other After Care Facilities, Inc.

★ 703 ★
CITY OF HOPE NATIONAL MEDICAL CENTER
208 West 8th Street   (213) 626-4611
Los Angeles, California 90014   Established 1913

Ben Horowitz, Executive Director
The Center is dedicated to the service of humanity through unsurpassed facilities for free patient care and pioneering programs in research and education in the major catastrophic diseases, namely, cancer and leukemia; heart, blood and lung maladies; diabetes and other disorders of metabolism and heredity. Its Consultation Service is also available at no cost to doctors and hospitals throughout the nation for diagnosis and treatment of their patients. Many thousands of original findings and discoverings have emerged from its staff and laboratories in recent years in its efforts to relieve pain, prolong life and effect cures. The City of Hope also seeks improvements in the quality, quantity, economy and efficiency in the delivery of health care. Finances: Supported by some 500 chartered auxiliaries, labor and management groups in 220 cities, 30 states and Washington, D.C.; Other Sources: Voluntary contributions, bequests, government grants, foundations, private grants. Publications: Pilot; President's Newsletter; City of Hope Medical Quarterly. Library: George Piness Medical and Scientific Library, 25,000 volumes.

★ 704 ★
CIVIL AVIATION MEDICAL ASSOCIATION
801 Green Bay Road
Lake Bluff, Illinois 60044   Established 1948

Albert Carriere, Business Counsel
To determine the basic mental and physical requirements of civil airmen and the proper methods for their assessment; to encourage research on the scientific status of civil aviation medicine to the end of safe-

guarding public safety. Membership: 1,200. Finances: Membership: $40. Awards: D. C. Henry Award and Tamislea Award, annually. Meetings: Annual, various locations. Publications: Bulletin, quarterly, Dale Ducommon, M.D., editor.

★ 705 ★
CLINICAL ORTHOPAEDIC SOCIETY
444 North Michigan Avenue   (312) 822-0970
Chicago, Illinois 60611   Established 1912

Dr. Einer W. Johnson, Jr., Secretary-Treasurer
Orthopaedic surgeons practicing in cities of Middle East. Sponsors annual clinical meeting for presentation of cases by local members.

★ 706 ★
CLINICAL SOCIETY OF GENITO-URINARY
    SURGEONS
c/o Dr. David Utz
Mayo Clinic
Department of Urology   (507) 284-3722
Rochester, Minnesota 55901   Established 1921

Dr. David C. Utz, Secretary-Treasurer
Professional education in the area of genito-urinary surgery. Membership: 50 active and senior (specialists in genito-urinary surgery who are affiliated with medical schools or clinics). Finances: Membership: Periodic dues. Meetings: Annual. Publications: Newsletter, 3 times annually; Program (includes directory), annually.

★ 707 ★
COALITION FOR A NATIONAL HEALTH SERVICE
1747 Connecticut Avenue, N.W.   (202) 483-3321
Washington, D.C. 20009   Established 1977

Lorin Kerr, Chairman; Leonard Rodberg, Co-Secretary/Treasurer; Barbara Mercado, Co-Secretary/
    Treasurer
To conduct education and other campaigns promoting a national health service for the United States. Membership: 8 local and regional coalitions, numerous national organizations; 300 indivudals. Finances: Membership: National organizations, $100; local and regional organizations, $25; individuals, $10 (low-income and students, $2); Other Sources: Contributions, publication sales. Meetings: National and regional conferences, semiannual Board meetings. Publications: National Health Service Action, quarterly, Kevin McNally, editor; It's Time for a National Health Service; National Health

Service and Women; brochures.   Affiliations:
Health Service Education Fund.   Former Name:
Health Service Action.

★ 708 ★
COALITION FOR THE ENVIRONMENT
6267 Delmar Boulevard   (314) 727-0600
St. Louis, Missouri 63130   Established 1969

David Wilson, Executive Director
Environmental education, watchdog organization for
St. Louis region.   Focus on safe energy alternatives
to nuclear power, reduction of air pollution, serves
as catalyst to bring scientific and technical personnel
together with lay public which needs information and
expertise.   Current work includes programs on occupational health.   Membership: 600 (individual and
groups).   Finances: Membership: $7.50 student/
senior citizen to $50 for sustaining; Other Sources:
Contributions (tax deductible); grants, contracts, fees
for service.   Publications: Alert, 10 times annually,
Linda Cohn, editor.

CODE – COMMITTEE ON DONOR ENLISTMENT
     See: Organ Recovery, Inc.

★ 709 ★
COLLEGE OF AMERICAN PATHOLOGISTS
7400 North Skokie Boulevard   (312) 677-3500
Skokie, Illinois 60077   Established 1947

Howard E. Cartwright, Executive Director
To foster the highest standards in education, research,
and the practice of Pathology; through study, education, and improvement of the economic aspects of the
practice of Pathology to advance the science of Pathology and to improve medical laboratory service to
patients, to physicians, to hospitals, and to the public; to enhance the dignity, scientific competence
and efficient practice of the specialty of Pathology
for the service of the common good.   Offers quality
control and laboratory management programs such as
the Surveys Program, Laboratory Accreditation Program,
Quality Assurance Service, Workload Recording Method, and Systematized Nomenclature of Medicine.
Sponsors regional seminars, various publications, and
resident workshops.   Membership: 8,100 (board-
certified pathologists).   Finances: Membership: Fellow, $150; junior, $25.   Meetings: Fall and
spring, various locations.   Publications: Pathologist,
monthly.

★ 710 ★
COLLEGE OF CHAPLAINS (OF THE APHA)
1701 East Woodfield Road, Suite 311 (312) 843-2701
Schaumburg, Illinois 60195   Established 1945

Kermit H. Smith, Executive Director
The College of Chaplains is a personal membership
division of the American Protestant Hospital Association (see separate entry).   The objectives of the
College are to associate chaplains in a professional
organization which serves as a means of ecumenical
cooperation in chaplaincy matters; to provide a professional identity for the chaplain and to interpret his
role to the other disciplines in the health field; to
provide for the effective communication and sharing of
concepts, experiences, and information related to the
chaplain's tasks; to promote excellence in the practice of pastoral care by developing and implementing
high standards of personal and professional competence
and by encouraging continuing education; to provide
professional certification of clergypersons who meet
high standards of chaplaincy service; to promote and
assist in the establishing of chaplaincy programs in institutions; to promote research and publication of
findings by chaplains; to publish literature and papers
designed to assist the chaplain and to contribute
toward the development of the body of literature on
pastoral care.   Membership: 1,500 personal members.
Finances: Membership: $55.   Meetings: Annual,
various locations.   Publications: Establishing Protestant Chaplaincy in Hospitals, Charles D. Phillips,
editor; Special Edition on Pastoral Care, annually;
Care Cassettes, monthly cassette tape, subscription
program; Bulletin, quarterly; The Tie, bimonthly
newsletter of the College; Annual Book of Papers.

★ 711 ★
COLLEGIUM MEDICORUM THEATRI
c/o Hans von Leden, M.D.
Institute of Laryngology and Voice Disorders
10921 Wilshire Boulevard   (213) 478-2100
Los Angeles, California 90024   Established 1969

Hans von Leden, M.D., Secretary
Encourage the scientific investigation of the physiology and pathology of the voice of singers and
actors and promote the professional care of enter-
tainers.   Membership: 50 (laryngologists and voice
scientists).   Finances: Membership: $10-$25.
Meetings: Symposia in various countries with major
operatic facilities, biennially.

COLLINS (JOSEPH) FOUNDATION
     See: Joseph Collins Foundation

★ 712 ★

COMMISSION ON ACCREDITATION OF REHABIL-
   ITATION FACILITIES
2500 North Pantano Road   (602) 886-8575
Tucson, Arizona 85715   Established 1966

Alan H. Toppel, Executive Director
Established by and for the field of rehabilitation to
adopt and apply standards in facilities throughout the
nation; to upgrade and improve the quality of services provided to disabled and disadvantaged people.
Membership: 5 sponsoring member organizations. Finances: Site survey and accreditation fees; members'
contributions; sale of Standards Manual. Meetings:
Board of Trustees, 3 times annually, Tucson, Arizona.
Publications: Standards Manual for Rehabilitation
Facilities, revised annually.

★ 713 ★

COMMISSION ON PROFESSIONAL AND HOSPITAL
   ACTIVITIES
1968 Green Road   (313) 769-6511
Ann Arbor, Michigan 48105   Established 1955

John G. Bassett, Chief Executive Officer
Major program is the Professional Activity Study, a
hospital medical records information system now involving nearly 1,900 hospitals.   In the PAS program
the Commission acts as a data processing, statistical
research, and educational center for the purpose of
assisting hospital, medical and administrative staffs in
their evaluation of quality of care and efficiency of
utilization. Membership: 16 Board members representing American College of Physicians, American
College of Surgeons, American Hospital Association,
Southwestern Michigan Hospital Council and 5 at-large
members. Finances: Professional Activity Study,
90¢ per patient discharge; Medical Audit program,
10¢ per patient discharge in addition to PAS; Other
Sources: Additional programs, grants and research con-
contracts. Meetings: Board, semiannually, Tutorial
Sessions, monthly, Commission Center, Ann Arbor;
regional workshops and training sessions. Publications: Reports, monthly, quarterly, semiannually, annually; various books and brochures. Affiliations:
American College of Physicians, American College of
Surgeons, American Hospital Association, Southwestern
Michigan Hospital Council.

★ 714 ★

COMMITTEE FOR AN EXTENDED LIFESPAN
Post Office Box 696   (714) 746-9430
San Marcos, California 92069   Established 1978

A. Stuart Otto, Chairman

A grassroots, non-profit organization engaged in the
dissemination of news gathered from various sources in
areas of aging research. To serve as a clearinghouse
for such information. Membership: Approximately
1,000 (about 10% M.D. and Ph.D.; 80% lay persons
of various walks of life, cross-sectional; 10% students). Finances: Membership: Voluntary annual
contribution, $10 to $1,000, with special rate of $5
for students. Awards: Award several plaques annually to prominent citizens for outstanding work in
improving the length and/or quality of the human
lifespan. Publications: Life Lines, quarterly, Sid
Ryan, editor; occasional bulletins reporting on specific topics. Former Name: Committee for Elimination of Death.

COMMITTEE FOR ELIMINATION OF DEATH
   See: Committee for An Extended Lifespan

★ 715 ★

COMMITTEE FOR THE PROMOTION OF MEDICAL
   RESEARCH
240 East 27 Street, Apt. 2A   (212) 288-3533
New York, New York 10016   Established 1944

Alma B. Helbing, Secretary-Treasurer
To support and administer research in medicine including projects in cancer, heart, drug pharmacology,
endocrinology, immunology, gastroenterology, hematology, etc. Membership: 9. Finances: Grants
from public and private agencies. Meetings: Annual, New York City.

★ 716 ★

COMMITTEE TO COMBAT HUNTINGTON'S
   DISEASE, INC.
250 West 57th Street, Suite 2016   (212) 757-0443
New York, New York 10107   Established 1967

Marjorie Guthrie, Founder/President Emeritus;
   Thomas House, Chairman of the Board; Robert K.
   Rusk, President; George Rosaler, Executive
   Director
National voluntary health organization whose goals
are fourfold in nature: identification of HD families;
education of the lay public and the professional; the
promotion and support of basic and clinical research
into the causes and cure of HD; and a patient services program, coordinated with various community
services, to assist families in meeting the social, economic, and emotional problems resulting from
Huntington's Disease.   CCHD has launched a nationwide legislative campaign in support of enacting

Federal and State legislation for the establishment of clinics, genetic counseling and screening centers, and diagnostic and treatment centers--not only for the care of the HD patient but also for the care of all those suffering from chronic, debilitating diseases. Its 31 chapters and 14 branches, and Friends of CCHD carry out the National goals at the local level; in addition, they act as a unique network of support groups and self-help groups for HD families. CCHD actively cooperates with many researchers in ongoing studies. At the present time, an HD roster is being set up. Membership: 20,000 (HD families, health professionals from all disciplines, interested individuals, organizations). Finances: Membership: $5-$10 minimum is requested, but not mandatory, for the receipt of the CCHD newsletter, published 3 times annually; Other Sources: Voluntary contributions: gifts, memorial contributions, gifts in honor of an occasion, bequests, special events, chapter assessments, corporate and foundation gifts. Awards: Applications for CCHD fellowships and grants, including the John R. Whittier Research Award (given to an outstanding researcher), accepted May 1-September 30, followed by National Science Council review in December. Upon ratification by the Board of Trustees of CCHD, award announcements are made in January, with the award commencing in July. Award amount - maximum, $15,000. Award period, 1 year only, with a second year application for outstanding proposal. Meetings: Annual, August, location selected by vote of Board of Trustees on bids submitted by chapters; National Science Council meeting in December. Publications: CCHD Newsletter, 3 times annually; CCHD Annual Report; Experiences of an HD Patient, Linda E. Nee and HD Patient, editor; Huntington's Disease, State of New York Department of Health, editor; Caring for the HD Patient at Home, Huntington's Disease, NIH Publication; Clinical Care of the Patient and Family with Huntington's Disease, Ira Shoulson, M.D., editor; Neurobiology and Pharmacology of Huntington's Disease, Enna, Stern, Wastek, and Yamamura, editors. Affiliations: Sister organizations in Canada, United Kingdom, the Netherlands, Australia, Scotland, Germany, France, Italy, New Zealand, Belgium, Ireland.

★ 717 ★
COMMONWEALTH AND INTERNATIONAL MEDICAL
    ADVISORY BUREAU
c/o British Medical Association
Tavistock Square
London WC1H 9JP, England,   Established 1947/
    United Kingdom   1948

Jill Draper, Executive Officer
Maintained by British Medical Association to advise members of BMA Branches overseas and members of

affiliated medical associations on postgraduate study and work in United Kingdom. Also advises United Kingdom members on work, study and visits to other countries of the world. Membership: All qualified medical practitioners registered with General Medical Council in United Kingdom. Finances: Depends on the National Medical Association fees; Other Sources: Maintained by British Medical Association. Library: Restricted use to members of BMA and Affiliated Medical Associations.

★ 718 ★
COMMONWEALTH FUND
1 East 75th Street   (212) 535-0400
New York, New York 10024   Established 1918

Margaret E. Mahoney, President
Founded to do something for the welfare of mankind, the foundation's present attentions are being focused upon education for medicine within the university. Attention is also being given to improvement of health care delivery and support for education of the allied health professions. Finances: Other Sources: Investment income. Award: Harkness Fellowships. Publications: Annual Report. Affiliation: Harkness Fellowships Program.

★ 719 ★
COMMONWEALTH SOCIETY FOR THE DEAF
105, Gower Street
London WC1E 6AH, England,   (01) 387-8033
    United Kingdom   Established 1959

Elisabeth Lubineska, Administrative Secretary
To promote the welfare, health and education of deaf persons - including those totally and partially deaf - throughout the Commonwealth and to help in the establishment of schools and organizations for this purpose in those parts of the Commonwealth where none now exist. Finances: Contributions, grants. Publications: The Commonwealth Society is Ten Years Old; Can We Be Deaf to this Appeal?; Reports From Seminars; Newsletter.

★ 720 ★
COMPLIMENT CLUB, INC.
Hopkins Building
Mellott, Indiana 47958   Established 1956

Cora E. Crane, Secretary
To aid in creating a better understanding between married persons by teaching and instructing them in methods of paying compliments to each other. Activities include sponsorship of local service clubs in coopera-

tion with churches, dating bureaus, personality clinics, study clubs and dissemination of literature. Membership: 20,000 (all races, colors and creeds). Finances: Membership: $50 permanent registration; Other Sources: Individual donors. Meetings: Semiannual, Mellott, Indiana. Publications: S.M.F. News, semi-annually, W. Irving Granville, editor.

★ 721 ★

CONFERENCE OF EDUCATIONAL ADMINISTRATORS
    SERVING THE DEAF, INC.
814 Thayer Avenue   (301) 585-4363
Silver Spring, Maryland 20910   Established 1869

Hubert D. Summers, Executive Director
To provide leadership for improvement and advancement of a continuum of educational opportunities which promote the general welfare of the deaf in North America and to encourage efficient management and operation of schools, programs, program service centers, and governmental units providing for the needs of the deaf. Membership: 300 Agencies (residential and day schools, day class programs, program service centers, governmental units, post secondary education programs for the deaf, teacher education programs; also associate members, honorary members). Finances: Membership: Agencies, $50-$250 annually; associate members, $20 annually; honorary members, no dues; Other Sources: Contract activities. Research Funds: Confers Award of Merit for outstanding contribution to field of deafness; confers Edward Allen Fay Award for significant publication. Meetings: Annually, various locations. Publications: American Annals of the Deaf, 6 to 9 annually, McCay Vernon, editor; Newsletter, 4 to 8 annually, Hubert D. Summers, editor; Proceedings of CEASD Convention, annually, Hubert D. Summers, editor. Former Name: Conference of Executives of American Schools for the Deaf, Inc.

CONFERENCE OF EXECUTIVES OF AMERICAN
SCHOOLS FOR THE DEAF, INC.
    See: Conference of Educational Administrators
         Serving the Deaf, Inc.

★ 722 ★

CONFERENCE OF PUBLIC HEALTH LABORATORY
    DIRECTORS
Post Office Box 9083   (512) 458-7318
Austin, Texas 78766   Established 1927

The objectives of the Conference are to promote the development, improvement and effectiveness of public health laboratory service; to coordinate public health

laboratory activities; to encourage inter-communications among members of the Conference; to develop and recommend the maintenance of adequate standards for the professional training of public health laboratory personnel; to encourage constant effort toward the improvement and standardization of technical methods; to collect and make accessible to all persons in official administrative positions in public health laboratories such information and data as might be of assistance to them in the proper fulfillment of their duties; to collaborate with the various public health organizations in matters pertaining to laboratory services; and to represent the members of the Conference in contacts with these organizations. Membership: Approximately 580 (regular, honorary and emeritus members). Finances: Membership: $10 annual dues; Other Sources: Registration for annual meeting. Award: Annual Kimble Methodology Award. Meetings: Annual, various locations in conjunction with the American Public Health Association. Publications: The Public Health Laboratory, quarterly.

★ 723 ★

CONFERENCE OF RESEARCH WORKERS IN ANIMAL
    DISEASES
Ohio Agricultural Research and
    Development Center
Department of Veterinary Science   (216) 264-1021
Wooster, Ohio 44691   Established 1920

Erwin M. Kohler, Secretary-Treasurer
To promote research in animal diseases and to provide a means of exchanging information on current and unpublished research work. Membership is limited to research workers in animal diseases whose application for membership has been approved by a committee which has reviewed the applicant's qualifications with respect to his publications and the nature of his research work. Membership: 600 (active, life members). Finances: Membership: $3. Meetings: Annual, Chicago, Illinois.

★ 724 ★

CONFERENCE OF STATE AND TERRITORIAL
    DIRECTORS OF PUBLIC HEALTH EDUCATION
301 Centennial Mall South
Post Office Box 95007   (402) 471-2101
Lincoln, Nebraska 68509   Established 1946

Stanley R. Miles, President
To improve the level of public health education; to recommend standards for recruitment and training in health education at the state level. Membership: 55 directors of public health education in state and territorial departments of health. Meetings: Annual

Convention, various locations. Publications: Proceedings, biennial; Roster of Members, irregular.

★ 725 ★

CONGRESS OF LUNG ASSOCIATIONS STAFF
1740 Broadway   (212) 245-8000
New York, New York 10019   Established 1912

Professional society of executives and staff members of voluntary lung associations. Membership: 550. Meetings: Annual, May, various locations. Publications: Newsletter, monthly. Affiliations: American Lung Association.

★ 726 ★

CONGRESS OF NEUROLOGICAL SURGEONS
Presbyterian University Hospital
230 Lothrop Street
Pittsburgh, Pennsylvania 15213   Established 1951

Joseph C. Maroon, M.D., Secretary
Association of contemporary neurosurgeons who meet annually for the purpose of expressing their views on various aspects of the principles and practice of neurological surgery; to exchange technical information and experience; to join in discussion and study of the developments in scientific fields allied to neurological surgery and to honor living leaders in the field of neurosurgery. Membership: 2,190 (active, honorary, senior, inactive). Finances: $60 annually for residents of the United States, Puerto Rico, Canada, and Mexico; $15 annually for international and service-connected members. Awards: Honored Guest; Resident Award Paper. Meetings: Annual, various locations. Publications: Clinical Neurosurgery, annual; Neurosurgery, monthly.

★ 727 ★

CONGRESS OF ORGANIZATIONS OF THE
    PHYSICALLY HANDICAPPED
6106 North 30th Street   (703) 532-4960
Arlington, Virginia 22207   Established 1958

Frances Lowder, National Chairman
To advance the welfare and well being of the physically handicapped nationwide. Membership: 15,000. Meetings: Annual, October, various locations. Publications: Bulletin, quarterly. Library: 150 volumes (publications by and for the physically handicapped).

★ 728 ★

CONSCIOUSNESS RESEARCH AND TRAINING
    PROJECT INC.
Box 9G
315 East 68th Street   (212) 879-9771
New York, New York 10021

Joyce Goodrich, Ph.D., Director
To develop theory, research, training in areas of human consciousness within a solidly grounded humanistic, scientific, philosophic framework at a level of excellence. Incorporating work in cross disciplinary fields. Training people of serious purpose from the professions, arts, sciences. Membership: 1,000. Finances: Other Sources: Seminar tuitions. Meetings: Seminars, bimonthly, nationally. Publications: Newsletter, quarterly, Joyce Goodrich, editor; American Society for Psychical Research Newsletter Article, July 1980, Marian Nestor, editor; The Medium, The Mystic and the Physicist, Lawrence LeShan, editor; How to Meditate, Lawrence LeShan, editor; Alternate Realities, Lawrence LeShan, editor; Healing, Its Implications for Psychotherapy, Fosshase and Olsen, editors (Chapter by Dr. Goodrich, entitled, The Psychic Healing Training and Research Project). Affiliations: Psi Lab, Syracuse University (New York); ASPR (New York); Parapsychology Foundation (New York). Former Name: Psychic Healing Training and Research Project.

★ 729 ★

CONSUMER COALITION FOR HEALTH
1751 N Street, N.W.   (202) 638-5828
Washington, D.C. 20036   Established 1977

Herbert Semmel, Esq., Board President;
    Mark Kleiman, Executive Director
CCH is a coalition of groups and individuals formed to aid consumer participation in the process of health planning. Provides technical assistance to health planning consumers (both health planning expertise and political and organizing advice), and serves as the consumers' voice in Washington on health planning matters. Membership: Approximately 1,000 on mailing list (consumer, senior citizen, labor, women's health, and civil rights groups, Health Systems Agencies (HSAs), many academics and other concerned individuals). Finances: Membership: Annual dues: National organizations, $180; Health Systems Agency/SHPDA, $90; institutional subscription, $40; community organization, $30; individual, $20; low income, $15; Other Sources: Campaign for Human Development. Publications: CHAN - Consumer Health Action Network, bimonthly, Mark Kleiman, editor; Planning, Politics and Power--A User's Guide to Taming the Health System, Mark Kleiman and Karen Glenn, editors.

★ 730 ★

CONSUMER COMMISSION ON THE ACCREDITATION
    OF HEALTH SERVICES
377 Park Avenue, South   (212) 689-8959
New York, New York 10016   Established 1972

Donald Rubin, President
The Commission's purpose is consumer health education, research and advocacy. Publications: Consumer Health Prospectives, 8 annually.

★ 731 ★

CONTACT LENS MANUFACTURERS ASSOCIATION
Tribune Tower
435 North Michigan Avenue   (312) 644-0828
Chicago, Illinois 60611   Established 1964

George K. Meszaros, President
To collect and disseminate information regarding contact lenses and accessories to the public; to recommend standards of nomenclature and manufacturing for
the improvement of the industry; to sponsor and
promulgate research related to contact lenses and accessories in hospitals, clinics, colleges and universities, and other persons or institutions; to provide information to the eye care field regarding contact
lenses and accessories by sponsoring or participating in
seminars, conferences and congresses related to education in the eye care field or field of health care;
to provide and disseminate information to the industry
regarding laws and regulations affecting the industry
and to promote the enforcement of same; to provide
industry statistics, to exchange knowledge among the
members for the improvement of the industry; to evaluate new inventions and ideas related to the industry;
to promote better understanding among its members in
their relations with each other, as well as with those
in the same or allied industries. Membership: 130
(regular, associate). Finances: Membership: $375-
$1,600 annually. Meetings: Annual, various loca-
tions. Publications: CLMA News and Views, periodically.

★ 732 ★

CONTACT LENS SOCIETY OF AMERICA, INC.
First National Building, Suite 301 (606) 233-1606
Lexington, Kentucky 40507   Established 1955

Thomas B. Stivers, Executive Secretary
A national organization of technicians who are interested in sharing their knowledge of contact lens technology and fostering the growth and ability of the
technician throughout the world. The Society works
to develop improvements in instrumentation, fitting
procedures and manufacturing processes; maintains a

scholarship fund for prospective contact lens technicians; provides a national public relations medium
through which information is disseminated to the laymen, governmental agencies, legislative bodies and
other professional groups. Membership: 1,000 (regular, affiliate, associate). Finances: Membership:
Regular, $100; affiliate, $50; associate, $200.
Meetings: Semiannual, various locations. Publications: CLSA Eyewitness Newsletter, monthly; Contact Lens Journal, annual; Membership Roster, annual.

★ 733 ★

CONVENTION OF AMERICAN INSTRUCTORS
    OF THE DEAF, INC.
814 Thayer Avenue   (301) 585-4363
Silver Spring, Maryland 20910 Established 1850

Howard M. Quigley, Executive Director
To secure the harmonious union in one organization of
all persons actively engaged in educating and counseling the deaf in North America; to provide for
general and local meetings of members from time to
time, with a view of affording opportunities for a
free interchange of views concerning methods and
means of educating the deaf; to promote the education of the deaf on the broadest, most advanced, and
practical lines by the publication of reports, essays,
and other information; as an association, to stand
committed to no particular theory, method, or system,
but seeking to develop more effective methods of
teaching hearing impaired children. Membership:
3,600 (classroom teachers, supervisors, administrators
of programs for the deaf). Finances: Membership:
$25. Meetings: Biennial, various locations. Pub-
lications: American Annals of the Deaf, 6 times annually (with special issues), McCay Vernon, editor.

★ 734 ★

COOLEY'S ANEMIA FOUNDATION, INC.
420 Lexington Avenue   (212) 697-7750
New York, New York 10017   Established 1954

Robert A. Ficarra, President;
    Alfred Addessi, Vice President
To find a cure for Cooley's Anemia (Thalassemia
Major). Total program includes research, public and
professional education and patient services. Membership: 8,000 family membership. Finances: Membership: $5; Other Sources: Memorials, chapter
fund raising. Meetings: Board meetings, monthly,
New York, New York. Publications: International
Symposium Reports; Educational Brochures.

COORDINATING COUNCIL ON MEDICAL
EDUCATION
See: Council for Medical Affairs

★ 735 ★

CORRECTIVE EYE CARE FOUNDATION
435 North Michigan Avenue
Suite 1717   (312) 644-0828
Chicago, Illinois 60611   Established 1973

W. William Applegate, President
To operate as an educational organization in conjunction with the health care industry and the public for
acquiring and disseminating information on eye care.
Finances: Other Sources: Contributions.

★ 736 ★

COUNCIL FOR CHRISTIAN MEDICAL WORK-
   THE LUTHERAN CHURCH-MISSOURI SYNOD
500 North Broadway   (314) 231-6969
St. Louis, Missouri 63102   ext. 248

Florence Montz, Staff Administrator
Advisor and consultant to the Lutheran Church-
Missouri Synod on all matters that have to do with
health and healing, including medical missions work
in developing countries. Membership: 7 members
on the Council (persons in health-related fields).
Meetings: Council meets semiannually. Publications:
Cross and Caduceus, semiannually, Elnora Briggeman,
editor. Affiliations: Lutheran Medical Mission Association.

★ 737 ★

COUNCIL FOR EXCEPTIONAL CHILDREN
1920 Association Drive   (703) 620-3660
Reston, Virginia 22091   Established 1922

Jeptha V. Greer, Executive Director
To further the education of handicapped and gifted
children. Maintains its own data base in both ma-
chine-readable and printed form; publishes its own
publications, conducts institutes and conventions, including annual convention; conducts federal and state
funded research and policy projects. Membership:
Approximately 63,000 (anyone interested in furthering
education of handicapped and gifted is welcome to
join, but most are teachers, administrators, and students preparing to teach). Finances: Membership:
From student fee of $16 to $25 (varies from state to
state). Meetings: CEC has annual International
Convention; state federations and local chapters also
hold meetings and conventions. Publications: Ex-

ceptional Children, 8 times annually, M. Angele
Thomas, editor; Teaching Exceptional Children, quarterly, June B. Jordan, editor; Exceptional Child
Education Resources, quarterly, June B. Jordan, editor; Insight (newsletter), monthly, Joseph Ballard,
editor. Library: Open to the public. Affiliations:
12 divisions.

COUNCIL FOR EXCEPTIONAL CHILDREN IN
CANADA
See: Canadian Council for Exceptional Children

★ 738 ★

COUNCIL FOR HEALTH AND WELFARE SERVICES
   (OF THE UCC)
132 West 31 Street   (212) 239-8700
New York, New York 10001   Established 1939

J. Robert Achtermann, Executive Secretary
To assist in providing the highest possible quality of
service; to stimulate the awareness and support of
agencies and programs at all levels of the UCC
(United Church of Christ); to assist United Church
Instrumentalities, Conferences, Associations and congregations in developing and carrying out institutional
as well as non-institutional health and welfare programs; to educate and influence the church with reference to social policies which affect the needs,
problems and conditions of people which Council
agencies encounter in the course of providing services
and to be an advocate for those persons; to stimulate
the development and use of new United Church of
Christ related health and welfare agencies and programs; to inspire innovation in the health and welfare
fields served by the United Church; to cooperate with
other health and welfare bodies in mutual concerns.
Finances: Membership: Minimum dues of $100 an-
nually, 1/2 mill for the first $5,000,000 expenses
plus 1/10 mill, on remaining expenses until maximum
dues $6,000 is attained; Other Sources: United
Church Board for Homeland Ministries. Meetings:
Annual, usually in late February or early March, various locations. Publications: Council for Health
and Welfare Services of the United Church of Christ
(Directory), biennial, J. Robert Achtermann, editor;
Speaking of Everything (newsletter), monthly, J.
Robert Achtermann, editor; That Something More
(filmstrip), J. Robert Achtermann, editor; More Than
a Hospital (filmstrip), J. Robert Achtermann, editor.
Affiliations: Protestant Health and Welfare Association.

★ 739 ★

COUNCIL FOR HOMEOPATHIC RESEARCH AND
    EDUCATION, INC.
c/o Constantine Sidamon-Eristoff, Esquire
551 Fifth Avenue, Suite 800   (212) 661-2820
New York, New York 10176   Established 1961

Claude H. Schmidt, Ph.D., President
The Council was organized as a non-profit New York
corporation for scientific and educational purposes.
Its aim is to advance homeopathic medical education,
teaching and knowledge. Its chief purposes are to
support homeopathic research and to further homeopathic education. The Council raises, accepts gifts
and donations which are tax deductible, for homeopathic research and education. It initiates research
and educational programs by making grants to individuals or by contracting with research laboratories or
universities under the guidance and supervision of the
Council. Membership: 9 trustees. Finances:
Other Sources: Gifts and donations. Research:
Research funds available as donated. Affiliations:
American Institute for Homeopathy; National Center
for Homeopathy.

★ 740 ★

COUNCIL FOR INTERNATIONAL ORGANIZATIONS
    OF MEDICAL SCIENCES
c/o World Health Organization
Avenue Appia   (022) 91.21.11
CH-1211 Geneva 27, Switzerland   Established 1949

Zbigniew Bankowski, Executive Secretary
Facilitate exchanges of view and scientific information in the medical sciences by securing continuity
and coordination between international associations of
medical sciences, by making their work known and by
furnishing to them material when necessary. Functions include coordination of international or regional
congresses to avoid overlap and duplication; multidisciplinary round table conferences to enable the
scientific community to express its views on topics of
immediate concern; and standardization of medical
nomenclature. Membership: 90 (international and
national organizations). Finances: Grants from
members, WHO and UNESCO. Publications: Calendar of International and Regional Congresses of Medical Sciences, annual; Proceedings of Round Table
Conferences; International Nomenclature of Diseases.
Affiliation: Consultative status with UNESCO and
WHO.

★ 741 ★

COUNCIL FOR MEDICAL AFFAIRS
Post Office Box 7586   (312) 751-6299
Chicago, Illinois 60680   Established 1980

Jackson W. Riddle, M.D., Ph.D., Secretary
To provide a forum for members of the organizations
represented to consider issues related to medical education and other matters of mutual concern, and to
initiate their consideration by the 5 parent organizations. Membership: 15 (2 elected officers and chief
executive officer from each of the following: Association of American Medical Colleges, American Board
of Medical Specialties, American Hospital Association, American Medical Association, and Council of
Medical Specialty Societies). Meetings: Quarterly
business meetings. Former Name: Coordinating
Council on Medical Education.

★ 742 ★

COUNCIL OF JEWISH FEDERATIONS
575 Lexington Avenue   (212) 751-1311
New York, New York 10022   Established 1932

Morton L. Mandel, President
Provides central services in fund raising, community
organization, health and welfare planning, personnel
recruitment and public relations for Jewish philanthropic federations, welfare funds and community
councils. Membership: 215 federations. Publications: Directory of Jewish Health and Welfare Agencies, periodically; Jewish Communal Services: Programs and Finances; Yearbook of Jewish Social Services, annually; Directory of Jewish Federations,
Welfare Funds and Community Councils, annually;
Council Publications, A Selected Bibliography, biennially. Former Name: Council of Jewish Federations and Welfare Funds.

COUNCIL OF JEWISH FEDERATIONS AND
WELFARE FUNDS
    See: Council of Jewish Federations

★ 743 ★

COUNCIL OF MEDICAL SPECIALTY SOCIETIES
    (CMSS)
Post Office Box 70   (312) 295-3456
Lake Forest, Illinois 60045   Established 1965

Richard S. Wilbur, M.D., Executive Vice President
To foster, promote, support, augment, develop and
encourage improved quality of medical care for all
patients; improved standards and systems of delivery

related to patient care, effective programs for continuing education; utilization of capabilities of physician members of specialty fields through their member societies to permit studied responses to health questions and to provide and promote communication among specialty organizations concerned with the principal disciplines of medicine. Activities include providing the secretariat and staff services for the Accreditation Council for Continuing Medical Education; advising third party payers regarding medical necessity through the CMSS Program on Clinical Procedure Review; professional liability through support of the National Association of Insurance Commissioner's Closed Claim Malpractice Study; monitoring manpower projections and trends. Membership: 24 national medical specialty societies representing 230,000 physicians (those specialties shall be recognized which have primary or conjoint examining boards recognized by voting membership in the American Board of Medical Specialties. A primary examining board is one which is a separate body to which members are elected or nominated by other organizations not themselves medical specialty boards. A conjoint examining board is a separate body established under the joint sponsorship of not less than 2 primary boards. For each such specialty, an organization representing the practicing specialists shall be selected as a member of the Council of Medical Specialty Societies). Finances: Membership: Primary income is derived from a prescribed amount per voting member of CMSS component societies; Other Sources: Grants. Meetings: Quarterly, March, July and November, Chicago, Illinois. Publications: Newsletter, Executive Report, monthly, Linda P. Johnson, editor; Proceedings of the Conference on Criteria for Accreditation of Continuing Medical Education, January 20-21, 1979; Proceedings of the National Conference on Physician Manpower Legislation, September 25-26, 1979. Affiliations: 24 member societies.

★ 744 ★
COUNCIL OF ROENTGENOLOGY OF THE AMER-
ICAN CHIROPRACTIC ASSOCIATION, INC.
Post Office Box 1072   (913) 722-2900
Mission, Kansas 66222   Established 1936

Brian M. Davis, O.C., Secretary-Treasurer
To encourage and promote the advancement of roentgenology by means of education, research, analysis and public relations; to establish and maintain the American Chiropractic College of Roentgenology. Membership: 3,000-3,250 (members of the American Chiropractic Association). Finances: Membership: Annual dues, $15; fee, $10; Other Sources: Donations, annual symposium. Meetings: Symposium, annual, various locations. Publications: Roentgenological Briefs, monthly. Affiliation: American

Chiropractic Association.

★ 745 ★
COUNCIL OF SOCIETIES IN DENTAL HYPNOSIS
c/o K. A. Bartlett
460 Bloomfield Avenue   (201) 746-1952
Montclair, New Jersey 07042   Established 1961

K. A. Bartlett, Secretary
To further the recognition of hypnosis in dentistry, and provide communication between the various hypnosis organizations having dentists in their membership, so that we may understand our common goals. Activities include annual meeting and projects. Membership: 10 (delegates from component societies). Finances: Contributions from member societies. Meetings: Annual. Publications: Reports to delegates. Affiliations: Various societies of hypnosis throughout the United States.

★ 746 ★
COUNCIL OF STATE ADMINISTRATORS OF
   VOCATIONAL REHABILITATION
1522 K Street, N.W., Suite 610 (202) 638-4634
Washington, D.C. 20005   Established 1940

Joseph H. Owens, Jr., Executive Director
To serve as an advisory body to federal agencies in the development of policies affecting rehabilitation of handicapped persons and to express the viewpoints of state rehabilitation agencies. Membership: 10 regional and 83 state groups. Meetings: Semiannual, spring and fall, various locations. Publications: Memorandum, biweekly; reports and manuals. Affiliation: American Coalition of Citizens with Disabilities.

★ 747 ★
COUNCIL OF TEACHING HOSPITALS
1 DuPont Circle, N.W., Suite 200 (202) 828-0490
Washington, D.C. 20036   Established 1966

Richard Knapp, Ph.D., Director
To develop, through the appointment of study groups, information concerning specific items or problems of hospital operation as they relate to the goals, purposes and functions of the Academic Medical Center. The Council conducts meetings for the presentation of papers and studies relating to education in hospitals. Membership: 420 teaching hospitals. Finances: Membership: $1,750. Meetings: Annual, various locations; regional educational programs.

★ 748 ★
COUNCIL OF WORLD ORGANIZATIONS
    INTERESTED IN THE HANDICAPPED
432 Park Avenue, South   (212) 679-6520
New York, New York 10016   Established 1953

Norman Acton, Chairman
To assist the United Nations and Specialized Agencies
and to enlist their cooperation to develop a well coordinated international program for the rehabilitation
of the handicapped and to serve as a permanent liaison body to develop cooperation between non-governmental organizations interested in the handicapped and
the United Nations and Specialized Agencies. Membership: 39 international organizations. Finances:
Grants from UNESCO. Meetings: Annual, usually
Geneva, Switzerland.

★ 749 ★
COUNCIL ON EDUCATION FOR PUBLIC HEALTH
1015 15th Street, N.W.   (202) 789-1050
Washington, D.C. 20005   Established 1974

Janet A. Strauss, M.P.H., Executive Director
Accreditation of graduate schools of public health and
graduate public health programs in the United States.
Currently there are 23 schools of public health, 21
of which are accredited. Five schools of public
health are reviewed annually by the Council and accreditation is granted to a school for a maximum period of 5 years. Membership: 10 counselors, appointed or approved by APHA and ASPH. Finances:
Funded by accredited schools and programs and by
APHA contribution. Meetings: Semiannual, various
locations. Publications: Listing of Accredited
Schools and Programs; Criteria Manuals; Procedures
Manual; Descriptive Brochure.

★ 750 ★
COUNCIL ON FAMILY HEALTH
633 Third Avenue   (212) 421-1090
New York, New York 10017   Established 1966

Frazier Cheston, President
A non-profit public service organization whose goals
are to promote the proper use of medicines, home
safety, and personal health. Membership: Over 80
manufacturers of prescription and non-prescription
medicines. Finances: The Council operates solely
from contributions by member companies. Publications: First Aid in the Home (chart); Women and
Health (booklet); The Care and Safety of Young
Children (booklet); Child's Mind, Child's Body (booklet); You and Your Health (booklet).

★ 751 ★
COUNCIL ON OPTOMETRIC EDUCATION
243 North Lindbergh Boulevard   (314) 991-4100
St. Louis, Missouri 63141   Established 1934

Brian Andrew, Administrative Director
Accreditation of schools and colleges of optometry and
para-optometric education programs and approval of
advanced optometric education programs. Member-
ship: 9 individuals (2 Association of Schools and
Colleges of Optometry; 2 International Association of
Boards of Examiners in Optometry; 3 American Op-
tometric Association; 2 public members). Finances:
American Optometric Association. Publications:
Various accreditation manuals.

★ 752 ★
COUNCIL ON PROFESSIONAL STANDARDS IN
    SPEECH-LANGUAGE PATHOLOGY AND
    AUDIOLOGY
c/o American Speech-Language-Hearing Association
10801 Rockville Pike   (301) 897-5700
Rockville, Maryland 20852   Established 1959

Tom Tillman, Ph.D., Chairman
Defines standards for clinical certification and for
accreditation of graduate educational programs and
professional services programs. Monitors interpreta-
tion and application of these standards to individuals,
institutions and organizations. Arbitrates appeals re-
garding certification and accreditation. Meetings:
Annual, November, various locations. Publications:
List of Accredited Clinical Service Programs, annual;
List of Accredited Training Programs, irregular; List
of Newly Certified Members, irregular. Affiliation:
American Speech-Language-Hearing Association.
Former Name: American Boards of Examiners in
Speech Pathology and Audiology.

★ 753 ★
COUNCIL ON SOCIAL WORK EDUCATION
111 Eighth Avenue   (212) 242-3800
New York, New York 10011   Established 1952

Arthur Katz, Executive Director
Formulates criteria and standards for all levels of social work education; accredits new graduate programs
of social work and reaccredits established programs;
accredits undergraduate social work programs; assists
in establishment of new graduate programs and undergraduate programs; provides service to social work
education on curriculum, faculty recruitment and development, students and admissions, teaching meth-
odologies and materials; publishes teaching materials,
conducts research and compiles data on social work

education.   Membership: Approximately 5,100.
Awards: Distinguished Service Award.   Meetings:
Annual, various locations.   Publications: Social
Work Education Reporter, 3 issues annually; Journal
of Education for Social Work, 3 issues annually; Statistics on Social Work Education, annual; lists of accredited graduate and undergraduate programs; books,
pamphlets, reports on special subjects and Catalog of
Publications.

★ 754 ★
CRANIAL ACADEMY
1140 West Eighth Street   (208) 888-1201
Meridan, Idaho 83642   Established 1947

Carl H. Rathjen, Executive Secretary-Treasurer
To promote a clearer understanding of the principles
of osteopathy in general and the cranio-sacral mechanism in particular; to stimulate further investigation,
research and dissemination of the philosophy and techniques taught by William Garner Sutherland, D.O.,
D.Sc.Hon.   The Academy conducts courses, study
groups and seminars in the United States and abroad;
publishes textbooks and other pertinent literature; and
offers scholarships in cranial osteopathy for qualifed
faculty members of osteopathic colleges.   Membership: 300 (regular and associate).   Finances: Membership: $25 annually; Other Sources: Income from
sale of literature, donations and bequests from osteopathic patients, interest on reserve funds.   Awards:
G. W. Sutherland Memorial plaque for meritorious
service to osteopathy; Honoary Life Membership
Award; funds to finance research projects.   Meetings: National, semiannual, various locations; frequency varies for regional groups.   Publications:
Cranial Academy Newsletter, quarterly, Carl H.
Rathjen, editor; various other pamphlets and manuals.
Affiliation: Sutherland Cranial Teaching Foundation.

★ 755 ★
CREDENTIALING COMMISSION
818 Olive Street, Suite 918   (314) 241-1445
St. Louis, Missouri 63101   Established 1962

David Birenbaum, Administrator
An independent, autonomous, credentialing agency.
Developed to establish the minimum qualifications for
certification.   The Commission also established the
minimum criteria for courses in Medical Laboratory
Technology.   Later the Commission dropped its accrediting activities and concentrated solely on the
credentialing of laboratory personnel.   The primary
purpose of the Credentialing Commission today is to
identify, on a non-discriminatory basis, those individuals who meet the minimum requirements of compe-

tency and who can establish their competency to perform as laboratory technicians and medical technologists.   These requirements do not discriminate against
any individual or group of individuals on the basis of
race, color, sex, religion, or source of national origin.   Finances: $65 fee for examination and initial
certification.   An annual fee is required for individuals to maintain their certification and registration.   Awards: Professional Merit Award.   Former
Name: National Accrediting Commission.

CURE
    See: Center for Ulcer Research and Education

★ 756 ★
CYSTIC FIBROSIS FOUNDATION
6000 Executive Boulevard, Suite 309 (301) 881-9130
Rockville, Maryland 20852   Established 1955

Henry V. Lione, National Director;
    Doris F. Tulcin, President
To find the means for the prevention, control and
effective treatment of cystic fibrosis.   This mission
is pursued through programs in research, care and ed-
ucation.   The Foundation supports 125 CF Medical
Centers across the United States.   Membership: 84
CFF Chapters and numerous branches across the United
States.   Finances: Other Sources: Annual Breath
of Life Campaign; special fund-raising events; contributions; grants; bequests; etc.   Awards:
Medical: Research Scholar; Research Grant; Research Fellowship; Clinical Fellowship; Student
Traineeship. Media: Communications Awards in
Print and Broadcast.   Publications: Perspective,
quarterly, Public Policy Department (editor); Focus,
quarterly, Medical Department (editor); The Commitment, quarterly, Public Relations Department (editor);
numerous pamphlets and brochures.   Affiliations:
National Health Council; International Cystic Fibrosis (Mucoviscidosis) Association.

D

★ 757 ★
DAMIEN-DUTTON SOCIETY FOR LEPROSY AID, INC.
616 Bedford Avenue   (516) 221-5829
Bellmore, New York 11710   Established 1944

Sister Mary Augustine, S.M.S.M., Director;
    Howard E. Crouch, Board President
The Society's main purpose is to raise funds to assist

in the treatment, rehabilitation, and research programs of leprosy hospitals in all parts of the world, regardless of race or creed, in order to promote the conquest of leprosy. Membership: 20,000 (priests and laity of all faiths). Finances: Other Sources: Contributions, fund-raising activities, legacies. Awards: The Damien-Dutton Award, given annually. Meetings: Bimonthly. Publications: The Damien-Dutton Call, quarterly, Sister Mary Augustine, S.M.S.M., editor. Affiliations: Catholic Press Association; International Leprosy Association.

★ 758 ★
DAMON RUNYON-WALTER WINCHELL CANCER
    FUND
33 West 56th Street   (212) 582-5400
New York, New York 10019   Established 1947

David W. Walsh, Executive Director
Invests in furthering research into the causes and control of cancer by supporting post-graduate fellowships in related research. Membership: 12 member Board of Directors; all members serve without compensation. Meetings: Scientific Advisory Committee, 3 times annually to grade applications for fellowships; Board, quarterly. Publications: Annual Report.

★ 759 ★
DEAFNESS RESEARCH FOUNDATION
342 Madison Avenue   (212) 682-3737
New York, New York 10173   Established 1958

T. E. Beck, Jr., Executive Director;
    Albert J. Levine, Director of Development
Founded to inform the public on deafness and ear disease, and to provide them a means of direct support for research on causes, treatment and prevention. The DRF has an active public education program, in its publications and through its support groups. Its major activity is the awarding of annual grants for new research at universities and hospitals in the United States and Canada. It was founded in 1960 and now directs and partially funds the National Temporal Bone Banks Program, a donor program serving ear research and medical training. Membership: Centurions, 1,716; DRF Auxiliary, 300. Finances: Membership: Centurions, variable $15-$100; DRFA: variable $25 and up; Other Sources: Public contributions (individual, corporation, foundation) are the major source of support. Meetings: Boart meeting, semiannually, New York, New York. Publications: Receiver, semiannual, T. E. Beck, Jr. and Nina Strong, editors; Centurion (newsletter), semiannual, T. E. Beck, Jr. and Nina Strong, editors; Inner Ear, semiannual, T. E. Beck, Jr., editor; DRFA (newsletter). Affiliations: New England Chapter of (Boston); Centurions of; DRF Auxiliary.

DEBAKEY, (MICHAEL E.) INTERNATIONAL
CARDIOVASCULAR SOCIETY
    See: Michael E. DeBakery International
        Cardiovascular Society

★ 760 ★
DEBBIE FOX FOUNDATION
Post Office Box 11082   (615) 266-1632
Chattanooga, Tennessee 37401 Established 1969

Mary Jane Torrance, Executive Director
A non-profit non-membership organization established for the purpose of assisting the craniofacially deformed of any age, sex, color, creed, or national origin. Serves as a liaison between medical centers and persons needing services; provides supportive services such as transportation costs and living expenses while at the medical center for those establishing eligiblity. Membership: Operated by a Board of Directors of 18 persons and an Executive Director. Finances: Other Sources: Contributions, gifts, pledges, endowments and bequests. Meetings: Board of Directors, quarterly, Chattanooga, Tennessee. Publications: Brochures. Affiliations: University of Virginia Medical Center; New York University Medical Center; Baylor Medical School. Former Name: The Debbie Fox Foundation for Craniofacial Deformities.

DEBBIE FOX FOUNDATION FOR CRANIOFACIAL
DEFORMITIES
    See: Debbie Fox Foundation

D.E.B.R.A. OF AMERICA, INC.
    See: Dystrophic Epidermolysis Bullosa Research
        Association of America, Inc.

★ 761 ★
DEFENCE MEDICAL ASSOCIATION OF CANADA
2111 Niagra Drive
Ottawa, Ontario K1H 6G9,   (613) 733-7389
    Canada   Established 1892

LCol. C. P. Smith, Secretary-Treasurer
To foster the development and efficiency of the Canadian Forces Medical Service by: bringing to the attention of the proper authorities recommendations and suggestions which in the opinion of the Association will improve the efficiency of the CFMS; maintaining liaison between the members of the CFMS and the medical and paramedical professions; and serving as a responsible body through which the Canadian Forces may disseminate knowledge on medical matters

pertinent to the defense of Canada. Membership: Approximately 200. Membership requirement: Service with the Medical Services of the Armed Forces of Canada or the Commonwealth. Finances: Membership: Annual fee variable; Other Sources: Grant from the Conference of Defence Associations. Awards: Best Medical Company Trophy; Best Medical Militia Section of Militia Medical Service Trophy. Meetings: Annual, various Canadian Military Bases.

★ 762 ★
DELTA DENTAL PLANS ASSOCIATION
211 East Chicago Avenue   (312) 337-4707
Chicago, Illinois 60611   Established 1965

F. Gene Dixon, D.D.S., Executive Vice President
Assists state dental societies in the formation of dental service corporations and assists dental service corporation in the development of dental care programs for application to multistate and national accounts. Membership: 50 (active, associate, constituent, affiliate). Meetings: Annual, various locations. Publications: DDPA Newsletter.

★ 763 ★
DELTA OMEGA - HONORARY PUBLIC HEALTH
     SOCIETY
Department of Environmental and Tropical Health
School of Health   (714) 796-7311
Loma Linda University   ext. 3736
Loma Linda, California 92350   Established 1924

Barbara Hulka, President
A national honorary public health fraternity established to recognize and encourage scholarship and research among those undertaking graduate study in Public Health and to recognize attainment in the field of Public Health. Membership: Approximately 2,800 (three types: graduating public health majors; faculty of schools of public health; and alumni of schools of public health in a ratio approximating 10:1:3. Finances: Membership: One-time payment of $10 national initiation fee. Awards: Annual National Merit Awards for outstanding contribution to professionalism in public health; three categories: student, faculty and alumni of schools of public health. Meetings: Annual, in conjunction with the American Public Health Association, various locations.

★ 764 ★
DELTA OMEGA NATIONAL SORORITY
226 West 39th Street
Kansas City, Missouri 64111   Established 1904

Dr. Sara Wheeler, Editor
Betterment of osteopathic women's groups. Educate women to study osteopathic medicine. Sponsors student women in osteopathic colleges. Membership: 510 (women osteopathic physicians and surgeons). Finances: Membership: $5; Other Sources: Alumni contributions. Awards: Annual award given to senior and junior women student with good scholastic average. Award given to 2 students of osteopathic colleges. Meetings: Annual, in conjunction with annual meeting of the American Osteopathic Association. Publications: The ALPHA, annually.

★ 765 ★
DELTA PSI KAPPA
c/o Mrs. John W. Schroll
6641 Lasley Shore Drive   (414) 582-4561
Winneconne, Wisconsin 54986   Established 1916

Mrs. J. Schroll, Executive Secretary
To recognize worthwhile achievement in health, physical education, and recreation and develop interest therein, and to promote greater fellowship among persons in these fields of activity. Membership: 11,000 (active and alumni chapters, students and graduates of health, physical education and recreation). Award: Research Award. Meetings: Biennial, with American Alliance of Health, Physical Education and Recreation. Publications: Foil, semiannually.

★ 766 ★
DELTA SIGMA DELTA
2317 Westwood Avenue
Box 6272   (804) 353-5004
Richmond, Virginia 23230   Established 1882

Dr. Charles L. Eubank, Supreme Scribe
To keep high the standards of dentistry by inculcating in the minds of dental students and practitioners a spirit of fraternal cooperation toward scientific, ethical and professional progress. Membership: 26,000 in undergraduate and graduate level chapters. Finances: Membership: Life, $90; undergraduate, $7; graduate, $10; Other Sources: Investments. Awards: Annual award to outstanding Delt; Award to top ranking junior in each undergraduate chapter, annually; first through fifth awards to leading undergraduate chapters. Meetings: Annually with a radium of 200 miles from American Dental Association Meetings. Publications: Desmos, quarterly; Campus Prospectus; freshman brochure.

★ 767 ★
DEMONSTRATOR'S ASSOCIATION OF ILLINOIS
2240 West Fillmore   (312) 733-5283
Chicago, Illinois 60612   Established 1885

Dr. Lincoln V. Domm, Executive Officer
To procure and prepare human bodies and to distribute
them to medical schools and colleges, either public
or private, in accordance with State law.   Membership: 1 director from each member school.   Finances:
Cost of services is assessed on a per unit basis.
Meetings: Quarterly, various locations.

★ 768 ★
DENTAL DEALERS OF AMERICA, INC.
1118 Land Title Building   (215) 563-2588
Philadelphia, Pennsylvania 19110   Established 1943

Edward B. Shils, Executive Secretary
An association of firms which trade in instruments,
equipment and supplies from dental offices.   Membership: 200.   Finances: Membership: $125-$350.

★ 769 ★
DENTAL GUIDANCE COUNCIL FOR CEREBRAL
     PALSY
122 East 23rd Street   (212) 677-7400
New York, New York 10010   Established 1948

To further the development of adequate programs for
the prevention and treatment of dental and oral disease and malformation in individuals affected by cerebral palsy; to promote the training of personnel for
the dental care of such individuals; to enlist the aid
of the dental profession and to coordinate all efforts
to meet the oral problems of the cerebral palsied and
persons with other handicapping conditions; to gain
new knowledge through studies and practical experience and to disseminate such knowledge to the dental
profession and others interested in the welfare of .the
cerebral palsied, and persons with other handicapping
conditions.   Membership: 40 dentists.   Finances:
Supported entirely by United Cerebral Palsy of New
York.   Meetings: Bimonthly, New York City.
Publications: Reprints on dentistry for the handicapped.

★ 770 ★
DENTAL HEALTH INTERNATIONAL
847 South Milledge Avenue   (404) 546-1715
Athens, Georgia 30605   Established 1973

Barry D. Simmons, DDS, Founder and President

To provide general dental care using hand-carryable
modular dental unit into areas without electricity or
water.   DHI uses a minimal fee structure that allows
self-continuity of a project.   All dentists serve a
voluntary period of 3 months.   Any pro-United
States country in the world may be served.   Membership: Dentists, dental hygienists, dental students
and dental technicians.   Finances: Other Sources:
Private contributions.

★ 771 ★
DENTAL MANUFACTURERS OF AMERICA, INC.
1118 Land Title Building   (215) 563-2588
Philadelphia, Pennsylvania 19110   Established 1933

Edward B. Shils, Executive Secretary
To advance the professional knowledge and public
careers of Dental Manufacturers by conducting activities with different associations.   Activities include
the operation of several committees, including trade
and professional relations; exhibits; specifications
and technology, etc.   Membership: 115.   Finances:
Membership: $330-$1,100.   Meetings: Quarterly,
various locations.

★ 772 ★
DERMATOLOGY BOARD OF THE AMERICAN COL-
     LEGE OF VETERINARY INTERNAL MEDICINE
Purdue University   (317) 494-8381
West Lafayette, Indiana 47907   Established 1974

James C. Blakemore, D.V.M., Past President,
     Contact Person
Organized to grant certification to trained Veterinary
Dermatologists, to establish training and to encourage
the development of training programs.   Membership:
19 Veterinary Dermatologists who meet criteria for
board certification and membership in ACVIM.   Finances: Membership: $50 annually.   Meetings:
Semiannual, in conjunction with the American Veterinary Medical Association and American Animal Hospital Association, various locations.

★ 773 ★
DERMATOLOGY FOUNDATION
820 Davis Street   (312) 328-2256
Evanston, Illinois 60201   Established 1966

Richard E. Blakley, Executive Director;
     Sandra Rahn Goldman, Associate Executive Director
To solicit and distribute funds for the advancement of
dermatology.   Support is available to strengthen the
capabilities of divisions of dermatology and initiate
research projects.   Post-doctoral fellowships are

awarded. <u>Membership:</u> 3,000 dermatologists. <u>Fi</u>nances: Membership: Regular, $50; Century Club, $100; life, according to age and on a scaled basis. <u>Awards:</u> C. W. Finnerud Award; Practitioner of the Year Award. <u>Meetings:</u> Annual, various locations. <u>Publications:</u> Progress in Dermatology, quarterly.

★ 774 ★

DES REGISTRY, INC.
5426   27th Street, N.W.   (202) 966-1766
Washington, D.C. 20015   Established 1978

Phyllis Wetherill, Executive Officer;
    Toni Mason, President
DES Registry maintains a file of persons exposed to diethylstilbestrol. Questions of exposed persons are answered and referrals made. <u>Finances:</u> Membership: Contributions (only $8 is suggested price for quarterly). <u>Publications:</u> DES National Quarterly, quarterly, P. Wetherill, editor.

★ 775 ★

DEVELOPMENTAL DISABILITIES CENTER
c/o Roosevelt Hospital
428 West 59th Street   (212) 554-6684
New York, New York 10019   Established 1965

Louis Z. Cooper, M.D., Director;
    Susan G. Gordon, M.D., Acting Clinical Director
Created to characterize the natural history of rubella and congenital rubella; to develop and evaluate methods of prevention, detection and treatment of rubella and congenital rubella; to develop and evaluate interdisciplinary health, education and social services for multi-handicapped children. <u>Member</u>ship: Physicians, nurses, social workers, special educators, psychologists, geneticists, dentists, and parents. <u>Publications:</u> Articles in journals and other forms of medical literature on rubella, rubella vaccines, congenital rubella, special education in child development. <u>Former Name:</u> Rubella Project.

★ 776 ★

DIRECT RELIEF FOUNDATION
404 East Carrillo Street
Post Office Box 1319   (805) 966-9149
Santa Barbara, California 93102   Established 1948

Robert G. McGill, President
    Dennis G. Karzag, Executive Director
Donates contributed pharmaceuticals, medical supplies and equipment to the needy in medically less-developed areas of the world. Arranges assignments for medical, dental and paramedical volunteer personnel in these areas. To date some 2,000 health facilities, in more than 80 countries, have been assisted. Also assists in emergency situations, providing medical assistance to refugees, victims of natural disasters, etc. Direct Relief's "New Directions in Agriculture for Health" places volunteers trained in organic high-yield farming methods in health facilities that request them. <u>Membership:</u> Approximately 100 (board of trustees, international advisory council, volunteer representatives in 18 countries). <u>Finances:</u> Contributions. <u>Meetings:</u> 6 annually, Santa Barbara, California. <u>Publications:</u> What's Up at DRF, quarterly, Margery Jarabin, editor; President's Report, annually, Margery Jarabin, editor. <u>Library:</u> Maintains small health library. <u>Affiliation:</u> Direct Relief International is a volunteer affiliate providing assistance in public relations and fund raising.

★ 777 ★

DISABLED AMERICAN VETERANS
Post Office Box 14301   (606) 441-7300
Cincinnati, Ohio 45214   Established 1920

Denvel D. Adams, National Adjutant
A society of wounded, gassed, injured or disabled military veterans devoted to the cause of improving the condition, health and interests of all disabled veterans. <u>Membership:</u> 669,491. <u>Publications:</u> DAV Magazine, monthly, Richard M. Wilson, executive editor.

★ 778 ★

DO IT NOW FOUNDATION
Post Office Box 5115   (602) 257-0797
Phoenix, Arizona 85010   Established 1967

W. Mark Clark, Executive Director
To publish public and professional information on all drug and health topics including alcohol, vitamins, food additives, etc., and also to use other forms of media to spread public awareness. Publications are distributed in the United States and Canada, with additional translations in Spanish. Radio spots on about 1,200 United States stations, press releases and other mass media efforts reached an estimated 35 million persons. <u>Finances:</u> Donations, about $1,000 annually; revenue from publications, about $300,000 in fiscal year 1979-80. <u>Publications:</u> Drug Survival News, bimonthly, Dario McDarby, managing editor; Standard publications: pamphlets, books, booklets, special packets, educational posters, games, etc. <u>Library:</u> Research Library, 800 periodicals, 85 published papers and 8,000 reprints. <u>Affiliations:</u> International Council on Alcohol and Addictions;

National Coordinating Council on Drug Abuse; Student Association for the Study of Hallucinogens, etc.

★ 779 ★
DOC (DOCTORS OUGHT TO CARE)
924 West Webster Street
Chicago, Illinois 60614

Dr. Allen Blum, President and Founder
DOC is a coalition of physicians, medical students, health care professionals, and other concerned citizenry, whose purpose is to promote good health and combat illness-producing habits and lifestyles.

DOCTORS OUGHT TO CARE
    See: D O C

★ 780 ★
DOOLEY FOUNDATION/INTERMED-USA, INC.
420 Lexington Avenue, Suite 2428   (212) 687-3620
New York, New York 10170   Established 1961

Verne E. Chaney, M.D., MPH, President and
    Founder
To provide technical, financial and material assistance on a self-help basis to the developing countries of the world in the fields of preventive medicine, health education and health manpower training. Health surveys and research on the use of technology for improvement of health delivery systems, paramedical manpower training, immunizations, patient education, and clinical care are all essential ingredients of its development assistance efforts.   Present programs areas include India and Nepal.   Membership: Domestic, 8; overseas, 12 (salaried employees [both Western and indigenous], Board of Directors, National Advisory Council).   Finances: Other Sources: Individual voluntary contributions; corporate and foundation grants; bequests.   Meetings: Board of Directors, annually.   Publications: Annual Report; The Intermed Journal, quarterly.   Affiliation: INTERMED, Geneva, Switzerland.   Former Name: Thomas A. Dooley Foundation, Inc.

★ 781 ★
DOWN'S SYNDROME CONGRESS
1640 West Roosevelt Road
Room 156E
Chicago, Illinois 60608   Established 1974

Diane M. Crutcher, President

To promote the welfare of persons with Down's Syndrome (DS), a chromosomal disorder that usually causes delays in physical and intellectual developments. Advises and aids parents on possible solutions to the needs of the DS child; acts as clearinghouse for information on DS.   Membership: Health professionals, educators, parents.   Meetings: Annual Convention. Publications: Down's Syndrome News, monthly; pamphlets, booklets and books on DS.

★ 782 ★
DRUG, CHEMICAL AND ALLIED TRADES
    ASSOCIATION, INC.
42-40 Bell Boulevard   (212) 229-8891
Bayside, New York 11361   Established 1890

Joseph D. Madden, Executive Vice President
To act as a nationwide forum for the exchange of useful information and the promotion of business contacts for members of the drug, chemical and allied trades. Activities include educational seminars; biweekly Bulletins; annual meetings and luncheon meetings. Membership: 500.   Meetings: Annual.   Publications: DCAT Bulletin, biweekly.

★ 783 ★
DRUG INFORMATION ASSOCIATION
Post Office Box 113   (215) 628-5177
Maple Glen, Pennsylvania 19002   Established 1967

Thomas W. Teal, Administrative Director
To provide mutual instruction in the technology of drug information processing in all its ramifications: collecting, selecting, abstracting, indexing, coding, vocabulary building, terminology standardizing, computerizing data storage and retrieval, tabulating, correlating, computing, evaluating, writing, editing, reporting and publishing.   Membership: 1,100 individuals who handle drug information in government, industry, the medical and pharmaceutical professionals, and allied fields.   Meetings: Annual, various locations.   Publications: Journal, irregular.

DUPONT (ALFRED I.) INSTITUTE OF THE NEMOURS
FOUNDATION
    See: Alfred I. Dupont Institute of the Nemours
        Foundation

★ 784 ★
DYSAUTONOMIA FOUNDATION, INC.
370 Lexington Avenue, Room 1504   (212) 889-0300
New York, New York 10017   Established 1951

Lenore Roseman, Executive Administrator
The Foundation was formed to stimulate, promote, and underwrite medical research into dysautonomia, a disease of autonomic nervous system; to provide and disseminate all possible information to the medical profession and lay people; and to raise the necessary funds to support the medical research and public education programs. Membership: 5,000 (parents, relatives, friends and benefactors of children afflicted with the disease) in 14 chapters in the United States, Canada, and Great Britain. Finances: Membership: $10; Other Sources: Fund-raising activities; public service radio and television advertising. Awards: Research grants and fellowship awards in medical schools in the United States, Canada, and Israel. Meetings: Annual Medical Symposium, May, New York City; Annual Membership Meeting, June, New York City. Publications: Dysautonomia Journal, annually; Dysautonomia Newsletter, quarterly; various publications to aid families and doctors.

★ 785 ★
DYSTROPHIC EPIDERMOLYSIS BULLOSA RESEARCH
    ASSOCIATION OF AMERICA, INC. (D.E.B.R.A.
    OF AMERICA, INC.)
2936 Avenue W   (212) 769-4568
Brooklyn, New York 11229   Established 1979

Arlene Pessar, R.N., Executive Director
A national organization working to solve some of the problems of EB patients and their families. Epidermolysis Bullosa (EB) is the name given to a group of inherited skin disorders characterized by the formation of blisters following mild trauma. The aims of the Association are: to raise funds to promote and support research into the causes, nature, treatment and cure of EB, in all its forms; to relieve the physical and mental distress among persons suffering from EB by the provision of practical advice, guidance and support; to provide EB patients and their families with information about the disorder and to assist them in finding medical, social and genetic counseling; to act as an information source for physicians and health workers on EB; to distribute educational material about EB to the public. Membership: Any persons or organizations interested in Epidermolysis Bullosa. Finances: Membership: $10 minimal (quarterly newsletter, other data); Other Sources: Individual donations. Meetings: Medical board meets in conjunction with scientific gatherings. Publications: D.E.B.R.A. Newsletter, quarterly, Arlene Pessar, R.N., editor.

E

★ 786 ★
EAST COAST MIGRANT HEALTH PROJECT
1234 Massachusetts Avenue, N.W.
Suite 623   (202) 347-7377
Washington, D.C. 20005   Established 1970

S. Cecilia Abhold, SO OP, Administrator;
    S. Margaret Ebbing, SC, Assistant Administrator
Sponsored by the women religious board (National Migrant Worker Council), it is financed on a yearly grant through Region III, DHHS to furnish health and allied health professionals to serve the migrant/seasonal farmworkers along the eastern coastline, using outreach as its chief methodology. Staff migrate twice a year with the migrants. Goals are accomplished through intense, practical health care delivery at peak seasons, with preservation of human dignity, and an emphasis of self-help techniques. Membership: ECMHP staff number between 12-15 in the winter months and as many as 20 during the summer months of operation in 7 states in 19 countries along the eastern seaboard (certified health professionals--physicians, all specialties, nurse extenders, allied health professionals). Finances: Federal funding and in-kind contributions from state, local and voluntary organizations. Meetings: Staff and Policy Board meetings, semiannually, preferably in Florida. Publications: SNAP (Staff, News and Publicity), for ECMHP staff distribution only. Library: 1,000 plus. Affiliations: East Coast Migrant Head Start Project; MHAP (Migrant Health Assurance Program).

★ 787 ★
ECRI (EMERGENCY CARE RESEARCH INSTITUTE)
5200 Butler Pike
Plymouth Meeting,   (215) 825-6000
    Pennsylvania 19462   Established 1955

Joel J. Nobel, M.D., Director
Evaluates and publishes monthly reports on comparative engineering and clinical tests of medical equipment; publishes twice-monthly abstracts of items in medical and technical literature related to medical device hazards and problems; publishes annual medical product directory; monthly newsletters for clinical specialists; conducts surveys of health care facilities which examine the safety, performance, cost-effectiveness, and utilization of clinical and support equipment systems; analyzes and/or prepares architectural plans for hospitals with emphasis on special care units,

emergency rooms, operating suites, and other technologically complex areas; undertakes management studies and provides supervisory services in biomedical engineering and conducts a variety of training programs. Membership: 2,200 hospitals. Finances: Membership: $610; Other Sources: Foundation grants, government grants and contracts. Publications: Health Devices, monthly, Robert Mosenkis, editor; Health Devices Alerts, semimonthly; Health Devices Sourcebook, annually; Health Devices Updates, monthly. Former Name: Emergency Care Research Institute.

★ 788 ★

EDUCATIONAL COMMISSION FOR FOREIGN
    MEDICAL GRADUATES
3624 Market Street   (215) 386-5900
Philadelphia, Pennsylvania 19104   Established 1956

Ray L. Casterline, M.D., Executive Director
To provide information to foreign medical graduates regarding entry into graduate medical education and health care systems in the United States; to evaluate their qualifications for such entry; to identify foreign medical graduates' cultural and professional needs; to assist in the establishment of educational policies and programs to meet the above-identified cultural and professional needs of foreign medical graduates; to gather, maintain, and disseminate data concerning foreign medical graduates; and to assist through cooperation and recommendation, other agencies concerned with foreign medical graduates. Membership: American Medical Association; American Hospital Association; Association of American Medical Colleges; Association for Hospital Medical Education; Federation of State Medical Boards of the United States; National Medical Association; American Board of Medical Specialties. Finances: Membership: Examination fees. Awards: Grants-in-Aid Program. Meetings: Quarterly, Board of Trustees, various locations. Publications: Annual Report; Information Booklet, semiannual; Handbook for Foreign Medical Graduates, periodically.

★ 789 ★

ELECTRON MICROSCOPY SOCIETY OF AMERICA
    (EMSA)
c/o Frances L. Ball
Oak Ridge National Lab
Post Office Box X   (615) 574-4877
Oak Ridge, Tennessee 37830   Established 1942

To increase and to diffuse, for scientific and educational purposes only, the knowledge of the science and practice of electron microscopy and the instruments and results relating to such activity in whatever fields of science and education they may be found applicable. Activities: education; certification of E. M. Technicians (Diology). Membership: 3,100 individuals; 21 local groups (member, student associate, sustaining member). Finances: Membership: Member, $20; student, $5; sustaining member, $50. Awards: Annual Scholarship to Graduate Students; Awards for Outstanding scientific contributions including the Burton Award to scientist under 35 years of age. Meetings: Annual, various locations nationwide. Publications: Proceedings--Annual Meeting, annual, G. W. Bailey, editor; Bulletin, semiannual, Linda C. Sawyer, editor; Ultramicroscopy (affiliated), 4 issues annually, Elmer Zerttin, editor; Analytical Electron Microscopy, Hren, Goldstein, and Joy, editors. Affiliations: AAAS; American Institute of Physics.

EMERGENCY CARE RESEARCH INSTITUTE
    See: ECRI

★ 790 ★

EMERGENCY DEPARTMENT NURSES ASSOCIATION
666 North Lakeshore Drive
Chicago, Illinois 60611   Established 1970

Robert J. Finnegan, C.A.E., Executive Director
As the national professional association of emergency nurses, it is the purpose of EDNA to promote improved emergency health care through the development and implementation of standards, research, continuing professional education, lay education, government relations and liaison activities with other health care groups. Activities at the local and state levels are encouraged and implemented by local chapters and state coordinating councils. Membership: 12,500 active (RN and LPN/LVN) and affiliate (EMT-A and paramedics). Finances: Membership: $50. Award: The President's Award for Extraordinary Service. Meetings: Annual scientific assembly, various locations. Publications: JEN, The Journal of Emergency Nursing, bimonthly, Gail Pisarcik, RN, MS, editor; EDNA Continuing Education Curriculum.

★ 791 ★

EMOTIONS ANONYMOUS
Post Office Box 4245   (612) 647-9712
St. Paul, Minnesota 55118   Established 1971

A fellowship of men and women who share their experience, strength and hope with each other that they may solve their common problem and help others

recover from emotional illness.   The only requirement for membership is a desire for serenity and peace
of mind.   Some EA members have had psychiatric
treatment, been hospitalized, or seen counselors while
others have not.   If you have gone the whole route
of other methods of treatment and have not achieved
inner peace and serenity, if your life is like a shoe
that pinches, if you are not as happy as you would
like to be or if your emotions interfer with or curtail
your daily activities and your wholesome relationships
with others, you are invited to discover as others
have, that the EA fellowship of weekly meetings is
warm and friendly and that it is also important in
achieving and maintaining emotional health.   Membership: Emotions Anonymous groups in most states,
Canada, and other foreign countries.   Finances:
Membership: Support solely from the voluntary contributions of the members.   Meetings: Weekly Self-
Help Support Meetings.   Publications: E/A Message
Magazine, monthly; Emotions Anonymous Book.

★ 792 ★

EMPHYSEMA ANONYMOUS, INC.
Post Office Box 66
1364 Palmetto Avenue   (813) 334-4226
Fort Myers, Florida 33902   Established 1965

Mrs. Myron F. Barkus, President
The organization is interested in helping victims of
emphysema (a condition affecting breathing capacity)
on a person-to-person basis.   They cooperate with
many emphysema groups throughout the country in o
order to achieve their goal of helping emphysema patients adjust to the strain and loneliness that may result.   EAI tries to bring encouragement as well as
education.   Membership: Approximately 12,000 individuals with emphysema and other breathing problems
and those interested and working professionally to help
them.   Finances: Membership: No membership fee
or other change for help; Other Sources: Volunteer
gifts, memorial gifts.   No fund raising.   Meetings:
Annual, various locations (last Saturday in February
of each year).   Publications: Batting the Breeze,
bimonthly, Mrs. Myron F. Barkus, editor.

★ 793 ★

ENDOCRINE SOCIETY
9650 Rockville Pike   (301) 530-9660
Bethesda, Maryland 20014   Established 1918

Nettie C. Karpin, Executive Secretary
Scientific purposes, for the advancement and promulgation of knowledge regarding the internal secretions
and for the facilitation of personal relationships among
investigators in the subject of endocrinology.   Mem-

bership: 4,000 (active, emeritus).   Finances: Membership: Active, $25; Other Sources: Annual meet-
ings, registration, postgraduate assembly and workshop
fees.   Awards: Fred Conrad Koch Award; Ernst
Oppenheimer Memorial Award; Edwin B. Astwood
Lectureship; Ayerst Award; Robert H. Williams Distinguished Leadership Award in Endoctrinology.
Meetings: Annual, various locations.   Publications:
Endocrinology, monthly, Jack L. Kostyo, Ph.D., editor; The Journal of Clinical Endocrinology and Metabolism, monthly, Delbert A. Fisher, M.D., editor;
Endocrine Reviews, quarterly, Donald S. Gann, M.D.,
editor; Annual Meeting Program Abstracts, annually,
Nettie C. Karpin, editor; Membership Roster, biennially, Nettie C. Karpin, editor.

★ 794 ★

EPILEPSY FOUNDATION OF AMERICA
1828 L Street, N.W., Suite 406   (202) 293-2930
Washington, D.C. 20036   Established 1968

William M. McLin, Executive Director
Devoted solely to the interests and needs of the person with epilepsy and to bringing about those changes
necessary for his medical, social and economic well-
being.   Represents the interests of people with epilepsy by initiating or responding to Federal programs
and by acting as an advocate for the rights of persons
with epilepsy.   EFA develops programs of national
significance; provides professional and public education on prevention and treatment.   Operates a low-
cost insurance and drug program for people with epilepsy and their families.   Membership: 12,000
(open to all people with epilepsy and their families,
regardless of age, sex, race, religion, or country of
origin).   Finances: Membership: General membership, $12 annually; Other Sources: Public contribu-
tions, various foundation and government grants and
contracts.   Research: Various medical research
grants.   Meetings: Semiannual Board of Directors
meetings, various locations; 1 annual National Conference, usually Washington, D.C.   Publications:
National Spokesman, 10 issues annually, Ann Scherer,
editor.   Affiliation: 100 local chapters.

★ 795 ★

EPISCOPAL CONFERENCE OF THE DEAF
504 West Hanover Street   (717) 632-0328
Hanover, Pennsylvania 17331   Established 1880

Rev. Robert Grinowod, Acting Executive Secretary
To spread the Gospel of Christ among the deaf.
Acts as a general clearinghouse concerning all aspects
of work among the deaf; encourages the establishment of missions, promotes recruitment, training and

placement of qualified workers and assists in the expansion, growth and perpetuation of the same; assists workers in the field to better serve God and his church both spiritually and temporally. Membership: 825 (clergymen and layman). Finances: Membership fees; contributions; gifts. Awards: Various awards for meritorious service. Meetings: Annual, various locations. Publications: The Deaf Episcopalian, bimonthly; Times (newsletter), quarterly; Convention Proceedings, annual. Library: Audio Visual Library, 49 volumes. Affiliation: Council of Organizations Serving the Deaf.

★ 796 ★
EPISCOPAL GUILD FOR THE BLIND
157 Montague Street   (212) 625-4886
Brooklyn, New York 11201   Established 1965

Harry J. Sutcliffe, Director
Provides tapes, cassettes, disc recordings for the blind.

ERICKSON EDUCATIONAL FOUNDATION
   See: Janus Information Facility

★ 797 ★
EUROPEAN ASSOCIATION FOR CANCER RESEARCH
c/o M. R. Price
Cancer Research Campaign Laboratories
University of Nottingham   (0602) 56101
Nottingham, NG7 2RD,   ext. 3401
   England, United Kingdom   Established 1968

M. R. Price, Secretary-General
To advance cancer research by facilitating communication between research workers including the organization of meetings. Membership: 661 (individual and national organizations). Finances: Membership: 25 D.Fl. Awards: 3 Fellowships of up to $500 are awarded annually to research workers who are members of the Association. Meetings: Biennial, various locations; The EACR also sponsors selected oncological meetings. Publications: Biology of the Cancer Cell--Proceedings of the Fifth Meeting of the EACR, K. Letnansky, editor.

★ 798 ★
EUROPEAN ASSOCIATION FOR THE STUDY OF DIABETES
10 Queen Anne Street   (01) 637-3644
London W1M 0BD, England   Established 1964
   United Kingdom

James G. L. Jackson, Executive Director
To encourage research in the field of diabetes mellitus, rapid diffusion of acquired knowledge, and facilitation of its application. The Association gives travel grants to young scientists and research workers to enable their attendance at Annual Meetings. Membership: 1,400. Finances: Membership: 10 pounds; Other Sources: Donations. Awards: Minkowski Prize; Claude Bernard Lecture. Meetings: Annual, various locations. Publications: Diabetologia, monthly, A. G. Cudworth, editor.

★ 799 ★
EUROPEAN ASSOCIATION FOR THE STUDY OF
   THE LIVER
Royal Free Hospital
Academic Department of Medicine
Pond Street
London NW3 2QG, England
   United Kingdom   Established 1966

Dr. Neil McIntyre, Secretary
To bring together European research workers in the field of liver disease. Membership: Individuals in various European countries.

★ 800 ★
EUROPEAN ASSOCIATION OF POISON CONTROL
   CENTRES   (02) 344 15 15
Rue Joseph Stallaert, 15   (02) 345 45 45
B-1060 Brussels, Belgium   Established 1964

Professor A. N. P. Van Heijst, President
To study all problems relating to poisons; to promote exchange of information on research work; to encourage surveys on human toxicological questions in Europe. Membership: 195 National Secretaries in 25 countries. Finances: 300 Belgian Francs. Publications: Bulletin de Médecine Légale et de Toxicologie Médicale, bimonthly, Masson and Company, editor. Affiliation: The Association is federate to World Federation of Poison Control Centers.

★ 801 ★
EUROPEAN ASSOCIATION OF PROGRAMMES IN HEALTH SERVICES STUDIES

1 Carlton Villas
Shelbourne Road   (01) 689642
Dublin 6, Ireland   Established 1966

Philip C. Berman, Director
The promotion and encouragement of the education and training of those with careers in Health Services Management, Health Services Research; the development of those engaged in education, training, and research in health services management; the exchange of information and documentation concerning education and training programmes in the health care field, faculty and students between the various European programmes. Other activities include faculty workshops, task forces, fellowships, annual conference. Membership: 29 corporate members (corporate membership, individual membership, associate membership). Finances: Membership: Corporate membership, IR/£60; individual membership IR/£ 20; associate membership, IR/£ 200; Other Sources: Grant from W. K. Kellogg Foundation. Awards: A number of Kellogg Fellowship awarded annually. Meetings: Annual Conference, various locations; workshops, various locations. Publications: Newsletter, quarterly, P. C. Berman, Director, editor. Former Name: European Association of Training Programmes in Hospital and Health Services Administration.

★ 802 ★
EUROPEAN ASSOCIATION OF SOCIAL MEDICINE

c/o H. Courbaire De Marcillat
6 Rond-Point-Winston-Churchill
F-92200 Neuilly Sur Seine, France

Dr. H. Courbaire De Marcillat, Secretary General
Studies medico-social problems in European countries and compares solutions adopted by national societies. Exchanges information in all problems of public health in the physical and psychic sense and from the social point of view. Membership: Individuals and organizations in 12 European countries. Finances: Membership: Dues; Other Sources: Donations. Meetings: General Assembly, triennially, various locations.

EUROPEAN ASSOCIATION OF TRAINING PROGRAMMES IN HOSPITAL AND HEALTH SERVICE ADMINISTRATION

     See: European Association of Programmes in Health Services Studies

★ 803 ★
EUROPEAN BRAIN AND BEHAVIOUR SOCIETY

c/o Dr. W. Singer
Max-Planck Institut für Psychiatrie
Kraepelinstrasse 2
D-8000, München 40   (089) 837-3611
Federal Republic of Germany   Established 1969

Dr. W. Singer, Secretary
To hold scientific meetings to report on research into interrelationships of brain mechanisms and behavior; to disseminate subsequent information and educational materials. Finances: Membership: 20 sF2. Meetings: Annual, various locations; workshop. Publications: Abstracts of papers presented at the annual meeting are published in Behavioural Brain Research.

★ 804 ★
EUROPEAN CHIROPRACTORS' UNION

Brockmanns Gate 9   (02) 15 31 98
Oslo 4, Norway   Established 1955

Dr. Arne Christensen, President
To promote the development of chiropractic in Europe as well as to pursue the interests of chiropractic as a science and a profession by research, teaching, publications and legal activities. It represents on a supranational scale the chiropractic profession in Europe as a whole. Membership: Approximately 550. Finances: Membership: Individual members, $120; associate members (outside Europe only), $30. Meetings: Annual, rotation within membership countries. Publications: The Bulletin, 4 times annually, Dr. R. Molloy, editor.

★ 805 ★
EUROPEAN COMMISSION FOR THE CONTROL OF FOOT-AND-MOUTH DISEASE

c/o Food and Agriculture Organization of the United Nations (FAO)
Viale delle Terme di Caracalla
I-00100 Rome, Italy   Established 1954

P. Stouraitis, Secretary
To promote national and international action with respect to control measures against foot-and-mouth disease in Europe; to collect information on national programs for the control of, and research on, FMD; to campaign against exotic FMD, especially in southeastern Europe; and to convene meetings for the examination of any problem, either administrative or technical, of special interest to Europe as a region. Membership: 24 (government representatives, usually chiefs of veterinary services). Finances: Membership: Based on head of cattle and FAO contribution.

Meetings: Biennial, Rome. Publications: Reports of the biennial sessions and of annual session of the Executive Committee and the Research Group.

★ 806 ★
EUROPEAN COMMITTEE FOR THE PROTECTION OF THE POPULATION AGAINST THE HAZARD OF CHRONIC TOXICITY
c/o Professor René Truhaut
Faculte des Sciences Pharmaceutiques et
    Biologiques de Paris-Luxembourg
4 Avenue de l'Observatoire   (01) 329 12.08
F-75006 Paris, France   Established 1957

Professor René Truhaut, Secretary-General
To study in the general interest the long term risks of intoxication due to exogenous agents and the possible means of protection from them; to create the necessary bases of research for the protection of public health and place these at the disposal of WHO and FAO as well as all international, European and national legislative authorities and other services which have need of them. Membership: 22 (full, corresponding, honorary). Meetings: Every 3 to 4 years, various locations. Publications: Reports of meetings.

★ 807 ★
EUROPEAN DIALYSIS AND TRANSPLANT
    ASSOCIATION (EDTA)
c/o Dr. S. T. Boen
Sint Lucas Hospital   (020) 5112233
Amsterdam, The Netherlands   Established 1964

S. T. Boen, Secretary-Treasurer
The Association aims to encourage and to report advances in the fields of haemodialysis, peritoneal dialysis, renal transplantation, and the broad field of nephrology, including clinical nephrology, renal physiology, and renal pathology. Membership: 1,200 (full, European and Mediterranean countries; associate, other countries). Finances: Annual membership fees. Research Funds: Subsistence allowances for full members to attend the annual Congress. Meetings: Congress, annually. Publications: Proceedings of the E.D.T.A., annually, Dr. B. H. B. Robinson, editor.

★ 808 ★
EUROPEAN LEAGUE AGAINST RHEUMATISM
Post Office Box 146   (061) 541122
CH-4011 Basel, Switzerland   Established 1947

H. Stulz, Executive Secretary
Coordinates all forms of research, treatment and education of rheumatic complaints initiated by scientific and social organizations in member countries. Membership: Approximately 5,000 (clinicians, general practitioners in rheumatology). Finances: Membership dues. Meetings: EULAR Congress, every 4-year regular; Symposias irregular, various locations. Publications: EULAR Bulletin, quarterly (education and information). Affiliations: Section of International League against Rheumatism, which is in consultative status with WHO, UNICEF.

★ 809 ★
EUROPEAN OPHTHALMOLOGICAL SOCIETY
c/o Professor H. E. Henkes
Eye Hospital
Schiedamse vest 180
3000 L M
Rotterdam, The Netherlands   Established 1960

Harold E. Henkes, Secretary-General
To bring together members of the European ophthalmological societies at a Congress every 4 years. Membership: All members of European national ophthalmological societies. Medals: Helmholtz Medal; Charamis Medal; Joseph Imre Prize. Meetings: Every 4 years, various locations.

★ 810 ★
EUROPEAN ORTHODONTIC SOCIETY
64 Wimpole Street
London W1M 8AL, England   (01) 935-2795
    United Kingdom   Established 1907

W. J. B. Houston, Secretary;
    M. A. Kettle, Treasurer
To advance the Science of Orthodontics and its relations with the collateral arts and sciences. Membership: 1,200 (active, honorary, associate, life). Finances: Membership: 90 Swiss francs; entry fee 45 Swiss francs. Awards: Professor Ernest Sheldon Friel Memorial Lecture; Research Essay Awards to members under 35. Meetings: Annual, European locations. Publications: European Journal of Orthodontics, quarterly, J. T. Cook, editor.

★ 811 ★
EUROPEAN SOCIETY FOR CLINICAL
    INVESTIGATION
c/o R. H. T. Edwards
Department of Human Metabolism
Rayne Institute
University College Hospital
University Street   (01) 388-2411
London WC1E 6JJ, England   ext. 262
    United Kingdom   Established 1967

R. H. T. Edwards, Honorary Secretary
To advance medical practice through science; to
cultivate clinical research by the methods of the natural sciences; to foster high standards of ethical practice and investigation. Membership: 820 (active,
senior). Finances: Membership: 75 Dutch Guilders;
Other Sources: Annual meeting. Awards: European
Mack-Forster Award for Clinical Investigation (10,000
D.M.). Meetings: Annual, various locations.
Publications: European Journal of Clinical Investigation, bimonthly, Dr. O. Paulson, editor.

EUROPEAN SOCIETY FOR EXPERIMENTAL SURGERY
    See: European Society for Surgical Research

★ 812 ★
EUROPEAN SOCIETY FOR PEDIATRIC NEPHROLOGY
Kliniek Voor Kinderziekten
Universitaire Insteeling Antwerpen
Universiteitsplein 1   (031) 282528
B-2610 Wilryk, Belgium   Established 1967

Karel J. Van Acker, M.D., Secretary
The Society's aim is to promote the knowledge of
pediatric nephrology and of research in this field, as
well as to disseminate such knowledge at meetings
and elsewhere. Membership: 91. Finances: Membership: 50 Swiss francs annually. Meetings: Annual, various locations.

★ 813 ★
EUROPEAN SOCIETY FOR SURGICAL RESEARCH
c/o Dr. T. V. Keaveny
St. Vincent's Hospital
Department of Surgery   (01) 639111
Dublin, Ireland   Established 1966

T. V. Keaveny, Secretary-General
To bring young European surgical research workers
together at an annual Congress to stimulate interlab-
oratory collaboration. Membership: 560 (associated,
full, foreign). Finances: Membership: 45 Swiss

francs. Awards: Annual Award for outstanding research project. Meetings: Annual, various locations. Publications: Abstracts of Meetings, annual,
S. Kanger, editor. Former Name: European Society
for Experimental Surgery.

EUROPEAN SOCIETY FOR THE STUDY OF DRUG
TOXICITY
    See: European Society of Toxicology

★ 814 ★
EUROPEAN SOCIETY OF CARDIOLOGY
Secretariat: Westzeedijk 118
3016 AH Rotterdam,   (010) 366988
    The Netherlands   Established 1950

Professor Paul G. Hugenholtz, Secretary
Contributes toward the development and teaching of
cardiology; promotes scientific collaboration through
18 working groups and facilitates personal contacts
between European cardiologists at various meetings
throughout the year and throughout Europe. Membership: Approximately 5,000 (member National Societies or individuals where there are no Societies).
in 31 countries. Finances: Membership: Membership dues through the National Society. Meetings:
Major congress every 4 years; joint meeting of the
working groups biennially. Publications: European
Heart Journal, 6 times annually, Professor D. G.
Julian, editor. Affiliations: Council for International Organization of Medical Sciences; International Society and Federation of Cardiology.

★ 815 ★
EUROPEAN SOCIETY OF CARDIOVASCULAR
    SURGERY
c/o Professor A. Senning
Universitatsspital   (01) 255-2300
CH-8091 Zurich, Switzerland   Established 1951

Professor A. Senning, President
To promote the art and science of cardiovascular
surgery. Membership: 750. Finances: Member-
ship: $35. Meetings: Congress. Publications:
Journal of Cardiovascular Surgery, 6 times annually,
Minerva Medica, editor. Affiliation: International
Cardiovascular Society.

★ 816 ★
EUROPEAN SOCIETY OF PATHOLOGY
c/o Laboratory of Pathological Anatomy
Université libre de Bruxelles   (02) 538 88 00
B-1000 Brussels, Belgium   Established 1964

Professor P. Dustin
The aims of the association are to unite the European
pathologists to organize meetings and congresses with
that view to publish works and to serve as a means of
communication between the members, eventually by
promoting the creation of an European Institute of
Pathology.   The term pathology includes general and
experimental pathology, pathological anatomy and
histology, surgical pathology, cytopathology, neuropathology and the morphological aspects of haematolo-
gy.   Europe has to be understood in the geographical
sense of the word.   Membership: About 600 (individual members, presented by members of national
Pathological Societies).   Lectureship: A special
"Symeonides Lecture" is organized at each Congress,
in honor of Professor Symeonides, from Thessaloniki
(Greece) who played an important role in the creation of the Society.   Meetings: Biennially; 1981:
Helsinki; 1983: probably Hamburg.   Publications:
Pathology Research and Practice, Gustav Fischer
Verlag (Stuttgart), editor.

★ 817 ★
EUROPEAN SOCIETY OF TOXICOLOGY
Dr. C. Hodel
c/o F. Hoffmann-La Roche & Company, Ltd.
Drug Safety Monitoring
Post Office Box 4002   (061) 27 56 20
Basle, Switzerland   Established 1962

Dr. C. Hodel, Secretary
To encourage and extend research in the field of drug
toxicity and other areas of toxicology;   to establish
working groups with a view to the scientific study of
the various aspects of toxicology;   to ensure, by
means of meetings, symposia, working groups and bulletins, a regular exchange of information hearing on
problems of toxicology;   to undertake any form of
scientific work connected with toxicology.   Membership: Approximately 900.   Finances: Membership:
40 hfl.   Awards: Young Scientists Award.   Meetings: Annual, various locations.   Publications: Proceedings of the European Society of Toxicology, as
Supplementum to Archives of Toxicology, annually.
Former Name: European Society for the Study of
Drug Toxicity.

★ 818 ★
EUROTRANSPLANT FOUNDATION
Rijnsburgerweg 10
2333 AA Leiden,   (071) 147222
     The Netherlands   Established 1967

Dr. B. Cohen, Administrative Director
An international collaboration between dialysis centers,
tissue typing laboratories, and transplantation centers
for the purpose of coordinating all activities, when
an organ for transplantation becomes available in a
participating centre, which will lead to the transplantation to the "best" waiting recipient.   Membership: Dialysis centers, transplantation centers tissue
typing laboratories.   Finances: Other Sources: Contracts with health insurance companies.   Meetings:
Annual, Leiden, The Netherlands.   Publications:
Articles, pamphlets, books on transplants.

★ 819 ★
EXOTIC PATHOLOGY SOCIETY
Institut Pasteur
25 rue du Docteur Roux   (01) 566-88-69
F-75015 Paris, France   Established 1908

Professor A. Dodin, Secretary-General;
     Professor L. Lamy, Secretary-General
To study the diseases of the tropics.   Activities include monthly meetings for the presentation and discussion of original research in the field.   Membership: 540 (associate, honorary, corresponding, titu-
lary).   Finances: 120 frs; Other Sources: Gifts,
donations, grants.   Awards: Gold Medal Laveran
Prize; Noury-Lemarié Prize.   Meetings: Congress,
biennial, various locations;   monthly meetings,
Paris, France.   Publications: Bulletin de la Société
de Pathologie Exotique, bimonthly; monographs.
Library: 1,200 volumes.

★ 820 ★
EYE BANK ASSOCIATION OF AMERICA, INC.
3195 Maplewood Avenue
Winston-Salem,   (919) 768-0719
     North Carolina   27103   Established 1961

Mrs. Charles A. Bunce, Executive Secretary
To promote and standardize the eye-bank movement;
to keep members in touch with advances in corneal
surgery thus promoting eye research.   Arranges for
individuals to donate their eyes for use in transplants.
Membership: 63 eye-banks.   Finances: Membership:
$300.   Meetings: Annual, with American Academy
of Ophthalmology and Otolaryngology.   Publications:
Newsletter, quarterly, Ruth Fisher, editor;   brochures.

★ 821 ★
EYE-BANK FOR SIGHT RESTORATION, INC.
210 East 64th Street   (212) 838-9200
New York, New York 10021   Established 1944

Mary Jane O'Neill, Executive Director
To make available to surgeons who are qualified to
perform the corneal graft and other sight-restoring
surgical techniques a fresh or preserved corneal tissue,
wherever and whenever needed; to encourage and extend, by teaching and research, the knowledge and
skill required to perform corneal graft operations; to
establish sources of supply of salvaged eyes and corneal tissue, and to provide the means for its collection, preparation, storage and redistribution; to stimulate interest in research work on blindness resulting
from corneal damage and other causes; to undertake
complete pathological studies of all eye tissue sent to
it.   Activities include informing the public on the
value of eye tissues and on the procedure to be followed in donating eyes, courses of instruction to
ophthalmologists on techniques of corneal transplantation and on other phases of eye surgery, research into
the cause and treatment of eye diseases, and the Corneal Clinic sponsored jointly with the Manhattan Eye,
Ear and Throat Hospital for patients with corneal disease or damage. Finances: Contributions, foundations, legacies, other. Meetings: Quarterly, New
York City. Publications: Every Day the Eye-Bank
Helps More People See, annually, Mary Jane O'Neill,
editor; Progress Report, annually. Library: The
Eye-Bank Library, 600 volumes. Affiliation: Eye-
Bank Association of America.

★ 822 ★
EYE RESEARCH INSTITUTE OF RETINA FOUNDATION
20 Staniford Street   (617) 742-3140
Boston, Massachusetts 02114   Established 1950

Charles L. Schepens, M.D., President
To support and conduct a broad program of biological
and medical research with respect to the eye and the
process of vision; to promote both laboratory and
clinical research; dissemination of knowledge concerning eye research and treatment; to conduct training in clinical techniques and research areas developed at the Institute. Membership: 203 staff members (research professional, research supporting, technicians, clerical, secretarial, maintenance). Finances: Other Sources: Research grants from government
agencies and private foundations; donations from individuals. Meetings: Annual, Boston, Massachusetts.
Publications: Sundial Newsletter, quarterly; monographs, conferences, International Congress. Library:
Approximately 3,000 volumes.

F

★ 823 ★
FAMILY SERVICES ASSOCIATION OF AMERICA
44 East 23rd Street   (212) 674-6100
New York, New York 10010   Established 1911

W. Keith Daugherty, General Director
To prevent family breakdown and promote family life
through counseling and other services. Membership:
Over 260 (accredited member agencies). Finances:
Membership dues; contributions, grants and contracts,
publication sales. Meetings: Biennial Conference,
various locations; board meeting, semiannual, New
York City. Publications: Social Casework, 10 times
annually, Jacqueline Atkins, editor; Highlights, bimonthly, Harold N. Weiner, editor.

FAUCHARD (PIERRE) ACADEMY
   See: Pierre Fauchard Academy

★ 824 ★
FEDERATION OF AMERICAN HOSPITALS
1405 North Pierce, Suite 311   (501) 661-9555
Little Rock, Arkansas 72207   Established 1966

John R. Walker, Director, Administrative Office
To promote the public welfare through the development of the best hospital care and service for all of
the people; to publicize and constantly strive to improve the service of the investor-owned hospitals; to
act as a spokesman and representative of the general
welfare and interest of investor-owned hospitals; to
foster, encourage and participate in the training of
all health personnel; to further the interest of com-
munity-supporting, investor-owned hospitals and related health facilities by stimulating and encouraging
participation in sound policies of management applicable to tax-paying private enterprises. Membership:
1,000 (regular, associate). Finances: Membership:
Regular, $14-$17 per licensed bed per month; associate, $100 or $350 annually. Publications: Investor-Owned Hospital Review; Annual Directory of
Investor-Owned Hospitals; Hospital Management
Companies.

★ 825 ★
FEDERATION OF AMERICAN SOCIETIES FOR
    EXPERIMENTAL BIOLOGY
9650 Rockville Pike   (301) 530-7000
Bethesda, Maryland 20014   Established 1912

Eugene L. Hess, Executive Director
To bring together investigators in biological and medical sciences represented by the member societies;
to disseminate information on the results of biological
research through publications and scientific meetings;
and to serve in other capacities in which the member
societies can function more efficiently as a group
than as individual units. Membership: 19,000
(members of 6 constituent societies). Finances:
Funds from the sale of journals and directories; advertising; annual meetings. Meetings: Annual,
various locations. Publications: Federation Proceedings, monthly, K. F. Heumann, editor. Affiliations:
American Physiological Society; American Society of
Biological Chemists; American Society for Pharmacology and Experimental Therapeutics; American Association of Pathologists; American Institute of Nutrition;
American Association of Immunologists.

★ 826 ★
FEDERATION OF FRENCH LANGUAGE
    GYNECOLOGISTS AND OBSTETRICIANS
123 Boulevard de Port-Royal   (01) 633 61 53
F-75014 Paris, France   Established 1945

C. Sureau, Secretary General
To promote professional and scientific activities among
French speaking gynecologists and obstetricians.
Membership: 1,700. Finances: Membership: 250
French francs. Meetings: Biennial, various loca-
tions. Publications: Journal de Gynécologie Ob-
stétrique et Biologie de la Reproduction, 8 volumes,
Masson, editor. Library: 8 volumes.

★ 827 ★
FEDERATION OF MEDICAL WOMEN OF CANADA
Box 9502
Ottawa, Ontario K1G 3U2,
    Canada   Established 1924

The Federation was founded with the object of pro-
moting the interest of medical women in Canada.
Membership: Approximately 450 medical women.
Award: Maude Abbott Scholarship Loan Fund. Meet-
ings: Annual, various locations. Publications:
Newsletter, quarterly. Affiliation: Medical Women's
International Association.

★ 828 ★
FEDERATION OF ORTHODONTIC ASSOCIATIONS
c/o Dr. David H. Watson
3953 North 76th Street   (414) 464-7440
Milwaukee, Wisconsin 53222   Established 1963

Dr. David H. Watson, Executive Director
To promote the advancement of orthodontic education;
to promote the exchange of ideas and experiences
between various associations interested in orthodontics;
to provide a better understanding between member associations; to protect the existing rights granted by
license to practice all phases of dentistry. Membership: 2,000 (general practitioners interested in ortho-
dontia). Meetings: Semiannual, various locations.
Publications: International Journal of Orthodontics,
quarterly, Dr. James Flatley, editor. Affiliations:
American Society for the Study of Orthodontics;
American Academy of Orthodontics for the General
Practitioner; American Academy of Gnathologic
Orthopedics; American Orthodontic Society.

★ 829 ★
FEDERATION OF PROSTHODONTIC
    ORGANIZATIONS
211 East Chicago Avenue, Suite 915
Chicago, Illinois 60611   Established 1955

Eric Bishop, Director of the Central Office
Organized to encourage and improve prosthodontic
service and to serve as a liaison to its member organizations. Membership: 20 organizations. Finances: Member organizations, $100; member of a
member organization, $25. Meetings: Annual,
Chicago. Publications: FPO Newsletter, Dr. Ells-
worth K. Kelly, editor; The Journal of Prosthetic
Dentistry, Dr. Judson Hickey, editor.

★ 830 ★
FEDERATION OF STATE MEDICAL BOARDS OF THE
    UNITED STATES, INC.
2626 B. W. Freeway   (817) 335-1141
Fort Worth, Texas 76102   Established 1912

H. E. Jervey, Jr., M.D., Executive Director
To promote higher standards of medical licensure and
uniformity between the states; to keep state boards
better informed of disciplinary actions taken by the
various boards; to keep state boards up to date
through correspondence on changes in licensure procedures, etc. Activities include the preparation of
the Federation Licensing Examination (FLEX), for administration by the participating state boards of medical examiners to insure uniform testing and the conduct of annual meetings open to attendance of every

board member for all the state boards of medical examiners. Membership: 52 medical boards (all 50 states, the District of Columbia, Puerto Rico); 8 separate osteopathic examining boards. Finances: Membership: States dues based on number of physicians licensed in each state. Award: Federation Certificate of Appreciation presented to retiring board members. Meetings: Approximately 3 annually, various locations. Publications: Federation Bulletin, monthly, Ray L. Casterline, M.D., editor.

FEDERATION OF THE EUROPEAN DENTAL INDUSTRY
See: FIDE

★ 831 ★
FEDERATION OF THE HANDICAPPED
211 West 14th Street   (212) 242-9050
New York, New York 10011   Established 1935

Milton Cohen, Executive Director
A non-profit, non-sectarian organization, providing vocational rehabilitation to the severely disabled - services on a non-fee basis provided to all disabled. Membership: 1,000. Finances: Contributions, foundations, government grants and self-sustaining work projects.

★ 832 ★
FEDERATION OF WORLD HEALTH FOUNDATIONS
Avenue Appia
CH-1211 Geneva 27   (022) 91-34-25
Switzerland   Established 1967

Anne-Marie Johannot-Meyer de Stadelhofen, Executive Director
To assist member Foundations in the pursuit of their objectives; to provide a liaison between World Health Foundations and the World Health Organization; to encourage the creation of additional World Health Foundations. Membership: 8 World Health Foundations. Finances: Support from W. K. Kellogg Foundation. Meetings: Steering Committee, annual, Geneva, Switzerland. Publications: Annual Report.

FELDMAN (RUTH RUBIN) NATIONAL ODD SHOE
EXCHANGE
See: Ruth Rubin Feldman National Odd Shoe
Exchange

★ 833 ★
FIDE - FEDERATION OF THE EUROPEAN DENTAL
INDUSTRY
Pipinstrasse 16
D-5000 Köln 1   (0221) 219458
Federal Republic of Germany Established 1957

Dr. Horst Herrmann, Secretary
Optimal and efficient arrangement of exhibition in connection with dental congresses of the FDI-Federation Dentaire International. Improvement of dental trade and industry relations to the dental profession. Membership: 8 member associations (European Dental Trade and Industry Associations in Great Britain, France, Sweden, Switzerland, Austria, Netherlands, Italy, West Germany). Finances: Membership: sfrs. 1.000, annually. Meetings: Semiannual, various locations.

★ 834 ★
FIGHT FOR SIGHT, INC.
139 East 57 Street   (212) 751-1118
New York, New York 10022   Established 1946

Mildred Weisenfeld, Executive Director
To provide funds for ophthalmic research through grants, postdoctoral research fellowships, student fellowships, occasional clinical service projects, and more recently, limited unrestricted awards to departments of ophthalmology. Finances: Membership: $5-$100 and over. Awards: Fight for Sight Citation, to encourage and recognize a major research contribution to the field of vision. Affiliations: Association for Research in Ophthalmology, Inc.; National Committee for Research in Vision and Ophthalmology and Blindness.

★ 835 ★
FLEISCHNER SOCIETY
c/o Norman Blank, M.D.
Department of Radiology
Stanford University
School of Medicine   (415) 497-6801
Palo Alto, California 94305 Established 1969

Norman Blank, M.D., Secretary
The Society works for the advancement of knowledge in the field of chest medicine. They offer an annual Instructional Course to further this goal. Membership: 65 individuals. Finances: $10 annually; Other Sources: Instructional Course proceeds. Lectureship: Annual Fleischner Lectureship. Meetings: Annual, various locations.

★ 836 ★

FLYING DENTISTS ASSOCIATION, INC.
5820 Wilshire Boulevard   (213) 937-5514
Los Angeles, California 90036   Established 1960

J. Replogle, Executive Director
To stimulate fraternal relations among flying dentists
and dental groups; to provide technical assistance
and consulting service on problems involving dental
materials, breathing apparatus, testing methods, products, etc.; to collect, evaluate and disseminate
technical information as dental flying problems are
related to aviation; to bring dental health service to
greater area and more people. Membership: 650.
Finances: Membership: Dues, $45; initiation, $15;
Other Sources: Journal subscriptions, convention activities. Meetings: Annual, various locations.
Publications: Flight Watch, quarterly.

★ 837 ★

FLYING PHYSICIANS ASSOCIATION, INC.
801 Green Bay Road   (312) 234-6330
Lake Bluff, Illinois 60044   Established 1954

Albert Carriere, Business Counsel
To promote aviation medicine and research; to promote general aviation safety by example and teaching;
to attain and promote more advanced proficiency and
knowledge in the operation of aircraft. Membership:
2,500. Meetings: Annual, semiannual, and regional, various locations. Publications: Flying Physi-
can, quarterly; Bulletin, monthly.

★ 838 ★

FOCUS
Loyola University Medical Center
Department of Ophthalmology
2160 South First Avenue   (312) 531-3048
Maywood, Illinois 60153   Established 1961

James E. McDonald, M.D., Director
To provide eye care for the needy in overseas areas
including Haiti, Guatamala, Colombia, and Nigeria.
Membership: About 150 ophthalmologists. Finances:
Donations.

★ 839 ★

FOOD AND DRUG LAW INSTITUTE
1200 New Hampshire Avenue, N.W. (202) 833-1601
Washington, D.C. 20036   Established 1949

Gary L. Yingling, Esquire, President
To improve understanding of the nature and scope of

laws and regulations applicable to the food, drug,
cosmetic and related industries. Membership: 120
firms (sustaining, associate). Finances: Membership:
Fee scale based on percentage of sales. Lectureship:
Food and Drug Law Courses at 5 universities through-
out the United States; Graduate Law Fellowships at
New York University Law School and the National
Law Center of the George Washington University.
Meetings: 8 annually, various locations. Publica-
tions: Food and Drug Cosmetic Law Journal, monthly,
Frank T. Dierson, editor; various casebooks and text-
books; legal research projects, annually.

★ 840 ★

FOOD AND NUTRITION BOARD
2101 Constitution Avenue   (202) 961-1366
Washington, D.C. 20418   Established 1940

Myrtle L. Brown, Executive Secretary
The Board functions as an advisory group on nutrition
to United States Agencies. It promotes needed research and helps interpret nutritional science in the
interests of public welfare. The Board may act on
its own initiative or on request from public or private
agencies. It is a part of the Division of Biology
and Agriculture of the National Academy of Sciences-
National Research Council. Specific activities are
carried on by committees composed of experts in each
field. Membership: 15 (leaders in sciences related
to food and nutrition). Finances: Foundation and
private industrial contributions, government contracts
and grants. Meetings: Semiannual, Washington,
D.C.

★ 841 ★

FORD FOUNDATION
320 East 43rd Street
New York, New York 10017   Established 1936

Franklin A. Thomas, President
A private, non-profit institution dedicated to the
public well-being. It seeks to identify and contribute to the solution of problems of national or international importance. The Foundation works mainly by
granting funds to institutions and organizations for experimental, demonstration, and developmental efforts
that give promise of producing advances in various
fields. The Foundation continues to support research
and training on promising ways of advancing knowledge of the reproductive process. Emphasis is on the
advancement of novel contraceptive approaches, fundamental research on the complex biochemical and hormonal processes that lead to reproduction. It also
supports other basic medical research.

★ 842 ★

FORUM FOR MEDICAL AFFAIRS
3935 North Meridian Street   (317) 925-7545
Indianapolis, Indiana 46208   Established 1944

Donald F. Foy, Secretary-Treasurer
An organization of officials of national, state and
local medical groups, sponsored by the Conference of
Presidents and Officers of State Medical Association.
Membership: 1,600.   Meetings: Annual, various
locations.

★ 843 ★

FOUNDATION FOR CHILDREN WITH LEARNING
    DISABILITIES
99 Park Avenue, 2nd Floor   (212) 687-7211
New York, New York 10016   Established 1977

Susan T. Vandiver, Executive Director
Provides direct financial support to various programs
which academically and sociably aid learning disabled
children and their families.

★ 844 ★

FOUNDATION FOR CHIROPRACTIC EDUCATION
    AND RESEARCH
3209 Ingersoll Avenue   (515) 274-2579
Des Moines, Iowa 50312   Established 1944

Brian E. Cartier, Executive Director
The Foundation for Chiropractic Education and Research, a non-profit organization, has a unique place
in the health community.   While it has close ties to
the chiropractic profession, its work is multi-disciplinary providing health education and research of benefit to all professions and all mankind.   FCER is a
philanthropic agency which seeks to improve chiropractic for the benefit of mankind.   The Foundation
provides motivation and funding necessary to produce
scientific information which will enhance the knowledge and treatment of physical disorders and encourage an individual's total good health.   Membership:
321 (general and partner in progress; doctors of
chiropractic and interested lay members).   Finances:
Membership: General, $25-$99.99; partner in progress, $100 and over; Other Sources: Individual and
corporate contributions.   Research Funds: Research
development, basic sciences, clinical sciences, education and training.   Meetings: Semiannual, in
January and June, various locations.   Publications:
Advance, bimonthly, Brian Cartier, editor; Chiropractic Health Care, Dr. R. C. Shafer, editor.   Affiliations: American Chiropractic Association.

★ 845 ★

FOUNDATION FOR CURE
12 Oriole Lane   (714) 757-4107
Oceanside, California 92054   Established 1969

Kyle E. Townsend, Chairman-Medical Director
The Foundation's purposes are to provide funds for
empirical/applied research in immunology; to cure
and prevent the common chronic bacterial diseases;
to cure and prevent the common acute bacterial diseases; to cure the carrier of the common bacterial
diseases; to assist the practicing physician to bring
his discoveries to the people; to provide an ambulatory chronic disease hospital and medical service center on the west coast where doctors can bring their
patients for study of clinical immunology; to provide
a biological laboratory to develop and make the
heterophile curative antigens/metabolites/vaccines;
to correlate clinical and immunochemistry to explain
the phenomenon of cure.   Meetings: Annual.   Publications: Immunity with Impunity, by Kyle E.
Townsend;   Patients Manual of Clinical Immunology,
Kyle E. Townsend, editor; To Get You Well and
Keep You Well, Kyle E. Townsend, editor; and
many other publications.

FOUNDATION FOR THE ADVANCEMENT OF
BIOMEDICAL SCIENCES (OFA)
    See: OFA Foundation for the Advancement of
          Biomedical Sciences

FOX (DEBBIE) FOUNDATION
    See: Debbie Fox Foundation

★ 846 ★

FRENCH LANGUAGE ASSOCIATION FOR RESEARCH
    ON DIABETES AND METABOLIC DISEASES
8 rue Anatole de la Forge
F-75017 Paris, France   Established 1956

Dr. Roland Lebouc, Secretary General
To bring together doctors, biologists and researchers
interested in diabetes and metabolism.   Membership:
400 doctors, biologists, and researchers interested in
diabetes and metabolic illnesses.   Finances: Membership: 110 francs annually.   Awards: Alfediam-
Maurice Uzan annual prize.   Meetings: Semiannually, spring, Paris; autumn, various locations.   Publications: Diabeté and Metabolisme, quarterly, in
French and English.   Former Name: Association of
French Speaking Diabetes and Metabolism Specialists.

★ 847 ★
FRENCH LANGUAGE ASSOCIATION OF SCIENTIFIC
      PSYCHOLOGY
c/o Marc Richelle
Lab. de Psychologie
32 Boulevard de la Constitution
B-4020 Liege, Belgium   Established 1952

Marc Richelle, Secretary-General
To promote the study and discussion of all the prob-
lems of scientific psychology; to unite French-speak-
ing researchers and psychologists. Membership: 630.
Finances: Membership: 20 French francs; Other
Sources: Donations. Meetings: Annual, various
locations. Publications: Proceedings of meetings;
Special Series, Presses Universitaires de France.

★ 848 ★
FRIENDS OF HISTORICAL PHARMACY, INC.
c/o Hugh Mercer Apothecary Shop
1020 Caroline Street
Fredricksburg, Virginia 22401   (703) 373-3362
                                     Established 1941

M. L. Neuroth, President
Maintains and operates the Virginia shrine to medicine and pharmacy, the Hugh Mercer Apothecary
Shop. Membership: 350 (individual, corporate,
life). Finances: Membership: Individual, $5;
corporate, $25; life, $75; Other Sources: Admission fees, souvenirs, contributions. Meetings: Annual, Fredricksburg, Virginia.

FULLER (ANNA) FUND
      See: Anna Fuller Fund

G

★ 849 ★
GAIRDNER FOUNDATION
255 Yorkland Boulevard, Suite 220
Willowdale, Ontario M2J 1S3,   (416) 493-3102
      Canada   Established 1957

T. V. Kenney, Executive Director
The Foundation's aim is to confer both signal and
tangible recognition on individuals who have made
significant contributions in the conquest of disease and
the relief of human suffering. Annual awards are
made to those selected from international nominations,
and recipients are then invited to Toronto to speak to
physicians and medical students on subjects of their

choice. Awards: Gairdner Foundation Award of
Merit, a $25,000 prize awarded irregularly; Gairdner
Foundation Annual Awards, a series of $15,000 prizes
awarded annually.

GENERAL SERVICE BOARD OF ALCOHOLICS
ANONYMOUS, INC.
      See: Alcoholics Anonymous, Inc.

★ 850 ★
GEORGIA WARM SPRINGS FOUNDATION
600 Third Avenue, Suite 2500   (212) 490-3361
New York, New York 10016   Established 1927

Makes grants for research and aid in rehabilitation of
afflicted individuals, and for the training of personnel
in the treatment of such diseases. Membership:
Board of Trustees. Finances: Investments. Meetings: Annual, New York City.

GERONTOLOGICAL SOCIETY
      See: Gerontological Society of America

★ 851 ★
GERONTOLOGICAL SOCIETY OF AMERICA
1835 K Street, N.W., Suite 305   (202) 466-6750
Washington, D.C. 20006   Established 1945

Janice Caldwell, Executive Director
To promote the scientific study of aging in the biological and social sciences; to stimulate communications
between scientific disciplines, and between researchers, teachers, professionals, and others; to broaden
education in aging; to foster application of research
to the field of practice; to advance the utilization
of research in the development of public policy; to
develop the qualifications of gerontologists by setting
high standards of professional ethics, conduct, education, and achievement. Membership: 5,400 (scientists and professionals in the field of aging). Finances: Membership: Regular, $55; student, $22.50.
Awards: Robert W. Kleemeier Award for outstanding
research in aging;   Donald P. Kent Award for outstanding application of research to practice; Brook-
dale Awards for research in gerontology. Meetings:
Annual, various locations. Publications: Journal of
Gerontology, bimonthly, Harold Brody, editor; The
Gerontologist, bimonthly, Elias S. Cohen, editor;
various monographs and pamphlets. Former Name:
Gerontological Society.

★ 852 ★
GOODWILL INDUSTRIES OF AMERICA, INC.
9200 Wisconsin Avenue   (301) 530-6500
Washington, D.C. 20014   Established 1902

Rear Admiral David M. Cooney, President and Chief
   Executive Officer; Andrea S. Heid, Associate
   Director, Public Relations
To provide rehabilitation services, training, employment and opportunities for personal growth for the
handicapped, disabled and the disadvantaged who are
not readily absorbed into the competitive labor market
or who are faced with social restraints. Through the
use of skilled techniques of rehabilitation and by providing work experience opportunity, Goodwill Industries organizational members strive to assist the handicapped, the disabled and the disadvantaged to their
maximum level of personal dignity and proficiency.
Membership: 167 autonomous Goodwill Industries and
35 branch workshops. Finances: Membership:
Monthly dues based on earned income (not total income) of the local Goodwill Industries. Awards:
National Goodwill Graduate of the Year Award;
Edgar J. Helms Award; Kenneth K. King Award;
National Employer of the Year Award (large and small
categories); National Goodwill Achiever of the Year
Award; local achievement awards. Meetings: Delegate Assembly, annually, various locations; Conference of Executives, annually. Publications: G.I.A.
News, bimonthly, Andrea Heid, editor. Affiliations:
167 autonomous Goodwill Industries and 35 branch
workshops.

★ 853 ★
GRAVITY AWARENESS CENTERS
Post Office Box 4490   (714) 327-1506
Palm Springs, California 92263   Established 1977

Larry Jacobs
Research and development of equipment for counter-
acting gravitational stress on the human body. Promoting information about people who utilize gravity
for enhancing their physical and mental well-beings.
Membership: 20,000 active participants. Finances:
Other Sources: From sales of literature and products.
Meetings: Seminars and workshops held in at least 8
major cities, annually. Publications: How to Live
on Earth in Harmony with Gravity, annually, Larry
Jacobs, editor; Cum Gravity, textbook, R. M.
Martin, M.D., editor. Former Name: Body Inversion Organization.

★ 854 ★
GRENFELL ASSOCIATION OF AMERICA
345 Park Avenue, Suite 4100   (212) 593-8725
New York, New York 10022   Established 1905

To promote medical and social service work in
Northern Newfoundland and Labrador by supporting
hospitals, nursing stations, a children's home, board-
ing school dormitories, hospitals, and supply vessels.
Publications: Among the Deep Sea Fisheries, quarterly.

★ 855 ★
GRENFELL REGIONAL HEALTH SERVICES BOARD
St. Anthony, Newfoundland   (709) 454-8881
   A0K 4S0, Canada   Established 1981

Dr. Peter Roberts, Executive Director
Established to continue the work begun by the International Grenfell Association in providing health services for the people of Northern Newfoundland and
Labrador. A non-profit health agency funded by the
Government of Newfoundland; operates 4 hospitals,
17 nursing stations and community health centres and
provides a full range of primary, secondary and
tertiary services. Presently, there are approximately
800 employees working with the Grenfell Regional
Health Services Board, including 35 medical doctors,
10 dentists and approximately 200 nurses. Affiliations: The International Grenfell Association and the
5 Supporting Associations of the IGA; Faculty of
Medicine, Memorial University of Newfoundland;
Newfoundland Hospital Association. Former Name:
International Grenfell Association.

★ 856 ★
GROUP FOR THE ADVANCEMENT OF PSYCHIATRY,
   INC.
1601 West Taylor Street   (312) 996-1451
Chicago, Illinois 60612   Established 1946

Jack Weinberg, M.D., President
To collect and appraise significant data in the field
of psychiatry, mental health and human relations; to
re-evaluate old concepts and to develop and test new
ones; to apply the knowledge thus obtained for the
promotion of mental health in good human relations.
Membership: Approximately 300 (active, contributing,
life, life consultant, Ginsburg Fellows). Finances:
Membership: Active, $250; contributing, $50;
Other Sources: Donations. Research Funds: Ginsburg Fellowship Funds; Maurice Falk Fellowship Funds
and others. Meetings: Semiannual, various locations. Publications: Various pamphlets on psychiatry
and related fields. Several during the fiscal year.

★ 857 ★
GROUP HEALTH ASSOCIATION OF AMERICA, INC.
1717 Massachusetts Avenue, N.W.
Suite 701   (202) 483-4012
Washington, D.C. 20036   Established 1959

James Doherty, Executive Director
To promote the health and well-being of the people
of North America, especially through application in
health care programs of the principles of prepayment
of the cost of health care, physician group practice
of medicine, comprehensive health care of high quality under the direction of qualified professional personnel, and control of policy and administrative functions in the interest of consumers of health services.
Activities include consultation services for the creation
and expansion of prepaid group practice health care
organizations; the production and distribution of publications; research and statistical reporting services.
Membership: 193 member organizations, 850 members.
Finances: Membership: Individual, $25 annually;
organizations pay by predetermined scale; Other
Sources: Sale of publications, contributions. Meet-
ings: Annual, various locations. Publications:
Group Health Journal; Group Health News, monthly;
GHAA News Briefs, irregular; Proceedings of Annual
Conference, annually.

★ 858 ★
GUIDE DOGS FOR THE BLIND, INC.
Post Office Box 1200   (415) 479-4000
San Rafael, California 94902   Established 1942

Benny Larsen, Executive Director
To provide mobility by means of dog guides to legally blind men and women who are physically and emotionally capable of undergoing the 4-week training
program. Membership: 15,000. Finances: Membership: Regular, $10; contributing, $25; sponsoring,
$50; sustaining, $100; patron, $500; benefactor,
$1,000; Other Sources: Bequests. Meetings: An-
nual, Guide Dogs for the Blind Campus. Publications: Guide Dog News, quarterly, Anne Hopkins,
editor.

★ 859 ★
GUIDE DOG FOUNDATION FOR THE BLIND, INC.
Training Center:
371 Jericho Turnpike
Smithtown, Long Island,   (516) 265-2121
   New York 11787   Established 1946
Main Office:
109-19 72nd Avenue   (212) 263-4885
Forest Hills, New York 11375

Richard Lehrfeld, President; E. M. Swanton,
   Executive Director; John Byfield, Director of
   Training
The Foundation serves to breed and train guide dogs
for the blind to provide more mobility for the handi-
capped. Finances: Other Sources: Contributions.

★ 860 ★
GUIDING EYES FOR THE BLIND, INC.
Yorktown Heights,   (914) 245-4024
   New York 10598   Established 1954

Donald Z. Kauth, Executive Director
Provides trained guide dogs and instruction in their
use to blind persons throughout the United States.
Received official accreditation of the National Accreditation Council for Agencies Serving the Blind
and Visually Handicapped in 1974. First guide dog
training school to be so recognized. Any blind
person who qualifies both physically and psycholog-
ically is eligible for guide dog training. The minimum age requirement is 16. There is no maximum
age and persons over 60 often derive great benefits
with a guide dog. Membership: Board of Directors,
33. Finances: Voluntary contributions. Meetings:
6 annually, New York City. Publications: Guide
Lines, quarterly; information pamphlets on guide dog
training.

GUTTMACHER (ALAN) INSTITUTE
   See: Alan Guttmacher Institute

H

★ 861 ★
HADASSAH MEDICAL RELIEF ORGANIZATION, INC.
50 West 58th Street   (212) 355-7900
New York, New York 10019   Established 1912

Aline Kaplan, Executive Director
In the United States Hadassah prepares its members to
help strengthen democracy, provides basic Jewish education and supports projects for American Jewish
youth; in Israel it aids medical and public health
systems, provides for child welfare and educational
training programs and supports land reclamation. Activities include the raising of funds to maintain the
Hadassah-Hebrew University Medical Center which includes schools of medicine, nursing, dentistry, pharmacology, public health and administration and occupational therapy. Membership: 370,000 women.

Finances: Membership: Regular, $10; life, $175;
Other Sources: Contributions, fundraising events,
special gifts, bequests, government and foundation
grants. Awards: National Henrietta Szold Award.
Meetings: Annual convention, various locations;
Mid Winter Conference of National Board; National
Board, alternate Thursdays, New York City. Publi-
cations: Hadassah Magazine, 10 times annually;
Headlines, regularly. Affiliations: National Council
of Women in U.S.A.; United Nations Association
of the U.S.A., Inc.; American Association for World
Health, Inc.; American Council of Voluntary Agen-
cies for Foreign Service, Inc.; Greater New York
Conference on Soviet Jewry; U.S. Mission to the
United Nations.

★ 862 ★

HARVEY SOCIETY
Rockefeller University
1230 York Avenue   (212) 360-1000
New York, New York 10021   Established 1905

Emil C. Gotschlich, M.D., Secretary
Via a series of eight lectures per year and a volume
of each year's lectures, the Society's main activity
is the dissemination of knowledge of current scientific
and medical themes. Membership: 1,600 members.
Finances: Membership: $12 annually; Other
Sources: Trust fund, the income to be used for the
expenses of the Society. Meetings: 3 times annually, Rockefeller University, New York. Publications:
Harvey Lectures, annual. Affiliation: New York
Academy of Medicine.

★ 863 ★

HEALING RESEARCH TRUST
Secretary: c/o Heseltine Moss & Company
3/4 Trump Street
London EC2V 8DH, England
     United Kingdom   Established 1974

To promote alternative medicine, encourage systematic
research in healing techniques and provide grants for
education. Finances: Donations. Awards: Bur-
series to students of natural therapeutics, some of
which are specifically reserved for those studying
radionics; research grants.

★ 864 ★

HEALTH AND EDUCATION RESOURCES, INC.
4733 Bethesda Avenue, Suite 7351   (301) 656-3178
Bethesda, Maryland 20014   Established 1969

Dallas Johnson, President
This non-profit organization is concerned with development and execution of studies, conferences, education and information programs and materials, as well
as with other instruments of communications in the
fields of health and education.   Current activities
include education programs and materials for medical
laboratory personnel, cancer education and information, and health education programs. Finances:
Other Sources: Contracts, grants. Publications:
Pamphlets, manuals, teaching guides, posters, magazine articles, and other printed media.

★ 865 ★

HEALTH CARE EXHIBITORS ASSOCIATION, INC.
90 Bagby Drive, Suite 222   (205) 870-5143
Birmingham, Alabama 35209   Established 1930

John W. Rousseau, Executive Director
The Association aims to assist both members and
health care associations in increasing the effectiveness
of the exhibit medium as a marketing experience.
Membership: 259 (firms which manufacture or distribute products to the medical, dental, nursing, hospital,
and allied health care professions). Publications:
Handbook Schedule of Conventions, semiannually;
Newsletter, quarterly.

★ 866 ★

HEALTH INSURANCE ASSOCIATION OF AMERICA
1750 K Street, N.W., Suite 400   (202) 331-1336
Washington, D.C. 20006   Established 1956

James L. Moorefield, President
Presentation of insurance company views on matters
affecting accident and health insurance; promotion
of ethical standards and conduct for observance of
member companies; promotion of public understanding
and confidence in the business; forums for discussion
and continued research in the development of insurance. Membership: 319 (insurance companies).
Meetings: Annual Meeting/Group Insurance Forum;
Individual Insurance Forum; Group Officers Round
Table; various locations.

★ 867 ★

HEALTH INSURANCE INSTITUTE
8750 K Street, N.W.   (202) 862-4122
Washington, D.C. 20006

Kenneth White, Vice President and General Manager;
     Jerry Miller, Assistant General Manager
Serves as a central source of information for the

public on private health insurance provided by the nation's health insurance companies. Major objectives are: to bring about better public understanding of progress and performance of private health insurance companies, to set forth among leadership publics the position of the business on relevant national health care issues, and to help keep insurance companies fully apprised and sensitive to the social environment. Membership: 310 (insurance companies responsible for 85% of health insurance written by insurance companies in the United States today). Publications: Numerous books, reports, and educational materials. Library: ACLI General Library. Affiliations: Health Insurance Association of America (HIAA); American Council of Life Insurance Companies (ACLI).

★ 868 ★

HEALTH LEAGUE OF CANADA
76 Avenue Road
Toronto, Ontario M5R 2H1,   (416) 923-8405
   Canada   Established 1920

Dr. Donald F. Damude, Director
Health education to prevent sickness, improve health and prolong life. Membership: 3,000 (interested professional groups, and general public). Finances: Membership: $6; Other Sources: Donations, grants. Meetings: Annual, Toronto, Ontario, Canada. Publications: Health, quarterly, Stanley E. Caldwell, editor; pamphlets on various aspects of health.

HEALTH/PAC
   See: Health Policy Advisory Center, Inc.

★ 869 ★

HEALTH PHYSICS SOCIETY
4720 Montgomery Lane, Suite 506   (301) 654-3080
Bethesda, Maryland 20014   Established 1955

Richard J. Burk, Jr., Executive Secretary
To promote the development of scientific knowledge and practical means for the protection of man and his environment from the harmful effects of radiation, while encouraging its optimum utilization for the benefit of mankind. Membership: 4,500 (plenary, associate, corresponding, students, emeritus, affiliate). Finances: Membership: Plenary, associate, $20; corresponding, student, $10; emeritus, $5; affiliates, $100-$1,200. Awards: Elda E. Anderson Award. Meetings: Annual, various locations; Topical Symposiums, various locations. Publications: Health Physics Journal, monthly, H. Wade Patterson, editor;

Newsletter, monthly, O. L. Cordes, editor.

★ 870 ★

HEALTH POLICY ADVISORY CENTER, INC.
   (HEALTH/PAC)
17 Murray Street   (212) 267-8890
New York, New York 10007   Established 1968

H. Alvin Strelnick, President;
   Catherine Pfordresher, Vice President
An independent, non-profit, public interest center, concerned with monitoring and interpreting the health system to change-oriented groups of health workers, consumers professionals and students. Its objectives include the provision of low-cost, high quality, accessible health services to all individuals. Membership: Approximately 2,000 subscribers to the Health/PAC Bulletin. Finances: Other Sources: Supported by sales of literature, royalties, combined with small foundation grants and individual contributions. Publications: Health/PAC Bulletin, monthly, Marilynn Norinsky, managing editor; Publicly Supported Preventive and Primary Care During the New York City Fiscal Crisis: 1974-1977; Double Indemnity: The Poverty and Mythology of Affirmative Action in the Health Professional Schools; Closing the Doors on the Poor: The Dismantling of California's County Hospitals; The Myth of Reverse Discrimination: Declining Minority Enrollment in New York City's Medical Schools; A Collection of Drawings by Bill Plympton; The Profit in Nonprofit Hospitals: A Health/Pac West Special Report; Coney Island Hospital: A Case of Study in the Politics of Health; American Health Empire; Prognosis Negative; Health Care is for People Not for Profit; Billions for Bandaids; A Critical Look at the Drug Industry; Washington Post Health Scenes by Ron Kessler; Health/PAC Back Issues. Library: Health/PAC Library, 1,500-2,000 volumes (by appointment). Affiliations: Health Planners Network; Nurses Network; Women and Alcoholism Film Project; Washington Heights Project.

HEALTH SCIENCES COMMUNICATIONS
ASSOCIATION
   See: HeSCA

HEALTH SCIENCES COMPUTING FACILITY
   See: BMDP Statistical Software

HEALTH SERVICE ACTION
    See: Coalition for a National Health Service

★ 871 ★
HEAR CENTER
301 East Del Mar Boulevard   (213) 681-4641
Pasadena, California 91101   Established 1954

Betty Petersen, M.A., Executive Director
    Ciwa Griffiths, Ed.D., Administrative Consultant
To serve those with communication problems due to
deafness through the development of auditory tech-
niques.   Early testing and early amplification vital.
Also offers audiological services for adults and speech
therapy for children.   Finances: Sliding scale ac-
cording to ability to pay; Other Sources: United
Way.   Publications: Conquering Childhood Deafness,
Ciwa Griffiths, editor; Proceedings of the Interna-
tional Conference on Auditory Techniques, Ciwa
Griffiths, editor (1974); Proceedings of the Second
International Conference on Auditory Techniques,
Ciwa Griffiths, editor (1980); Effectiveness of Early
Detection and Auditory Stimulation on the Speech and
Language of Hearing Impaired Children (1978).

★ 872 ★
HEART DISEASE RESEARCH FOUNDATION
50 Court Street   (212) 649-9003
Brooklyn, New York 11201   Established 1962

Robert R. Peters, Chairman of the Board of Trustees;
    Yoshiaki Omura, M.D., Sc.D., Director of
    Medical Research
To promote prevention, early diagnosis and treatment
of cardiovascular disease.   Multi-disciplinary research
has been particularly encouraged in the areas of
cardiovascular research, which are often neglected,
such as effects of acupuncture on the micro-circula-
tory system and blood chemistries, or measurement of
minute notches and slurrings appearing in the QRS
complex of ECG's as early diagnostic signs, pain and
tingling sensation associated with hypertension, lower
extremity hypertension, cephalic hypertension syndrome
and its treatment, normal and abnormal relationship
between transmembrane action potentials of single
cardiac cells and corresponding surface electrograms.
Finances: Other Sources: Donations. Meetings:
Every 2 or 3 months, the Foundation co-sponsors continued medical education programs for licensed physicians and dentists. Publications: Basic and Clinical
Medical Science Series of the Heart Disease Research
Foundation, Biennial, Y. Omura, M.D., Sc.D., editor.

★ 873 ★
HELEN HAY WHITNEY FOUNDATION
450 East 63rd Street   (212) 751-8228
New York, New York 10021   Established 1947

Barbara M. Hugonnet, Administrative Director
To stimulate and support research on the problem of
rheumatic fever and rheumatic heart disease and later
expanded its interests to include diseases of connective tissues.   The current program of Postdoctoral Research Fellowships, established in 1957, to which the
Foundation's funds are now totally committed, is
based on the recognition that research training in the
relevant basic biomedical sciences is an essential pre-
requisite to the attainment of the Foundation's ultimate goal - an increase in the number of imaginative,
well-trained, and dedicated medical scientists.
Membership: 9 (Board of Trustees plus 1). Finances:
Endowment. Awards: 18-20 postdoctoral research
fellowships awarded each year. Publications: Annual Report.

★ 874 ★
HELEN KELLER INTERNATIONAL, INC.
22 West 17 Street   (212) 620-2115
New York, New York 10011   Established 1915

Ronald F. Kozusko, Public Information Officer
A voluntary non-profit, non-sectarian organization
devoted to the worldwide conquest of blindness
through its prevention, education and rehabilitation
programs in Africa, Asia, Latin American and the
Middle East.   HKI's global blindness prevention effort is directed at eradicating xerophthalmia, a serious eye disease caused by malnutrition and vitamin A
deficiency that is the world's leading cause of child
blindness.   HKI helps in the distribution of massive
dose capsules of vitamin A, advocates breast feeding
and nutrition education programs to encourage mothers
to provide their children with vitamin A-rich food to
prevent nutritional blindness.   Program services
geared to the integration of blind children and adults
into community life.   Field workers trained by HKI
are at work in rural areas to help blind persons
achieve full integration in their communities.   HKI
projects reach out to all age groups: to infants,
through parent counseling to prevent blindness and
encourage normal development for blind youngsters;
to school-age children, through providing formal and
non-formal educational opportunities; and to blind
adults, by on-the-spot training in basic living skills
and simple trades.   HKI field workers travel to rural
villages to seek out blind people, check for signs of
eye diseases, treat simpler problems such as conjunc-
tivitis, and refer more serious cases to clinics or
hospitals. Membership: 16-member Board of Directors and two 11-member Advisory Committees on

Blindness Prevention and Services for the Blind. Awards: Annual Helen Keller International Award. Publications: HKI Report (newsletter), semiannually; periodic monographs and project reports. Affiliations: World Council for the Welfare of the Blind; American Council of Voluntary Agencies for Foreign Service; HKI is affiliated with the United Nations Department of Public Information. Former Name: American Foundation for Overseas Blind.

★ 875 ★
HELP HOSPITALIZED VETERANS
708 West Redwood Street   (714) 291-5846
San Diego, California 92103   Established 1971

Roger Chapin, Executive Director;
    Lola Tracey, National Coordinator
To provide therapeutic arts and crafts materials to hospitalized veterans through the recreational and occupational rehabilitation departments of 275 veteran and military hospitals. Finances: Voluntary contributions.

HELPERN (MILTON) INSTITUTE OF FORENSIC MEDICINE
    See: Milton Helpern Institute of Forensic Medicine

★ 876 ★
HeSCA - THE HEALTH SCIENCES COMMUNICA-
    TIONS ASSOCIATION   (days) (414) 963-5438
2343 North 115th Street   (414) 258-2525
Wauwatosa, Wisconsin 53226   (eve., Sat./Sun.)
                                 Established 1959

Phyllis Duke, Association Manager
To carry out scientific, educational, catalytic, and research activities with the aim of furthering knowledge and use of educational technology and television in the health sciences. Membership: 700. Finances: Membership: Individual, $40; sustaining, $100; institutional, $160; student, $20. Meetings: Annual, various locations. Publications: HeSCA Feedback (newsletter), 6 times annually, Corki Wilson, editor; Journal of Biocommunication, 3 times annually.

★ 877 ★
HOLISTIC HEALTH HAVENS (HHH)
13615 Victory Boulevard, Suite 114 (213) 988-5710
Van Nuys, California 91401   Established 1980

Joseph M. Kadans, Executive Director
The ever-increasing cost of living and the trend toward healthful living to avoid high hospital and medical costs has triggered the need for health education and the establishments of retreats for the study of healthful health practices, especially the adoption of programs to serve nutritional needs of the body, relief of mental strains and learning the wisdom of the Bible. Membership: Organization member; individual member. Finances: Membership: Dues, $18; Other Sources: Advertising in quarterly journal. Meetings: Quarterly, various locations. Publications: Holistic Health Quarterly, quarterly, Dr. Joseph M. Kadans, editor. Library: Preventive Medicine Library, 2,000 volumes.

HOPE'S INSTITUTE FOR HEALTH POLICY STUDY
    See: People-to-People Health Foundation, Inc.

★ 878 ★
HOSPITAL BUREAU, INC.
80 Wheeler Avenue   (914) 769-6800
Pleasantville, New York 10570   Established 1910

Peter B. Terenzio, President;
    Barry M. Gilman, Executive Vice President
Shared Services Organization with primary effort in joint purchasing for not-for-profit health institutions. Membership: 1,000 hospitals. Finances: Membership: $200 to $500; Other Sources: Educational Institutes fees, advertising, etc. Meetings: 4 Board of Directors Meetings, 1 Annual Meeting of Members, annually, held primarily in the New York City Metropolitan Area. Publications: HBI Report, 6 times annually, Laurie Yarnell, editor. Affiliations: Hospital Bureau Research Institute, Inc.; Shared Services of America, Inc.; Hospital Energists, Inc.

★ 879 ★
HOSPITAL FINANCIAL MANAGEMENT
    ASSOCIATION
1900 Spring Road, Suite 500   (312) 655-4600
Oak Brook, Illinois 60521   Established 1946

Robert M. Shelton, FHFMA, Executive Director
To improve financial management in hospitals and allied patient care institutions; to foster and increase knowledge of and proficiency in financial management; to conduct and participate in educational programs and activities concerning financial management; to provide media for the interchange of ideas and dissemination of material relative to financial management; to establish standards of performance for

individuals and institutions in the various areas of financial management; to do research in areas of financial management to help achieve these objectives. Membership: Over 18,000 (members, affiliates, associates, students, advanced). Finances: Membership: Member, $75 annual dues; students, $15 annual dues. Awards: Graham L. Davis Award; Frederick C. Morgan Individual Achievement Award; William G. Follmer Merit Award; Robert H. Reeves Award; Frederick T. Muncie Award for individual service at chapter level; life memberships for meritorious service at national level. Meetings: Annual, Chicago, Illinois; Chapter Presidents, annual, Boulder, Colorado. Publications: Hospital Financial Management, monthly, Tim Murnane, editor; numerous books and manuals on financial management.

★ 880 ★
HOSPITAL FOOD DIRECTORS ASSOCIATION, INC.
Mercer Medical Center
446 Bellevue Avenue   (215) 947-3000
Trenton, New Jersey 08607   Established 1964

Frank Germaine
Conceived and organized by a dedicated group of hospital food directors to achieve a common goal-- efficient dietary service to patients. The Association is achieving its goal by sharing ideas, experiences and techniques; by developing employee training programs through its Correspondence Course for Food Service Supervisors; by Educational Seminars held at regular intervals; by sharing the benefits of increased buying power and by holding its members to a code of ethics insuring tangible and intangible benefits to all. Membership: Over 1,500 hospital food directors or assistants. Finances: $20. Meetings: Monthly, at various members' hospitals. Publications: Cornucopia, monthly. Affiliation: American Society for Hospital Food Administrators.

★ 881 ★
HOSPITAL INFORMATION SYSTEMS SHARING
    GROUP
2415 South 2300 West   (801) 972-6099
Salt Lake City, Utah 84119   Established 1967

W. V. Rosqvist, Executive Director
To promote the sharing of ideas, system designs, software implementation, and management techniques; to provide conferences, seminars, committee research and other appropriate means to broaden member representatives' understanding of the health care industry - especially as related to information processing; to provide a continuing information processing forum for the management of member institutions. Membership:

About 100 (membership is institutional, though self-employed consultants may obtain individual memberships). Finances: Membership: $285 institutional (a portion of which is credited toward seminar registration fee); $125 individual; Other Sources: Seminar fees. Meetings: Semiannual, January and July, various locations. Publications: HISSG Communique, monthly, John A. Tvedtnes, editor; special publications, irregular.

★ 882 ★
HOSPITAL, INSTITUTION AND EDUCATIONAL
    FOOD SERVICE SOCIETY
4410 West Roosevelt Road   (312) 449-2770
Hillside, Illinois 60162

Jean Denwood, Executive Director
To provide educational opportunities for the membership and to offer a voluntary certification program. The membership consists of dietetic assistants and dietetic technicians. Membership: 13,000 (dietetic assistants and dietetic technicians). Finances: Membership: $25 annual dues; $20 annual certification fee. Awards: 2 annual scholarships, $500 each. Meetings: Nationally, 1 annual meeting; each state society holds 2 annual meetings. Publications: Issues, bimonthly, Carolyn Isch, editor; Weathervane, bimonthly, Carolyn Isch, editor.

★ 883 ★
HOSPITAL MANAGEMENT SYSTEMS SOCIETY
840 North Lake Shore Drive   (312) 280-6023
Chicago, Illinois 60611   Established 1961

Richard P. Covert, Ph.D., Director
The thesis on which the founding of the Society is based shall be that an organized exchange of experiences among members and with other organizations can promote a better understanding of existing principles and can develop new principles for improving hospital management systems. The major purpose of the Society shall be to help develop its members in the areas of professional career enhancement, recognition, and effectiveness in the field of health care management systems. The function of HMSS in meeting this purpose involves coordinating national and regional conferences and providing educational programs, timely newsletter publications, and similar communications. It is to be the vehicle whereby the role of its multidisciplined membership is defined and promoted to administrators, government agencies, and other "Client" groups throughout the system. Membership: 1,300 (personal members mainly management engineers, administrators, some data processing managers). Finances: Membership: $40 annually for

employees of AHA members; $70 for employees of non-members; $20 for students; Other Sources: Annual Conference. Meetings: Annual Meeting and Conference, various locations. Publications: Health Care Systems, 6 times annually, Suzanne Hogg, editor; Proceedings of Annual Conference, annually, Sandra Weiss and Suzanne Hogg, editors; Roster of Members, annually. Affiliation: American Hospital Association.

★ 884 ★
HOSPITAL RESEARCH AND EDUCATIONAL TRUST
840 North Lake Shore Drive   (312) 280-6000
Chicago, Illinois 60611   Established 1944

Gerald E. Bisbee, Jr., Ph.D., Vice President and
    Director
To stimulate, support and conduct research and educational programs designed to improve the organization and delivery of health services. Finances: Other Sources: Mainly grant funds. Publications: Health Services Research, quarterly, G. E. Bisbee, Jr., Ph.D., editor; hospital training manuals and health care research publications. Affiliation: American Hospital Association.

★ 885 ★
HOSPITALIZED VETERANS WRITING PROJECT, INC.
5920 Nall, Room 117
Mission, Kansas 66202   Established 1946

Margaret Sally Keach, President
To encourage patients and outpatients to Veterans Administration Medical Center and domiciliaries to try creative writing for recreation and therapy. The organization assists with writing contests in local VA facilities, coordinates activities of volunteer writing aides and typists, and publishes Veterans Voices, a national magazine devoted exclusively to the writings of hospitalized veterans. Finances: Membership: Associate, from $10; family, from $15; contributing, from $25; sponsor, from $50; sustaining, from $100; patron, from $500; life, from $1,000; Other Sources: Memorial gifts; foundations. Awards: Cash prizes for writings appearing in Veterans Voices: $5 per poem, $10 per essay, article, or short story; Joseph Posik Talen Award; Gladys Feld Helzberg Memorial Award. Publications: Veterans Voices, 3 times annually, Margaret C. Clark, editor; HVWP in Action, Sharon L. Smith, editor. Affiliation: Disabled American Veterans Auxiliary; Women's Overseas Service League; WAC Veterans Association.

★ 886 ★
HUMAN GROWTH FOUNDATION
4930 West 77th Street
Post Office Box 20253   (612) 831-2780
Minneapolis, Minnesota 55420   Established 1965

Thomas R. Pressler, President
A national health organization of volunteers which is concerned with the ways that children grow, and with the reasons why some children do not become average-sized adults. HGF strives to keep parents informed of current research in the field of growth retardation. Through its local chapters Human Growth provides members with the opportunity to meet other parents of short-statured children and to share the everyday problems of family life. They also provide research funds for scientists who are trying to learn more about the growth process and, especially, dwarfism. Membership: 800 parents, physicians and people concerned with children who have growth disorders. Finances: Other Sources: Donations. Research: Grants for research in growth disorders. Publications: Human Growth Ink, 5 times annually, Roger Passman, editor.

★ 887 ★
HUNTINGTON CLINICAL FOUNDATION, INC.
1149 4th Avenue
Huntington, West Virginia 25701   Established 1948

Dr. J. Bernard Poindexter, Jr., President
To expend funds for the treatment, study and research of human disease. Membership: Board of Trustees consisting of 15 members, with 5 to be physicians. Finances: 1/3 of residuary of estate of late Honorable Rufus Switzer, one of Huntington's late capitalists and one of the first mayors. Meetings: Board, quarterly, Huntington, West Virginia.

I

★ 888 ★
IAMFES, INC. (INTERNATIONAL ASSOCIATION OF
    MILK, FOOD AND ENVIRONMENTAL SANI-
    TATIONS)
413 Kellogg Avenue, Suite 3
Post Office Box 701   (515) 232-6699
Ames, Iowa 50010   Established 1911

Earl O. Wright, Executive Secretary
The Association works to promote an atmosphere in which professionals can achieve personal goals by learning about new research developments; widening

perspectives; enhancing professional status, interacting with other professionals in the field; becoming more proficient in work, sharpening investigatory skills. IAMFES offers many opportunities to work for the improvement of milk, food and environmental sanitation through an extensive committee structure. The work of these committees has produced 3A Sanitary Standards for milk and egg processing equipment, as well as other key publications in the field. IAMFES members represent the Association and are actively involved in the National Mastitis Council, the National Conference on Interstate Milk Shipments, National Labeling Committee, Intersociety Council on Standard Methods for the Examination of Dairy Products, and the Sanitarians Joint Council. Membership: 10,000 (individual membership, 1 person only; subscription membership, organizations, institutions, agencies). Awards: Sanitarian of the Year; Educator Industry Award; Citation Award; Shogren Award. Meetings: Annual, June or June, various locations in United States or Canada. Publications: Journal of Food Protection, monthly, Dr. Elmer Marth, editor; Dairy and Food Sanitation, monthly, Jan Richards, editor; Procedures to Investigate Foodborne Illness; Procedures to Investigate Waterborne Illness; 3-A Sanitary Standards.

★ 889 ★
IBERO LATIN-AMERICAN COLLEGE OF DERMA-
    TOLOGY
Avenida da Liberdade 90-1°
1298 Lisbon, Portugal   Established 1948

Francisco da Cruz Sobral, Secretary-General
The College aims to increase relations between members and to develop Ibero Latin-American dermatology. Membership: 2,000 dermatologists and interested doctors. Finances: Membership: $30; Other Sources: Sale of publications. Awards: Vilanova and Gay Prieto prize for the best dermatological work presented at conference. Meetings: Every 4 years, various locations. Publications: Medicina Cutanea Ibero-Latino-Americana, 6 issues annually; monographs.

★ 890 ★
INDOOR SPORTS CLUB, INC.
1145 Highland Street   (419) 592-5756
Napoleon, Ohio 43545   Established 1936

Georgean Davis, Executive Secretary
To establish a social, benevolent and rehabilitative organization for physically disabled persons; to provide and furnish entertainment to such disabled persons and shut-ins and to work for the betterment and pensions for all needy disabled persons. Membership: 2,500. Finances: Membership dues; donations. Awards: Certificate of appreciation for service to the handicapped. Meetings: Annual, various locations. Publications: National Hookup, monthly, Ruth Meyette, editor.

★ 891 ★
INDUSTRIAL HEALTH FOUNDATION, INC.
5231 Centre Avenue   (412) 687-2100
Pittsburgh, Pennsylvania 15232 Established 1935

Daniel C. Braun, M.D., President
To promote the advancement of healthful working conditions. Membership: 160 industrial firms. Finances: Membership: Scale based on number of employees. Meetings: Annual, Pittsburgh, Pennsylvania. Publications: Industrial Hygiene Digest, monthly, Jane Brislin, editor; Technical Bulletins, as needed. Library: Industrial Health Foundation, 1,500 volumes.

INDUSTRIAL MEDICAL ADMINISTRATORS'
ASSOCIATION
    See: Occupational Medical Administrators'
          Association

★ 892 ★
INFORMED HOMEBIRTH, INC.
Box 788   (313) 484-8337
Boulder, Colorado 80306   Established 1977

Rahima Baldwin, President;
    Marianne Schroeder, Director
To educate couples interested in childbirth alternatives--home, hospital birth-centers; to prepare women or couples wanting to become childbirth educators. Offers childbirth classes. Membership: Approximately 900 (annual membership, made up primarily of interested couples/individuals and those taking the class from our teachers). Finances: Membership: $10 annual; Other Sources: Books sales, tape series, various workshops. Publications: Special Delivery, quarterly, Penny Camp, editor.

★ 893 ★
INHALATION TOXICOLOGY RESEARCH INSTITUTE -
    LOVELACE BIOMEDICAL AND ENVIRONMENTAL
    RESEARCH INSTITUTE, INC.
Post Office Box 5890   (505) 844-6835
Albuquerque, New Mexico 87115 Established 1976

Roger O. McClellan, D.V.M., President-Director;
   Robert K. Jones, M.D., Vice President/Associate
   Director
Started in 1960 as Fission Product Inhalation Laboratory, a subunit of the Lovelace Foundation for Medical Education and Research. Initial research on toxicity of fission product radionuclides. Research program expanded in 1970's to include transuranic radionuclides and research on health effects of airborne materials associated with other energy technologies such as fluidized bed combustion of coal, coal gasification, use of insulating materials and use of diesel vehicles. Since 1976 operated as a subsidiary corporation of the Lovelace Medical Foundation. Finances: Research contracts and grants from the United States Government. Library: 6,400 books, 4,400 bound jouranls, 8,000 documents.

INSTITUTE FOR ADVANCED STUDY IN RATIONAL
PSYCHOTHERAPY
   See: Institute for Rational-Emotive Therapy

INSTITUTE FOR BIO-ENERGETIC ANALYSIS
   See: International Institute for Bioenergetic
   Analysis

★ 894 ★
INSTITUTE FOR CANCER RESEARCH
7701 Burholme Avenue   (215) 342-1000
Philadelphia, Pennsylvania 19111   Established 1924

Alfred G. Knudson, Jr., M.D., Ph.D., Director
Conducts research in the field of cancer. Membership: 400. Library: Library Institute for Cancer Research, 19,000 volumes.

INSTITUTE FOR HEALTH POLICY STUDY
   See: People-to-People Health Foundation, Inc.

★ 895 ★
INSTITUTE FOR RATIONAL-EMOTIVE THERAPY
45 East 65th Street   (212) 535-0822
New York, New York 10021   Established 1968

Albert Ellis, Ph.D., Executive Director
A comprehensive facility, offering clinical services, professional training, and research in rational-emotive psychotherapy and counseling, as well as public education, consultative services, and an emotional edu-

cation curriculum service for schools and community agencies. Finances: Private grants. Meetings: 8 times annually, New York City. Affiliation: World Federation of Mental Health. Former Name: Institute for Advanced Study in Rational Psychotherapy.

★ 896 ★
INSTITUTE FOR RATIONAL LIVING
45 East 65th Street   (212) 535-0822
New York, New York 10021   Established 1959

Albert Ellis, Ph.D., Executive Director
Founded for the purpose of professional training and research in the theory and practice of Rational psychotherapy, and for public education in rational living. Membership: Approximately 1,200 (lay persons, professionals). Finances: Membership: Student, $5; regular, $10; professional, $15; fellows, $25; sustaining, $50; sponsor, $100; life, $500; Other Sources: Contributions, publications. Meetings: Approximately 6 annually, New York City. Publications: Rational Living, semiannual, Richard Wessler, editor.

★ 897 ★
INSTITUTE FOR REALITY THERAPY
11633 San Vicente Boulevard   (213) 826-2690
Los Angeles, California 90045

William Glasser, M.D., President
To promote the understanding and use of reality therapy through the teaching of concepts and practice in intensive seminars leading to certification in reality therapy. Membership: Approximately 600 graduates, 50 faculty associates. Finances: Membership: Intensive weeks cost $300 for registration. Meetings: Annual, various locations. Publications: Journal of Reality Therapy. Affiliation: Educator Training Center.

★ 898 ★
INSTITUTE FOR SEX RESEARCH
Indiana University, Morrison 416   (812) 337-7686
Bloomington, Indiana 47401   Established 1947

Dr. Paul H. Gebhard, Director
Officially founded in 1947 by Dr. Alfred C. Kinsey, the primary purpose of the Institute is to conduct research on the social and behavioral aspects of human sexual behavior by gathering data, analyzing it and making the resultant information available to those who need it. Findings are disseminated through lectures and publishing, and by means of an Information

Service established in 1971 by a grant from the National Institute of Mental Health. The Institute's Library contains the world's largest collection of material relating to human sexuality, and its resources are made available for scholarly and research purposes through prepared bibliographies and literature searches conducted by the Information Service, or for on-site use by application. A seminar for psychiatrists, physicians, educators, social workers and other professionals is conducted by Institute staff and visiting experts each summer. Publications: International Directory of Sex Research and Related Fields; Social and behavioral sciences portion of the Library catalog; several major books and numerous journal articles and chapters have been authored by Institute staff members. Library: Institute for Sex Research Library, 44,000 volumes.

★ 899 ★
INSTITUTE OF ADVANCED SANITATION RESEARCH
      INTERNATIONAL
106 Drury Lane   (317) 463-9203
West Lafayette, Indiana 47906   Established 1963

Dr. Robert Howe, Program Secretary
To encourage advanced sanitation research and communication in interdisciplinary scientific fields and activities among individuals of all nations, on the doctoral and professorial levels. Membership: 54 elected fellows (doctoral and professorial scientists elected by the Council of Fellows). Finances: Membership: Expenses shared by members of host country. Awards: Buswell-Porges Scientific Achievement Award; Buswell-Porges Lecture Series; Buswell-Porges Junior Scientific Achievement Award-Prize. Meetings: Semiannual, various countries. Publications: Proceedings of annual symposiums on Hazardous Chemicals, Handling and Disposal, Dr. Howe, editor; special monographs.

★ 900 ★
INSTITUTE OF ENVIRONMENTAL SCIENCES
940 East Northwest Highway   (312) 255-1561
Mount Prospect, Illinois 60056   Established 1953

Betty Peterson, Executive Director
To promote and encourage the acquisition and dissemination of knowledge pertaining to environmental sciences, environmental engineering, and related areas of interest for industry, science, and government; to develop and promote standards, research, simulation, testing, and design criteria in the environmental field; to sponsor or otherwise encourage courses or curricula in the environmental sciences in institutions of higher education; to encourage and recognize outstanding

achievement in the environmental sciences, environmental engineering, and related areas of interest. Membership: Approximately 1,600 (students, associates, members, senior members, fellows, honorary fellows). Finances: Membership: Members, senior members, fellows, $40; students, $10; associates, $33; Other Sources: Meetings, publications, seminars. Awards: Irwin Vigness Award; Monroe Seligman Award; Ostrander Award. Meetings: Annual, various locations. Publications: Journal of Environmental Sciences, bimonthly, B. Peterson, editor; Technical Publications catalog.

★ 901 ★
INSTITUTE OF GERONTOLOGY
The University of Michigan
520 East Liberty   (313) 764-3493
Ann Arbor, Michigan 48109   Established 1965

Harold R. Johnson, Director
The Institute was established to conduct research, training and services benefiting older citizens. It is involved in extensive educational programming which includes both graduate level certification and in-service training in health-related and other fields. Current health-related research includes projects examining models of advocacy for older people in health care situations, the evaluation of elderly patients' understanding of prescription instructions, the development of training and competency testing for nurse aides in nursing homes, and the development and evaluation of community councils in proprietary nursing homes. The Institute's involvement with training, consultation, and advocacy extends into many states. Finances: Appropriations from the State of Michigan; federal and private grants. Publications: Books; pamphlets; bibliographies; films; cassettes; monographs. Library: Institute of Gerontology Learning Resources Center, 8,000 volumes.

INSTITUTE OF HYPERTENSION, SCHOOL OF
RESEARCH
      See: National Institute of Hypertension Studies

★ 902 ★
INSTITUTE OF LOGOPEDICS
2400 Jardine Drive   (316) 262-8271
Wichita, Kansas 67219   Established 1934

Dr. Frank R. Kleffnor, Director
The Institute is dedicated to the alleviation of communicative disorders through a three-fold program of (1) habilitation/residential rehabilitation of children

and adults; (2) professional training of students in the fields; and (3) research. Opportunities are provided to individuals for rehabilitation in order that they may function at their maximum level of potential in society. An intra/inter-disciplinary approach is designed to meet the physical, emotional, and social needs of the patient in a coordinated program. Finances: Other Sources: Local United Way; school district and state agency contracts; contributions; grants from businesses, organizations, and foundations; partial parent and patient financing. Award: Martin F. Palmer Humanitarian Award, presented annually to an individual who has made an outstanding contribution to the field of hearing and speech rehabilitation. Meetings: Quarterly, various locations. Publication: DiaLOGue, quarterly, Cathy Hall, editor; brochures. Library: Technical Library, 6,000 volumes. Affiliations: Wichita State University; National Association of Private Schools for Exceptional Children; National Association of Private Residential Facilities for the Mentally Retarded; International Association for Rehabilitation Facilities.

★ 903 ★

INSTITUTE OF MEDICINE OF THE NATIONAL
    ACADEMY OF SCIENCES
2101 Constitution Avenue   (202) 389-6891
Washington, D.C. 20418   Established 1970

Frederick C. Robbins, M.D., President
To bring together persons from a variety of backgrounds for consideration of the complex problems of health care in the United States. The Institute is concerned with policies affecting the delivery of health care, education for the health professions, and conduct of biomedical research. Membership: 399 to expand to 400 through annual elections. Finances: Federal contracts, private and public grants. Meetings: Annual, National Academy of Sciences. Publications: Institute Newsletter, bimonthly, W. K. Waterfall, editor.

★ 904 ★

INSTITUTE OF NUTRITION OF CENTRAL AMERICA
    AND PANAMA (INCAP)
Carretera Roosevelt, Zona 11
Aptdo. Postal 1188   43762-7
Guatemala City, Guatemala   Established 1949

Carlos Tejada, Director
To study the problems of human nutrition, to seek means for their solution and to assist the member countries (Costa Rico, El Salvador, Guatemala, Honduras, Nicaragua and Panama) in the effective application of solutions. Its academic program comprises:

a School of Nutrition with a 4-year curriculum at the graduate level and 4 postgraduate courses: in public health with emphasis in nutrition and maternal and child care; in food sciences and animal nutrition; in food science and technology; and in biochemistry and human nutrition. Its training programs also include opportunities for specialized tutorial training through active participation in relevant basic, applied or operational research and academic activities in all areas of INCAP's competence. Through agreement signed by PASB and the United Nations University, in 1976 INCAP became the first Associated Institution of the UNU. An academic tutorial program was thus established for the training of fellows from any part of the world who have completed their university advanced studies at the Doctoral or Master of Science level. Publications: More than 2,200 articles published in both Spanish and English in recognized scientific journals; 12 monographs and 15 books.

★ 905 ★

INSTITUTE OF OCCUPATIONAL AND ENVIRON-
    MENTAL HEALTH
1130 Sherbrooke, Suite 410   (514) 844-4955
Montreal, Quebec, Canada   Established 1966

The Institute was founded with the principal aim to organize and support scientific research of biological effects of asbestos. Prospective research of some other problems of occupational and environmental health is envisaged. Finances: Sponsored by Quebec Asbestos Mining Association. Research Funds: Research grants were given by the Institute to support to date 40 research projects of epidemiologic, experimental and clinical nature in Canada, U.S.A., United Kingdom, Italy and Finland. Publications: Proceedings of 1973 Conference on Fibres for Biological Experiments, Premysl V. Pelnar, M.D., editor. Library: Institute of Occupational and Environmental Health Collection, over 4,000 documents.

★ 906 ★

INSTITUTE OF PERSONALITY ASSESSMENT AND
    RESEARCH
University of California   (415) 642-5050
Berkeley, California 94720   Established 1949

Harrison G. Gough, Ph.D., Director
Aims of the Institute are to conduct studies of the normal or effectively functioning individual and to develop and improve methods for the assessment of the healthy personality. Finances: Other Sources: Grants from philanthropic foundations and governmental agencies.

INSTITUTE OF RECONSTRUCTIVE PLASTIC SURGERY
OF THE NEW YORK UNIVERSITY MEDICAL CENTER
    See: Society for the Rehabilitation of the
          Facially Disfigured, Inc.

INSTITUTE OF SCIENTIFIC INVESTIGATION
    See: OFA Foundation for the Advancement of
          Biomedical Sciences

★ 907 ★
INSTITUTES FOR THE ACHIEVEMENT OF HUMAN
     POTENTIAL
8801 Stenton Avenue   (215) 233-2050
Philadelphia, Pennsylvania 19118   Established 1955

Glenn Doman, Chairman; Gretchen Kerr, Director
The purpose of The Institutes is to multiply the abilities of all children in intellectual, physical and social
realms.   This is done by courses which teach parents
of both brain-injured and average children how to
treat and teach their children at home.   The Institutes, which operate internationally, are a group of
seven non-profit, federally tax-exempt institutes.
Four of these institutes are devoted to the actual
teaching of parents and to serving the children of the
world.   Three of these institutes provide vital information for the entire organization through research
and information gathering.   Finances: Membership:
Payment for services, individual donations and foundation grants.   Publications: The In-Report, bimonthly,
Pearl LeWinn, editor; New Parentage, bimonthly,
Lee Pattinson, editor.   Affiliations: World Organization for Human Potential.

★ 908 ★
INTERAFRICAN BUREAU FOR ANIMAL RESOURCES
     OF THE OAU
Post Office Box 30786   Nairobi 338544
Nairobi, Kenya   Established 1951

Dr. P. Atang, Director
A Bureau for Animal Health and Production, catering
for the interests of the Member States of the Organization of African Unity (OAU) collects and collates
information on animal health and production in Africa;
publishes this information, conducts symposia seminars,
training courses, etc. and undertakes studies and exe-
cutes international projects on Animal Production and
Animal Diseases control.   Membership: 50 (Member
States of the Organization of African Unity).   Finances: Membership: Annual contributions by Member States; Other Sources: Sales of contribution and
project frunds from donor countries.   Meetings:

Conference of Heads of Animal Health and Production
Services of Africa, biennial; Meetings of Internation-
al Scientific Council for Trypanosomiasis Research and
Control, biennial; IBAR Advisory Committee, annual;
Meetings held in different African capitals.   Publi-
cations: Bulletin of Animal Health and Production in
Africa, quarterly, P. Atang, editor; Information
Leaflets, monthly, K. Adeniji, editor; Animal Health
Statistics, monthly and annually, A. Tall, editor;
IBAR Annual Report, annually, P. Atang, editor;
Proceedings of Symposia seminars, meetings, workshops,
etc.   Library: IBAR Library, approximately 1,650
volumes.   Affiliation: Scientific, Technical and
Research Commission of the OAU.

INTERAMERICAN ASSOCIATION OF SANITARY
ENGINEERING
    See: Interamerican Association of Sanitary
          Engineering and Environment

★ 909 ★
INTERAMERICAN ASSOCIATION OF SANITARY
     ENGINEERING AND ENVIRONMENT
18729 Considine Drive   Office (301) 492-7686
Brookeville, Maryland   Home (301) 774-6534
                                   Established 1946

Harold Shipman, President;
     Dr. Richard F. Cole, Secretary/Treasurer
To obtain through common agreement within the Inter-
American Association of Sanitary Engineering the solution of sanitation problems and to establish uniform
standards for the continuous protection of the population of this hemisphere.   Membership: Approximately 400 in United States of America section; approximately 2,500 located in 23 American Republics (individual and corporate).   Finances: Membership: Individual, $12; corporate, $75.   Awards: Hemi-
spheric Award to persons who have provided outstanding service to the Association and to the goal of
better hemisphere through sanitary engineering.
Meetings: Biennial, various locations.   Publications:
Journal of the Interamerican Association of Sanitary
Engineering, quarterly.   Former Name: Interamerican Association of Sanitary Engineering.

★ 910 ★
INTER-AMERICAN SAFETY COUNCIL
33 Park Place   (201) 871-0004
Englewood, New Jersey 07631   Established 1938

F. E. Fernandez, President;
     Rafael Roman, Administrative Manager

A nonprofit, nongovernmental, privately supported, educational service organization dedicated to the furthering of accident prevention and health care awareness among the Spanish and Portuguese speaking people of the world. Its aims are to gather, analyze and distribute accident prevention and health care information internationally through its various publications and programs. Membership: 2,600 (industrial plan, associated plan, airline plan). Finances: Membership: $110-$2,300 based on membership plan; Other Sources: Sale of publications, visual aids, technical consultations and training programs. Meetings: Annual, New York City. Publications: Noticias de Seguridad, monthly, Santiago G. Egaña, editor; El Supervisor, monthly, Santiago G. Egaña, editor; Spanish/English Catalog, annually, Santiago G. Egaña, editor. Library: Technical Library, 2,000 plus volumes. Affiliation: National Safety Council.

★ 911 ★
INTERAMERICAN SOCIETY OF PSYCHOLOGY
Spanish Speaking Mental Health Research Center
University of California   (213) 825-8886
Los Angeles, California 90024   Established 1951

Gerardo Marin, Ph.D., Secretary General
To provide avenues of direct communication among behavioral scientists in North, Central and South America; to promote the development of the behavioral sciences in the Western Hemisphere; and to further the hope of contributing to international understanding through a greater comprehension of cultural differences and the meeting of minds across national boundaries. To further these aims the Society helps to promote cross-cultural research and the exchange of scholars and information among the nations in the Americas and holds the Interamerican Congresses of Psychology. Membership: 1,200 (honorary, life, regular). Finances: Membership: $25 residents of Canada and United States; $20 for all others. Awards: Interamerican Psychology Award, biennial. Meetings: Interamerican Congress of Psychology, biennial; Interamerican Seminar on Community Psychology, biennial. Publications: Interamerican Journal of Psychology, semiannual, Dr. Gordon Finley, editor; Spanish Language Psychology, quarterly, Dr. Gerardo Marin, editor; Interamerican Psychologist, quarterly, Dr. Gerardo Marin, editor; Membership Directory. Remarks: Affiliated to the International Union of Psychological Science IUPS.

★ 912 ★
INTERCHURCH MEDICAL ASSISTANCE, INC.
Brethren Service Center   (301) 635-6464
New Windsor, Maryland 21776   Established 1961

W. Eugene Grubbs, Th.D., Executive Director
Organized by Mission Boards and agencies of major Protestant denominations to procure and distribute pharmaceutical, medical and hospital supplies to medical mission programs and projects. Currently assisting 400 hospitals in 60 countries. Membership: 16 (14 Protestant denominations, 2 relief agencies). Finances: Membership: Percentage of operating costs based on 3 year use of service; Other Sources: Some donations by corporations and charges for services to non-member organizations. Meetings: Board of Directors, 3 times annually; members, annually. Publications: The Bridge, occasional, W. Eugene Grubbs, editor.

★ 913 ★
INTERNATIONAL ACADEMY OF AVIATION AND
     SPACE MEDICINE
935 La Gauchetiere West
Post Office Box 8100
Montreal, Quebec H3C 3N4,   (514) 877-5742
Canada   Established 1959

Peter Vaughan, Secretary General
To promote the development of science and to foster research in the realm of aviation and/or space medicine; to help to improve and develop the exchange of information and ideas in all these fields; to contribute to the search for new knowledge and its practical scientific application; to improve the teaching of these sciences and their corollaries and to foster the training of experts in aviation and/or space medicine; to facilitate international cooperation and relations among persons dedicated to such cooperation; to foster, coordinate, and develop the international cooperation and relations among organizations dedicated to aviation and/or space medicine. The Academy pursues its objectives through sponsoring and/or organizing of conferences, meetings, congresses, study groups; through presenting views to national and international organizations; investigations; research and publications. Membership: Full, maximum 200; associate, maximum 50 (in 37 countries). Finances: Full, $100; Other Sources: Voluntary contributions by members and National Societies of Aviation and Space Medicine. Meetings: Annual, various locations.

★ 914 ★
INTERNATIONAL ACADEMY OF CYTOLOGY
1050 Chemin Ste-Foy
Quebec, Quebec G1S 4L8,   (418) 688-3640
Canada   Established 1957

Alexander Meisels, M.D., Secretary-Treasurer

To encourage cooperation among those persons who are actively engaged in the practice of cytology; to foster and facilitate the international exchange of knowledge and information on specialized problems of clinical cytology; to standardize terminology; to stimulate the development of all phases of clinical cytology and to encourage research in cytology. Membership: 1,579 (honorary fellows, fellows, members, professional members, cytotechnologist fellows, cytotechnologist members). Finances: Membership: $64 (United States); Cytotechnologist, $25 (United States). Awards: Maurice Goldblatt Cytology Award. Meetings: Triennially, various locations. Publications: ACTA Cytologica, bimonthly, George L. Wied, M.D., editor; Analytical and Quantitative Cytology, bimonthly, George L. Wied, M.D., editor.

★ 915 ★

INTERNATIONAL ACADEMY OF PREVENTIVE
    MEDICINE
10409 Town and Country Way
Suite 200   (713) 468-7851
Houston, Texas 77024   Established 1971

Joseph A. Nowell, Executive Director
Founded to further the ideals of preventive medicine through education and research on the professional level. The Academy is particularly concerned about the increasing incidence of chronic degenerative diseases and believes that keeping patients healthy is preferable to crisis diagnosis and treatment. Membership: 1,300 physicians and other health related professionals. Special categories for those in training. Finances: Membership: Active and associate, $90; student/intern, $24; resident, retired and foreign, $48; supporting, $360; Other Sources: Conference registration fees and sales of publications. Awards: Tom Spies Memorial Award, annual. Meetings: Semiannual, various locations. Publications: Journal of IAPM, semiannual, Leon R. Pomeroy, Ph.D., editor; New Dynamics of Preventive Medicine, 5 volumes in print, Leon R. Pomeroy, Ph.D. editor; IAPM Memorandum, monthly, Lyle A. Baker, D.V.M., editor; Your Health, monthly, Steven Cordas, D.O., editor.

★ 916 ★

INTERNATIONAL ACADEMY OF PROCTOLOGY
c/o Alfred J. Cantor, M.D.
North Shore Towers, 271-17V
Grand Central Parkway   (212) 631-5291
Floral Park, New York 11005   Established 1948

Alfred J. Cantor, M.D., International Secretary and
    Founder
To unite in one association those who are engaged in the specialty of proctology or its allied fields. To advance the practice and study of diseases of the colon and accessory organs of digestion, including those of nutrition. To stimulate and encourage research in proctology. To promote the practical application of all recent advances in proctology and to help correlate clinical and experimental studies. To encourage proctology as a specialty. To formulate the highest standards and principles for the practice of proctology. Membership: 1,200 (international and United States medical affiliation for M.D.'s only). Finances: Membership: $100. Fellowships and Research Grants: For leading 8 universities. Meetings: Annual, various locations. Publications: American Journal of Proctology; Gastroenterology and Colon and Rectal Surgery, monthly, Alfred Cantor, M.D., editor. Affiliation: International Board of Proctology.

★ 917 ★

INTERNATIONAL AGENCY FOR RESEARCH ON
    CANCER
150 cours Albert Thomas   (078) 75-81-81
F-69372 Lyon, France   Established 1965

John Higginson, Director
To promote international collaboration in cancer research, including the organization of specific research programs in environmental carcinogenesis. Membership: 11 countries. Finances: Membership: $600,000-$1,000,000. Awards: Research fellowships. Publications: Annual Report, Technical and Scientific Reports, irregularly, W. Davis, editor; Library Bulletin, irregularly. Library: 17,000 volumes. Affiliation: World Health Organization.

★ 918 ★

INTERNATIONAL AGENCY FOR THE PREVENTION
    OF BLINDNESS
3885 Round Top Drive
Honolulu, Hawaii 96822   Established 1974

Dr. W. John Holmes, Executive Vice President
The Agency is dedicated to the prevention of impaired vision and blindness around the world. Membership: Approximately 67 Prevention of Blindness societies around the world. Finances: Membership: Individual, $10; organizational, $100; Other Sources: Fund raising. Affiliations: WHO; UNICEF.

★ 919 ★
INTERNATIONAL ANESTHESIA RESEARCH SOCIETY
3645 Warrensville Center Road   (216) 295-1124
Cleveland, Ohio 44122   Established 1922

B. B. Sankey, M.D., Executive Secretary
To foster and promote progress and research in the
specialty of anesthesiology, through publication of a
journal and sponsorship of annual scientific meeting.
Membership: 10,000 (practicing anesthesiologists,
dentists, doctors of veterinary medicine, nurse anesthetists, clinical and research workers in the specialty).
Finances: Membership: $35 (for U.S. members);
$40 (for foreign members). Meetings: Annual, var-
ious locations. Publications: Anesthesia and Analgesia, monthly, Nicholas M. Greene, M.D., editor.

★ 920 ★
INTERNATIONAL ASSOCIATION FOR ACCIDENT
     AND TRAFFIC MEDICINE
Post Office Box 10043
S-10055 Stockholm 10, Sweden   Established 1960

Rune Andreasson, Executive Director
The organization groups national associations for accident and traffic medicine. Membership: Physicians
and others interested in motor vehicle and traffic related accidents. Meetings: Annual, in conjunction
with the World Health Organization, Geneva,
Switzerland. Publications: Journal of Traffic Medicine, quarterly.

★ 921 ★
INTERNATIONAL ASSOCIATION FOR ANALYTICAL
     PSYCHOLOGY (IAAP)
Postfach 115
CH-8042 Zurich, Switzerland   Established 1958

Adolf Guggenbühl-Craig, M.D., President;
     Yvonne Trüeb-Teucher, Secretariat
To encourage the maintenance of high standards of
training and practice of Analytical Psychology, to
promote the study and to disseminate knowledge of
Analytical Psychology, and to hold Congresses. Membership: 780 (junior and senior members). Finances:
Membership: Junior members, Sw. francs, 100 annually; senior members, Sw. francs, 120 annually.
Meetings: Triennially, various locations. Publications: Congress papers.

★ 922 ★
INTERNATIONAL ASSOCIATION FOR CHILD AND
ADOLESCENT PSYCHIATRY AND ALLIED PRO-
FESSIONS
The Maudsley Hospital
Denmark Hill
London SE5 8AZ, England
     United Kingdom   Established 1948

Lionel Hersov, M.D., President;
     Richard Lansdown, Ph.D., Secretary-General
To promote the study, treatment, care and prevention
of mental and emotional disorders and deficiencies of
children, adolescents and their families in practice
and in research through effective collaboration among
child psychiatrists and the allied professions of psychology, social work, pediatrics, public health,
nursing, education, social sciences and other relevant
professions. Membership: 32 member organizations;
22 affiliate member organizations; 131 associate members. Finances: Membership: Full members, $25;
affiliate, $25; associate, $10. Meetings: International Congress, every 4 years; Study Group meetings, annually. Affiliations: World Health Organization; World Psychiatric Association; World Federation for Mental Health. Former Name: International Association for Child Psychiatry and Allied
Professions.

INTERNATIONAL ASSOCIATION FOR CHILD
PSYCHIATRY AND ALLIED PROFESSIONALS
     See: International Association for Child and
         Adolescent Psychiatry and Allied Professions

★ 923 ★
INTERNATIONAL ASSOCIATION FOR COMPARATIVE
     RESEARCH ON LEUKEMIA AND RELATED
     DISEASES
400 West 12th Avenue
Secretariat: Suite 302   (614) 422-5022
Columbus, Ohio 43210   Established 1963

David S. Yohn, Secretary General
The intent of the Association is to promote and stimulate the exchange of ideas and knowledge among
research workers interested in comparative leukemia
research. This intent is carried out by organizing
and conducting an International Symposium every 2
years; by publishing the Proceedings of this Symposium; and by encouraging cooperative activities between institutions, organizations and societies having
common interests in the comparative approach to the
study of leukemia and related diseases. Membership:
325. Finances: Membership: $10 dues, paid bi-
ennially; Other Sources: Supporting memberships:

Benefactor, $1,000 plus; patron, $500 to $1,000; donor, $100 to $500. Publications: Proceedings of the Symposium, biennially.

★ 924 ★
INTERNATIONAL ASSOCIATION FOR DENTAL
    RESEARCH
734 15th Street, N.W., Suite 809   (202) 638-1515
Washington, D.C. 20005   Established 1920

John A. Gray, Ph.D., Executive Director
To advance dental research and dental health on an international level. Membership: 5,000 from over 50 countries. Finances: Membership: Active, associate, $8-$46; sustaining, $46. Awards: Edward Hatton Awards; Wilmer Souder Award; H. Trendley Dean Memorial Award; Isaac Schour Memorial Award; commercially supported awards. Meetings: Annual, various locations; Triennial conferences. Publications: Journal of Dental Research, monthly.

★ 925 ★
INTERNATIONAL ASSOCIATION FOR LIFE-SAVING
    AND FIRST AID TO THE INJURED
Statenlaan 81
The Hague, The Netherlands   Established 1908

W. van der Slikke, M.D., President
To promote life-saving and first aid throughout the world; to serve as a medium for deliberation, research, exchange of ideas, know-how and experiences; and for compilation and dissemination of information on life-saving/first aid. Membership: ca. 75 (800 technical contacts on a global level [single persons, organizations]). Finances: Membership: Individual 50 dfl; associations 100 dfl. Publications: Inter-rescue Information IRI, 2-3 times annually, Aage Rørmark, editor. Library: Interrescue Denmark, 5,000 plus reprints/small prints.

★ 926 ★
INTERNATIONAL ASSOCIATION FOR MEDICAL
    ASSISTANCE TO TRAVELLERS
Empire State Building
350 Fifth Avenue, Suite 5620   (212) 279-6465
New York, New York 10001   Established 1960

Vicenzo Marcolongo, M.D., President;
    Maria-Assunta Uffer, Executive Vice President
To aid international travelers in need of medical assistance when outside their countries of residence. Membership: 4,000,000 (individual travelers and corporations with traveling executives and employees).

Finances: Other Sources: Donations from members. Publication: Annual directory of participating physicians and medical institutions abroad and telephone numbers where travelers can reach an English-speaking physician who is on call for 24 hours a day.

★ 927 ★
INTERNATIONAL ASSOCIATION FOR
    ORTHODONTICS
645 North Michigan Avenue   (312) 642-2602
Chicago, Illinois 60611   Established 1961

Joanna Carey, Executive Director
Continuing education in orthodontic technique for general dentists and pedodontists. Membership: 800 (practicing dentists). Finances: Membership: Annual dues, $80; students, $25; Other Sources: Annual meeting, exhibits, course tuitions. Awards: Leon J. Pinsker Merit Award; Membership Recruitment Award; Diplomate, International Board of Orthodontics. Meetings: Annual, usually September, various locations. Publications: Bandelette, monthly, J. Carey, editor; Directory and Referral Guide, Biannually, J. Carey, editor.

★ 928 ★
INTERNATIONAL ASSOCIATION FOR SUICIDE
    PREVENTION
c/o Charlotte P. Ross
1811 Trousdale Drive   (415) 877-5604
Burlingame, California 94010   Established 1961

Charlotte P. Ross, Secretary-General
To bring together individuals and agencies concerned with suicide prevention; to disseminate information and encourage research in the field. Membership: 850. Finances: Membership: Dues, contributions, subsidies. Meetings: Biennial, various locations. Publications: VITA, quarterly; Congress proceedings. Affiliation: World Federation of Mental Health.

INTERNATIONAL ASSOCIATION OF AGRICULTURAL
MEDICINE
    See: International Association of Agricultural
        Medicine and Rural Health

★ 929 ★
INTERNATIONAL ASSOCIATION OF AGRICULTURAL
    MEDICINE AND RURAL HEALTH
c/o Professor Toshikozu Wakatsuki
Saku Central Hospital
197 Usuda-machi,
Minamisaku-Gun
Nagano Pref 384-03, Japan   Established 1961

To study the problems of agricultural medicine; to
seek cures for diseases caused by agricultural work
and rural environment. Membership: 300. Finances: Dues, contributions. Meetings: Triennially,
various locations. Publications: Agricultural Medicine and Rural Health, T. Wakatsuki, editor.
Former Name: International Association of Agricultural Medicine.

INTERNATIONAL ASSOCIATION OF ALLERGOLOGY
    See: International Organization of Allergology
        and Clinical Immunology

★ 930 ★
INTERNATIONAL ASSOCIATION OF APPLIED
    PSYCHOLOGY
Montessorilaan 3,
Nijmegen-6500 HE,   (080) 512639
The Netherlands   Established 1920

Professor C. J. De Wolff, Secretary General
The Association's aims are to establish contact between those who, in different countries, devote themselves to scientific work in the various fields of applied psychology, and to advance the study and
achievement of means likely to contribute to scientific and social development in these fields. Membership: 2,567 members in 77 countries (full, associate,
honorary and life). Finances: Membership: Full
membership, $15; associate, $14; Other Sources:
Occasional grants from international foundations.
Lectureship: Congress lectureships. Meetings: Every
4 years, various locations. Publications: International Review of Applied Psychology, semiannual,
C. Levy-Leboyer, editor. Affiliation: International
Union of Psychological Science.

★ 931 ★
INTERNATIONAL ASSOCIATION OF CANCER
    VICTIMS AND FRIENDS, INC.
7740 West Manchester Avenue   (213) 822-5032
Suite 110   (213) 822-5132
Playa del Rey, California 90291 Established 1963

Ann Cinquina, Executive Director
Founded for the purpose of disseminating information
and helping fund research on the subject of non-toxic
or natural cancer therapies. Its membership is interested in alternative therapies to radiation, chemotherapy and surgery. It maintains a list of physicians
and clinics for referrals to members. Membership is
approximately 16,000 including regional chapters and
affiliates throughout the nation and abroad. Membership: Approximately 16,000 (regular membership,
$15; sustaining, $25; life, $250; perpetual, $1,000;
members can be affiliated with chapters). Finances:
Membership: Donations, memorials, wills and bequests,
various small non-governmental grants; Other Sources:
Private donations and chapter support. Awards:
Humanitarian Award. Meetings: Regional Seminars
and Annual Convention, locations determined by
chapters for regional seminars; conventions usually
in Los Angeles. Publications: Cancer News Journal,
quarterly, Ann Cinquina, editor; One Answer to
Cancer, William Donald Kelley, DDS, editor; A
Solution to the Cancer Problem, Dr. Moerman, editor.

★ 932 ★
INTERNATIONAL ASSOCIATION OF CORONERS
    AND MEDICAL EXAMINERS
2121 Adelbert Road   (216) 721-5610
Cleveland, Ohio 44106   Established 1938

S. R. Gerber, M.D., Executive Secretary-Treasurer
To meet annually for a working seminar to discuss
changes in state laws and changes in Forensic Sciences in general. Membership: 550 (coroners,
medical examiners, staff investigators). Finances:
Membership: $25. Meetings: Annual, various lo-
cations in the United States, Canada and Mexico.
Publications: Seminar Proceeding, triennially, S. R.
Gerber, M.D., editor.

★ 933 ★
INTERNATIONAL ASSOCIATION OF DENTAL
    STUDENTS
Central Office
c/o Dr. John Seear
Medical Protection Society
50 Hallam Street
London W1N 6DE, England,   (01) 637 0541
    United Kingdom   Established 1951

Dr. John Seear
To promote international contact among dental students,
to facilitate exchange of students between member
countries, develop international programs. Committees: Dental Education, Public Dental Health.
Membership: 36 schools and countries (national

membership, school membership, individual supporting membership). <u>Finances:</u> Membership: Individual supporting membership, 20 Swiss francs annually. Meetings: Annual Congress. <u>Publications:</u> Newsletter, bimonthly; Newsbulletin, 6 annually.

★ 934 ★
INTERNATIONAL ASSOCIATION OF DENTISTRY
    FOR CHILDREN
Department of Child Dental Health
University of Newcastle upon Tyne
Dental School, Framlington Place   (0632) 28511
Newcastle upon Tyne, NE2 4BW,   ext. 4242
    England, United Kingdom   Established 1970

Professor J. J. Murray, Honorable Secretary
The purpose of the Association is to support the concept of international dentistry for children. <u>Membership:</u> 250 individuals who possess a recognized dental qualification in their country of residence (29 member nations). <u>Finances:</u> Membership: Supporting membership £3 annually. <u>Awards:</u> Astra Prize in child dental health, biennially. <u>Publications:</u> Journal of IADC, semiannual, Dr. G. Falcolini, editor; Newsletter of IADC, semiannual.

★ 935 ★
INTERNATIONAL ASSOCIATION OF FORENSIC
    TOXICOLOGISTS
Home Office Forensic Science Laboratory
Aldermaston-Reading RG7 4PN,   Tadley 4100
    England, United Kingdom   Established 1954

N. Dunnett, Secretary
Promotes cooperation and coordination of effort among members and encourages research in chemical toxicology. <u>Membership:</u> 900 individuals. <u>Finances:</u> Membership: $5. <u>Meetings:</u> Congresses, triennially, various locations. <u>Publications:</u> Bulletin, 3 times annually, John Jackson, case notes editor; Toxicological Abstracts.

★ 936 ★
INTERNATIONAL ASSOCIATION OF FRENCH
    SPEAKING ANAESTHETIST-REANIMATORS
La Closerie   (020) 03 52 36
F-59126 Linselles, France   Established 1963

Dr. Claude Laniez, Administrator
To bring together the anaesthetists of the French-speaking cultural community; to promote the exchange of scientific information among the members; to reunite entire French-speaking community of the world.

Membership: 1,000 (anaesthetists and reanimators). <u>Finances:</u> Subscriptions and dues. <u>Meetings:</u> Annual congress, various locations in the French-speaking community. <u>Publications:</u> Bulletin, Proceedings of Congress, annual.

★ 937 ★
INTERNATIONAL ASSOCIATION OF GROUP
    PSYCHOTHERAPY
Post Office Box 327   (201) 788-6903
Three Bridges, New Jersey 08887 Established 1954

Malcolm Pines, M.D., President;
    Jay W. Fidler, M.D., Secretary-Treasurer
To provide the free flow of communication between those persons professionally interested in the practice and study of group psychotherapy throughout the world and to provide periodic organization of international meetings. The Association is incorporated according to the Swiss Law. <u>Membership:</u> 550 individuals, 40 organizations. <u>Finances:</u> Membership: Dues and Congress registration. <u>Meetings:</u> Triennially, different countries. <u>Publications:</u> Newsletter, semiannual, Guillermo Ferschtut, M.D., editor; Proceedings of Congresses. <u>Former Name:</u> International Council of Group Psychotherapy.

INTERNATIONAL ASSOCIATION OF HEALTH
UNDERWRITERS
    See: National Association of Health Underwriters

★ 938 ★
INTERNATIONAL ASSOCIATION OF HOSPITAL
    CENTRAL SERVICE MANAGEMENT
875 North Michigan Avenue
Suite 3342   (312) 440-0078
Chicago, Illinois 60611   Established 1958

Betty Hanna, Executive Director
Only independent, non-profit association in health care field with the sole aim of improving the quality of Central Service Departments. Established to define the functions of hospital central service management and to promote standards of professional practice in hospital central service; to promote an exchange of ideas among hospital central service supervisors; to develop and apply more efficient methods and practice in hospital central service. <u>Membership:</u> 1,000 (active, associate, affiliate). <u>Finances:</u> Membership: Active and associate, $30 annually; affiliate, $10 annually; Other Sources: Educational seminars, dues. <u>Awards:</u> 2 AMSCO John J. Perkins Memorial Scholarships. <u>Meetings:</u>

3 annually, various locations across country. Publications: Communique (newsletter), quarterly, Betty Hanna, editor. Library: IAHCSM Library, 200 volumes.

★ 939 ★
INTERNATIONAL ASSOCIATION OF HUMAN
   BIOLOGISTS
c/o Professor D. F. Roberts
Department of Human Genetics
19 Claremont Place   (0632) 28511
Newcastle upon Tyne, NE2 4AA,   ext. 3464
   England, United Kingdom   Established 1967

Professor D. F. Roberts, Secretary-General
To advance research, education and facilitate communication in all aspects of human biology on an international basis. Membership: 430 individuals (honorary, active and associate) and 6 national societies. Finances: Membership: £2.50 p.a. (membership fee). Publications: Newsletter, irregular, D. F. Roberts, editor. Affiliations: Society for the Study of Human Biology; Society for the Study of Social Biology; Polish Anthropological Association; Indian Society of Human Genetics; International Union of Biological Sciences.

★ 940 ★
INTERNATIONAL ASSOCIATION OF INDIVIDUAL
   PSYCHOLOGY
37 West 65th Street   (212) 874-2427
New York, New York 10023   Established 1922

Marvin O. Nelson, Ed.D., Secretary-General
A federation of organizations in various countries which attempts to provide a forum for exchange of ideas among those interested in individual psychology. The Association grew out of the work of Alfred Adler, M.D., the founder of individual psychology. Membership: 20 member organizations (no individual membership). Finances: Organizations contribute 10% of their dues to IAIP; Other Sources: Fees for congress registration. Meetings: Triennially, various locations. Publications: Individual Psychology Newsletter, bimonthly, Paul Rom, editor.

★ 941 ★
INTERNATIONAL ASSOCIATION OF INDUSTRIAL
   ACCIDENT BOARDS AND COMMISSIONS
Post Office Box 2917   (206) 754-3793
Olympia, Washington 98507   Established 1914

Phillip T. Bork, Executive Director

To bring representatives of the various jurisdictions together at least once a year to discuss problems and experiences arising out of the administration of workmen's compensation laws, to develop and recommend standards for improving and strengthening workmen's compensation laws and their administration based on the experience of the states and provinces, and to approve and promote the acceptance of such standards. Membership: 400 (active, associate, honorary, life). Finances: Membership: Active, $400; associate, $150. Meetings: Annual, various locations. Publications: Newsletter and Journal, 8 times annually, Phillip Bork, editor; Convention Proceedings, annually, Phillip Bork, editor. Affiliations: Canadian Association of Workmen's Compensation Boards; Central, Eastern, Western Sections; Southern Association of Workmen's Compensation Administrators.

★ 942 ★
INTERNATIONAL ASSOCIATION OF
   LARYNGECTOMEES
c/o American Cancer Society
777 Third Avenue   (212) 371-2900
New York, New York 10017   Established 1952

Paul J. Scriffignano, Executive Secretary
To help in the speech retraining of persons who have lost their natural voices through surgery to cancer; to assist in total rehabilitation of such persons; to coordinate activities of the clubs; to disseminate information to the clubs regarding programs and activities. Activities include an international convention, voice rehabilitation institute to help train teachers of esophageal voice, registry of teachers, educational program for safety and artificial respiration for laryngectomees. Membership: 20,000 (laryngectomees and interested non-laryngectomees). Finances: Support from the American Cancer Society and from the 296 IAL member clubs. Meetings: Annual, various locations. Publications: IAL News, bimonthly, Robin Frames, editor; Annual Directory of Clubs, Officers; technical papers; speeches; other. Affiliation: American Cancer Society.

★ 943 ★
INTERNATIONAL ASSOCIATION OF LOGOPEDICS
   AND PHONIATRICS
c/o Dr. André Muller
Av. de la Gare 6
CH-1003 Lausanne, Switzerland   Established 1924

Dr. André Muller, General Secretary
To establish a center of information as to the state of Logopedics and Phoniatrics in various countries and to

keep records thereof; to promote standards of training and medical, educational and scientific research in the field of Logopedics and Phoniatrics, i.e., human communication disorders (speech pathology, speech therapy, orthophony, phono-audiology, deaf-mutism, language pathology, etc.), in all countries and at all levels of the educational system; to organize periodical international congresses for exchanging the most recent knowledge in the field of Logopedics and Phoniatrics; to establish contact with kindred scientific and therapeutical organizations and to assist in the establishment of such organizations in countries where there are none; to encourage and promote a scientifically accurate and internationally recognized terminology in the field of Logopedics and Phoniatrics. Membership: 650 individuals; 41 affiliated societies. Finances: Membership: Individual, $45; affiliated societies, fee based on membership. Award: Manuel Garcia Prize, triennially. Meetings: Triennial, various locations. Publications: Folia Phoniatrica, bimonthly, Ernst Loebell, editor. Affiliations: 41 affiliated societies.

★ 944 ★
INTERNATIONAL ASSOCIATION OF MILK
    CONTROL AGENCIES
c/o R. C. Pearce
New York Department of Agricultural
    and Markets   (518) 457-5731
Albany, New York 12235   Established 1934

R. C. Pearce, Secretary-Treasurer
To promote effective, efficient and improved administration of economic milk regulations through cooperation, coordination, research, education and other activity mutually beneficial to its member agencies and to the public. Membership: 34 (state and provincial milk control agencies in the United States, Canada, and Puerto Rico). Finances: Membership: $100 annually for each member agency; Other Sources: Occasional contributions by member agencies for conduct of meetings or special projects. Meetings: Annual, various locations. Publications: Report of Annual Meeting, annual, R. C. Pearce, editor. Affiliation: National Association of State Departments of Agriculture.

INTERNATIONAL ASSOCIATION OF MILK, FOOD
AND ENVIRONMENTAL SANITATIONS
    See: IAMFES, Inc.

★ 945 ★
INTERNATIONAL ASSOCIATION OF PACEMAKER
    PATIENTS, INC.   (800) 241-6993
Post Office Box 54305   (404) 523-3379
Atlanta, Georgia 30308   Established 1977

Carroll Reddic, President;
    Mari Schaarschmidt, Secretary/Treasurer
A non-profit service organization dedicated to supporting the emotional and psychological needs of pacemaker recipients and their families by giving them the opportunity to share experiences, problems, solutions and information. Through PULSE, the official journal of IAPP, the organization is able to communicate directly to its members. Local chapters have been established throughout the country for those members wishing to participate actively. The Association also provides a 24-hour telephone EKG pacemaker monitoring service, PULSELINE, enabling those members enrolled to have their pacemaker checked. The EKG report is intercepted by a cardiologist and forwarded to the patient's physician. Should there be a problem with the pacer, the patient and physician are notified immediately. Membership: 1,800 active (pacemaker recipients); associate (those interested in the pacemaker patient); membership comprises pacemaker recipients, doctors, nurses, hospitals and libraries, along with pacemaker engineers and other industry personnel. Finances: Membership: $12 annually. Meetings: Annual, each summer. Publications: PULSE, quarterly, William C. Maloy, M.D., editor.

★ 946 ★
INTERNATIONAL ASSOCIATION ON WATER
    POLLUTION RESEARCH
c/o Ronald Fairall
Chichester House
278 High Holborn
London WC1V 7HE, England   (01) 405-4552
    United Kingdom   Established 1965

Ronald Fairall, Secretary-Treasurer
To encourage international exchange of information on water pollution research and water quality management; to sponsor regular international meetings and conferences where reports on important research in water pollution are presented; to provide a scientific medium for the publication of research reports and activities of the Association; and to shorten the time lag between development of research findings and their application in engineering design. Membership: 1,200 (associate, individual, national). Finances: Membership: Individual, $30; associate, $200; sustaining, $400; student, $15; Other Sources: Sale of proceedings. Meetings: Biennial, and specialized various locations. Publications: Water Research,

monthly, S. H. Jenkins, editor; Progress in Water Technology, bimonthly, S. H. Jenkins, editor.

★ 947 ★
INTERNATIONAL BRAIN RESEARCH ORGANIZATION
c/o Dr. Mary A. B. Brazier, Secretary-General
Department of Anatomy
University of California, Los Angeles   (213) 825-9555
Los Angeles, California 90024   Established 1958

Dr. Mary A. B. Brazier, Secretary-General
Cultivates a strong, flexible, worldwide network of scientific intercommunication in the 9 principal branches of brain research: neuroanatomy, neuroendocrinology, neurochemistry, neuropharmacology, neurophysiology, the behavioral sciences, neurocommunications and biophysics, brain pathology and clinical and health-related science.   Activities include fellowships and exchange of scientific workers; temporary working parties; traveling teams of instructors to supplement local teaching facilities; and the sponsorship of international neuroscience symposia.   Membership: 1,700 individuals and 18 national corporate members. Finances: Supported by funds from the national corporate members.   Meetings: Biennial, Central Council.   Publications: IBRO News; Neuroscience; IBRO Monograph Series.

★ 948 ★
INTERNATIONAL BRONCHOESOPHAGOLOGICAL
      SOCIETY
3401 North Broad Street
Philadelphia, Pennsylvania 19140   Established 1951

Charles M. Norris, Executive Secretary-Treasurer
The Society aims to (1) promote by all possible means the progress of bronchoesophagology; (2) permit specialists of different branches of the science to meet and exchange their points of view.   Membership: Approximately 500.   Finances: Membership: United States, $10; foreign, $5.   Meetings: Annual, various locations.   Publications: Transactions, annual. Affiliation: American College of Chest Physicians; American Society for Gastrointestinal Endoscopy.

★ 949 ★
INTERNATIONAL BUNDLE BRANCH BLOCK
      ASSOCIATION
6631 West 83rd Street   (213) 670-9132
Los Angeles, California 90045   Established 1979

Rita Kurtz Lewis, Founder
Bundle Branch Block (BBB) is a rare heart condition caused by an "electrical malfunction" resulting in heart failure, heart attacks and fatigue.   This organization is designed to cultivate and promote interest in the study and dissemination of information about BBB, later about cardiomyopathy, and possibly other conditions accompanying BBB in some patients; to provide a fount of ready information for professionals and concerned laity.   Report information, not advise, as laity.   Our medical advisors are the only ones to advise.   Records from members, clippings, other printed material will be kept to aid research, and for information to concerned laity.   Membership: 700 letters of interest; no formal membership as yet. Finances: Membership: Proposed fee, $10 annually or whatever the member can afford;   Other Sources: Donations.   Meetings: Annual, various locations. Publications: The International Bundle Branch Block Association Publication, quarterly, R. Kurtz Lewis, editor; The International Bundle Branch Block Association (fact sheet), sent once to inquirers, R. Kurtz Lewis, editor; Newsletter, sent once to inquirers, R. Kurtz Lewis, editor.

★ 950 ★
INTERNATIONAL CARDIOLOGY FOUNDATION
7320 Greenville Avenue   (214) 750-5429
Dallas, Texas 75231   Established 1965

J. Keith Thwaites
A small foundation whose main function is to assist developing countries with their cardiovascular needs. The Foundation directs the role the American Heart Association will play in assisting Heart Associations in foreign counties to get organized; identifies the areas of international need and recommend programs that will fulfill those needs; directs and promotes the Visiting Teacher Program of the P. D. White Fund; provides Cardiovascular Public and Professional Education Material to developing countries.   Membership: 10 (physicians, nurses and laymen).   Finances: Other Sources: P. D. White Fund.

★ 951 ★
INTERNATIONAL CARDIOVASCULAR SOCIETY
13 Elm Street
Post Office Box 1565   (617) 927-8330
Manchester, Massachusetts 01944   Established 1950

William T. Maloney, Executive Director
To promote investigation and study of the art, science and therapy of vascular diseases.   Finances: Dues, gifts.   Meetings: Biennial, various locations.   Publications: Journal of Cardiovascular Surgery; Congress proceedings.

★ 952 ★

INTERNATIONAL CATHOLIC DEAF ASSOCIATION,
 INC. (301) 588-4009
814 Thayer Avenue (TDI only-no Voice)
Silver Spring, Maryland 20910 Established 1949

Irene Hodock, Secretary-General
To promote a friendly and cultural bond of union
among the Catholic Deaf throughout the world, and
to extend this union to our other brothers of other
religious beliefs; to be interested and actively engaged in all good works pertaining to the education,
social and ethical advancement of any deaf persons.
First Home Office set up on September 5, 1978. The
Association also employs a full time priest to do missionary work among the deaf in United States and
Canada, and occasionally abroad. Membership:
8,000 (active, associate, honorary, junior). Finances: Membership: Single, $6.50; couple, $10;
Other Sources: Donations. Awards: Member of the
Year Award; Ecumenical Service Award; Newsletter
Contest; Chapter Poster Contest. Meetings: Annual, various locations. Publications: Deaf Cath-
olic, bimonthly, George Wilson, editor; pamphlets.

★ 953 ★

INTERNATIONAL CENTER OF INFORMATION ON
 ANTIBIOTICS
32 Boulevard de la Constitution (041) 430525
B-4020 Liege, Belgium Established 1961

M. Welsch, Director
To gather and disseminate information on antibiotics
and strains producing them; to establish contacts
between research workers in view of helping them to
identify quickly supposed new antibiotics, in order to
avoid duplication of investigation and confusion in
scientific literature. Membership: 600 correspond-
ents. Publication: Information Bulletin, annual,
L. Delcambe, editor.

★ 954 ★

INTERNATIONAL CHILDBIRTH EDUCATIONAL
 ASSOCIATION
Post Office Box 20048 (612) 854-8660
Minneapolis, Minnesota 55420 Established 1960

Joan C. Bowen, President
The Association exists as an interdisciplinary organization to represent a federation of groups and individuals, both parents and professionals, who share a
genuine interest in education for childbearing and
family-centered maternity care. Activities include
publication of newsletters and other communications;
sponsorship of meetings and conferences on interna-

tional and state/province levels; maintenance of a
mail order book store; and support of a referral system for couples to find medical care and education
opportunities. Membership: 13,000 (member groups:
325 with contributing professionals, 325; members of
member groups, 9,200; individual members, 3,100).
Finances: Membership: Member group, $30 plus $3
per member; contributing professional, $35; individ-
ual membership, $15; lifetime membership, $300;
Other Sources: Conferences and conventions; sale of
publications; operation of mail order book store.
Meetings: International Convention, biennially; Regional Conferences, biennially; state/province
workshops. Publications: ICEA News, quarterly,
Joanne Dunne, editor; ICEA Review, 3 issues an-
nually; Rosemary Cogan, editor; ICEA Sharing, 3
issues annually, Phyllis Williams, editor; ICEA
Forum, 3 issues annually, Jayne Polliard, editor;
ICEA Bookmarks, 3 issues annually, Sharon C. Bulger,
editor; Bonding--How Parents Become Attached to
Their Baby, Diony Young, editor; Unnecessary Cesar-
eans--Ways to Avoid Them, Diony Young and Charles
Mahan, editors; Outreach Teaching, Barbara
McCormick, editor; The Pregnant Patient's Bill of
Rights--The Pregnant Patient's Responsibilities, Doris
Haire and Members of ICEA, editors; ICEA Position
Paper on Planning Comprehensive Maternal and New-
born Services for the Childbearing Year.

★ 955 ★

INTERNATIONAL CHILDREN'S CENTRE
c/o Professor Michel Manciaux
Chateau de Longchamp
Carrefour de Longchamp
Bois de Boulogne (01) 506 79-92
F-75016 Paris, France Established 1950

Professor Michel Manciaux, Director
To encourage in all countries, training of specialized
staff, study of problems affecting childhood, diffusion
of data concerning physical, mental and social development of the child. WHO collaborative center
for Family Health. Finances: Grants from the
French government, UNICEF, WHO. Publications:
Le Courrier, bimonthly; L'Enfant en Milieu Tropical,
bimonthly; seminar reports, specialized bibliographic
bulletins.

★ 956 ★

INTERNATIONAL CHRISTIAN FEDERATION FOR THE
 PREVENTION OF ALCOHOLISM AND DRUG
 ADDICTION
4 Southampton Row
London WC1B 4AA, England (01) 242 6511
 United Kingdom Established 1980

Rev. J. Kenneth Lawton, Honorable General Secretary (United Kingdom); Bishop James K. Mathews, President (United States)
Present constitution and newly established Federation developed out of consultations with the World Council of Churches, church leaders from around the world and representatives of WHO. Purposes are to promote world-wide educational and remedial work through the Churches, teaching the wisdom of sobriety for the welfare of society; to be the agency for drawing together the Christian concern related to alcohol and drug abuse and thus sharing research, educational work and experience; to be the agency whereby informed Christian thought and experience is related to the WHO and is expressed in the concerns of the world Church. Membership: 21 churches and member organizations are committed to active membership but a large number of others attending the 1980 consultation represented 25 countries and 30 churches (Membership of the International Christian Federation with the approval of the Executive Committee (1) Churches and Federations of Churches in membership with the World Council of Churches; (2) Other Churches or Federations of Churches accepting the aims and purposes set out above; (3) National Temperance Councils or regional groups working ecumenically in the field of alcohol and drugs supporting the above purposes; (4) The International Federation of the Temperance Blue Cross Societies and any similar international Christian body; (5) Individuals shall be entitled to associate personal membership on receipt of an agreed annual contribution). Meetings: Biennial, World Consultation with members of the Council, various locations throughout the world.
Former Name: World Christian Temperance Federation.

★ 957 ★
INTERNATIONAL CHRISTIAL LEPROSY MISSION
(IN CANADA)
Post Office Box 91564
West Vancouver, British Columbia   (604) 926-1390
V7V 3P2, Canada   Established 1943

Violet T. Habershon, Executive Secretary for Canada; Dr. Ben Gullison, General Director, ICLM Board-Canada
To support the preaching of the Gospel to the leperous patients and to provide physical care and healing for them; to encourage and aid in the training and support of indigenous Christian leaders and workers in leper work on Mission Fields; to compliment the general missionary programs of the cooperative Missions and Societies; to exercise due economy in the conduct of the business affairs of the Mission, consistent with efficient operation of the Lord's work. Membership: 9 Board Members; 25 on card Membership List; 350 contributers, free-will all over Canada.

Finances: Other Sources: All free-will offerings to the work. Meetings: Quarterly Prayer Meetings, Annual Board Meeting. Publications: Global Missions, 3 times annually, Mrs. Hattie Metcalf, editor; monthly letter from the office to contributers in Canada.

★ 958 ★
INTERNATIONAL CHRISTIAN LEPROSY MISSION, INC. (IN THE UNITED STATES)
6917 Southwest Oak Drive
Box 23353   (503) 244-5935
Portland, Oregon 97223   Established 1943

Hattie A. Metcalf, General Director
To assist those with leprosy and their children. A faith missionary organization. Membership: 20. Finances: Contributions. Meetings: Annual, Portland, Oregon, or Vancouver, British Columbia. Publications: Global Missions, 3 times annually, Hattie A. Metcalf, editor. Affiliation: International Christian Leprosy Mission (in Canada).

★ 959 ★
INTERNATIONAL COLLEGE OF ACUPUNCTURE AND ELECTRO-THERAPEUTICS
800 Riverside Drive (8-1)   (212) 781-6262
New York, New York 10032   Established 1979

Yoshiaki Omura,,M.D., Sc.D., F.A.C.A., F.I.C.A.E., President
To maintain highest universally acceptable medical and scientific standards in practice and research and education of acupuncture and electro-therapeutics. To inform medical profession and public about the beneficial as well as adverse effects of acupuncture and electro-therapeutics. To publish the official journal, Acupuncture and Electro-Therapeutics Research, The International Journal (Pergamon Press) and encourage research and give New York State Boards of Medicine and Dentistry accredited seminars and workshops every 2 or 3 months for licensed physicians and dentists. The College is duly chartered by the University of the State of New York, New York State Educational Department, since 1979. Membership: About 100, including 80 non-paying fellows (licensed physicians and dentists). Full Founding Members must have the New York State certificate to practice acupuncture; Fellows must be M.D., Ph.D., or DDS who are outstanding researchers, clinicians or educators. Finances: Fellows: Free (free for editorial board members of the official journal or for those who regularly teach the accredited courses) or $100; full founding members, $65; members, $65. Awards: Awards of Fellow of the International College of

Acupuncture and Electro-Therapeutics. Meetings: New York State Boards of Medicine and Dentistry accredited courses for the 100 credit hour requirement to obtain the certificate to practice acupuncture are given every 2 or 3 months by inviting internationally reknowned researchers to lecture or demonstrate. Publications: Acupuncture and Electro-Therapeutics Research, The International Journal, quarterly, Yoshiaki Omura, M.D., Sc.D., editor.

★ 960 ★
INTERNATIONAL COLLEGE OF APPLIED
    NUTRITION
Post Office Box 386   (213) 697-4576
La Habra, California 90631   Established 1960

Mrs. H. Stone, Executive Secretary
An organization of physicians, veterinarians, dentists, and scientists in fields related to nutrition which was organized to promote the study of nutrition and encouragement of research in the nutritional aspects of disease. Sponsors spring lecture series. Membership: 1,026. Meetings: Annual, various locations. Publications: Journal of Applied Nutrition; Newsletter, bimonthly.

★ 961 ★
INTERNATIONAL COLLEGE OF SURGEONS
1516 North Lake Shore Drive   (312) 642-3555
Chicago, Illinois 60610   Established 1935

Luis Graña, International Secretary-General
The College aims to cultivate a spirit among surgeons that facilitates the international exchange of surgical knowledge, not only among surgeons who speak a common language or who share a common ideology, but between the largest possible number of surgeons of diverse nationalities and varied political, social and religious alignments throughout the world. Membership: 12,000. Awards: Research grants; scholarships for undergraduate and postgraduate medical students. Meetings: International Biennial Congresses, Hemisphere and Federation Congresses, National Section Meetings. Publications: International Surgery, 6 times annually, Professor Giuseppe Pezzuoli, editor in chief. Library: International Museum of Surgical Sciences Library.

★ 962 ★
INTERNATIONAL COLLEGIUM OF NEUROPSY-
    CHOPHARMACOLOGY
Tennessee Neuropsychiatric
    Institute   (615) 741-7431
Nashville, Tennessee 37217   Established 1957

Dr. Paul Janssen, President
Object is to establish an organization whose members shall meet from time to time to consider and discuss matters related to neuropsychopharmacology and who through this organization shall encourage and promote international scientific study, teaching and application of neuropsychopharmacology. The CINP shall also provide consultation and advice for the better evaluation of the biochemistry, pharmacology, safety and therapeutic efficacy of neuropsychiatric drugs and may act as an advisory body to educational institutions, governmental agencies, and such other organizations and bodies as determined by the Council. Membership: 600 founding and supporting members, fellows, honorary and emeritus fellows. Meetings: Biennially, various locations. Publications: Roster of Members, annually.

★ 963 ★
INTERNATIONAL COMMISSION FOR OPTICS
c/o Professor H. J. Frankena
Département of Applied Physics,
Lorentzweg 1   (015) 785309
2628 C J Delft, The Netherlands Established 1958

Professor H. J. Frankena, Secretary-General
To contribute, on an international basis, to the progress and knowledge of theoretical and instrumental optics, the applications of optics, and physiological optics; to facilitate the rapid exchange of information, by encouraging and regulating the organization of, congresses, symposia, and summer schools; and to promote international agreement on nomenclature, units, symbols, and similar subjects. Membership: 24 national committees. Finances: Membership: Member dues; Other Sources: Grants from organizations; sale of journals. Meetings: General Assembly, triennial; symposia, annual; sponsored meetings, 2 to 3 annually. Publications: Report from the ICO Bureau, every 1 1/2 years, Professor H. J. Frankena, editor; ICO, Its Constitution, History and Status, once in 5 years, Professor H. J. Frankena, editor. Affiliation: ICO is affiliated to IUPAP.

★ 964 ★

INTERNATIONAL COMMISSION FOR THE PRE-
VENTION OF ALCOHOLISM

6830 Laurel Street, N.W.   (202) 723-0800
Washington, D.C. 20012   Established 1950

Ernest H. J. Steed, Executive Director
Sponsors institutes and seminars on the prevention and
treatment of alcoholism.   Meetings: Quadrennial.
Publications: ICPA Quarterly Bulleting.

★ 965 ★

INTERNATIONAL COMMISSION ON MICRO-
BIOLOGICAL SPECIFICATIONS FOR FOODS
c/o D. S. Clark
Bureau of Microbial Hazards
Health Protection Branch
Tanney's Pasture   (613) 593-7071
Ottawa, Ontario K1A 0L2, Canada   Established 1962

Dr. D. S. Clark, Secretary-Treasurer
The Commission was founded to assemble and correlate
evidence about the actual microbiological quality of
foods; to consider whether specifications are necessary for any particular food; where necessary, to
propose suitable specifications; and to suggest appropriate methods of examination.   Its purpose is to aid
in providing comparable standards of judgment among
countries with sophisticated facilities for food control,
and to offer useful procedures to the developing
countries; to foster safe movement of foods in international commerce; and to dissipate difficulties
caused by disparage microbiological standards and
methods of analysis.   Membership: 24 leading scientists in food microbiology from 15 different countries.   Finances: Funds raised from the food industry
in several countries, government agencies, and the
International Union of Biological Societies.   Meetings: Annual, various locations.   Publications: Microorganisms in Foods, 2nd edition; Microorganisms in
Foods 2; Microorganisms in Foods 3; several scientific papers.   Affiliations: Balkan and Danubian
Subcommission; Latinamerican Subcommission; Middle East-North African Subcommission.

★ 966 ★

INTERNATIONAL COMMISSION ON RADIATION
UNITS AND MEASUREMENTS
7910 Woodmont Avenue, Suite 1016 (301) 657-2652
Bethesda, Maryland 20014   Established 1928

R. S. Caswell, Secretary
To develop internationally acceptable recommendations
regarding: quantities and units of radiation and rad-
ioactivity, procedures suitable for the measurement

and application of these quantities in medicine and
biology, physical data needed in the application of
these procedures, the use of which tends to assure
uniformity in reporting.   Membership: 93.   Finances: Contributions, grants, contracts.   Awards:
ICRU Gray Medal.   Publications: ICRU Reports,
irregularly; reports and reprints.

★ 967 ★

INTERNATIONAL COMMISSION ON RADIOLOGI-
CAL PROTECTION
Clifton Avenue   Telex 895 1244 ICRP G
Sutton Surrey SM2 5PU, England,   (01) 642-4680
United Kingdom   Established 1928

Dr. F. D. Sowby, Scientific Secretary
The Commission aims to familiarize itself with progress in the whole field of radiation protection and
to publish recommendations in radiation safety standards, mainly dealing with basic principles of radiation protection.   Membership: Individuals in 18
countries.   Finances: Grants from official and private bodies.   Meetings: Irregular, various locations.
Publications: Reports and papers.   Affiliations: Official relations with WHO and IAEA.

★ 968 ★

INTERNATIONAL COMMITTEE AGAINST MENTAL
ILLNESS
Post Office Box 898 Ansonia Station
1990 Broadway   (914) 359-8797
New York, New York 10023   Established 1957

Nathan S. Kline, M.D., President;
Irving Blumberg, Executive Vice President
The Committee concerns itself with promoting research, services, rehabilitation, and data information
systems in relation to mental health care.   Its activities include conducting symposia, international conferences, and research projects.   Finances: Contributions from private sources, foundations, businesses.

INTERNATIONAL COMMITTEE FOR HISTOCHEMIS-
TRY AND CYTOCHEMISTRY
See: International Federation of Societies for
Histochemistry and Cytochemistry

★ 969 ★

INTERNATIONAL COMMITTEE FOR LIFE
    ASSURANCE MEDICINE
c/o Professor E. Tanner, M.D.
Swiss Reinsurance Company
Mythenquai 50/60   (01) 208.21.21
CH-8022 Zurich, Switzerland   Established 1932

Professor E. Tanner, M.D., General Secretary
The Committee's aim is the advancement of medical
science in relation to Life Assurance.   It seeks to
achieve this aim by organizing International Congresses
for Life Assurance Medicine; by establishing societies of Life Assurance Medicine in countries where
none as yet exist; by promoting the teaching of Life
Assurance Medicine and encouraging the scientific research into problems related thereto; and by fostering
the personal relations of its members.   Membership:
50 observers and delegates (the number of observers
is limited to 3 per country).   Finances: National
insurance companies of the country, where the congress is being held.   Meetings: Bureau, annual;
committee, triennially.   Publications: Proceedings
of the International Congress of Life Assurance Medicine, triennially.

★ 970 ★

INTERNATIONAL COMMITTEE OF CATHOLIC
    NURSES
Palazzo S. Calisto
00120-Vatican City   Established 1933

Liliana Fiori, General Secretary
To encourage, in all countries, the organization and
the development of catholic professional associations
capable of giving moral and spiritual support to Catholic Nurses (and Public Health Nurses) as well as
helping them perfect their techniques;   to coordinate
the efforts of Catholic Professional Associations while
respecting their autonomy, in order to study and to
represent christian thought in the profession in general;
to participate in the general development of the nursing profession and to promote health and social welfare measures along the lines of scientific progress
and following christian principles, thereby ensuring
the health and welfare to which every human being
is entitled, and at the same time respecting the religious convictions of every individual.   Membership:
65 (full and corresponding member associations).
Finances: Membership fees.   Meetings: Every 4
years, various locations; Regional Congress, biennially.   Publications: Ciciams-News, quarterly; circular letters.

★ 971 ★

INTERNATIONAL COMMITTEE OF MILITARY
    MEDICINE AND PHARMACY
c/o Dr. J. Mathieu
Hôspital Militaire
rue Saint-Laurent, 79   (04) 32.21.83
B-4000 Liege, Belgium   Established 1921

Dr. J. Mathieu, Secretary General
To maintain and contribute to collaboration in the
care of the sick and wounded among medical and
pharmaceutical personnel during peace and war.   The
Committee organizes periodic international congresses
and publishes material relating to its purposes.
Membership: 90 (health services of member nations
are each represented by a delegate).   Finances:
Contributions of member nations.   Meetings: Congress, biennially, various member nations.   Publications: Revue Internationale des Services de Santé des
Armees, monthly, J. Mathieu, editor.

★ 972 ★

INTERNATIONAL COMMITTEE OF THE RED CROSS
17 avenue de la Paix   (022) 34.60.01
CH-1211 Geneva, Switzerland   Established 1863

Alexander Hay, President
In time of war, civil war or internal disturbances; to
act as a neutral institution or intermediary in order
to ameliorate the condition of victims; to take any
humanitarian initiative in conformity with its role as
a specifically neutral and independent institution; to
contribute to the training and equipping of voluntary
medical personnel; to work for the development of
international humanitarian law, for the understanding
and dissemination of the Geneva Conventions.   Membership: 20, all Swiss, plus several hundred of col-
laborators at Geneva headquarters or delegates abroad.
Finances: Contributions.   Publications: International
Review of the Red Cross, bimonthly; ICRC Bulletin,
monthly;   Annual Report and many other publications.

★ 973 ★

INTERNATIONAL COMMITTEE OF THE SILENT
    SPORTS
Langaavej 41
DK-2650 Hvidovre, Denmark   Established 1924

Knud Sondergaard, Secretary-General
To develop and control the physical education in
general and the practice of sports in particular among
the deaf of the world; to encourage relations between
the countries practice sports for the deaf and using its
influence to initiate and then give guidance to the
practice of these sports in countries, where this is

unknown; to supervise the regular celebration of the World Games for the Deaf. Membership: 30,000-40,000 members in 43 countries. Finances: Membership: Countries with 1-10 clubs, $60; with 11-30 clubs, $90; with over 30 clubs, $120. Awards: Gold, silver, bronze medals. Meetings: Biennial, various locations. Publications: CISS-Bulletin, quarterly; Yearbook, every 8 years.

★ 974 ★

INTERNATIONAL COMMITTEE ON ALCOHOL,
    DRUGS AND TRAFFIC SAFETY
Sycamore Hall 302
Bloomington, Indiana 47401

Robert F. Borkenstein, President
To assess the state of knowledge in the field of alcohol, drugs, and traffic safety; to identify and draw attention to new developments in the field; to provide an interdisciplinary forum for the exchange of information; to draw public attention to the severity and magnitude of problems resulting from driving while impaired by alcohol and other drugs. Membership: 48 (elected by proposal from members). Awards: Widmark Award. Meetings: Every 4 years, various locations. Publications: Blutalkohol (Blood Alcohol), 6 times annual, Gerchow, editor; Proceedings of the International Conferences, published after each conference.

★ 975 ★

INTERNATIONAL CONFEDERATION FOR PLASTIC
    AND RECONSTRUCTIVE SURGERY
40 rue Bichat   (01) 206-62-44
F-75010 Paris, France   Established 1955

Roger Mouly, General Secretary
To promote plastic surgery, both scientifically and clinically; to further education; and to encourage friendship between physicians in all countries. Activities include international meetings. Membership: 48 national societies. Finances: Membership: $10 or equivalent per member from each national society covering a 4-year period. Meetings: Every 4 years, various locations.

★ 976 ★

INTERNATIONAL CONFEDERATION OF MIDWIVES
57 Lower Belgrave Street
London SW1W 0LR, England   (01) 730 6137/8
    United Kingdom   Established 1954

Aims of the Confederation are to (1) further among its member groups knowledge and good understanding of all problems relating to reproduction and childbirth; (2) assist the national groups in working together for the purpose of promoting family health, improving

the standard of maternal care and advancing the training of midwives and their professional status; (3) provide means of communication between midwives of various nationalities and with other international organizations, to improve the standards of maternal and child care; (4) create opportunities for discussion of questions relating to the social aspects of midwifery and the advancement of midwives; (5) maintain facilities for the promotion of international understanding and the interchange of international hospitality; (6) provide a center of information, documentation and liaison and to promote the study of problems which affect the health of mothers and babies and also the professional life of the midwife. Membership: 51 (midwifery associations throughout the world with a combined membership of 100,000 professional midwives). Finances: Dues; Other Sources: Profits from triennial congresses. Meetings: Triennial Congress, various locations. Publications: Congress Reports, triennially; Working Party Reports; Maternity Care in the World. Affiliations: International Federation of Gynaecology and Obstetrics; European Economic Community; WHO; IAMANEH.

★ 977 ★

INTERNATIONAL CORRESPONDENCE SOCIETY OF
    ALLERGISTS
350 East Broad Street   (614) 221-2457
Columbus, Ohio 43215   Established 1934

N. M. Newport, M.D., Director-General
Dissemination of information relating to the practice of allergy. Membership: 750 (allergists throughout the world). Finances: Membership: Dues, $20 annually. Publications: The Letters, monthly, N. M. Newport, M.D., editor.

INTERNATIONAL COUNCIL OF GROUP
PSYCHOTHERAPY
    See: International Association of Group Psychotherapy

★ 978 ★

INTERNATIONAL COUNCIL OF NURSES
37, rue de Vermont
Post Office Box 42
CH-1211 Geneva 20, Switzerland (022) 33.64.00
                                Established 1899

Executive Director (appointment pending)
To assist national nurses' associations to improve the standards of nursing and the competence of nurses; to promote the development of strong national nurses' associations; to serve as the authoritative voice for nurses and nursing internationally; to assist national nurses' associations to improve the professional, social

and economic position of nurses. Through its meetings, programme and publications, ICN aims to develop and improve health services for the public; nursing education, practice and research; and the social and economic welfare of nurses. Membership: 93 national nurses association (ICN is a federation of national nurses associations; only one national association per country may be admitted to ICN). Finances: Membership: Annual dues of Swiss francs, 2.20 per individual member, paid by each national association; Other Sources: Sale of publications, bequests, donations. Awards: 2 ICN/3M International Nursing Fellowships of United States $6,000 each awarded annually. Meetings: Congress, once every 4 years; Council of National Representatives (governing body), biennial; seminars and workshops organized in line with current programs. Publications: International Nursing Review, 6 times annually, Merren Tardivelle, editor; Basic Principles of Nursing Care; Code for Nurses; ICN Policy Statements; The Nurse's Dilemma: Ethical Considerations in Nursing Practice; Proceedings of Congresses: A Bio-Bibliography of Florence Nightingale; A History of the International Council of Nurses; Introducing the ICN; Principles of Legislation for Nursing Education and Practice; An Underestimated Problem in Nursing: The Effect of the Economic and Social Welfare of Nurses on Patient Care.

★ 979 ★

INTERNATIONAL COUNCIL OF PSYCHOLOGISTS, INC.
Secretariat
2772 North Lake Avenue   (213) 794-0337
Altadena, California 91001   Established 1960

Dr. Georgia S. Adams, Secretary-General
A network of psychologists with international interests, dedicated to advancing psychology and the application of its scientific findings around the world, by deeping and clarifying channels of communication between individuals. Membership: Approximately 1,300 (members are psychologists who hold membership in, or are eligible for, their national psychological association, affiliated with the International Union of Psychological Sciences. Social workers and psychologists who do not fully meet requirements are associates, affiliates, student members). Finances: Membership: Canada and United States, $22; Mexico, $12; countries of Western and Northern Europe, Mediterranean region, OPEC countries, Japan, $15; developing countries, $10; Other Sources: Contributions, subscriptions to journals, convention registration fees. Meetings: Annual conventions, in odd-numbered years. ICP meets at or near site of convention of American Psychological Association. In eve- even-numbered years, the convention is held overseas, preceding quadrennial conventions of IUPS and IAAP.

Publications: International Psychologist, quarterly, Dr. Carleton Shay, editor; ICP Yearbook-Directory, biennial, Dr. Helen Nicklin, editor.

★ 980 ★

INTERNATIONAL COUNCIL OF SOCIETIES OF
       PATHOLOGY
c/o Dr. F. K. Mostofi
7001 Georgia Street   (301) 654-0095
Chevy Chase, Maryland 20015   Established 1962

F. K. Mostofi, M.D., Secretary
To provide an international medium for the exchange of information among pathologists; to aid and cooperate in the development of uniformity in the criteria for the definition and diagnosis of disease; to encourage research and education in the field of pathology; to promote relations with national organizations concerned with health problems. Membership: 65 national associations. Finances: Dues, contributions. Meetings: Biennial, various locations. Affiliations: WHO; PAHO.

★ 981 ★

INTERNATIONAL COUNCIL ON ALCOHOL AND
       ADDICTIONS
Case Postale 140   (021) 29.64.85
CH-1001 Lausanne, Switzerland   Established 1907

Archer Tongue, Executive Director;
    Eva Tongue, LL.D., Deputy Director
To stimulate and facilitate the exchange of experience and research in the prevention and treatment of alcoholism and drug dependence. Membership: 750 individual, 210 organizations. Finances: Membership: Individual 100 Swiss francs; full 1,000 Swiss francs; Other Sources: Organizational and governmental donations. Awards: Jellinek Award; Browning Award. Meetings: Annual, various locations; Congresses, triannual, various locations. Publications: Selected articles and reports.

★ 982 ★

INTERNATIONAL COUNCIL ON HEALTH, PHYSICAL
       EDUCATION AND RECREATION
1900 Association Drive   (703) 476-3462
Reston, Virginia 22091   Established 1959

Carl A. Troester, Jr., Secretary-General
To advance the profession of health, physical education, recreation, and related areas throughout the world; to develop new and better programs for children and youth; to encourage and conduct practical research in these fields; to publish reports, studies and pamphlets needed in professional activities.

Membership: 1,800 (individual, institutional, national, contributing, international). Finances: Membership: Individual, $15; institutional, $25; national, $25; contributing, over $25; international, $25. Meetings: International Congress every other odd year; Geographical and specialized meetings even years; both in various locations. Publications: International Journal of Physical Education, quarterly, Verlag Karl Hoffman, editor; ICHPER Congress Proceedings, annual; various booklets and papers.

★ 983 ★
INTERNATIONAL COUNCIL ON SOCIAL WELFARE
Koestlergasse 1/29   (0222) 57-81-64
A-1060 Vienna, Austria   Established 1928

Miss Ingrid Gelinek, Secretary-General
To provide an international forum for the discussion of social work, social welfare and related issues; to promote the exchange of information and experiences among members; and to facilitate and promote cooperation among international organizations related to the field of social welfare. Membership: National Committees in 73 countries; 21 international non-governmental organizations. Finances: Membership: Each National Committee pays a quota which varies from $150 to several thousand dollars. Meetings: International Conferences, biennially, various locations; National Conferences; Regional Seminars and Workshops. Publications: International Social Work, quarterly; Proceedings, newsletter.

★ 984 ★
INTERNATIONAL DENTAL FEDERATION
64 Wimpole Street
London W1M 8AL, England,   (01) 935.7852
    United Kingdom   Established 1900

J. E. Ahlberg, Executive Director
To represent the profession of dentistry on a voluntary, international basis; to sponsor a World Dental Congress and to establish and encourage international programs which will advance the science and art of dentistry and the status of the profession of dentistry in the interest of improved dental and general health for all peoples. Activities includes 4 standings commissions active in various dental fields. Membership: 78 associations, 13,700 supporting members. Finances: Membership: Regular pay fees based on per capita income of own country; supporting, $18; Other Sources: Sale of journals, registration fees for Congress. Awards: Georges Villain International Prize, International Miller Prize, Jessen Fellowship in Children's Dentistry, Johnson & Johnson International Preventive Dentistry Awards. Meetings: Annual, various locations. Publications: International Dental Journal, quarterly, F. E. Lawton, editor; Newsletter, bimonthly; manuals and monographs.

★ 985 ★
INTERNATIONAL DIABETES FEDERATION
10 Queen Anne Street
London W1M 0BD, England,   (01) 637-3644
    United Kingdom   Established 1950

James G. L. Jackson, M.D., hc, Secretary-General
To further the acquisition and dissemination of useful and accurate information regarding diabetes mellitus and to undertake such activities as will improve the physical and socio-economic welfare of persons afflicted with the disorder. Membership: 64 member associations in 55 countries, 250 individual members (national member associations; individual members, supporting members (firms). Finances: Membership: 7 1/2 pence per capita membership of each national association; minimum £75 p.a.; individual members, £15 p.a.; supporting members, £ 500 p.a.; Other Sources: Donations. Lectureships: Bernardo A. Houssay Memorial Lecture; Solomon Berson Lecture; Alan D. N. Nabarro Lecture. Meetings: Triennial International Congress, various locations. Publications: IDF Bulletin, 3 times annually, James G. L. Jackson, editor. Remarks: NGO with WHO; Member of Executive of CIOMS.

★ 986 ★
INTERNATIONAL DOCTORS IN ALCOHOLICS
    ANONYMOUS   (216) 782-6216
1950 Volney Road   (216) 788-7357
Youngstown, Ohio 44511   Established 1949

Lewis K. Reed, M.D., Secretary-Treasurer
The aims of International Doctors in Alcoholics Anonymous are essentially those of Alcoholics Anonymous in general. The organization educates and assists not only physicians, but anyone suffering from the disease of alcoholism in hope to better cope with and understand the problems of medical profession and those of the patients. All doctors are active in their local A.A. Membership: There is no formal membership. The Secretary-Treasurer holds one strictly confidential mailing list of more than 2,000 names; the majority are medical doctors, there are also dentists, psychologists, veterinarians, and medical scientists, such as biochemists and microbiologists. Among corresponding members are doctors in Canada, Australia, New Zealand, South America, South Africa and Japan. When members request the names of other A.A. doctors in their locality, this is given only with the consent of all parties involved. Finances: Other Sources: Modest registration fee at the annual meeting, contributions. Meetings: Annual, held in the first weekend of August, usually from Friday evening through Sunday morning, various locations.

★ 987 ★

INTERNATIONAL EPIDEMIOLOGICAL ASSOCIATION
c/o Edward H. Kass, M.D.
Harvard Medical School   (617) 732-2280
Boston, Massachusetts 02115   Established 1954

Edward H. Kass, M.D., Treasurer
The Association's aim is to support and further the development of the science of epidemiology on a world basis, and to secure the application of this knowledge for the benefit of mankind. Membership: 1,000. Finances: Membership: $24 or equivalent in other currencies. Meetings: Annually, every 3 years, various locations; regional meetings. Publications: Journal, quarterly, W. W. Holland, editor; also publishes books and manuals and Membership Directory. Affiliations: World Health Organization; Council for International Organizations of Medical Sciences.

★ 988 ★

INTERNATIONAL EYE FOUNDATION
7801 Norfolk Avenue   (301) 986-1830
Bethesda, Maryland 20014   Established 1961

J. H. King, Jr., M.D., Medical Director
To support and assist with the prevention and cure of blindness throughout the world including the design and implementation of integrated blindness prevention and primary eye care programs delivering low-cost primary eye health care services to the poor majority in specific developing countries. Membership: Through the Society of Eye Surgeons, over 1,000 ophthalmologists. Finances: Membership: $75; Other Sources: Donations, foundations, industry, governments. Awards: McLean Medallion; Vail Medal; Atkinson Lectures. Meetings: Biennial, various locations. Publications: Newsletter, quarterly.

★ 989 ★

INTERNATIONAL FEDERATION FOR MEDICAL
    AND BIOLOGICAL ENGINEERING
National Research Council of Canada
Ottawa, Ontario K1A 0R6,   (613) 993-9287
    Canada   Established 1959

Dr. John A. Hopps, Secretary-General
To promote the application of engineering theory and techniques to biological and medical research and practice on an international basis. Activities include the organization of conferences and the establishment of aid to developing countries. Membership: 14,000 within societies in 22 countries. Finances: Membership: For societies with up to 10 members, $42; up to 100 members, $220; and up to 1,100

members, $600; Other Sources: Revenues from publication sales and conferences. Awards: Nightingale Prize, awarded biennially. Publication: Medical and Biological Engineering, bimonthly, D. W. Hill, editor.

★ 990 ★

INTERNATIONAL FEDERATION FOR MEDICAL
    PSYCHOTHERAPY
Post Office Box 26, Vindern   (02) 14 61 90
Oslo 3, Norway   Established 1947

Dr. Finn Magnussen, President;
    Dr. Truls-Eirik Mogstad, Secretary-General
To further research and teaching of psychotherapy, especially through both practical and theoretical cooperation between medical psychotherapists of all countries. Organizes international congresses for medical psychotherapy usually every third year and supports publication of scientific papers. Membership: Nearly 4,000 collective (psychotherapeutic societies), individual. Finances: Membership: Collective members: $2, United States; individual, $5, United States. Meetings: Triennially, various locations. Publications: Psychotherapy and Psychosomatics, 6 times annually.

★ 991 ★

INTERNATIONAL FEDERATION OF ANTI-LEPROSY
    ASSOCIATIONS (ILEP)
234 Blythe Road   Telex 894241 ILEPCB
GB - London W14 OHJ, England   (01) 602-6925
    United Kingdom   Established 1966

Pierre Van den Wijngaert, General Secretary
The aims of the Federation are to foster the campaign against leprosy in the world, medically and scientifically, and on the social and humanitarian planes. It carries out these aims by encouraging the coordination of leprosy activities and cooperation between its members, while recognizing their autonomy in accordance with their own individuality. It pursues these aims without regard to political, religious, social or other grounds. Membership: 25 non-governmental associations (full members and associate members). Finances: Membership: £ 400; Other Sources: Gifts. Research Funds: More than 5% of the grants distributed by the member-organizations are for research in leprosy. Meetings: Semiannual, various locations. Publications: ILEP Flash, variable; Coordinate Budgets, 3 times annually; Analytic and Financial Directory, annually; all edited by The Coordinating Bureau.

★ 992 ★
INTERNATIONAL FEDERATION OF CATHOLIC
    PHARMACISTS (F.I.P.C.)
59, Bergstrasse   (087) 55 20 54
B-4700 Eupen, Belgium

Manfred Schunck, Secretary-General
To uphold the principles of Catholic faith and morality
as related to the profession and practice of pharmacy.
Membership: All members of national Catholic Guilds
throughout the world.   Meetings: Biennial, various
locations.   Publications: F.I.P.C. Acta, quarterly;
Cahier Albert le Grand; Albertus Magnus Blaetter.

★ 993 ★
INTERNATIONAL FEDERATION OF CLINICAL
    CHEMISTRY
Department of Clinical Chemistry
Karolinska Sjukhuset   (08) 736 1943
S-10401 Stockholm 60, Sweden   Established 1952

A. Kallner, Secretary
To advance the science and practice of clinical chemistry and to enhance its service to health and medicine.   Membership: 42 national societies.   Finances: Dues, private contributions.   Awards: Awards
to distinguished clinical chemists.   Meetings: Every
3 years, various locations; executive board, semiannual, various locations.   Publications: Newsletter,
irregularly, Dr. J. G. Lines, editor; IFCC pages in
Clinica Chimica Acta.

★ 994 ★
INTERNATIONAL FEDERATION OF DISABLED
    WORKMEN AND CIVILIAN CRIPPLES
Amthausquai 11   (062) 211037
CH-4600 Olten, Switzerland   Established 1963

Dr. Manfred Fink, President
To bring together representatives of disabled workmen
and civilian cripples; to promote medical and vocational rehabilitation and employment for the disabled.
Membership: 16 national organizations.   Finances:
Contributions.   Meetings: Biennial, various locations.   Publications: Bulletin, quarterly; Newsletter; Proceedings.

★ 995 ★
INTERNATIONAL FEDERATION OF GYNECOLOGY
    AND OBSTETRICS
27 Sussex Place, Regent's Park
London NW1 4RG, England
    United Kingdom   (01) 723-2951
                                    Established 1954

J. S. Tomkinson, Secretary-General
To promote the development of science and assist in
scientific research work relating to all the fields pertaining to gynecology and obstetrics; to further the
attainment, by all appropriate means, of a higher
level of physical and mental health of women, mothers
and their children; to develop and improve the exchange of information and ideas in this field; to contribute to the research of fresh knowledge in this field;
to contribute to the improvement of teaching standards
in the profession; to promote international cooperation and facilitate relationships between national
bodies of the profession.   Membership: 83 constituent
national societies.   Finances: Membership: Constituent societies pay $1.25 per active member, an-
nually.   Meetings: World Congress, triennial, various continents; Executive Board, annual.   Publication: International Journal of Gynecology and Obstetrics, bimonthly, H. A. Kaminetzky, editor.

★ 996 ★
INTERNATIONAL FEDERATION OF HEALTH
    PROFESSIONALS
8 West 40th Street   (212) 689-7040
New York, New York 10018

Vincent A. Delman, D.D.S., President
Created in response to a need for protection of the
professional individual (in the health field) and the
public since the introduction of third and fourth party
involvement.   Membership: 3,500 (physicians, dentists, podiatrists, optometrists, paraprofessionals).
Finances: Membership: $125 annually.   Meetings:
Biennial, New York City.   Affiliations: ILA;
AFL-CIO.

★ 997 ★
INTERNATIONAL FEDERATION OF MEDICAL
    STUDENTS ASSOCIATIONS
Liechtensteinstrasse 13   (0222) 31 55 66
A-1090 Vienna, Austria   Established 1951

Gunter Schultes, Secretary-General
To be a forum for medical students throughout the
world to discuss topics of interest to themselves and
to formulate policies arising from such discussions; to
act as a means whereby medical student professional
exchange program can be carried out; to be the body
through which contacts with other worldwide organizations are made; to act as a means by which member associations can exert influence in fund raising
activities for IFMSA recognized projects and contact
other medical student associations throughout the
world.   Membership: 29 full member associations,
36 corresponding member associations (National

Medical Students Associations). <u>Finances:</u> Membership: Associations, less developed countries approximately 200, SFR; developed countries, approximately 600, SFR. <u>Meetings:</u> General Assembly, annual, various locations; Technical meetings (on Medical Education, Population Activities, Professional Exchange, Environment). <u>Publications:</u> IFMSA-Information Service, monthly; Intermedica, annual; Medical Student How to go Abroad, annual.

★ 998 ★
INTERNATIONAL FEDERATION OF MULTIPLE
    SCLEROSIS SOCIETIES
Stubenring 6   (0222) 52 88 64
A-1010 Vienna, Austria   Established 1968

Sidney Lamont O'Donoghue, Secretary-General
To coordinate and further the work of national multiple sclerosis organizations throughout the world; to stimulate and encourage scientific research respecting multiple sclerosis and related neurological diseases; to aid individuals who are in any way disabled as a result of multiple sclerosis and related diseases; to collect and disseminate scientific and educational information relating to multiple sclerosis. <u>Membership:</u> 21 societies; 3 affiliated medical groups (National Multiple Sclerosis Societies). <u>Finances:</u> Dues, contributions, donations. <u>Awards:</u> Charcot Award. <u>Meetings:</u> Annual, various locations. <u>Publications:</u> Newssheet, quarterly, S. L. O'Donoghue; Annual Report; Working manuals of various types.

★ 999 ★
INTERNATIONAL FEDERATION OF
    OPHTHALMOLOGICAL SOCIETIES
15 Philips van Leyden   (080) 513138
Nijmegen, The Netherlands

Professor A. F. Deutman, Secretary-General
To promote the science of ophthalmology among all peoples and nations, and in furtherance of this, to ensure permanent cooperation between representative ophthalmological societies of different countries and with their governments and the various international bodies concerned with the organization of educational, scientific and cultural matters. <u>Membership:</u> 80 Societies. <u>Finances:</u> Membership: 50 Swiss francs. <u>Medals and Awards:</u> Gonin Medal; Sir Stewart Duke-Elder Medal. <u>Meetings:</u> Every 4 years, various international locations. <u>Publications:</u> Concilium Ophthalmologicium, every 4 years; ACTA, P. Henkind, editor (1982). <u>Affiliation:</u> WHO, Geneva, Switzerland.

★ 1000 ★
INTERNATIONAL FEDERATION OF PHYSICAL
    EDUCATION
c/o Dr. Pierre Seurin
F-65240 Arreau, France   Established 1923

Dr. P. Seurin, President
To encourage the development of activities concerned with movement, sport and the outdoors in all countries and to contribute to international cooperation in this field; to provide a means of communication and contact between physical educational organizations in various countries. <u>Membership:</u> 90 countries. <u>Finances:</u> Membership: Individual, $12; collective, $20. <u>Meetings:</u> Periodically, various locations. <u>Publications:</u> FIEP Bulletin, quarterly, published in English, French, Spanish and Portuguese.

★ 1001 ★
INTERNATIONAL FEDERATION OF PHYSICAL
    MEDICINE AND REHABILITATION
"Zonhove", Nieuwstraat 70   1241
Son (NB1), The Netherlands   Established 1952

Dr. A. P. M. van Gestel, Secretary-General
To advance all aspects of Physical Medicine and Rehabilitation by the linking on an international level of existing local societies of physical medicine and rehabilitation; the organization of International Congresses every 4 years; the collection and exchange of information between members of the Federation. <u>Membership:</u> 30 national societies of physical medicine and rehabilitation. <u>Finances:</u> Dues based on total membership of society. <u>Meetings:</u> Every 4 years, various locations.

★ 1002 ★
INTERNATIONAL FEDERATION OF SOCIETIES FOR
    ELECTROENCEPHALOGRAPHY AND CLINICAL
    NEUROPHYSIOLOGY
Nebraska Psychiatric Institute
602 South 44th Avenue   (402) 541-4509
Omaha, Nebraska 68105   Established 1949

Robert J. Ellingson, Secretary
A confederation of some 41 national organizations which supports and arranges periodic international congresses and disseminates information on research progress in the fields of its major interest. Sponsors courses in electroencephalography and fosters research, investigation and demonstrations in the field. <u>Membership:</u> Consists of memberships of the national societies which comprise it. <u>Finances:</u> Based upon membership size of constituent societies and journal subscriptions. <u>Meetings:</u> International congress

every 4 years, various locations. Publication: Electroencephalography and Clinical Neurophysiology. Affiliations: Maintains liaison with International Brain Research Organization; World Federation of Neurology; CIOMS.

★ 1003 ★
INTERNATIONAL FEDERATION OF SOCIETIES FOR
    HISTOCHEMISTRY AND CYTOCHEMISTRY
Department of Anatomy
Kyoto University
Faculty of Medicine
Yoshida, Sakyoku   (075) 751-7727
Kyoto 606, Japan   Established 1960

Kazuo Ogawa, Secretary-General
It shall be the task of the IFSHC to promote communication and co-operation among scientists throughout the world who are interested in these fields of study. In support of these aims, the IFSHC will arrange International Congresses to provide a forum for scientists interested in histo- and cytochemistry. Membership: 18 (national societies). Finances: Membership: Annual dues (from Class I, $100 United States to Class IV, $250 United States) from national societies. Grants: 1 annually for young histochemists not older than 32 years to attend the International Congress. Meetings: International Congress, every 4 years, various locations. Publications: Histochemical Journals published in respective countries such as: J. Histochem Cytochem, monthly, P. J. Anderson, editor; Histochemistry, 18 issues annually, T. H. Schiebler, editor; Histochemical J., bimonthly, P. J. Stoward, editor; ACTA Histochem. Cytochem, bimonthly, K. Ogawa, editor; Proceedings of the International Congress, every 4 years. Former Name: International Committee for Histochemistry and Cytochemistry.

★ 1004 ★
INTERNATIONAL FEDERATION OF SPORTS
    MEDICINE
c/o Allan J. Ryan, M.D.
5800 Jeff Place   (612) 922-0156
Edina, Minnesota 55436   Established 1928

Allan J. Ryan, M.D., Secretary-General
To encourage education and research in the applications of exercise and sports to health and physical fitness. Affiliated with international olympic committee, United Nations cultural and scientific organization, international council on physical education and sport. Membership: 55 Member National Associations and individual (honorary, full, associate, and collegiate members). Meetings: Council of

Delegates on member associations, meets semiannually; General Congress, quadrennial. Publications: The Journal of Sports Medicine and Physical Fitness, quarterly, G. LaCava, M.D., editor.

★ 1005 ★
INTERNATIONAL FEDERATION OF SURGICAL
    COLLEGES
Royal College of Surgeons of Edinburgh
18 Nicolson Street
Edinburgh EH8 9DW, Scotland   (031) 667-0865
    United Kingdom   Established 1957

Johnathan E. Rhoads, President
Activities include open discussions on surgical topics, and defining and maintaining standards for the training of surgeons. The Federation encourages the interchange of young surgeons between countries and give support to World Health Organization and allied bodies. Membership: 42 national surgical colleges and and associations. Finances: Membership: $30 per member of each association. Meetings: Annual meeting, various locations. Publications: News Bulletin, John Cook, Honorary Secretary, editor; reports from symposia. Affiliations: International Society for Burn Injuries; World Federation of Neurosurgeons; Societe Internationale de Chirurgie; International Cardiovascular Society; SICOT; World Federation of Pediatric Surgeons; The Medical Commission on Accident Prevention; Societe Internationale d'Urologie; International Federation of Otorhinolaryngological Societies.

★ 1006 ★
INTERNATIONAL FEDERATION OF THE TEMPERANCE
    BLUE CROSS SOCIETIES
Kermély, 10   (022) 47 20 88
CH-1206 Geneva, Switzerland   Established 1877

Jean-Paul A. Widmer, President
To help rescue the victims of alcohol with the help of God; to organize international meetings and keep close touch with other world organizations working in the same field. Membership: 250,000. Finances: Membership: Varies by country; Other Sources: Contributions, fund-raising. Meetings: Conference, every 4 years, various locations; Board, monthly, in Switzerland.

★ 1007 ★

INTERNATIONAL FEDERATION OF THERMALISM
  AND CLIMATISM
Post Office Box 142   (085) 9.01.61
CH-7310 Bad Ragaz, Switzerland   Established 1947

Guy Ebrard, President;
  Dr. U. Lisowsky, Secretary-General
The advancement of theoretical and practical collaboration in the field of balneology and climatology
from scientific, medical, technical, social and economic standpoints. Membership: 26 countries.
Finances: Membership: Dues set each year by convention of delegates. Awards: A fund exists for
scientific research. Meetings: Annual convention
of delegates; and International Congress for Balneology and Climatology, every 4 years.

★ 1008 ★

INTERNATIONAL FEDERATION ON AGING
1909 K Street, N.W., Suite 500   (202) 872-4885
Washington, D.C. 20049   Established 1973

William M. Kerrigan, General Secretary
The Federation seeks to facilitate the transfer and
dissemination of information that has practical application to the problems of the aged.   Their objectives
are to: advance the well-being of the elderly around
the world; provide a world-wide forum for the discussion of problems of aging and preparation for retirement; promote the exchange of information and
experiences among associations of the aging and organizations serving them as well as interested individuals; foster the development of associations that represent or serve the elderly; and facilitate and promote cooperation among international organizations
related to the field of aging. Membership: 52
member organizations from 29 countries. Finances:
Membership: Full, $250; associates, $100; Other
Sources: Sale of publications and the National Retired Teachers Association and Association of Retired
Persons provide additional administrative and logistics
support. Meetings: Executive Board, annual; Membership Conference, biennial. Publications: Ageing,
International, quarterly, Charlotte Nusberg; Home
Help Services for the Ageing Around the World; The
Voluntary Agency as an Instrument of Social Change
on Behalf of the Elderly; Survey of Periodicals in
Geriatrics and Gerontology: An International Di-
rectory; Mandatory Retirement: Blessing or Curse?;
Crime Against the Elderly; Planning for the Aging
in Local Communities: An International Perspective;
Social Services for the Aged, Dying and Bereaved in
International Perspective; Comparative Gerontology:
A Selected Annotated Bibliography.

INTERNATIONAL FOUNDATION FOR CHILDREN'S
HEARING EDUCATION AND RESEARCH
  See: CHEAR

INTERNATIONAL GRENFELL ASSOCIATION
  See: Grenfell Regional Health Services Board

★ 1009 ★

INTERNATIONAL GROUP FOR PHARMACEUTICAL
  DISTRIBUTION IN THE COUNTRIES OF THE
  EUROPEAN COMMUNITY
K. Astridlaan 55
B-3290 Diest, Belgium   Established 1960

D. P. L. Borgeis, Secretary-General
To promote and defend the interests of the pharmaceutical distribution companies in the European community. Membership: 13 national associations.
Finances: Membership: Varies by country. Meetings: Semiannual, various locations.

★ 1010 ★

INTERNATIONAL GUIDING EYES, INC.
Post Office Box 18   (213) 849-5439
North Hollywood,   (213) 845-0203
  California 91603   Established 1948

To provide scientifically trained guide dogs to the
blind free of any charge whatsoever. A sightless
persons, 16 years of age or older, regardless of
nationality, color or religion, may make application
for training providing he or she desires, needs and
can use a Dog Guide. Finances: Other Sources:
Voluntary contributions.

★ 1011 ★

INTERNATIONAL GUILD DISPENSING OPTICIANS
1250 Connecticut Avenue, N.W.
Washington, D.C. 20036   Established 1951

Peter Lancaster, Secretary
The Guild aims to provide dispensing opticians in all
countries with the opportunity of exchanging information about their profession and to enhance their status
in every way, and to ensure to the public and the
medical profession the supply of skilled and competent dispensing opticians. Activities include biennial convention, issuing of Directory of Members,
giving advice to organizations and legislatures on
matters relating to the supply and fitting of optical
appliances. Membership: 5 National Associations

(representing established groups of dispensing opticians) covering member firms. Finances: Membership: $1 for each address of a National Association member. Meetings: Biennial Convention and council meetings, America, Britain. Affiliations: Guild of British Dispensing Opticians, Limited; Guild of Dispensing Opticians (Australia) Limited; Guild of Irish Dispensing Opticians; Guild of Prescription Opticians of Canada, Limited; Opticians Association of America, Inc.

★ 1012 ★
INTERNATIONAL HEALTH FOUNDATION
8 avenue Don Bosco   (02) 771-9598
B-1150 Brussels, Belgium   Established 1969

P. A. van Keep, M.D.
The Foundation aims to contribute to a better understanding of possibilities and problems concerning today's health by doing studies in the medical/sociological field, by facilitating communications between experts, and by distributing information to everyone who might be interested. In practice they limit their scope at present to problems of aging, all aspects of the menstrual cycle and contraception. Finances: Legs, donations, research contracts and fees. Publication: IHF News, 3 times annually; congress and workshop reports.

★ 1013 ★
INTERNATIONAL HEALTH SOCIETY, INC.
c/o Franklin L. Bowling, M.D., M.P.H.
1001 East Oxford Lane
Cherry Hills Village
Englewood, Colorado 80110   (303) 789-3003
                             Established 1944

Franklin L. Bowling, M.D., M.P.H., Secretary-
    Treasurer
To bring together individuals who have the interest in and capability of promoting international health. The Society is an internationally recognized educational organization dedicated to the continuing education of physicians and all other health science professionals, worldwide. This non-profit, non-political and non-sectarian organization works toward the improvement of the health of all the people. Membership: 500 (regular, life, emeritus, honorary for M.D.'s, Ph.D.'s, R.N.'s, and other scientifically trained persons interested in public health). Finances: Membership: Regular, $20; honorary depends upon age; emeritus, free after 10 years membership and age 65, honorary, free; Other Sources: Dues, CME courses, donations, grants for CME. Meetings: Annual Scientific Assembly in the United States. Publications: Quarterly Bulletin, quarterly, Franklin L.

Bowling, editor. Affiliation: Continued affiliation with APHA. Periodic affiliation with other organizations during co-sponsorship; ACME programs.

★ 1014 ★
INTERNATIONAL HOSPITAL FEDERATION
Headquarters: (01) 267-5176
126 Albert Street   Established 1947
London NW1 7NX, England, United Kingdom
U.S. Office:
444 North Capitol Street, N.W., Suite 500
Washington, D.C. 20001   (202) 638-1100

Allen J. Manzano, Director;
    Jose Gonzales, M.D., Secretary
Maintains an Information Service for members on hospital and health service matters; offers advice and assistance to members; organizes a Study Tour biennially to give members first-hand knowledge of hospital work in different countries; offers courses in hospital and health service administration; and sponsors projects on different aspects of hospital and health services. Membership: 2,000 plus (membership is divided into 4 main classes: 'A' members, which are national hospital and health service organizations; 'B' members, which are other organizations, associations and institutions directly concerned with hospitals and health services; 'C' members, who are individuals from all disciplines concerned with health services; 'D' members, which are professional firms or commercial or industrial companies involved in health services. The combined membership forms the General Assembly of the Federation). Finances: Membership: $40 to $2,750 according to membership category. Meetings: General Assembly, every second year during a Congress; Regional and Special Conferences, 5 to 10 a year, various locations around the world. Publications: World Hospitals, quarterly, Leslie Paine, editor.

★ 1015 ★
INTERNATIONAL INSTITUTE FOR BIOENERGETIC
    ANALYSIS
144 East 36th Street, #1A   (212) 532-7742
New York, New York 10016   Established 1956

Alexander Lowen, M.D., Executive Director
To promote research and education in the fields of emotional and physical health; to coordinate and further projects which relate the findings of psychoanalysis to a knowledge of the energy principles applicable to biological structure and function. Activities include public lectures, clinical seminars, and clinical workshops. Membership: 750 (active, associate, supporting, honorary); membership includes

psychiatrists, M.D.'s, social workers, nurses, psychologists, dentists and others who work with the human body or mental diseases). Finances: Membership: Supporting, $10; associate, $25; active, $50; Other Sources: Public lectures, contributions, workshops. Meetings: Monthly, New York City. Publications: Books and pamphlets on bioenergetics. Former Name: Institute for Bio-Energetic Analysis.

INTERNATIONAL INSTITUTE FOR MENTAL
HEALTH RESEARCH
    See: American Mental Health Foundation, Inc.

INTERNATIONAL INSTITUTE OF MEDICAL
SOPHROLOGY
    See: International Sophrology Institute

★ 1016 ★
INTERNATIONAL LEAGUE AGAINST RHEUMATISM
Executive Secretariat
Post Office Box 145
CH-4011 Basle, Switzerland   Established 1927

H. Stulz, Executive Secretary
To promote international cooperation for the study, control, and treatment of rheumatic diseases. Membership: Approximately 8,000 (3 Regional Leagues and 62 National Leagues). Finances: Membership dues. Meetings: Every 4 years, various locations.

★ 1017 ★
INTERNATIONAL LEAGUE OF DERMATOLOGICAL
    SOCIETIES
Department of Dermatology
Karolinska Sjukhuset
S-104 01 Stockholm 60, Sweden   Established 1952

Professor Nils Thyresson, M.D., Secretary-
    General Treasurer
The International League of Dermatological Societies (I.L.D.S.) is an association of national and international dermatology societies. The aims of the League are: to stimulate the cooperation of societies of dermatology or within in the field of dermatology throughout the world; to encourage the advancement of dermatology and dermatologic sciences and education; to promote personal and professional relations among the dermatologists of the world; to represent dermatology in other international organizations; to hold a world congress of dermatology every 5 years and to sponsor additional international activities.

Membership: Approximately 12,000. Finances: Membership: Society pays $.60 per member. Meetings: Every 5 years, various locations.

★ 1018 ★
INTERNATIONAL LEAGUE OF SOCIETIES FOR
    THE MENTALLY HANDICAPPED
13 rue Forestiere   (02) 647 6180
B-1050 Brussels, Belgium   Established 1960

To advance the interests of the mentally handicapped without regard to nationality, race or creed; to secure on their behalf from all possible sources the provision of efficient remedial, residential, educational training, employment and welfare services. Membership: 80 associations (full, affiliate, subscribing). Finances: Membership: Dues based on membership; Other Sources: Donations. Awards: ILSMH International Award. Meetings: Congress, every 4 years; Assembly, biennially, various locations. Publications: News, variable, Rosemary Dybwad, editor; Congress proceedings; reports and conclusions of symposia (list available upon request).

★ 1019 ★
INTERNATIONAL LEPROSY ASSOCIATION
16 Bridgefield Road
Sutton, Surrey SM1 2DG, England (01) 642 1656
    United Kingdom   Established 1931

Dr. S. G. Browne, Secretary
The Association encourages and facilitates collaboration between persons of all nationalities concerned in leprosy work, coordinates their efforts, and spreads knowledge of leprosy and its control. Membership: 500 in 70 countries (regular and sustaining). Finances: Membership: $40. Meetings: Congress every 5 years, various locations. Publications: International Journal of Leprosy and other Mycobacterial Diseases, quarterly. Affiliations: Founder member of Council for International Organizations of Medical Sciences; World Health Organization.

★ 1020 ★
INTERNATIONAL MEDICAL AND RESEARCH
    FOUNDATION
833 United Nations Plaza   (212) 949-6421
New York, New York 10017   Established 1956

Dr. Michael S. Gerber, Executive Director
The purpose of the Foundation is to support, engage in, and promote health delivery, surgical services, and research in Africa and to apply the knowledge

therefrom to the causes and prevention of human diseases. Program areas include health education, training of health auxiliaries, mobile medical teams and Flying Doctors Services, research, and two-way medical radio communications. Membership: 10 member organizations (affiliated foundations in Kenya, Tanzania, United Kingdom, Germany, Holland, Denmark, Sweden, Canada, France, United States). Finances: Other Sources: Project funding from governments, foundations, corporations, individuals. Meetings: Annual Board Meeting, Annual International Board Meeting, Executive Committee meets at regular intervals. Publications: Defender, quarterly; AFYA, 6 times annually; Rural Health Manuals on: Child Health, Diagnostic Pathways in Clinical Medicine, Health Education, Obstetric Emergencies, Pharmacology and Therapeutics, Mental Health, Design for Medical Buildings, Immunology Simplified, Communicable Diseases, The Hand, Epidermiology in Community Health. Former Name: African Medical and Research Foundation.

★ 1021 ★
INTERNATIONAL MEDICAL SOCIETY OF
    PARAPLEGIA
c/o Dr. H. L. Frankel
National Spinal Injuries Centre
Stoke Mandeville Hospital
Aylesbury, Bucks, England   (0296) 84111
    United Kingdom   Established 1962

Professor V. Paeslack, President
    H. L. Frankel, Honorary Secretary
To link specialists in different countries who are interested in the study and treatment of spinal cord lesions. Meetings: Annual, various locations. Publications: Paraplegia.

★ 1022 ★
INTERNATIONAL MYOMASSETHICS FEDERATION,
    INC.
c/o Morton E. Bissell, M.T.
196 West Main Street   (216) 767-3297
Brewster, Ohio 44613   Established 1971

Morton E. Bissell, M.T., President
The Federation was founded in response to a need for teaching more aspects and methods of therapeutic massage. It is composed of affiliating state associations and members at large. States have one local seminar annually at which they unite to study and promote the natural healing arts. Membership: 350 (active, retired, student, associate, auxiliary, meritorious and honorary). Finances: $8; Other Sources: Donations for pins and decals; profits of

annual meetings. Awards: Meritorious Service Awards. Meetings: Annual, various locations. Publications: IntraMyomassethics Forum, bimonthly, Dorothy Westphal, editor; Membership Roster, annually, Veva Hicks, editor; Convention Book, annually. Affiliations: 10 State associations.

★ 1023 ★
INTERNATIONAL NARCOTICS CONTROL BOARD
Vienna International Centre   (0222) 34-60-11
A-1400 Vienna, Austria   Established 1968

A. Bahi, Secretary
The Board is entrusted with the overall supervision of the national implementation of the existing drug control treaties throughout the world. Membership: 13. Finances: United Nations Budget. Meetings: Semiannual, Vienna, Austria. Publications: Annual reports on activities, statistics and estimates.

★ 1024 ★
INTERNATIONAL NARCOTIC ENFORCEMENT
    OFFICERS ASSOCIATION
112 State Street, Suite 1310   (518) 463-6232
Albany, New York 12207   Established 1960

John J. Bellizzi, Executive Director
To promote and foster mutual interest in the problems of narcotic control; to provide a medium for the exchange of ideas; to conduct seminars, conferences, and study groups; and to issue publications. Membership: 7,500. Finances: Membership: $15; Other Sources: Contributions. Awards: Honor Award to persons supporting narcotic enforcement. Meetings: Annual, various locations. Publications: International Drug Report, monthly, Celeste Morga, editor; Proceedings of Annual Conference; Directory of Membership, annual.

★ 1025 ★
INTERNATIONAL NATURIST FEDERATION
St. Thomasstraat 24   (031) 391287
B-2000 Antwerp, Belgium   Established 1953

R. Lambrechts, Secretary
The aim of INF and its national associations is health combined with sports. In support of this aim the organizations represented by INF will tolerate, promote, or practice, as far as circumstances permit, mixed nude bathing in air, water, and sunshine for the purpose of improving physical, mental, and moral health. In addition the Federation (1) opposes the misuse of alcohol and tobacco; (2) advocates the

suppression of pornography;   (3) favors the extension
of naturist ideas throughout the world;   (4) facilitates
and coordinates the naturist activities of affiliated
organizations;   (5) collects and issues accurate information regarding naturism;   (6) organizes periodical
gatherings of naturists of different countries;   (7) facilitates mutual visits to naturist camps abroad;   (8)
aids in the creation of naturist groups throughout the
world and the foundation of camps for naturism;   (9)
furnishes legal protection to naturists in lawsuits concerning naturism;   (10) campaigns for recognition of
naturism by public authorities and churches;   and (11)
supports the cultural organizations of the United Nations.   Membership: 250,000 (members of affiliated
naturist federations in 22 countries;   individual members in 30 countries).   Finances: Federations S.Fr.
0.60 per member plus S.Fr. 2.00 per naturist club;
individual members S.Fr. 12.00 (one person), S.Fr.
25.00 (couple);   Other Sources: Sale of INF Camp
Guide, donations.   Awards: Special fund for INF
Literary Prize.   Meetings: World Congress, biennially, various locations.   Publications: Press Bulletin, bimonthly, Karl Dressen, editor;   INF Guide,
biennial;   Naturist Holiday Centres;   Naturism and
Sport;   Naturism and Sexuality.

INTERNATIONAL NATUROPATHIC ASSOCIATION,
INC.
    See: International Society of Preventive Medicine,
        Inc.

★ 1026 ★
INTERNATIONAL ORGANIZATION FOR MEDICAL
    PHYSICS
c/o Dr. R. E. Walstam
Department of Radiation Physics
Post Office Box 60204   (08) 736 1359
S-104 01 Stockholm, Sweden   Established 1963

Dr. R. E. Walstam, Secretary-General
To organize international cooperation in medical physics;   to promote communication between the various
branches of medical physics and allied subjects.
Membership: 22 national groups.   Meetings: Triennial, various locations.   Affiliations: International
Organization for Pure and Applied Biophysics.

★ 1027 ★
INTERNATIONAL ORGANIZATION FOR THE STUDY
    OF HUMAN DEVELOPMENT
c/o Dwain Walcher, M.D.
1330 West Michigan Street   (317) 633-8481
Indianapolis, Indiana 46206   Established 1969

Dwain N. Walcher, M.D., Executive Secretary-
    Treasurer
The International Organization for the Study of Human
Development was established to promote and facilitate,
on an international basis, the interdisciplinary study
of human development over the entire life cycle.
Membership: 100 (M.D.;   Ph.D.;   Biology;   Behavioural Sciences).   Finances: Contributions.   Meetings: Biennial, USA or Europe.   Publications:
Papers and congress proceedings.

★ 1028 ★
INTERNATIONAL ORGANIZATION OF ALLERGOL-
    OGY AND CLINICAL IMMUNOLOGY
350 Sparks Street, Suite 602
Ottawa, Ontario K1R 7S8,   (613) 238-8120
    Canada   Established 1951

R. W. Neal, Executive Secretary
To advance the knowledge of allergy and of related
field;   to foster the dissemination of this knowledge
through international congresses and by other means.
Membership: 6,430 from 38 national member societies.
Finances: Membership: 2.50 Swiss francs;   Other
Sources: Congress fees, contributions from pharmaceutical firms.   Meetings: Triennially, various locations.   Publications: Proceeding of Congress, triennial.   Former Name: International Association
of Allergology.

★ 1029 ★
INTERNATIONAL PARENTS' ORGANIZATION (OF
    THE ALEXANDER GRAHAM BELL ASSOCIATION
    FOR THE DEAF)
3417 Volta Place, N.W.   (202) 337-5220
Washington, D.C. 20007   Established 1958

Peter Illing, Executive Chairperson
The International Parents' Organization, the parents'
section of The Alexander Graham Bell Association (see
separate entry) enables parents of hearing-impaired
children to speak with unified strength.   Through its
central office in Washington, D.C., IPO serves as a
clearinghouse for the exchange of ideas, coordinates
the efforts of parents with those of professionals who
deal with hearing-impaired children, and spearheads
action in such areas of national interest and concern
as parent surveys, scholarships, public information
projects, and legislative action.   IPO not only assists
groups of parents to organize and function locally,
but also arranges special sessions for parents at regional and national meetings of the Alexander Graham
Bell Association.   In this way, parents exchange
ideas and experiences and learn of new training techniques and resources from the professionals who meet

with them.   A primary concern of all IPO affiliated
groups is continuing parent and public education regarding the necessity of early diagnosis, auditory
training, and language and speech training for the
hearing-impaired child.   Through its support of local
groups, IPO offers to the parents of hearing-impaired
children the opportunity to participate in concentrated
and coordinated efforts that are of both immediate and
ultimate benefit to their own child, themselves, and
hearing-impaired children throughout the world.
Membership: 14,000 parents in affiliated groups
(group membership in IPO includes a group membership in the Bell Association).   Finances: Membership: Annual dues of $40 per group;   Other Sources:
Donations.   Awards: Honors Award, semiannually
to an outstanding parent of a deaf child; Scholarship
Award of $250 annually for oral deaf student at regu-
lar college.   Meetings: Biennially, at Bell Association convention.   Publications: IPO News Briefs,
quarterly, Virginia Gilmer, editor.

★ 1030 ★
INTERNATIONAL PEDIATRIC ASSOCIATION
Secretariat:
Château de Longchamp
Bois de Boulogne   (01) 772.15.90
F-75016 Paris, France   Established 1910

Professor Ihsan Dogramaci, Director General
To promote the friendship between pediatricians of all
countries for the benefit of children everywhere; to
promote the child health throughout the world; to
organize seminars, symposia and conference on topics
of interest to pediatricians; to encourage regional
and international scientific meetings of pediatricians;
to hold a triennial international congress of pediatrics
for its members; to encourage pediatric research; to
promote the dissemination of pediatric knowledge.
Membership: 91 members (89 active members); members are National Pediatric Societies whose combined
memberships exceed 56,000); Member societies: National Pediatric Societies; Affiliate socities: International Societies of Pediatric Specialties and Regional
Pediatric Societies.   Finances: Membership: 2 Swiss
francs per member based on total membership at the
end of the preceding year; Other Sources: Contributions and an assessment for participants in the international congresses.   Medals: Medal for oustanding
contributions to pediatrics.   Meetings: Triennial
international pediatric congresses, 1983 in Manila.
Publications: Bulletin of the I.P.A., quarterly, Professor I. Dogramaci, editor; Proceedings of the international congresses, triennially.

★ 1031 ★
INTERNATIONAL PHARMACEUTICAL FEDERATION
(F.I.P.)
11, Alexanderstraat
2514 JL The Hague,   (070) 631925
The Netherlands   Established 1912

A. Bédat, President; L. G. Félix-Faure, Administrative Director; J. M. H. A. Martens, General
Secretary
The development of pharmacy at international level
both in the professional and in the scientific fields
and the extension of the role of the pharmacist in the
field of health care.   Activities include organizing
congresses, development of activities of specialized
sections, collaboration with the World Health Organization, publication of a journal.   Membership: 60
national associations (ordinary members), 103 companies, colleges, etc. (associate collective members),
3,500 individuals (associate members);   pharmaceutical associations representing pharmacy in the broadest
sense, companies, schools of pharmacy, libraries,
individual pharmacists.   Medal: Høst-Madsen Medal;
awarded biennially.   Meetings: Annual, various
locations; 1981 Vienna (Austria); 1982 Copenhagen
(Denmark).   Publications: Pharmacy International
(with Elsevier North Holland), monthly, Professor F.
Merkus, editor; F.I.P. Bulletin (as supplement to the
above), monthly, L. Félix-Faure, editor.

★ 1032 ★
INTERNATIONAL PLANNED PARENTHOOD
   FEDERATION
18-20 Lower Regent Street
London SW1Y 4PW, England   (01) 839-2911
   United Kingdom   Established 1952

Carl Wahren, Secretary-General
Aims are based on the belief that knowledge of family planning is a basic human right and that a balance
between the population of the world and its natural
resources and productivity is a necessary condition of
human happiness, prosperity and peace.   Encourages
the formation of national family planning associations
to pioneer family planning services in each country of
the world and to bring about a favorable climate of
public opinion in which governments can be persuaded
to accept responsibility; helps FPA's offer contraceptive services, set and maintain high clinical standards
and train all levels of personnel; promotes population
and sex education and marriage counseling; and
stimulates research in the fields of biology, demogra-
phy, sociology, economics, human reproduction and
sex education.   Membership: 95 National Associations.   Finances: Contributions from foundations,
individuals, government grants.   Publications: People,
quarterly; Medical Bulletin, bimonthly; Research in

Reproduction, quarterly; IPPF Co-operative Information Bulletin, quarterly; IPPF in Action, annual; conference proceedings; manuals; case studies; medical, legal, educational and information publications and materials. Library: IPPF Central Office Library, 7,000 volumes; 20,000 reports; 350 periodicals.

★ 1033 ★
INTERNATIONAL PRIMATOLOGICAL SOCIETY
Brown University
Department of Psychology (401) 863-2727
Providence, Rhode Island 02912   Established 1966

Dr. Allan Schrier, Secretary-General
To encourage all areas of primate research and to facilitate cooperations between workers of all nationalities who are engaged in such research; also to intercede for the preservation and protection of primates. Membership: 750. Finances: Membership: $5. Meetings: Biennial, various locations.

★ 1034 ★
INTERNATIONAL RESCUE AND EMERGENCY CARE ASSOCIATION
8107 Ensign Curve (612) 941-2926
Bloomington, Minnesota 55438   Established 1948

Executive Director
An international organization with worldwide goals. Constantly working for the improvement of standards and techniques, with wide dissemination of information to rescue and emergency medical care personnel. Membership: 1,500 (individual, family, unit, association). Finances: Membership: Individual, $15; family, $40; unit, $50; association, $100. Meetings: Annual, various locations in United States and Canada. Publication: Rescuer, quarterly, Executive Director. Affiliation: All rescue and emergency care associations. Former Name: International Rescue and First Aid Association.

INTERNATIONAL RESCUE AND FIRST AID ASSOCIATION
See: International Rescue and Emergency Care Association

★ 1035 ★
INTERNATIONAL RORSCHACH SOCIETY
c/o Professor A. Friedemann
Chemical des Pecheurs 6 (032) 27889
CH-2503 Biel-Bienne, Switzerland   Established 1949

Professor Dr. med. A. Friedemann, Chairman
To develop international contacts between Rorschach specialists and other interested individuals; to promote theoretical and practical knowledge of Rorschach and other projective techniques. Membership: About 400. Meetings: Every 3 or 4 years, various locations. Publications: Rorschachiana Communications, Verlag Hans Huber, editor. Former Name: International Society for Rorschach Research.

★ 1036 ★
INTERNATIONAL SOCIETY AND FEDERATION OF CARDIOLOGY
34, rue de l'Athénée
Post Office Box 117 (022) 476755
CH-1211 Geneva 12, Switzerland   Established 1978

H. N. Neufeld, M.D., President
To stimulate development of cardiology, improve scientific exchanges and contribute to scientific development of members. Activities include organizing scientific and professional meetings, organizing and promoting world congresses every 4 years. Membership: 60 National Members. Finances: Fees of National Members vary. Publications: Heartbeat, quarterly. Affiliations: National Societies and Foundations; Continental and Individual Members.

★ 1037 ★
INTERNATIONAL SOCIETY FOR AUTISTIC CHILDREN
1A Golders Green Road
London NW11 8EA, England,
United Kingdom   Established 1972

Monica White, General Secretary
To stimulate understanding of the problems of autism; to exchange information; to keep individual member organizations in touch with research and developments in the field. Meetings: Every 4 years. Publications: Communication, quarterly; International Newsletter, biennial.

★ 1038 ★
INTERNATIONAL SOCIETY FOR BURN INJURIES
4200 East Ninth Avenue
Box C 309
Denver, Colorado 80262   Established 1965

John A. Boswick, Jr., M.D., General Secretary
To disseminate knowledge and to stimulate prevention
in the fields of burns; to promote and coordinate
scientific, clinical and social research in burns; to
promote education in all phases of burn care, including first aid and nursing; to encourage higher standards of care in all countries and to make available
active help where needed by whatsoever means are
possible; to encourage co-operation among all countries by sharing available information in all ways possible. Membership: 1,200 (members, associate,
friends). Finances: Membership: 20 Swiss francs
annually. Meetings: International Congress, every
4 years, various locations; Regional seminars held
periodically.

★ 1039 ★
INTERNATIONAL SOCIETY FOR CLINICAL
    LABORATORY TECHNOLOGY
818 Olive Street, Suite 918   (314) 241-1445
St. Louis, Missouri 63101   Established 1962

David Birenbaum, Administrator
ISCLT is a professional society dedicated to serving
the needs of allied health professionals working in the
clinical laboratory field. Laboratorians look to the
ISCLT for continuing education opportunities, information about advancements in the field, and a chance
to discuss important issues and ideas with colleagues.
The Society fills these needs through educational programs, publications, meetings, and seminars. In addition, ISCLT closely follows both state and federal
health care activity dealing with the clinical laboratory, and promotes better government understanding
and support of the professions. Membership: 10,000
(medical technologists, laboratory technicians, supervisors, directors). Finances: Membership: $60 reg-
istrant class; $40 regular class. Awards: At least
3 $500 scholarships annually. Meetings: Annual
convention, various locations throughout the United
States. Publications: Newsletter, bimonthly,
Lisa A. Mooradian, editor. Affiliation: Credentialing Commission. Former Name: International
Society of Clinical Laboratory Technologists.

★ 1040 ★
INTERNATIONAL SOCIETY FOR ELECTROSLEEP AND
    ELECTROANAESTHESIA
Chirurgische Universitatsklinik
Auenbruggerplatz
A-8036 Graz, Austria   Established 1966

F. M. Wagender, M.D., President
To exchange ideas and coordinate research in the
areas of cerebral electrotherapy, electroanesthesia and
related subjects. Membership: 200 (medical doctors,
biologists, engineers, bioengineers, physiologists,
psychologists, psychiatrists; corporate members: pharmaceutical and electronics firms). Meetings: Congress every four years. Publications: Information,
quarterly.

★ 1041 ★
INTERNATIONAL SOCIETY FOR HEART RESEARCH
University of Manitoba, Faculty of Medicine
Department of Physiology
770 Bannatyne Avenue
Winnipeg, Manitoba R3E OW3,   (204) 786-3735
    Canada   Established 1967

R. J. Bing, Life President
The Society is devoted to research and education on
heart disease. Membership: 1,250 members interested in heart research. Finances: Membership:
$15 to $30 annually. Award: R. J. Bing Award.
Meetings: Annual, various locations. Publication:
Journal of Molecular and Cellular Cardiology, monthly; Advances in Myocardiology; Proceedings of International Meetings.

★ 1042 ★
INTERNATIONAL SOCIETY FOR HUMAN AND
    ANIMAL MYCOLOGY (ISHAM)
c/o Professor Dr. Wolfgang Loeffler
Gellertstrasse 11a
CH-4052 Basle, Switzerland   Established 1954

Professor Dr. Wolfgang Loeffler, General Secretary
Activities of the Society are concentrated on promoting
medical veterinary and general mycology. International congresses are held at least once in 5 years.
Membership: Individual - 800 from 70 different countries (honorary, emeritus, active, associate) and affiliated organizations, 14. Finances: Membership:
United States, $30 (until 1983). Awards and Medals:
ISHAM Award at International Congresses; The Lucille Georg Medallion. Meetings: International
Congresses at least once in 5 years, different locations. Publications: Sabouraudia, 1 volume annually in 4 parts, F. C. Odds, editor; The ISHAM

Mycoses Newsletter, semiannual, D. W. R. Mackenzie, editor; List of Members, biennial, J. Müller (Zentrum Hygiene Postfach 820, D-7800 Freiburg, West Germany), editor. Remark: The present Council will be in office until February 12, 1982.

★ 1043 ★

INTERNATIONAL SOCIETY FOR PEDIATRIC
    NEUROSURGERY
303 East Chicago Avenue   (312) 649-8143
Chicago, Illinois 60611   Established 1972

Maurice Choux, Secretary
The Society was established to contribute to the advance of pediatric neurosurgery. Its objectives are: (1) to serve as a forum for effective communication among neurosurgeons devoted to paediatric neurosurgery and for communication between paediatric neurosurgeons and basic scientists and specialists in related fields; (2) to serve as a medium for development of scientific knowledge, medical care, rehabilitation and prevention of disease within the area of paediatric neurosurgery; (3) to serve as a workshop to promote active cooperation among members of the Society; and (4) to encourage high standards of training in the specialty at an international level for present or prospective neurosurgeons. Membership: 168 (active, candidate, associate and senior). Finances: Membership: $110 includes subscribing to Child's Brain. Meetings: Annual, various locations. Publications: Child's Brain, bimonthly, Anthony J. Raimondi, M.D., editor.

INTERNATIONAL SOCIETY FOR RORSCHACH
RESEARCH
    See: International Rorschach Society

★ 1044 ★

INTERNATIONAL SOCIETY FOR SKI TRAUMA-
    TOLOGY AND MEDICINE OF WINTER SPORTS
c/o Dr. Med. Klaus Herwig
Chalet Erosen
CH-7050 Arosa, Switzerland

Dr. Med. Klaus Herwig, Secretary-General
Biennial 3-day conference in one of the Alpine countries (Germany, France, Italy, Austria, Switzerland). Next conference April 22, 1982 in Austria.

★ 1045 ★

INTERNATIONAL SOCIETY OF ACUPUNCTURE
86 rue de l'Université   (01) 705.86.61
F-75007 Paris, France   Established 1943

Dr. Jean Schatz, President
To develop knowledge of acupuncture in the world by means of courses (congresses, lectures, etc.). Membership: 1,800 M.D. acupuncturists. Finances: Membership: 400 FF.; Other Sources: Sale of publications. Meetings: Biennial, various locations. Publication: Revue de la Societe Internationale D'Acupuncture, quarterly.

★ 1046 ★

INTERNATIONAL SOCIETY OF ART AND
    PSYCHOPATHOLOGY
SIPE, Clinique de la Faculté
100 rue de la Santé   (01) 589.55 21
F-75014 Paris, France   Established 1959

Dr. Wiart, Secretary-General
Group specialists interested in the problem of expression and artistic activities in relation to psychiatric, sociological and psychological research including the application of methods employed in fields other than those of neurology and mental illness. Membership: Doctors and specialists from other disciplines: anestheticians, critics, artists and writers, psychologists, ethnologists, linguists, criminologists. Individuals (522) in 37 countries. Finances: Membership dues. Meetings: General Assemblies, irregular, various locations. Publication: Confinia Psychiatrica, quarterly, Kargerl Bale, editor. Affiliations: Associate Member of the Council for International Organizations of Medical Sciences; World Psychiatry Association.

★ 1047 ★

INTERNATIONAL SOCIETY OF AUDIOLOGY
330 Gray's Inn Road
London WC1, England   (01) 837.8855
    United Kingdom   Established 1952

Professor Ronald Hinchcliffe, Secretary-General
To promote research into and to disseminate knowledge of hearing disorders. Membership: About 350. Finances: Membership: $59.35 which includes subscription to Journal Audiology. Meetings: Biennial, various locations. Publication: Audiology, bimonthly, E. König, editor.

★ 1048 ★

INTERNATIONAL SOCIETY OF BLOOD
       TRANSFUSION
6 rue Alexandre Cabanel
F-75739 Paris, France   Established 1937

C. Salmon, Secretary-General
To contribute to the solution of scientific, technical,
social and ethical problems related to the transfusion
of blood; to standardize methods and equipment; to
establish closer relations among individuals dealing
with the problem related to the transfusion of blood.
Membership: 1,510 (individuals 1,432; organizations, 78). Meetings: Biennial, various locations.
Publications: Newsletter, quarterly; ISBT Guides,
irregular.

★ 1049 ★

INTERAMERICAN SOCIETY OF CARDIOLOGY
Juan Badiano No. 1   (905) 573-2911
Mexico 22, D.F., Mexico   Established 1946

Dr. M. Cárdenas, Secretary-Treasurer
To stimulate development of cardiology, improve scientific exchanges, contribute to scientific development of members, and establish scholarships for the
purpose of developing specialists in cardiology.
Membership: 24 national socities. Finances: Membership: $2 annually; Other Sources: Subsidies,
donations. Meetings: World Congresses, every 4
years, various locations. Publications: Bulletin of
the ISC, semiannual.

★ 1050 ★

INTERNATIONAL SOCIETY OF CHEMOTHERAPY
c/o Professor Dr. med. H. P. Kuemmerle
Gustav-Adolf-Strasse 6
D-8192 Geretsried, Federal   (08171) 31132
     Republic of Germany   Established 1961

Professor H. P. Kuemmerle, President;
     Professor J. D. Williams, Secretary General
     (United Kingdom)
The Society conducts congresses and symposia on an
international basis; also workshops and awards.
Membership: Approximately 6,500 (national societies
and individual members), and 25,000 corresponding
members. Finances: Membership: Calculated per
unit. Awards: The ISC Award. Publications: International Journal of Clinical Pharmacology, Therapy
and Toxicology. Affiliations: 15 national organizations.

★ 1051 ★

INTERNATIONAL SOCIETY OF CHRONOBIOLOGY
c/o Professor L. E. Scheving, Ph.D.
College of Medicine
University of Arkansas for Medical Sciences
4301 West Markham   (501) 661-5138
Little Rock, Arkansas 72205   Established 1937

Professor Franz Halbert, M.D., President;
     Professor L. E. Scheving, Ph.D., Secretary-
     Treasurer
Aims of the Society are to promote the development
of research in the field, to facilitate contact among
investigators, and to organize international conferences on topics pertaining to the basic and applied
study of temporal parameters of physiologic functions,
i.e., chronobiology. Membership: 575. Finances: Membership: Supporting, $20; regular, $10;
student, $5; Other Sources: Grants. Meetings:
Biennial, various locations. Publications: International Journal of Chronobiology, quarterly, Dr. Hugh
W. Simpson, managing editor; Chronobiologia, quarterly, Dr. F. Carandente, managing editor.

INTERNATIONAL SOCIETY OF CLINICAL
LABORATORY TECHNOLOGISTS
     See: International Society for Clinical Laboratory
          Technology

★ 1052 ★

INTERNATIONAL SOCIETY OF CLINICAL
       PHARMACOLOGY
c/o Professor Dr. med. H. P. Kuemmerle
Gustav-Adolf-Strasse 6
D-8192 Geretsried, Federal   (08171) 31132
     Republic of Germany   Established 1971

Professor Dr. T. K. Shibuya, President (Japan);
     Professor Dr. H. P. Kuemmerle, Executive Vice
     President
The Society conducts congresses and symposia on an
international basis; also workshops and journal publication. Membership: Approximately 350 (national
societies and individual members). Finances: Membership: $20 (United States). Publications: Inter-
national Journal of Clinical Pharmacology, Therapy
and Toxicology, monthly, Professor Dr. H. P.
Kuemmerle, editor and editor-in-chief.

★ 1053 ★
INTERNATIONAL SOCIETY OF CYBERNETIC
    MEDICINE
348 Via Roma   (081) 41.32.84
I-80134 Naples, Italy   Established 1958

Professor Aldo Masturzo, President
    P. Battarra, Secretary-General
The Society aims to promote the use of cybernetic
methods in biological and medical sciences, with special concern to medimatics (mathematical medicine),
computer sciences, medical automation, bioengineer-
ing, and systems in medicine.   Membership: Individ-
ual and collective members.   Finances: Membership:
Individual, 5,000 lire; collective, 25,000 lire.
Meetings: Biennial, various locations.   Publications:
Cybernetic Medicine (journal); Congress and Sym-
posia reports.   Affiliations: World Organizations for
Research on the Informational Triangle; Rheumatism-
Cancer Mental Disease; World Organization for the
Science Power.

★ 1054 ★
INTERNATIONAL SOCIETY OF DEVELOPMENTAL
    BIOLOGISTS
Secretariat: Department of Biological Sciences
Dartmouth College   (603) 646-2324
Hanover, New Hampshire 03755   Established 1911

Professor Melvin Spiegel, Secretary-Treasurer
The Society's intent is to promote international cooperation among developmental biologists.   Activities
include the sponsorship of international symposia, as
well as conferences on embryology and developmental
biology.   Membership: 800.   Finances: Membership: $15 annually; Other Sources: Administrative
support from the International Union of Biological
Sciences.   Meetings: Once every 4 years, various
locations.   Affiliation: International Union of Biological Sciences.

★ 1055 ★
INTERNATIONAL SOCIETY OF ELECTRO-
    PHYSIOLOGICAL KINESIOLOGY
c/o Gunnar Andersson
Department of Orthopaedic Surgery I
Sahlgren Hospital
S-413 45 Goteborg, Sweden   Established 1965

Dr. Gunnar Andersson, Secretary
To advance research and teaching in electrophysiology,
kinesiology and bio-engineering.   Membership: 500
(doctors, dentists, physiotherapists, psychologists,
biological scientists, biomedical engineers).   Finances: Membership: $10 annually.   Meetings: An-

nual National meetings; International meetings,
every 3 to 4 years.   Publications: ISEK Newsletter,
quarterly, Robert P. Lehr, Jr., editor; Proceedings
of the 4th Congress of the International Society of
Electrophysiological Kinesiology, Carlo J. de Luca,
editor.

★ 1056 ★
INTERNATIONAL SOCIETY OF ENDOCRINOLOGY
9650 Rockville Pike   (301) 656-4133
Bethesda, Maryland 20014   Established 1960

Mortimer B. Lipsett, M.D., Secretary-General
To disseminate knowledge of endocrinology by coordinating and organizing international congresses and
conferences of endocrinology, by facilitating collaboration among national endocrinological societies and
qualified persons interested in endocrinology, and by
publication of books, reports and other papers relating
thereto.   Membership: 43 national societies.
Meetings: International Congress, every 4 years,
various locations.   Publication: Abstracts of Congresses.

★ 1057 ★
INTERNATIONAL SOCIETY OF GENERAL PRACTICE
    (SIMG)
Secretariat: Bahnhofstrasse 22/I   (04222) 70615
A-9020 Klagenfurt, Austria   Established 1959

Mrs. Sigrid Taupe, Secretary
The International Society of General Practice, also
known under its Latin name as Societas Internationalis
Medicinae Generalis (SIMG) was founded in 1959 as
a society for individual members with scientific interests.   Since then the corporative membership of national institutes and societies in Europe has been made
possible.   The SIMG wishes to provide the general
practitioners of Europe with a scientific basis which
enables them to offer patients and their families improved continuous integrative primary medical care.
Membership: Approximately 750 (single members and
scientific associations of G.P.'s).   Finances: Membership: Swiss Fr. 75 annually.   Awards: Hippoc-
rates Medal; Jansseen SIMG Research Award.
Meetings: Semiannually, in springtime, various locations in Europe; in autumn, Klagenfurt, Austria.
Publications: General Practice International, quarterly, Dr. E. Sturm, editor.

★ 1058 ★

INTERNATIONAL SOCIETY OF HEMATOLOGY
c/o Dr. Sanchez Medal
Apartado Postal 41-711
Mexico 10, D.F. Mexico   Established 1946

Dr. Sanchez Medal, Secretary-General
To promote the exchange and diffusion throughout the
world of information and ideas concerning blood and
blood-forming tissues. Membership: Individuals in
69 countries. Finances: Membership: $10; Other
Sources: Grants. Meetings: Biennial, various locations.

★ 1059 ★

INTERNATIONAL SOCIETY OF INTERNAL MEDICINE
c/o Professor P. C. Frei
Centre Hospitalier Universitaire
    Vaudois   (021) 41.22.25
CH-1011 Lausanne, Switzerland   Established 1948

Professor Philippe C. Frei, Secretary General
Promotes scientific knowledge in internal medicine;
encourage friendship between physicians in all countries. Membership: Individual and collective.
Acts as a federation of the national societies of internal medicine. Finances: Membership: Dues.
Meetings: Congresses, biennially, various locations.
Affiliations: Member of Council for International Organizations of Medical Sciences, which is in consultative status with UNESCO, WHO.

★ 1060 ★

INTERNATIONAL SOCIETY OF NEUROPATHOLOGY
c/o Professor Hume Adams
Department of Neuropathology
Institute of Neurological Sciences
Southern General Hospital   (041) 445.2466
Glasgow GS1 4TF, Scotland   ext. 767
    United Kingdom   Established 1967

Professor Hume Adams, Secretary-General
To further the science of neuropathology by initiating
and maintaining permanent co-operation between national and regional societies of neuropathology; encouraging the exchange of information and the publication of matters relevant to the science of neuropathology. Membership: Over 1,000 from national
societies. Finances: Membership: Societies pay fee
based on membership. Meetings: International Congress every 4 years, various locations. Publication:
Newsletter, semiannual.

★ 1061 ★

INTERNATIONAL SOCIETY OF PAEDIATRIC
    ONCOLOGY (S.I.O.P.)
c/o Dr. M. G. Mott
Department of Child Health
Royal Hospital for Sick Children
St. Michael's Hill
Bristol BS2 8BJ, England,
    United Kingdom   Established 1968

Dr. M. G. Mott, Secretary
This Society aims to promote research, treatment and
clinical review of malignant tumors in children.
Non-European people, interested in paediatric oncology, are also members of the Society.   Their purpose
is to exchange information about treatment and research of children with cancer and to perform studies.
Membership: 154 full members (paediatric oncologists,
paediatric surgeons dealing with oncology, radiother-
apists, pathologists and research workers in the field
of oncology). Finances: Other Sources: The Dutch
Cancer Fund; Institut National de la Santé et de la
Recherche Médicale Paris Grant 714.413, A.T.P. no.
1; Contract for Clinical Research FC72 A6 of the
Institut Gustave-Roussy Villejuif/Paris. Meetings:
Annual.

★ 1062 ★

INTERNATIONAL SOCIETY OF PREVENTIVE
    MEDICINE, INC.
3419 Thom Boulevard   (702) 873-4542
Las Vegas, Nevada 89106   Established 1970

Joseph M. Kadens, Executive Director
To establish and promote methods of improving health
by prophylactic means through education in nutrition,
sanitation and hygiene. Membership: Professional,
public. Finances: Membership: Professional members, $25 annually; public members, $10 annually;
Other Sources: Sales of publications; holding of
seminars and workshops; convention registration fees.
Meetings: Annual convention, first week-end in
June of each year, various locations. Publications:
Journal of Preventive Medicine, quarterly, Joseph M.
Kadans, editor; Newsletter for members, monthly.
Library: Preventive Medicine Library, 2,500 volumes
(special permission for researchers only). Affilia-
tion: Bernadean University (College of Health Sci-
ences). Former Name: International Naturopathic
Association, Inc.

★ 1063 ★

INTERNATIONAL SOCIETY OF RADIOGRAPHERS
   AND RADIOLOGICAL TECHNICIANS
159 Gabalfa Avenue
Cardiff CF4 2PB, Wales   (0222) 62371
   United Kingdom   Established 1959

E. R. Hutchinson, Secretary-General
To promote and encourage improved standards and
training in radiography, radiotherapy and nuclear
medicine; to facilitate exchange of information
among member societies. Charitable status granted
to society in 1979. Membership: 57 societies in
51 countries (national societies; individual associate
members, since 1979); Other Sources: Donations
support from some commercial companies. Meetings:
World Congress, every 4 years; other conferences in
regions, average 1 every 18 months. Publications:
Newsletter, semiannual, D. Van Dijk, editor. Affiliation: World Health Organization.

★ 1064 ★

INTERNATIONAL SOCIETY OF RADIOLOGY
c/o Professor W. A. Fuchs
Department of Diagnostic Radiology
University Hospital
CH-3010 Bern, Switzerland   Established 1953

Professor Med. W.A. Fuchs, Secretary-Treasurer
Contribute to coordination of progress in medical radiology; act as the continuing body between International Congresses of Radiology. Membership: National radiological societies. Meetings: Congresses,
irregular, various locations. Affiliations: Member
of Council for International Organizations of Medical
Sciences, which is in consultative status with
UNESCO, WHO.

★ 1065 ★

INTERNATIONAL SOCIETY OF SURGERY (UNITED
   STATES CHAPTER)
Cornell University Medical College
1300 York Avenue, Room F-739   (212) 472-6561
New York, New York 10021

G. Tom Shires, M.D., Secretary
The aim of the Society is to make contributions to
the progress of science by research into and discussion
of surgical problems. Membership: 780 (honorary,
emeritus, titular). Finances: Membership: Chapter
assessment, $12; initiation fee, $11; titular members,
$80 biennially; Other Sources: Publications.
Awards: Annual award to the surgeon making the most
outstanding contribution during the year. Meetings:
Congress, biennially, various locations. Publications:

World Journal of Surgery; Bulletin of the Interna-
tional Society of Surgery; Proceedings of the Biennial
Congress. Affiliation: Societe Internationale de
Chirurgie.

★ 1066 ★

INTERNATIONAL SOCIETY OF THE HISTORY OF
   MEDICINE
Lotissement Les Rêves
22, Rue François Villeneuve
F-34000 Montpellier, France   Established 1921

Dr. Louis Dulieu, Secretary-General
To study all aspects of the history of medicine and
related sciences. Membership: 752 representing 54
nations. Finances: Membership: 40 F.F. Meetings: Congress, biennially, various locations. Publication: Proceedings of Congress, biennially. Affiliation: CIOMS.

★ 1067 ★

INTERNATIONAL SOCIETY ON TOXINOLOGY
c/o Dr. Philip Rosenberg
University of Connecticut School
   of Pharmacy   (203) 486-2213
Storrs, Connecticut 06268   Established 1962

Dr. Philip Rosenberg, Secretary;
   B. Uvnas, President
The Society's purpose is to advance knowledge on the
properties of toxins and antitoxins and to bring together scholars interested in these substances through
a common society. Membership: Several hundred
(regular and associate). Finances: Membership:
$25 annually. Awards: Redi Award (Plaque and
Illuminated Manuscript), triennially. Meetings:
Triennial, various locations. Publications: Toxicon,
bimonthly, Dr. Philip Rosenberg, editor.

★ 1068 ★

INTERNATIONAL SOCIETY OF TROPICAL
   DERMATOLOGY
c/o S. A. Muller, M.D.
200 First Street, S.W.
Rochester, Minnesota 55901   Established 1966

S. A. Muller, M.D., Secretary-General;
   Orlando Canizares, M.D., President
To promote and encourage investigations and to facilitate mutual acquaintance and collaboration between
persons of all nationalities concerning the field of
tropical dermatology and geographic ecology. Membership: 1,500. Finances: Membership: $35;

Other Sources: Grants from pharmaceutical industry; publications. Awards: Caslallani-Reiss Medal and Award ($1,000) for best paper. Meetings: Every 5 years, various locations. Publications: International Journal of Dermatology. Affiliation: International League of International Societies.

★ 1069 ★
INTERNATIONAL SOCIETY ON THROMBOSIS AND
    HAEMOSTASIS
Post Office Box 5847
Washington, D.C. 20014   Established 1969

James M. Stengle, M.D., Executive Officer
This Society is devoted to research and education on subjects relating to thrombosis and hemorrhagic disease. Membership: 900. Finances: Membership: $25; Other Sources: Gifts and bequests. Awards: Shirley Johnson Memorial Lecture; Wright-Schulte Lecture; Robert P. Grant Medal. Meetings: Biennial, various locations. Publications: Thrombosis and Haemostasis, 6 issues annually, F. H. Duckert, editor.

★ 1070 ★
INTERNATIONAL SOPHROLOGY INSTITUTE
Grand Central Station
Post Office Box 2567   (212) 849-9335
New York, New York 10163   Established 1978

Lisa Curtis, Director of Communications
Sophrology was founded in Europe in 1962 to train doctors and help people to manage and direct stress for dynamic self improvement. Managing stress creatively means either neutralizing it without developing any psychosomatic illness, or better still, turning a given situation to our advantage. Membership: 2,000 in Europe. Finances: Membership: Seminars given throughout the country; 3-day public seminar, $350; 4-day Doctors' seminar, $500. Meetings: Local centers in New York, New Jersey, California, Colorado. Publications: Sophrology: Information and Newsletter, quarterly, Dr. Robert Lichtenstein, editor (to be published). Also Known As: International Institute of Medical Sophrology.

★ 1071 ★
INTERNATIONAL TEMPERANCE ASSOCIATION
6830 Laurel Street, N.W.   (202) 722-6000
Washington, D.C. 20012   (202) 723-0800
                                         ext. 501

Dr. E. H. J. Steed, Executive Director

To encourage an individual choice toward a non-drug way of life--alcohol, tobacco, narcotics, etc. Membership: Over 500,000. Finances: Membership: Local society membership fees to local projects; Other Sources: Donations and gifts.

★ 1072 ★
INTERNATIONAL TEMPERANCE BLUE CROSS UNION
Kermély, 10   (022) 47 20 88
CH-1206 Geneva, Switzerland   Established 1877

Jean-Paul A. Widmer, President
To combat the evil of intemperance, prevention of alcoholism, rehabilitation of alcoholics and drug addicts, education on drugs and alcohol problems on a Christian basis. Conducts social gatherings, runs clinics, halfway-homes, cure-homes, farms for alcoholics, vacation-homes, offices for social treatment of alcoholics. Membership: 200,000 (co-operators and rehabilitated alcoholics); societies in Europe and Africa (20). Finances: Membership: $4 annual average; Other Sources: Governments subsidies, church subsidies, grants by private persons. Meetings: Every 4 years, various locations. Publications: Report of the Chairman; Quarterly Information Bulletin; conference reports.

★ 1073 ★
INTERNATIONAL TRANSACTIONAL ANALYSIS
    ASSOCIATION
1772 Vallejo Street   (415) 885-5992
San Francisco, California 94123   Established 1961

Muriel James, Ed.D., President
To encourage the advancement and development of transactional analysis as a method of psychotherapy and to encourage its application in businesses, organizations, and governments. Membership: 7,000. Finances: Membership: $35; Other Sources: Conferences. Awards: Eric Berne Scientific Award; Research grants for projects in Transactional Analysis. Meetings: Semiannual, various locations. Publications: Transactional Analysis Journal, quarterly, John McNeel, Ph.D., editor; Script (newsletter), bimonthly. Library: Eric Berne Memorial Library, 3,000 volumes.

★ 1074 ★
INTERNATIONAL UNION AGAINST CANCER
3 rue de Conseil General
CH-1205 Geneva, Switzerland   Established 1935

Dr. J. F. Delafresnaye, Director

To carry forward the campaign against cancer by research, therapy and control measures. The Union facilitates the exchange of information between national cancer organizations, holds international cancer congresses, symposia and conferences, publishes an international journal, stimulates and encourages national efforts in research, therapy and control, and establishes working groups for such problems as tumor nomenclature and clinical stage classification and applied statistics. Membership: Official governmental departments, voluntary organizations. Finances: Membership: 6 categories - $500-$120,000; Other Sources: Grants, legacies, etc. Awards: Administration of the American Cancer Society--Eleanor Roosevelt International Cancer Fellowships. Meetings: Congresses, every 4 years, various locations. Publications: International Journal of Cancer, 12 times annually, E. A. Saxen, editor; Bulletin, quarterly, P. T. Rentchnick, editor; annual reports, etc. Affiliations: WHO, CIOMS, IARC, ICLAS.

★ 1075 ★

INTERNATIONAL UNION AGAINST THE VENEREAL
    DISEASES AND THE TREPONEMATOSES
James Pringle House
The Middlesex Hospital   (01) 636-8333
London W1N 8AA, England   ext. 7497
    United Kingdom   Established 1923

R. D. Catterall, FRCPE, FRCP, President
To encourage, in all countries, in co-operation with national organizations, all preventive measures, both medical and social to promote the campaign against venereal diseases and treponematoses. Membership: National organizations in 14 countries. Finances: Membership: $10. Meetings: Biennial, various locations.

★ 1076 ★

INTERNATIONAL UNION AGAINST TUBERCULOSIS
    (IUAT)
3 Rue Georges Ville   (01) 501 70 73
F-75116 Paris, France   Established 1920

Dr. Annik Rouillon, Executive Director
The IUAT is a non-governmental, non-profit, voluntary organization which was founded in 1920. It currently federates national voluntary antituberculosis associations or governmental tuberculosis or health services of 113 countries throughout the world. It is dedicated to the fight against tuberculosis, respiratory diseases and the promotion of community health. The IUAT fulfills its objectives through dissemination of scientific knowledge; exchange of experience and conferences; operational and applied research; field

projects under the mutual assistance programme; collaboration with other agencies (WHO, UICC, UNESCO). Membership: 113 constituent members, (affiliated countries); 6,000 individual members; members of honor and benefactors. Finances: Membership: According to a quota share system (the same system as in the United Nations and WHO). Quota shares range from 21 to 0,05 for constituent members; membership fees of individual members; Other Sources: Donations. Meetings: Annual Meetings, various locations; World Conferences, triennially, in different Members' countries. Publications: Bulletin of the International Union Against Tuberculosis (3 languages), quarterly, IUAT, editor. Affiliations: WHO, UICC, UNESCO.

★ 1077 ★

INTERNATIONAL UNION OF ANGIOLOGY
Via Bonifacio Lupi 11   (055) 499020
I-50129 Florence, Italy   Established 1952

Professor Marcello Tesi, General Secretary
Study of vascular diseases. Activities include international congresses every 3 years. Cooperates with UNESCO and is a member of CIONS. Membership: 20 National Societies of Angiology. Finances: Membership: Variable. Meetings: Biennially, various locations. Publications: Proceedings of each congress. Affiliations: Angiological societies in various countries.

★ 1078 ★

INTERNATIONAL UNION OF ASSOCIATIONS OF
    DOCTOR-MOTORISTS
Johanna-Melber-Weg 8
D-6000 Frankfurt/Main 70   (0611) 622007
    Federal Republic of Germany   Established 1933

Dr. Alban Becker, President
Promotion of the interest of the Associations affiliated with the Union on an international ground in the most extensive meaning of the word, collectively as well as individually, exclusive of all national and political problems, without discrimination between race, creed, or political inclinations, and without the purpose of making profits. Membership: 10 associations of doctor-motorists. Finances: Membership: DM 200 per country; DM 25 per member. Meetings: Annual, various locations.

★ 1079 ★

INTERNATIONAL UNION OF BIOLOGICAL
　　SCIENCES
51, Boulevard de Montmorency
F-75016 Paris, France　　　　　　Established 1919

Dr. Talal Younès, Executive Secretary
To promote biological studies and research through the
exchange of ideas and the discussion of scientific
findings.　The Union plays a very important role in
providing financial assistance to scientific activities
organized by the scientific members who rely totally
or partially on IUBS support for their functioning.
Membership: 47 national members;　80 scientific members (each national member, or country, adheres
through its Academy of Science, National Research
Council, national science associations or similar organizations.　The 80 scientific members come from international scientific organizations).　Meetings: Triennially, General Assembly;　next one will be in
1982 in Canada.　Publications:　Biology International,
semiannual, IUBS Executive Secretary, editor;　Proceedings of General Assemblies.

★ 1080 ★

INTERNATIONAL UNION OF MICROBIOLOGICAL
　　SOCIETIES
CNRS/LCB
31 Chemin Joseph Aiguier　　　　(091) 75 90 42
F-13009 Marseille, France　　　　Established 1927

Professor Jacques C. Senez, Secretary-General
To maintain contact with microbiological societies
throughout the world;　to foster and sponsor meetings,
symposia, and conferences as needed to ensure the
dissemination of new or pertinent knowledge in the
field;　to maintain contact between microbiologists;
to foster organization of the discipline;　to encourage
research in microbiology and related fields;　and to
encourage the highest standard of training of microbiologists of all nations and by all means so that
microbiology may be used for the fullest benefit of
mankind.　Membership:　62 national societies or
committees.　Finances:　Membership: Based on membership of society;　basic fee, $100;　Other Sources:
grants, UNESCO, IUBS.　Meetings: Congress,
every 4 years, various locations.　Publications: International Journal of Systematic Bacteriology, quarterly, E. F. Lessel, editor;　Intervirology, monthly,
J. L. Melnick, editor;　Proceedings of Congresses,
symposia;　reports.

★ 1081 ★

INTERNATIONAL UNION OF NUTRITIONAL
　　SCIENCES
c/o Institute of Biology
41 Queen's Gate
London SW7 5HU, England　　　(01) 589 9076
　　United Kingdom　　　　　　Established 1946

Joyce Harrison, Executive Secretary
To promote international cooperation in the scientific
study of nutrition and its applications;　to encourage
research and the exchange of scientific information in
the nutritional sciences, by the holding of international congresses and conferences, by publication, and
by other suitable means;　to establish such commissions, committees, and other bodies as may be required;　to provide a means of communication with
other organizations, and to encourage participation in
the activities of the International Council of Scientific Unions, of which the Union is a member;　to
develop activity regarded as helpful and appropriate
in achieving the objectives of the Union.　Membership:　42 national societies.　Finances:　Sfrs 600-
9600;　Other Sources:　Grants from International
Council of Scientific Unions.　Meetings:　General
Assembly in conjunction with an International Con-
gress of Nutrition every 4 years;　next one in 1981.
Publications:　IUNS Newsletter, irregularly, D. F.
Hollingsworth, editor;　Directory, quarterly;　reports.
Affiliations:　Group of European Nutritionists (GEN);
International Committee of Dietetic Associations
(ICDA);　International Society of Parenteral Nutrition
(ISPN);　The Latin American Society of Nutrition
(SLAN).

★ 1082 ★

INTERNATIONAL UNION OF PHARMACOLOGY
University of Heidelberg
Department of Pharmacology
Im Neuenheimer Feld 366
D-6900 Heidelberg, Federal　　　(06221) 563900
　　Republic of Germany　　　　Established 1959

Professor F. Gross, Secretary-General
Stimulates international coordination of research in
pharmacology by organizing and supporting congresses,
symposia, discussions, publications.　Promotes international cooperation between national and regional
pharmacological societies.　Contributes to the advancement of pharmacology in all its international
aspects.　Cooperates with WHO in all matters concerning drugs and drug research.　Membership:　43
national, regional and international societies of pharmacology and related disciplines.　Finances:　Membership:　$200-$2,000 annually;　Other Sources:　Royalties from Congress Proceedings, balances left at end
of Congress, yearly contribution from International

Council of Scientific Unions. Meetings: Triennial International Congress. Publications: Congress Proceedings, triennially; Newsletter, semiannually. Affiliation: Sections of Clinical Pharmacology and on Toxicology.

★ 1083 ★

INTERNATIONAL VEGETARIAN UNION
10, King's Drive, Marple
Stockport SK6 6NQ, England   (061) 427-5850
    United Kingdom   Established 1908

Dr. Gordon Latto, President;
    Maxwell Lee, Honorary General Secretary
To further vegetarianism worldwide and to disseminate information about the vegetarian cause. To support national vegetarian societies and to encourage the establishment of vegetarian societies where none exist. Activites include holding the holding of Congresses, maintaining an information service on vegetarianism, issuing Congress reports and lectures, developing interest in vegetarianism among international bodies, representing the vegetarian viewpoint. Membership: Members and associates in all the major inhabited continents; some 50 or more worldwide; full members (any society advocating vegetarianism which is controlled by vegetarians); associate members (sympathetic bodies which might not be vegetarian). Finances: Membership: £ 5 minimum for up to 150 members and £ 10 per 500 members above this up to a maximum subscription of £ 75; associates £ 7.50 annually; Other Sources: Donations, sale of literature and badges, organized events, Congresses. Awards: Manker Memorial Foundation provides grants to further vegetarianism and to enable participation in events. Meetings: World Vegetarian Congress, biennial, various countries; Regional Congresses, biennial, various locations. Publications: Scientific Information Bulletin, 6 times annually, Dr. Alan Long, editor.

★ 1084 ★

INTERNATIONAL VETERINARY ASSOCIATION FOR
    ANIMAL PRODUCTION
c/o Carlos Luis de Cuenca
Facultad de Veterinaria
Ciudad Universitaria   (01) 243-9459
Madrid-3, Spain   Established 1951

Carlos Luis de Cuenca, Secretary-General
To develop interest in animal production sciences. Membership: 1,500. Finances: Membership: $10; fees, $8; Other Sources: Donations. Awards: Gold, Silver Medals. Meetings: Biennial, Madrid, Spain. Publications: Zootechnia, bimonthly;

Congress proceedings (1st, 2nd, and 3rd World Congresses on Animal Feeding, Madrid, 1966, 1972, 1978, 3 volumes each; 1st World Congress on Genetics Applied to Animal Breeding, Madrid, 1974; 1st World Congress on Ethology Applied to Livestock Production, Madrid, 1978; IXth World Congress on Animal Reproduction and Artificial Insemination, Madrid, 1980, 2 volumes). Library: 4,000 volumes. Affiliation: World Veterinary Association.

★ 1085 ★

INTER-SOCIETY COMMISSION FOR HEART
    DISEASE RESOURCES
7320 Greenville Avenue   (214) 750-5352
Dallas, Texas 75231

Leonard Scherlis, M.D., National Chairman;
    Curtis Nelson, Ph.D., National Project Director
The ICHD was begun to provide optimal recommendations and guidelines for the care of patients with cardiovascular diseases. Finances: Other Sources: American Heart Association. Publications: Recommendations are published in Circulation, a journal of the American Heart Association, irregular. Affiliation: 16 cooperating organizations. Remarks: The ICHD recommendations are revised on a regular basis; outstanding scientists make up the panels charged with the review and revision of each report.

★ 1086 ★

INTERSOCIETY COMMITTEE ON PATHOLOGY
    INFORMATION, INC.
4733 Bethesda Avenue, Suite 735   (301) 656-2944
Bethesda, Maryland 20014   Established 1957

Judy Graves, Information Counsel;
    Kenneth M. Brinkhous, M.D., Chairman
To inform the public of the role of pathology in medical practice and research and pathologists' contributions to medical knowledge and patient care. To keep pathologists informed of events and developments in fields bearing on their specialty; to provide informational and recruitment aids for the use of pathologists; to facilitate press coverage of member societies' professional meetings by providing press rooms, etc. Membership: 4 national pathology societies. Finances: Membership on a contract fee basis; Other Sources: Contributions for individual projects; sales of informational materials; subscriptions to the annual Directory of Pathology Training Programs. Meetings: Semiannual, various locations. Publications: Pathology Daily News, daily through annual meetings; Directory of Pathology Training Programs, annually; Pathology: The Science of Diseases, a career pamphlet.

★ 1087 ★
INTERSTATE POSTGRADUATE MEDICAL ASSOCIA-
　TION OF NORTH AMERICA
Post Office Box 1109　　　　　　　(608) 257-6781
Madison, Wisconsin　53701　　　Established 1916

H. B. Maroney, Executive Director
Founded to "up date" practicing physicians in all
phases of their medical practice.　Annually presents
a high-quality instructional program, primarily directed to Family Physicians.　Attendance from all
parts of the United States and Canada.　Not a
"membership" organization, but rather a distinctive
teaching service available to any licensed MD in the
United States and Canada.　Membership: Approximately 3,000 physicians who attend annually or once
every 2 or 3 years.　Finances: Other Sources: Proceeds of annual instructional program; sale of exhibit
space to ethical pharmaceutical houses and others who
are members of Health Care Exhibitors Association.
Awards: $2,000 to $3,000 annually to young researchers in the medical school where meeting is
held; $1,500 Teaching Award.　Meetings: Annual,
various locations.

J

★ 1088 ★
J. P. BICKELL FOUNDATION
21 King Street East
Toronto, Ontario M5C 1B3, Canada　Established 1951

P. J. Sewell, Secretary, Foundation Committee
By the terms of the will left by the late John Paris
Bickell, the Foundation was created to provide a per-
petual subsidy for The Hospital for Sick Children in
Toronto to the extent of 1/2 the annual net income
of the Foundation; to support research by recognized
leaders in the various fields of medical science; to
support charitable and/or educational organizations.
Grants from the Foundation are restricted to organizations operating solely within the Province of Ontario.　Research Funds: Funds are available to Ontario Universities and Hospitals for research projects.
Application forms are available and are forwarded to
Secretary when completed.　Meetings: Semiannual,
in February and July at National Trust Company,
Toronto, Ontario, Canada.　Publications:　J. P.
Bickell Foundation Report, biennially, P. J. Sewell,
editor.

★ 1089 ★
JANE COFFIN CHILDS MEMORIAL FUND FOR
　MEDICAL RESEARCH
333 Cedar Street　　　　　　　　(203) 432-4503
New Haven, Connecticut　06510　Established 1937

F. M. Richards, Director
To further research into the causes, origins and treatment of cancer through fellowship program and grant-
in-aid for the support of specific investigators.　Priority is given to fellowship program with only 5-10
percent of money available to grant program.　Meetings: Annual, Board of Scientific Advisors.

★ 1090 ★
JANUS INFORMATION FACILITY
1952 Union Street　　　　　　　(415) 567-0162
San Francisco, California　94123　Established 1976

Paul A. Walker, Ph.D., Director
Medical research foundation engaged in research in
the area of gender dysphoria and in particular, gender
identity orientation and transsexualism.　(Transsexual
is defined as the condition being genetically, gon-
adally and morphologically of one sex but physically
of the other sex, with a desire for sex reassignment).
Provides referrals and distributes literature on transsexualism and gender dysphoria.　Finances: $7.50
charge to cover printing and mailing costs; donations.
Publications: Information pamphlets: Legal Aspects
of Transsexualism; Religious Aspects of Transsexualism;
Guidelines for Transsexuals; Information for the Family of the Transsexual; Counseling the Transsexual,
J. Money and P. Walker, editors.　Former Name:
Erickson Educational Foundation.

JEFFERSON (THOMAS) RESEARCH CENTER
　See: Thomas Jefferson Research Center

★ 1091 ★
JERUSALEM INSTITUTIONS FOR THE BLIND,
　KEREN OR, INC.
1133 Broadway, Suite 1227/1228　(212) 255-1180
New York, New York　10010　　Established 1956

Jacob Igra, Executive Director
Funds as special program at the Jewish Institute for
the Blind in Jerusalem, Israel, that houses, feeds,
clothes, educates and trains blind multi-handicapped
from childhood into adulthood.　Membership: Contributors.　Finances: Contributions, bequests, legacies.　Meetings: When necessary, New York City.
Affiliation: Keren Or, Inc., Chapter in California.

★ 1092 ★
JEWISH BRAILLE INSTITUTE OF AMERICA, INC.
110 East 30th Street   (212) 889-2525
New York, New York 10016   Established 1931

Gerald M. Kass, Executive Vice President
To serve the cultural and religious needs of the
Jewish blind and visually disabled and to provide
Jewish resources to all blind and visually disabled
through free circulation of books in braille, sound
records and large type. Publications: The Jewish
Braille Review, monthly; The Jewish Braille Institute
Voice, monthly, Jacob Freid, editor. Library:
55,000 braille volumes, 40,000 tapes and cassettes,
a growing resource of large print.

★ 1093 ★
JEWISH GUILD FOR THE BLIND
15 West 65th Street   (212) 595-2000
New York, New York 10023   Established 1914

John F. Heimerdinger, Executive Director
The Guild's basic goal is, as far as possible, to help
the blind or visually handicapped person to participate
in the community on a self-supporting basis. It provides a large variety of rehabilitation services and
mental health to blind and visually handicapped persons of all ages, races and creeds. It also operates
a Home for Aged Blind with 172 beds, a sheltered
workshop providing gainful employment to about 150
persons, and a community residence for multiple
handicapped young adults. Finances: Sources:
Voluntary contributions, government fees, foundation
gifts, bequests. Publication: Insight, quarterly,
Irving Leon, editor. Library: Cassette Library, 500
volumes.

★ 1094 ★
JOHN MILTON SOCIETY FOR THE BLIND (IN
    CANADA)
40 St. Clair Avenue East,
Suite 201
Toronto, Ontario M4T 1M9,   (416) 921-4152
    Canada   Established 1970

Ruth F. Banko, Executive Secretary
The Society provides large type, cassette and braille
literature for blind and visually handicapped individuals in Canada. Its name honors the 17th Century
Christian man of letters who became blind in middle
life. Finances: Contributions. Publications: Insight (large print magazine), 11 issues annually; In-
sound (cassette magazine for those unable to read
large print); In Touch (Braille magazine for adults);
Mostly for Children (Braille magazine for children);

Love in Doing; and other publications for individual
or study groups.

★ 1095 ★
JOHN MILTON SOCIETY FOR THE BLIND (IN THE
    UNITED STATES)
29 West 34th Street   (212) 736-4162
New York, New York 10001   Established 1928

Chenoweth J. Watson, General Secretary
Serves persons prevented from reading by visual and
physical handicaps through its program of publication
and free distribution of Christian literature in braille,
on records, and in large type form on behalf of many
Protestant churches; provides financial assistance to
church-related homes and schools for blind children in
Africa and Asia. Finances: Contributions, gifts,
bequests. Publications: John Milton Magazine
(braille and large type), monthly; John Milton Talking Book Magazine, bimonthly; John Milton Sunday
School Lessons (braille and talking book), quarterly;
Discovery, monthly; other.

JOHNSON (ROBERT WOOD) FOUNDATION
    See: Robert Wood Johnson Foundation

★ 1096 ★
JOINT COMMISSION ON ACCREDITATION OF
    HOSPITALS
875 North Michigan Avenue   (312) 642-6061
Chicago, Illinois 60611   Established 1951

John E. Affeldt, M.D., President
The Commission's purpose is to establish standards for
the operation of hospitals and other health-related
facilities and services; to conduct survey and accreditation programs which will encourage and promote a
high quality of patient care; and to recognize compliance with standards by issuance of certificates of
accreditation. Membership: Organizations (appoint-
ees from these organizations make up the 21 member
Board of Commissioners). Finances: Membership:
Each member organization pays that proportion of the
total budgeted members' contributions which its number of commissioners on the Board bears to the total
number of commissioners; Other Sources: Accreditation survey fees, grants. Meetings: 3 times annually, Chicago. Publications: Perspectives on Accreditation, bimonthly, Susan Zivich, editor; Quality
Review Bulletin, monthly, Barbara Wendorf, executive editor; many other publications. Affiliations:
American College of Physicians; American College
of Surgeons; American Dental Association; American

Hospital Association; American Medical Association.

★ 1097 ★
JOSEPH COLLINS FOUNDATION
153 East 53 Street
New York, New York 10022   Established 1951

Mark F. Hughes, President;
   Augusta L. Packer, Secretary
Established for the purpose of aiding needy medical
students to complete their medical education without
sacrificing all other interests in the broad field of
learning.   The Foundation makes annual grants in
sums not exceeding $2,000 to men and women for the
purpose of enabling them to attend the medical schools
of their choice.

★ 1098 ★
JOURNAL OF NUTRITIONAL MICROBIOLOGY
Post Office Box N   (408) 338-2544
Boulder Creek, California 95006   Established 1980

Christopher B. Hills, Ph.D., DSc., Editor
Membership: 1,600 (general subscribers).   Finances:
$10; Other Sources: Sale of journals.   Meetings:
Annual Meeting, 1981 in Mexico.   Affiliations:
Microalgae International Union; University of the
Trees Press.

JUNG (C. G.) FOUNDATION FOR ANALYTICAL
PSYCHOLOGY, INC.
   See: C. G. Jung Foundation for Analytical
   Psychology, Inc.

★ 1099 ★
JUNIOR NATIONAL ASSOCIATION OF THE DEAF
814 Thayer Avenue   (301) 587-1788
Silver Spring, Maryland 20910   Established 1960

Melinda C. Padden, National Director
The Junior National Association of the Deaf is an organization of, by, and for deaf youth with chapters
in day and residential schools for the deaf throughout
the United States.   The Association emphasizes self-
discipline in motivating deaf youth to utilize their
potentials on their own in becoming all that they can
be.   The Junior NAD programs provide the young
deaf people a training in citizenship, leadership and
scholarship, an opportunity to contribute to community
growth and development.   Membership: 5,000 members (teenagers).   Finances: Membership: $4 for

members from a chapter; $6 for individual member-
ship; Other Sources: Mostly self-supporting, but do
receive help financially from the parent organization,
the National Association of the Deaf.   Meetings:
Every odd number year, 2 conferences, 1 east and
1 west; every even-number year, a Convention which
is held at a school for the deaf.   Publications:
Junior Deaf American, quarterly, Melinda C. Padden,
editor; Junior NAD Newsletter, monthly, Melinda C.
Padden, editor.   Affiliations: National Association
of the Deaf; International Year of Disabled Persons.

★ 1100 ★
JUST ONE BREAK, INC.
373 Park Avenue South   (212) 725-2500
New York, New York 10016   Established 1952

Paul G. Hearne, Executive Director
Established for purposes of evaluating, placing and
relating research in the employment of physically disabled men and women.   Used extensively by agencies in rehabilitation field and by commerce and industry as a prime source of recruitment of employees
who have a disability.   Membership: Approximately
1,000 members (contributors of $15 or more).   Fi-
nances: Other Sources: Grants received from Federal and private foundations to undertake specific research or projects.   Meetings: Annual, at the
J.O.B. office.   Publications: JobAids, quarterly;
Research monographs and reports.

★ 1101 ★
J W B
15 East 26th Street   (212) 532-4949
New York, New York 10010   Established 1917

Arthur Rotman, Executive Vice President
JWB is the Association of Jewish Community Centers
and the Young Men-Young Women Hebrew Associations and camps in the United States and Canada, and
is the United States government-authorized agency for
serving cultural, religious, welfare and morale needs
of Jewish personnel and their dependents in the United
States Armed Forces, as well as of hospitalized veterans.   JWB provides professional and technical
guidance and help to affiliated centers; recruits,
trains and places professional personnel in centers;
publishes and distributes materials and program literature; provides books and organized lectures by Jewish
cultural activity.   Membership: 447 affiliated centers, major branches, and camps with a membership of
800,000.   Finances: Membership: Allocations from
local Jewish Federations, Welfare Funds, the Greater
New York United Jewish Appeal Federation Campaign,
annual JWB Associates memberships, and affiliated

centers. Awards: Frank L. Weil Award; awards for best Jewish fiction, juvenile, and poetry books in English and for Hebrew and Yiddish poetry. Meetings: Biennial, various locations. Publications: JWB Circle, bimonthly, L. Koppman, editor; Zarkor, monthly, L. Rubin, editor; Personnel Reporter, quarterly, B. Pine, editor. Affiliation: Area councils of centers and Armed Services committees. Former Name: National Jewish Welfare Board.

K

★ 1102 ★
KAPPA EPSILON FRATERNITY
Executive Office, Box 11
Boonvile, Missouri 65233   Established 1921

Mrs. Sherri Kempf, Executive Secretary
To unite women students of pharmacy, to cooperate with the faculties of the colleges where chapters are established, to stimulate in its members a desire for high scholarship, to foster a professional consciousness... Membership: 10,000 collegiate and alumnae members; other professionals, associate, and honorary. Finances: Membership: $10 initiation fee plus 1 year's dues of $6 (student) or $7 (alumnae); Other Sources: Donations. Awards: Zada M. Cooper Scholarship; Nellie Wakeman Fellowship; Key of Excellence; Individual High Grade Average Award (for final 3 year period); Individual High Grade Average Award (annually in each chapter); Merit Award Citation. Meetings: Convention, biennially, various locations; province meetings; biennially in alternate years. Publications: The Bond, 3 times annually, Teresa G. Bridge, editor; career brochures. Affiliations: Professional Fraternity Association; International Pharmaceutical Student's Federation; College Fraternity Editors Association.

★ 1103 ★
KAPPA PSI PHARMACEUTICAL FRATERNITY
College of Pharmacy
University of Oklahoma Health Science Center
644 N.E. 14th Street   (405) 271-6942
Oklahoma City, Oklahoma 73190   Established 1879

Dr. Robert A. Magarian, Executive Director
To provide all the benefits of a professional fraternal affiliation and offer, in addition, the opportunity for attainment of greater professional competency and achievement in the field of pharmacy. Membership: 45,000 (collegiate, graduate, honorary); there are 63 collegiate chapters and 30 graduate chapters;

honorary membership awarded only by the Executive Committee. Finances: Membership: Collegiate dues, $2.75 monthly (for 8 months a year), $11 a semester or $22 a year; graduate chapters, $10 a year (voluntary). Awards: Honorary membership; Certificate of Appreciation. Meetings: Annual, Regional meetings; National Convention, biennially, various locations. Publications: The Mask, quarterly, Dr. Anthony Palmieri, editor; Handbook and Pledge Manual, revised biennially.

KELLER (HELEN) INTERNATIONAL, INC.
    See: Helen Keller International, Inc.

★ 1104 ★
KELLOGG FOUNDATION
400 North Avenue   (616) 965-1221
Battle Creek, Michigan 49016   Established 1930

Russell G. Mawby, President
A philanthropic organization with grant making priorities for educational programs in the areas of health, education and agriculture in the United States, Canada, Australia, Europe and Latin America. The Foundation is interested in the application of existing knowledge rather than research per se. Publications: Annual Report; occasional publications on specialized subjects, Robert Hencey, Communications Director.

KENNY (SISTER) INSTITUTE
    See: Sister Kenny Institute

★ 1105 ★
KENYA ASSOCIATION FOR THE PREVENTION OF
        TUBERCULOSIS
Post Office Box 47855   332466
Nairobi, Kenya   Established 1958

Founded in 1958 by the then Governor of Kenya, Sir Everlyin Baring. Aims are to assist in the prevention and control of tuberculosis in Kenya with a view to erradicate it by fostering interest of the people, dissemination of knowledge, providing facilities to patients or their dependents and adopt-measures to achieve aims and supplement government efforts through health authorities to provent and control TB. Membership: Life membership, ordinary membership, corporate membership, student membership, open to all. Finances: Membership: Life membership, K.Sh. 100 F; Other Sources: Donations, membership fees, fund-drive activities, etc. Awards: Some members of the Association do research in tuberculosis and respiratory disease centers and give lectures to medical students, post-graduate doctors, etc. at the University of Nairobi Medical School. Meetings: Annual, in Nairobi; Executive Committee meets more often as need arises. Publications: Information Booklet on TB in the Country. Library: Medical School Library.

L

★ 1106 ★
LA LECHE LEAGUE INTERNATIONAL, INC.
9616 Minneapolis Avenue   (312) 455-7730
Franklin Park, Illinois 60131   Established 1956

Betty Wagner, Chief Executive Officer;
    Edwina Froehlich, Executive Secretary
Founded for the purpose of giving help and encouragement, primarily through personal instruction, to those mothers who want to breastfeed their babies. The League believes that breastfeeding is the ideal way to initiate good mother-child relationships and strengthen family ties. Membership: 50,000 (supporting membership, mothers membership, contributing membership, benefactor membership, sustaining membership). Finances: Membership: Mothers membership, $12; supporting membership, $20; contributing membership, $100; benefactor membership, $500; sustaining membership, $1,000; Other Sources: Yearly appeal letter, AID Grant for building centers in El Salvador. Meetings: Series of 4 monthly meetings, various locations. Publications: LLLI Newsletter, bimonthly, Judy Torgus, editor; Leaven, bimonthly, Judy Torgus, editor; Womanly Art of Breastfeeding, 1,000,000 printed, La Leche League, International (editor). Remarks: International Conferences, biennially.

LAMAZE BIRTH WITHOUT PAIN EDUCATION
ASSOCIATION
    See: Childbirth Without Pain Education Association

★ 1107 ★
LAMBDA KAPPA SIGMA - INTERNATIONAL
    PHARMACY FRATERNITY
c/o International Office
2025 Andrew   (314) 335-4902
Cape Girardeau, Missouri 63701   Established 1913

Avis J. Ericson, Grand Secretary
To provide for the training of young women studying pharmacy in reaching social, intellectual, cultural

and professional goals. Membership: Over 11,000 (collegiate, alumnae, honorary). Finances: Membership: $20; initiation fee, $25; Other Sources: Chapter assessments. Awards: 10 Cora E. Craven Grants, $250, given annually; B. Olive Cole Graduate Educational Grant, $300; Ethel J. Heath Scholarship Keys; Biennial Award of Merit; Distinguished Service Citation; Lambda Kappa Sigma Educational Trust. Meetings: Biennial Conventions and Regional Meetings, various locations. Publications: Blue and Gold Triangle, quarterly, Sue Corkum, grand editor; Manual, pledge handbook, prospectus, etc. Affiliations: Professional Fraternity Association; International Pharmaceutical Students Association; Interfraternity Research and Advisory Council; International Council of Pharmacy Fraternities, College and Fraternity Editors Association.

★ 1108 ★
LATIN AMERICAN ASSOCIATION OF PHYSIOLOG-
    ICAL SCIENCES
Instituto Politecnico National
Departamento de Fisiologia
Apartado Postal 14-740   (905) 754-0200
Mexico 14, D.F. Mexico   Established 1957

Dr. Juan Garcia Ramos, President
To stimulate experimental research work in Physiological Sciences. Membership: 22 biological societies. Finances: Membership: $30. Meetings: Biennial, various locations. Publications: ACTA Physiologica Latino Americana, bimonthly, Alvaro Gimeno, editor.

★ 1109 ★
LATIN AMERICAN SOCIETY FOR PEDIATRIC
    RESEARCH
Rúa Cardoso de Almeida 2144   (11) 62-4062
01251-São Paulo, Brazil   Established 1962

Professor Benjamin Jose Schmidt, M.D., General
    Secretary
The Society was founded with the goal of promoting and activating new research in pediatric fields and promoting relationships between their own members from Latin America and with other pediatric research societies. They provide meetings where the research can be discussed openly and constructively, and they aim to influence the medical correspondence in teaching and assistential pediatrics. Membership: 122 (active, with right to vote and discuss; and honorary, right to discuss but not to vote). Finances: Membership: Active, $20; honorary, no charge; Other Sources: Multinational pharmaceutical companies. Meetings: Annual, various locations.

★ 1110 ★

LATIN AMERICAN SOCIETY OF PATHOLOGY
Apartado Postal 12-923   (905) 574-12 35
Mexico 12, D.F. Mexico   Established 1955

Founded in 1955 for the advancement of the practice,
teaching and research in pathology in Latin American
countries. Membership: 580 (honorary, actives,
associated and junior members). Finances: Membership: Active members pay $15 Dlls. annually;
Other Sources: Short courses in Pathology. Awards:
Awards and diplomas to outstanding members. Meetings: Biennial, various locations in Latin America.
Publications: Patologia, quarterly, Dr. Luis Benitez-
Bribies, editor; Information Boletin, semiannually,
President in charge (editor).

★ 1111 ★

LATIN-MEDITERRANEAN MEDICAL UNION
c/o Professor J. Hureau
Hospital de Vaugirard
389 Rue de Vaugirard
F-75015 Paris, France

Professor J. Hureau, Secretary;
   Professor R. Bourgeon, President
To meet biennially in one of the following countries:
France, Italy or Spain for the purpose of discussing
new developments in surgery. Membership: Approximately 150 (teaching and practicing doctors). Finances: Other Sources: Contributions from pharmaceutical firms. Meetings: Biennially, various locations in France, Italy, Spain.

★ 1112 ★

LATIN-MEDITERRANEAN SOCIETY OF PHARMACY
Via Belmeloro 6   (051) 28 89 82
Bologna, Italy   Established 1953

Elisa Ghigi, Italian Group President;
   Professor Antonio Timbesi, Secretary General
To establish scientific, professional and cultural links
between member pharmacists. Membership: Individuals in France, Italy, Spain. Finances: Dues,
donations, legacies. Meetings: Biennial, various
locations. Affiliation: Mediterranean Medical
Union.

★ 1113 ★

LEADER DOGS FOR THE BLIND
1039 Rochester Road   (313) 651-9011
Rochester, Michigan 48063   Established 1939

Harold L. Pocklington, Executive Director
To train dogs to serve as guides for the blind and to
coordinate blind persons and Leader Dogs as operating
units. Finances: Lions Club, Community Chests,
Sororities, individual contributions. Meetings: Annual, Leader Dog School.

★ 1114 ★

LEAGUE OF RED CROSS SOCIETIES
Post Office Box 276   (022) 34 55 80
CH-1211 Geneva 19, Switzerland   Established 1919

Henrik Beer, Secretary General
To increase the strength of all National Red Cross,
Red Crescent and Red Lion and Sun Societies, serve
as their medium of liaison, coordination and study,
represent them at the international level and protect
their moral and material interests at all times. Activities include the administration and coordination of
international relief actions, coordination and advice
in the fields of health and social service, nursing,
Red Cross Youth and Development of National Societies. Membership: 122 (all National Red Cross,
Red Crescent and Red Lion and Sun Societies internationally recognized). Finances: Membership: Annual quota fixed on basis of resources and membership
of each Society and national per capita income of
country concerned; Other Sources: Interest on investment of reserve funds, supplementary contributions
from National Societies, donations. Meetings:
Executive Committee, biennial, usually Geneva;
Board of Governors, biennial. Publications: Pano-
rama, 6 issues annually, League of Red Cross Societies, editor; Annual Report.

★ 1115 ★

LEUKEMIA SOCIETY OF AMERICA, INC.
800 Second Avenue   (212) 573-8484
New York, New York 10017   Established 1949

Meade P. Brown, Executive Director
Dedicated to the conquest of leukemia through medical research. Supports patient-aid, and public and
professional education programs. Membership:
783,000 volunteers. Finances: Contributions.
Awards: DeVilliers Award for outstanding Leukemia
research; Dameshek Award. Research: Grants,
scholarships, fellowships and special fellowships.
Publications: Annual Report; pamphlets on leukemia.

★ 1116 ★
LIAISON COMMITTEE ON MEDICAL EDUCATION
1 DuPont Circle   (202) 828-0670
Washington, D.C. 20036   Established 1942

James R. Schofield, M.D., Secretary;
    Edward S. Peterson, M.D., Secretary
The Committee, established by the American Medical
Association and the Association of American Medical
Colleges, acts as the recognized accreditation agency
for programs leading to the M.D. degree in the
United States and Canada. Membership: 15. Finances: Other Sources: Funded by the 2 sponsoring
organizations as a public service. Affiliations:
American Medical Association; Association of American Medical Colleges; Committee for the Accreditation of Canadian Medical Schools.

★ 1117 ★
LISTER HILL NATIONAL CENTER FOR BIOMEDICAL
    COMMUNICATIONS
8600 Rockville Pike   (301) 496-4441
Bethesda, Maryland 20209   Established 1968

Lionel M. Bernstein, M.D., Ph.D., Director
The Lister Hill Center was created by act of Congress
in 1968 and placed within the National Library of
Medicine (see separate entry). The Center's mission
is to explore the uses of advanced computer and communications technology to improve health education,
biomedical research, and health care delivery. Current developmental efforts include the use of mini-
computers to develop integrated library services in
health-science libraries, the design of a series of
computerized "knowledge bases" to provide current
information to health practitioners, and the development of videodisc technology for application in biomedical communications. Finances: Other Sources:
Under the Congressional appropriation for the National Library of Medicine. Publications: Series of
technical reports available from the National Technical Information Service. Affiliation: A component
of the National Library of Medicine.

★ 1118 ★
LIVING BANK INTERNATIONAL
Hermann Professional Building
Post Office Box 6725   (713) 528-2971
Houston, Texas 77005   Established 1968

Glen W. Karsten, President
The group is dedicated to helping those persons who,
after death, wish to donate a part or all parts of
their bodies for the purposes of transplantation, therapy, medical research or anatomical studies. The

primary function of The Living Bank is to educate the
public so that being a donor is the usual rather than
the unusual thing. It functions as a service through
which you can make your wishes known. When
called at the time of death, The Living Bank immediately contacts the appropriate facility and cooperates
fully with Eye Banks, Kidney Transplant Centers, etc.
When a body has been donated for anatomical study,
the nearest medical school is notified. Membership:
Over 75,000 potential donors (sustaining, supporting,
participating, contributing). Finances: Foundation
grants, contributions. Meetings: Quarterly board
meetings.

★ 1119 ★
LOUIS BRAILLE FOUNDATION FOR BLIND
    MUSICIANS, INC.
215 Park Avenue South   (212) 982-7290
New York, New York 10003   Established 1951

Sheldon Freund, Executive Director
Auditions, evaluates and counsels blind musicians and
composers; provides a dictation, transcription and
copyright (as well as placement) service for blind
composers; produces demonstration recordings to help
secure work and performances for blind musicians and
composers; obtains paid engagements for qualified
blind musicians; sponsors "showcase" concerts to
present talented blind musicians (under conditions in
which they can be judged on merit alone) in day-care
centers, old age homes and hospitals; where necessary, provides the blind musician with such essentials
for carrying on his activity as professional wardrobe,
payment of telephone bills, paying back dues to the
Musicians' Union, extra transportation costs, special
personal incidentals and emergency aid; provides
theatrical photographs, publicity, and promotional
help for the professional blind musician; offers professional guidance in stage deportment and grooming,
to make sure the artist is well dressed and attractive
in appearance so his blindness does not become a
distraction; provides hand-produced braille transcrip-
tions for both amateur and professional blind musicians
(when unavailable from existing sources); provides
musical instruments and any special equipment needed
by the blind for individuals who cannot meet such
costs themselves; arranges for appropriate training;
provides scholarship aid (when available) to supplement
other resources. Finances: Contributions and endowment.

★ 1120 ★

LOVELACE FOUNDATION FOR MEDICAL EDUCA-
 TION AND RESEARCH
5200 Gibson Boulevard Southeast   (505) 842-7000
Albuquerque, New Mexico 87108   Established 1947

David J. Ottensmeyer, M.D., President
To further the advancement of medical science through
an integrated center of biomedical research, medical
education and clinic-hospital patient care.   Finances: Patient fees, private donations, endowment income and research grants and contracts.   Library:
Lassetter-Foster Memorial Library, 25,200 volumes.
Affiliations: Inhalation Toxicology Research Institute-
Lovelace Biomedical and Environmental Research Institute, Incorporated, a wholly-owned subsidiary.

★ 1121 ★

LUTHERAN BRAILLE EVANGELISM ASSOCIATION
660 East Montana Avenue   (612) 772-1681
St. Paul, Minnesota 55106   Established 1952

Carl C. Sunwall, Executive Director
Christian literature for the blind and others with impaired vision.   Membership: Approximately 4,000.
Meetings: Annual, Minneapolis, Minnesota.   Publications: Christian Megnifier (large print), monthly,
Carl C. Sunwall, editor; Tract Messenger (Braille),
monthly, Carl C. Sunwall, editor; books, hymnals
for the blind, tape cassettes.

★ 1122 ★

LUTHERAN HOSPITAL ASSOCIATION OF AMERICA
7649 N. Eastlake Terrace, 2-F   (312) 465-1282
Chicago, Illinois 60626   Established 1948

Adeline Lavers, Administrative Secretary
To assist in promoting, improving and extending the
services of all hospitals associated with the Lutheran
Church; to study the problems which are specifically
related to Lutheran hospitals, insofar as possible
avoiding duplication of activities sponsored by other
hospital associations; to encourage Lutheran young
people to seek professional training in hospitals of
their own denomination; to foster the maintenance of
a chaplaincy service and continuing program of
Christian service for patients, student nurses and other
personnel so that the spirit of Christ may prevail; to
evaluate unmet needs and to suggest ways and means
of meeting same through existing hospitals as well as
assisting with advice and counsel in the establishment
of Lutheran Hospitals in other localities; to cooperate
with other national hospital associations in promoting
the highest standards of service and to cooperate in
the solution of all problems affecting the hospital

field; to cooperate with all Lutheran agencies in the
development of health and hospital services.   Membership: Lutheran hospitals.   Finances: Membership:
Personal, $3; hospitals, $20-$80.   Meetings: An-
nual, various locations.   Publications: LHA Newsletter; Health Directory, 1972.

★ 1123 ★

LUTHERAN HOSPITALS AND HOMES SOCIETY OF
 AMERICA
Post Office Box 2087   (701) 293-9053
Fargo, North Dakota 58107   Established 1938

Robert A. Anderson, President
To lease, purchase, erect or acquire by device or
bequest, real and personal property essential for the
operation and maintenance of Christian hospitals and
homes, used and needed in the caring for the sick,
infirm, crippled and aged persons, and to do and perform charitable acts incidental to such tasks and other
works of charity.   To operate hospitals and schools
for crippled children and multiple handicapped; operate general hospitals, hospitals for chronically ill,
nursing homes and homes for the aged.   Membership:
7,500.   Finances: Membership: $1 and $25;
Other Sources: Contributions, operating revenue.
Meetings: Annual, various locations.   Publications:
Light of Faith, bimonthly, Marilyn Anstett, editor.

M

MCLAUGHLIN (R. SAMUEL) FOUNDATION
 See: R. Samuel McLaughlin Foundation

★ 1124 ★

MAP INTERNATIONAL
327 Gundersen Drive   (312) 653-6010
Carol Stream, Illinois 60187   Established 1965

Larry E. Dixon, President
MAP International is a worldwide health development
organization serving as a channel through which concerned individuals can respond to human need throughout the developing world.   MAP works with existing
Christian mission organizations and national churches
in a ministry to the whole man, physical and spiritual,
through programs of medical assistance, emergency relief, community development and short-term overseas
personnel.   Finances: Other Sources: Individuals,
churches, foundations.   Publications: Articles on
Community Health, periodically; MAP International

Report, quarterly.

★ 1125 ★
MARCH OF DIMES BIRTH DEFECTS FOUNDATION
1275 Mamaroneck Avenue   (914) 428-7100
White Plains, New York 10605   Established 1938

George S. Dillon, Chairman, Board of Trustees;
    Charles L. Massey, President
Founded in 1938 by President Franklin D. Roosevelt
to support research, medical services and public and
professional education in poliomyelitis. Totally supported development of the Salk killed-virus vaccine
and the Sabin oral vaccine against polio. With
polio conquered, this uniquely successful partnership
of scientists and laymen turned its attention to a
greater unmet need--that of birth defects and improving the outcome of pregnancy. The Foundation supports research and services which offer the best scientific information on the beginning of human life, on
human development before and after birth, and on
those factors believed to insure healthy development
of the unborn and the newborn. Not a membership
organization. Finances: Contributions, bequests.
Former Name: The National Foundation--March of
Dimes.

★ 1126 ★
MARIO NEGRI INSTITUTE FOR PHARMACOLOGICAL
    RESEARCH
Via Eritrea 62   (02) 355 45 46
I-20157 Milan, Italy   Established 1961

Professor Silvio Grattini, Director;
    Professor Alfredo Leonardi, General Secretary
The Mario Negri Institute for Pharmacological Research is a scientific organization for biomedical research. Based in Milan, Italy, where its founder
lived, the Institute operates with the basic aim of
helping to improve the quality of health and life.
It aims to reach this goal by investigating the inner-
most mechanisms of living organisms, by discovering
why certain diseases occur, and by learning what hap-
pens in a body when a "foreign" substance, such as a
drug or a medicine enters it. The Institute's research
path starts at the molecular level and extends to
studies involving the whole body. The results of this
research help in the development of new drugs and in
improving the efficacy of those already in use. The
Institute works in three main fields - cancer, mental
and nervous system disorders, and diseases of the heart
and blood vessels. There are also research programs
on the toxic effects of environmental pollutants and
on several rare diseases. In addition to research,
the Institute arranges training for laboratory techni-

cians, and offers postgraduate courses. It disseminates scientific knowledge and encourages improved
medical practice and the rational use of drugs.
Membership: 320 (members of the institute plus post-
doctoral training fellows, foreign fellows, laboratory
school students, etc.). Finances: Contributions,
grants, national and foreign foundations, international
agencies. Awards: Scholarships to post-doctoral
training fellows. Meetings: International and national congresses, seminars. Publication: Congress
Proceedings. Library: Gustavus A. Pfeiffer Memorial Library. Affiliation: Mario Negri Institute
Foundation, Inc., New York City (U.S.).

★ 1127 ★
MATERNITY CENTER ASSOCIATION
48 East 92nd Street   (212) 369-7300
New York, New York 10028   Established 1918

Ruth Watson Lubic, General Director
Devoted to the improvement of maternity care, the
Association maintains a childbearing center for low-
risk families; conducts classes on pregnancy, childbearing and baby care for expectant mothers and
fathers; responds to requests for information on childbearing and family life problems from parents, community agencies, city and state health departments,
and the communications media; conducts conferences
and seminars on maternity care for doctors, nurses,
nurse-midwives, and other interested professionals;
conducts parent-education institutes for nurses who
teach expectant parent classes; and sponsors research
to investigate problems in maternity and infant care
and to help resolve them. Membership: Approximately 1,000. Finances: Membership: $20 and
over; Other Sources: Foundations, grants, benefits.
Awards: Scholarships to nurse-midwives. Meetings:
Monthly from October to May, New York City.
Publications: Briefs, monthly, Martin Kelly, editor;
Annual Report; educational books and pamphlets.

★ 1128 ★
MAYNARD LISTENER LIBRARY
171 Washington Street   (617) 823-3783
Taunton, Massachusetts 02780   Established 1960

Merrill A. Maynard, Librarian
Free loan of tape recorded books for the Blind and
Physically Handicapped. Membership: Handicapped.
Library: 7,000 titles.

★ 1129 ★
MEDIC ALERT FOUNDATION INTERNATIONAL
1000 North Palm Street   (209) 632-2371
Turlock, California 95380   Established 1956

Alfred A. Hodder, President
Dedicated to educating and encouraging the public to
wear on their person a device for identification of
any medical problems that should be known in an
emergency. Membership: 1,660,000 (United States
and International). Finances: Membership: $15;
Other Sources: Members and charitable organizations.
Meetings: Biennial, various locations. Publications:
Newsletter, bimonthly, Dennis Brennan, editor. Affiliations: Organizations in 14 countries.

★ 1130 ★
MEDICAL COUNCIL OF CANADA
1867 Alta Vista Drive
Post Office Box 8234   (613) 733-3761
Ottawa, Ontario K1G 3H7, Canada   Established 1912

J. W. B. Barr, M.D., Registrar
The registration of medical practitioners in Canada is
a provincial rather than a national responsibility and
every province has a medical council authorized to
decide upon the suitability of candidates for such
registration. The Medical Council of Canada, here-
inafter called the Council, was established in 1912 to
examine professionally, on behalf of the provincial
medical councils, persons certified by the latter as
eligible for examination. The examinations of the
Council lead to enrollment on the Canadian Medical
Register as Licentiate of the Medical Council of Canada and consequent eligibility for registration as a
practitioner by the provincial medical council sponsoring the candidate's admission to examination or by
any other provincial medical council or territorial
registration authority regarding him as suitable for
such registration. Membership: 39 (3 members appointed by the Governor in Council, 2 elected by
each of the provincial medical councils, and 1 from
each university having a medical school). Meetings:
Annual, Ottawa. Publications: Annual Announce-
ment and Information Pamphlet, restricted distribution.
Affiliation: Provincial Medical Councils.

MEDICAL ELECTRONICS AND DATA SOCIETY
    See: Medical Electronics Society

★ 1131 ★
MEDICAL ELECTRONICS SOCIETY
2994 West Liberty Avenue   (412) 343-9666
Pittsburgh, Pennsylvania 15216   Established 1970

Milton H. Aronson, President
The Society's purpose is to improve the quality and
quantity of both products and services available to
all by application of electronic techniques wherever
possible. The group conducts seminars, sponsors
numerous home study courses and issues a Certificate
of Course Completion. Membership: 5,500 (medical
electronics engineers, scientists). Publications:
Medical Electronics, bimonthly. Former Name:
Medical Electronics and Data Society.

★ 1132 ★
MEDICAL GROUP MANAGEMENT ASSOCIATION
4101 East Louisiana   (303) 753-1111
Denver, Colorado 80222   Established 1926

Richard V. Grant, Ph.D., Executive Director
To improve business administration in medical groups
in order to serve better the members of the Association, the medical groups they represent, and medical
group practice. Membership: Active, associate,
honorary, inactive, life, international. Finances:
Membership: Active, $195 plus $50 initiation fee;
associate, $65; international, $75 plus $50 initiation
fee. Meetings: Annual, various locations. Publications: Journal of the M.G.M.A., bimonthly;
Directory; Clinic Manager's Manual; special reports.
Affiliations: American College of Medical Group
Administration; Center for Research in Ambulatory
Health Care Administration.

★ 1133 ★
MEDICAL GROUP MISSIONS OF THE CHRISTIAN
      MEDICAL SOCIETY
1616 Gateway Boulevard
Post Office Box 689   (214) 783-8384
Richardson, Texas 75080   Established 1960

Louisa Haughton, Secretary
A Medical Group Mission is a short-term group outreach of the Christian Medical Society (see separate
entry). Through this means the Christian Medical
Society members from all over the United States and
Canada help to meet the medical and spiritual needs
of the people in the countries where projects are
conducted. The Missions have been held regularly
in the Dominican Republic and Honduras with occasional visits to Columbia, Guatemala, Haiti, Liberia
and Taiwan. About 10-12 projects are held each
year. All projects are clinical/surgical/dental.

Membership: 60-100 participants per project, including medical and non-medical participants. Finances: MGM is a self-supported ministry of CMS. Participants pay all their own expenses, including MGM fees and air fare. The registration fee of $50 covers administrative costs. The project fee covers accommodations and food for participants, local transportation while on a project, and the costs of medications and other supplies. Project fees are $145 for a 1-week project, $175 for a 10-day project, and $250 for a 2-week project; Other Sources: Donations. Publications: Hope, quarterly, Louisa Haughton, editor. Affiliation: Christian Medical Society.

★ 1134 ★
MEDICAL LETTER, INC.
56 Harrison Street   (914) 235-0500
New Rochelle, New York 10801   Established 1959

Mark Abramowicz, M.D., Editor and Chief
    Executive Officer
To publish unbiased critical evaluation of drugs in terms of effectiveness, adverse effects and possible alternative medications. Membership: 125,000 subscribers. Finances: Subscription fees. Publications: Medical Letter on Drugs and Therapeutics, biweekly, Mark Abramowicz, editor; handbooks on drugs. Library: Medical Letter Library, over 1,370 volumes.

★ 1135 ★
MEDICAL LIBRARY ASSOCIATION, INC.
919 North Michigan Avenue
Suite 3208   (312) 266-2456
Chicago, Illinois 60611   Established 1898

Shirley Echelman, Executive Director
The Association aims for the fostering of medical and allied scientific libraries, the exchange of medical literature among its institutional members, and the improvement of the professional qualifications and status of medical librarians. Activities include an exchange program for duplicate copies of books, a certification program, continuing education programs, and an employment referral service. Membership: 5,000 (active, associate, honorary, fellow, life, student, sustaining, institutional). Fellow and honorary are categories elected by the Board of Directors. Finances: Membership: Annual fees: Active, $45; associate, $45; emeritus, $45; student, $10; sustaining, $150; institutional, $75-$175; life members, $900; Other Sources: Sale of publications. Awards: Janet Doe Lecture, Rittenhouse; Ida and George Eliot Prize Award; Marcia C. Noyes Award; Murray Gottlieb Prize Award. Meetings: Annual,

various locations. Publications: Bulletin of the Medical Library Association, quarterly, Robert French Lewis, editor; Current Catalog Proof Sheets, weekly; Vital Notes on Medical Periodicals, 3 times annually, William Beatty, editor; Directory of the Medical Library Association, annually; Index to Audiovisual Serials in Health Sciences, quarterly; MLA News, monthly, Cecile Kramer, editor; monographs and brochures.

★ 1136 ★
MEDICAL PASSPORT FOUNDATION, INC.
Post Office Box 820   (904) 734-0639
DeLand, Florida 32720   Established 1957

Vivian T. Doerr, Secretary-Treasurer
Promotes better medical care through the use by physicians, hospitals and patients of a standardized system of records. Informs the public of the advisability of recording and maintaining uniform individual medical records. Provides individuals, on request, with portable forms for recording their medical history, which are the keys for implementing medical passports. Is engaged in the study of early life (pre-conception, conception, pregnancy, labor and delivery and neonatal period) in an effort to learn the environmental causes of congenital defects. Finances: Gifts, bequests. Meetings: Annual board of directors meeting, usually New York City. Publications: Questions and Answers; The Medical Passport; medical records books.

★ 1137 ★
MENDED HEARTS, INC.
7320 Greenville Avenue
Dallas, Texas 75231   (214) 750-5442
                                 Established 1950

Darla Donhan, Executive Secretary
An affiliation of persons throughout the world who have undergone heart surgery. Its objectives are: to visit and encourage, with the approval of the physician, persons anticipating or recovering from heart surgery; to distribute information of specific educational value to Mended Hearts and potential heart surgery patients; to provide advice and services to families of patients, undergoing heart surgery where possible; to establish a program of assistance to surgeons, physicians and hospitals in their work with heart patients; to cooperate with other organizations which engage in educational and research activities pertaining to heart illnesses; to assist established rehabilitation programs for Mended Hearts and their families; and to plan and conduct a suitable program of social and educational events. Membership:

12,000 (active, associate). <u>Finances:</u> Membership:
$7.50 single; $12 family; $100 single life; $150
family life; Other Sources: Contributions. <u>Meet-</u>
<u>ings:</u> Annual. <u>Publications:</u> Heartbeat, quarterly,
Mari Schaarschmidt, editor; information bulletin.

★ 1138 ★
MENNINGER FOUNDATION
Post Office Box 829   (913) 234-9566
Topeka, Kansas 66601   Established 1925

Roy W. Menninger, M.D., President
A non-profit center for treatment, research, professional education, and prevention in psychiatry. The
Foundation provides inpatient and outpatient psychiatric and neurological treatment, an alcoholism recovery program, a halfway house program, and a Children's Division. <u>Membership:</u> 6,000 (individuals,
corporations, corporate foundations, philanthropic
foundations). <u>Meetings:</u> Annual, Topeka, Kansas.
<u>Publications:</u> Bulletin of the Menninger Clinic, bi-
monthly, Paul W. Pruyser, Ph.D., editor; Menninger
Perspective, quarterly, Sherry Levy-Reiner, Ph.D.,
editor. <u>Library:</u> 35,000 volumes.

★ 1139 ★
MENTAL HEALTH MATERIALS CENTER, INC.
30 East 29th Street   (212) 889-5760
New York, New York 10016   Established 1953

Alex Sareyan, President
To develop new audiences and new distribution techniques for mental health materials; to promote and
distribute mental health materials, including, but not
limited to, books, pamphlets, information, plays,
films, recordings, radio and television manuscripts,
and all other materials designed to increase public
information on mental health; to provide services to
assist organizations in planning, producing, promoting
and distributing their mental health materials; to
create, produce, edit, publish and distribute informational and promotional material in the field of mental
health; to provide a service for consultation and
evaluation of methods of distributing and using mental
health materials. The MHMC is a resource center
for information about authoritative educational materials in the areas of mental health and family life education. Its services are available to a wide range
of community and state programs through a newly established Human Services Educational Resource System.
<u>Membership:</u> Restricted to past and present board
members--approximately 35. <u>Finances:</u> Fees for services rendered to other agencies; contracts and grants
projects carried out for federal, state and local programs; sale of publications; grants and contributions.

<u>Meetings:</u> Annually, New York City. <u>Publications:</u>
Selective Guide to Materials for Mental Health and
Family Life Education; Sneak Previews, bimonthly;
Best in Print, bimonthly.

★ 1140 ★
MENTAL PATIENTS LIBERATION FRONT
Post Office Box 514   (617) 628-8438
Cambridge, Massachusetts 02238 Established 1971

Judi Chamberlin, Contact Person
Completely composed of present and former psychiatric
inmates and outpatients. The Front works for the
human rights of its members through dissemination of
information to the public, a limited amount of advocacy, and alternative ways of supporting one
another without using coercion, forcible drugging,
electroshock, etc. There are no professionals in the
organization. <u>Finances:</u> Other Sources: Donations.
<u>Meetings:</u> 3 times a week, Boston, Massachusetts;
former "consumers" are invited to Sunday night meetings, at 6:00 P.M.; the public is invited to first
and third Monday nights at 7:30 P.M. <u>Publications:</u>
Acting Out, quarterly, collective editing; Legal
Handbook--4th Edition, unfunded. <u>Affiliation:</u>
There are 50 similar grassroots organizations in United
States and Europe.

★ 1141 ★
MENTAL RESEARCH INSTITUTE
555 Middlefield Road   (415) 321-3055
Palo Alto, California 94301   Established 1958

Carlos E. Slvzki, M.D., Director
To promote advanced research and training in the
fields of family interaction, communication, and other
social systems involving human behavior. MRI has
pioneered the study of the processes of communication
and conflict resolutions within the family. The research interests of the organization have broadened
recently to include how the family relates to other
families and to the institutions of society. <u>Finances:</u>
Voluntary donations. <u>Publications:</u> Articles in professional journals and books. <u>Library:</u> 700 volumes.

★ 1142 ★
MENTAL RETARDATION ASSOCIATION OF AMERICA
211 East Third Street, Suite 212 (801) 328-1575
Salt Lake City, Utah 84111   Established 1974

Dr. Ernest H. Dean, President
Independent volunteer organization of state and local
associations, working for the improvement of the

quality of life for the mentally retarded; promoting research aimed at preventing mental retardation in future generations. Membership: 22 groups. Meetings: Annual Convention, June, various locations.

★ 1143 ★
METROPOLITAN COLLEGE MENTAL HEALTH
   ASSOCIATION
c/o Rachel R. Aubrey
Columbia University Health Service
519 West 114th Street   (212) 280-2878
New York, New York 10027   Established 1969

Rachel R. Aubrey, M.S.W., Secretary
To promote high standards in the delivery of mental health services to students, and in the training programs of those persons working with students; to stimulate continuing education to professionals in the college mental health field; to further research, and to provide a forum for exchange and discussion of college mental health problems. Membership: 150. Finances: Membership: Individual, $15; full-time graduate student, $10; institution, $25. Meetings: Quarterly. Publications: Newsletter, quarterly.

★ 1144 ★
MICHAEL E. DEBAKEY INTERNATIONAL CARDIO-
   VASCULAR SOCIETY
1200 Moursund   (713) 790-5720
Houston, Texas 77030   Established 1977

Yousif Al-Naaman, M.D., President; Patricio
   Welsh, M.D., Vice President; Charles H.
   McCollum, M.D., Secretary-Treasurer
To encourage, advance, and promote scientific research relating to the treatment of cardiac and cardiovascular defects and diseases through cardiovascular surgery, by means of awarding fellowship grants for the purpose of allowing promising young surgeons to study experimental and clinical cardiovascular surgery, and providing annual awards to persons who have made significant contributions to the field of cardiovascular surgery; and to educate the medical community by correlating information relating to cardiovascular care of patients and disseminating such information by means of scientific meetings and symposia. Membership: 525. Finances: Membership: $25 annual dues; Other Sources: Contributions by drug companies and registration at meetings support the cost of the meeting. Awards: The Michael E. DeBakey Award is given every other year, it consists of a substantial cash award plus a miniature statue of Dr. DeBakey. Meetings: Biennial, various locations.

★ 1145 ★
MICHAEL FUND/INTERNATIONAL FOUNDATION
   FOR GENETIC RESEARCH
400 Penn Center   (412) 325-3801
Pittsburgh, Pennsylvania 15235   Established 1978

Robert Vogel, Chairman of the Board;
   Randy Engel, President
Formed in 1978 in Pennsylvania to raise funds for prolife genetic research especially in the area of Down's Syndrome. Membership: The organization is a non-membership group managed by a 9 member Board of Directors; in addition, there are various committees of an advisory nature to assist in foundation work. Finances: Other Sources: Direct donations from public solicitations and grant money from foundations. Meetings: Board Meetings only in Pittsburgh, approximately once a month for total board. Remarks: As an organization, The Michael Fund which has a 501 Tax Status, is fairly young; the organization intends to develop a newsletter and information on research in the near future.

★ 1146 ★
MICROALGAE INTERNATIONAL UNION
University of the Trees
Post Office Box 644   (408) 338-2544
Boulder Creek, California 95006   Established 1965

Christopher B. Hills, President
The Union was originally established for the purpose of promoting development of Chlorella in 1965 in all parts of the world. A new edible microalgae, called Spirulina, was discovered and the Union subsequently changed its emphasis to promoting Spirulina as a future world food for health and protein-starved countries. Membership: Individuals in various countries. Publications: Newsletter (occasional). Affiliation: With Journal of Nutritional Microbiology. Former Name: Chlorella International Union.

★ 1147 ★
MICROSCOPICAL SOCIETY OF CANADA
150 College Street, Room 79
University of Toronto
Toronto, Ontario M5S 1A1,   (416) 978-8896
   Canada   Established 1972

G. H. Haggis, President;
   N. Anderson, Executive Secretary
The Society's purpose is to promote the advancement of microscopy and its application in the physical and life sciences. Membership: 480. Finances: Membership: Ordinary, $12; corporate, $125; student, $6. Awards: President's Award for Graduate

Students, 2 awards annually, 1 in Material Science and 1 in Biological Science. Meetings: Annual, various locations. Publications: Bulletin, quarterly, F. W. Doane, editor; Proceedings of the Annual Meeting.

★ 1148 ★
MIDDLE ATLANTIC HEALTH CONGRESS
760 Alexander Road, CN 1   (609) 452-9280
Princeton, New Jersey 08540   (609) 924-0049
                                 Established 1948

Jack W. Owen, Convention Manager, Secretary
This non-profit arm of the state hospital associations of Delaware, New Jersey, New York and Pennsylvania has as its purpose the planning and execution of an annual educational and exhibit health convention held in May. Meetings: Annual, Atlantic City, New Jersey.

★ 1149 ★
MID-WEST HEALTH CONGRESS
208 Nichols Road   (816) 561-6202
Kansas City, Missouri 64112   Established 1927

Thomas W. Waters, Executive Director
To promote professional education and to encourage higher standards of health care. Membership: 15 state health-care organizations. Finances: Exhibits. Meetings: Annual.

★ 1150 ★
MIDWESTERN PSYCHOLOGICAL ASSOCIATION
c/o Judith P. Goggin
Department of Psychology   (915) 747-5478
El Paso, Texas 79968   Established 1926

Judith P. Goggin
To meet annually to exchange scientific information. Has functions in the areas of job placement, scientific and publishing exhibits, social activities and the application of psychology. Membership: 4,000 (life members; members; student members). Finances: Members, $6 annually; students, $3 annually; Other Sources: Non-member registration at the Annual Meeting; exhibit fees; placement fees; program advertising. Lectureship: Invited addresses and symposium at Annual Meeting. Meetings: Annual, various locations. Publications: Program of the Annual Meeting, annual, Secretary-Treasurer, editor.

★ 1151 ★
MIGRAINE FOUNDATION
390 Brunswick Avenue   (416) 920-4916
Toronto, Ontario M5R 2Z4, Canada

Rosemary Dudley, Executive Vice President
The Foundation is a non-profit organization dedicated to helping Canada's migraine sufferers. It aims to make available to the public, migraine sufferers, medical, education and other agencies, information concerning migraine; to encourage and sponsor research into various aspects of migraine--causes, effects, treatment--and to evaluate findings; and to establish clinics to serve migraine sufferers across Canada and to serve as training centres for medical and para-medical personnel in the treatment and recognition of migraine. Finances: Contributions and dues.

★ 1152 ★
MILTON HELPERN INSTITUTE OF FORENSIC
   MEDICINE
520 First Avenue   (212) 340-0102
New York, New York 10016   Established 1962

Ellen Brenner, Librarian
To promote medical-legal research and education, to collect material and provide a reference source for the use of medical examiners and related professionals. Membership: 300 (annual, sustaining, contributing, life). Finances: Membership: Annual, $25; sustaining, $50; contributing, $100; life, $500; Other Sources: Random donations from various institutions. Awards: Annual Memorial Award for contributions to the field of Legal Medicine. Meetings: Annual spring symposium for coroners, medical examiners, and law enforcement officers; annual memorial awards dinner. Publications: International Microform Journal of Legal Medicine and Forensic Sciences, quarterly, Dr. William Eckert, editor. Library: Milton Helpern Library of Legal Medicine, 3,000 volumes (open to members, and to the public by appointment). Affiliation: New York University and the City of New York.

MILTON (JOHN) SOCIETY FOR THE BLIND
   See: John Milton Society for the Blind

★ 1153 ★
MONTREAL NEUROLOGICAL INSTITUTE
3801 University Street
Montreal, Quebec H3A 2B4,   (514) 284-4500
   Canada   Established 1934

William Feindel, M.D., Director
Research and teaching in neurology, neurosurgery and the neurosciences. Membership: 60 staff, 30 research fellows, 50 support staff (neuroscientists, associate neuroscientists and fellows). Finances: Other Sources: External research grants (1×10^6), donations and endowments. Awards: Killam Scholarships. Publications: Annual Report, annual. Library: Fellows' Library, Montreal Neurological Institute, 4,000 volumes (inter-library loans only; photocopies are supplied wherever possible).

★ 1154 ★
MORENO ACADEMY, WORLD CENTER OF PSY-
    CHODRAMA, GROUP PSYCHOTHERAPY AND
    SOCIOMETRY, INC.
259 Wolcott Avenue   (914) 831-2318
Beacon, New York 12508   Established 1968

Zerka T. Moreno, Secretary
To promote and stimulate interest and knowledge of these sciences among both professionals and laymen on an international scale; to coordinate research and training; to serve as a central source of information and assistance. Membership: Professionals in the fields of psychodrama and group psychotherapy. Finances: Fellow, $100; associate, $50; founder over $10,000; sponsor over $100; member $15; Other Sources: Contributions. Meetings: Annual or biennial, various locations. Publications: Group Therapy; International Journal of Sociometry and Sociatry.

MOTT (C.S.) CENTER FOR HUMAN GROWTH &
DEVELOPMENT
    See: C. S. Mott Center for Human Growth &
    Development

★ 1155 ★
MULTIPLE SCLEROSIS SOCIETY OF CANADA
130 Bloor Street West, Suite 700   (416) 922-6065
Toronto, Ontario M5S 1N9, Canada Established 1948

Sheila Kieran, Executive Director
The Society works to promote and fund research into multiple sclerosis, to increase public awareness of the problems of MS and patient service. Finances: Membership: $2 annually; Other Sources: Donations from national corporations and foundations; fund raising drives. Awards: Research Grants; Postdoctoral Fellowships; Research Studentships; Career Development Awards; MS Research Clinics. Meetings: Annual, various locations. Publication: MS Canada, 4 to 5 times annually, Deanna Groltzinger, editor.

Affiliation: 4 divisional offices; 96 chapters.

★ 1156 ★
MUSCULAR DYSTROPHY ASSOCIATION, INC.
810 Seventh Avenue   (212) 586-0808
New York, New York 10019   Established 1950

Robert Ross, Vice President and Executive Director
To foster scientific research into the cause and cure of muscular dystrophy and related neuromuscular diseases; to provide specific assistance to individuals through a program of patient and community services, administered locally through affiliated chapters and nationally through establishment of clinics, and medical and paramedical conferences; to carry on a program of education among physicians, members of paramedical professions, patients, and the general public. Membership: 28,000 affiliate chapter members; 17 member board of directors; 80 national corporate members. Finances: Contributions. Awards: Post doctoral fellowships; research awards and grants. Publications: M.D. News, bimonthly, various publications. Affiliation: 269 affiliate chapters.

★ 1157 ★
MYASTHENIA GRAVIS FOUNDATION, INC.
15 East 26th Street   (212) 889-8157
New York, New York 10010   Established 1952

Daniel Morris, Executive Director
To foster, coordinate and support research into the cause, prevention, alleviation and cure of myasthenia gravis; to voluntarily aid and assist sufferers of this disease; to disseminate among members of the medical profession, information concerning the results of research in myasthenia gravis; to disburse research funds to institutions and individuals for the purpose of finding the cause and cure of the disease, as well as improved treatment techniques; to disseminate information on the disease and the work of the Foundation and its chapters to the general public. Membership: Patients and their relatives and friends, medical professionals and other interested persons. Finances: Membership: $5; Other Sources: Contributions, memorials, honors, bequests, special events. Awards: Grants-in-Aid Clinics; Henry R. Viets Student Fellowships; Kermit E. Osserman Post-Doctoral Fellowships; Special Research Projects. Publications: Update (newsletter), 8 annually; handbooks, brochures, manuals, public service ads, films, etc.

★ 1158 ★

MYOPIA INTERNATIONAL RESEARCH FOUNDATION,
    INC.

415 Lexington Avenue, Suite 705   (212) 867-1888
New York, New York 10017   Established 1963

Sylvia N. Rachlin, Executive Vice President
To sponsor research into the causes, treatment and
prevention of nearsightedness and blindness due to
myopia. Finances: Membership: $5; Other
Sources: Contributions. Meetings: 10 to 20 annually, usually New York City. Publications: Com-
plimentary distribution of research reports to doctors.

N

★ 1159 ★

NARCOTICS EDUCATION, INC.
6830 Laurel Street, N.W.
Post Office Box 4390   (202) 723-4774
Washington, D.C. 20012   Established 1954

E. H. J. Steed, Executive Director
To prepare and place educational and research materials in the hands of educators, schools, libraries,
churches and other organizations carrying on educational programs dealing with the study of tobacco,
alcohol and narcotics. Finances: Sale of materials;
donations. Publications: Listen, monthly; Smoke
Signals, monthly, F. A. Soper, editor; The Winner,
monthly; books, films, reprints, posters, Audio Visual aids.

★ 1160 ★

NATIONAL ACADEMY OF OPTICIANRY
Post Office Box 19391   (202) 659-7672
Washington, D.C. 20036   Established 1973

Floyd H. Holmgrain, Jr., Ed.D., Executive Director
The Academy is a non-profit corporation devoted to
promoting opticianry education. Membership: 2,500
licensed certified opticians and master opticians.
Finances: $47.50; initiation fee, $15. Awards:
Beverly Myers Achievement Awards. Meetings: An-
nual, various locations; seminars, various locations,
about 20 annually. Publications: Archives of the
National Academy of Opticianry; Book Review on
Opthalmic Subjects.

★ 1161 ★

NATIONAL ACCREDITATION ASSOCIATION AND
    THE AMERICAN EXAMINING BOARD OF
    PSYCHOANALYSIS

80 Eighth Avenue, Suite 1210   (212) 741-0515
New York, New York 10011   Established 1972

Phyllis W. Meadow, Ph.D., President
Establishes standards for psychoanalytic training and
works to improve its quality by evaluating and accrediting psychoanalytic training institutes which may
train medical doctors, psychologist, social workers,
counselors and others.   Sets standards for certification of individual psychoanalysts and psychoanalytic
psychotherapists; certifies as competent those who
meet its standards. Membership: 1,120 (1,100 individuals and 20 psychoanalytic training institutes).
Meetings: Annual Convention, various locations.
Publications: Newsletter, semiannual; Directory,
annual; National Registry of Psychoanalysts, annual;
Manual on Accreditation and Standards.

★ 1162 ★

NATIONAL ACCREDITATION COUNCIL FOR
    AGENCIES SERVING THE BLIND AND VISUALLY
    HANDICAPPED

79 Madison Avenue, Suite 1406   (212) 683-8581
New York, New York 10016   Established 1967

Richard W. Bleecker, Ed.D., Executive Director
Established to encourage improvements in services and
to give public recognition to agencies and schools for
the blind which demonstrate substantial compliance
with national standards for management, services and
public accountability. Membership: 152 representing 84 accredited organizations; 33 sponsors and
supporters and 35 individual members of the Board of
Directors. Finances: Membership: Accredited and
sponsoring members, $50-$1,500; supporters, $50;
Other Sources: Grants and contributions. Meetings:
Annual, various locations. Publications: The Stand-
ard-Bearer, 3 times annually, Carl R. Augusto, editor; Annual Report, annually, Cheryl Sandler, editor; List of Accredited Members, semiannually,
Ann F. Barber, editor; Self-Study and Evaluation
Guides, Huesten Collingwood, editor.

★ 1163 ★

NATIONAL ACCREDITING AGENCY FOR CLINICAL
    LABORATORY SERVICES

222 South Riverside Plaza
Suite 1512   (312) 648-0270
Chicago, Illinois 60606   Established 1974

Carol M. Elkins, M.T., (ASEP) M.Ed., Executive Director

The Agency's aim is to maintain high educational and ethical standards in accredited programs which educate medical technologists, medical laboratory technicians, certified laboratory assistants, and those specializing in histotechnique. The organization collaborates on accreditation matters with the Committee on Allied Health Education and Accreditation of the American Medical Association by surveying, evaluating and reporting to the CAHEA on every program accredited by the AMA CAHEA at least once every 5 years or more often as needed. Membership: 16 Review Board members (4 pathologists, 4 medical technologists, 1 medical laboratory technician, 1 certified laboratory assistant, 2 educators holding earned doctorates, 1 clinical microbiologist, 1 histologic technologist, and 2 consumers). Publications: NAACLS News, quarterly. Affiliations: American Society of Clinical Pathologists; American Society for Medical Technology; American Society of Microbiology; and National Society of Histotechnology.

NATIONAL ACCREDITING COMMISSION
See: Credentialing Commission

★ 1164 ★
NATIONAL AMPUTATION FOUNDATION, INC.
12-45 150th Street   (212) 767-8400
Whitestone, New York 11357   Established 1919

Frank Ruzika, President; Sol Kaminsky, Secretary
The National Amputation Foundation (NAF) has for over 50 years been offering valuable assistance to veterans of World War I, II, Korea and the Vietnam Conflict. The new civilian amputee has become a major concern to the Foundation. Unlike the new veteran amputee who is generally a male and relatively young, the new civilian amputee is older and includes many female amputees. The amputee population has been increasing due to accidents (this category includes both young and old and male and female), diabetes, cancer and circulatory diseases. In many cases the civilian amputee suffers a greater psychological trauma than the young soldier. The services provided by the Foundation include legal counsel, vocational guidance and placement, social activities, liaison with outside groups, psychological aid, training in the use of prosthetic devices. Through vocational guidance an amputee is encouraged to enter the training program for suitable employment. The Foundation works with other agencies as well as the private section in their effort to find jobs. The Foundation sponsors an "Amp to Amp" program. An Amp member of our organization who has returned to

a normal life visits the new amputee. This has proved to be a terrific morale builder. Membership: 2,000 (amputees, veterans and civilians; honorary membership, not amputees). Finances: Membership: $10 annually; Other Sources: Solicitation from the public sector. Awards: Amp of the Year Award. Meetings: Second and fourth Tuesday of the month; other special meetings called from time to time; quarterly meetings; Whitestone, New York. Publications: Amp, 10 months annually (except July and August), Don Sioss, editor. Affiliations: Join Handicapped Council; Disabled American Veterans.

★ 1165 ★
NATIONAL ASSEMBLY OF NATIONAL VOLUNTARY HEALTH AND SOCIAL WELFARE ORGANIZATIONS, INC.
291 Broadway   (212) 267-1700
New York, New York 10007   Established 1923

Vernon M. Goetcheus, Ph.D., Executive Director
The National Assembly is an association of national voluntary health and social welfare organizations concerned with human services. The organization's purpose is to facilitate communication and cooperation among member agencies and thereby enhance the capacity of each one to accomplish its own goals and objectives. Membership: 36 (national voluntary organizations). Finances: Membership: Dues formula; Other Sources: Government grants, individual contributions, foundation and corporate support. Meetings: Annual, alternating between New York and Washington, D.C. Publications: National Assembly News, quarterly; Public Policy Perspectives, quarterly; Service Directory of National Voluntary Health and Social Welfare Organizations, biennial.

★ 1166 ★
NATIONAL ASSOCIATION FOR DOWN'S SYNDROME
Post Office Box 63   (312) 543-6060
Oak Park, Illinois 60303   Established 1960

Sheila Hebein, Executive Secretary
NADS acts as a clearinghouse of information on Down's Syndrome. It attempts to keep its membership informed on such areas as education, recreation, occupation, rehabilitation, research and legislation. Membership: 1,500 (families, professionals in medicine, special education). Finances: Membership: $10; Other Sources: Fund raising events, donations. Meetings: Quarterly, Chicago, Illinois.

★ 1167 ★
NATIONAL ASSOCIATION FOR HOSPITAL
    DEVELOPMENT
1700 K Street, N.W., Suite 605   (202) 857-0107
Washington, D.C. 20006

Richard A. Strano, Executive Director
To advance the interests and knowledge of hospital
development; to assist in providing for continuing education; to work toward constantly improved professional standards; to encourage and stimulate better
understanding of hospital needs; to accomplish common goals through an exchange of ideas and information; to promote the importance and prestige of the
hospital development field. Membership: 1,200
(active, 1,084; associate, 12; institutional, 69;
affiliate, 35). Finances: Membership: Active,
$100-$150; associate, $75-$100; institutional, $150;
affiliate, $250-$400. Awards: Annual Si Seymour
Award to an active member; Annual NAHD Governmental Affairs Achievement Award to an individual in
government. Meetings: Annual National Conference,
1981 Denver; 1982, Cincinnati; 1983, New York;
1984, San Francisco; 1985, Atlanta; 1986, Phoenix;
1987, Boston; 1988 (Open); 1989, Seattle plus 12
Regional Conferences. Publications: NAHD News,
10 times annually; NAHD Journal, semiannually.

★ 1168 ★
NATIONAL ASSOCIATION FOR INDEPENDENT
    LIVING
c/o National Rehabilitation Association
633 South Washington   (703) 836-0850
Alexandria, Virginia 22314

A Division of the National Rehabilitation Association
(see spearate entry). The purpose of NAIL is to
stimulate public and professional awareness of the
meaning of independent living and the necessity of it
in regard to dealing with homebound and institutionalized persons, most of whom are severly disabled; to
build stronger communications between the homebound
and institutionalized people and the rehabilitation
professionals to insure steps are taken to guarantee a
total rehabilitation plan--an important plan of which
is independent living; to initiate, expedite and foster
research, demonstration and innovation for homebound
and institutionalized persons to live to their fullest
capacity; to develop, disseminate and foster the utilization of information, skill, knowledge, and ability
needed to more effectively serve homebound and institutionalized persons; to promote through advocacy
and related efforts, social policy for the betterment
of homebound and institutionalized persons; and to
work closely with Legislators to assure legal rights for
the severely handicapped to live. Membership: All
members of NAIL must be members of the National

Rehabilitation Association.

NATIONAL ASSOCIATION FOR MENTAL HEALTH
    See: National Mental Health Association

★ 1169 ★
NATIONAL ASSOCIATION FOR MUSIC THERAPY,
    INC.
Post Office Box 610   (913) 842-1909
Lawrence, Kansas 66044   Established 1950

Margaret S. Sears, Executive Director
The progressive development of the use of music in
medicine, through advancement of research, distribution of helpful information, establishment of qualifications and standards of training for therapists and
perfection of techniques of music programming which
aid medical treatment most effectively. Membership:
2,776 (active, associate, student, patron, affiliate
organization). Finances: Membership: Active, $50;
associate, $40; student, $15; patron, $100 minimum;
affiliated organization, $50; Other Sources: Dona-
tions. Awards: Gaston Writing Award. Meetings:
Annual, various locations. Publications: Journal of
Music Therapy, quarterly, Janet Gilbert, editor;
Handbook; Bulletins; films, other. Affiliations:
New England, Mid-Atlantic, Southeastern, Southwestern, Western, Midwestern, Great Lakes, and
South Central Regional Chapters.

NATIONAL ASSOCIATION FOR PHYSICAL
EDUCATION FOR COLLEGE WOMEN
    See: National Association for Physical Education
        in Higher Education

★ 1170 ★
NATIONAL ASSOCIATION FOR PHYSICAL
    EDUCATION IN HIGHER EDUCATION
c/o Mary O. Bowman
San Jose State University
Department of Human Performance
San Jose, California 95192   Established 1978

Promotes physical education in higher education.
Membership: 1,300 (active, student, emertus, honorary). Finances: Membership: Active, $25;
emeritus, $25; student, $15. Meetings: Annual,
held in early January each year. Publications:
Quest, semiannual, E. Dean Ryan, editor; Annual
Proceedings, annually; Action Line (Newsletter),
3 times annually, Ron Feingold, editor. Former

Name: National College Physical Education Association for Men and National Association for Physical Education for College Women.

★ 1171 ★

NATIONAL ASSOCIATION FOR PRACTICAL NURSE
    EDUCATION AND SERVICE, INC.
254 West 31st Street   (212) 736-4540
New York, New York 10001   Established 1941

Lucille L. Etheridge, R.N., Executive Director
To promote and maintain high educational standards
for the licensed practical/vocational nurse through national accreditation of basic practical nurse programs
and continuing education.   Recognized by United
States Commissioner of Education and The Council on
Postsecondary Accreditation as accrediting agency for
schools and programs of practical nursing.   Provides
consultation service to aid practical nursing programs
during the planning stages, to advise on facilities,
equipment, policies, curriculum staffing, etc.   Prepares and publishes informational and educational materials for use in practical nursing education and service.   Prepares and publishes annually a list of approved schools of practical nursing in the United
States and its territories.   Conducts regional workshops on practical nurse education and service and
provides materials and resource personnel.   Membership: 30,000.   Finances: Membership: $20-$300;
Other Sources: Contributions from foundations, corporations and individuals; sale of publications.
Awards: Scholarships; Awards of Distinction; Membership Awards.   Meetings: Annual, various locations.   Publications: Journal of Practical Nursing,
monthly, Freda Friedman, editorial director; Direct
Lines, bimonthly, Ellen Rosen, editor.   Affiliations:
State licensed practical/vocational nurse association.

NATIONAL ASSOCIATION FOR RETARDED CITIZENS
    See: Association for Retarded Citizens of the
        United States.

★ 1172 ★

NATIONAL ASSOCIATION FOR SEARCH AND
    RESCUE
Post Office Box 2123   (714) 268-3266
La Jolla, California 92038   Established 1970

George Wesley Reynolds; Lois Clark McCoy;
    Scott Ruby
The National Association for Search and Rescue
(NASAR) is a nonprofit organization actively working
toward the development of improved communications

and coordination between Federal, State, local and
volunteer Search and Rescue (SAR) groups.   NASAR's
primary goal is aiding in the development and implementation of a total, coordinated emergency response,
rescue, and recovery system.   SAR can probably be
best defined as "finding and aiding people in distress –
relieving trauma and suffering."   Membership: 2,400
(state member, organization member, individual member, corporate member, sustaining member); distinguished professionals and volunteers, all active in the
fields of search and rescue, disaster aid, emergency
medicine, and awareness education.   Finances:
Membership: State, $150; organization, $50; individual, $25; corporate, $500; sustaining, $100;
Other Sources: Membership sales, contributions,
catalog sales.   Meetings: Semiannual Board and
Trustees Meetings, various locations; Annual Conferences, various locations.   Publications: Briefings,
quarterly, Louis J. Levinson, editor; Update, quarterly, Louis J. Levinson, editor.

★ 1173 ★

NATIONAL ASSOCIATION FOR VISUALLY HANDI-
    CAPPED
305 East 24 Street   (212) 889-3141
New York, New York 10010   Established 1954

Lorraine H. Marchi, Executive Director
Only national voluntary health agency serving the
partially seeing, not the totally blind.   Offers large
print textbooks, testing material and reading material,
providing counsel and guidance to parents of partially seeing children, adults with impaired vision, the
professionals, and paraprofessionals, who work with
the partially seeing, medical facilities, retirement
communities, libraries, educational facilities, hospitals
and nursing homes.   Serves as the "umbrella organization" for information about sources of assistance
from public and private sources, and refers individuals
to local agencies for service.   Offers Youth Group
activities in New York and San Francisco, as well
as Adult Discussion Groups in both cities.   Distributes
and publishes informational literature about partial
vision throughout the country and in many foreign
countries.   Serves as consultant to commercial publishers who are considering entering the large print
field.   Membership: 3,000 (individuals, clubs, organizations and foundations).   Finances: Membership:
Regular, $15; sponsor, $50; sustaining, $100; pa-
tron, $250; life clubs, $1,000; organizations, $50;
Other Sources: Greeting Cards, stock investments--
no government or united drive monies received.
Meetings: Approximately 10 annually, New York
City.   Library: Loan Library, 251 volumes (individual partially seeing persons).

★ 1174 ★

NATIONAL ASSOCIATION OF ANOREXIA NERVOSA
AND ASSOCIATED DISORDERS, INC. (ANAD)
Box 271   (312) 831-3438
Highland Park, Illinois 60035   Established 1976

Vivian Meehan, President
A national non-profit educational and self-help organization dedicated to alleviating problems of eating
disorders. Founded by Vivian Meehan, R.N., in
response to limited information on anorexia nervosa
and bulimia. Counseling, referral, self-help groups
and educational programs are the activities of ANAD.
Membership: Membership in ANAD is shared by victims of eating disorders, their families, health professionals and others concerned with eating disorders.
Finances: Membership: Voluntary contributions;
Other Sources: Contributions. Awards: J. B.
Lippincott National Creative Nursing Award. Lectureships: Mrs. Meehan is a frequent lecturer on the
subject of eating disorders. Meetings: ANAD endorses support group meetings nationwide, held at
hospitals, clinics and other locations convenient to
those leading and attending them. Former Name:
Anorexia Nervosa and Associated Disorders, Inc.

NATIONAL ASSOCIATION OF BLUE SHIELD PLANS
    See: Blue Shield Association

★ 1175 ★

NATIONAL ASSOCIATION OF BOARDS OF
    PHARMACY
1 East Wacker Drive, Suite 2210   (312) 467-6220
Chicago, Illinois 60601

Fred T. Mahaffey, Executive Director
The National Association of Boards of Pharmacy is an
organization composed of 57 boards of pharmacy whose
founding purpose was to provide for interstate recip-
rocity of licensure. Over 75 years later, NABP still
provides American pharmacists and the public with the
only reciprocal licensure system in the health profes-
sions--and much more. NABP today has ongoing
activities in every facet of modern pharmacy from
computerized recordkeeping to nuclear pharmacy practice. In every instance, the state boards of pharmacy, through their national association, produce collectively what they cannot accomplish individually.
Membership: 57 boards of pharmacy (active, associate). Finances: Membership: $100 for both active
and associate membership: Other Sources: Reciproc-
ity fees. Awards: Distinguished Service Award, 1
annually. Meetings: Annual committee meetings,
held between the second week in April and the second
week in May. Publications: NABP Newsletter,

monthly, D. J. Lambert, editor; NABP Proceedings,
annually, D. J. Lambert, editor; Survey of Pharmacy Law, annually, D. J. Lambert, editor; State
Board Newsletters, quarterly, D. J. Lambert, editor;
NABPLEX and FDLE Candidates Guide, annually,
D. J. Lambert, editor (Director of Communications
and Meetings). Affiliation: Federation of Associations of Health Regulatory Boards.

★ 1176 ★

NATIONAL ASSOCIATION OF CHAIN DRUG
    STORES, INC.
413 North Lee Street   (703) 549-3000
Alexandria, Virginia 22314   Established 1933

Robert J. Bolger, President
To help members improve their services to the public;
to study all problems incident to the operation of
chain drug stores; to keep standards of service by
chain drug stores high while improving operation and
reducing expenses; to disseminate information to assist in operation of chain drug stores; and to promote
the general welfare of chain drug stores. Membership: 175 chain drug corporations with 12,000 stores;
associate, 470 manufacturers, advertising agencies and
publications. Finances: Membership: Chain Drug -
sales volume; associate, sales volume through chain
members' stores. Meetings: Annual, various locations. Publications: Executive Newsletter, biweekly.

NATIONAL ASSOCIATION OF COORDINATORS OF
STATE PROGRAMS FOR THE MENTALLY RETARDED
    See: National Association of State Mental Re-
    tardation Program Directors, Inc.

★ 1177 ★

NATIONAL ASSOCIATION OF COUNCIL OF
    STUTTERERS
c/o Speech and Hearing Clinic
Catholic University of America   (202) 635-5556
Washington, D.C. 20064   Established 1974

Michael Hartford, Executive Secretary
The Association is a national coalition of local self-
help groups for stutterers. The chief purpose of
these groups is to put stutterers, who tend to isolate
themselves, in contact with each other. Members
share insights and experiences, learning from each
other's mistakes and exhilarating in each other's suc-
cesses. Members learn from each other's adaptive
speech behaviors. No formal therapy is given; all
participants are peers. By forming a national

association these councils intend to enhance their public information work, to generate support for clinical research in stuttering therapy, and to encourage the formation of new councils. Membership: Council, individual (persons not affiliated with a council), association (associations sympathetic to the council's aims). Finances: Membership: Councils, $1 per member; individuals and associations, $5. Publication: Newsletter, bimonthly, Sandra Wagner, editor. Affiliations: Charter councils around the United States and Canada.

★ 1178 ★
NATIONAL ASSOCIATION OF DENTAL
   LABORATORIES, INC.
3801 Mount Vernon Avenue   (703) 683-5263
Alexandria, Virginia 22305   Established 1951

Robert M. Gregory, Executive Director
To uphold and advance the dignity and efficiency of those engaged as operators of dental laboratories, to advance their standards of service to the dental profession, and to establish cooperation among its members. Membership: 2,950 dental laboratories; 10,000 certified dental technicians. Finances: Membership: $132 per laboratory annually; Other Sources: Certification program, publications. Meetings: Annual, various locations; seminars. Publications: NADL Journal, monthly, Audrey J. Calomino, editor; manuals, handbook, directory. Affiliations: 48 state component associations.

★ 1179 ★
NATIONAL ASSOCIATION OF FEDERAL
   VETERINARIANS
1522 K Street, N.W., Suite 836   (202) 223-3590
Washington, D.C. 20005   Established 1918

Clarence H. Pals, D.V.M., Executive Vice President
To promote the welfare of its members, having as a primary purpose the improvement of working conditions among veterinarian employees of the Federal Government and to promote a continuing improvement in the standards of training, levels of conduct and conditions of safety for professional veterinarians. Membership: 1,937 (active, associate, honorary). Finances: Membership: $104; Other Sources: Subscriptions. Meetings: Semiannual, with American Veterinary Medical Association and with the United States Animal Health Association. Publications: Federal Veterinarian, monthly, Edward L. Menning, D.V.M., M.P.H., editor. Affiliation: Constituent body of the American Veterinary Medical Association.

★ 1180 ★
NATIONAL ASSOCIATION OF HEALTH AND
WELFARE MINISTRIES OF THE UNITED
METHODIST CHURCH
1200 Davis Street   (312) 869-9600
Evanston, Illinois 60201   Established 1941

Charles P. Kellogg, Executive Secretary
In cooperation with the Health and Welfare Ministries Division, helps lift the spiritual, scientific and financial standards of United Methodist agencies. Membership: 500-600 (administrators of United Methodist hospitals, homes for the aging, agencies serving children and youth, chaplains, conference board chairpersons, other key personnel affiliated with agencies, and individual members). Finances: Membership: Fee varies according to budget of institution; standard fee for individual members. Meetings: Annual, various locations. Publications: Annual Directory; Health and Welfare News. Affiliations: Health and Welfare Ministries Division, Board of Global Ministries, the United Methodist Church.

★ 1181 ★
NATIONAL ASSOCIATION OF HEALTH UNDER-
   WRITERS
145 North Avenue   (414) 367-3248
Hartland, Wisconsin 53029   Established 1930

John K. Pardee, CAE, RHU, Executive Vice President
A professional association involving persons engaged in the sale and service of disability income and health care insurances. NAHU promotes excellence in the industry and its representatives through information, education and leadership. Membership: 5,000 (active, life, honorary). Finances: Membership: $25 national dues; each state and local chapter sets their own dues; Other Sources: Magazine advertising; annual meeting; Disability Insurance Training Council seminars; Registered Health Underwriter "RHU" and Leading Producers Round Table "LPRT" professional designations. Awards: Registered Health Underwriter "RHU" designation; Leading Producers Round Table "LPRT" designation; Health Insurance Man of the Year Award. Meetings: Annual. Publications: Health Insurance Underwriter, 11 annually, John K. Pardee, CAE, RHU, editor. Former Name: International Association of Health Underwriters.

★ 1182 ★
NATIONAL ASSOCIATION OF HUMAN SERVICES
   TECHNOLOGIES
1127 11th Street, Suite 321   (916) 444-3772
Sacramento, California 95814   Established 1961

William Grimm, Executive Director
Organized for the professional development and utilization of psychiatric technicians. (Psych techs are the line-level personnel in mental health programs who directly deliver services to recipients). From the beginning, the Association has existed to develop the profession of psychiatric technology through licensure or certification programs, development of community college programs, development of career ladders, and continuing education programs. Membership: 6,000 psychiatric technicians and mental health workers. Finances: Membership: $12 annually. Publications: ESPRIT, quarterly, Gregory Alterton, editor; booklets.

★ 1183 ★
NATIONAL ASSOCIATION OF JEWISH HOMES
FOR THE AGED
2525 Centerville Road   (214) 327-4503
Dallas, Texas 75228   Established 1960

Dr. Herbert Shore, Executive Vice President
To represent the best interests of aged served in nonprofit homes; to exchange information and share publications among members. Membership: 105 homes. Finances: Dues based on size of home. Lectureship: Jerome Hammerman Memorial Lecture. Meetings: Annual, various locations. Publications: Newsletter, quarterly, Herbert Shire, editor; Directory, biennial; reports of special conferences. Affiliation: Conference of Jewish Communal Services.

★ 1184 ★
NATIONAL ASSOCIATION OF MAIL SERVICE
PHARMACIES, INC.
1750 K Street, N.W., Suite 1190A (202) 293-2424
Washington, D.C. 20006   Established 1975

John R. McHugh, President;
    James R. Ball, Executive Director
To assist and inform consumers in obtaining the maximum health benefits from the nation's pharmaceuticals through more economical purchasing of highest quality prescription drugs and the proper use of medication. Mail service pharmacies are primarily used by the elderly and retired persons, often chronically ill, immobile, isolated or heavily burdened by drug expense. Membership: 4 (licensed pharmacies which have filled a minimum of 25,000 prescriptions annually for 2 years and which have received and filled by mail a majority of all prescriptions serviced by them during such period). Finances: Membership: Initiation fee, $2,000, plus $1,000 annual assessment. Meetings: Annual, Washington, D.C.

★ 1185 ★
NATIONAL ASSOCIATION OF MEDICAL EXAMINERS
200 South Adams Street   (302) 571-3420
Wilmington, Delaware 19801   Established 1966

William G. Eckertun, President
To improve and make more effective the official investigation under the medical examiner's system of medically unattended, sudden, suspicious and violent deaths; to strengthen the administration and operation of medical examiner offices; to assist and encourage the establishment of the medical examiner system in areas where such system is not now in effect; to establish, maintain and promote proper standards for a model medical examiner system; to disseminate accurate information regarding the medical examiner system and its contributions to the administration of justice and the health of the community; to advance the professional interests of medical examiners, including those relating to the administrative and career aspects of their work; to conduct studies, sponsor publications and undertake activities or projects that would assist medical examiners in improving the quality of their work; to establish and maintain a Code of Ethics. Membership: 400 (medical examiners, pathologists, and other licensed physicians who have responsibilities in related fields). Finances: Membership: $50. Publications: Standards for Inspection and Accreditation of a Modern Medicolegal Investigative System. Affiliation: American Journal of Forensic Medicine and Pathology.

★ 1186 ★
NATIONAL ASSOCIATION OF PATIENTS ON
HEMODIALYSIS AND TRANSPLANTATION, INC.
505 Northern Boulevard   (516) 482-2720
Great Neck, New York 11021   Established 1969

I. Gilbert Willix, President
The Association aims to help patients on a personal basis to adjust to the emotional impact of their illnesses. Activities include programs concerned with education, organ donation, travel, children's summer camps, and rehabilitation. Membership: 9,500 (patients, professional, friends). Finances: Membership: $8.50; Other Sources: Fund-raising campaigns. Publications: NAPHT News, quarterly, June Crowley, editor; Living With Renal Failure; Dialysis World-Wide for the Traveling Patient; Transplant Kidneys, Don't Bury Them; Renal Failure and Diabetes.

★ 1187 ★

NATIONAL ASSOCIATION OF PHARMACEUTICAL
    MANUFACTURERS
747 Third Avenue   (212) 838-3720
New York, New York 10017

George Dowden, President;
    George Schwartz, Executive Director
Legislative, legal and technical activities as affecting
the industry and membership. Membership: 115
(regular and associates). Awards: Man of the Year
Awards; Public Service Award. Meetings: Annual,
Puerto Rico; Regional, East and West Coast.

★ 1188 ★

NATIONAL ASSOCIATION OF PHYSICIANS'
    NURSES
9401 Lee Highway, Suite 210   (703) 273-6262
Fairfax, Virginia 22031   Established 1973

John H. Swain, Executive Director;
    Sara P. Johnson, Membership Director
To bring professional stature through continuing education to physicians' nurses, supplemented with group
benefits. Membership: 2,500 (R.N.'s and LPN's
primarily, some other personnel employed by physicians). Finances: Membership: $34 annually; $24
annual renewals; Other Sources: Conference fees
($125 average). Meetings: Annual, spring, various
resort locations. Publications: The Nightingale,
monthly, Sara P. Johnson, editor.

★ 1189 ★

NATIONAL ASSOCIATION OF PRIVATE PSYCHIA-
    TRIC HOSPITALS
1701 K Street, N.W., Suite 1205   (202) 223-6691
Washington, D.C. 20006   Established 1933

Robert L. Thomas, Executive Director
The National Association of Private Psychiatric Hospitals (NAPPH) is a nonprofit organization devoted to
the improvement of psychiatric hospital treatment and
to the advancement of professional education in psychiatric and hospital administration and allied fields.
The NAPPH works to foster cooperation of all concerned with psychiatric, administrative, legal and related aspects of private and other psychiatric hospitals;
to gain strength of unity in community actions that
discriminate against private psychiatric hospitals or
jeopardize their existence; to assist in the development of research and teaching programs in private psychiatric hospitals. Activities include annual meeting, international conferences, seminars, committees,
public information, personnel recruitment, consulting
services, and publications. Membership: 185 private psychiatric hospitals. Finances: Membership:
Hospitals pay fee based on number of beds; Other
Sources: Education. Meetings: Annual, various

locations; seminars, various locations. Publications:
Newsletter, monthly; Journal, quarterly; Political
Action Reports.

★ 1190 ★

NATIONAL ASSOCIATION OF REHABILITATION
    FACILITIES
5530 Wisconsin Avenue, Suite 955 (301) 654-5882
Washington, D.C. 20015   Established 1954

James Allen Cox, Jr., Executive Director
The purpose of the Association is to strengthen the
resources of rehabilitation facilities so that they may
provide high quality services to disabled persons and
the community at large. Membership: 900 (institutional members, rehabilitation facilities; group and
individual associates). Finances: Membership:
Individual, $25; group, state agencies, $50; national agencies, $100; Other Sources: Government
and grants and contracts. Meetings: Quarterly
Board of Director's meetings; Annual Conference,
various locations. Publications: Newsletter, monthly; NARF State Chapter Legislative Coordination
Program; Code of Ethics: Vocational Rehabilitation
Facilities; A Client Is... Definition of a Client in
a Vocational Rehabilitation Facilities; Communications and Community Relations. Former Name: As-
sociational of Rehabilitation Facilities.

★ 1191 ★

NATIONAL ASSOCIATION OF REHABILITATION
    INSTRUCTORS
c/o National Rehabilitation Association
633 South Washington   (703) 836-0850
Alexandria, Virginia 22314

A Division of the National Rehabilitation Association
(see separate entry). The purpose of NARI is to
promote the rehabilitation of all handicapped persons
by providing a medium through which all Rehabilitation Instructors may coordinate and combine their
teaching interests with other instructors, facilities,
workshops, centers, individuals, or organizations engaged in instructional services to the handicapped;
and to encourage and stimulate professional growth of
instructors through education, in order that they may
be continually prepared to meet the needs of changing
times. Membership: All members of N A R I must
be members of the National Rehabilitation Association.

★ 1192 ★

NATIONAL ASSOCIATION OF REHABILITATION
    SECRETARIES
c/o National Rehabilitation Association
633 South Washington
Alexandria, Virginia 22314   (703) 836-0850

A Division of the National Rehabilitation Association (see separate entry). The purpose of NARS is to promote the highest ethical conduct and practices in respecting the dignity, rights, and uniqueness of rehabilitation clients served, maintaining strict confidence of information and records; to discuss and exchange ideas concerning the specialized skills and knowledge needed by secretaries; and to encourage recruitment of qualified persons for secretarial-clerical work in the field of rehabilitation. NARS' program of services includes the identification, organization, and dissemination of knowledge and skills, in-service training for rehabilitation secretaries, development of regional and annual conference programs, encouragement of achievement through presentation of an annual award, and publication of a newsletter unique to secretarial-clerical persons employed in a rehabilitation setting. Membership: All members of NARS must be members of the National Rehabilitation Association.

★ 1193 ★
NATIONAL ASSOCIATION OF RESIDENTS AND
    INTERNS
292 Madison Avenue   (212) 949-5960
New York, New York 10017   Established 1959

George J. Arden, Executive Director;
    Bernadette Surak, Executive Secretary
The Association is dedicated to advancing the economic welfare and education of medical and dental students, residents, interns and fellows by providing group financial benefits such as major merchandise discount privileges, insurance and loan programs, educational, travel, and special services. Membership: 100,000. Finances: Membership: $12.50 annually. Publications: Stethoscope, newsletter, bimonthly.

★ 1194 ★
NATIONAL ASSOCIATION OF RETAIL DRUGGISTS
1750 K Street, N.W., Suite 1200   (202) 347-7495
Washington, D.C. 20006   Established 1898

William E. Woods, Executive Vice President
To protect and promote the commercial interests of the Independent Retail Pharmacies in the United States. Provides legal services, professional advice, scientific assistance in the field of pharmacy, business promotion activities. Membership: Approximately 30,000 (proprietors of retail drug stores, registered pharmacists employed in retail drug stores). Finances: Membership: Active, $80; associate, $60; Other Sources: Advertising in journal and almanac; sale of exhibit space at Drug Show. Meetings: Annual, various locations. Publications: N.A.R.D. Journal, semimonthly, William E. Woods, editor; N.A.R.D. Almanac, annual. Members: State Pharmaceutical Associations.

★ 1195 ★
NATIONAL ASSOCIATION OF SCHOOL
    PSYCHOLOGISTS
1629 K Street, N.W., Suite 520   (202) 347-3956
Washington, D.C. 20006

Mary St. Cyr, Executive Manager; Jean Ranage,
    Executive Manager; Mike Chrin, Executive Manager; Sharon Petty, Executive Manager
To advance the standards of the profession of school psychology; to promote actively the interests of school psychology; to help secure conditions necessary to the greatest effectiveness in the practice of psychology in the schools; to serve the mental health and educational needs of children and youth. Membership: 6,000 (regular and student). Finances: Membership: Regular, $49; student, $16. Meetings: Quarterly, various locations. Publications: School Psychology Review, quarterly; Communique, 8 times annually.

★ 1196 ★
NATIONAL ASSOCIATION OF SEVENTH-DAY
    ADVENTIST DENTISTS
Post Office Box 101
Loma Linda, California 92354   Established 1943

Gerald Muncy, D.D.S., Secretary-Treasurer
To promote the spirit of Christian missionary service and scientific interest among Seventh-Day Adventist dentists. The Association supports and helps establish missionary dentists in foreign countries, provides loans for dental students at Loma Linda University, and helps financially with the operation of the School of Dentistry at Loma Linda University. Membership: Approximately 500-550 (active, life, affiliate, associate, junior, and honorary). Finances: Membership: Active, $30; affiliate, associate, $20; junior, $7; Other Sources: Voluntary contributions. Meetings: Semiannual, in conjunction with the ADA meeting and the Chicago Mid-Winter Clinics. Publications: NASDAD Newsletter, quarterly; SDA Dentist Annual Directory. Affiliations: 10 local chapters throughout the United States.

★ 1197 ★
NATIONAL ASSOCIATION OF SOCIAL WORKERS
1425 H Street, N.W., Suite 600   (202) 628-6800
Washington, D.C. 20005   Established 1955

Chauncey A. Alexander, Executive Director
To promote activities that stimulate, strengthen and unify the social work profession; to contribute to the improvement of social and working conditions. Membership: 85,000. Finances: Membership: $22-$90 depending on status; Other Sources: Foundations

and government grants. <u>Awards:</u> Research and education fund; awards in research, continuing education, community service, social work practice. <u>Meetings:</u> Biennial, various locations; 55 State and territorial chapters meet monthly. <u>Publications:</u> Social Work, bimonthly, Scott Briar, editor; NASW News, monthly, Rae Hamilton, editor; Encyclopedia of Social Work; Directory of Social Workers; Health and Social Work, quarterly; Registry of Clinical Social Workers, annual; Directory of Agencies (United States Voluntary, International Voluntary, Intergovernmental); Social Work Research Abstracts, quarterly; Practice Digest, quarterly; Social Work in Education, quarterly; monographs, books, pamphlets. <u>Library:</u> 4,000 volumes. <u>Affiliations:</u> International Federation of Social Workers; Council on Social Work Education; National Conference on Social Welfare; American Association for the Advancement of Science; and many coalitions.

★ 1198 ★
NATIONAL ASSOCIATION OF STATE MENTAL
    HEALTH PROGRAM DIRECTORS
<u>Main Office:</u>
1001 Third St., S.W., Suite 114   (202) 554-7807
Washington, D.C. 20024   Established 1963
<u>Hall-of-States-Annex</u>
444 N. Capitol St., N.W.
Suite 347   (202) 624-5837
Washington, D.C. 20001

Harry C. Schnibbe, Executive Director; Susan Manduke, Deputy Director; Roy Praschil, Program Staff; James Finley, Program Staff; Charles Gabriel, Program Staff
The Association (1) provides a vehicle for exchange of information between state agencies for the mentally disabled on state programs, laws, plans, needs, and practices; (2) provides a channel for quick information reports on news of federal agencies and the Congress; (3) provides a means of communicating the objectives and needs of the state mental health agencies to the federal government; (4) coordinates the actions of the state mental health agencies with other state agencies, national citizen voluntary associations, national professional associations, city and county government associations, consumer and patient advocacy groups, and national health and mental health provider groups; and (5) provides a means for state mental health administrators to meet on a regular and organized basis to exchange program and administrative ideas and to develop a national consensus and policy for public mental health programs. <u>Membership:</u> The 54 directors of mental health agencies. <u>Finances:</u> Membership: Dues vary; Other Sources: Sale of Publications, conferences. <u>Publications:</u> Federal Funding News, monthly. <u>Affiliation:</u> Cooperating Agency--Council of State Governments.

★ 1199 ★
NATIONAL ASSOCIATION OF STATE MENTAL
    RETARDATION PROGRAM DIRECTORS, INC.
2001 Jefferson Davis Highway
Suite 806   (703) 920-0700
Arlington, Virginia 22202   Established 1964

Robert M. Gettings, Executive Director
To improve and expand public services to mentally retarded children and adults; to facilitate the exchange of information between states on the most advanced and efficacious methods of providing care and training for the retarded; to represent the interests of state program officials in the development and implementation of programs of the federal government. <u>Membership:</u> 53. <u>Finances:</u> Membership: Sliding fee scale with a fixed minimum. <u>Publications:</u> New Directions, monthly, Deborah Mitchell Yerrings, editor; Capitol Capsule, monthly, Stephanie Mensh, editor. <u>Former Name:</u> National Association of Coordinators of State Programs for the Mentally Retarded.

★ 1200 ★
NATIONAL ASSOCIATION OF STATE PUBLIC
    HEALTH VETERINARIANS
Post Office Box 13528   (301) 383-2678
Baltimore, Maryland 21201   Established 1941

Dr. Kenneth L. Crawford
The control of animal related matters of human health concern. <u>Membership:</u> 50 (1 per state). <u>Meetings:</u> Annual, various locations.

★ 1201 ★
NATIONAL ASSOCIATION OF THE DEAF
814 Thayer Avenue   (301) 587-1788
Silver Spring, Maryland 20910   Established 1880

Albert T. Pimentel, Executive Director
To improve educational opportunities and social and economic problems of deaf persons; to serve as an information and referral center for deafness; to represent the deaf consumer in all areas in which he has an interest and to protect civil rights of deaf people. <u>Membership:</u> 18,000 (deaf consumers, educators and professionals in the field). <u>Finances:</u> Membership: Individual, $15; husband/wife, $25; family, $35; affiliate, $25; Other Sources: Sale of books, materials, and equipment for or about the deaf. <u>Awards:</u> International Solidary Medal of the World Federation of the Deaf. <u>Meetings:</u> Biennial Convention, even-numbered years. <u>Publications:</u> The Deaf American, 11 times annually, Muriel Strassler, editor; The NAD Broadcaster, 11 times annually, Muriel Strassler, editor; The Interstate, 6 times annually, Muriel Strassler, editor; numerous textbooks

on American Sign Language and other systems of manual communication; over 200 books on various aspects of deafness (parent education, psychology, mental health, children's books, etc.). Affiliations: 47 affiliated State Associations of the Deaf.

★ 1202 ★
NATIONAL ASSOCIATION OF THE PHYSICALLY
    HANDICAPPED, INC.
76 Elm Street   (614) 852-1664
London, Ohio 43140   Established 1958

Helen Lee Roudebush, Administrative Assistant
The purpose of the organization is to advance the social, economic and physical welfare of the physically handicapped. Membership: Varies from year to year. Members may belong to Chapters, or join National as Member-At-Large. Finances: Membership: Dues; chapter application fee, $10; member-at-large dues, $6 annually; Other Sources: Contributions; newsletter advertising. Meetings: Annual, various locations. Publications: NAPH National Newsletter, quarterly (subscription, $3 annually to non-members); brochures. Affiliations: National Congress of Organization of the Physically Handicapped; President's Committee on Employment of the Handicapped.

★ 1203 ★
NATIONAL ASSOCIATION ON STANDARD
    MEDICAL VOCABULARY
c/o Lee Wollman, M.D.
2802 Mermaid Avenue   (212) 372-4569
Brooklyn, New York 11224   Established 1962

Leo Wollman, M.D., Secretary
To work for a standard medical vocabulary. Membership: Over 7,000. Finances: Grants.

NATIONAL ASTHMA CENTER
    See: National Jewish Hospital/National
    Asthma Center

★ 1204 ★
NATIONAL ATAXIA FOUNDATION
6681 Country Club Drive   (612) 546-6220
Minneapolis, Minnesota 55427   Established 1957

Julie Schuur, President
Organized to offer help and information to persons affected by hereditary ataxia, ataxia telangiectasia, spastic paraplegia, Charcot-Marie Tooth and hereditary tremor. Services include clinics at which a variety of services are offered free of charge. Membership: Annual, sponsoring, lifetime. Finances:

Membership: Annual, $10; sponsoring, $25; lifetime, $100; Other Sources: Private contributions. Research: Information on research grants available from Foundation headquarters. Meetings: Annual Membership Meeting. Publications: Generations, quarterly; Informational Literature.

★ 1205 ★
NATIONAL BOARD FOR RESPIRATORY THERAPY
11015 West 75th Terrace   (913) 384-0282
Shawnee Mission, Kansas 66203   Established 1960

Steven K. Bryant, Executive Director
The Board serves as the national certifying organization for respiratory therapists and respiratory therapy technicians. Membership: 36,000 (registered respiratory therapists, certified respiratory therapy technicians). Finances: Membership: Annual fee, $8; examination application fee, $150 (for registry); $60 (for certification). Publications: Directory of Registered Respiratory Therapists and Respiratory Therapy Technicians, annually; NBRT Newsletter, monthly.

★ 1206 ★
NATIONAL BOARD OF EXAMINERS FOR OSTEO-
    PATHIC PHYSICIANS AND SURGEONS, INC.
22 South Washington, Suite 102   (312) 825-4938
Park Ridge, Illinois 60068   Established 1934

Roderick Cannatalla, D.O., Secretary-Treasurer
To test applicants as to qualifications and competency for serving the public as osteopathic physicians and surgeons through the preparation and administration of examinations; to provide examinations for colleges of osteopathy; to provide state boards with examinations which will meet their specific requirements. Membership: 6,900 (osteopathic physicians and surgeons, holding diplomate certificate). Finances: Registration and examination fees. Meetings: Annual, Chicago, Illinois. Affiliation: American Osteopathic Association.

★ 1207 ★
NATIONAL BOARD OF MEDICAL EXAMINERS
3930 Chestnut Street   (215) 349-6400
Philadelphia, Pennsylvania 19104   Established 1915

Edithe J. Levit, M.D., President and Director
The National Board of Medical Examiners is a voluntary and unofficial examining agency, the purpose of which is to prepare and to administer qualifying examinations of such high quality, that legal agencies governing the practice of medicine within each state may in their discretion grant successful candidates a license without further examination for those who have successfully completed the examinations of the National Board and have met such other requirements as

the National Board may establish for certification of its Diplomates; to consult and cooperate with examining boards of the states; to consult and cooperate with medical schools; and to study and develop methods of testing and evaluating medical knowledge and competence. Membership: 72 (elected); staff, 140. Finances: Fees from candidates for examinations. Meetings: Annual, always spring, Philadelphia, Pennsylvania. Publications: Annual Report, issued March for preceding year; The National Board Examiner, quarterly newsletter; Bulletins of Information; Policy Statements.

★ 1208 ★
NATIONAL BRAILLE ASSOCIATION, INC.
654A Godwin Avenue   (201) 447-1484
Midland Park, New Jersey 07432   Established 1945

Sister Anne Columba, CSJ, President
To bring together all those interested in the production and distribution of braille, large type and material recorded on tape for blind and partially sighted readers; to furnish reading material for the blind in all media. Membership: 2,500. Finances: Membership: Regular, $15; regular outside the U.S., $20; sustaining, $50; patron, $100; life, $300; Other Sources: Grants, gifts, contributions. Meetings: 3 times annually, January, May and October, various locations. Publications: Bulletin, quarterly, Mrs. I. Richman, editor; manuals and other materials to aid transcribers. Library: Braille Book Bank, over 10,000 (includes college level and career materials, music braille, over 300 most commonly used technical tables, daily living material).

★ 1209 ★
NATIONAL BRAILLE PRESS, INC.
88 St. Stephen Street   (617) 266-6160
Boston, Massachusetts 02115   Established 1927

William M. Raeder, Managing Director
Publishes books and magazines in braille; prints adult and children's books; reprints music braille, booklets on cooking, handicraft, public information topics, and braille business cards. Sponsors a braille reader's short story competition. Membership: 29, staff, 39. Finances: Gifts and legacies. Meetings: Quarterly, trustees; annual corporate meeting, second Wednesday of April, Boston, Massachusetts. Publications: Our Special, in braille, monthly; Luminary (newsletter), 2 to 3 times annually.

★ 1210 ★
NATIONAL CANCER CYTOLOGY CENTER
88 Sunnyside Boulevard, Suite 204   (516) 349-0610
Plainview, New York 11803   Established 1953

Ann L. Ayre, Executive Director
To further the use of cytological techniques in cancer control by supporting research, publications and educational material. Publications: Cancer Cytology, semiannual, Ann L. Ayre, editor; numerous scientific reports. Affiliations: Pan American Cancer Cytology Society.

★ 1211 ★
NATIONAL CANCER FOUNDATION
1 Park Avenue   (212) 679-5700
New York, New York 10016   Established 1944

Irene G. Buckley, Executive Director
A voluntary social agency, the National Cancer Foundation is a parent organization for Cancer Care, Inc. (see separate entry). The Foundation provides aid for the development of social services to patients and their families to help them cope with the emotional and psychological consequences of advanced cancer when the patient can be cared for at home. The Foundation together with Cancer Care, Inc. conduct programs of professional consultation and education, social research, public affairs and public education on a national and worldwide basis.

★ 1212 ★
NATIONAL CANCER INSTITUTE OF CANADA
401-77 Bloor Street West   (416) 961-7223
Toronto, Ontario M5S 2V7, Canada   Established 1947

Dr. R. A. Macbeth, Executive Vice President;
    Dr. P. G. Scholefield, Executive Director
The Institute was formed on the joint initiative of the Department of National Health and Welfare and the Canadian Cancer Society, to co-ordinate and correlate the efforts of individuals and organized bodies with a view to reducing the morbidity and mortality from cancer. It fulfills this role by support of clinical and fundamental research activities and research personnel, as well as through programs of professional education, statistical and epidemiological studies. The Institute is dedicated to a maximum effort to conquer cancer. The main hope of achieving this goal lies in enlisting intelligent and imaginative men and women into the cancer research field and in providing them with the material assistance required to explore their ideas in the laboratory and in hospital clinic. Membership: Members at large, 26; representative members, 16 (members at large are

appointed by the Board of Directors on the basis of continuing lay or professional interest in the subject of cancer). Finances: Other Sources: Canadian Cancer Society. Research: Research Funds, 1980-1981, $15,000,000. Medals and Awards: R. M. Taylor Award. Meetings: Most meetings held in Toronto, Canada; 1 annual meeting of the Institute; 4 meetings annually of the Board of Directors. Publications: Annual Report, annually; Manual, annually. Affiliation: Canadian Cancer Society.

★ 1213 ★
NATIONAL CATHOLIC PHARMACISTS GUILD OF
    THE UNITED STATES
1012 Surrey Hills Drive   (314) 645-0085
St. Louis, Missouri 63117   Established 1962

John P. Winkelmann, President and Executive Director
The purposes of the Guild are to uphold the principles of the Catholic faith, of all laws of the country and especially those pertaining to the profession of the practice of pharmacy; to assist the ecclesiastical authorities in the diffusion of Catholic Pharmacy ethics; to oppose the sale of pornographic and indecent literature, especially that being sold in pharmacies; to promote donations of funds and supplies to catholic charitable groups; to take active participation in all possible projects in which a love of God and neighbor policy is pursued through the profession of pharmacy; to foster brotherhood and good will among all pharmacists. Membership: 400 Catholic pharmacists, pharmacy graduates and students. Finances: Membership: Annual, $7; life $75. Awards: Catholic Pharmacist of the Year; "For Church and Profession" Plaque; Award of Merit Certificates; Honorary President of the Year. Meetings: Biennial, various locations. Publication: The Catholic Pharmacist, quarterly, John P. Winkelmann, editor. Affiliation: National Council of Catholic Laity; International Federation of Catholic Pharmacists.

NATIONAL CITIZENS COMMITTEE FOR THE
WORLD HEALTH ORGANIZATION
    See: American Association for World Health:
    U.S. Committee for the World Health
    Organization

★ 1214 ★
NATIONAL CLEARINGHOUSE FOR ALCOHOL
    INFORMATION
U.S. Department of Health and Human Services
Post Office Box 2345   (301) 468-2600
Rockville, Maryland 20852

Terry Bellicha, Director
The National Clearinghouse for Alcohol Information (NCALI) has been established as a service of the National Institute on Alcohol Abuse and Alcoholism (see separate entry) to make available current knowledge on alcohol-related programs and subjects. NCALI collects and disseminates information pertaining to prevention, treatment, and research aspects of alcohol abuse and alcoholism. Publications: Numerous books, posters, brochures, pamphlets.

NATIONAL COLLEGE PHYSICAL EDUCATION
ASSOCIATION FOR MEN
    See: National Association for Physical Education
    in Higher Education

★ 1215 ★
NATIONAL CONSORTIUM FOR CHILD MENTAL
    HEALTH SERVICES
1424 16th Street, N.W.
Suite 201-A   (202) 462-3754
Washington, D.C. 20036   Established 1971

Frank Rafferty, M.D., Chairman;
    Virginia Q. Bausch, Executive Director
To serve as a forum for the exchange of information on child mental health services and to bring concerns regarding child mental health services to appropriate local, state, and federal agencies. Committees include: Education for All Handicapped Children Act; Implementation of the President's Commission on Mental Health; Insurance. Membership: 18 (national psychiatry, psychology, medical, social welfare, educational, parent and teacher, and consumer organizations). Finances: Other Sources: Grants and contributions from the American Academy of Child Psychiatry. Meetings: Quarterly, Washington, D.C. Affiliations: American Academy of Child Psychiatry; American Academy of Pediatrics; American Association of Children's Residential Centers; American Association of Psychiatric Services for Children; American Association on Mental Deficiency; American Medical Association; American Psychiatric Association; American Psychological Association; American Society for Adolescent Psychiatry; Child Welfare League of America; Children's Defense Fund; Mental Health Association; National Association for Retarded Citizens; National Association of School Psychologists; National Association of State Mental Health Program Directors; National Congress of Parents and Teachers; National Council of Community Mental Health Centers; Society of Professors of Child Psychiatry.

NATIONAL COUNCIL FOR HOMEMAKER - HOME
HEALTH AIDE SERVICES, INC.
  See: National Home Caring Council

NATIONAL COUNCIL OF HEALTH CARE SERVICES
  See: National Council of Health Centers

★ 1216 ★
NATIONAL COUNCIL OF SENIOR CITIZENS
1511 K Street, N.W.   (202) 347-8800
Washington, D.C. 20005   Established 1961

William R. Hutton, Executive Director
To provide health legislation information and the exchange of information pertinent to senior citizens; to
promote the interest of senior citizens through clubs
linked in a statewide and national structure. Membership: 4,000 clubs (about 4,000,000 senior citizens
in these clubs). Finances: Membership: Individual
membership, $6; member of affiliated club, $5;
Other Sources: Contributions. Awards: Aime J.
Forand Award. Meetings: Board, quarterly and biennial convention, off-year legislative conference,
Washington, D.C. Publications: Senior Citizens
News, monthly, William R. Hutton, editor.

★ 1217 ★
NATIONAL COUNCIL ON ALCOHOLISM, INC.
733 Third Avenue, Suite 1405   (212) 986-4433
New York, New York 10017   Established 1944

The National Council on Alcoholism, Inc., has been
established to combat the disease of alcoholism, specifically to educate the general public to three facts:
alcoholism is a disease; the disease of alcoholism is
treatable; the victims of this disease are worth treating. NCA stimulates and coordinates medical research; encourages development of effective treatment
facilities; assists management and labor in initiating
and implementing effective employee alcoholism programs; provides technical information and expert
testimony for legislative hearings on alcoholism; provides material for and stimulates programs of education
and prevention; conducts major public information
campaigns and provides technical information to the
media, and provides support and technical assistance
in the development and maintenance of local alcoholism councils. Membership: Over 350 members, including 223 Councils, 15 State Associations, 65 non-
service agency members, 50 individuals, 3 major components, listed under "Affiliated Organizations" below.
Finances: Membership: Categorical membership plan,
varies; Other Sources: Contributions, from individu-

als, corporations, and foundations. Awards: Gold,
Silver, Bronze Key Awards for outstanding contribu-
tions to the field; Meany-Roche Awards for outstanding contributions to the occupational alcoholism field.
Meetings: Annual Meeting, various locations; Board
meets 3 times annually, various locations. Publications: Labor-Management Alcoholism Journal, bimonthly, William S. Dunkin, editor; Alcoholism:
Clinical and Experimental Research, quarterly,
Marcus A. Rothschild, M.D., editor; Currents in
Alcoholism, annually, Marc Galanter, M.D. editor.
Library: Yvelin Gardner Memorial Library, over
1,500 volumes (by permission only). Affiliations:
Over 220 affiliated local councils; 15 State Voluntary Alcoholism Associations; American Medical Society on Alcoholism (AMSA); Research Society on
Alcoholism (RSA); National Nurses Society on Alco-
holism (NNSA).

★ 1218 ★
NATIONAL COUNCIL OF HEALTH CENTERS
2600 Virginia Avenue, N.W.
Suite 915   (202) 298-7393
Washington, D.C. 20037   Established 1969

Jack A. MacDonald, Executive Vice President
A select group of tax-paying health care companies
owning and/or managing hospitals, nursing homes,
psychiatric facilities, clinics, pharmacies, home
health agencies, surgical supply companies, homemaker services, and day care centers dedicated to
seeking innovative approaches to providing quality
patient care in the appropriate cost-effective setting.
Membership: 1,200 licensed nursing centers. Finances: Membership: Agency fee based on number
of beds. Meetings: Bimonthly, Washington, D.C.
Former Name: National Council of Health Care
Services.

★ 1219 ★
NATIONAL COUNCIL ON RADIATION PROTECTION
  AND MEASUREMENTS
7910 Woodmont Avenue
Suite 1016   (310) 657-2652
Washington, D.C. 20014   Established 1929

W. R. Noy, Executive Director
To collect, analyze, develop and disseminate information and recommendations about radiation protection and measurements. Membership: 320. Finances: Contributions, grants, contracts. Publications: Scientific reports.

★ 1220 ★

NATIONAL COUNCIL ON THE AGING, INC.
1828 L Street, N.W., Suite 504   (202) 223-6250
Washington, D.C. 20036   Established 1950

Jack Ossofsky, Executive Director
Central, national resource for planning, information,
consultation and materials in the field of aging. The
Council provides a national information and consultation center; maintains a special library; keeps current on activities in the field; holds conferences and
workshops; serves as a medium for interchange of information and ideas; encourages experimentation in
programs and services; stimulates studies and research;
conducts special projects and studies. Offers training,
technical assistance and consultation to local, state
and regional bodies. Membership: 4,000 (representatives of national, state, regional organizations in
the following fields, as well as individual professionals working in the field: education and research,
labor, business and industry, social work, government,
health, religion, lay and professional). Finances:
Foundation and government grants, contributions,
memberships and publications. Awards: The Ollie
A. Randall Award; The NCOA Community Service
Award. Meetings: Annual, various locations.
Publications: Perspective on Aging, bimonthly;
Senior Centers MEMO, 10 times annually; Aging and
Work, quarterly; National Voluntary Organizations
for Independent Living for the Aging, Newsletter, 10
times annually; Current Literature on Aging, quarter-
ly. Library: 10,000.

★ 1221 ★

NATIONAL COUNCIL ON WHOLISTIC THERA-
        PEUTICS & MEDICINE
GPO Box H   (212) 683-4793
Brooklyn, New York 11202   Established 1978
        and
271 Fifth Avenue, Suite 3
New York, New York 10016

Leslie Kaslof, Chairman
Federation of groups interested in the emergency of
responsible and integrated systems of healing. Ex-
plores new and innovative therapeutic techniques in
the field. Has mailing list available of over 2,000
groups throughout the country in the field of (w)hol-
istic health. Maintains speakers bureau and other
services. Library: Barnabe Memorial Library (non-
circulating research library), 3,000 volumes.

★ 1222 ★

NATIONAL DAIRY COUNCIL
6300 North River Road   (312) 696-1020
Rosemont, Illinois 60018   Established 1915

Marion F. Brink, Ph.D., President
To contribute to the achievement of optimal health
by providing leadership in nutrition research and nutrition education based on the concept of a balanced
diet, including milk and milk products, in accordance with scientific recommendations, thus strengthening the dairy industry and American agriculture.
Serves as a national resource agency in nutrition education, maintaining cooperative relations with government, professional, educational and consumer group
leaders on the national level. Program plans orig-
inate from sponsored research and are implemented by
a staff of professionally trained nutritionists and health
educators. Nutrition research is directed, authentic
literature is prepared and distributed, educational exhibits are developed, films produced, factual and professional advertising placed in professional and educational publications, and food and news releases provided editors of newspapers, magazines and programs
directors of radio and television. Membership:
3,000 (dairy farmers, processors and distributors of
dairy foods and manufacturers and jobbers of dairy
equipment and supplies). Finances: Membership:
$500 and up. Awards: Approximately $259,000 is
budgeted annually for nutrition research; McCollum
Award, $1000 annually. Meetings: Annual, and
program conference, various locations. Publications:
Dairy Council Digest, bimonthly; Nutrition News,
quarterly; Focus, biweekly; Food News, semiannually; Paradigms, monthly. Library: Research Library,
3,100 volumes. Affiliations: 37 affiliated Dairy
Council units.

★ 1223 ★

NATIONAL DENTAL ASSOCIATION
5506 Connecticut Avenue, N.W.
Suite 24   (202) 244-7555
Washington, D.C. 20015   Established 1913

Dr. Elisha Richardson, President
A national professional society designed to improve
public health and to promote the art and science of
dental practice. Membership: 700-1,000 (active
and honorary). Finances: Membership: $125;
Other Sources: Exhibits. Awards: Educational
Scholarships; Dentist of the Year Award. Meetings:
Annual, various locations. Publications: Quarterly,
quarterly, Dr. T. E. Bolden, editor; Newsletter.

★ 1224 ★

NATIONAL DENTAL EXAMINING BOARD OF
　　CANADA
100 Bronson Avenue, Suite 807
Ottawa, Ontario K1R 6G8, Canada Established 1952

Dr. G. Kravis, Registrar
The National Dental Examining Board of Canada was
incorporated by an Act of Parliament in 1952 for the
purpose of establishing qualifying conditions for a
national standard for dentists.   All 10 Canadian provincial licensing authorities recognize and participate
in the activities of the Board.   Membership: 12
(1 member from each Provincial Licensing Authority
and 2 members from Council on Education of the Canadian Dental Association).   Finances: Membership:
Non-profit organization, financed by certificate and
examination fees.   Fees: current graduate, $225;
written examination, $400; preclinical, $500; clinical, $1,100.   Meetings: Annual, Board; semian-
nual meetings of the Executive.

★ 1225 ★

NATIONAL EASTER SEAL SOCIETY
2023 West Ogden Avenue　　　　(312) 243-8400
Chicago, Illinois 60612　　　　Established 1921

John Garrison, Executive Director
The National, State and Local Societies are organized
to carry out a program of direct services benefiting
crippled children and adults; education of the public,
the professions, and parents; and research into the
causes and prevention of crippling conditions and improved methods of care, education and treatment.
Membership: Member societies in all 47 states, Puerto
Rico, and the District of Columbia; 2,000 local affiliates.   Finances: Major source of support is the
annual Easter Seal Campaign; Other Sources: Special gifts, bequests, capital fund contributions, fees,
and grants.   Awards: Easter Seal Research Foundation has made grants for other 400 projects; Distinguished Service Medal for outstanding achievement on
behalf of the handicapped.   Meetings: Annual,
Chicago, in alternate years; otherwise various locations.   Publications: Rehabilitation Literature, bimonthly; Easter Seal Communicator, bimonthly;
series of pamphlets; professional monographs; annual
report.   Library: 3,000 volumes.   Former Name:
National Easter Seal Society for Crippled Children and
and Adults.

NATIONAL EASTER SEAL SOCIETY FOR CRIPPLED
CHILDREN AND ADULTS
　　See: National Easter Seal Society

★ 1226 ★

NATIONAL ENVIRONMENTAL HEALTH
　　ASSOCIATION
1200 Lincoln Street, Suite 704　　(303) 861-9090
Denver, Colorado 80203　　　　Established 1937

Nicholas Pohlit, Executive Director;
　　Lawrence J. Krone, Ph.D., R.S.
To control environmental hazards and permit attain-
ment of the highest possible human health standards.
Membership: 6,000 (active, associate, student, agen-
cy, sustaining, honorary, fellow, life).   Finances:
Membership: Active, $25; student, $7; agency,
$35; sustaining, $250; Other Sources: Sale of
journal, advertising in journal.   Awards: Mangold
Award; Walter Snyder Award; LaReine A. Hatch
Memorial Scholarship.   Meetings: Annual, various
locations.   Publications: Journal of Environmental
Health, bimonthly, Ida Frances Marshall, editor-in-
chief; Association Newsletter.   Library: A Harry
Bliss Library, 1,200 volumes.

★ 1227 ★

NATIONAL EXECUTIVE HOUSEKEEPERS ASSOCIA-
　　TION, INC.
201 Business and Professional
　　Building　　　　　　　　　(614) 446-4800
Gallipolis, Ohio 45631　　　　Established 1930

Elaine Rees, Executive Director
To provide leadership in the development of institutional housekeeping management in hospitals, hotels,
motels, schools and industrial establishments; to promote education in the institutional housekeeping
management field.   Membership: Over 4,200 (certified, associate, active).   Finances: Membership:
$65 annual dues; entrance fee, $20.   Publications:
Executive Housekeeping Today, monthly, Elaine Rees,
editor.

★ 1228 ★

NATIONAL EYE RESEARCH FOUNDATION
18 South Michigan Avenue　　　(312) 726-7866
Chicago, Illinois 60603　　　　Established 1956

Dr. Allen Prechtel, President;
　　Waneta Reynolds, Executive Secretary
Founded in 1956 by Dr. Newton K. Wesley and Dr.
George Jessen, the Foundation is a non-profit organization with an international and interprofessional
membership.   It has two main objectives: to improve the quality of eye care for the general public
and to meet the professional needs of eye care practitioners.   The Foundation is engaged in vision research (developed pioneering knowledge in contact

lens application) and sponsors educational seminars, conventions and congresses on national and international level. Membership: 3,000 (optometrists, ophthalmologist oculists and opticians). Finances: Membership: $50 professional; $20 laity. Publications: Contacto, bimonthly, Albert D. Geller, editor; Eyes Right, monthly (Newsletter).

★ 1229 ★
NATIONAL FEDERATION OF LICENSED PRACTICAL
    NURSES, INC.
888 Seventh Avenue, 18th Floor   (212) 246-6629
New York, New York 10106   Established 1949

Sammy K. Griffin, President
To preserve and foster the nursing ideal of comprehensive care for the ill and aged; to promote the economic and general welfare of all licensed practical nurses; to uphold the standards and ethics of all licensed practical nurses and to interpret them to the public; and to cooperate with all members of health groups and with organizations interested in better patient care. Provides services of skilled specialists and consultants on organizational, legal, and nursing problems. Activities include leadership conferences; promotional activities on recruitment; field work; and provision of speakers. Membership: 20,000. Finances: Membership: Individual (in states with no affiliation); regular, student affiliates. Meetings: Annual, various locations. Publications: Nursing Care, monthly. Affiliations (Cooperating Organizations): American Nurses Association; American Medical Association; American Hospital Association; National League for Nursing; American Nursing Home Association.

★ 1230 ★
NATIONAL FEDERATION OF THE BLIND
1800 Johnson Street   (301) 659-9314
Baltimore, Maryland 21230   Established 1940

Kenneth Jernigan, President
To work for the complete integration of the blind into society on a basis of quality. This involves the removal of legal, economic, and social discriminations; the education of the public to new concepts concerning blindness; and the achievement by each and every blind person of the right to exercise to the fullest his individual talents and capacities. Membership: 50,000. Awards: Howard Brown Rickard Scholarship Fund for Blind College Students; Newel Perry Award for outstanding service to the blind. Dr. Isabel Goant Scholarship to deserving blind female college students. Publications: Braille Monitor, monthly, James Gashely, Acting Editor; num-

erous articles and research materials on blindness. Affiliations: 51 (state and the District of Columbia organizations).

★ 1231 ★
NATIONAL FIRE PROTECTION ASSOCIATION
470 Atlantic Avenue   (617) 482-8755
Boston, Massachusetts 02210   Established 1896

Robert W. Grant, President
NFPA's general mission is the safeguarding of man and his environment from destructive fire, using scientific and engineering techniques and education. The basic technical activity involves development, publication and dissemination of timely consensus standards intented to minimize the possibility and effects of fire in all aspects of contemporary activity. Membership: Approximately 31,600 individuals and 154 national trade and professional organizations (85 nations are represented). Finances: Membership: $225 organizational; $50 individual; Other Sources: Sale of publications, audio-visual materials, advertising space; research contacts; contributions. Meetings: Annual, in May; Fall Meetings, November. Publications: Fire Command, monthly, Joyce Keefe, editor; Fire Journal, bimonthly, Paul E. Teague, editor; Fire News, monthly, Paul R. Sawin, editor; Fire Technology, quarterly, Charles A. Tuck, Jr., editor; Fire Protection Handbook, every 6 weeks, Gordon P. McKinnon, editor; National Fire Codes, annual; books, audio-visual materials, flyers, folders, reports, posters, etc. Library: NFPA Technical Reference Library, 27,000 titles, including 16,000 technical reports, 5,000 books, 500 audio-visuals and 5,000 items on microforms. Affiliations: 10 sections within the NFPA membership; NFPA itself is a member of the Joint Council of National Fire Service Organizations.

★ 1232 ★
NATIONAL FOUNDATION FOR ASTHMA, INC.
Transamerica Building, Suite 511
Post Office Box 50304   (602) 624-7481
Tucson, Arizona 85703   Established 1949

Nita Sersain, Executive Director
The purpose of this organization is to care for those who suffer from allergies, asthma and chronic pulmonary lung diseases and cannot affort private specialized care. Activities include provision of outpatient services, emergency room care and ambulatory pulmonary care. Finances: Other Sources: Contributions and bequests. Awards: Encourages research in the area of Chronic Pulmonary Lung Disease, has furnished Fellowships in Allergy at the

University of Arizona and numerous research programs. Publications: Weeds 'N Things, Linda Alpert, R.N., editor; Dust 'N' Stuff, Linda Alpert, R.N., editor; booklet containing general information for Asthmatics. Remarks: Patients in the Outpatient Allergy Clinic, funded by this organization must provide a "written referral" from their attending physician. They are screened for eligibility (financial). If patients are able to pay for private specialized care, they are furnished with the names of doctors who specialize in this field.

★ 1233 ★

NATIONAL FOUNDATION FOR CANCER RESEARCH
7315 Wisconsin Avenue   (301) 654-1250
Bethesda, Maryland 20014

Franklin C. Salisbury, J.D., Executive Director; Albert Szent-Gyorgyi, M.D., Ph.D., Scientific Director

NFCR is a non-profit cancer foundation which conducts bio-electronic research and has assembled a number of interrelating research laboratories (workshops) at distinguished universities throughout the world--in the United States, Great Britain, Ireland, France, Germany, Italy, Hungary, Japan, etc. To date, there are 20 laboratories working under the auspices and support of the Foundation. The Foundation pays for the materials, the post graduates and Ph.D. candidates working under their supervision, for the equipment and a small percentage to the University for administrative overhead. Membership: 1,000,000 (donors). Finances: Membership: $7.50 average; Other Sources: Direct mail solicitations. Awards: 35 NFCR Workshops at Universities and other institutions, 5 grants, 2 scholarships, in 1981 3 Fellowships. Meetings: Annual meeting for all research investigators; 2 to 4 mini-meetings for investigators in specialized fields. Publications: Numerous reports and scientific articles.

★ 1234 ★

NATIONAL FOUNDATION FOR ILEITIS AND
   COLITIS, INC.
295 Madison Avenue, Suite 519   (212) 685-3440
New York, New York 10017   Established 1965

Lyn Meyerhoff, President
To support research seeking the cause and cure for ileitis and colitis (intestinal inflamation), and to inform the public of the nature and prevalence of the diseases. Membership: 15,000 (regular, life). Finances: Membership: $15, $25, $50, $100; Other Sources: Fund riasing, contributions, journal sales, annual dinner. Awards: National Humanitarian

Award; National Achievement Award. Meetings: Board, quarterly; chapters, monthly, various locations; professional and lay educational seminars. Publications: National Newsletters; research bibliographies; reports; brochures.

★ 1235 ★

NATIONAL FOUNDATION FOR INFECTIOUS
   DISEASES
Box 459, MCV Station   (804) 786-9714
Richmond, Virginia 23298   Established 1973

Larry Hoff, Chairman, Board of Trustees; Richard J. Duma, M.D., Ph.D., President, Board of Directors; H. Jean Shadomy, Ph.D., Secretary-Treasurer, Board of Directors
To encourage and support research, prevention and education (both public and professional) in the field of Infectious Diseases and in special circumstances to aid patients with numeral infectious disease problems. Membership: 3,000 (philanthorpic and based on voluntary contribution). Finances: Other Sources: Contributions from industry and organizations. Lectureships: Supports entirely Annual Lectureship in Young Investigator Matching Grant; NFID Fellowships (2); supports entirely Annual Lectureship in Hospital Infection Control or Epideimology for the American Practitioners of Infection Control (APIC). Meetings: 4 Executive Committee Meetings annually, and an Annual Board of Directors and Board of Trustees Meetings; various locations. Publications: The Double Helix, quarterly, Richard J. Duma, M.D., Ph.D., and Robin H. Doran, editors; brochures, Rocky Mountain Spotted Fever, Annual Reports.

NATIONAL FOUNDATION FOR SUDDEN INFANT
DEATH, INC.
   See: National Sudden Infant Death Syndrome
         Foundation, Inc.

NATIONAL FOUNDATION - MARCH OF DIMES
   See: March of Dimes Birth Defects Foundation

★ 1236 ★

NATIONAL FOUNDATION OF DENTISTRY FOR
   THE HANDICAPPED
1726 Champa, Suite 422   (303) 573-0264
Denver, Colorado 80202   Established 1954

The National Foundation of Dentistry for the Handicapped, a public non-profit corporation, was created to decrease the need for dental care among handicapped people by controlling the incidence and severity of oral disease and by sensitizing dental caregivers to the needs of disabled individuals. Most NFDH efforts have focused on development and administration of its "Campaign of Concern." This program is predicated on the philosophy that dentistry must reach out in an organized manner into the schools, workshops, and homes where many handicapped people learn, work, and live if they are to enjoy the dignity and comfort of good oral health instead of the offtimes crisis care not provided. The support of the American Dental Association and federal government has enabled NFDH to establish a number of "Campaign of Concern" programs nationwide.

★ 1237 ★

NATIONAL FRATERNAL SOCIETY OF THE DEAF
1300 West Northwest Highway   (312) 592-9282
Mount Prospect, Illinois 60056   Established 1901

To unite fraternally all able-bodied deaf men and women, their relatives and others involved in the field of deafness, all of whom are not more than 60 years of age at the time of becoming members and are possessed of good bodily and mental health, and are of good moral character and industrious habits; to give moral aid and support to its members in time of need; to establish and disburse endowments, annuities, cash surrender, loan values, paidup insurance and income options; and, on demise of members, to pay death benefits to those persons who have been named as beneficiaries in accordance with the laws of the society. Membership: 14,000 (applicants for membership who are under 18 years of age must have written consent of a parent or guardian). Meetings: Quadrennial. Publication: The Frat, bimonthly, F. B. Sullivan, editor. Library: A. L. Roberts Memorial Library, 1,200 volumes. Affiliation: National Fraternal Congress of America.

★ 1238 ★

NATIONAL FUND FOR MEDICAL EDUCATION
999 Asylum Avenue   (203) 278-5070
Hartford, Connecticut 06105   Established 1949

John G. Freymann, M.D., President
Organized in 1949 and was granted a Federal Charter in 1954. Since 1954, NFME has awarded over $53 million in grants to institutions and organizations dedicated to medical education. Prior to 1965, this amount was in unrestricted support; since then, $13 million has been awarded for specific projects in educational research and innovation and for postgraduate

fellowships for medical educators. NFME objectives are to promote the best possible health care for the American people through improvement in medical education. Finances: Other Sources: Contributions from corporations, foundations, and individuals. Awards: Innovative projects, fellowships, postgraduate and undergraduate, special tutorial program for minority students, Lahey Award. Meetings: Annual, Washington, D.C. Publications: News About Medical Education, semiannually, Helen Charov, editor; Special Reports, occasionally, Helen Charov, editor; Annual Report, annually--May, Helen Charov, editor.

★ 1239 ★

NATIONAL GENETICS FOUNDATION, INC.
555 West 57th Street   (212) 586-5800
New York, New York 10019   Established 1953

Ruth Y. Berini, Executive Director
To provide diagnostic, treatment, and counseling services for people suffering from genetic diseases. Sponsors a network of 60 genetic counseling and treatment centers at medical teaching institutions throughout the United States and Canada. The Foundation headquarters serves as a clearinghouse and directs patients or their physicians to appropriate centers with the most comprehensive facilities for a particular problem. It also conducts educational programs to provide genetic information to both professionals and the lay public, as well as research programs for improving techniques for the delivery of care in medical genetics. Membership: Local chapters. Finances: Funds from private foundations; contributions from corporations, fraternal organizations, chapters, and the public; bequests.

★ 1240 ★

NATIONAL GERIATRICS SOCIETY, INC.
212 West Wisconsin Avenue   (414) 272-4130
Milwaukee, Wisconsin 53203   Established 1952

Thomas J. Bergen, Executive Director
To promote the advancement of techniques of care for aged, infirm, chronically ill, handicapped and convalescent patients; to promote the exchange of experience, techniques and research among professionals concerned with geriatric care, from a broad spectrum of institutions which care for the aged; to promote a multi-discipline dialogue, and provide a means for geriatrics professionals to keep in touch with developments in medicine, nursing, rehabilitation, pharmacology, psychology and the social sciences. Membership: 500. Finances: Membership: Individual, $25; institutional fee based on number of beds; sustaining varies; Other Sources: Seminars,

workshops, programs. <u>Meetings</u>: Annual, various locations. <u>Publications</u>: Aging and Leisure Living, monthly, Eugene E. Tillock, editor; Survey of Nursing Care Requirements in Nursing Homes in the State of the Union, update to January 1979, $5 a copy.

★ 1241 ★

NATIONAL HEALTH AND WELFARE MUTUAL LIFE INSURANCE ASSOCIATION

666 Fifth Avenue	(212) 399-1600
New York, New York 10019	Established 1945

William J. Flynn, President and Chief Executive Officer
To provide pension, tax-deferred annuities, and insurance benefits for the employees of non-profit health and welfare organizations and voluntary hospitals. <u>Membership</u>: 3,700. <u>Finances</u>: From both employers and employees. <u>Meetings</u>: Annual, New York City. <u>Publications</u>: NHW Report; Participant Newsletter; Investment Report. <u>Former Name</u>: National Health and Welfare Retirement Association.

NATIONAL HEALTH AND WELFARE RETIREMENT ASSOCIATION
    See: National Health and Welfare Mutual Life Insurance Association

★ 1242 ★

NATIONAL HEALTH COUNCIL, INC.

70 West 40th Street	(212) 869-8100
New York, New York 10018	Established 1920

Edward H. Van Ness, Executive Vice President
National membership association of voluntary and professional societies in the health field, federal government agencies concerned with health, and national organizations and business groups with strong health interests. Seeks to improve the health of the nation. <u>Membership</u>: Over 80 national organizations. <u>Finances</u>: Membership: Dues and service fees, $250-$24,000; Other Sources: Contributions from business and industry, federal and private contracts, grants from foundations. <u>Awards</u>: Certificates of Active Membership. <u>Meetings</u>: Annual Health Forum and Membership Meeting, various locations. <u>Publications</u>: Annual Report and list of members, as well as special publications on health topics such as: antitrust, credentialing, financial reporting, budgeting, health careers. Prints directories of health groups in Washington, Congress and Health, etc.

★ 1243 ★

NATIONAL HEALTH FEDERATION

212 West Foothill Boulevard	(213) 357-2181
Monrovia, California 91016	Established 1955

Kurt W. Donsbach, Chairman;
    Betty Lee Morales, Secretary
NHF is a non-profit consumer oriented organization devoted exclusively to health matters. In action, the NHF is a health-rights organization advocating the absolute right of the people to enjoy the civil liberty of "Freedom of Choice" in matters of personal health where such choices do not infringe upon the liberties of others. Although the Federation encourages everyone to live a health-oriented life by adopting a sensible, health-promoting program, it does not advocate any particular system of therapy of health philosophy. Rather, its work is in the preservation of the freedom which permits personal choice. <u>Membership</u>: Approximately 30,000 (physicians, dentists, chiropractors, osteopathic phsycians, naturopaths, pharmacists, pharmaceutical and food supplement manufacturers, health food distributors and dealers and average citizens). <u>Finances</u>: Membership: $12 regular membership annually; Other Sources: Donations, bequest and limited profit from some of the larger NHF conventions. <u>Meetings</u>: Annual Convention, various locations; seminars. <u>Publications</u>: The Journal of the NHF-Public Scrutiny, monthly. <u>Affiliation</u>: Local chapters of the NHF.

★ 1244 ★

NATIONAL HEARING AID SOCIETY

20361 Middlebelt	(313) 478-2610
Livonia, Michigan 48152	Established 1951

Anthony Di Rocco, Executive Vice President
The National Hearing Aid Society (NHAS) consists of individual members throughout the United States and Canada who are engaged in the testing of hearing for the selection, adaptation, fitting, sale and servicing of hearing aids. The National Institute for Hearing Instruments Studies, the educational arm of the hearing aid health field, is structured as a division of the Society. NHAS is the certifying body which grants the title "Certified Hearing Aid Audiologist" to those who meet certain standards and requirements, serves as a data resource center, sponsors and conducts educational programs, cooperates with government agencies and service organizations concerned with hearing health care, and sponsors and administers the national toll-free Hearing Aid Helpline (1-800-521-5247), which provides information and assists with problems about hearing loss and hearing aids. <u>Membership</u>: 3,100 hearing aid health professionals (1,750 certified members, 50 registered members, 1,300 state chapter members [dues paid to state chapters]).

Finances: $150 annually per individual member; Other Sources: Annual convention and educational materials. Meetings: Annual Convention, various locations. Publications: Audecibel, quarterly, Anthony DiRocco, editor; Directory of NHAS Members, annual, Anthony DiRocco, editor. Affiliation: There are 50 state and provincial chapters affiliated with NHAS.

★ 1245 ★
NATIONAL HEARING ASSOCIATION
1010 Jorie Boulevard, Suite 308   (312) 323-7200
Oak Brook, Illinois 60521   Established 1977

J. William Wright, Jr., President;
    Jack D. Beem, Secretary
The National Hearing Association is a charitable organization dedicated to the prevention and cure of deafness through finding solutions to clinical problems, and the rehabilitation of all hearing-impaired age groups through educational programs.   NHA provides a holistic approach to hearing.   The programs and services of NHA offers funding of intensive hearing research studies, preparation and distribution of specialized medical education materials for professionals, workshops on hearing health for parents, professionals and community members, funding of equipment for learning and speech therapy centers, public distribution of special educational materials, lecture series to increase public awareness, public information source for hearing problem inquiries, scholarship award to hearing-impaired students.   Membership: Approximately 50,000 nationwide (all age groups, majority of adults, medical and professional people, educators, and those with a vested interest in hearing across the nation).   Finances: Membership: Associate member, $10, $25, $50; contributing member, $100; professional member (physician or medical specialist), $100; sustaining member, $500; patron, $1,000; benefactor, $5,000; Other Sources: Private contributions: individuals, foundations and corporations.   Research Funds: Ear Research Institute and the Wright Institute of Otology.   Scholarship: 1980 American Field Service (AFS) foreign exchange student scholarship to Australia.   Meetings: Quarterly, Board of Directors. Meetings of the Scientific Advisory Committee, Fund Development Committee, Executive Committee and Program and Education Committee throughout the year. Publications: Hear, Hear (educational journal), quarterly, Sarah R. Melvin, editor; brochures regarding NHA and its work; brochures/pamphlets for the hearing-impaired.

★ 1246 ★
NATIONAL HEMOPHILIA FOUNDATION
19 West 34th Street   (212) 563-0211
New York, New York 10001   Established 1948

Deidre Kaylor Richardson, Acting Executive Director
To award grants for research and the clinical study of hemophilia and other blood-clotting deficiencies; to provide information relating to the prevention and treatment of these diseases for patients, their families, and professional health care providers and the general public; to raise money for the foregoing, philanthropic purposes.   Membership: 10,000-15,000 persons. Finances: Other Sources: Dues, special events, fund raising, grants, voluntary contributions.   Awards: Lee Ferguson Henry Memorial Scholarship Award; Judith Graham Pool Research Fellowship in Hemophilia.   Meetings: Annual, various locations.   Publications: over 30 various educational material. Affiliations: World Federation of Hemophilia; 50 local chapters; National Health Council; American Blood Commission.

★ 1247 ★
NATIONAL HERBALIST ASSOCIATION
271 Fifth Avenue, Suite 3   (212) 683-4793
New York, New York 10016   Established 1979

Leslie Kaslof, Chairman, Funding Board of Directors
To promote the use of whole plant substances for hearing and in the field of medicine.   To educate and develop standards of practice through certification programs in Herbal Medicine.   Speakers bureau, Seminars and Conferences and training programs are among some of the services being developed.   Membership: 95 (member and associate member). Meetings: Annual, various locations.   Publications: Newsletter, intermittently.   Library: 3 libraries: New York, New York; San Francisco, California; Melbourne, Arkansas, a total of 4,000 volumes (non-circulating research libraries for members only).

★ 1248 ★
NATIONAL HOME CARING COUNCIL
67 Irving Place   (212) 674-4990
New York, New York 10003   Established 1962

Florence Moore, Executive Director
To promote the development of homemaker-home health aide services throughout the country.   Membership: 610 (agencies, organizations, individuals). Finances: Membership: Agencies, $125-$2,700 (based on homemakers' salaries; individuals, $25 and up; organizations, $100 and up; Other Sources: Contracts; donations from foundations and corporations.

Meetings: Occasionally, various locations. Publications: Homemaker-Home Health Aide News, quarterly; papers and reprints; policy and legislative statements; pamphlets; brochures and books. Affiliation: Homemaker-Home Health Aide Agencies throughout the country. Former Name: National Council for Homemaker-Home Health Aide Services, Inc.

★ 1249 ★
NATIONAL HOSPICE ORGANIZATION
1311A Dolley Madison Boulevard
Suite 3B   (703) 356-6770
McLean, Virginia 22101   Established 1978

Josefina B. Magno, M.D., Executive Director;
    Daniel Hadlock, M.D., President, Board of
    Directors
NHO was established as a non-profit organization in April 1977 to promote the hospice concept of care for the terminally ill in the United States and to establish a mechanism by which to monitor existing and emerging programs, develop standards, conduct research problems, seminars and workshops, promote reimbursement and licensure by the health care system in the United States. It has become the major clearinghouse for information and referral to individuals seeking hospice care throughout the country. Its Board of Director has representation from 10 regions of the United States. It is currently engaged in increasing its membership, educating its members and the public, supporting legislative efforts for reimbursement and licensure and improving its data base. Membership: 1,620 (providers, cooperating, institutional, individual, senior citizens, students). Finances: Membership: $15 annually to $500 annually. Other Sources: Contributions, grants, sale of publications. Meetings: Full Board Meetings, quarterly, held in various locations of the United States; Executive Committee Meetings, 3 times annually, Washington Metropolitan area. Publications: Delivery and Payment of Hospice Services: Investigative Study: Final Report, 1979, reprinted as needed, NHO (editor); Hospice in America (brochure), reprinted as needed, NHO (editor); Standards of a Hospice Program of Care, 6th Revision, reprinted as needed, NHO (editor); Locator Directory of the National Hospice Organization, periodic update, NHO (editor); NHO Newsletter, quarterly, Eilene Dorf, editor; Frequently Most Asked Questions About Hospice, reprinted as needed, NHO (editor); Volunteers in Hospice, reprinted as needed, NHO (editor). Library: National Hospice Organization, 150 volumes (by appointment).

★ 1250 ★
NATIONAL INDUSTRIES FOR THE BLIND
1455 Broad Street   (201) 338-3804
Bloomfield, New Jersey 07003 Established 1938

George J. Mertz, Executive Vice President
To develop gainful industrial employment opportunities for blind and multihandicapped blind persons throughout the United States with appropriate rehabilitation and supportive services; professional assistance to nonprofit agencies serving the blind in the manufacture and marketing of blind-made products; allocating agency for orders for blind-made products received from the Federal Government. The organization is composed of a national network of workshops operated by agencies serving the blind in 37 states. Membership: 104 associated workshops. Finances: Membership: Sales from workshops. Publications: Annual Report.

★ 1251 ★
NATIONAL INSTITUTE FOR REHABILITATION
    ENGINEERING
97 Decker Road   (201) 838-2500
Butler, New Jersey 07405   Established 1967

Donald Selwyn, Executive Vice President
Multidisciplinary research, training and service organization providing custom-designed and custom-made tools and devices along with intensive personal task-performance and driver training to aid the handicapped person in becoming more self-sufficient and independent. Membership: Staffed by electronics engineers, physicians, physicists, psychologists, optometrists. Finances: Fees (based on each person's income and means); no handicapped person is denied the Institut's services due to an inability to pay; Other Sources: Grants and donations. Publications: News on Rehabilitation, semiannual.

★ 1252 ★
NATIONAL INSTITUTE OF HYPERTENSION STUDIES
12007 Linwood Avenue   (313) 867-1400
Detroit, Michigan 48206

Dr. H. R. Lockett, Executive Director and President
To assist in the nationwide effort to find the causes of psychosocial and occupational stresses related to essential hypertension; to conduct research projects; to provide techniques to alter attitudes conducive to new lifestyle concepts, an open door clinic for the purpose of reducing stress and the aging process; to design new educational programs for the consumer; to provide education and training for people of all ages. Finances: Other Sources: Donations, grants.

Meetings: Monthly, Detroit, Michigan. Affiliations: H.E.W., Metropolitan Hospital - Detroit tip program; National Kidney Foundation of Michigan; National Conference on High Blood Pressure. Remarks: Future plans: Television productions, publication; applied research projects. Former Name: Institute of Hypertension, School of Research.

★ 1253 ★
NATIONAL INSTITUTE OF MEDICAL HERBALISTS
c/o Hein Zeylstran
148 Forest Road
Turnbridge Wells   Established 1864
Kent TN2 5EY, England, United Kingdom

Hein Zeylstran, General Secretary
To conduct research on and administer non-poisonous medicine of plant extraction to the sick. Patients consult members as their sole medical practitioner. Membership: 150 members and honorary members (individuals become members by examination after 4 years of full time or part time tutorial study). Awards: Henry Potter Award; Arthur Baker Award; T. Bartram Award and Herb Society Award, to the best students after final examination. Meetings: Annual. Publications: The Herbal Practitioner, quarterly; Newsletter, irregular.

★ 1254 ★
NATIONAL INSTITUTE ON ALCOHOL ABUSE
   AND ALCOHOLISM
U.S. Department of Health and Human Services
Post Office Box 2345   (301) 468-2600
Rockville, Maryland 20852   Establshed 1971

Ernest P. Noble, Ph.D., M.D., Director
The National Institute on Alcohol Abuse and Alcoholism (NIAAA) has been established by the Federal Government to meet the challenge of coping with the rapid proliferation of alcoholism, the third greatest health problem in this country. The Institute has addressed this problem in a number of ways including research, prevention, treatment, rehabilitation, and training. The National Clearinghouse for Alcohol Information (see separate entry) is a service of NIAAA to make available current knowledge on alcohol-related programs and subjects.

★ 1255 ★
NATIONAL INTERAGENCY COUNCIL ON
   SMOKING AND HEALTH
291 Broadway   (212) 227-4390
New York, New York 10007   Established 1964

Louis Cenci, Executive Director
Seeks to be a cooperative and independent force to inform the public regarding the harmful effects of tobacco use, especially cigarette smoking. Membership: 32. Meetings: Quarterly, New York City. Publication: Newsletter, quarterly.

NATIONAL JEWISH HOSPITAL AND RESEARCH CENTER
   See: National Jewish Hospital/National Asthma Center

★ 1256 ★
NATIONAL JEWISH HOSPITAL/NATIONAL
   ASTHMA CENTER
3800 East Colfax   (303) 388-4461
Denver, Colorado 80206   Established 1899

Richard N. Bluestein, President
NJH/NAC is the world's largest medical center devoted to treatment, research and education in chronic respiratory diseases and immunological disorders. It provides hospitalization and outpatient services for patients of all ages with the following conditions: asthma; pulmonary and extra pulmonary tuberculosis and infections caused by atypical mycobacteria; other chest conditions including cystic fibrosis, chronic bronchitis, bronchiectasis, sarcoidosis, emphysems, fungus disease of the lung and pulmonary disorders in which the diagnosis has not been established; selected cases of connective tissue disorder with altered immune mechanisms such as systemic lupus erythematosis, juvenile rheumatoid arthritis and polyarteritis: certain other immune deficiency disorders. Membership: 12,000 auxiliary members in 78 local chapters. Finances: Other Sources: 55-60% of total operating budget is raised through development. Awards: Humanitarian awards, annual, for outstanding civic and community service. Meetings: Annual, Auxiliary Meeting, July, Denver, Colorado; Annual Board of Trustees meeting, September, Denver, Colorado. Library: Jerry Tucker Memorial Library, 11,000 volumes. Former Name: In 1978, National Jewish Hospital and Research Center merged with· the National Asthma Center.

NATIONAL JEWISH WELFARE BOARD
   See: J W B

★ 1257 ★
NATIONAL KIDNEY FOUNDATION
2 Park Avenue   (212) 889-2210
New York, New York 10016   Established 1950

Paul Archambault, Executive Director
To work for the prevention, treatment and cure of
diseases of the kidney. Programs include research,
patient services, nationwide organ donor program,
professional training and education, public information,
and community services. Finances: Voluntary contributions. Meetings: Annual, various locations.
Publications: The Kidney, bimonthly, William B.
Blythe, M.D., editor; KF Newsletter, quarterly,
Jim Warren, editor; Annual Report; brochures.
Affiliations: 54 affiliated division.

★ 1258 ★
NATIONAL LEAGUE FOR NURSING
10 Columbus Circle   (212) 582-1022
New York, New York 10019   Established 1952

Margaret E. Walsh, CAE, Executive Director
The League was founded to work with health care
agencies, of which nursing services are a basic component, with nursing educational institutions and with
communities to improve health care services and nursing education programs needed by society through services in accreditation, consultation, testing, continuing education, research and publications. Membership: 18,000 individuals; 1,800 agencies. Finances: Membership: Individual, $30 plus local con-
stituent league dues; agency, varying according to
size; Other Sources: Grants and services. Awards:
Nutting Award, for contribution to nursing; NLN
Distinguished Service Award; Lucile Petry Leone
Award; Linda Richards Award; Anna Fillmore Award;
Long Term Care Award. Meetings: Convention,
biennially; Education and Service Council meetings,
annually; workshops, conferences. Publications:
Nursing and Health Care, monthly, except July and
August, Susan Kennedy, editor; State-Approved
Schools of Nursing-LPN/LVN, annual; State-Approved
Schools of Nursing-RN, annual; NLN Data Book,
annual; Employment, Mobility and Personal Characteristics of Nurses Newly Licensed in (Year), annual;
several council bulletins. Affiliations: Constituent
leagues for nursing in 45 states, District of Columbia
and Puerto Rico.

★ 1259 ★
NATIONAL LIBRARY OF MEDICINE
8600 Rockville Pike   (301) 496-6095
Bethesda, Maryland 20209   Established 1836

Martin D. Cummings, M.D., Director; Albert
    Berkowitz, Chief of Reference Services; Robert B.
    Mehnert, Public Information Officer
Collects, organizes, and disseminates published biomedical literature; operates computerized literature
retrieval services; performs research and development
pertaining to biomedical communications through
NLM's Lister Hill National Center for Biomedical
Communications (see separate entry); conducts programs to improve the quality and use of medical
audiovisual materials through NLM's National Medical
Audiovisual Center (see separate entry); and provides
grant assistance for medical library resources, research, training, and publications. Operates specialized information services in toxicology/pharmacol-
ogy and environmental health and operates a network
of Regional Medical Libraries to provide document
delivery and other health science information services.
Finances: Other Sources: Congressional appropriation.
Publications: Index Medicus, monthly and annual,
C. A. Bachrach, M.D., editor; Abridged Index
Medicus, monthly and annual, C. A. Bachrach,
M.D., editor; NLM Current Catalog, quarterly and
annual; NLM Audiovisual Catalog, quarterly and
annual; Health Sciences Serials, quarterly (micro-
fiche only); National Library of Medicine Classification; Bibliography of the History of Medicine; Index of NLM Serial Titles; List of Journals Indexed
in Index Medicus; Medical Subject Headings. Library: 2.5 million items (for health professionals and
students). Affiliations: NLM is a component of the
National Institutes of Health, Public Health Service,
Department of Health and Human Services.

★ 1260 ★
NATIONAL MEDICAL AND DENTAL ASSOCIATION,
    INC.
c/o Dr. Arthur J. Wolski
5450 Sunnyside Avenue   (312) 777-5450
Chicago, Illinois 60630   Established 1910

Arthur J. Wolski, D.D.S., President
The National Medical and Dental Association, Inc.,
is an organization of physicians and dentists of Polish
heritage. It is the parent organization of several
smaller local units or chapters. Membership: 2,500
(honorary and active); active membership is available
to ethnical dentists and physicians of Polish heritage,
licensed to practice medicine or dentistry (also allied
professionals) and eligible for membership to the AMA
or ADA. Finance: Membership: $20 plus scholar-
ship donation; Other Sources: Annual Meetings.
Awards: Man of the Year or Woman of the Year
Award, annual, to an outstanding man or woman of
Polish heritage who has distinguished him (her) self
in his/her field of work; Scholarships to needy medical or dental students. Meetings: Annual

Convention with local chapters, various locations; Board meetings, semiannually. Publications: Bulletin, annual, Raymond S. Dziejma, D.D.S., and John J. Kraw, M.D., editors. Affiliations: Chicago Polish Medical Society; Medical and Dental Arts Chief of Detroit; Dental Arts Clubs of Chicago; Medical Arts Society of Buffalo; Chapters in Boston, Buffalo, Chicago, Cleveland, Detroit, New York City, Newark, Philadelphia, Pittsburgh.

★ 1261 ★
NATIONAL MEDICAL AUDIOVISUAL CENTER
8600 Rockville Pike   (301) 496-3547
Bethesda, Maryland 20209   Established 1967

James Woods, Ph.D., Director
The audiovisual facility, originally located in Atlanta, Georgia, was transferred organizationally to the National Library of Medicine (see separate entry) in 1967 and renamed the National Medical Audiovisual Center. The goal of the Center is to develop a national program to improve the quality and use of medicalaudiovisuals in schools of the health professions and throughout the biomedical community. The Center has developed an online retrieval system for audiovisuals, lends medical motion pictures, designs, develops and tests instructional media materials, and assists schools in planning and designing facilities for using instructional media. NMAC also conducts AV training programs through field training sites. Finances: Other Sources: Under the Congressional appropriation for the National Library of Medicine. Publications: National Medical Audiovisual Center Catalog. Affiliation: A component of the National Library of Medicine.

★ 1262 ★
NATIONAL MENTAL HEALTH ASSOCIATION
1800 North Kent Street   (703) 528-6405
Arlington, Virginia 20009   Established 1909

Jack McAllister, Executive Director
The National Mental Health Association is a nationwide, voluntary, non-governmental organization dedicated to the promotion of mental health, the prevention of mental illnesses, and the improved care and treatment of the mentally ill. Its 850 chapters and divisions and more than 1,000,000 citizen volunteers work toward these goals through a wide range of activities in social action, education, advocacy and information. Membership: Over 1,000,000 volunteers. Finances: Membership: Private donations. Awards: The Mental Health Employer of the Year Award; The Lela Rowland Award; The Clifford W. Beers Award; The Mental Health Research Achieve-

ment Award (McAlpin Award); The Mental Health Media Awards; The NMHA Film Festival Awards; The Katherine Hamilton Volunteer of the Year Award. Publications: Focus, bimonthly, Lynn Schultz Writsel, editor; In Touch, bimonthly; a variety of booklets and pamphlets on mental health topics and issues. Library: The Clifford W. Beers Memorial Library (for members and staff). Former Name: National Association for Mental Health.

★ 1263 ★
NATIONAL MIGRAINE FOUNDATION
5214 North Western Avenue   (312) 878-7715
Chicago, Illinois 60625   Established 1970

Arnold Friedman, President;
    Seymour Diamond, Executive Director
To provide a channel for funds for research into the cause of severe headache; to provide educational information for both physicians and the lay public. Functions as a referral service for those who need help finding medical aid and also as an educational facility to provide the most up-to-date information worldwide in the area of headache. Membership: 6,000. Finances: Membership: $10 for Newsletter sent out quarterly; Other Sources: Donations. Meetings: Annual, in June, various locations. Publications: NMF Newsletter, quarterly, Sidney Gimpel, editor. Affiliation: American Association for the Study of Headache.

★ 1264 ★
NATIONAL NUTRITION CONSORTIUM, INC.
1635 P Street, N.W., Suite 1   (202) 234-7760
Washington, D.C. 20036

Dr. Mahlon A. Burnette, III, Executive Officer
Professional societies in the fields of nutrition, food and dietetics. To provide information to the public on food and health; to provide leadership in the development and coordination of food and nutrition policies at national and local levels in the public interest. Serves as a clearinghouse of information on nutrition food and health. Membership: 9 member organizations (professional organizations, food scientists, dietitians, nutritional educators, physicians).

★ 1265 ★
NATIONAL OSTEOPATHIC FOUNDATION
212 East Ohio Street   (312) 280-5850
Chicago, Illinois 60611   Established 1949

Howard W. Baldock, President;
    Lee Stein, Executive Vice President
To acquire funds for student loans, osteopathic research, college support, and education grants; to
provide for a better understanding of the fundamental
principles and practice of osteopathic medicine and to
promote and support research activities.   Membership:
160 full, 2,000 supporting members (industry, individual and patron).   Finances: Membership: $25
individual; $100 patron; $1,000 industry.   Awards:
Mead Johnson Fellowship Grant Program; Burroughs-
Wellcome Osteopathic Research Fellowship.   Meetings: Semiannual, various locations.   Affiliation:
Philanthropic Affiliate of American Osteopathic Association.

★ 1266 ★
NATIONAL OSTEOPATHIC GUILD ASSOCIATION
930 Busse Highway   (312) 944-2713
Park Ridge, Illinois 60068   Established 1954

The organization was formed for the following objectives: to correlate the activities of the guilds
serving non-profit osteopathic hospitals as classified
by the American Osteopathic Association; to maintain
a clearinghouse for guild information; to assist with
the formation of new guilds; and to function as an
allied organization of the Auxiliary to the American
Osteopathic Associations.   Membership: 35 Guilds
representing 1,500 members (regular and associate).
Finances: Membership: $2 per person for the guild;
associate guilds pay a flat fee of $10; Other Sources:
Grants from the Auxiliary of the American Osteopathic Association.   Awards: Guild Volunteer of the
Year; Scrapbook and Craft Awards.   Meetings: Annual.   Publication: N.O.G.A. Newsletter, quarterly.   Affiliation: Auxiliary of the American Osteopathic Association.

NATIONAL PARAPLEGIA FOUNDATION
    See: National Spinal Cord Injury Foundation

★ 1267 ★
NATIONAL PHARMACEUTICAL ASSOCIATION
Howard University, College of
    Pharmacy and Pharmacal Science (202) 636-7963
Washington, D.C. 20059   Established 1947

James N. Tyson, Executive Secretary
To unite minority pharmacists and to provide a means
whereby these pharmacists could contribute to their
common improvement, share their experiences, and
contribute to the public good.   Membership: 350

full; 600 affiliated.   Finances: Membership: $30.
Meetings: Annual, various locations.   Publications:
Journal, quarterly, Edward D. Miller, editor.   Affiliations: Student National Pharmaceutical Association; 22 local associations.

★ 1268 ★
NATIONAL PHARMACEUTICAL COUNCIL, INC.
1030 15th Street, N.W.,
Suite 468   (202) 659-2121
Washington, D.C. 20005   Established 1953

Mark R. Knowles
The National Pharmaceutical Council is dedicated to
the enhancement of the quality and integrity of pharmaceutical services in the manufacturing, distributing,
and dispensing of prescription medications and other
pharmaceutical products.   Toward this end, NPC
undertakes educational activities and provides services
for providers, professional associations, government
offices, and consumers concerning such aspects of
health care as the quality and cost/effectiveness of
pharmaceutical products, the economics of drug programs, and the contributions of research-oriented manufacturers.   Membership: 21 Research Intensive
Pharmaceutical Manufacturers.   Finances: Membership: Dues based upon domestic pharmaceutical sales.
Meetings: Internal committee meetings, board sessions
and seminars.

★ 1269 ★
NATIONAL PSYCHOLOGICAL ASSOCIATION FOR
    PSYCHOANALYSIS, INC.
150 West 13th Street   (212) 924-7440
New York, New York 10011   Established 1946

Annabella B. Nelken, Executive Administrator;
    Joel Gold, Secretary
An association of psychoanalysts dedicated to the advancement of psychoanalysis as a science and as a
profession.   The Association maintains a training institute for preparing qualified analysts, conducts public lecture programs and maintains a psychoanalytic
library as well as a non-profit community referral
service, known as The Theodor Reik Consultation
Center.   Membership: 229 (senior, associate, honorary, special).   Finances: Membership: $75;
Other Sources: Tuition fees, contributions.   Meetings: New York City.   Publications: Psychoanalytic
Review, quarterly, Leila Lerner, editor; Annual
Bulletin of courses and membership directory.   Library: George Lawton Memorial Library, approximately 4,000 volumes.

★ 1270 ★

NATIONAL PSYCHOLOGICAL ASSOCIATION, INC.
Post Office Box 2436
West Palm Beach, Florida 33402   Established 1947

Dale Halle, Secretary
To provide a professional association for persons involved in behavioral sciences or other pertinent specialities who do not qualify for membership in the
major association, such as clergymen involved in
counseling, etc.   Membership: 200 (full, associate,
student, honorary).   Finances: Membership: Full,
$25, plus initiation fee, $25; associate and student,
$25.   Awards: Award of Excellence for outstanding
contribution to behavioral science field; Award of
Honor for outstanding contribution toward NPA growth.
Meetings: Annual, various locations; board meeting,
quarterly.   Publications: NPA Newsletter, quarterly,
R. L. Bair, editor; NPA Journal, annually, R. L.
Bair, editor; Bulletins.   Affiliation: American
Psychotherapy Association.

★ 1271 ★

NATIONAL RECREATION AND PARK ASSOCIATION
1601 North Kent Street   (703) 525-0606
Arlington, Virginia 22209   Established 1906

John H. Davis, Executive Director
The National Recreation and Park Association is dedicated to promoting the leisure movement in America.
Parks and recreation services provide a zestful,
heartening environment for individuals to refresh themselves physically and mentally.   The Association
seeks to build public understanding of its mission, it
has embarked on a major plan to illustrate to Americans the value of recreation and keeping active.
NRPA works with more than 65,000 indoor and out-
door park and recreation assets encompassing millions
of acres of publicly owned land and thousands of private facilities.   Membership: 18,000 (individual and
institutional).   Finances: Individual Membership:
Professional, $40-$100; retired professional, $35;
associate, $35; student, $25; Institutional Membership: Citizen and Board (policy and advisory boards,
commission, councils and committees concerned with
parks recreation and conservation), $150-$400; Agency (public and private agencies, departments, bureaus
and other districts and authorities with no individual
board or commission members), $150-$400; organiza-
tion/institution (national, state and local organizations,
hospitals, colleges, universities, libraries, clubs,
etc.), $150; affiliate, $200; commercial firm, $200;
friend, $35; friend/contributor, $50; friend/support-
ing, $100; friend/benefactor, $250; friend/patron,
$500; friend/fellow, $1,000.   Finances: Other
Sources: Contributions.   Meetings: Annual Congress, various locations; annual meetings of the 5

regional offices in their respective districts.   Publications: Park and Recreation, monthly; Washington
Action Report, biweekly; The Journal of Leisure Research, quarterly; Therapeutic Recreation Journal;
Catalog of NRPA Publications; Dateline: NRPA,
bimonthly; other technical and management publications like Management Aids and Park Practice Program.   Library: 2,000 volumes.

★ 1272 ★

NATIONAL REGISTRY IN CLINICAL CHEMISTRY
1155 16th Street, N.W.   (202) 659-9660
Washington, D.C. 20036   Established 1967

Irma D. Campbell, Executive Secretary
To identify chemists and technologists qualified by
education and experience to provide essential health
services of a chemical nature in the nation's clinical
laboratories; to provide an annual evaluation of
clinical laboratory specialists in the chemical field
who voluntarily present their credentials to the Registry, and to certify persons who meet the Standards for
Certification.   Membership: 1,200 certified chemists and technologists.   Finances: Examination and
application fees.   Affiliations: American Chemical
Society; American Board of Clinical Chemistry;
American Association for Clinical Chemistry; American Institute of Chemists; American Society of Biological Chemists; American Society of Clinical Pathologists.

★ 1273 ★

NATIONAL REHABILITATION ADMINISTRATION
   ASSOCIATION
c/o National Rehabilitation Association
633 South Washington   (703) 836-0850
Alexandria, Virginia 22314

A Division of the National Rehabilitation Association
(see listing below).   The purpose of NRAA is to develop, improve and strengthen practices and skills of
administrators and supervisors in both public and private rehabilitation organizations.   Membership: All
members of NRAA must be members of the National
Rehabilitation Association.   Publications: Journal of
Rehabilitation Administration, quarterly; Administration and Supervision in Rehabilitation, quarterly.

★ 1274 ★

NATIONAL REHABILITATION ASSOCIATION
633 South Washington   (703) 836-0850
Alexandria, Virginia 22314   Established 1925

David L. Mills, Executive Director
Private, non-profit organization whose purpose is to advance the rehabilitation of all handicapped persons. The Association is an effective advocate of handicapped people, articulating their rights and needs, and pursuing the best possible means to meet these needs. The Association's Job Placement Division assists in the placement of handicapped persons in employment. The other six divisions are: National Association for Independent Living; National Association of Rehabilitation Instructors; National Association of Rehabilitation Secretaries; National Rehabilitation Administration Association; National Rehabilitation Counseling Association; Vocational Evaluation and Work Adjustment Association (see separate entries for further information). Membership: Approximately 25,000 (full, associate, student, sustaining). Finances: Membership: Full, $30; associate, $15; student, $15; sustaining, $50. Meetings: Annual conferences, various locations. Publications: NRA Newsletter; Journal of Rehabilitation. Affiliations: Chapters in each state (except Vermont) and in Puerto Rico.

★ 1275 ★
NATIONAL REHABILITATION COUNSELING
    ASSOCIATION
c/o National Rehabilitation Association
633 South Washington   (703) 836-0850
Alexandria, Virginia 22314   Established 1958

A Division of the National Rehabilitation Association (see listing above). The purpose of NRCA is to identify the nature of the needs of disabled persons and the nature of rehabilitation counseling knowledge and skills necessary to respond to client needs; to discover and develop means whereby client needs will be adequately met through rehabilitation counseling; to share the results of these discoveries through its publications, branch meetings, national conferences, and its liaison with other interested professionals and professions; to gain a higher degree of recognition for the profession of rehabilittation counseling. NRCA is the largest professional association in the field of rehabilitation counseling. Its programs and services include the maintenance of a governmental relations programs, promotion of awards and scholarships, sponsorship of continuing education programs, and promotion of a professional code of ethics. Membership: Professional member (a master's degree in rehabilitation counseling and a minimum of one year's experience); Member (baccalaureate degree from an accredited college, employment in a rehabilitation setting); Student member (enrollment in an accredited college); Affiliate member (employment in a supporting, ancillary, or helping capacity at a technical level in support of rehabilitation counseling

practice). All members of NRCA must be members of the National Rehabilitation Association. Publications: The Professional Report; The Journal of Applied Rehabilitation Counseling.

★ 1276 ★
NATIONAL RETINITIS PIGMENTOSA FOUNDA-
    TION, INC. (U.S.)
Rolling Park Building
8331 Mindale Circle   (301) 655-1011
Baltimore, Maryland 21207   Established 1971

Dennis L. Hartenstine, Executive Director
To determine through laboratory research the cause, treatment, and cure for retinitis pigmentosa and allied diseases; to solicit funds from the public, corporations, civic organizations, private and public foundations, and other philanthropic individuals and groups; to inform the public of the magnitude and symptoms of the disease. Finances: Other Sources: Contributions. Awards: Research grants and fellowships for the study of retinitis pigmentosa. Affiliation: National Retinitis Pigmentosa Foundation of Canada.

★ 1277 ★
NATIONAL RETINITIS PIGMENTOSA FOUNDA-
    TION OF CANADA
1 Spadina Crescent, Suite 115   (416) 368-3809
Toronto, Ontario M5S 2J5, Canada Established 1974

Leon E. Weinstein, Chairman;
    Jay N. Martin, President
To find, through research programs, the causes and the cure for retinitis pigmentosa (retinitis pigmentosa is an inherited retinal degenerative disease usually beginning with night blindness in children which may result in blindness by age of 25-50); to educate people of the magnitude and the symptoms of RP; to raise funds from the public, corporations and other charitable organizations to continue and expand research efforts. Membership: 500-550 families. Finances: No membership fee; Other Source: Donations. Meetings: Semiannual, wherever chapters have been formed. Publication: Newsletter, semiannual, National Headquarters. Affiliation: National Retinitis Pigmentosa Foundation, Inc. (U.S.).

★ 1278 ★
NATIONAL SAFETY MANAGEMENT SOCIETY
6060 Duke Street   (703) 751-6416
Alexandria, Virginia 22304   Established 1966

Philip H. Bolger, Executive Director;

Joseph C. Caldwell, Chairman, Board of Directors
The mission of the Society is devoted to education and scientific research for the purpose of better managed accident prevention activities. Among other activities, the Society promotes the development of safety management studies leading to undergraduate and graduate degrees as well as the inclusion of sa-safety management studies into programs of business administration. Membership: 1,800 (no restrictions-members in all States of the United States and 10 foreign countries). Finances: Membership: Initial registration fee, $25; annual dues, $25; applicants outside of North America, $35 (United States); student rates available; Other Sources: Solicitation of corporate memberships, donations and grants. Meetings: Various State and Chapter meetings, monthly; Annual general membership meeting and quarterly executive committee meetings. Publications: Journal of Safety Management, quarterly, Robert LeClerg and William C. Pope, editors; Focus (a quarterly insert into Occupational Hazards Magazine).

★ 1279 ★

NATIONAL SANITATION FOUNDATION
3475 Plymouth Road
Post Office Box 1468   (313) 769-8010
Ann Arbor, Michigan 48105   Established 1944

Nina I. McClelland, President; Edward L. Stockton, Executive Vice President; Tom S. Gable, Senior Vice President
NSF affords a method for developing uniform nationally accepted standards which are based on scientific facts, sound engineering and good public health practices. NSF provides a methodology which brings together people with mutual interests to study a problem, define the need and carry out the necessary research to arrive at a standard suitable for nationwide application. A by-product of this process, often as valuable as the standard itself, is the mutual respect and confidence that arises in this new cooperation between public health officials, industrial managers and consumer representatives. Research efforts by the NSF testing laboratory have played an important role in the development of many standards. Finances: Other Sources: Fees for services, research and educational grants and contracts, gifts. Awards: Walter F. Snyder Award; Spes Hominum Awards. Meetings: Annual meeting of Joint and Advisory Committees and the Council of Public Health Consultants. Publications: News from NSF, quarterly, D. L. Lancaster, editor; numerous educational materials reports, brochures, booklets, posters. Library: N.S.F., 500 volumes (staff and committee members).

★ 1280 ★

NATIONAL SAVE-A-LIFE LEAGUE
815 Second Avenue, Suite 409   (212) 736-6191
New York, New York 10017   Established 1906

Robert Amoury, President; Duane C. DeLair, Suicidologist; Eric Hadar, Director of Training
Non-profit organization providing befriending service, practicing crisis intervention, dealing mainly with suicide, but also receives calls about loneliness, alcoholism, drug abuse, child abuse, old age. Volunteers are trained with an eclectic approach. Membership: Varies (anyone passing training program and internship is given certified volunteer status). Finances: Other Sources: Donations. Lectureship: Lectures are given as a public service by qualified members of the League. Meetings: Monthly, at New York office. Publications: Plans for research publications are under way, projection date 1982. Library: League has its own library, 50 volumes (in facility). Affiliation: National Save-A-Life Northern New Jersey, Irma Cohn, Director. Remarks: Save-A-Life is the oldest suicide Center in the United States.

★ 1281 ★

NATIONAL SOCIETY FOR AUTISTIC CHILDREN
1234 Massachusetts Avenue, N.W.
Suite 1017   (202) 783-0125
Washington, D.C. 20005   Established 1965

Harold A. Benson, Jr., Executive Director
Dedicated to the education, welfare and cure of children and adults with severe disorders of communication and behavior. Membership: 5,000 (parent and professional). Finances: Membership: Family, $22.50; individual, $15; student, $7.50; contributing, $45; supporting, $75; sponsoring, $300; patron, $1,500; life, $3,000. Awards: Plaques, Pendants, Certificates of Appreciation, and Certificates of Commendation, all presented at the annual meeting. Meetings: Annual, various locations. Publications: Newsletter, bimonthly, Carol Hansen, editor; Conference Proceedings; pamphlets. Library: Combined with bookstore, 3,000 volumes. Affiliation: 187 local chapters.

★ 1282 ★

NATIONAL SOCIETY FOR MEDICAL RESEARCH
1029 Vermont Avenue, N.W.
Suite 700   (202) 347-9565
Washington, D.C. 20005   Established 1946

Dr. W. Doyne Collings, Executive Director
The purpose of the Society is to assure continued

progress in the United States biomedical research effort by protecting the scientific investigators right to use laboratory animals whenever he feels it is necessary. Activities include exhibits at scientific meetings and a data bank. Membership: 1,193 (scientific and professional societies; medical, dental, and veterinary medical schools; pharmaceutical companies; individuals). Finances: Membership: Dues; individual memberships starting at $15; Other Sources: Contributions. Meetings: Annual, November, Washington, D.C. Publications: NSMR Bulletin, monthly; Annual Report, annually; miscellaneous educational publications.

NATIONAL SOCIETY FOR THE PREVENTION OF BLINDNESS
See: National Society to Prevent Blindness

★ 1283 ★
NATIONAL SOCIETY OF CARDIOPULMONARY
    TECHNOLOGISTS, INC.
1 Bank Street, Suite 307   (301) 258-9050
Gaithersburg, Maryland 20760   Established 1967

John L. Acuff, Executive Director
To encourage the training and education of cardiopulmonary technologists; to raise the educational requirements of such technologists and to assist them in improving and maintaining a high standard of performance; to provide the technologist with a greater opportunity for employment by cultivating an awareness on the part of the medical profession, of our standards, and professional capabilities; to aid the physician in his service to the patient and in the promotion of medical research; and to collect and disseminate information of value to all members, and to the public at large, to be realized in part by publishing and circulating books, pamphlets and periodicals in connection with the activities of this society. Membership: 2,900 (technologist, technician, affiliate, student and sustaining). Finances: Membership: $35 annually; Other Sources: Journal advertising, Trade Shows and registration fees at meeting. Meetings: Semiannual, various locations. Publications: Analyzer, quarterly, L. Acuff, editor; C. P. Digest, monthly, L. Acuff, editor.

★ 1284 ★
NATIONAL SOCIETY TO PREVENT BLINDNESS
79 Madison Avenue   (212) 684-3505
New York, New York 10016   Established 1908

Virginia S. Boyce, Executive Director

To prevent blindness and to conserve sight through a nationwide comprehensive program of public and professional education, research, industrial and community services. Services include promotion and support of local glaucoma screening programs, preschool vision testing, industrial eye safety, and seminars for professional education and public information programs through mass media and communications. Serves as a clearinghouse on matters pertaining to the prevention of blindness and conservation of vision; assembles statistical and other data about the nature and extent of causes of blindness and defective vision to serve as a basis for preventive programs; assists educational authorities in the improvement of environmental conditions affecting eye health in schools and colleges; provides guidance and consultation to industry in the adoption of eye health and safety procedures; promotes eye care and safety programs in vocational shops, manual arts and chemistry laboratories in schools and colleges; disseminates information on preventive aspects of eye conditions to professional groups; provides public education on positive eye care and prevention of blindness; supports basic research and special projects, such as preschool vision testing and glaucoma screening demonstration. Finances: Mail campaign, corporation and foundation gifts, contributions, legacies and bequests. Awards: Annual grants are made by the Society to scientists conducting eye research. The Pan American Gold Medal for distinguished service in the eye field at quadrennial meetings of the Pan American Congress of Ophthalmology; periodically, Mason Huntington Bigelow Award, for an outstanding contribution to prevention of blindness by a non-medical person, agency or organization. Meetings: Biennial, National Conference; annual membership, New York City. Publications: Sightsaving Review, quarterly; Prevent Blindness News and Wise Owl News, quarterly; Annual Report and many publications, films, and audio-visual aids for professional and lay audiences. Library: Conrad Berens Library, 2,955 volumes. Affiliations: The National Society to Prevent Blindness is represented by local societies throughout the United States. Former Name: National Society for the Prevention of Blindness.

★ 1285 ★
NATIONAL SPINAL CORD INJURY FOUNDATION
369 Elliot Street
Newton Upper Falls,   (617) 964-0521
    Massachusetts 02164   Established 1948

Robert J. McHugh, Executive Director;
    Ann Ford, Secretary
Purpose is to address the needs of persons with spinal cord injuries; activities in the area of resource identification and documentation, information and referral,

professional education and research.   Membership:
4,000 (membership is open to all who wish to join;
available through chapters or "at-large").   Finances:
Membership: At-large membership - Participating,
$10; contributing, $15; supporting, $25; sustaining,
$50; century club, $100; life, $500;   Other
Sources: Public contributions, sale of literature.
Awards: 2 to 4 fellowships awarded annually for
basic spinal cord injury research.   Meetings: Annual
Convention, location changes each year.   Publica-
tions: Paraplegia Life (internal newsletter), quarterly,
James Smittkamp, editor; Convention Journal and
Annual Report, annually, Judith C. Gilliom, editor.
Former Name: National Paraplegia Foundation.

★ 1286 ★
NATIONAL STUDENT NURSES' ASSOCIATION, INC.
10 Columbus Circle   (212) 581-2211
New York, New York 10019   Established 1952

Mary Ann Tuft, CAE, Executive Director
To aid in the development of the individual student
and to urge students of nursing, as future health professionals, to be aware of and to contribute to, improving the health care of all people.   The organization is active in promoting student participation in
community affairs toward improved health care; in
promoting and encouraging student participation in
interdisciplinary activities in legislation; in recruitment and retention of minority students in schools of
nursing.   Membership: 30,000.   Finances: Membership: $15; Other Sources: Advertising; exhibits.
Meetings: Annual, various locations.   Publications:
Imprint, quarterly; NSNA News.

NATIONAL STUDENT SPEECH AND HEARING
ASSOCIATION
     See: National Student Speech Language Hearing
            Association

★ 1287 ★
NATIONAL STUDENT SPEECH LANGUAGE HEARING
     ASSOCIATION
10801 Rockville Pike   (301) 897-5700
Rockville, Maryland 20852   Established 1972

Jane B. Franklin, National Office
The official organization of students interested in
speech and hearing governed by a council of ten students and five professor-consultants; provides student
representation on ASHA's Legislative Council, Scientific and Professional Meeting Board and Publication
Board.   Membership: Approximately 9,000 under-

graduate and premasters students interested in the
field of normal and disordered human communication
behavior.   Finances: Membership: $25; Other
Sources: Royalties from publications.   Meetings:
Semiannual.   Publications: Journal of the National
Student Speech Language Hearing Association, annually; NSSLHA Clinical Series, biennially; NSSLHA
Newsletter, semiannual, John Bernthal, Ph.D., Administrative Consultant, editor, and Jane B. Franklin,
National Office Coordinator.   Former Name: National Student Speech and Hearing Association.

★ 1288 ★
NATIONAL SUDDEN INFANT DEATH SYNDROME
     FOUNDATION, INC.
310 South Michigan Avenue
Suite 1904   (312) 663-0650
Chicago, Illinois 60604   Established 1962

Executive Director
Founded by Mr. and Mrs. E. Jedd Roe, Jr. in memory of their son, Mark Addison, a SIDS victim.
Programs for research, service to families of SIDS
victims and educational services for first responders
have developed into a network across the country.
While the ultimate objective remains the elimination
of SIDS, both research and services now have been
extended to infants at high risk and their parents.
The NSIDSF operates a clearinghouse for SIDS literature and plays a strong parent advocate role.   Education of the general public through literature dis-
persal and workshops follows the Foundation's programs
for professional in importance.   Membership: 57
Chapters in 35 states; volunteers are listed in various
categories according to their relation to the Chapter
or the organization nationally.   Finances: Membership: Multiple combination from voluntary offering to
specific annual fees varying from chapter to chapter;
Other Sources: Contributions from the private sector;
foundations, corporations and multiple volunteer organizations.   Research Funds: Restricted funds for
research make up the core of research funding for the
national organization; Chapters conduct fundraising
activities for specific research projects in their locale.
Meetings: Boards of Trustees, NSIDSF, annual;
Executive Committee of Board of Trustees, NSIDSF,
quarterly.   Publications: National Newsletter, The
Tree of Hope, semiannual, National Office Staff
(editor); Regional newsletter, semiannually, more
frequent on occasion, editing directed by respective
regional directors; Facts About Sudden Infant Death
Syndrome (revised approximately every 5 years);
Counseling of Families in the Professional Management
of SIDS; The Subsequent Child; SIDS: Siblings
and Grief; SIDS for Police Officers.   Former Name:
National Foundation for Sudden Infant Death, Inc.

★ 1289 ★
NATIONAL TAY-SACHS AND ALLIED DISEASES
    ASSOCIATION, INC.
112 East 42nd Street   (212) 661-2780
New York, New York 10168   Established 1958

Jane Birnbaum, Executive Director
National Tay-Sachs and Allied Diseases Association,
Inc. is a National health organization dedicated to
the eradication of fatal genetic diseases, specifically
Tay-Sachs disease and its over 40 allied disorders.
NTSAD's main purpose is to educate the Jewish com-
munity (a heterozygote frequency in the American
Jewish Population of 1 in 29.7 has been determined)
and the larger community about Tay-Sachs disease and
its prevention, to help conduct Tay-Sachs screening
programs, to help establish an International Tay-Sachs
Disease screening, reference standard and Quality
Control Center in order to maintain the highest possible technical quality and accuracy in Tay-Sachs
Disease screening programs throughout the world.
Membership: Professional and lay leadership. Finances: Membership: $15; Other Sources: Grants
and fundraising activities. Research: An international quality control program. Meetings: Annual,
various locations. Publications: What Every Family
Should Know, annual; The Killer is Cornered, annual; Are you Gamblin With Your Family's Future?,
annual.

★ 1290 ★
NATIONAL THERAPEUTIC RECREATION SOCIETY
c/o National Recreation and Park Association
1601 North Kent Street   (703) 525-0606
Arlington, Virginia 22209   Established 1966

Ms. Y. A. Washington, Staff Liaison
The national professional organization for those individuals concerned with the provision of recreation and
leisure services for the ill, handicapped, disabled
and other special populations in hospitals, institutions,
and in the community. Membership: 2,200 (professional, associate). Finances: Membership; Other
Sources: Voluntary contributions, foundation support.
Meetings: Annual with the National Recreation and
Park Association. Publications: Parks and Recreation, monthly; Therapeutic Recreation Journal,
quarterly; NTRS Year Book; TR Annual.

★ 1291 ★
NATURAL FOOD ASSOCIATES, INC.
Post Office Box 210   (214) 796-3612
Atlanta, Texas 75551   Established 1952

Dr. Joe D. Nichols, M.D., Chairman of the Board;

Martha H. Andrews, Secretary-Treasurer
To teach all people the importance of conservation of
soil; water and environment, the values of natural,
poison-free food grown on fertile soil; to expose the
evils of chemical contamination of food, water, and
environment; to convince all people that prevention
of metabolic disease is necessary to save our civilization. Membership: Approximately 8,000 (all types).
Finances: Membership: $12 annually; Other Sources:
Donations and bookstore sales (mail order). Meetings: Annual convention, various locations; approximately 4 seminars annually, usually held locally.
Publications: Natural Food and Farming, monthly,
Marvin Steffins, acting editor; Natural Food News,
monthly, Marvin Steffins, acting editor; various reprints (usually taken from Natural Food and Farming),
public demand. Affiliation: Various State Chapters.

NEGRI (MARIO) INSTITUTE FOR PHARMACOLOGICAL
RESEARCH
    See: Mario Negri Institute for Pharmacological
        Research

★ 1292 ★
NEUROELECTRIC SOCIETY
8700 West Wisconsin Avenue   (414) 258-8460
Milwaukee, Wisconsin 53226   Established 1967

Anthony Sances, President
To study the effects of electrical currents on biological systems; to establish scholarships in the areas
related to neuroelectric investigations for the endowment of education in the field of neuroelectricity and
for the advancement of clinical systems and research
in the field of neuroelectricity. Membership: 200.
Finances: Membership: $25. Meetings: Annual,
various locations. Publications: Neuroelectric
News, quarterly, Arsen Iwanovsky, editor.

★ 1293 ★
NEUROSURGICAL SOCIETY OF AMERICA
7703 Floyd Curl Drive   (512) 691-6136
San Antonio, Texas 78284   Established 1948

Jim L. Story, M.D., Secretary
Dissemination of the information in the field of neurosurgery, and stimulation and promotion of fellowship
among young neurosurgeons. Activities include annual meeting, special meetings, executive committee
meetings. Membership: 162 (active, associate,
senior members). Finances: Membership: $35;
Other Sources: Special assessments. Meetings: Annual, various locations.

★ 1294 ★
NEUROTICS ANONYMOUS INTERNATIONAL
    LIAISON, INC.
Post Office Box 4866
Cleveland Park Station   (202) 628-4379
Washington, D.C. 20008   Established 1964

Grover Boydston, Chairman
A non-profit, charitable, educational organization
offering help to the mentally and emotionally disturbed.   Modeled after Alcoholics Anonymous, N.A.
uses the A.A. 12 step program to help its members.
Membership: 350 groups, 10,000 members.   Finances: Voluntary contributions; sale of publications.
Meetings: Groups meet weekly.   Publications:
Journal of Mental Health, quarterly, Grover Boydston,
editor; books; pamphlets.

★ 1295 ★
NEW ENGLAND COUNCIL OF OPTOMETRISTS
101 Tremont Street, Suite 614   (617) 542-1233
Boston, Massachusetts 02108

David J. Schurgin, O.D., Secretary
To bring together in annual education congresses the
optometrists of New England; to publish educational
material relative to the profession; to cooperate with
other health professions.   Membership: 1,350 (active, life, student and honorary).   Finances: Membership: $25 annually; Other Sources: Journal ad-
vertising and subscriptions, exhibitor's fees. Meetings:
Annual, Boston, Massachusetts.   Publications: New
England Journal of Optometry, monthly, Diane Gunn,
editor.   Affiliation: American Optometric Association.

★ 1296 ★
NEW ENGLAND HOSPITAL ASSEMBLY
Post Office Box 736
Osterville, Massachusetts 02655   Established 1921

John L. Quigley, Executive Director
To improve quality of patient care through educational
programs for hospital personnel.   Membership: Hospital employees, trustees, and auxiliaries - all personal members of the 6 New England state hospital
associations.   Finances: Exhibitors of hospital supplies and equipment at annual meeting.   Meetings:
Monthly, officers and trustees and program committee,
Boston, Massachusetts; annual.

★ 1297 ★
NEW ENGLAND SOCIETY OF PATHOLOGISTS
c/o E. Tessa Hedley-Whyte, M.D.
New England Deaconess Hospital
185 Pilgrim Road   (617) 732-9006
Boston, Massachusetts 02215   Established 1929

President
To foster and maintain through education and research
high standards of practice.   Sponsors bimonthly
meetings consisting of 1 1/2 hours of Seminar followed
by a 2-hour slide seminar.   Sponsors a Spring all-
day meeting.   Membership: Approximately 416 members.   Finances: Membership: Dues, $20 annually;
$12 extra to have slides mailed to members.   Lec-
tureship: Annual Shields Warren Lectureship.
Meetings: Bimonthly, mostly Boston, Massachusetts.

★ 1298 ★
NEW ENGLAND SURGICAL SOCIETY
13 Elm Street
Manchester, Massachusetts 01944

Richard E. Wilson, M.D., Secretary
The Society promotes the science of surgery and kindred arts and sciences and the welfare of the profession of surgery in New England by holding professional
and social meetings and publishing transactions.   Activities include a spring meeting, with a 1-day presentation of papers, at one of the medical center hospitals in New England, as well as a fall meeting,
consisting of 2 full days with presentation of papers
at a New England resort hotel.   Membership: 456
(active, senior, associate).   Finances: Membership:
$100 annually.   Meeting: Semiannual, various lo-
cations.   Publications: Transactions of the Society
are contained in the program of the annual meeting
printed in the April issue of the American Journal of
Surgery.

★ 1299 ★
NEW EYES FOR THE NEEDY, INC.
549 Millburn Avenue   (201) 376-4903
Short Hills, New Jersey 07078   Established 1932

Mrs. Mark O'Donnell, President
To provide new prescription eyeglasses and artificial
eyes for the needy in the United States, and send
reusable plastic eyeglasses to missions and hospitals
overseas upon specific requests.   Activities include
collection of old eyeglasses, scrap jewelry, etc.
Funds received from melting of precious metals are
used to provide the eyeglasses.   Membership: Approximately 300 volunteers.   Finances: Donations,
sale of good jewelry, gifts.   Meetings: Quarterly

board meetings, Short Hills, New Jersey.

NEW YORK STATE COUNCIL ON ALCOHOL
PROBLEMS
    See: Alcohol Education for Youth, Inc.

★ 1300 ★
NORTH AMERICAN ACADEMY OF MANIPULATIVE
    MEDICINE
5021 Seminary Road, #125   (703) 931-0233
Alexandria, Virginia 22311   Established 1965

David A. Rubin, M.D., Third Vice President and
    Resident Vice President
Physicians of varied backgrounds interested in the
science and art of manipulation.   All physicians interested in manipulative techniques no matter what
their skill level are welcome as the major purpose of
the organization is one of the education.   During our
annual meeting there is usually an associated course
teaching the techniques of manipulation.   Membership: 225 (orthopaedic surgeons, osteopathic physicians, general practitioners, family practitioners,
internists, etc.).   Finances: Membership: $35 an-
nually.   Meetings: Annual, various locations.
Publications: Newsletter, quarterly, Scott Haldeman,
M.D., editor.   Library: Stephen M. Levin, M.D.,
(holder), 20 volumes; also a film and tape library,
re: manipulation, etc. (available to members for cost
of postage and handling).

★ 1301 ★
NORTH AMERICAN CLINICAL DERMATOLOGIC
    SOCIETY
510 Commonwealth Avenue   (617) 536-8910
Boston, Massachusetts 02215   Established 1959

E. F. Finnerty, M.D., Secretary-General
To bring together clinical dermatologists at an annual
meeting to exchange ideas and experiences.   Mem-
bership: 175.   Finances: Membership: $75; Other
Sources: Investments.   Awards: Research grants.
Meetings: Annual, various locations.

★ 1302 ★
NORTH AMERICAN SOCIETY OF ADLERIAN
    PSYCHOLOGY
159 North Dearborn   (312) 346-3458
Chicago, Illinois 60601   Established 1952

Neva L. Hefner, Executive Secretary

Further professional knowledge, training, teaching and
research in the theory and practice of Individual Psychology (I.P.);   acquaint the public in its theories
and practical application.   Membership: 1,300 professional and lay persons interested in Individual Psychology.   Finances: Membership: Regular, $30-$50;
student, $20.   Meetings: Annual, semiannual, var-
ious locations.   Publications: Journal of Individual
Psychology, semiannual, Guy J. Manaster, Ph.D., editor;
Individual Psychologist, semiannual, Jon Carlson,
Ed.D., editor; NASAP Newsletter, monthly, Neva
L. Hefner, editor.   Affiliations: International Association of Individual Psychology.   Former Name:
American Society of Adlerian Psychology.

★ 1303 ★
NURSES ASSOCIATION OF THE AMERICAN COL-
    LEGE OF OBSTETRICIANS AND GYNECOLOGISTS
1 East Wacker Drive, Suite 2700   (312) 222-1600
Chicago, Illinois 60601   Established 1969

Sharon A. Birk, R.N., Acting Director
To promote, in conjunction with the College, the
highest standards of obstetric, gynecologic and neonatal nursing practice and education; to cooperate at
all levels with qualified physicians and nurses; and
to stimulate interest in obstetric, gynecologic and
neonatal nursing.   Membership: 20,000 (registered
nurses and allied health workers in obstetric, gynecologic and neonatal nursing).   Finances: Dues
based on class of membership.   Awards: Fellowships
for continuing education.   Meetings: District and
Section Meetings, various locations.   Publication:
Journal of Obstetric, Gynecologic and Neonatal
Nursing, bimonthly, Mark Hobbs, editor; Bulletin,
monthly, Gordon Briggs, editor.   Library: Resource
Center, 600 volumes.   Affiliation: American College of Obstetricians and Gynecologists.

★ 1304 ★
NURSES CHRISTIAN FELLOWSHIP INTERNATIONAL
42 Station Road, Penge
London SE20, England   (01) 659-7788
    United Kingdom   Established 1957

Ruth E. Lichtenberger, R.N., BSNEd.,MRE,
    General Director
NCFI's purposes are to maintain, strengthen and extend the interests of Christ's church among nurses
everywhere; to awaken and deepen personal faith in
the Lord Jesus Christ among nurses worldwide; to
strengthen the existing National Nurses Christian Fellowships, encourage those that are small, and assist
in forming new fellowships where none at present
exist; to encourage the application of Christian

principles in professional life.   Membership: 21
countries which have a national Nurses Christian Fellowship are member countries in NCFI, and NCFI
serves as a link with 64 non-member countries as well;
(as national Nurses Christian Fellowships develop,
they may apply for membership in NCFI).   Finances:
Membership: Gifts from the member countries and
individuals.   Meetings: Annual executive meeting,
various member countries; Quadrennial General committee meetings, along with a Quadrennial General
Conference.   Publications: Highway, quarterly,
Ruth Lichtenberger, editor; Bible study guides:
Building Where You Are Who You Are;   Standing
Orders;   Rough Edges of the Christian Life;   Provided
We Suffer.

★ 1305 ★
NURSES CHRISTIAN FELLOWSHIP (U.S.)
233 Langdon Street   (608) 257-0263
Madison, Wisconsin 53703   Established 1948

F. Grace Wallace, R.N., M.A., Director
To assist both students and nurses in being prepared
to minister to the whole person in health and illness;
to help students to become increasingly aware of their
potential as Christians in the practice of nursing and
to recognize their responsibilities for active participation in the profession.   Membership: Contact with
over 300 schools of nursing.   Finances: Gifts.
Meetings: Local meetings held regularly.   Publications: Nurses Lamp, bimonthly; Bible Study Guides.

★ 1306 ★
NURSES' EDUCATIONAL FUNDS, INC.
555 West 57th Street, 13th Floor   (212) 582-8820
New York, New York 10019   Established 1941

Michael J. Feeley, Secretary-Treasurer
To establish, maintain, and administer funds to provide financial assistance to undergraduate students preparing for professional nursing and to professional
nurses studying toward advanced degrees; to formulate
and develop policies and plans for awarding scholarships, fellowships, loans, and other suitable aid to
individuals of approved qualifications in institutions of
higher education where there are programs of appropriate character; to solicit, collect, receive, hold
in trust, invest, re-invest, and utilize funds contributed to it.   Awards: Educational Scholarships.
Meetings: Board, annual, New York City; Executive
Committee; semiannual, New York City.   Affiliation: American Journal of Nursing Company.

★ 1307 ★
NUTRITION FOUNDATION, INC.
489 Fifth Avenue   (212) 687-4830
New York, New York 10017   Established 1941

W. J. Darby, President
Provides support for basic research and education in
the science of nutrition.   Activities include research,
grants to universities in support of basic research projects.   Education, publication of nutrition education materials and support of cooperative education
projects with qualified professional groups.   Membership: 51 (companies within the food and related industries).   Finances: Membership: Dues, $1,000 to
$40,000 determined by capitalization; grants and
gifts.   Awards: Osborne-Mendel, administered by
American Institute of Nutrition; Babcock-Hart, administered by Institute of Food Technologists; Mary
Schwartz Rose Fellowship, administered by American
Dietetic Association; J. George Harrar Research
Award and William C. Rose Lectureship.   Meetings:
Board of Trustees meets semiannually, usually in New
York City.   Publications: Nutrition Reviews, month-
ly, Robert E. Olson, editor; Present Knowledge in
Nutrition (4th edition); Nutritional Requirements of
Man: A Conspectus of Human Research; books and
pamphlets for professional use in nutrition.

★ 1308 ★
NUTRITION SOCIETY OF CANADA
Box 276
Macdonald Campus of McGill University
Ste. Anne de Bellevue   (514) 457-2000
Quebec H9X 1CO, Canada   Established 1957

Dr. Florence A. Farmer, Secretary
To extend knowledge of nutrition by the encouragement of research; to provide opportunities for the
presentation and discussion of reports of research; to
promote application of nutrition knowledge; to facilitate interchange of nutrition information and to represent the interests of its members.   Membership:
341 (29 emeritus; 284 ordinary; 28 student members);
human nutritionists, medical doctors, dietitians, public health nutritionists, animal nutritionists, and biochemists.   To be eligible for membership in the Society, applicants must have obtained a Bachelor's degree and have spent at least 3 subsequent years in
research and/or teaching at the university level or
have held a position of responsibility for scientific
aspects of nutrition programs.   Finances: Membership: Members are required to pay annual membership
levies, both of the Society and of CFBS; emeritus
members pay no fees; ordinary members, $14 plus $20;
student members, $2.50 plus $5.   Lectureships:
Hoffmann-LaRoche Lecture, sponsored annually at 2
centres in Canada, topic of lecture usually appeals

to colleagues in science and medicine, and possibly to the general public. Awards: The Borden Award, annually to a member of the Society who has not yet attained the age of 45 years, and is based on research done during the previous 5 years; the recipient presents the Borden Award Lecture at the annual meeting of the Society; The Earle Willard McHenry Award for Distinguished Service in Nutrition, funded by Canada Packers Limited, also awarded annually by the Society; A Graduate Student Award, for the best paper presented at the CFBS meetings awarded annually, provided the paper is of sufficiently high standard as judged by the Awards Committee. Meetings: Annual, in conjunction with the Canadian Federation of Biological Societies, various locations. Publications: Nutrition Forum de Nutrition, semiannual, Dr. S. Atkinson and Mrs. S. Innes, editors. Affiliation: Canadian Federation of Biological Societies, Inc.

★ 1309 ★
NUTRITION TODAY SOCIETY
703 Giddings Avenue
Post Office Box 1829   (301) 267-8616
Annapolis, Maryland 21404   Established 1974

Cortez F. Enloe, Jr., M.D., Executive Vice
     President
The Society was founded by an interdisciplinary group of health professionals for the increase and dissemination of nutrition knowledge. Its activities include journal publication, continuing education activities, tours in conjunction with major nutrition and dietetic meetings, information services, and numerous other member services. Membership: 27,850 health care professionals and laymen. Finances: Membership: Regular, $14.75 (United States), $17.11 (Canada), $16.75 (elsewhere); associate, $7.40 (student or retiree). Publication: Nutrition Today, bimonthly, Cortez F. Enloe, Jr., M.D., editor. Library: Nutrition Today Library, 2,000-2,500 volumes.

O

★ 1310 ★
OCCUPATIONAL MEDICAL ADMINISTRATORS'
     ASSOCIATION
c/o Robert F. Gaglione
New York Telephone Company, Medical Department
1095 Avenue of the Americas
Room 2557   (212) 395-2183
New York, New York 10036   Established 1959

Robert F. Gaglione, Secretary-Treasurer
To stimulate interest in and provide a forum for the discussion of problems in the field of industrial medical administration; to develop principles and promote standards relating to sound administration of industrial medical programs and facilities; to promote research and educational activities in the field of industrial medical administration; to constitute the recognized professional association of individuals engaged in the field of medical administration in industry, business or government; to raise the level of professional standards of individuals engaged in industrial medical administration. Membership: 32 (full-time administrators of medical departments in industry or government). Meetings: Annual, various locations. Publications: News Letter, 3 annually, Keith R. Eady, editor. Former Name: Industrial Medical Administrators' Association.

★ 1311 ★
OFA FOUNDATION FOR THE ADVANCEMENT
     OF BIOMEDICAL SCIENCES
Carrera 7 No. 29-34, Piso 3   232-1154
Bogota, Colombia   Established 1979

José Felix Patiño, M.D., Director;
     Gustavo Roman Campos, M.D., Deputy Director
To support, develop, promote and stimulate scientific research, teaching and medical practice in the biomedical field. Finances: Organización Farmacéutica Americana, S.A. (OFA). Awards: José Celestino Mutis Award in Biomedical Sciences, biennially, to individuals and institutions. Meetings: Annual Francisco José de Caldas Conference. Publications: Las Bases Moleculares de la Vida y la Enfermedad, J. F. Patiño and G. Roman Campos, editors. Library: Cenro de Documentación de la Fundación OFA (open to researchers and students). Former Name: Institute of Scientific Investigation.

★ 1312 ★
OMEGA EPSILON PHI
1041 Hamilton Street   (215) 437-3507
Allentown, Pennsylvania 18101   Established 1919

Dr. Alvin H. Freedman, President
To promote and elevate the standards and educational level of optometry. Membership: 4,712 optometrists. Finances: Membership: $10; Other Sources: Undergraduate affiliate fee. Awards: O. E. Phi International Award. Meetings: Monthly, New York City; Annual with American Optometric Association. Publication: Optist, bimonthly, Dr. Norbert Kastner, editor.

★ 1313 ★
OMICRON KAPPA UPSILON
College of Dentistry
University of Nebraska   (402) 472-1375
Lincoln, Nebraska 68583   Established 1914

William S. Kramer, D.D.S., Secretary-Treasurer
To promote scholarship and honor character among
students of dentistry.   Component Chapters at the
individual dental schools may elect to alumni membership 12 percent of the graduating class.   Faculty
membership and honorary membership may be bestowed
upon individuals who have made outstanding contributions to the art, science or literature of the profession.   The Supreme Chapter consists of a delegate
from each Component Chapter plus 5 officers.   Honorary membership may also be bestowed by the Supreme Chapter.   Membership: 17,000.   Meetings:
Annual, various locations, in conjunction with the
meeting of the American Association of Dental
Schools.

★ 1314 ★
OPTICAL LABORATORIES ASSOCIATION
6935 Wisconsin Avenue, Suite 200   (301) 986-9470
Washington, D.C. 20015   Established 1939

Irby N. Hollans, Jr., Executive Director
To help optical laboratories and supply houses with
industry information and techniques, and to foster
good relations with the ophthalmic professions.   Membership: 309 optical laboratories, 28 optical supply
houses, and 38 foreign optical laboratory members.
Finances: Fees paid quarterly and based on gross
sales.   Meetings: Annual, various locations.   Publications: OLA Newsletter, bimonthly; Bulletins as
needed.   Affiliations: National Association of
Wholesalers-Distributors; American National Standards Institute; Chamber of Commerce of the United
States.   Former Name: Optical Wholesalers Association.

★ 1315 ★
OPTICAL MANUFACTURERS ASSOCIATION
1901 North Fort Myer Drive
Suite 1104   (703) 525-3514
Arlington, Virginia 22209   Established 1916

Eugene A. Keeney, Executive Vice President
A general trade association of manufacturers, this
agency's activities include rendering ethical services
of value to the manufacturers, the industry and professions and the public.   Membership: 46 regular
members (manufacturers of ophthalmic products); 36
associate members (suppliers of parts and materials to

regular members).   Finances: Membership: Percent
of sales for regular members; flat fee for associate
members.   Meetings: Spring, Arlington, Virginia;
fall, various locations.

★ 1316 ★
OPTICAL SOCIETY OF AMERICA
1816 Jefferson Place, N.W.   (202) 223-8130
Washington, D.C. 20036   Established 1916

Jarus W. Quinn, Executive Director
To increase and diffuse the knowledge of optics in
all its branches, pure and applied, to promote the
mutual interests of investigators of optical problems,
of designers, manufacturers, and users of optical instruments and apparatus of all kinds, and to encourage cooperation among them.   Membership: 8,560
(regular, student, fellow, corporation, emeritus,
honorary).   Finances: Membership: Regular, $45;
student, $10; fellow, $45; corporation, $400.
Awards: Distinguished Service Award; Lippincott
(Ellis R.) Award; Meggers (William F.) Award;
Tillyer (Edgar D.) Award; Townes (Charles Hard)
Award; R. W. Wood Prize; Frederic Ives Medal;
Adolph Lomb Medal; C. E. K. Mees Medal; David
Richardson Medal.   Meetings: Annual, various locations.   Publications: Applied Optics, semimonthly, John N. Howard, editor; Journal of the Optical
Society of America, monthly, Joseph W. Goodman,
editor; Optics Letter, monthly, Robert W. Terhune,
editor; other publications: Uniform Color Scales.

OPTICAL WHOLESALERS ASSOCIATION
   See: Optical Laboratories Association

★ 1317 ★
OPTICIANS ASSOCIATION OF AMERICA, INC.
1250 Connecticut Avenue, N.W.
Suite 330   (202) 659-3620
Washington, D.C. 20036   Established 1925

J. A. Miller, Executive Director
To provide the vision care doctor and the public with
an efficient optical dispensing service; to establish
and maintain standards of competence; to foster the
use of qualified opticians in the dispensing of eye-
wear and other optical products to the public.
Membership: 800 firms operating 2,500 of retail optical stores and 37 state societies.   Finances: Membership: Company fee based on sales volume; State
Societies pay a per capita fee; Other Sources:
Annual Meeting.   Meetings: Annual, various locations.   Publications: The Dispensing Optician,

monthly, James H. McCormick, editor. Affiliations: American Board of Opticianry; National Contact Lens Examiners; Canadian Guild of Dispensing Opticians; International Guild of Dispensing Opticians.

★ 1318 ★
OPTION, INC.
3502 Hancock Street
Post Office Box 81122   (714) 299-1534
San Diego, California 92138   Established 1963

C. Robert Cronk, Executive Director/Vice President
The organization functions as an international clearinghouse directing both salaried and volunteer medical professionals into developing regions of extreme medical need. Option seeks to correct the maldistribution of the world's health care personnel by arranging short and long term medical assignments around the world and in the United States for all medical and allied health care professionals. Any hospital, clinic or health care group is welcome to utilize their services. Placement services are performed at no expense to either the individual placed or the facility served. Finances: Donations and gifts. Meetings: Quarterly, various locations. Affiliation: Project Concern International.

★ 1319 ★
OPTOMETRIC EXTENSION PROGRAM FOUNDATION,
    INC.
Post Office Box 850   (405) 255-2230
Duncan, Oklahoma 73533   Established 1928

Homer Hendrickson, O.D., D.O.S., President
The Foundation is devoted exclusively to education, including educational research, in the field of human vision. To further education in this field, the group arranges and conducts extended study courses, meetings, congresses, seminars and other study groups for those interested in the discovery and dissemination of knowledge relating to human vision and optometry. Membership: 3,000 optometrists; 1,000 optometric assistants. Finances: Membership: Clinical associates, $9 monthly; overseas clinical associates, $5 monthly; optometric assistants, $5 monthly; reduced dues for first year following passing of State Board. Awards: Research funds allocated as approved by Board of Directors. Publications: Optometric Extension Program News, monthly, Mary Kay Aufrance, M.A., editor; Continuing Education Course Texts released monthly. Library: Optometric Extension Program Archives, complete file of all course texts since 1928.

★ 1320 ★
ORGAN RECOVERY, INC.
1991 Lee Road   (216) 371-8455
Cleveland, Ohio 44118   Established 1977

Robert S. Post, M.D., President
Organ Recovery, Inc., is designed to increase the number of useful body organs available for transplant by encouraging individuals to consider the possibility of donating their body organs for use after death. The Agency also is involved in the coordination, administration and implementation of organ donation and recovery efforts in Northeastern Ohio, as well as the coordination of public and professional education programs in conjunction with the overall effort. Organ Recovery, Inc., carries out the actual recovery of donated organs within the community, and cooperates with other similar organ recovery programs throughout the country. Finances: Other Sources: Funding is primarily through the Medicare program related to End Stage Renal Disease program of the Social Security Administration, the Transportation Society of Northeastern Ohio and the Kidney Foundation of Ohio, Inc. Former Name: CODE - Committee on Donor Enlistment.

★ 1321 ★
ORGANIZATION FOR COORDINATION IN CONTROL OF ENDEMIC DISEASES IN CENTRAL AFRICA
B. P. 268   (237) 22.22.32
Yaounde, Cameroon   Established 1965

Dr. Louis Sentilhes, Secretary-General
To harmonize and coordinate the activities of the national health services in the member states in their control of endemic diseases. Membership: 5 (Cameroon, Central African Republic, Congo, Gabon and Chad). Finances: Membership: Dues from member states. Meetings: Technical Conference, biennial, Yaounde. Publications: Bulletin OCEAC EPI-Notes, monthly, OCEAC (editor); Le Bulletin de l'OCEAC; Technical Conference Report; Activities Report, annual. Library: Documentation Center of OCEAC.

★ 1322 ★
ORTON SOCIETY, INC.
8415 Bellona Lane, Suite 113   (301) 296-0232
Towson, Maryland 21204   Established 1949

William Ellis, President;
    Linda M. Frank, Executive Secretary
To promote the study, treatment and prevention of the problems of specific language difficulty, often

called developmental dyslexia. Membership: 5,000. Finances: Membership: Individual, $25; full-time student, $10; Other Sources: Sale of publications; contributions. Meetings: Annual, various locations. Publications: Bulletin of the Orton Society, annual, Alice Ansara, editor; monographs; reprints; Index of Past Bulletins; free brochure available on request.

★ 1323 ★
OSTEOPATHIC COLLEGE OF OPHTHALMOLOGY
    AND OTORHINOLARYNGOLOGY
Academy Office
405 Grand Avenue   (513) 222-4213
Dayton, Ohio 45405   Established 1916

G. Joseph Strickler, C.A.E., Executive Director
To improve the practice of ophthalmology and oto-rhinolaryngology, to develop osteopathic concepts in these fields, to study and to promote such arts and sciences as may directly improve the practice of oph-thalmology and otorhinolaryngology. The College determines and prescribes standards for training qual-ifications in the specialty training programs, sponsors approved graduate training programs in the specialty, seeks to maintain and promote the highest moral and ethical standards in the practice of ophthalmology and otorhinolaryngology, sets up educational programs for members at the Annual Clinical Assemblies. Mem-bership: 246 (members, candidates, fellows, honorary and life members). Finances: Membership: $200 annual dues; $175 annual candidate validation fee; Other Sources: Registration from annual assemblies. Awards: Award of Fellow in the Osteopathic College of Ophthalmology and Otorhinolaryngology. Meet-ings: Annual, various locations. Publications: Newsletter, quarterly; Manual of Postgraduate Train-ing Programs; Membership Director.

★ 1324 ★
OTOSCLEROSIS STUDY GROUP
662 South Henderson   (817) 332-4060
Fort Worth, Texas 76104 Established 1947

W. P. Anthony, M.D., Secretary-Treasurer
To exchange ideas, promote research and foster fel-lowship for those interested in otosclerosis. Mem-bership: 117 (active, senior, emeritus, associate). Meetings: Annual, various locations.

★ 1325 ★
OXFAM
274 Banbury Road
Oxford OX2 7DZ, England   (0865) 56777
    United Kingdom   Established 1942

Brian W. Walker, Director General
The agency exists to relieve poverty, distress and suffering primarily in developing countries. It helps over 1,000 projects in about 80 countries at any one time. Oxfam achieves its goal by appropriating funds to relief and disasters, medical projects, agri-culture, training and welfare schemes. The majority of its funding goes to long term development projects. They are a funding rather than an operational group. Overseas programs are carried out by the most appro-priate group on the spot with funds from Oxfam. Finances: Funds raised by volunteer. Publications: Information sheets and educational materials on third world topics; booklets, newsheets and leaflets. Affiliations: Sister organizations in the United States, Canada, Belgium and Australia, and maintains con-tacts with a wide range of new governmental organi-zations in various countries.

P

★ 1326 ★
PACIFIC COAST SOCIETY OF ORTHODONTISTS
18 Second Avenue, Suite 209
San Mateo, California 94401   (415) 344-3795

Raymond E. Morris, Executive Secretary
Advancement of orthodontics. Activities include annual meetings. Membership: 1,350 (active). Finances: Membership: $100; other sources - advertising in Bulletin. Meetings: Annual, various locations, plus regional meetings. Publica-tions: Bulletin, quarterly, David Turpin, editor. Affiliation: American Association of Orthodontists.

★ 1327 ★
PACIFIC DERMATOLOGIC ASSOCIATION
180 Mark Twain Avenue   (702) 323-2461
Reno, Nevada 98509   Established 1948

Florence Beardsley, Executive Secretary
For charitable, educational, and scientific purposes, and to provide opportunities to exchange information for advancement of knowledge of dermatology and syphilology among physicians within the Pacific Rim. Membership: 1115 (fellow, associates, affiliates,

special affiliates, honorary members, honorary corresponding members, and inactive members). Finances: $50 for members within the United States and Canada; $20 outside this area; other sources - pharmaceutical exhibits at annual meeting, donations. Awards: The Nelson Paul Anderson memorial essay contest each year awards $500 plus expenses to, from and during the annual meeting for the best essay relating to the field of dermatology. Meetings: Annaul, various cities in the Pacific Rim area. Publications: Transactions, annually, Dr. Elizabeth Ringrose, editor; Membership Directory, published biennially.

★ 1328 ★
PAN AMERICAN ASSOCIATION OF OPHTHALMOLOGY
1 Tara View Road
Tiburon, California 94920   Established 1939

H. Dunbar Hoskins, Jr., M.D., Secretary-Treasurer
    for North America
An organization of ophthalmologists of the Western Hemisphere promoting the improvement and dissemination of ophthalmic knowledge in scientific meetings, and mutual respect through its social activities. Membership: 4,000 (opthalmologists practicing in the Western Hemisphere). Finances: $100 per year. Awards: Gradle Medal; Medal for the Prevention of Blindness; Gradle Lecturer; A.J.O. Lecturer. Meetings: Annual meetings of Council during American Academy of Ophthalmology convention; biennial, Pan American Congresses, various locations in the Western Hemisphere.

★ 1329 ★
PAN AMERICAN ASSOCIATION OF OTO-RHINO-
    LARYNGOLOGY AND BRONCHO-ESOPHA-
    GOLOGY
c/o Dr. Hans von Leden
10921 Wilshire Boulevard   (213) 478-2100
Los Angeles, California 90024   Established 1946

Hans von Leden, Secretary-General
To promote through all the means in its power the progress of oto-rhino-laryngology and broncho-esophagology; to assist in the union and cultural exchange among the American countries, and to arrange Pan American Congresses of these specialties every two years. Membership: 2,000. Finances: Membership: $10. Meetings: Biennially, various locations. Publications: Revista Panamericana de Otorrinolaringologia y Broncoesofagologia, 3 times a year, Dr. Pedro Andrade Pradillo, editor. Affiliations: World Health Organization; Pan American Health Organization.

★ 1330 ★
PAN AMERICAN FEDERATION OF ENDOCRINE
    SOCIETIES
Primeira Clinica Medica
Hospital das Clinicas, C.P. 8091
Saõ Paulo, S.P, Brazil   Established 1968

Professor Emilio Mattar, President
To bring together endocrine societies of America. Membership: 16 Latin American Society of Endocrinology. Finances: Membership: $20-$100.

★ 1331 ★
PAN AMERICAN HEALTH ORGANIZATION
525 23rd Street, N.W.   (202) 861-3200
Washington, D.C. 20037   Established 1902

Dr. Hector R. Acuna, Director
To promote and coordinate Western Hemisphere efforts to combat disease, lengthen life, and promote physical and mental health of the people. Membership: 33 countries. Finances: Contributions. Meetings: Conference, every four years, various locations; Council, annual. Publications: PAHO Reports, bimonthly; Bulleting of PAHO, quarterly; Boletin de la OSP, monthly; Educación médica y salud, quarterly; Epidemiological Bulletin, bimonthly; Annual Report; Health Conditions in the Americas, quadrennial; Technical publications. Affiliations: Specialized agency of Organization of American States; Regional Office for World Health Organization.

★ 1332 ★
PAN AMERICAN MEDICAL ASSOCIATION,
    INCORPORATED
222 Kent Terrace   (305) 832-0296
West Palm Beach, Florida 33407   Established 1925

Joseph J. Eller, M.D., Director General; Horoshi Washio, M.D., Secretary; Harry Tebrock, M.D., Trustee
To interchange medical knowledge and research among the physicians of the Western Hemisphere countries; to hold Inter-American Congresses covering all branches of medicine and surgery; to establish a Postgraduate Medical School and to grant postgraduate scholarships; to sponsor regional seminars; and to further, through its medical activities, goodwill and understanding among the physicians, peoples and countries of the Western Hemisphere, always avoiding, however, any political policy. Membership: 10,000. Finances: Membership: $35.00; other sources - contributions and annual dues.

★ 1333 ★
PAN AMERICAN MEDICAL WOMEN'S ALLIANCE
c/o Dr. Helen Cannon Bernfield
Post Office Box 9822, Northside Station
Jackson, Mississippi   39206   (601) 362-5685
                                      Established 1947

Dr. Helen Cannon Bernfield, Treasurer
The purpose of this Alliance is to bring medical
women of North, South and Central America, and
the Caribbean Area into an Association with each
other for mutual improvements, for encouragement of
their participation in all branches of medical public
welfare work; for the exchange of ideas; to facilitate social and cooperative relations; to assist in
the further education of its members and to generally
forward such constructive movements as may be
mutually beneficial and properly endorsed by the
medical associations of our several countries.   Loan
Fund has been established to promote attendance at
Congresses, post graduate education and establishment
of medical practice for those requiring such aid.
Membership: 700 (medical doctors representing many
specialties, practicing in countries of North, Central
and South America, and the Caribbean area).
Finances: Membership: Dues - $4.00 each year;
other sources - donations from members and others.
Meetings: Biennial, alternating between English
speaking and Spanish speakking countries.   Publications: Newsletter; Journal of the American Medical
Women's Association; PANMA's Reports of Congress
and other materials.

★ 1334 ★
PAN PACIFIC SURGICAL ASSOCIATION
Alexander Young Building, Room 236 (808) 536-4911
Honolulu, Hawaii 96813   Established 1929

To bring together surgeons so as to permit the exchange of scientific knowledge and techniques relating to medicine and surgery, to provide funding
for various educational programs that further the
progress and improvement of surgical and health
care in the Pacific.   Membership: 3,200 (regular
and associate, senior, emeritus, honorary).   Finances:
Membership: United States and Canada; regular
and associate $50; other countries, regular and
associate $25; senior, emeritus, honorary - no dues;
other sources - Congress registration fees and donations to the Living Endowment Fund.   Meetings:
Biennial, in January, always in Holoulu, Hawaii.

★ 1335 ★
PAPER SOCIETY FOR THE OVERSEAS BLIND, INC.
219 West 16th Street   (713) 861-3089
Houston, Texas   77008   Established 1969

Johnathan Quinn, President
The Paper Society provides braille stationery and
plastic slate-and-stylus to write braille to blind individuals in underdeveloped countries, without
charge.   This is the only society for the blind which
is specifically chartered to provide individuals with
slates and paper.   Besides supplying paper, the
group exchanges braille letters, recipes, gardening
tips and sports news with blind individuals abroad.
The stationery consists of recycled manila file
folders.   Membership: 100 donors and/or volunteers; 500 blind individuals overseas.   Finances:
Free membership; other sources - donations from
the public.   Meetings: Annual (January 3rd),
Houston.

★ 1336 ★
PARAPSYCHOLOGICAL ASSOCIATION
Post Office Box 7503   (703) 768-2809
Alexandria, Virginia   22307   Established 1957

Howard M. Zimmerman, Executive Secretary
To advance parapsychology as a science, to dissem-
inate knowledge of the field, and to integrate the
findings with those of other branches of science.
Membership: 250 (full, associate).   Finances:
Membership: Full United States $20; other $15;
associate United States $15; other $7; other
sources - registration at convention, royalties from
publications.   Meetings: Annual, various locations.
Publications: Research in Parapsychology, annually,
W. Roll, editor; Psi News, quarterly newsletter,
Hoyt Edge, editor.   Affiliation: A.A.A.S.

★ 1337 ★
PARENTERAL DRUG ASSOCIATION, INC.
1240 Western Savings Bank Building
Broad and Chestnut Streets   (215) 735-9752
Philadelphia, Pennsylvania 19107 Established 1946

Solomon C. Pflag, Executive Director
To foster and advance, in the interest of public
health, the art and science of parenteral therapy,
and to preserve and improve the integrity and
standards of the parenteral drug industry; to provide and disseminate information relating to parenteral drugs, parenteral therapy, sterile products and
relating processes; to encourage research projects
into matters of scientific and technical interest in
the field of parenteral medication; to promote

higher standards in the production of parenteral drugs, sterile products and related processes; to encourage the education and training of personnel for the parenteral and related industries. Membership: 1700 (manufacturers and suppliers of parenteral products and faculty members of colleges of pharmacy). Finances: Membership: individual, $45; corporate $250. Awards: Parenteral Drug Association Award, $1,000. Meetings: 3 times a year; 2 regional meetings. Publications: PDA Letter, monthly; Journal of the Prenteral Drug Association, bimonthly, Joseph R. Robinson, editor.

★ 1338 ★
PARENTS OF DOWN'S SYNDROME CHILDREN
c/o Montgomery County Association for Retarded
   Citizens
10730 Connecticut Avenue   (301) 949-8140
Kensington, Maryland 20795   Established 1966

Marilyn Trainer, Maryland Coordinator
To help parents of Down's Syndrome Children to raise money for Down's Syndrome research. The organization distributes Parent Information Kits, acts as a resource coordinator in helping new parents to find programs and information to help themselves and their children, and works closely with local associations for retarded citizens. Membership: 125. Finances: Other sources: Donations. Meetings: Monthly, various locations. Publications: Parent Information Kit ($1.00 charge), Marilyn Trainer, editor.

★ 1339 ★
PARKINSON'S DISEASE FOUNDATION, INC.
William Black Research Building
Columbia Presbyterian Medical Center
640-650 West 168th Street   (212) 923-4700
New York, New York 10032   Established 1957

Dinah T. Orr, Executive Director
To support research and training in the field of Parkinson's Disease. Maintains a registry of Parkinson patients and conducts a range of activities designed to assist patients and physicians in relation to this disease. Finances: Donations; publication solicitations. Awards: Research grants; Post doctoral student fellowships. Meetings: Annual.

★ 1340 ★
PATHFINDER FUND
1330 Boylston Street   (617) 731-1700
Chestnut Hill, Massachusetts 02167   Established 1957

Richard B. Gamble, Chairman; Howard K. Gray, Jr., Executive Director
The Fund encourages and helps developing countries to initiate family planning programs and to limit their population growth. It has three principal goals: to increase the recognition that population growth must be limited; to make contraception available and people willing to use it; and to accelerate the social changes that will bring population stabilization. Currently supporting 150 projects in 40 countries, they sponsor a wide range of research, development and demonstration work. Finances: Other sources: USAID population funds, and private gifts and grants. Publications: Occasional Manuals.

★ 1341 ★
PEOPLE-TO-PEOPLE COMMITTEE FOR THE
   HANDICAPPED
1526 K Street, N.W., Suite 1130 (202) 638-2487
Washington, D.C. 20005   Established 1956

James R. Burress, Executive Director
Disseminates information; acts as consultant in promoting exchange activities; coordinates special assistance projects in developing countries. Membership: 250 individuals. Meetings: Annual, May, Washington, D.C. Publications: Newsletter, quarterly; Directory of Organizations Interested in Handicapped, biennial; reports and surveys.

★ 1342 ★
PEOPLE-TO-PEOPLE HEALTH FOUNDATION, INC.
PROJECT HOPE
Health Sciences Education Center   (703) 837-2100
Milwood, Virginia 22646   Established 1958

William B. Walsh, President
To teach modern techniques of medical science to medical, dental, nursing and allied health personnel in developing areas through Project HOPE; to conduct international conferences and other studies of health policy issues through HOPE's Institute for Health Policy Study. Membership: 22 board members. Finances: Contributions and government grants. Publications: Annual Report, Anson Campbell, editor; HOPE News, quarterly, Anson Campbell, editor; various publications about HOPE.

★ 1343 ★
PERMANENT COMMISSION AND INTERNATIONAL
   ASSOCIATION ON OCCUPATIONAL HEALTH
Quality House, Quality Court   (01) 353-0518
Chancery Lane   Established 1906
London WC2A 1HP, England, United Kingdom

Dr. Robert Murray, Secretary-Treasurer
To foster the scientific progress, knowledge and
development of occupational health in all its aspects
on an international basis through international congresses, special meetings and training courses.
Membership: 926 (active, associate, honorary,
affiliate, sustaining). Finances: Membership: Per
3 years, active Sw. Fr. 150; associate Sw. Fr. 40;
affiliate Sw.Fr. 300-500; sustaining Sw. Fr. 1,500
and up. Meetings: Every three years.

★ 1344 ★
PHARMACEUTICAL MANUFACTURERS ASSOCIATION
1155 15th Street, N.W.   (202) 463-2000
Washington, D.C. 20005   Established 1958

Lewis A. Engman, President; Bruce J. Brennan,
Vice President and General Counsel
The Association is a nonprofit scientific and professional organization. Its active membership is
composed of firms that discover, develop and produce
prescription drugs, medical devices and diagnostic
products. Companies must be significantly engaged
in research for the advancement of medical science
to qualify for membership. Present membership,
which is voluntary, accounts for most human-use
pharmaceutical sales in the United States and about
one-half of the free world's supply as well as a
substantial portion of devices and diagnostics.
Membership: 149 members; 37 associates. Finances:
based on yearly pharmaceutical sales. Awards:
Doctoral dissertation program. Meetings: Annual,
also section meetings throughout the year. Publications: PMA Newsletter, weekly, Duffy Miller,
editor; State Capital Report, weekly, Christine
Solomon Budd, editor; Trademark Bulletin, weekly,
Nancy Nugent, editor; Devices and Diagnostic
Digest, monthly, Thomas X. White. Library: 700
volumes.

★ 1345 ★
PHI ALPHA SIGMA MEDICAL FRATERNITY
Jefferson Medical College
313 South Tenth Street   (215) 627-8821
Philadelphia, Pennsylvania 19107   Established 1886

Robert Good, M.D., Scribus Magnus
Social, professional and academic fraternity for the
benefit of medical students and alumni. Membership:
Approximately 1,200. Finances: Membership: $5;
other sources - contributions. Awards: Distinguished
Teaching Award to member of Jefferson faculty.
Meetings: Annual, Philadelphia, Pennsylvania.
Publication: Bubbling Rales, annual.

★ 1346 ★
PHI CHI MEDICAL FRATERNITY
103 West Brookwood Drive
Post Office Box 2035   (912) 242-4841
Valdosta, Georgia 31601   Established 1889

Albert F. Saunders, M.D., Secretary
A professional fraternity for male and female medical
students, dedicated to promoting excellence in
scholarship, attainment of the high ethical ideals of
the medical profession and providing, at the same
time, opportunities for increased sociability and close
friendships. Enduring ties of brotherly assistance
throughout each member's professional lifetime is
perpetuated by affiliated alumni associations.
Membership: 55,404 (a candidate must be a student
of a medical school). Awards: Eben J. Carey
Memorial Award in Anatomy; Michael J. Carey
Outstanding Service Award; Chapter Chatter Award;
various chapter awards. Meetings: Grand Chapter,
biennially, various locations. Publication:
Quarterly, Jacob E. Reisch, M.D., editor.
Affiliation: The Phi Chi Welfare Association, Incorporated, to provide assistance to needy student
members.

★ 1347 ★
PHI DELTA CHI FRATERNITY
School of Pharmacy
Auburn University   (205) 826-4740
Auburn, Alabama 36830   Established 1883

Archie Jay Beebe, Ph.D., Executive Director
To advance the science of pharmacy and its allied
interest, and to foster and promote a fraternal spirit
among its members. Membership: 28,000 initiated
since 1883 (active, graduate and honorary). Finances:
Membership: $10 per year; $27 initiation fee;
other sources - alumni dues, $12. Awards:
Scholarship awards to undergraduate chapters;
Achievement Award for organizational activity;
Publication Awards; Window Display Awards;
Service Project Awards; Brotherhood Award; Alumni
Organization Awards. Meetings: Biennial; regional meetings annually. Publications: Communicator,
quarterly, Robert E. Henry, editor.

★ 1348 ★
PHI DELTA EPSILON MEDICAL FRATERNITY
145 East 52nd Street   (212) 753-1185
New York, New York 10022   Established 1904

Myer H. Stolar, M.D., Executive Director
A charitable and educational fraternity which gives
assistance to undergraduate medical students and

recent graduates. Membership: 20,000 (physicians in practice, interns, residents and undergraduate medical students). Finances: Membership: Life, $125, $25 per member annually; graduate club dues, $10 per member annually; chapter dues, $10 per member annually. Awards: 25-Year Service Scrolls; 50-Year Citation; Phi Delta Epsilon Fraternity Distinguished Service Award; 60-Year Plaques; 40-Year Service Scrolls; Student Loans for tuition; Higher Education Loans for recent graduates and members going into practice. Meetings: Annual, various locations; Executive Committee, semiannually. Publication: Phi Delta Epsilon News and Scientific Journal, quarterly, Matthew Ross, M.D., editor. Affiliations: Phi Delta Epsilon Fraternity Foundation, Incorporated; Aaron Brown Educational Foundation, Incorporated.

★ 1349 ★
PHI RHO SIGMA MEDICAL SOCIETY
Post Office Box 10886   (412) 655-2161
Pittsburgh, Pennsylvania 15236   Established 1890

Don E. Morehead, Secretary-Treasurer
To promote good fellowship among congenial men of medical schools and colleges; to encourage a high standard of professional work; to assist the advancement of its members. Conducts various professional and social programs among the undergraduate chapters, lectureships, and community Service Projects. Membership: 28,880 (alumni groups and undergraduate chapters). Finances: Membership: Initiation fee, $30; life membership, $200; $25 yearly dues to Chapter International. Awards: Cutter Award to a member who has made an outstanding contribution to medicine; Griffin Award to a member who has made an outstanding contribution to the Society; nationally - 2 gold medals; various local chapter scholarship awards. Meetings: Biennial convention, various locations. Publications: The Journal of Phi Rho Sigma, quarterly, C.H. William Ruhe, M.D., editor; Careers in Medicine; Manual of Chapter Operations. Former Name: Phi Rho Sigma Fraternity.

★ 1350 ★
PHYSICIANS FORUM, INC.
510 Madison Avenue   (212) 688-3290
New York, New York 10022   Established 1944

Elaine B. Zinner, Executive Secretary
To work for a national overhaul of medical care delivery by preparing statements on health care, testifying before government bodies, providing speakers and acting in coalition with other organiza-

tions to develop a consumer cominated health constituency in the United States. Membership: 1,000 physicians, dentists, health professionals, and lay people interested in the reform of medical care delivery. Finances: Membership: Sustaining, $100; regular $35; residents, $15; non-physicians, $10; medical students, $5; other sources - fund raising events. Publications: The Physicans Forum Newsletter, 3 times a year; Position papers.

★ 1351 ★
PHYSICIANS' SERVICES INCORPORATED
    FOUNDATION
4881 Yonge Street, Suite 304
Willowdale, Ontario M2N 5X3,   (416) 226-6323
Canada   Established 1970

C.A. Bond, Executive Director
A public charitable foundation awarding grants and fellowships in the health field in the Province of Ontario. Finances: Investment income of approximately $2.2 million annually.

★ 1352 ★
PIERRE FAUCHARD ACADEMY
c/o Dr. Walter A. Cyhel
1003 Central Avenue
Kansas City, Kansas 66102   Established 1936

Dr. Walter A. Cyhel, Secretary
To promote the advancement of dentistry through all forms of service, with particular emphasis laid on the progress of the profession through postgraduate education of all kinds; to provide the dental practitioner with a simplified literature of the latest developments in dentistry; to establish a high plane of competence in contributions to the literature of the profession; to aid in dentistry's development by encouraging practitioners to contribute to its literature. Membership: Approximately 4,000 (dentists in the United States and abroad). Finances: Membership: $20. Awards: Contribution to AFDE Fund; Elmer S. Best International Award; Fauchard Gold Medal; Memorial Luncheon honoring a deceased contributor to dentistry. Meetings: Annual, Chicago, Illinois. Publication: Dental World, bimonthly, Hamilton B.G. Robinson, editor.

★ 1353 ★
PILOT DOGS, INC.
625 West Town Street   (614) 221-6367
Columbus, Ohio 43215   Established 1950

Clyde R. Tipton, Jr., President; John L. Gray,
Executive Manager
Pilot Dogs is one of eight organizations in the United
States which trains pilot dogs to guide the blind.
It receives students from all over the United States,
but the majority of the applicants reside in the
Midwest.   Any sightless person who is physically
and mentally capable of receiving benefit from the
Pilot Dog may apply.   There is no charge to the
blind people.   Finances: Contributions and be-
quests.   Affiliation: Pilot Guide Dog Foundation.

★ 1354 ★
PILOT GUIDE DOG FOUNDATION
625 West Town Street   (614) 221-6367
Columbus, Ohio 43215   Established 1945

Clyde R. Tipton, Jr., President; John L. Gray,
Executive Manager
Dedicated to providing guide dogs to blind persons.
Finances: Contributions from individuals, clubs,
business organizations and philantropic groups which
either make regular donations or set up scholarship
funds.   Affiliation: Pilot Dogs, Inc.

★ 1355 ★
PLANNED PARENTHOOD FEDERATION OF
    AMERICA
810 Seventh Avenue   (212) 541-7800
New York, New York 10019   Established 1921

Faye Wattelton, President; Frederic C. Smith,
Chairman
To provide leadership in making effective means of
voluntary fertility regulation, including contraception,
abortion, sterilization, and infertility services,
available and fully accessible to all as a central
element of reproductive health care; in achieving
through informed individual choice, a United States
population of stable size in an optimum environment;
in stimulating and sponsoring relevant biomedical,
socio-economic and demographic research; in
developing appropriate information, education and
training programs, and to support and assist efforts
to achieve similar goals in the United States and
throughout the world.   Operates over 700 clinics
in the major cities which provide medically supervised family planning services.   Established the
Justice Fund in 1977 to regain for poor women the
right to the use of Medicaid funds for abortion and
to relieve the disadvantage that poor women have
in obtaining safe, legal abortions.   Membership:
188 affiliates.   Finances: Contributions, corporate
and government grants.   Awards: Margaret Sanger
Award, annually.   Meetings: Annual, in Fall,

various locations.   Publications: News, 5 times a
year; Affiliates Directory, annual; Annual Report;
also publishes Washington Memi, Medical Digest,
books and pamphlets.   Former Name: Planned
Parenthood/World Population.

★ 1356 ★
PLANNED PARENTHOOD FEDERATION OF CANADA
1226A Wellington Street
Ottawa, Ontario K1Y 3A1,   (613) 722-3484
Canada   Established 1969

Marilyn M. Wilson, Executive Director
The Federation's objectives include (1) promoting the
understanding and adoption of family planning and
encouraging good citizenship through responsible
family life;   (2) providing a national organization
for societies and associations with similar objects and
representing such societies and associations before any
international planned parenthood association;   (3)
promoting research and education on population problems, both domestic and international; and (4) informing the public on the problems arising from un-
controlled population growth.   Membership: 60
organizations (provincial, territorial, local, affiliate,
associate).   Finances: Government grants, private
donations.   Awards: Ortho Family Planning Volunteer
Award for an outstanding contribution by a volunteer
to the family planning movement in Canada.   Meetings: General meeting, annually, Board meetings,
three times a year, all at Ottawa, Ontario, Canada.

PLANNED PARENTHOOD/WORLD POPULATION
    See: Planned Parenthood Federation of America

★ 1357 ★
PLASTIC SURGERY RESEARCH COUNCIL
Division of Plastic Surgery
University of Oregon
Health Science Center   (503) 225-7824
Portland, Oregon 97201   Established 1956

Stephen H. Miller, M.D., Secretary-Treasurer
The Council founded as information forum for plastic
surgeons from around the country.   The forum was
established with the belief that the personal discipline
of reviewing one's own activities in the laboratory
once a year and describing these to one's professional colleagues would prove to be a genuine stimulus
to completing worthwhile work.   Each year abstracts
are solicited from the membership on their current
laboratory research.   A committee of the membership selects what they feel to be the most worthwhile

of these abstracts and informs the authors to prepare a formal paper for deliver at the Annual Meeting in the Spring of each year. Membership: 160 (active, senior, associate). Finances: Membership: Active members, $100; Associate members, $25; other sources - Registration fee at meeting. Meetings: Annual, various locations.

★ 1358 ★
PLAY SCHOOLS ASSOCIATION, INC.
19 West 44th Street   (212) 921-2940
New York, New York 10036   Established 1917

Mrs. Richard S. Aldrich, President
The Association aims for the promotion of children's play as an educational tool vital to the healthy development of children and youth. Such an aim is carried out by (1) consultation to and affiliation with community groups, institutions, hospitals, and day care centers; (2) sponsorship of studies and pilot projects; (3) provision of training, workshops, and discussions for teachers, group leaders, parents, nurses, students, volunteers, and paraprofessionals; and (4) production of films and pamphlets. Finances: Membership: Contributing members on a sliding scale; other sources - voluntary contributions. Meetings: Board meeting, monthly, New York City. Publications: staff written pamphlets on science, parent education, music activities in children's education and play programs, pilot studies with retarded and brain-injured children, hospital play programs, etc.

POB
    See: Prevention of Blindness Society of
         Metropolitan Washington

★ 1359 ★
POSTGRADUATE CENTER FOR MENTAL HEALTH
124 East 28th Street   (212) 689-7700
New York, New York 10016   Established 1945

Harry Sands, Ph.D., Executive Director
Provides low cost mental health treatment, psychoanalysis, individual and group psychotherapy, social and vocational rehabilitation; postgraduate training for psychiatrists, psychologists and social workers; mental health research; community services and education to community agencies, individuals and industry in mental health subjects. Membership: 200 (psychiatrists, psychologists, psychiatric social workers). Finances: Patient fees, contributions from foundations and general public, government grants and contracts. Publications: Transnational

Mental Health Research Newsletter, quarterly, Bernard F. Riess, editor. Library: Emil A. Gutheil Memorial Library, 10,000 volumes.

★ 1360 ★
PRADER-WILLI SYNDROME ASSOCIATION
5515 Malibu Drive   (612) 933-0113
Edina, Minnesota 55436   Established 1975

Marge A. Wett, Executive Director
The Association was formed in order to provide a vehicle or communication for parents, professionals and other interested citizens. It is an organization dedicated to the sharing of experiences in how to cope with the syndrome. It is a nonprofit group working together to solve the many attendant problems associated with the Prader-Willi Syndrome. Membership: 570 (parents, educators, doctors and other medically related individuals, schools, hospitals, residential and vocational type training centers). Finances: Membership: United States, $10; Canada and Overseas, $15 annually; other sources - donations. Awards: $1,000 grant from the March of Dimes. Publications: The Gathered View, bimonthly, Marilyn Jorgensen, editor; Prader Willi Syndrome - A Handbook for Parents, Shirley Neason, editor; National Conference papers, yearly, Marge Wett, editor; Therapy Informational Sheets, irregular, Marge Wett, editor. Affiliations: Chapters in some States.

★ 1361 ★
PREVENTION OF BLINDNESS SOCIETY OF
    METROPOLITAN WASHINGTON
1775 Church Street, N.W.   (202) 234-1010
Washington, D.C. 20036   Established 1936

Arnold Simonse, Executive Director
The Society is a regional nonprofit corporation formed to prevent the needless loss of sight; conducts about 15,000 glaucoma screening tests each year and also tests about 15,000 preschool children annually; offers educational programs to make people aware of resources available to them and provides free classes for those who are in financial stress and who would otherwise have to go without. Staff members answer telephone calls requesting information on eye health. Membership: 1,500. Finances: Membership: Annual, $10; associate, $25; affiliate, $50; other sources - United Way, foundations, grants, endowment, thrift shops, contributions. Also Known As: POB.

★ 1362 ★
PRICE-POTTENGER NUTRITION FOUNDATION
6035 University Avenue   (714) 582-4168
San Diego, California 92115   Established 1969

Pat Connally, Executive Administrator; Granville
Knight, M.D., President
A nonprofit organization, the Foundation produces
educational books, slides, videotapes and films for
rent and sale, for mass distribution in order to spread
the message of optimal health through sound nutrition.
Through these materials, as well as seminars and
lectures for both lay and professional audiences, it
promotes the physical, emotional, mental, and nutritional aspects of natural health through researching
and implementing the optimal restoration of living
soil, pure water and air, and improved growth of
plants and animals.   The association maintains nutrition exhibits which are shown at meetings of scientific societies.   It also has reference and research
archives, a library, and photograph collection, all
on health subjects.   In addition it provides professional speakers for meetings and media appearances.
Membership: 1,000 (fellows, associates - both
classes include supporting, sustaining, patron and
life membership).   Finances: Membership: donations,
fellows, $25; associates, $15; special limited
introductory, $7.50; supporting, $50-$100; patron,
$1,000 and up; life, $2,500 and up; Other Sources:
Donations.   Publications: Bulletin, quarterly, James
Winer, editor; Newsletter, quarterly, Linda Clark,
editor;   Nutrition and Physical Degeneration, by
Weston Price, D.D.S.; Secrets of Dental Health, by
James Winer; Films, Slides, etc.   Library: 1,000
volumes - restricted to members or researchers - no
borrowing privileges.

★ 1363 ★
PRIORY OF CANADA OF THE MOST VENERABLE
    ORDER OF THE HOSPITAL OF SAINT JOHN OF
    JERUSALEM (ST. JOHN AMBULANCE)
312 Laurier Avenue, East   (613) 236-7461
Ottawa, Ontario K1N 6P6, Canada Established 1895

D.W. Cunningham, Secretary
The Priory is an independent national charitable cor-
portion devoted to the teaching of First Aid (over
300,000 were trained in 1979) and related health care
subjects, and to the provision of First Aid services
wherever crowds gather.   The Priory also contributes
to the support of and maintains a Canadian surgeon at
the St. John Ophthalmic Hospital in Jerusalem which
is a Foundation of the Order.   Membership: Order,
4,000; uniformed brigade, 14,000; non-uniformed
volunteers, 22,000.   Finances: Dues, revenue from
first aid training and supplies, donations, government
grants and fees for service.   Awards: Bursary for

nursing students.   Meetings: Priory Council, quarterly; Priory Chapter, annual, usually in Ottawa.
Publications: Multi-Media First Aid Courses including
film and self-instruction workbooks; Joint home care
course in multi-media format, with Canadian Red
Cross Society; First aid, home care and child care
texts.

★ 1364 ★
PROFESSIONAL EXAMINATION SERVICE
475 Riverside Drive, Room 740   (212) 870-3167
New York, New York 10115   Established 1941

Craig G. Schoon, Ph.D., President
The Service aims to advance the nation's health by
developing methods of assessing the qualifications of
human service personnel in health and health-related
fields.   Examinations are developed and administered
in the areas of certification and licensure, training,
self-assessment, employment, and the determination
of proficiency.   Finances: Other sources: Fees
from member agencies.

PROFESSIONAL REHABILITATION WORKERS WITH
    THE ADULT DEAF
        See: American Deafness and Rehabilitation
              Association

PROJECT HOPE
    See: People-to-People Health Foundation, Inc.

★ 1365 ★
PROPRIETARY ASSOCIATION
1700 Pennsylvania Avenue, N.W. (202) 393-1700
Washington, D.C. 20006   Established 1881

James D. Cope, President and Treasurer
The Association acts as the voice of self-medication
by speaking for manufacturers of over-the-counter
medicines which are prepackaged and labeled in accordance with the Federal Food, Drug and Cosmetic
Act and which are intended for use in self-care, and
by communicating the message of self-medication to
various publics, including academia, the professions,
legislations, and the home.   Specifically, its objects are to (1) preserve and improve the integrity
and stability of the over-the-counter medicine industry;   (2) preserve and improve the integrity and
stability of the trademarks its members own or control
and pursuant to and under which they conduct business;   (3) acquire and disseminate for the use of

members such business and scientific information as may prove of value to them; (4) assist its members in the preparation of labels and advertising copy complying with the requirements of law; (5) foster and encourage a spirit of friendly cooperation among its members and between its members and the general public; (6) participate in cooperative enterprises with the various branches of the industry and related industries worldwide. Membership: 85 active members, 125 associates. Finances: Membership: Active based on sales volume; associate, flat fee. Meetings: Annual, various locations; specialized conferences and informal briefing sessions. Publications: Executive Newsletter, weekly; Legislative News Bulletin; Proceedings of meetings; Compilation of Law Affecting the Proprietary Drug and Allied Industries, updated annually; Compilation of OTC Drug Regulations.

★ 1366 ★

PROPRIETARY ASSOCIATION OF CANADA
350 Sparks Street, Suite 504   (613) 238-1814
Ottawa, Ontario K1R 7S8, Canada   Established 1896

J. Donald Harper, President
The Association speaks for the manufacturers of the majority of proprietary and over-the-counter medicines. Members of P.A.C. are dedicated to making available to the public, quality non-prescription products which are both safe and effective for use as labeled. The Association's active membership is composed of firms which manufacture and distribute medicines. Associate members are companies which are interested, as suppliers of various materials and services, in such manufacture and distribution. Membership: 136 (active, 68; associate, 68). Finances: Membership: Active: percentage of proprietary sales; Associate: $250 annually. Meetings: Mid-Year and Annual, various locations. Publications: P.A.C. Update, monthly, J.D. Harper, editor; Code of Consumer Advertising Practices for Non-Prescription Medicines; Telling it Like it is; Excerpts from "Symposium on Self-Care."

★ 1367 ★

PROPRIETARY ASSOCIATION OF EUROPE
18 Rue Jean Giraudoux
F-75116 Paris, France   Established 1963

Werner Sedlag, Director-General
To assist responsible participation of the pharmaceutical industries united in AESGP within the framework of the health systems of the various countries by appropriate initiatives and by supporting similar activities; to promote the highest standards for the production, distribution and advertising of proprietary

medicines through the adoption of the ethical rules of good practices and to secure their observance through methods of voluntary control; to define and defend the principle of self-medication through the use of safe and efficacious medicines which are lawfully available without prescription; to be concerned with all aspects of existing or proposed legislation on pharmaceutical matters and to ensure that the views and interests of the proprietary medicines industry are recognized by international bodies concerned with such legislation; to promote cooperation and exchange of information, not only among its members, but also on their behalf with international professional and governmental organizations concerned with health matters; to represent its member national associations within the World Federation of Proprietary Medicines Manufacturers. Membership: 550 pharmaceutical firms. Finances: Membership: Decided annually for the membership meeting; other sources - sale of publications. Meetings: Annual, various locations. Publications: Proceedings, annually; Advertising Code; Annual Report. Affiliations: Other Proprietary Medicines Associations through the World Federation of Proprietory Medicine Manufacturers.

★ 1368 ★

PSI CHI NATIONAL HONORS SOCIETY IN
     PSYCHOLOGY
1400 North Uhle, Suite 102   (703) 522-2538
Arlington, Virginia 22201   Established 1929

Ruth Cousins, Executive Director
To advance the science of psychology; and to encourage, stimulate, and maintain scholarship of the individual members in all fields, particularly in psychology. Membership: 500 active chapters. Finances: Initiation fees. Meetings: Annual, with American Psychology Association; regional conventions. Publications: Psi Chi Newsletter, 4 times a year, Ruth Cousins, editor; Psi Chi Handbook; Psi Chi Information Booklet. Affiliations: American Psychology Association; Association of College Honor Societies.

★ 1369 ★

PSI OMEGA FRATERNITY
1030 Lincoln Avenue   (215) 532-2330
Prospect Park, Pennsylvania 19076 Established 1892

Edward M. Grosse, Executive Director
A fraternity of dental practitioners and students engaged in the study of dentistry. Membership: 30,000. Publications: Frater of Psi Omega.

★ 1370 ★
PSORIASIS RESEARCH ASSOCIATION, INC.
107 Vista Del Grande   (415) 593-1394
San Carlos, California 94070   Established 1952

Diane Mullins, Executive Secretary
To support research on psoriasis, provide patient help
through educational materials and referrals.   Member-
ship: 200 ($12, $25, $50, $75, $100).   Finances:
Other sources - Drug companies, donations. Meetings:
Annual, San Mateo, California.   Publications:
Psoriasis "Top to Bottom", Diane Mullins, editor;
Food for Thought; Excerpts from International Psoriasis
Research Association Magazine.

PSYCHIATRIC HOSPITAL PATIENTS' WELFARE
    ASSOCIATION
        See: Canadian Association for the Welfare
              of Psychiatric Patients

PSYCHIATRIC INSTITUTE
    See: Psychiatric Institute Foundation

★ 1371 ★
PSYCHIATRIC INSTITUTE FOUNDATION
4460 MacArthur Boulevard, N.W.   (202) 467-4663
Washington, D.C. 20007   Established 1968

Howard Hoffman, M.D., President
The Foundation is a non-profit community service
organization dedicated to extending knowledge in
the mental health field and bringing that knowledge
to bear on pressing social problems.   The Foundation has sponsored well over 500 separate mental
health training, education, research and service
projects.   Some of the problems that have been
worked on include the plight of the aged; problems
of the changing family; drug dependency and
alcoholism; and crime and violence.   Awards:
Mental Health Achievement Awards, offered in the
categories of service, legislation and communication,
to recognize outstanding efforts to improve mental
health.   Former Name: Psychiatric Institute.

★ 1372 ★
PSYCHIATRIC NURSES ASSOCIATION OF CANADA
1854 Portage Avenue
Winnipeg, Manitoba R3J OG9,   (204) 786-6879
Canada   Established 1951

Aurelia Rust, President; Marlene Fitzsimmons,
Secretary
The Association's objectives are to promote and
maintain an enlightened and progressive standard of
psychiatric nursing throughout Canada; to promote
the upholding of the psychiatric nursing profession's
code of ethics in order to render high standards of
professional service to the public; to encourage
educational programs of the highest possible standard
for the purpose of providing well-qualified psychiatric
nurses; to promote better understanding throughout
the nation of the work and the importance of the
psychiatric nurse; to work in cooperation with other
approved bodies having similar interests in the promotion of mental health; to formulate policies and
express the opinions of psychiatric nurses on the
national level; and to foster the formation of psychiatric nurses' associations throughout Canada and
to unite them under the Psychiatric Nurses Association of Canada for the common good, common interest and common advancement of all.   Membership:
5,000 individuals; provincial member associations.
Finances: Membership: per capita $16.   Meetings:
Annual conferences, various provinces; board and
executive meetings, semiannually; Committee
meetings, as necessary.   Publications: Canadian
Journal of Psychiatric Nursing, quarterly, C. Martin,
editor.   Library: National Office Library.
Affiliations: 7 provincial psychiatric nurses associations.

★ 1373 ★
PSYCHIATRIC SERVICES SECTION OF THE
    AMERICAN HOSPITAL ASSOCIATION
840 North Lake Shore Drive   (312) 280-6000
Chicago, Illinois 60611   Established 1969

Victoria V. Smaller, Director
The basic goal of the American Hospital Association,
(see separate entry #311) is to promote the public
welfare through better health care for all the people.
The Psychiatric Services Section under the umbrella
of the AHA Center for Mental Health and Psychiatric Services, in representing the views of its members, is committed to the development and implementation of policies and programs designed to promote recognition of, support for, and improvement
in all aspects of hospital related mental health and
services.   Membership: Approximately 2,800 institutional (all hospitals and hospital-related programs
providing mental health/psychiatric/chemical dependency services).   Finances: Based on American
Hospital Association membership fee.   Meetings:
Annual, various locations; occasional educational
conferences/workshops.   Publications: Psychiatric
Services Newsletter, 3 times a year, Victoria V.
Smaller, editor; Psychiatric Services in Institutional

Settings: Selected Conference Papers. Library: 1,000 periodicals; 30,000 books. Affiliations: American Psychiatric Association, Joint Commission on Accreditation of Hospitals.

PSYCHIC HEALING TRAINING AND RESEARCH PROJECT
        See: Consciousness Research and Training Project, Inc.

★ 1374 ★
PSYCHOLOGY SOCIETY
100 Beekman Street   (212) 285-1872
New York, New York 10038   Established 1960

Dr. Pierre C. Haber, Executive Director
The Society is composed of psychologists who treat people primarily (practicing psychologists) as opposed to those who engage only in research and teaching (commonly called "clinical psychologists"). Membership: 2,000 (full - psychologists who practice; associate - research and teaching psychologists; student - graduate students in psychology). Finances: Full, $50; associate, $40; student $25; other sources - bequests, grants, subscriptions from non-members. Awards: Funds programs that deal with people who have mental problems (child abuse, drug use, crime and criminals, marital and other person-ality conflicts). Meetings: Annual, various locations. Publications: The Psychology Society, quarterly, Richard Scharff, editor; PS Newsletter, monthly, Mildred Steiner, editor; Proceedings of the annual meetings; selected papers; policy state-ments; recommendations to legislators.

★ 1375 ★
PSYCHONOMIC SOCIETY, INC.
University of Minnesota
Department of Psychology   (612) 373-2851
Minneapolis, Minnesota 55455   Established 1960

J. Bruce Overmeier, Secretary-Treasurer
To further the scientific study of psychology. Membership: 2,000. Finances: Membership: $25. Meetings: Annual, various locations. Publications: Bulletin of the Psychonomic Society, monthly; Animal Learning and Behavior, quarterly; Physiological Psychology, quarterly; Memory and Cognition, quarterly; Perception and Psychophysics, bimonthly; Behavior Research Methods and Instrumentation, bimonthly.

R

★ 1376 ★
R. SAMUEL MCLAUGHLIN FOUNDATION
c/o National Trust Company, Limited
21 King Street East
Toronto, Ontario, Canada   Established 1951

To use, apply and devote the net income of the Foundation for the improvement of the health and welfare of the people within Canada. Membership: 4 trustees.

★ 1377 ★
RADIATION THERAPY ONCOLOGY GROUP
Radiation Oncology Study Center
925 Chestnut Street, 7th Floor   (215) 574-3150
Philadelphia, Pennsylvania 19107 Established 1971

Luther L. Brady, M.D., Chairman; Lawrence W. Davis, M.D., Associate Chairman
Instituted as a group of research and clinical centers dedicated to conducting joint clinical trials and other studies to improve the management of patients with cancer. Membership: 37 full, provisional. Finances: Other sources: Funded by a grant from the National Cancer Institute. Meetings: Semi-annual, various locations. Publications: Members have published numerous journal articles.

★ 1378 ★
RADIOLOGICAL SOCIETY OF NORTH AMERICA, INC.
1415 West 22nd Street   (312) 920-2670
Oak Brook, Illinois 600521   Established 1915

Adele Swenson, Executive Director
To promote the study and practical application of radiology in all of its aspects; to provide meetings for the reading and discussion of papers and the dissemination of knowledge and to maintain a journal. Membership: 11,877 (active, junior, corresponding, associate, and honorary). Finances: Membership: $50. Awards: Memorial Fund; Memorial Fund Lecture; New Horizons Lecture; Gold Medal. Meetings: Annual, various locations. Publications: Radiology, monthly, William R. Eyler, M.D., editor.

★ 1379 ★
RADIONIC ASSOCIATION
16A North Bar   (0295) 3183
Banbury, Oxfordshire OX16 OTF,   Established 1943
England, United Kingdom

Anita J. Dunn, Secretary
The Association's aims are to protect and promote
the practice of Radionics as an honorable and skilled
profession, to foster research into the science of
Radionics and, by establishing contacts with responsible organizations and individuals thinking on similar
lines throughout the world, to provide a clearinghouse
for the collection and dissemination of relevant information.   The Association also supports the School
of Radionics which provides education and training
in Radionics.   Membership: 700 (fellows, members,
licentiates, associates).   Finances: Membership:
Fellows and members, 20 pounds; licentiates, 10
pounds; associates, 5 pounds; other sources - donations, money-raising events.   Meetings: Conference,
annually; two general meetings per year, London.
Publications: Radionic Quarterly, Vicki Roberts,
editor; various pamphlets and monographs.   Library:
The Radionic Association Library, 800 volumes -
restricted to United Kingdom members only.

★ 1380 ★
RECORDING FOR THE BLIND, INC.
215 East 58th Street   (212) 751 -0860
New York, New York 10022   Established 1951

Stuart Carothers, Executive Director
To record textbooks and educational material for the
blind and physically handicapped, free of charge and
at their specific request.   Membership: Not a
membership organization, but have 20 chartered
Recording Units.   Finances: Supported by contributions from foundations and from individuals.
Meetings: Annual conference of Unit Officers, New
York City.   Publications: Newsletter, biennially.

★ 1381 ★
REGISTRY OF INTERPRETERS FOR THE DEAF
814 Thayer Avenue   (301) 588-1025
Silver Spring, Maryland 20910   Established 1964

Richard Dirst, Executive Director
The Registry functions to professionalize interpreting
for deaf people; to educate the public concerning
interpreting process and interpreting services available; and to certify and evaluate interpreters
throughout the United States.   Membership: 4,500
(55 individuals in state chapters).   Finances:
Membership: $10; other sources - evaluation fees.

Meetings: Biennial, various locations.   Publications:
Interprenews; information pamphlets.

★ 1382 ★
REHABILITATION INTERNATIONAL
432 Park Avenue South   (212) 679-6520
New York, New York 10016   Established 1922

Norman Acton, Secretary-General
To collect and disseminate information relative to
rehabilitation of the disabled; to encourage research,
stimulate and assist the development of national
organizations in the field, assist in the development
inall countries for disability prevention and rehabilitation; to ensure adequate attention to the problems
of the disabled by governments and intergovernmental
organizations through legislation, technical assistance
programs and other means.   Membership: 115 organizations in 64 countries.   Finances: Membership:
Based on UN percentages; other sources - grants,
contributions.   Awards: Albert Lasker Awards for
Distinguished International Contributions to services
for the disabled.   Meetings: Congress, every 4
years, various locations.   Publications: International
Rehabilitation Review, Norman Acton, editor; Newsletter; International Journal of Rehabilitation Research; miscellaneous publications.

★ 1383 ★
RESEARCH AND EDUCATION FOUNDATION FOR
   CHEST DISEASE
911 Busse Highway
Park Ridge, Illinois 60068   (312) 698-2200

Alfred Soffer, M.D., Executive Director
An association of physicians and surgeons which
seeks to support investigations in the field of chest
medicine.   Membership: 10,500.   Affiliation:
American College of Chest Physicians.

★ 1384 ★
RESEARCH DISCUSSION GROUP
c/o Dr. Jeffrey Fedan
West Virginia University
Department of Pharmacology and Toxicology
Morgantown, West Virginia 26505   Established 1957

Jeffrey Fedan, Ph.D., Secretary-Treasurer
To encourage the exchange of ideas and promote free
discussion among medical research scientists.   Finances:
Payment for Annual Dinner.   Meetings: Annual, with
Federation of American Societies for Experimental
Biology.

★ 1385 ★
RESEARCH INSTITUTE FOR SUPERSENSONIC
     HEALING ENERGIES (RISHE)
Post Office Box 644   (408) 338-2161
Boulder Creek, California 95006   Established 1975

Christopher Hills, Ph.D., D.Sc., President; Victor
R. Beasley, Ph.D., Director
The Institute aims to bring together the research of
over 150 authors of the last 75 years on the application of radiesthesia, radiational paraphysics, radionics
and the divining ability of insects, animals and
humans, for the purpose of detecting health patterns,
analysis of biological and atomic structures and
nutrition needs both in human and plant life. The
work of the organization is based upon a series of
volumes available through University of the Trees
Press. Membership: 25 founding members (health
care researchers and practitioners, nutritional researchers, sub-atomic physicists). Finances: Other
sources: Fees from seminars and lectures, book sales,
grants from the University of the Trees. Library:
Museum of Radiesthesia and Radiational Physics, 750
volumes. Affiliations: University of the Trees;
Mankind Research Foundation. Former Name:
Supersensonics International Divining Association.

★ 1386 ★
RESOLVE, INC.
Post Office Box 474   (617) 484-2424
Belmont, Massachusetts 02178   Established 1973

Barbara Eck Menning, Executive Director
To educate and support couples dealing with infertility through training professionals, educating the
general public, offering individual or marital counseling, offering referral to infertility specialists,
adoption resources, therapists, etc., writing and
publishing educational materials, and setting up
support groups. Membership: Approximately 4,000
(individuals, couples or health/social services
professionals dealing with infertility). Finances:
Membership: $10, $15, or $25 annually; other
sources - donations, sale of literature, counseling
on a sliding scale fee for service basis, consultation
and training, grants. Publications: The Resolve
Newsletter, 5 times a year, Barbara Eck Menning,
editor; Directory of Infertility Resources, annually.

★ 1387 ★
RETARDED INFANTS SERVICES
386 Park Avenue, South   (212) 889-5464
New York, New York 10016   Established 1953

Peter P. Gorham, Executive Director

Service agency devoted to the physical well-being
and development of the retarded child and the sound
mental health of the parents. Helps families with
retarded children. First Hope Program offers intervention for parents at the birth of a retarded child
with in-home support, guidance and infant stimulation. Operates Step One Children's Center to
prevent development of functional retardation of the
pre-school children from disadvantaged families.

★ 1388 ★
RHO CHI SOCIETY
Massachusetts College of Pharmacy and
     Allied Health Sciences   (617) 732-2929
Boston, Massachusetts 02115   Established 1922

Douglas H. Kay, Ph.D., National Secretary
To promote the advancement of the pharmaceutical
sciences through the encouragement and recognition
of scholarship; to promote scholarly fellowship in
pharmacy by bringing undergraduate and graduate
students and faculty members together in fraternal
and helpful fellowships; to increase the awareness
of the ethical and social responsibilities of the profession and thereby enhanve the prestige of the profession; and to encourage research in the pharmaceutical sciences. Membership: 33,000 in 70
chapters (active, alumni, honorary). Finances:
Initiation fee $7.50; other sources - interest from
fund. Awards: Chapter Award; Lecture Award;
Graduate Scholarship. Meetings: Annual, with American
Pharmaceutical Association, various locations.
Publications: Report of Rho Chi, annual, Douglas
H. Kay, editor; Directory of Membership, every
5 years; History and Bylaws, biennial, Douglas
H. Kay, editor.

★ 1389 ★
RHO PI PHI INTERNATIONAL PHARMACEUTICAL
     FRATERNITY
5351 South West 35 Manor   (305) 792-0642
Ft. Lauderdale, Florida 33314   Established 1919

Murray Wolfe, Ph.D., Director, Continuing Education
Formed in 1919 Boston College of Pharmacy. Now
international in scope. Dedicated to the improvement of the profession of Pharmacy through leadership guidance and continuing education programs
both domestically and internationally. Maintains
one of the world's most complete libraries of continuing education tapes on pharmacy for use by any
pharmacist. Membership: Approximately 4,000
undergraduates at colleges of pharmacy, alumni
organizations. Finances: $8; other sources -
Jewelry, Convention journal, programs for scholar-

ships.   Awards: Annual scholarships to undergraduate chapters; research grants for Tay-Sachs disease.
Meetings: Annual, various locations; chapter meetings, weekly, monthly, semi-monthly.   Publications:
ROPE Newsletter, bimonthly, Gerald Arywitz, editor;
Supreme Scribes Newsletter, monthly, Nancy Frank,
editor.   Library 26 volumes on continuing education
for pharmacists.   Affiliation: Professional Intrafra-
ternity Council.

★ 1390 ★
ROBERT WOOD JOHNSON FOUNDATION
Post Office Box 2316   (609) 452-8701
Princeton, New Jersey 08540   Established 1936

David E. Rogers, M.D., President
The Foundation is a private philanthropy which makes
grants to institutions interested in improving individual
access to primary medical care, and in improving the
quality of the care received.   The Foundation also
uses its resource to develop ways to objectively
analyze alternative public policies in health.   Its
grants are only made to institutions and agencies
seeking to improve ambulatory health care in the
United States.

★ 1391 ★
ROLF INSTITUTE
302 Pearl Street   (303) 449-5803
Boulder, Colorado 80302   Established 1971

Richard Stenstadvold, Executive Director; Anne
Hyder, Director of Admissions
To train Rolfers and to help educate the general
public about Rolfing.   (Rolfing is a technique
devised by Dr. Ida P. Rolf for reordering the body
to bring its major segments toward a vertical align-
ment).   Membership: 260 (certified Rolfers,
certified Rolfing movement teachers).   Finances:
Varies geographically; other sources - training,
tuition.   Meetings: Annual, Boulder, Colorado.
Publications: Bulletin of Structural Integration,
biannually, Gary Horvitz, editor; Rolf-Lines,
monthly, Anna Hyder, editor.

★ 1392 ★
ROYAL COLLEGE OF PHYSICIANS AND SURGEONS
    OF CANADA
74 Stanley Avenue   (613) 746-8177
Ottawa, Ontario K1M 1P4, Canada   Established 1929

James H. Darragh, Executive Director
To contribute to the improvement of health care of

Canadians through the provision of designations for
specially trained physicians and surgeons whereby it
may be known that they are properly qualified.
The Members of the College are known as "Fellows,"
admission being attained almost exclusively by way of
the Certification examination taken after the prescribed period of 4 to 5 years of graduate training.
Certification examinations are conducted in 40 medical, surgical and laboratory specialties.   Membership: Approximately 15,000 fellows.   Finances:
Membership: $80. Meetings: Annual, various loca-
tions.   Publications: Annals of the Royal College
of Physicians and Surgeons of Canada, quarterly,
James H. Darragh, editor. Library: Raddick
Memorial Library, historical only.

RUBELLA PROJECT
    See: Developmental Disabilities Center

★ 1393 ★
RUTGERS CENTER OF ALCOHOL STUDIES
Rutgers University   (201) 932-3510
New Brunswick, New Jersey 08903 Established 1940

John A. Carpenter, Ph.D., Director
The Center is a multidisciplinary research, training
and documentation-publications institute which seeks
to discover and make available valid information
about drinking - biological, psychological, behavioral, sociological facts relevant to alcohol use and
drinking problems.   Publications: Journal of Studies
on Alcohol, monthly, Timothy G. Coffey, editor;
International Bibliography of Studies on Alcohol;
Monographs of the Rutgers Center of Alcohol Studies;
NIAAA – Rucas Alcoholism Treatment Series.
Library: R.C.A.S. Library, 7,500 volumes.

★ 1394 ★
RUTH RUBIN FELDMAN NATIONAL ODD SHOE
    EXCHANGE
3100 Neilson Way - 220
Santa Monica, California 90405   Established 1944

Ruth Rubin Feldman, Founder-Director
Service organization to bring together persons with
mutual shoe problems (e.g., persons having feet
that are not mates due to disease, injury or accident,
and persons who have had a foot amputated).   The
Exchange supplies names of persons of similar ages
and tastes in shoe styles who have extra shoes or
who are seeking someone with whom to exchange
mismated footwear.   Finances: Minimal fees.

S

★ 1395 ★
SACRO OCCIPITAL RESEARCH SOCIETY
   INTERNATIONAL
Post Office Box 358   (316) 725-3173
Sedan, Kansas 67361   Established 1925

Dr. M.L. Rees, Executive Secretary; M.B.
DeJarnette, President
Research development in the field of spinal and
structural abnormalities pertaining to the practice
of chiropractic. The Society conducts seminars to
teach structural corrective techniques to members of
the chiropractic profession. Membership: 1,855.
Finances: Membership: $60 a year. Awards: Re-
search funds are derived from the $60 per year mem-
bership fee; awards made each September during
clinical seminar. Meetings: Annual, various
locations. Publications: Sacro Occipital Seminar
Notes, annually, M.B. Dejarnette, editor; Research
findings.

★ 1396 ★
ST. JUDE CHILDREN'S RESEARCH HOSPITAL
332 North Lauderdale   (901) 522-0300
Memphis, Tennessee 38101   Established 1962

Danny Thomas, Founder; Dr. Alvin M. Mauer,
Director
To study catastrophic childhood disease, SJCRH has
become the leading center for childhood cancer research since opening in 1962. It currently treats
over 4,000 patients without charge. Admission is
by physician referral of a child diagnosed with an
illness being studied at SJCRH. These include
cancer, muscle disorders, rare blook diseases, and
other catastrophic illnesses of children. Membership: 2,500 (American Lebanese Syrian Associated
Charities; annual, family and life in ALSAC, the
fund-raising arm of the hospital). Finances: $10
annual, $20 family, $100 life ALSAC; other sources-
Individual donations provide three quarters of operating budget, 18% from grants and balance from
other sources. There is no charge to patients.
Awards: Karnofsky Fellowship in Cancer Research;
Leon Journey Fellowship in Biomedical Research;
Robbie Simpson Fellowship in Cancer Nursing; other
post-graduate training awards. Meetings: Regular
medical and scientific meetings. Publications:
Scientific Annual Report, John Gilbert, editor;
Over 100 papers annually in scientific media.

★ 1397 ★
SALVATION ARMY
National Headquarters
120 West 14th Street   (212) 620-4900
New York, New York 10011   Established 1865

Colonel G. Ernest Murray, National Chief Secretary
To operate as a religious and charitable corporation
with the following purposes: the spiritual, moral and
physical reformation of all who need it; the reclamation of the vicious, criminal, dissolute and degraded;
visitation among the poor and lowly and sick; the
preaching of the Gospel and the dissemination of
Christian truth by means of open-air and indoor
meetings. Today the Salvation Army's religious and
social service activities have made allies of millions
of men and women in over 80 nations. In the
United States there are almost 10,000 centers of
operation including corps community centers, service
extension units and social service centers. Membership: 414,035. Finances: Public support. Publications: The War Cry, weekly, Major Henry
Gariepy, editor; other publications: The Young
Soldier; Say; Elgrito de Guerra (a Spanish language
edition of The War Cry); The Deliverer; All the
World; The Officer, The Home League Exchange;
newsletters and pamphlets.

★ 1398 ★
SCANDINAVIAN ASSOCIATION FOR THORACIC
   AND CARDIOVASCULAR SURGERY
c/o Professor Karl Victor Hall
Rikshospitalet
The National Hospital of Norway
University Hospital   (02) 201050
Oslo 1, Norway   Established 1949

Professor Karl Victor Hall, Secretary-General
Annual meetings on topics related to Thoracic,
Cardial and Vascular surgery. Membership:
Approximately 150 (surgeons, cardiologists, radiolo-
gists - open to Scandinavians and invited members).
Finances: Annual fees 40 Norwegian Kroner.
Awards: Two awards for outstanding scientific work
by young surgeons. Meetings: Annual, various
locations. Publication: Scandinavian Journal of
Thoracic and Cardiovascular Surgery, quarterly.

★ 1399 ★
SCANDINAVIAN ASSOCIATION OF GENETICISTS
c/o Hans Doll
Risö National Laboratory
DK-4000 Roskilde, Denmark

Professor B. Rasmuson

Association for Geneticists in Iceland, Norway, Sweden, Finland and Denmark. Membership: 250. Finances: 5 Swedish Kroner per year. Meeting : Biennial, in one of the Scandinavian countries.

★ 1400 ★
SCANDINAVIAN ASSOCIATION OF OBSTETRICIANS
  AND GYNECOLOGISTS
University of Turku
Department of Obstetrics and Gynecology
SF-20520 Turku 52, Finland   (021) 611611
                                     Established 1934

Dr. Matti Grönroos, Secretary-General
The Association was founded to further the science and practice in the area of obstetrics and gynecology. Membership: Approximately 800 individuals from Scandinavian countries. Finances: Dues. Meetings: Biennial, various locations. Publications: Acta Obstetricia et Gynecologica Scandinavica, quarterly, Professor Ingemar Joelsson, chief editor; supplements.

★ 1401 ★
SCANDINAVIAN ASSOCIATION OF UROLOGY
Karolinska Hospital
Department of Urology
Post Office Box 60 500   (08) 7361543
S-10401 Stockholm, Sweden   Established 1956

Doc. Per Olov Hedlund, General-Secretary
Scandinavian Association of Urology is the Association of the National Urological Societies of Denmark, Finland, Iceland, Norway and Sweden. Its purpose is to promote collaboration and progress in Scandinavian urology. Special interest is paid to post graduate education and to the communication between different clinics and colleagues. The aim is also to some extent to promote multicentre collaborative research. Membership: 400 (mostly urological surgeons of Scandinavia). Finances: Membership: $4 per year. Awards: The Leo Fennica Prize to the best presentation at the Congress of the Scandinavian Association of Urology. Meetings: Biennial Congress, alternately in the different Scandinavian countries. Publications: NUF-bulletinen (in Swedish), 2-3 times a year.

★ 1402 ★
SCANDINAVIAN NEUROSURGICAL SOCIETY
c/o Jakob Husby, M.D.
Post Office Box 365
Neurosurgical Department   ext. 2294
Aalborg Sygehus   (08) 131111
DK-9100 Aalborg, Denmark   Established 1946

Jacob Husby, M.D., Secretary
To further neurosurgery in Scandinavia. Membership: 250 (active, junior, honorary, corresponding, associate). Finances: Membership: Fee for active members, 100 skr. Meetings: Annual, various locations in Scandinavia. Publications: Acta Neurochirurgica, Springer, Vienna.

★ 1403 ★
SCANDINAVIAN ORTHOPAEDIC ASSOCIATION
c/o Jan Goldie, M.D.
Sahlgrenska Sjukhuset
S-41345 Göteborg, Sweden   Established 1919

Dr. Jan Goldie, Secretary General
The Association aims to promote skill in orthopaedic surgery and to bring orthopaedic surgeons from Scandinavian countries together. Membership: 685. Finances: Membership: $10 per year. Meetings: Congress, biennially, various locations in Scandinavia; Post-graduate course in orthopaedic surgery, alternate years, various locations in Scandinavia. Publication: Acta Orthopaedica Scandinavica, 6 times per year, Knud Jansen, editor.

★ 1404 ★
SCANDINAVIAN PSYSIOLOGICAL SOCIETY
Institute of Medical Physiology C
Panum-Institute
3c Blegdomsvej   (01) 357900
DK-2200 Copenhagen N, Denmark   Established 1926

Niela A. Thorn, Secretary-General
Consists of scientists in Denmark, Finland, Iceland Norway and Sweden working in the field of physiology and related sciences. Membership: About 900 (honorary and ordinary members). Finances: Membership: Annual subscription, 45 Swedish kroner. Meetings: Congress, every 3 years; annual and semiannual, various locations. Publications: Acta Physiologica Scandinavica, bimonthly, U.S. von Euler, editor.

★ 1405 ★
SCANDINAVIAN RADIOLOGICAL SOCIETY
c/o Dr. Tor Drevvatne
Det Norske Radiumhospital
Montebello   (02) 55 40 80
Oslo 2, Norway   Established 1919

Dr. Tor Drevvatne, Secretary General
The Society aims to promote research as well as

friendship between the radiologists in the Scandina-vian countries. Membership: 2,200 (radiologists, oncologists, scientists – other related fields). Finances: Membership: 2 Swedish krone. Awards: Prize for best research, annually. Publications: Kongress Program, annually. Affiliations: Radiological Society of Finland, Radiological Society of Iceland, Danish Society of Diagnostic Radiology, Swedish Society of Medical Radiology, Norwegian Society of Radiology.

★ 1406 ★
SCANDINAVIAN SOCIETY OF ANESTHESIOLOGISTS
Ulleväl Hospital
Department of Anesthesia
Oslo, Norway   Established 1950

Andreas Skulberg
Work for the scientific development of Anaesthes-iology in the Scandinavian countries and promote collabroation between Scandinavian anaesthesiologists. Membership: Scandinavian specialists in anaesthesia (ordinary members) and anaesthetists from other countries (extraordinary members) totaling 687 in 22 countries. Finances: Membership dues. Meetings: Congresses, biennial, various locations. Publication: Acta Anaesthesiologica Scandinavica, quarterly.

★ 1407 ★
SCANDINAVIAN SOCIETY OF FORENSIC
        ODONTOLOGY
Department of Forensic Odontology
Statens Rättsläkarstation, Fack
S-17120 Solna, Sweden   Established 1961

Docent Gunnar Johanson, Chairman
To promote research, education and practice of forensic odontology in Scandinavia and internationally; to increase the cooperation and understanding between forensic odontology and allied forensic sciences and professions. Membership: 40 forensic odontologists and dentists interested in this field. Finances: Membership: 10 Swedish crowns per year. Meet-ings: Periodically, various locations. Affiliation: Scandinavian Society of Forensic Medicine.

★ 1408 ★
SEEING EYE, INC.
Washington Valley Road
Post Office Box 375   (201) 539 4425
Morristown, New Jersey 07960   Established 1929

Stuart Grout, Executive Vice President

The Seeing Eye is a non-profit philanthropic organiza-tion whose purpose is to supply blind persons with dogs trained to act as guides for such blind persons or to obtain dogs for such purpose by purchase, gifts, or breeding; to train such dogs to guide the blind and to furnish such trained dogs to blind persons needing them; and to instruct such blind persons in the proper use and handling of such trained dogs. Finances: Currently supported by annual and deferred gifts and by income derived from investments, lega-cies. Meetings: Board, 4 times a year, New York City or Seeing Eye Headquarters. Publications: Seeing Eye Guide, quarterly; other literature re-lating to mobility of blind persons and other aspects of their rehabilitation.

★ 1409 ★
SEX INFORMATION AND EDUCATION COUNCIL
        OF THE U.S. (SIECUS)
84 Fifth Avenue, Suite 407   (212) 929-2300
New York, New York 10011   Established 1964

Mary S. Calderone, M.D., M.P.H., President
Barbara Whitney, R.N., M.S., Executive Director
SIECUS was founded in order to establish human sexuality as a health entity. Its primary focus is information and education on human sexuality for all health and educational disciplines, to reach the primary provider of services. In 1979, the SIECUS Resource Center and Library was opened at New York University. Membership: 28 (voting member-ship consists of the elected Board), associate, non-voting. Finances: Membership: $30, associate; other sources - public contributions, foundation grants, royalties, bequests. Meetings: Semiannual, New York City. Publications: SIECUS Report, bimonthly, Mary S. Calderone; monographs, study guides, film resource guides, special publications, bibliographies. Library: SIECUS Resource Center and Library, 2,000 volumes, 60 journals; user fee for non-Associates, noncirculating. Affiliations: Department of Health Education of the School of Education, Health, Nursing, and Arts Professions of New York University; and the Sex Information and Education Councils of Indiana and Connecticut (SIECIND, SIECCONN).

★ 1410 ★
SHARE, INC.
Post Office Box 1342   (213) 274-5361
Beverly Hills, California 90213 Established 1953

Anne Jeffries Sterling, President
A volunteer organization of individuals to raise funds for the mentally retarded under the direction of the Exceptional Children's Foundation. Projects

include: pre-school training and special education classes for mentally retarded children not accepted by public schools; sheltered workshops for the older retarded; an art center for the gifted retarded; an infant development program and a residential home for the retarded. Provides internship opportunities for graduate students from local colleges and universities.

SIECUS
See: Sex Information and Education Council of the U.S.

★ 1411 ★
SISTER KENNY INSTITUTE
Chicago Avenue at 27th Street   (612) 874-4463
Minneapolis, Minnesota 55407   Established 1942

Sy Schlossman, Executive Director
The Institute is a 48-bed comprehensive rehabilitation hospital (a division of Abbott-Northwestern Hospital) that provides rehabilitation services for the medical center complex and serves patients throughout the upper midwest region. The Institute continues to pioneer in innovative treatment techniques, disability prevention, research and education, which assist disabled persons to reach optimal functions and independence. Membership: Board of Directors, 24. Finances: other sources - fees for service, United Way and other philanthropic donations. Publications: numerous educational books and audiovisual materials. Affiliations: American Hospital Association, Section on Rehabilitation; Joint Commission on Accreditation of Hospitals; National Association of Rehabilitation Facilities.

SMITHERS (CHRISTOPHER D.) FOUNDATION, INC.
See: Christopher D. Smithers Foundation, Inc.

★ 1412 ★
SOCIAL PSYCHIATRY RESEARCH INSTITUTE, INC.
150 East 69th Street   (212) 628-4800
New York, New York 10021   Established 1970

Ari Kiev, M.D., Director
To further study the social impact of psychiatric illness and to develop videotape and film training materials in psychiatry and transcultural psychiatry. Membership: 15 collaborating physicians. Finances: Other sources - government grants; private contributions. Publications: Producers of Videotape seminars

in psychiatry and Perspectives in Mental Health videotape series.

★ 1413 ★
SOCIETY FOR ADOLESCENT MEDICINE
Post Office Box 3462   (213) 368-5996
Granada Hills, California 91344   Established 1968

Edie Moore, Business Manager
To promote the development, synthesis, and dissemination of scientific and scholarly knowledge unique to the developmental and health care needs of adolescents. Membership: 850 (active - membership in SAM is open to health care professionals throughout the world who are involved in health services, teaching, or research that is concerned with the welfare of adolescents). Finances: Membership: $50 annually regular; $35 annually affiliate (individual in training); other sources - donations and research awards. Awards: Currently in developmental stages of Research Awards annually. Meetings: Annual Business Meeting and Clinical and Experimental Research Meetings and Workshops held in the fall preceding the American Academy of Pediatric fall sessions. Publication: Journal of Adolescent Health Care, quarterly, H. Verdain Barnes, M.D., editor-in-chief. Affiliations: Regional Chapters: New Jersey, Northern California, Northwest, Rocky Mountain, Southeast, Washington, D.C., (Mid-West Chapter in the developmental stages).

★ 1414 ★
SOCIETY FOR ADVANCED MEDICAL SYSTEMS
4405 East-West Highway, Suite 404 (301) 657-4142
Bethesda, Maryland 20014   Established 1969

Patricia I. Horner, Executive Director
Aims of the Society are to bring together medical personnel, physical scientists, engineers, and others to foster cooperation in advancing technology for medical care; to develop standards, terminology, and guidelines for the evaluation and employment of technological systems for detection and treatment of disease states, to promote training and development of professional and allied health manpower needed for advanced medical systems; and to assist in integration of advanced technological health care systems into the practice of medicine while maintaining high standards of professional ethics. Membership: Approximately 400 members and fellows; student members are registered students, interns and residents at reduced rates (members - any person with interest in advanced medical systems is eligible upon payment of dues; fellows - elected by the Board -

should have competently engaged in administration, development, implementation, research, planning, or teaching for two years and have a degree, relevant publications, inventions, processes, etc. Finances: Membership: Members, $25; Fellows, $50; Student, $10; subscription to Journal of Medical Systems, $15 per year; - other sources - conference fees, publications, contracts, contributions. Meetings: Board, 2-3 times year; annual conference, various locations. Publications: Algorhythm - Newsletter, quarterly, Douglas Mackintosh, editor; Journal of Medical Systems, semiannually; Proceedings of Annual Conferences, annually; Membership Directory, annually; Allied Health Apprenticeship Standards, Training Guides; Instructors Manual. Library: More than 200 volumes. Affiliation: Member of the Alliance for Engineering in Medicine and Biology.

★ 1415 ★

SOCIETY FOR CLINICAL AND EXPERIMENTAL
    HYPNOSIS, INC.
129-A Kings Park Drive   (315) 652-7299
Liverpool, New York 13088   Established 1949

Marion Kenn, Administrative Director
To stimulate and support the professional pursuit of research in this field (hypnosis) and its boundary areas; to encourage cooperation among members of professional and scientific disciplines with regard to the utilization of hypnosis both in research and in practice; to support communication by scientific meetings as well as by publications; to set up standards of adequacy and ethics for those making use of hypnosis; and to strive toward the establishment of formal and standardized training facilities for those who qualify. Membership: 950 (dentists, physicians and psychologists - must be members of ADA, AMA or APA). Finances: Membership: Student, $20; regular, $40; other sources - subscriptions to International Journal of Clinical and Experimental Hypnosis. Awards: Best research paper in hypnosis; best clinical paper; best theoretical paper; best book on hypnosis; Bernard B. Raginsky Award; Shirley Schneck Award; Sherry K. and Harold B. Crasilneck Award; Morton Prince Award. Meetings: Annual, various locations. Publications: International Journal of Clinical and Experimental Hypnosis, quarterly, Martin T. Orne, M.D., Ph.D., editor; SCEH Newsletter, quarterly.

★ 1416 ★

SOCIETY FOR GOODWILL SERVICES
234 Adelaide Street East   (416) 362-4711
Toronto, Ontario M5A 1M9, Canada   Established 1935

J. Philip Gandon, Executive Director

To provide remunerative employment for persons with emotional, sociological, physical and mental handicaps; to provide assessment, work adjustment and training to clients referred from government, private and public sources; to provide supplementary social services to employees and clients, including community service referrals, appliances and counselling. Membership: 32 board members. Finances: Sale of donated recyclable materials; government grants and private donations. Meetings: 5 times a year, Toronto. Publications: The Goodwill Quarterly, Raymond Byrnes, editor; Annual Report. Affiliations: International Council of Goodwill Industries of America, Incorporated; Canadian Rehabilitation Council for the Disabled; Social Planning Council of Metropolitan Toronto; and Ontario Rehabilitation Workshop Council.

★ 1417 ★

SOCIETY FOR HEALTH AND HUMAN VALUES
925 Chestnut Street, 6th Floor   (215) 928-2793
Philadelphia, Pennsylvania 19107 Established 1969

The Society is a professional association whose primary objective is to encourage and promote informed concern for human values as an essential, explicit dimension of education for the health professions. To accomplish this objective, the Society seeks through a variety of endeavors to facilitate communication and cooperation among the professionals from diverse disciplines who share such an objective; to support critical and scholarly efforts to develop knowledge, concepts and programs dealing with the relation of human values to education for the health professions. Membership: 925 (faculty and students in health professional schools, faculty in humanities, theologians, ethicists, etc.) Finances: Membership: $30 per year; $15 students; other sources - grants. Awards: Annual Award; Annual Oration. Meetings: Annual, Washington, D.C.; Regional Meetings, annually. Publications: Notes, quarterly, E.A. Vastyan, editor; Annual Oration; Nourishing the Humanistic in Medicine: Interactions with the Social Sciences; Medicine and Religion: Strategies of Care. Affiliations: Member of Council of Academic Societies; Association of American Medical Colleges.

★ 1418 ★

SOCIETY FOR INVESTIGATIVE DERMATOLOGY
14435 Southwest Uplands Drive (503) 636-9890
Lake Oswego, Oregon 97034   Established 1937

Kirk D. Wuepper, M.D., Secretary-Treasurer
The Society publishes a monthly Journal and provides an annual and four regional meetings for the

exchange of information and ideas. Membership: 2,700 (active, $75; patron, $150; corporate sustaining, $1,000). Awards: Rothman Award, presented at Annual Meeting; Research Fellowship of $16,000, annually. Meetings: Annual, Spring, various locations. Publications: The Journal of Investigative Dermatology, monthly, Ruth K. Freinkel, M.D., editor. Affiliation: ESDR European Society for Dermatological Research.

★ 1419 ★
SOCIETY FOR NEUROSCIENCE
9650 Rockville Pike   (301) 530-8955
Bethesda, Maryland 20014   Established 1969

Marjorie G. Wilson, Executive Secretary; Gerry Gurvitch, Publications Director
To advance the understanding of nervous systems, including the part they play in determining behavior, by bringing together scientists of varying backgrounds, and by facilitating the integration of research directed at all levels of biological organization; to promote education in the neurosciences; to inform the general public on the results and implications of current research in this area. Membership: 4,000 (regular, affiliate, student). Finances: Membership: $35-$60; other sources - grants from private foundations; The Journal of Neuroscience. Awards: Grass Foundation Lectureship. Meetings: Annual, various locations. Publications: The Journal of Neuroscience, quarterly; Neuroscience Newsletter, quarterly, Geraldine Gurvitch, assistant editor; Abstracts Volume; Symposia Volume. Affiliations: International Brain Research Organization; World Health Organization; British Brain Research Association; European Brain and Behavior Society.

★ 1420 ★
SOCIETY FOR PEDIATRIC RADIOLOGY
Post Office Box 648
University of Rochester Medical Center
601 Elmwood Avenue   (716) 275-2298
Rochester, New York 14642   Established 1958

Beverly P. Wood, M.D., Secretary
The purposes are scientific, education, and professional and include the study of problems and diagnostic methods related to pediatric radiology. Each annual meeting consists of presentation of scientific material as formal papers and short informal presentations. Membership: 417 (active, associate, emeritus, corresponding). Finances: Membership: $55 - active and associate members. Awards: Neuhauser Lectureship in Pediatric Radiology, annually; John Caffey Award Paper in Pediatric

Radiology, selected by the Society and presented to the American Roentgen Ray Society, annually. Meetings: Annual, Spring, usually in conjunction with the American Roentgen Ray Society, various locations.

★ 1421 ★
SOCIETY FOR PEDIATRIC RESEARCH
University of New Mexico
School of Medicine
Department of Pediatrics   (505) 277-4361
Albuquerque, New Mexico 87131   Established 1929

John D. Johnson, M.D., Secretary-Treasurer
Established as a non-profit charitable corporation to foster pediatric investigation and to provide a forum and an opportunity for younger investigators to present their work before an audience of their peers. For this purpose the Society holds an annual meeting for the presentation of new, original investigation into the disorders of childhood. Membership: 900 (active and emeritus members); members become emeritus at age 45. Finances: Membership: Yearly dues, $60. Meetings: Annual, various locations in the continental U.S.A. Publication: Pediatric Research, monthly, Joseph A. Bellanti, M.D., editor. Affiliations: American Pediatric Society; Ambulatory Pediatric Association.

★ 1422 ★
SOCIETY FOR PSYCHOPHYSIOLOGICAL RESEARCH, INC.
University of Rochester
Department of Psychology   (716) 275-2595
Rochester, New York 14627   Established 1960

Dr. Rafael Klorman, Secretary-Treasurer
The Society's intent is to foster research on the interrelationships between the physiological and psychological aspects of human behavior. Membership: 900 (psychologists, physiologists, physicians, and engineers). Finances: Membership: Member, $27; student, $16. Meetings: Annual, various locations. Publication: Psychophysiology, bimonthly, David Shapino, editor.

★ 1423 ★
SOCIETY FOR PUBLIC HEALTH EDUCATION, INC.
703 Market, Suite 535   (415) 546-7511
San Francisco, California 94103   Established 1950

James P. Lovegren, Executive Director
To promote, encourage and contribute to the

advancement of the health of all people through education. Membership: 1,200. Finances: Membership: Sustaining, $100; active $50; student, $25. Meetings: Annual, various locations. Publications: Health Education Quarterly, Marshall Becker, editor; Newsletter, bimonthly, Phyllis Hecker, editor.

★ 1424 ★
SOCIETY FOR RESEARCH IN CHILD DEVELOPMENT, INC.
University of Chicago
5801 South Ellis Avenue   (312) 753-3370
Chicago, Illinois 60637   Established 1933

Dorothy Eichorn, Executive Director
To provide opportunity for people from different disciplines to extend their horizons, to become cognizant of the techniques and tools of research in allied fields, to critically evaluate their own approaches to the study of children in the light of knowledge in related areas. Membership: 4,000. Finances: Membership: Member, $50; student, $25; other sources - subscriptions to non-members. Meetings: Biennial, various locations. Publications: Child Development, quarterly, E. Mavis Hetherington, editor; Child Development Abstracts and Bibliography, 3 times a year, Hoben Thomas, editor; Monographs of SRCD, irregularly, Frances D. Horowitz, editor.

★ 1425 ★
SOCIETY FOR SURGERY OF THE ALIMENTARY TRACT
c/o R. Scott Jones, M.D.
Duke University Medical Center
Department of Surgery   (919) 684-6437
Durham, North Carolina 27710   Established 1961

R. Scott Jones, M.D., Secretary
To stimulate and foster the study of, and research in, the function and diseases of the alimentary tract; to provide a forum for the presentation of such knowledge; to provide funds and training opportunities for surgeons interested in these diseases; and to edit, sponsor, or encourage publications pertaining to the foregoing activities. Membership: 909 (active, senior, honorary). Finances: $60. Awards: Annual Resident Lecture Award; Annual Founders' Lecture Award. Meetings: Annual, various locations.

★ 1426 ★
SOCIETY FOR THE PROTECTION OF THE UNBORN THROUGH NUTRITION
17 North Wabash, Suite 603   (312) 332-2334
Chicago, Illinois 60602   Established 1972

Tom Brewer, M.D., President
To promote education and information on nutrition during gestation including counseling, the coordination of classes and panels on nutrition during pregnancy and the publication and distribution of educational pamphlets on this subject; to encourage the medical profession to adopt nutritional standards for pregnant women and to discourage low-salt, low-calorie regimens, weight control programs and the use of drugs during pregnancy; to receive and maintain funds, the income from which shall be applied within the United States exclusively for the charitable benevolent, social and educational purposes listed above. Membership: 21 associate members. Finances: Membership: $10 a year - other sources - individual contributions and occasional governmental and foundations grants. Meetings: Annual, various locations. Publications: The Pregnant Issue: Medicate or Educate?, bimonthly; What Every Pregnant Woman Should Know: The Truth About Diets and Drugs in Pregnancy, by Gail Sforza Brewer and Tom Brewer, M.D.; and other books, pamphlets, reprints of newspaper, magazine and journal articles; bibliography.

★ 1427 ★
SOCIETY FOR THE PSYCHOLOGICAL STUDY OF SOCIAL ISSUES
Post Office Box 1248   (313) 662-9130
Ann Arbor, Michigan 48106   Established 1936

Caroline Weichlein, Administrative Associate
Major concern is the application of the behavioral science research to the major social dilemmas of modern man. Membership: Approximately 3,000. Finances: Membership: Dues based on total income; contributions; sale of journal. Awards: Gordon Allport Intergroup Relations Prize; Kurt Lewin Memorial Award. Meetings: Annual with American Psychological Association. Publications: Journal of Social Issues, quarterly, Joseph E. McGrath, editor; Newsletter.

★ 1428 ★
SOCIETY FOR THE REHABILITATION OF THE FACIALLY DISFIGURED, INC.
550 First Avenue   (212) 340-5400
New York, New York 10016   Established 1951

Henry Steeger, President

The Society's purposes are to provide facilities for the treatment and assistance of individuals who are unable to afford private reconstructive surgical care, to assist in the training and education of personnel engaged in reconstructive plastic surgery, to initiate, stimulate and encourage research in this field, and to carry on a public education program to make more people aware of the problems of facial disfigurement and the treatment methods currently available. The major activity of the Society has been sponsorship of the Institute of Reconstructive Plastic Surgery of the New York University Medical Center. Membership: 650 individuals. Finances: Patron, $1,000; participating, $500; sustaining, $100; supporting, $50; contributing, $25; annual, $10. Meetings: Annual. Publications: Case Booklet, annual, Robert E. Bochat, editor; SFD News, periodic, Robert E. Bochat, editor.

★ 1429 ★
SOCIETY FOR THE SCIENTIFIC STUDY OF SEX, INC.
208 Daffodil Road   (301) 766-4556
Glen Burnie, Maryland 21061   Established 1957

Mary Westervelt, Executive Secretary
The Society was organized to foster interdisciplinary exchange in the field of sexual knowledge. The aim of the Society is to bring together individuals working in the biological, medical, anthropological, psychological, sociological, and allied fields who are conducting sexual research, whose profession involves problems relating to sex, or who are vitally concerned with sexual science. The Society holds periodic scientific meetings for the presentation of studies and research papers. It organizes symposia, seminars, workshops and conferences to consider theoretical and practical aspects of sexuality. It publishes a scientific journal devoted to original studies, abstracts of the relevant literature, reports, comments, and book reviews. Membership: 500 plus, individuals. Finances: Regular and associate, $60; student, $25; Other Sources: Profit, if any, from meetings; journal sales to non-members. Awards: Annual Award for outstanding contribution to the understanding of sexuality, Hugo G. Beigel Research Award. Meetings: Annual, various locations. Publications: The Journal of Sex Research, quarterly, Clive M. Davis, Ph.D., editor; Newsletter, annual, Andrew E. Behrendt, editor.

★ 1430 ★
SOCIETY FOR THE STUDY OF BLOOD, INC.
New York University Medical Center
Department of Medicine   (212) 679-3200
New York, New York 10016   Established 1945

Michael Freedman, M.D., Secretary-Treasurer
To further research and disseminate knowledge concerning the allied fields of hematology, blood grouping and transfusion. Membership: 300. Finances: Membership: $18. Meetings: Quarterly, New York City.

★ 1431 ★
SOCIETY FOR THE STUDY OF HUMAN BIOLOGY
c/o C. J. Turner
University of Surrey
Department of Human Biology and Health
Guilford, Surrey, England,   (0483) 71281
   United Kingdom   Established 1958

C. J. Turner, Secretary
To advance the study of biology of human populations and of man as a species, in all its branches, particularly human variability, human genetics and evolution, human adaptability and ecology. Membership: 500. Finances: Membership: Full, 10 pounds or $24; student, 1 pound. Meetings: Semiannual, various locations. Publications: Annals of Human Biology, bimonthly, J. M. Tanner, editor.

★ 1432 ★
SOCIETY FOR THE STUDY OF REPRODUCTION
309 West Clark Street   (217) 356-3182
Champaign, Illinois 61820   Established 1967

Claude Cruse, Executive Secretary
To promote the study of reproduction by fostering interdisciplinary communication within the science, by holding conferences, and publication of meritorious studies. Membership: 1,300 (profession, associate, students, sustaining). Finances: Membership: Professional, $35; associate, $35; student, $26; sustaining, $500. Meetings: Annual, various locations. Publication: Biology of Reproduction, 2 volumes annually, A. V. Nalbondov, editor.

★ 1433 ★
SOCIETY FOR VASCULAR SURGERY
c/o Wesley S. Moore, M.D.
U.C.L.A. Medical Center
Department of Surgery   (213) 825-9641
Los Angeles, California 90024   Established 1947

Wesley S. Moore, Secretary
To promote the study of and research in vascular diseases; to define more clearly the role of surgery in these diseases; to pool the experience and knowledge of studying and managing these diseases; to stand-

ardize the nomenclature of these diseases. Membership: 358. Meetings: Annual, various locations. Publication: Surgery, annual, C. V. Mosby Company, editors. Affiliation: North American Chapter, International Cardiovascular Society.

★ 1434 ★
SOCIETY OF AIR FORCE ANESTHESIOLOGISTS
4499 Medical Drive, Suite 306   (512) 692-0101
San Antonio, Texas 78229   Established 1970

Francis J. Dannemiller, M.D.
Provides postgraduate medical education and review of the specialty of anesthesiology. Membership: 75 active duty Air Force anesthesiologists and nurse anethetists (M.D. anesthesiologists, dentists, nurse anesthetists and registered nurses in anesthesia training). Finances: Membership: Student nurse anesthetists, $100; resident M.D. anesthesia and nurse anesthetists, $150; CRNA, $175; certified M.D. anesthesiologists, $200; Other Sources: Exhibitors at meeting. Meetings: Annual M.D. meeting, June, San Antonio, Texas; Semiannual Nurse Anesthesia Review Courses, Spring and Fall, San Antonio, Texas. Publications: AnesthesiaFile, monthly abstract, F. J. Dannemiller, M.D., editor; Annual Review Course Lecture Outlines (meeting lecture notes), F. J. Dannemiller, M.D., editor.

★ 1435 ★
SOCIETY OF BIOLOGICAL PSYCHIATRY
2010 Wilshire Boulevard, Suite 607 (213) 483-7863
Los Angeles, California 90057   Established 1945

George N. Thompson, M.D.
To encourage research in the common areas of the biological and psychiatric fields and to relate the activities of psychiatry and neurology. Activities include annual meetings to disseminate information and present scientific papers and exhibits. Membership: 600 (active, honorary, senior, corresponding). Finances: Membership: Annual dues, $15; Other Sources: Foreign guest speaker grants. Awards: A. E. Bennett Research Awards; Gold Medal Award. Meetings: Annual, various locations. Publication: Biological Psychiatry, 6 issues, 2 volumes annually, Joseph Wortis, M.D., editor.

★ 1436 ★
SOCIETY OF CRITICAL CARE MEDICINE
Post Office Box 3158   (714) 870-5243
Anaheim, California 92803   Established 1971

Norma Shoemaker, R.N., Executive Director
To improve care for acute life-threatening illnesses and injuries; to promote the development of optimal facilities for this purpose; to engage in any and all lawful activities incidental to the aforegoing purposes. Membership: 1,200 (physicians, scientists, engineers, paramedics, nurses, allied health scientists, technologists). Finances: Membership: Physicians, $125; paramedics, nurses, scientists, technicians, $60; foreign and corresponding, $25. Meetings: Annual, various locations. Publication: Critical Care Medicine, bimonthly, William C. Shoemaker, editor.

★ 1437 ★
SOCIETY OF EYE SURGEONS
International Eye Foundation
7801 Norfolk Avenue   (301) 986-1830
Bethesda, Maryland 20014   Established 1969

John Harry King, Jr., M.D., Executive Secretary
To promote the science of ophthalmic surgery among all peoples and nations. Activities include sponsoring fellowships in eye surgery for young ophthalmologists now in training and those who have completed training; sponsoring eye surgical meetings; sponsoring teaching teams and Visiting Professors to and from certain countries to present lectures, courses and operating demonstrations to upgrade eye surgical care and for the interchange of scientific knowledge; fostering social intercourse among physicians and scientists interested in and skilled in ophthalmic surgery and surgical research; sponsoring the International Eye Foundation programs, such as the International Eye Bank, for the prevention and treatment of blindness. Membership: Over 1,000. Finances: Membership: $75; dues, $35. Awards: Vail Medal; Atkinson Lectures. Meetings: Biennial, various locations. Publication: Newsletter, quarterly.

★ 1438 ★
SOCIETY OF FRENCH-SPEAKING NEUROSURGEONS
Domus Medica - 60 Boulevard de la
   Tour Maubourg
F-75007 Paris, France   Established 1950

Pr. Janny
The organization is a scientific society that conducts annual congresses and meetings. Membership: 450 (titular, correspondant associate and honor). Finances: Other Sources: Subscriptions, research funds, grants. Meetings: Annual Meeting, Paris; Annual Congress, various locations. Publications: Neurochirurgie, 9 issues annually, Masson and Cie, editors. Library: Masson, 9 volumes.

★ 1439 ★

SOCIETY OF GENERAL PHYSIOLOGISTS
Marine Biological Laboratory
Woods Hole, Massachusetts 02543   Established 1946

To promote and disseminate knowledge in the field of general physiology and otherwise to advance understanding and interest in the field of general physiology, and to engage in general scientific research in any field relating to general physiology. Membership: Approximately 700 (regular membership: physiologists holding their doctorate degree; associate membership: students and those with the doctorate degree for less than 2 years). Finances: Membership: Dues are $10 annually for all members; Other Sources: Annual symposium (registration fees and royalties from publication of the symposium). Awards: The Society provides scholarships to 2 or 3 students annually who wish to take courses at the Marine Biological Laboratory, and also provides a distinguished lectureship at various international meetings. Meetings: Annual, Marine Biological Laboratory at Woods Hole, Massachusetts. Publications: Journal of General Physiology, monthly, Paul F. Cranefield, editor; the annual symposium is published annually (1981 will be the 35th annual symposium.

★ 1440 ★

SOCIETY OF HEAD AND NECK SURGEONS
The Johns Hopkins Hospital
811 Harvey Building   (301) 955-3190
Baltimore, Maryland 21205   Established 1954

Elliot W. Strong, M.D., President; John M. Lore, M.D., President-Elect; Alvin L. Watne, M.D., Vice President; Darrell A. Jaques, M.D., Secretary; Dwight C. Hanna, M.D., Treasurer
The Society was founded in order to serve as a medium for the exchange and advancement of scientific knowledge relative to the management of head and neck tumors, exclusive of lesions of the brain, with particular reference to the surgery of cancer. Membership: Approximately 600 (active, senior, foreign corresponding, consulting, and honorary). Finances: Membership: Active, $150; senior, honorary, consulting, no fee; foreign corresponding, $50; initiation fee, $100; Other Sources: Annual Scientific Meeting. Awards: Hayes Martin Lecture Award and Resident/Fellow Essay Award. Meetings: Annual, usually in the spring months (March, April, May), various locations. Publications: Proceeding annual meeting, papers presented in the American Journal of Surgery.

★ 1441 ★

SOCIETY OF MEDICAL FRIENDS OF WINE
Post Office Box 218
Sausalito, California 94965   Established 1939

Leon D. Adams, Executive Secretary
To encourage research on wine, develop understanding of its beneficial effects. Membership: 350 (active resident, active non-resident, associate, honorary). Finances: Membership: Resident, $60; non-resident, $10. Awards: $1,000 award for original research on wine, biennial. Meetings: Quarterly, San Francisco Bay Area. Publication: Bulletin of the Society, semiannual, Leon D. Adams, editor.

★ 1442 ★

SOCIETY OF NEUROLOGICAL SURGEONS
c/o W. Kemp Clark, M.D.
University of Texas Health
    Science Center   (214) 688-3530
Dallas, Texas 75235   Established 1920

W. Kemp Clark, M.D., Secretary
To further development of the field of neurological surgery; to carry on the traditions of the founding members who were the first in the world to appreciate the need for a society for neurological surgery. To bestow recognition upon men of outstanding ability and excellence in their work and teaching--both in universities and clinics in the United States and Canada. Such recognition may be bestowed by appointment to membership or by appearance on the programs at appropriate time. Membership: 200 (active, senior, honorary). Finances: Membership: $100; Other Sources: Annual meeting assessment. Meetings: Annual, various locations.

★ 1443 ★

SOCIETY OF PATIENT REPRESENTATIVES OF THE
    AMERICAN HOSPITAL ASSOCIATION
840 North Lake Shore Drive   (312) 280-6424
Chicago, Illinois 60611   Established 1972

Alexander B. Gekas
The Society is organized exclusively for charitable, scientific, and educational purposes as a not-for-profit association. The objectives of the Society are to promote the improvement and extension of adequate health service for all persons and to advance the development of effective patient relations programs in health care institutions by: conducting educational programs and activities to strengthen and develop patient relations programs; providing a medium for the interchange of ideas among members and dissemination of information to members; and disseminating

information on patient representative programs to health care institutions and agencies. Membership: 830 members (individuals employed by a health care institution or a health related public or private agency whose primary assignment is to represent patients in their relationship with health care institutions and services). Finances: Membership: $40. Meetings: 2 Spring Workshops and a Fall Annual Meeting and Conference. Publication: Newsletter, 4 to 5 times annually, Alexandra B. Gekas, editor; Essentials of a Patient Representative Program in Hospitals; Development and Implementation of a Patient's Bill of Rights in Hospitals; The Patient Representative's Participation in Risk Management. Affiliation: 19 Chapters affiliated with the Society of Patient Representatives.

★ 1444 ★
SOCIETY OF PELVIC SURGEONS
c/o George W. Morley, M.D.
Department of Obstetrics and Gynecology
University of Michigan
   Medical Center   (313) 764-8125
Ann Arbor, Michigan 48109   Established 1952

George H. Morley, M.D., Secretary-Treasurer
To bring together individuals whose special interest is the surgical treatment of diseases of the pelvis. Membership: Not to exceed 55 active members. Finances: Membership: $25. Meetings: Annual, various locations.

★ 1445 ★
SOCIETY OF PROSPECTIVE MEDICINE
4405 East-West Highway, Suite 404   (301) 657-4142
Bethesda, Maryland 20014   Established 1964

Patricia I. Horner, Executive Director
A Society for the promotion and maintenance of positive health practices through accurate and effective risk assessment and reduction programs. Goals are to advocate the concept of extending useful life expectancy by precursor recognition and reduction, to provide a forum for dissemination of risk reduction knowledge and encourage widespread use of this knowledge in risk reduction programs, to participate in the identification of appropriate precursors of disability and death, to advance the teaching of Prospective Medicine in medical and nursing schools, health departments, community hospitals and other appropriate educational forums, and to promote research and evaluation in the field of Prospective Medicine which provides guidance in risk reduction motivation. Membership: Approximately 400 (members and student members). Finances: Membership: Members, $35;

students, $15; Other Sources: Conferences, publications, contributions. Awards: Lewis C. Robbins Award given to persons who have contributed to the useful life expectancy of their fellowman. Meetings: Annual, various locations. Publications: Newsletter, usually every 3 to 4 months, Dr. Bill Hetler, editor; Proceedings, annually.

★ 1446 ★
SOCIETY OF REMEDIAL GYMNASTS
Kingston General Hospital
Beverley Road, Hull
N. Humberside, HU3 1UR, England (0482) 28631
   United Kingdom   Established 1946

W. R. Knight, Honorary Secretary
The Society of Remedial Gymnasts consists of Gymnasts who are qualified in rehabilitation treatment by exercise therapy. It's purpose is to advise and help members in their working environment, to circulate journals, literature, and other information, and to organize postgraduate courses, Congresses and meetings. Membership: Approximately 600 (full members who have taken the recognized training and examinations; associate membership is granted to a limited number of unqualified persons who have a proven ability and accepted level of experience). Finances: Membership: Full, 14 pounds sterling; associate, 12.75 pounds sterling (under review); Other Sources: Journal advertising and subscriptions to Journal. Awards: Fellowship of the Society for outstanding services. Publications: Remedial Gymnastics and Recreational Therapy, quarterly, Mrs. J. King, editor; Monthly Appointments; Circular (advertising vacancies for remedial gymnasts).

★ 1447 ★
SOCIETY OF TEACHERS OF FAMILY MEDICINE
1740 West 92nd Street   (816) 333-9700
Kansas City, Missouri 64114   Established 1967

Edward J. Shahady, M.D., President;
   F. Marian Bishop, Ph.D., MSPH, President-Elect
Formed to meet the needs of the multi-disciplined educators in family medicine, which is the academic arm of family practice. Purposes are to support the principles of family medicine as an academic discipline and to maintain and improve the quality of education in family medicine. Activities include a DHEW Pilot Program in Faculty Development, two academic meetings annually, co-sponsorship with AAFP in the Medical School Workshop, co-sponsorship with AAFP, ABFP and the Family Health Foundation of America in the Residency Assistance Program. Membership: 2,000 (physician, non-physician, resident/

fellow). Finances: Membership: Physician, $100; non-physician, $70; resident/fellow, $30. Awards: Past President Plaque; Recognition Award. Meetings: Annual, various locations; Fall Scientific Session in conjunction with the Association of American Medical Colleges. Publications: Family Medicine, bimonthly, Robert Martin, managing editor.

★ 1448 ★
SOCIETY OF THORACIC SURGEONS
111 East Wacker Drive   (312) 644-6610
Chicago, Illinois 60601   Established 1964

Walter G. Purcell, Business Manager
To improve the quality and practice of thoracic and cardiovascular surgery as a specialty; to strengthen and establish basic standards in the training programs of thoracic and cardiovascular surgery; to encourage clinical as well as basic research in the field of thoracic and cardiovascular surgery; to promote the professional development of those surgeons specializing in the field of thoracic and cardiovascular surgery and to encourage, represent, and sponsor those surgeons who have recently entered this field; and to provide a forum and publication for scientific presentations and discussions. Membership: 1,920 (active, senior). Finances: Membership dues; exhibition fees. Meetings: Annual, various locations. Publications: Annals of Thoracic Surgery, monthly, Herbert Aloan, editor.

★ 1449 ★
SOCIETY OF TOXICOLOGY
c/o William E. McCormick
475 Wolf Ledges Parkway   (216) 762-2289
Akron, Ohio 44311   Established 1961

William E. McCormick, Executive Secretary
The Society aims to promote the extension of knowledge in toxicology and to facilitate the exchange of information among its members as well as among investigators of other scientific disciplines. The activities primarily concern the planning and sponsorship of an annual scientific meeting, but the Society is also regularly involved in major toxicological issues of the time. Membership: 1,250. Finances: Membership: $85. Awards: Arnold J. Letiman Award; Achievement, Education Meritorious Award. Meetings: Annual, various locations. Publications: Toxicology and Applied Pharmacology (Academic Press), monthly; Fundamental and Applied Toxicology, bimonthly.

★ 1450 ★
SOCIETY OF UNIVERSITY SURGEONS
Department of Surgery, SUNY Downstate
   Medical Center
450 Clarkson Avenue   (212) 270-1975
Brooklyn, New York 11203   Established 1938

Bernard M. Jaffe, M.D., Secretary
To advance the art and science of surgery by the encouragement of members to pursue original investigations both in the clinic and in the laboratory; the development of methods of graduate teaching of surgery with particular reference to the resident system; free and informal interchange of ideas pertaining to the above subjects as a limited membership and common aims make possible. Membership: 825 (active, senior). Finances: Membership: $50. Meetings: Annual, various locations.

★ 1451 ★
SOUTHEASTERN SURGICAL CONGRESS
315 Boulevard Northeast   (404) 681-3636
Atlanta, Georgia 30312   Established 1930

A. H. Letton, M.D., Secretary-Director
To establish and maintain an association of surgeons and allied specialties not for pecuniary profit, but for benefit of humanity by advancing the education of its membership in the science of surgery and the ethical and competent practice of its arts. Membership: 2,750 (honorary, regular, inactive). Finances: Membership: Regular, $50. Awards: Certificate and paperweight awarded for most outstanding paper submitted for a Forum on Progress in Surgery. Meetings: Annual, various locations in Southeastern states. Publication: American Surgeon, Arlie R. Mansberger, M.D., editor.

★ 1452 ★
SOUTHERN COUNCIL OF OPTOMETRISTS
2030 Pernoshal Court   (404) 451-8206
Atlanta, Georgia 30338   Established 1924

Sam J. Galloway, Jr., Executive Director
To promote the continuing education of optometrists. Membership: 3,500 (optometrists). Finances: Membership: $2. Awards: Optometrist of the Year; Award of Merit. Meetings: Annual, Atlanta, Georgia. Publication: Southern Journal of Optometry, monthly, Frank Gibson, editor. Affiliation: 12 southern state associations.

★ 1453 ★

SOUTHERN MEDICAL ASSOCIATION
2601 Highland Avenue
Post Office Box 2446   (205) 323-4400
Birmingham, Alabama 35201   Established 1906

William J. Ranieri, Executive Vice President
To develop and foster scientific medicine. It shall
have no direct connection with or control over any
other society or organization, nor shall it at any time
be controlled by any other society or organization.
All meetings of the Association shall be for the sole
purpose of reading and discussing papers pertaining to
the science of medicine, to public health and to medical education. The Association shall not at any
time take active part in any economic, political or
sectarian questions, or concerted movements for securing legislative enactments. Membership: 25,000
(active, practicing physicians). Finances: Membership: $50 annually. Awards: Distinguished Ser-
vice Award; Research Medal; Seale Harris Medal.
Meetings: Annual, various locations. Publications:
Southern Medical Journal, monthly, John B. Thomison,
M.D., editor; Southern Medicine.

★ 1454 ★

SOUTHERN PSYCHIATRIC ASSOCIATION
800 St. Mary's Street
Post Office Box 10387   (919) 821-2226
Raleigh, North Carolina 27605

Annette S. Boutwell, Executive Secretary;
   Robert L. Green, Jr., M.D., Secretary-Treasurer
To further the study of all subjects pertaining to the
cause, treatment, and prevention of psychiatric disorders; to promote the interests, maintenance, and
the advancement of standards in public and private
hospitals for psychiatric disorders, or outpatient clinics, and of all other agencies concerned with the
medical, social, and legal aspects of these disorders;
to further psychiatric education and research; and to
increase psychiatric knowledge in other branches of
medicine and in other sciences and to furnish the
public with the proper concept of psychiatric disease.
Membership: Up to 300 members and fellows; also
have honorary, life fellows, associate and corresponding members (these are members who live outside the
area of SPA). Finances: Membership: Dues, $40
annually. Awards: Resident Training Research
Award presented to deserving and qualifying residents,
a committee reviews abstracts and papers, the winning
paper is presented at the annual meeting as part of
the scientific programs. Meetings: Annual, early
October, various locations (selected 5 years in advance and approved by the membership). Publication: Newsletter to Members, July and December,
Annette S. Boutwell, Executive Secretary, editor.

Affiliation: Affiliated with the American Psychiatric
Association.

★ 1455 ★

SOUTHERN SOCIETY FOR CLINICAL INVESTI-
GATION
University of Texas Health Science Center
Department of Medicine
7703 Floyd Curl Drive   (512) 691-6511
San Antonio, Texas 78284   Established 1946

Jay H. Stein, M.D., Secretary-Treasurer
The encouragement of research in the various medical
sciences and the establishment of a forum from which
new ideas may be presented to the medical profession at large. Membership: 538 (active, emeritus,
honorary). Finances: Membership: Active, $15;
emeritus, $7.50; Other Sources: Contributions for
support of annual meeting. Awards: Founders
Medal; Student Research Awards. Meetings: Annual.

★ 1456 ★

SOUTHERN SOCIETY OF CLINICAL SURGEONS
1 Cross Creek
901 West Faris Road   (803) 233-4349
Greenville, South Carolina 29605 Established 1926

J. D. Ashmore, Jr., M.D., Secretary
For interchange of professional thought and study of
surgery. Each year the Society meets in a Surgical
Center in the United States or Canada for a 3-day
meeting. Operative clinics are attended in the
morning and surgical papers are presented by the
Department of Surgery of the institution visited in the
afternoon. Membership: 50 (general, thoracic and
vascular surgeons). Finances: Membership: $45;
Other Sources: Assessments. Meetings: Annual,
various locations.

★ 1457 ★

SOUTHERN SOCIETY OF ORTHODONTISTS
3355 Lenox Road, N.E., Suite 1120 (414) 261-5528
Atlanta, Georgia 30326   Established 1921

John K. Ottley, Jr., Executive Director
To advance the science and art of orthodontics; to
encourage and sponsor research; to strive for higher
standards of excellence in orthodontic education and
practice; to contribute its part in dental health service; and to promote fraternal relationship among its
members. Membership: 1,184 (active, affiliate,
honorary, retired). Finances: Membership: $110.

Awards: Distinguished Service Award. Meetings: Annual, various southern cities. Publication: Newsletter, semiannual. Affiliation: Constituent of American Association of Orthodontists.

★ 1458 ★
SOUTHERN SURGEONS CLUB
c/o Harlan Stone, M.D.
Department of Surgery
69 Butler Street
Atlanta, Georgia 30303   Established 1940

A small organization composed of surgeons which meets once yearly at various medical centers. A scientific program is presented by the staff of the medical school where the meeting is held each year and various social functions are also planned. Membership: 46. Finances: Membership: $100 annually. Meeting : Annual, various locations.

★ 1459 ★
SOUTHERN THORACIC SURGICAL ASSOCIATION
University Station   (205) 934-3202
Birmingham, Alabama 35294   Established 1953

Richard B. McElvein, M.D., Secretary-Treasurer
To disseminate knowledge and information and to stimulate progress in the field of Thoracic and Cardiovasculary Surgery in the states comprising the organization. Membership: 595 (active, honorary and senior). Finances: Membership: $65 annually; Other Sources: Registration and exhibits at Annual Meeting. Meeting : Annual, November, various locations. Publications: Papers presented at annual meeting are presented to the Annals of Thoracic Surgery.

SPRINGS (GEORGIA WARM) FOUNDATION
See: Georgia Warm Springs Foundation

★ 1460 ★
STROKE CLUB INTERNATIONAL
805 12th Street   (713) 762-1022
Galveston, Texas 77550   Established 1968

Ellis Williamson, President
The Club has been established to provide a special kind of group therapy for stroke victims, with members helping each other in overcoming their handicaps. Stress is placed on what stroke victims can do as opposed to what they are unable to do, and in line with this philosophy, only stroke victims can vote,

hold office, or serve on committees. Membership: 5,000 (active, stroke victims; associate, family members and friends). Finances: Other Sources: Contributions. Publication: International Stroke Club Bulletin, monthly, Ellis Williamson, editor. Library: Galveston Stroke Club Library, 200 volumes. Former Name: Stroke Club of America.

STROKE CLUB OF AMERICA
See: Stroke Club International

★ 1461 ★
STUDENT AMERICAN PHARMACEUTICAL
ASSOCIATION (SAPhA)
2215 Constitution Avenue, N.W.   (202) 628-4410
Washington, D.C. 20037   Established 1954

Ronald L. Williams, Pharmacist, Executive Secretary; Donna J. Walker, Pharmacist, Special Assistant for Subdivision Activities
Aims are to (1) aid and support the objectives of the American Pharmaceutical Association; (2) improve the public health; (3) foster and encourage interprofessional relations for the promotion of public health; (4) improve the science of pharmacy for the general welfare of the public; and (5) provide direct methods for pharmacy students to carry out the above objectives, as well as to enhance interprofessional programs and health conditions on their own campuses and in the communities of this nation. Membership: 14,000 (undergraduate students regularly enrolled in pre-pharmacy or pharmacy programs in a university or college of pharmacy accredited by the American Council on Pharmaceutical Education). Finances: Membership: $10; Other Sources: Contributions from pharmaceutical companies. Meetings: Annual with the American Pharmaceutical Association, 8 midyear meetings for the SAPhA Regions held in the fall. Publication: The Pharmacy Student, quarterly. Affiliation: American Pharmaceutical Association.

SUPERSENSONICS INTERNATIONAL DIVINING
ASSOCIATION
See: Research Institute for Supersensonic Healing Energies

SURGICAL TRADE FOUNDATION
See: American Surgical Trade Association

★ 1462 ★
SWEDISH CANCER SOCIETY
Sturegatan 14   (08) 63 58 40
S-11436 Stockholm, Sweden   Established 1951

Dagmar von Walden Laing, General Secretary;
    Bengt Gustafsson, Professor, Chairman of Scientific
    Board; Erling Norrby, Professor, Chairman of
    Public Education Committee
To support, organize and coordinate cancer research,
the main emphasis dealing with attempts to clarify
mechanisms behind the appearance of cancer; to
promote the development of new methods of detections
and treatment of cancer; to provide information about
cancer research, prevention, symptoms and treatment
of malignant diseases. Membership: 4,500 individual members; 150 associations and societies (38 nationwide organizations, affiliated to the Society ap-
point principals who elect the Society's Board of
Directors). Finances: Membership: 20 Skr annually, individual members; 100 Skr annually, associations, etc.; Other Sources: Gifts and bequests-
donations amounted to Skr 21.7 million in 1979;
government grant Skr 3 million annually. Research
Funds: In 1979, research grants were awarded to 130
scientists, total amount Skr 30 million. Publications:
Cancer (in Swedish), semiannually, Erling Norrby,
editor; Current Projects, annual, Bengt Gustafsson,
editor.

★ 1463 ★
SYNANON CHURCH
6055 Marshall
Petaluma Road
Marshall, California 94940
Mailing Address:
Post Office Box 786   (415) 663-8111
Marshall, California 94940   Established 1958

Cecilia Jason Dederich, Chairman of the Board;
    Ronald V. Cook, Chief Executive Officer;
    Lawrence H. Akey, President
Synanon was established in 1958 by Charles E.
Dederich. It's earliest work was to develop methods
for re-education and re-orientation of drug addicts
and other character disordered persons. Synanon
continues to maintain religious communities in which
this work is carried on. More recently, Synanon has
established the Synanon Distribution Network. This
charitable arm of the Synanon Church secures donations of materials which manufacturers and farmers
have produced in surplus. These products are distributed to other charitable organizations and needy
individuals throughout the United States and the world.
In 1980, Synanon provided 9 million meals for needy
individuals. Membership: Synanon Distribution Network reaches many thousands of people. Finances:

Other Sources: Synanon's operating funds come from
donations and proceeds from its operational operations;
there is no fee for membership. Publications: The
Synanon Story, quarterly; I Am Betty D.; Betty
Dederich "No Time for Yeah, But". Former Name:
Synanon Foundation, Inc.

SYNANON FOUNDATION, INC.
    See: Synanon Church

T

★ 1464 ★
TAPES FOR THE BLIND, INC.
7852 Cole Street   (213) 923-3388
Downey, California 90242   Established 1968

Harold C. Barnett, President;
    Dr. Ben L. Pacheco, Jr., Secretary
To supply recording tapes and cassettes to the Blind
or physically handicapped throughout the world.
Sources of the magnetic tapes include major aerospace
companies so the tapes are extremely well suited for
recording the entire range of audio frequencies, from
voice through the range of instrumental music. State
Rehabilitation Centers throughout the United States
are major customers. The U.S. Government provides
free postage anywhere in the world and in some
countries shipments of the tapes are admitted free of
custom's duties.

★ 1465 ★
TERATOLOGY SOCIETY
c/o A. G. Hendrick, Ph.D.
University of California
California Primate Research Center   (916) 752-3045
Davis, California 95616   Established 1961

Andrew G. Hendrick, Ph.D., Secretary
The objective of the Society is to stimulate scientific
interest in and to promote the exchange of ideas and
information about problems of abnormal biological development and malformation at the fundamental or
clinical level. Membership: 562 (medical doctors
and scientists internationally). Finances: $25 an-
nually; Other Sources: Sustaining memberships.
Meetings: Annually, various locations. Publications: Teratology, The International Journal of Abnormal Development, bimonthly, Robert Brent, editor.

THOMAS A. DOOLEY FOUNDATION, INC.
  See: Dooley Foundation/INTERMED-USA, Inc.

★ 1466 ★
THOMAS JEFFERSON RESEARCH CENTER
1143 North Lake Avenue   (213) 798-0791
Pasadena, California 91104   Established 1963

Frank Goble, President
The Center exists to conduct interdisciplinary study in
the social and behavioral sciences with particular
emphasis on practical applications.   Other activities
include the publication of books, pamphlets, reports,
and magazine articles; and the promotion of seminars,
lectures, and consultation in applied psychology
(management, therapy, rehabilitation, motivation,
communications, and the development of personal potential).   Membership: 646.   Finances: Membership: Regular, $15; associate, $25; sustaining, $50;
life, $5,000; Other Sources: Contributions from in-
dividuals, corporations, and foundations; publication
sales; lecture fees; consultation fees.   Publication:
Thomas Jefferson Research Letter, monthly, Frank
Goble, editor.

★ 1467 ★
TISSUE CULTURE ASSOCIATION, INC.
1 Bank Street, Suite 210   (301) 869-2900
Gaithersburg, Maryland 20760   Established 1946

William G. Momberger, Executive Director
To promote scientific knowledge concerning the growth,
maintenance and experimental use of tissue cells in
vitro.   Membership: 2,300.   Finances: Membership: Regular, $50; students, $15; Other Sources:
Meetings.   Awards: Wilton Earle Award.   Meetings: Annual, various locations.   Publications: In
Vitro, monthly, M. K. Patterson, editor; Report,
bimonthly, N. Beales, editor; Journal of Tissue Culture Methods, L. R. Murrell, editor.

★ 1468 ★
TRANSPLANTATION SOCIETY
State University of New York at Stony Brook
T-19, Room 040   (516) 246-2209
Stony Brook, New York 11794   Established 1964

Felix T. Rapaport, M.D., President
Intent of the Society is to foster and encourage research and exchange of information on experimental
and clinical transportation and experimental immuno-
biology.   Membership: 2,000.   Finances: Membership: $15.   Publications: Transplantation, monthly,

E. Eichwald, editor;   Transplantation Proceedings,
F. Rapaport, editor.

U

★ 1469 ★
UKRAINIAN ACADEMY OF MEDICAL SCIENCES
c/o Roman S. Oryshkevich, M.D.
University of Illinois Hospital
Department of Physical Medicine & Rehabilitation
Post Office Box 6998
Chicago, Illinois 60680   Established 1979

Roman S. Oryshkevich, M.D., Secretary
Academic-Scientific Organization consisting of scientists of Ukrainian descent, who are diplomats of
their specialty boards, have faculty position at the
minimum rank of assistant professor and actively engaged in clinical, educational and scientific work in
all aspects of medicine and surgery.   Membership:
50 (active).   Finances: Membership: $8.   Meet-
ings: Annual, various locations; Newsletter, semiannually.

★ 1470 ★
UKRAINIAN MEDICAL ASSOCIATION OF NORTH
  AMERICA
2316 West Chicago Avenue   (312) 235-8883
Chicago, Illinois 60622   Established 1950

M. Charkewych, M.D., President;
   M. Kolenskyi, D.D.S., Secretary
Sponsors continuing education, conventions; helps
students financially.   Membership: 1,000 (physicians,
dentists, pharmacists in USA and Canada).   Finances:
$100 annually; Other Sources: Voluntary donations.
Meetings: Annual.   Publications: Journal of Ukrain-
ian Medical Association of North America, quarterly,
Paul J. Dzul, M.D., editor; History of Ukrainian
Medicine.

★ 1471 ★
UNDERSEA MEDICAL SOCIETY, INC.
9650 Rockville Pike   (301) 530-9225
Bethesda, Maryland 20014   Established 1967

Charles W. Shilling, M.D., Executive Secretary
The Society has been organized to aid the advancement of undersea medicine and its supporting sciences
and to develop channels of scientific communications
among all researchers dedicated to the safe penetration

of the oceans by man.   Membership: 1,750.   Finances: Membership: Regular, $40; associates, $15; corporate, $500; students, $15; Other Sources: Contracts with federal agencies.   Awards: Albert R. Behnke Award;   Link Foundation Stover-Link Award; Oceaneering International Award.   Publications: Undersea Biomedical Research, quarterly; Pressure, 6 times annually.   Library: Hyperbaric Information Center Library, 8,000 documents.   Affiliation: European Undersea Biomedical Society.

★ 1472 ★

UNITED CANCER COUNCIL, INC.
1803 North Meridian Street   (317) 923-6490
Indianapolis, Indiana 46202   Established 1963

Helen L. Clayton, Executive Director
The Council works to promote and encourage programs of research...public and professional education and service; to coordinate efforts of member agencies; to facilitate exchange of ideas, plans, programs and procedures among similar associations, and to recognize at all times that each member agency retains complete autonomy in the conduct of local affairs and programs and associates in and with the Council on a completely voluntary basis.   The Council's three main interests are service to cancer patients and their families; public and professional education; and research to find a cure for cancer.   Membership: 50 United Way Agencies.   Finances: Percentage of United Way Allocations.   Publications: Coordinator, quarterly, Helen L. Clayton, editor; monographs and pamphlets.

★ 1473 ★

UNITED CEREBRAL PALSY ASSOCIATIONS, INC.
66 East 34th Street   (212) 889-6655
New York, New York 10016   Established 1949

Earl H. Cunerd, Executive Director
The group was founded as a national movement by parents of children with cerebral palsy.   Its purposes are to provide community services to persons with cerebral palsy and their families which will aid in rehabilitation and life enrichment, to educate the public about cerebral palsy and its prevention, and to foster research and scientific training of care personnel. Membership: 276 representatives of state and local affiliates.   Finances: Public contributions, government grants.   Awards: Funds for research and professional training related to Cerebral Plasy; Weinstein-Goldenson Award; Isabelle and Leonard H. Goldenson Award for Technology; Roger S. Firestone Award; Distinguished Service Award; President's Award; Awards for Campaign; Consumer Activities; Man-Made Environment Program Services; Public Relations;

Women's Activities and Youth Activities.   Meetings: Annual, various locations.   Publications: UC People, quarterly; Word from Washington, monthly, E. Clarke Ross, editor.   Affiliations: 247 state and local organizations.

★ 1474 ★

UNITED OSTOMY ASSOCIATION, INC.
2001 West Beverly Boulevard   (213) 413-5510
Los Angeles, California 90057   Established 1962

Donald P. Binder, Executive Director
Dedicated to helping every ostomy patient return to normal living through mutual aid and moral support; education in proper ostomy care and management; exchange of ideas; assistance in improving ostomy equipment and supplies; advancement of knowledge of gastro-intestinal diseases; cooperation with other organizations having common purposes; exhibits at medical and public meetings; and public education about ostomy.   Membership: Approximately 43,000. Finances: Membership: $5; Other Sources: Fund raising, publication sales.   Awards: San Dubin Award.   Meetings: Annual, regional, various locations.   Publications: Ostomy Quarterly, quarterly; care and management manuals.

★ 1475 ★

UNITED PARKINSON FOUNDATION
220 South State Street   (312) 922-9734
Chicago, Illinois 60604   Established 1963

Edgar N. Greenebaum, Jr., Chairman
The Foundation is dedicated to promote and support scientific research in Parkinson's disease and related illnesses and to assist patients through educational materials, such as newsletters, and also referrals to competent medical care.   Membership: Approximately 20,000 individuals.   Finances: Contributions. Research Funds: Presently supporting the work of several clinical research neurologists, as recommended by Medical Advisory Board.   Meetings: Quadrennial, various locations.   Publication: Newsletters, 3-4 annually, Judy Rosner.

★ 1476 ★

UNITED STATES CONFERENCE OF CITY HEALTH
    OFFICERS
1620 Eye Street, N.W.   (202) 293-7306
Washington, D.C. 20006   Established 1961

John J. Gunther, Executive Director
Founded by the United States Conference of Mayors

as an affiliated organization to promote public health administration, exchange information on public health, foster intergovernmental relations in the health field. Activities include publication of a bimonthly newsletter and other forms of communication with federal, state, county, and city public health agencies and other public and private providers and organizations concerned with preventive and curative health services. Membership: Directors of city and city-county health departments. Finances: Membership: Cities 2 million and over, $1,500; 650,000 to 2 million, $1,000; 500,000 to 650,000, $600; 250,000 to 500,000, $500; 250,000 to 100,000, $250; below 100,000, $100. Meetings: Semiannual roundtables; Annual, in conjunction with the American Public Health Association. Publication: City Health Officers News, bimonthly, Deborah E. Lamm, editor. Affiliations: United States Conference of Mayors.

★ 1477 ★
UNITED STATES PHARMACOPEIAL CONVENTION, INC.
12601 Twinbrook Parkway   (301) 881-0666
Rockville, Maryland 20852   Established 1820

William M. Heller, Ph.D., Executive Director
To develop and publish for medicinals and drugs objective standards of purity, potency, identify, and packaging and labeling; to participate in programs having the object of establishing names and standards for drugs on the national and international levels; and to encourage and promote the science and art of medicine and pharmacy. Membership: Approximately 300 (1 delegate from each school of medicine and pharmacy, each national and state medical and pharmaceutical association, and some departments of the U.S. Government). Finances: Sale of publications and sale of USP Reference Standards. Meetings: Every 5 years, usually in Washington, D.C. Publications: Pharmacopeial Forum, Bimonthly, USP Headquarters staff, including editorial department; USP DI Review, bimonthly, USP Drug Information Division; USP Dispensing Information, annual, William M. Heller, Ph.D., editor; USAN and the USP Dictionary of Drug Names, annual, Mary C. Griffiths, Chief, editorial department; The United States Pharmacopeia and The National Formulary, every 5 years, USP Headquarters staff, including editorial department; About Your Medicines (abridged Consumer edition of USP DI), USP Drug Information Division; USP DI About Your Medicines (complete reference edition), USP Drug Information Division. Library: USPC Library, about 400 volumes.

★ 1478 ★
UNITED WAY OF AMERICA
801 North Fairfax Street   (703) 836-7100
Alexandria, Virginia 22314   Established 1918

William Aramony, National Executive
To raise funds efficiently, to allocate the funds effectively and to plan and coordinate health and welfare programs. Provides its membership with services to strengthen local fund raising and community planning. Membership: Approximately 2,200 local groups. Publications: Community Focus Magazine, 10 times annually; Directory, annually; Digest of Selected Current Reports, semiannually; Publications Catalog, annually; Executive Newsletter, weekly. Library: Information Center, 3,000 reports, 300 books.

★ 1479 ★
UNIVERSITIES ASSOCIATED FOR RESEARCH AND
     EDUCATION IN PATHOLOGY
9650 Rockville Pike   (301) 530-7130
Bethesda, Maryland 20014   Established 1965

Benjamin F. Trump, M.D., President
To initiate, sponsor and encourage biomedical research and educational projects; to assist in the development of research and educational programs in the natural and biological sciences in the Universities and Colleges of the United States and in all foreign countries; to foster, encourage and conduct research and education for the United States of America or any of its departments or agencies, for any state or municipal governmental body and for any foreign government or subdivision thereof in all branches of science, including but not limited to those sciences associated with the field of pathology; to seek and receive grants, bequests, gifts, devices and loans of property of whatever kind or nature from any source whatsoever to promote the state objectives of this corporation; and to establish, maintain and operate medical, research, training, and other facilities in any locality where and as required for the achievement and advancement of the foregoing purposes. Finances: Other Sources: Research grants. Publications: Various monographs.

UNIVERSITY ASSOCIATION FOR EMERGENCY
MEDICAL SERVICES
     See: University Association for Emergency
          Medicine

★ 1480 ★
UNIVERSITY ASSOCIATION FOR EMERGENCY
    MEDICINE
900 West Ottawa
Post Office Box 17037   (517) 485-5484
Lansing, Michigan 48915   Established 1970

W. Kendall McNabney, M.D., President;
    Mary Ann Dye, Executive Manager
The University Association for Emergency Medicine
(UREM) has as its primary objective improving the
quality and delivery of care to the acutely ill and injured through educational programs centered in teaching hospitals.   Objective is pursued by collecting
and disseminating information concerning the operation
of emergency medical services; providing a forum for
the discussion of problems in emergency medicine;
aiding the university physician in the planning, administration and provision of emergency medical services and developing guidelines for those activities;
recommending appropriate changes in emergency medical services legislation at the local, regional and national levels; and encouraging academic recognition
for work in this field by teaching physicians. Membership: 503 (emergency physicians with faculty appointments are eligible for active membership; associate membership is designed for resident physicians in
emergency medicine). Finances: Active membership,
$100 annually. Meetings: Annual, usually in the
spring, various locations. Publications: Annals of
Emergency Medicine, monthly, Ronald L. Krome,
M.D., editor. Former Name: University Association for Emergency Medical Services.

★ 1481 ★
UPPER MIDWEST HOSPITAL CONFERENCE
2221 University Avenue, S.E.   (612) 331-5571
Minneapolis, Minnesota 55414   Established 1945

Sylvia Sodman, Conference Coordinator
Conducts an educational program in all phases of hospital administration and its allied groups.   Promotes
educational exhibits and commercial and industrial
exhibits so that member hospitals and invited allied
groups may be acquainted with all of the latest information regarding hospital techniques and equipment.
Membership: Approximately 1,500 hospitals and
health care facilities in upper midwest. Finances:
Exhibition fees. Meetings: Annual, Minneapolis,
Minnesota.

V

★ 1482 ★
VETERANS HOSPITAL RADIO AND TELEVISION
    GUILD
1841 Broadway   (212) 757-8659
New York, New York 10023

Alex F. Courtney, Executive Director
A recreation kind of service to the vet-patients.   To
encourage and train hospitalized veterans to perform
in their own radio and television programs for broadcast over closed circuit networks in the hospitals.
Membership: 650 (professional actors, writers, producers, musicians and others who serve as volunteers
in Veterans Administration hospitals).

★ 1483 ★
VICTORIAN ORDER OF NURSES OF CANADA
5 Blackburn Avenue
Ottawa, Ontario K1N 8A2,   (613) 233-5694
    Canada   Established 1897

Ada E. McEwen, National Director
To establish and maintain visiting nursing services in
Canada; to engage and direct the activities of nurses
to undertake the care of the sick in their own homes,
to demonstrate nursing methods and to aid in the prevention of disease and the maintenance of health; to
assist with the education of nurses; to assist in establishing and maintaining the highest possible standard of efficiency in all nursing services. Membership: Approximately 800 nurses, local boards comprised of lay and professional members. Finances:
Other Sources: Government payments, United Fund
Appeals, government grants, local campaigns, patients' fees. Awards: VON bursaries of $2,500 are
awarded annually to assist nurses in taking preparation
in nursing at a Canadian university; VON bursaries
of up to $9,000 are awarded for 2 years of study for
a Master's or post-Master's degree in an approved
area of study. Meetings: Annual, various locations.
Library: National Office, over 600 volumes.

VISION INSTITUTE OF AMERICA
    See: Vision Service Plan

★ 1484 ★
VISION SERVICE PLAN
7711 Carondelet Boulevard
Suite 807   (314) 725-6500
St. Louis, Missouri 63105   Established 1964

Robert E. Atwood, President
A non-profit corporation created by the optometric
profession to bring vision care to groups by coordinating the services and operations of state and regional corporations.   Membership: 44 vision service
plans in 48 states.   Meetings: Annual, various locations.   Former Name: Vision Institute of America.

★ 1485 ★
VITAMIN INFORMATION BUREAU, INC.
664 North Michigan Avenue   (312) 751-2223
Chicago, Illinois 60611   Established 1967

Caryl M. Wright, President
The Bureau was formed by several pharmaceutical
manufacturers to promote a better public and professional understanding of the role of vitamins and minerals in nutrition.   Present emphasis is on the sale
of nutrition education materials.   Finances: Other
Sources: Publication sales.   Publications: Wall
Charts on vitamins and minerals; filmstrips; school
and adult leaflets.

★ 1486 ★
VOCATIONAL EVALUATION AND WORK
    ADJUSTMENT ASSOCIATION
c/o National Rehabilitation Association
633 South Washington   (703) 836-0850
Alexandria, Virginia 22314

A Division of the National Rehabilitation Association
(see separate entry).   The purpose of VEWAA is to
improve and advance the field of vocational evaluation and work adjustment training of handicapped persons by use of simulated and/or real work in order to
enhance the habilitation or rehabilitation of said persons.   Membership: Professional member; associate
member; student member (enrolled in accredited college program related to vocational evaluation or work
adjustment training of handicapped persons).   All
members of VEWAA must be members of the National
Rehabilitation Association.   Awards: Mini-grants for
research projects.   Publications: VEWAA Newsletter,
quarterly; VEWAA Bulletin.

★ 1487 ★
VOLUNTEER SERVICES FOR THE BLIND (VSB)
919 Walnut Street   (215) 627-0600
Philadelphia, Pennsylvania 19107   Established 1920

Richard B. Wathey, Ph.D., Executive Director
Volunteer Services for the Blind began 60 years ago
as a chapter of the American Red Cross to held
blinded World War I veterans become self-supporting.
Today the organization is expanded and provides worldwide services to the blind and visually impaired with
Braille, large type and sound recordings.   Membership: Approximately 1,200 contributors.   Finances:
Other Sources: Foundation grants, corporate support.
Meetings: Monthly, from February to November,
Philadelphia, Pennsylvania.   Publications: Blind
Data Processor, bimonthly; Consumers' Research,
monthly; Jack & Jill, 10 issues annually; Journal
of Rehabilitation, quarterly; Ladies Home Journal,
monthly; Seventeen, monthly; Teen Magazine,
monthly; numerous periodicals and textbooks, including mathematics and language texts; pamphlets;
novels and other materials for students, professional
people and all others who may have need--braille or
recorded on cassette.   Remarks: Cassette - 4 track,
15/16 i.p.s. playable on the Library of Congress 4
track, 2 speed player available at your Regional Library at no charge to USA citizens.   Others may
purchase a machine from The American Printing House
f/t Blind, Inc., 1839 Frankfort Avenue, Louisville,
Kentucky 40206.   Inquiries concerning other ma-
chines may be made to SFB Products, Box 385,
Wayne, Pennsylvania 19087.

W

★ 1488 ★
WATER POLLUTION CONTROL FEDERATION
2626 Pennsylvania Avenue, N.W.   (202) 337-2500
Washington, D.C. 20037   Established 1928

Robert A. Canham, Executive Director
The Water Pollution Control Federation is a membership organization devoted to the development and
dissemination of technical information concerning the
nature, collection, treatment, and disposal of domestic and industrial wastewater.   The Federation has
held as an integral part of its mandate the pledge to
act as a source of education to the general public as
well as to individuals engaged in the field of water
pollution control.   Membership: 30,000 (active
membership, corporate membership, student membership, consultant membership, associate membership).
Finances: Membership: $35 annually; Other Sources:
Journal subscriptions and advertising.   Meetings:

Annual, various locations. Publications: Journal Water Pollution Control Federation, monthly, Peter J. Piecuch, editor; Highlights, monthly, Peter J. Piecuch, editor.

★ 1489 ★
WESTERN ASSOCIATION OF PHYSICIANS
c/o Allen Goldfein, M.D.
School of Medicine
University of California   (415) 666-9000
San Francisco, California 94102   Established 1956

Allen Goldfein, M.D., Secretary-Treasurer
To bring together for the purpose of discussion and presentation of observations and ideas, persons residing in the Western region of the United States and Canada who have achieved and sustained distinction in clinical research or creative scholarship in the bio-medical sphere. Membership: 258. Finances: Membership: $14. Awards: Kroc Foundation Distinguished Lectureship, awarded annually. Meetings: Annual, Carmel, California.

★ 1490 ★
WESTERN PHARMACOLOGY SOCIETY
Department of Pharmacology
UCLA School of Medicine   (213) 825-5447
Los Angeles, California 90024   Established 1953

Peter Lomax, M.D., D.Sc., Treasurer-Editor
To promote pharmacological knowledge and to facilitate its utilization among scientists. Membership: 250 (residents living west of the Mississippi, in Western Canada, or in Mexico with a record of investigative work in the broad field of the action of drugs on life processes). Finances: Membership: $10; Other Sources: Donations. Awards: Award for Distinguished Service to Pharmacology, irregular intervals. Meetings: Annual, West Coast. Publication: Proceedings of the Western Pharmacology Society, annually, Peter Lomax, editor.

★ 1491 ★
WESTERN SURGICAL ASSOCIATION
c/o R. Dale Liechty, M.D.
University of Colorado, Department of Surgery
Health Sciences Center B-192
4200 East 9th Avenue   (303) 394-8055
Denver, Colorado 80262   Established 1891

R. Dale Liechty, M.D., Secretary
Established for the cultivation, promotion, and diffusion of knowledge of the art and science of surgery

and the sponsorship and maintenance of the highest standards of practice. Membership: 550 (active, senior, honorary). Finances: Membership: $40 annually. Meetings: Annual, in November, various locations. Publications: Abstracts presented at annual meeting in November are then published in Archives of Surgery the following spring.

WHITNEY (HELEN HAY) FOUNDATION
   See: Helen Hay Whitney Foundation

★ 1492 ★
WILKINSON FOUNDATION, INC.
1812 Carlton Road, S.W.
Roanoke, Virginia 24015   Established 1948

Robert J. Wilkinson, Jr., President
To expand funds for medical research, medical education, treatment of indigent sick, and furtherance of the well-being of mankind. Membership: Board of Trustees consisting of 7 members. Finances: Contributions. Meetings: Board, quarterly, Huntington, West Virginia. Publications: Findings of 2 studies on medical indigency and recreation in the South.

WOMEN'S VETERINARY MEDICAL ASSOCIATION
   See: Association for Women Veterinarians

★ 1493 ★
WORLD ASSOCIATION FOR BUIATRICS
c/o Dr. M. Stöber
Rinderklinik, Bischofshder Damm 15
D-3000 Hannover, Federal Republic (0511) 8113243
   of Germany   Established 1960

Dr. M. Stöber, Secretary General
The objectives of the Association to organize meetings on cattle diseases in order to report the results of research work and practical experiences in this field, and to discuss the topics on an international basis and thus promote buiatrics in science and practice. Membership: 700 individual members and 4,100 collective members. Finances: Fees of the meetings. Meetings: Biennial, various locations. Publications: The Bovine Practitioner, annual, Dr. Eric Williams, editor; Proceedings of meetings. Affiliations: Deutsche Gruppe fur Buiatrik in der Deutschen Veterinarmedizinischen Gesellschaft; American Association of Bovine Practitioners; Societa Italiana di Buiatria; Sociedad Latinoamericana de Buiatria; L'Société Francaise de Buiatrie; British Cattle

Veterinary Association; Australian Association of Cattle Veterinarians; Asociación Mexicana de Medicos Veterinarios Especialistas en Bovinos; Asociación de los Veterinarios Españoles de Buiatria; Indian Society for Buiatrics; Nederlandse Groep Geneeskunde van het Rund; Israel Association for Buiatrics; Rural (Bovine) Practitioners' Group of the South African Veterinary Association; Irish Cattle Association.

★ 1494 ★

WORLD ASSOCIATION FOR THE ADVANCEMENT
    OF VETERINARY PARASITOLOGY
Secretariat, c/o Department Appl. Helminth.
    and Entomology
Veterinary School
Aristotelian University   (031) 991-2655
Thessaloniki, Greece   Established 1963

Professor S. M. Gaafar, President (West Lafayette,
    Indiana); Professor C. A. Himonas, Secretary-
    Treasurer (Thessaloniki, Greece)
To encourage research in veterinary parasitology and
to promote exchange of information and material between individuals and organizations interested in this
field; to organize meetings for the study of parasites
of veterinary importance.   WAAVP is not a federation of national societies but is operating on a basis
of individual interest.   Membership: 301 members
from 50 countries (active and honorary).   Finances:
Membership: $5 annual fee.   Awards: Honorary
memberships.   Meetings: Biennial Conferences, various locations.   Every 4 years the conference follows
the World Veterinary Congress (same place, 1 week
before or after it).   Publication: Proceedings of the
Conferences, biennially, Dr. E. J. L. Soulsby, editor (Cambridge, England).   Affiliations: World Veterinary Association; World Federation of Parasitologists.

★ 1495 ★

WORLD ASSOCIATION OF SOCIETIES OF
    PATHOLOGY
c/o Dr. A. C. Ritchie
Department of Pathology
Toronto General Hospital, EC4-305
Toronto, Ontario M5G 1L7,   (416) 595-3136
    Canada   Established 1947

H. A. Sissons, President;
    A. C. Ritchie, Secretary
The World Association of Societies of Pathology has
as its principle objects the promotion of anatomical
and clinical pathology in all their branches, by World
Congresses and other means; to encourage cooperation between the national societies of pathology com-

prising the association; and to present the views of
pathologists and to advance the interest on the international level.   Membership: 35 Societies of Pathology (National Societies of Pathology).   Finances:
Membership: Dues are assessed according to the
number of members of the National Societies; Other
Sources: Contributions.   Awards: The World Foundation of Pathology established to support the World
Association awards annually a Gordon Signy Foreign
Fellowship in Pathology.   Meetings: World Congresses, every 2 or 3 years.   Publications: Directory,
2 to 3 years, Utz Merten, editor; News Bulletin,
quarterly, Utz Merten, editor.

★ 1496 ★

WORLD ASSOCIATION OF VETERINARY FOOD
    HYGIENISTS
Post Office Box 1   (030) 789111
Bilthoven, The Netherlands   Established 1955

Dr. M. van Schothorst, Secretary-Treasurer
The Association aims to exchange, on the international level, the results of scientific research pertaining to food products of animal origin and to promote
co-operation in this direction.   To accomplish this,
international scientific meetings (symposia, round table
conferences, etc.) are organized.   In co-operation
with the World Veterinary Association, the
W.A.V.F.H. organizes the section "Food-Hygiene"
for World Veterinary Congresses.   Membership: 35
countries.   Finances: Membership: $50 annually.

★ 1497 ★

WORLD ASSOCIATION OF VETERINARY MICRO-
    BIOLOGISTS, IMMUNOLOGISTS AND SPECIAL-
    ISTS IN INFECTIOUS DISEASES
Ecole Nationale Veterinaire d'Alfort
7 avenue du General de Gaulle
F-94704 Maisons-Alfort ,   (01) 375-9211
    France   Established 1967

Professor C. Pilet, President, Secretary-Treasurer
To facilitate international contacts, exchange of information and research data; to promote and develop
basic and applied research in microbiology, immunology and infectious diseases in animals.   Membership:
222 Veterinarians, microbiologists, immunologists,
Professors in Veterinary School and specialists in infectious diseases.   Finances: Membership: 50 F.F.
annually.

★ 1498 ★

WORLD ASSOCIATION OF VETERINARY
       PATHOLOGISTS
c/o Professor Dr. Hans Winter
Veterinary School
University of Queensland
Sta Lucia, Queensland 4067,
       Australia   Established 1967

Coordination of national associations of veterinary
pathologists; coordination of study programs; periodical meetings. Membership: ca 1,000. Finances:
Membership: 2 $. Meetings: Quadrennially, in
conjunction with the World Veterinary Association,
various locations; biennially, together with a national association.

WORLD CHRISTIAN TEMPERANCE FEDERATION
       See: International Christian Federation for the
              Prevention of Alcoholism and Drug Addiction

★ 1499 ★

WORLD COUNCIL FOR THE WELFARE OF THE BLIND
58 avenue Bosquet   (01) 555-6754
F-75007 Paris, France   Established 1951

Dorina de Gouvea Nowill, President (Brazil);
       Hilary Gohier, Assistant Secretary General
The international, non-governmental organization
which groups the representatives of associations of and
for the blind. To achieve its aims, the Council provides the means of consultation between those organizations, encourages the exchange of experience, collects and disseminates information, keeps its members
informed about all social and legislative matters relating to blindness and its prevention. It also carries out studies in the field of service to the blind
and prevention of blindness, provides guidance in the
fields of education, rehabilitation, vocational training
and employment, promotes the creation of national
coordinating bodies. One of the main objectives of
the WCWB, however, is to represent the blind and
those who work in their service at the international
level and to place the needs and aspirations of the
blind before the United Nations and its Specialized
Agencies, to recommend measures for improving their
standards of living and to encourage all social and
legislative action to achieve the full integration of
the blind in the general community. Membership:
209 national members in 76 countries; 66 associate,
4 international members; 2 sponsoring members and
7 honorary life members. Finances: Membership:
National member, $250; associate member, $75; international member, $1,000; sponsoring member,
$1,250. Meetings: General Assembly, every 5

years, various locations. Publications: Newsletter,
quarterly, Hilary Gohier, editor; reports of World
Assemblies; monographs. Affiliations: Consultative
status with the Economic and Social Council of the
United Nations, UNESCO, UNICEF, and official relations with WHO. On the special list of ILO.
Also a member of the Council of World Organizations
interested in the Handicapped and a member of the
Board of the International Agency for the Prevention
of Blindness. Consultative status with the International Federation of Library Associations. WCWB
also has a permanent observer status with the Intergovernmental Copyright Committee.

★ 1500 ★

WORLD FEDERATION FOR MENTAL HEALTH
107-2352 Health Sciences Mall
University of British Columbia
Vancouver, British Columbia   (604) 228-2332
       V6T 1W5, Canada   Established 1948

Roberta L. Beiser, Executive Director
To promote among all peoples and nations the highest
possible standard of mental health, in its broadest
biological, medical, educational and social aspects;
to work with the United Nations Economic and Social
Council, UNESCO, WHO and UNICEF and with all
other international agencies in so far as they may
promote mental health help and encourage member associations in the improvement of mental health services in their own countries; to promote communications and understanding through meetings and international congresses; and to further the establishment of
better human relations in all possible ways. Membership: 88 member associations in 36 countries; 100
affiliated organizations in 23 countries; 1,300 individuals in 45 countries. Finances: Membership:
Member association: Category 1: $150 U.S. funds;
Category 2: $500; Category 3: $1,000; affiliated:
Category 1: $50; Category 2: $150; Category 3:
$500 U.S.; Individual: $15, $50 or life member-
ship of $500. Meetings: World Congress on Mental
Health, biennial, various locations. Publications:
Newsletter, quarterly, WFMH, editor; Proceedings
of World Congresses; Monograph Series from the
World Congresses.

★ 1501 ★

WORLD FEDERATION OF HEMOPHILIA
1155 Dorchester Boulevard, West, Suite 2902
Montreal, Quebec H3B 2L3,   (514) 866-0442
       Canada   Established 1963

Frank Schnabel, President
To assist hemophiliacs and persons with related

disorders in every possible way and to contribute by all means placed at its disposal to the advancement of the scientific, technical, social and ethical problems related to such disorders.   An important function of WFH is to provide the know-how that will assist in the formation of national member organizations.   The knowledge and experience of others, gained by comparing methods, techniques and procedures, enable a hemophilia organization to improve its services and to find solutions.   WFH supports International Hemophilia Centers which are involved in the following functions: to training visiting physicians and technologists is the major objective, particularly those from the developing nations; to organize regional workshop programs--with theoretical lectures and practical demonstrations on the care of hemophilia (laboratory diagnosis: orthopedic, dental and general surgery; physical therapy, etc.); to send experts to underdeveloped countries officially requesting help in setting up facilities for the treatment of hemophilia.   Membership: Approximately 700 (individual, corporate, associate) and national member organizations in 53 countries.   Finances: Membership: Individual U.S., $30; corporate U.S., $350; associate U.S., $300; National Member Organizations-Assessments.   Meetings: Biennial, Congress, various locations; symposia and workshops, all over the world.   Publications: Bulletins, semiannually, Marthe Schnabel and Professor P. M. Mannucci, editors.

★ 1502 ★
WORLD FEDERATION OF NEUROLOGY
Århus Kommunehospital
Neurofysiologisk afd.
DK-8000 Århus C, Denmark   Established 1957

Dr. Palle Juul-Jensen, M.D., Secretary-Treasurer
    General
To advance the development of clinical neurology and neurological science throughout the world by the dissemination of information and scientific knowledge, stimulating, encouraging and developing programs of clinical and basic neurological research throughout the work and providing a means for close professional and personal appreciation of neurologists and neurological scientists.   Membership: 65 societies.   Finances: Membership: $2 per member of each national society. Meetings: Biennial, various locations.   Publications: Journal of Neurological Sciences, bimonthly, John Walton, editor.

★ 1503 ★
WORLD FEDERATION OF NEUROSURGICAL
        SOCIETIES
c/o Professor W. Luyendÿk
Academic Hospital
Leiden, The Netherlands   Established 1955

Professor William Luyendÿk, Secretary
Advance neurological surgery in all its aspects by facilitating personal association of neurosurgeons throughout the world; aid exchange and dissemination of knowledge and ideas in the field of neurosurgery; encourage research and investigation in neurosurgery and allied sciences.   Membership: National or international societies of neurological surgery whose membership is 25 or more (if less, the membership must represent the available and/or neurosurgical talent of the nation); 17 founder members; in all, 48 continental and member societies representing 42 countries.   Finances: Membership: $2 dues annually for each member of the societies.   Meetings: Congresses, quadrennially, various locations.   Affiliations: Special liaison committee with the World Federation of Neurology and the International Congress of Neurology.

★ 1504 ★
WORLD FEDERATION OF OCCUPATIONAL
        THERAPISTS
11 Slalom Drive, Wembley Downs,
Perth, Western Australia 6019
        Australia

Joanne Barker, Secretary-Treasurer
To advance the standards of professional practice for the benefit of the physically and mentally disabled; to promote international co-operation among occupational therapy associations, occupational therapists, and between them and other allied professional groups; to be involved in matters where occupational therapy expertise can contribute to policy making in general preventative, curative and rehabilitative health matters.   Membership: 28 full organization members, 8 associate organization members, 3,600 individual members (organization member, 1 per sovereign state; full organization member--national professional association where accredited occupation therapy course exists; associate organization member--national professional association where no accredited occupational therapy course exists; individual professional membership-- qualified occupational therapist in good standing as member of own national association; contributing member--persons professional association or corporations interested in development of occupational therapy.   Finances: Membership: Full organization, Sw.F. 25-Sw.F. 2,500 according to per capita assessment; associate organization, Sw.F. 7.50; individ-

ual membership, Sw.F. 10; Other Sources: Donations. Awards: Honorary Fellow: Persons who have
performed distinguished service for occupational therapy. Meetings: International Congress, quadrennially; Council meetings, biennially. Publications:
Bulletin, semiannual, Moya Kinnealey, editor (Philadelphia, Pennsylvania); Proceeding--International
Congresses, quadrennial, available from WFOT Secretary; Recommended Minimum Standards Education
of Occupational Therapists, available from WFOT Secretary; Bibliography on Occupational Therapy, available from WFOT Secretary; Requirements for Employment of Occupational Therapists Among WFOT Member Countries, available from WFOT Secretary.

★ 1505 ★
WORLD FEDERATION OF PUBLIC HEALTH
       ASSOCIATIONS
c/o APHA Secretariat
1015 15th Street, N.W.   (202) 789-5691
Washington, D.C. 20005   Established 1967

Dr. N. Sotoodeh, President (Iran); Dr. Susi Kessler,
       Executive Secretary (United States)
The WFPHA is a union of national public health associations joining efforts to strengthen the public health
professions and to improve personal and community
health throughout the world. Membership: 32 national public health associations from developing and
industrialized countries (full membership; limited
membership; associate membership; sustaining membership). Finances: Membership: Full membership,
U.S. $50 plus $.05 multiplied by the number of members of the association (annually); limited membership, U.S. $50; associate membership, U.S. $25;
sustaining membership, U.S. $500; Other Sources:
Grants. Lectureships: Annual High R. Leavell
Lectureship. Meetings: Annual meeting and technical discussions in Geneva every May; triennial International Congress, hosted by a different member association. Publications: Salubritas, quarterly, Ina
Selden, editor; WFPHA News, quarterly, Susan
Brems, editor; occasional monographs. Affiliations:
WHO; UNICEF.

★ 1506 ★
WORLD FEDERATION OF THE DEAF
120 via Gregorio VII   (06) 637-7041
I-00165 Rome, Italy   Established 1951

Dr. Cesare Magarotto, General Director
Organized to conduct social rehabilitation of the deaf
and the fight against deafness, the Federation (1) collects data concerning the education, the legal and
social position, the organization of assistance, the

professional rehabilitation of the deaf in all countries,
the prevention and treatment of deafness and informs
its members on the scientific and practical results
achieved; (2) promotes in the various countries the
unification of associations, federations and national
societies which represent the deaf or favors their establishment where they do not yet exist; (3) obtains
information, report and studies on social legislation
concerning the deaf; (4) organizes international
meetings for the purpose of studying various problems
and organizes and coordinates the prevention and
treatment of deafness; (5) arranges for participation
at meetings interesting the deaf and cooperates with
other international organizations which deal with
problems of disabled; (6) defends the rights of the
deaf and promotes their social rehabilitation; (7) promotes the international exchange of specially trained
people in the assistance, education and rehabilitation
of the deaf; and (8) promotes the inclusion of the
problems concerning the deaf among those which are
to be dealt with by international bodies in cooperation with the United Nations Organization, its bodies
and its specialized Agencies. Membership: 86 national associations. Finances: Membership: Ordinary, $120; associate, $80; individual, $15.
Awards: International Solidarity Merit Award.
Meetings: International Conference, quadrennial,
various locations. Publications: The Voice of Silence, 3 issues annually, Cesare Margarotto, editor;
Proceedings of World Congresses.

★ 1507 ★
WORLD HEALTH ORGANIZATION
CH-1211 Geneva 27   (022) 912111
       Switzerland   Established 1948

H. Mahler, Director-General
To fulfill tasks which require and justify the existence
of a single international organization to collate, unify, codify where necessary, standardize, and disseminate data and information on health; to assist
member countries in improving their national public
health services and raise their standards of health.
Membership: 155 member states, 1 associate member.
Finances: Membership: Fee scale similar to United
Nations assessment; Other Sources: United Nations
bodies, voluntary funds from groups and individuals.
Meetings: Annual, Geneva, Switzerland. Publications: WHO Chronicle, monthly; World Health,
monthly; International Digest of Health Legislation,
quarterly; Bulletin of the World Health Organization;
World Health Statistics Annual; monographs and reports.

★ 1508 ★
WORLD MEDICAL ASSOCIATION
28 avenue des Alpes
F-01210 Fenrey-Voltaire, France   Established 1947

Dr. Andre Wynen, Secretary-General
To promote closer ties among medical organizations and doctors of the world; to study professional problems in different countries. Membership: 50 national medical associations. Meetings: Biennial, World Medical Assembly, various locations. Publications: World Medical Journal, bimonthly.

★ 1509 ★
WORLD MEDICAL RELIEF, INC.
11745 12th Street   (313) 866-5333
Detroit, Michigan 48206   Established 1953

Mrs. L. G. Auberlin, President
A philanthropic organization which contributes free medical equipment, supplies and medicine to the sick and indigent in all parts of the free world, based upon contributions from any who wish to support its program.

★ 1510 ★
WORLD ORGANIZATION OF GASTROENTEROLOGY
c/o Dr. E. A. Vallejo
Londres 17   (01) 255-6808
Madrid 28, Spain   Established 1958

Dr. E. Arias Vallejo, President
To promote the free exchange of knowledge of all branches of gastroenterology amongst its members; to organize quadrennial Congresses. Membership: 8,000 individuals, representing 54 societies. Finances: Membership: $1 per member per society. Awards: Brohee Lectureship and Medal. Meetings: Quadrennial, various locations. Publication: O.M.G.E. Bulletin, annually, G. Watkinson and F. Vilardell, co-editors.

★ 1511 ★
WORLD VETERINARY ASSOCIATION
70 Route du Pont Butin
CH-1213 Petit-Lancy/Ge,   (022) 93 03 57
     Switzerland   Established 1959

Max Leuenberger, Secretary-Treasurer
To unify the veterinary profession throughout the world by providing a central link for national veterinary associations; to organize and hold World Veterinary Congresses; to promote all branches of veterinary science by all appropriate means, including the exchange of information on matters of veterinary interest, the collection and distribution of information on films, the establishment of a uniform nomenclature; to help improve veterinary education; to promote the standing of the veterinary profession; and, to establish relations with organizations whose interests are related to the purposes of the Association. Membership: 65 national societies, 14 associate. Finances: Membership: U.S. $75 per member per society; Other Sources: Donations, income from Congresses; sale of publications. Awards: John Gamgee Gold Medal. Meetings: Congress, quadrenially, various locations; Permanent Committee, annual, Paris. Publications: WVA News, 7 times annually; World Catalogue of Veterinary Film and Films of Veterinary Interest. Affiliations: World Veterinary Poultry Association; International Veterinary Association for Animal Production; World Small Animal Veterinary Association; World Association of Veterinary Anatomists; World Association of Veterinary Pathologists; World Association of Veterinary Food Hygienists; World Association for Buiatrics; World Association for the Advancement of Veterinary Parasitology; World Association of Veterinary Microbiologists, Immunologists and Specialists in Infectious Diseases; World Association of Veterinary Physiologists, Pharmacologists and Biochemists; International Pig Veterinary Society; World Association for the History of Veterinary Medicine; World Veterinary Epidemiology Society and International Association of Teachers of Veterinary Preventive Medicine.

★ 1512 ★
WORLD VETERINARY POULTRY ASSOCIATION
c/o Dr. P. M. Biggs
Houghton Poultry Research Station,
Houghton
Huntingdon, Cambridgeshire,   St.Ives 64101
     England, United Kingdom   Established 1959

Dr. P. M. Biggs, Secretary-Treasurer
The Association's aims are to organize meetings for studying diseases and conditions relating to the avian species, to encourage research in this field and to promote the exchange of information and material for study between individuals and organizations interested in the avian species. Membership: Approximately 600 veterinary surgeons. Finances: Membership: 1 pound sterling annually. Meetings: Quadrennial, various locations. Publications: AVIAN Pathology, quarterly, Dr. P. M. Biggs, editor; Proceedings of Quadrennial Congresses. Affiliation: World Veterinary Association.

X

★ 1513 ★
XI PSI PHI
1005 East Main Street, Suite 7   (503) 772-6011
Medford, Oregon 97501   Established 1889

William L. Barnum, Secretary-Treasurer
To further the moral code, professional ethics, individual high ideals for professional dentists. Membership: 25,000 (22 college chapters, 35 alumni chapters). Meetings: Board of Directors Meeting, annual, various locations. Publications: Quarterly.

Y

★ 1514 ★
YOUNG ADULT INSTITUTE AND WORKSHOPS
251 Park Avenue, South   (212) 982-4600
New York, New York 10010   Established 1957

Joel M. Levy, Executive Director
To provide comprehensive program that enables mentally handicapped young adults with mental retardation, emotional disturbance or brain damage to progress from a state of isolation and dependency to financial and social independence. Offers an alternative to institutionalization and focuses on the development of a series of supportive services to maintain individuals within the community. Certain programs serve the multiple handicapped including those who are deaf, blind or have other physical disabilities. Institute's programs include adjustment counseling, recreational activities, classes in employment skills, remedial/reading, money handling, budgeting and sex education. Finances: The Institute is supported by tuition fees, government agencies, foundations and private donations.

SELECTED KEYWORD INDEX OF ORGANIZATIONS

A

Broncho-Esophagological Association. American 213

Bronchoesophagological Society. International 948

Broncho-Esophagology. Pan American Association of Oto-Rhinolaryngology and 1329

Buiatrics. World Association for 1493

Bundle Branch Block Association. International 949

Burn Association. American 215

Burn Injuries. International Society for 1038

C

Canada. Acupuncture Foundation of 15

Canada. Association of Faculties of Pharmacy of 530

Canada. Catholic Health Association of 677

Canada. Defence Medical Association of 761

Canada. Federation of Medical Women of 827

Canada. Health League of 868

Canada). International Christian Leprosy Mission (in 957

Canada). John Milton Society for the Blind (in 1094

Canada. Medical Council of 1130

Canada. Microscopical Society of 1147

Canada. Multiple Sclerosis Society of 1155

Canada. National Cancer Institute of 1212

Canada. National Dental Examining Board of 1224

Canada. National Retinitis Pigmentosa Foundation of 1277

Canada. Nutrition Society of 1308

Canada of the Most Venerable Order of the Hospital of St. John of Jerusalem (St. John Ambulance). Priory of 1363

Canada. Planned Parenthood Federation of 1356

Canada. Proprietary Association of 1366

Canada. Psychiatric Nurses Association of 1372

Canada. Royal College of Physicians and Surgeons of 1392

Canada. Victorian Order of Nurses of 1483

Canadian Association for Health, Physical Education, and Recreation. 602

Canadian Association for the Mentally Retarded. 603

Canadian Association for the Welfare of Psychiatric Patients. 604

Canadian Association for Treatment of Offenders. 605

Canadian Association of Anatomists. 606

Canadian Association of Electroencephalograph Technologists, Inc. 607

Canadian Association of Gastroenterology. 608

Canadian Association of Medical Radiation Technologists. 609

Canadian Association of Optometrists. 610

Canadian Association of Pathologists. 611

Canadian Association of Radiologists. 612

Canadian Association of Social Workers. 613

Canadian Biochemical Society. 614

Canadian Board of Registration of Electroencephalograph Technologists. 615

Canadian Cardiovascular Society. 616

Canadian Chiropractic Examining Board. 617

Canadian Coordinating Council on Deafness. 618

Canadian Council for Exceptional Children. 619

Canadian Council of the Blind. 620

Canadian Council on Health Education. 621

Canadian Council on Hospital Accreditation. 622

Canadian Council on Social Development. 623

Canadian Cystic Fibrosis Foundation. 624

Canadian Dental Association. 625

Canadian Dental Research Foundation. 626

Canadian Dermatological Association. 627

Canadian Diabetes Association. 628

Canadian Dietetic Association. 629

Canadian Faculties of Dentistry. Association of 525

Canadian Federation of Biological Societies. 630

Canadian Federation of Voluntary Health Plans. 631

Canadian Foundation for Ileitis and Colitis. 632

Canadian Health Record Association. 633

Canadian Hearing Society. 634

Canadian Heart Foundation. 635

Canadian Hospital Association. 636

Canadian Institute of Public Health Inspectors. 637

Canadian Lung Association. 638

Canadian Medic Alert Foundation, Inc. 639

Canadian Medical Association. 640

Canadian Medical Colleges. Association of 526

Canadian Medical Colleges: Special Resource Committee on Instructional Media. Association of 527

Canadian Mental Health Association. 641

Canadian Nurses' Association. 642

Canadian Ophthalmological Society. 643

Canadian Orthoptic Council. 644

Canadian Orthoptic Society. 645

Canadian Osteopathic Aid Society. 646

Canadian Osteopathic Association. 647

Canadian Otolaryngological Society. 648

Canadian Paediatric Society. 649

Canadian Paraplegic Association. 650

Canadian Parks/Recreation Association. 651

Canadian Pharmaceutical Association. 652

Canadian Physiological Society. 653

Canadian Physiotherapy Association. 654

Canadian Psychiatric Association. 655

Canadian Red Cross Society. 656

Canadian Rheumatism Association. 657

Canadian Save the Children Fund. 658

Canadian Schizophrenia Foundation. 659

Canadian Society for Cell Biology. 660

Canadian Society of Clinical Chemists. 661

Canadian Society of Cytology. 662

Canadian Society of Dentistry for Children. 663

Canadian Society of Electroencephalographers,

M

Keyword Index of Organizations

W

Keyword Index
of Organizations

LIST OF SUBJECTS AND CROSS REFERENCES

SUBJECT INDEX OF ORGANIZATIONS

Accreditation and Certification

Acupuncture

Administration
See: Health Administration

Aging

Aid, Medical
See: Emergency Health Services;
Foundations and Grant-
Making Organizations

Alcoholism

Allergy

Amputation
See: Handicapped; Orthopedics.

Analgesia
See: Anesthesiology

Anatomy

Anemia
See: Blood

Anesthesiology

Angiology

Animal Health
See: Veterinary Medicine

Anorexia Nervosa

Aphasia
See: Deafness and Speech
Corrections

Athritis

Assistance, Medical
See: Medical Assistance

Asthma

Aviation Medicine
See: Space and Undersea
Medicine

Bacteriology

Baptist Organizations

Bariatrics

Behavior

Biology

Birth Control

Blindness

Blood

Braille
See: Blindness

Brain

Bronchitis
See: Chest Diseases; Internal
Medicine; Respiratory
Diseases

Burns
See: Emergency Health Services

Cancer

Cardiac Diseases
See: Heart Diseases

Cardiology
See: Heart Diseases

Catholic Organizations

Cerebral Palsy

Certifying Boards
See: Accreditation and
Certification

Chemistry

Chest Diseases

Child Health

Childbirth
See: Obstetrics and Gynecology

Chiropody
See: Podiatry

Chiropractics

Christian Organizations

Church of the Brethren

Climatology

Clinical Medicine

Contraception
See: Birth Control

Cooley's Anemia
See: Blood

Crippling Diseases
See: Cerebral Palsy; Handi-
capped; Orthopedics;
Polio; Rehabilitation

Cystic Fibrosis

Cytology

Dance Therapy
See: Physical Education and
Recreation

Deafness and Speech Corrections

Dental Administration
See: Health Administration

Dentistry

Dermatology

Diabetes

Dialysis
See: Kidney Diseases

Dietetics
See: Nutrition

Digestive Diseases
See: Gastroenterology

Disabilities
See: Handicapped

Down's Syndrome
See: Mental Retardation

Drugs
See: Narcotics; Pharmacy

Ear Diseases
See: Deafness and Speech
Corrections; Otolaryngology;
Otology; Otorhinolaryngology

Electrodiagnosis

Electroencephalography

Electromyography

Emergency Health Services

Endocrinology

Endodontics
See: Dentistry

Environmental Health

Epidemiology

Epilepsy

Episcopal Organizations

Ethnic Organizations

Eugenics
See: Genetics

Examining Boards
See: Accreditation and Certification

Eyesight
See: Blindness; Ophthalmology;
Opticianry and Optics;
Optometry

Family Planning
See: Birth Control; Parenthood

Family Practice

Fertility

First Aid
See: Emergency Health Services

Food Sanitation
See: Sanitation

Foot Diseases
See: Podiatry

Forensic Sciences

Foundations and Grant-Making
Organizations

Fraternities

Fund Raising
See: Foundations and Grant-
Making Organizations

Gastroenterology

Gastroscopy
See: Gastroenterology;
Internal Medicine

Genetics

Geriatrics
See: Aging

Germs
See: Gnotobiotics

Gerontology
See: Aging

Gnotobiotics

Grant-Making Organizations
See: Foundations and Grant-
Making Organizations

Gynecology
  See: Obstetrics and Gynecology

Hard of Hearing
  See: Deafness and Speech
    Corrections
Handicapped
Hay Fever
  See Allergy
Headache
  See: Neurology
Health Administration
Health Care Plans
Health Insurance
  See: Health Care Plans
Health Journalism
Health Records and Statistics
Hearing Defects
  See: Deafness and Speech
    Corrections; Otolaryngol-
    ogy; Otology; Otorhinol-
    aryngology
Heart Diseases
Hematology
  See: Blood
Hemophilia
  See: Blood
Hepatology
  See: Liver Diseases
Heredity
  See: Genetics
Histochemistry
  See: Cytology
Histology
  See Cytology
Homeopathy
  See: Natural Healing and
    Living
Homosexuality
  See: Human Sexuality
Hospital Administration
  See: Health Administration
Hospital Insurance
  See: Health Care Plans
Hospitals
Human Sexuality
Huntington's Disease
Hygiene
  See: Industrial and Occupational
    Medicine; Natural Heal-
    ing and Living: Public
    Health; Sanitation
Hypnosis

Immunology
Industrial and Occupational
  Medicine
Infectious Diseases
  See: Public Health
Information Centers
  See: Libraries and Information
    Centers
Insanity
  See: Mental Health; Mental
    Retardation; Psychiatry
    and Psychology
Insurance, Health
  See: Health Care Plans
Instrumentation, Medical
  See: Medical Instrumentation
Internal Medicine

Jewish Organizations
Journalism
  See: Health Journalism

Kidney Diseases

Laboratories
Laryngology
Legal Aspects
Leprosy
Leukemia
  See: Blood
Libraries and Information Centers
Liver Diseases
Lung Diseases
  See: Chest Diseases; Internal
    Medicine; Respiratory
    Diseases; Tuberculosis
Lutheran Organizations

Malaria
  See: Tropical Diseases
Management
  See: Health Administration
Manufacturing and Trade
  Organizations
Massage
  See: Natural Healing and
    Living
Maternity
  See: Obstetrics and Gyne-
    cology; Parenthood
Medical Administration
  See: Health Administration

Medical Assistance
Medical Care Plans
  See: Health Care Plans
Medical Climatology
  See: Climatology
Medical Instrumentation
Medical Journalism
  See: Health Journalism
Medical Jurisprudence
  See: Legal Aspects
Medical Records
  See: Health Records and Statistics
Medical Research
  See: Research
Medical Statistics
  See: Health Records and Statistics
Medical Women
  See: Women in Medicine
Mental Deficiency
  See: Mental Health; Mental Re-
    tardation; Psychiatry and
    Psychology
Mental Health
Mental Retardation
Microbiology
  See: Biology
Microscopy
Midwifery
  See: Obstetrics and Gynecology;
    Nursing
Migraine
  See: Neurology
Motherhood
  See: Obstetrics and Gynecology;
    Parenthood
Multiple Sclerosis
Music Therapy
  See: Mental Health
Mycology

Naprapathy
  See: Natural Healing and Living
Narcotics
Natural Healing and Living
Naturopathics
  See: Natural Healing and
    Living
Nephrology
  See: Kidney Diseases
Nervous Diseases
  See: Mental Health; Neurology;
    Psychiatry and Psychology
Neurology
Nose Diseases
  See: Otorhinolaryngology;
    Rhinology
Nursing
Nursing Homes
Nutrition

Obesity
    See: Bariatrics
Obstetrics and Gynecology
Occupational Medicine
    See: Industrial and Occupational
        Medicine
Oncology
    See: Cancer
Ophthalmology
Opticianry and Optics
Optometry
Organ Donations
    See: Post Mortem and Organ
        Donations
Orthodontics
    See: Dentistry
Orthopedics
Orthoptics
    See: Ophthalmology
Orthotics
    See: Orthopedics
Osteopathy
Otolaryngology
Otology
Otorhinolaryngology

Paraplegia
    See: Handicapped
Parasitology
Parenthood
Parkinson's Disease
Pathology
Pediatrics
Pedodontics
    See: Dentistry
Periodontology
    See: Dentistry
Pharmacology
    See: Pharmacy
Pharmacy
Physical Disabilities
    See: Handicapped
Physical Education and Recreation
Physical Therapy
    See: Rehabilitation
Physics
Physiology
Planned Parenthood
    See: Birth Control; Parenthood
Plastic Surgery
    See: Surgery
Podiatry
Poetry Therapy
    See: Mental Health
Poisoning
Polio
Pollution
    See: Environmental Health

Post Mortem and Organ Donations
Proctology
Prosthetics
Prosthodontics
    See: Dentistry
Psychiatry and Psychology
Psychoanalysis
    See: Psychiatry and Psychology
Psychology
    See: Psychiatry and Psychology
Psychosomatic Medicine
Psychotherapy
    See: Psychiatry and Psychology
Public Health
Public Health Administration
    See: Health Administration

Radiation and Radiology
Radiology
    See: Radiation and Radiology
Records, Medical
    See: Health Records and Statistics
Recreation
    See: Physical Education and
        Recreation
Red Cross
Rehabilitation
Renal Failure
    See: Kidney Diseases
Reproduction
    See: Birth Control; Fertility; Human
        Sexuality; Sterilization
Research
Respiratory Diseases
Rheumatism
    See: Athritis
Rhinology
Roentgenology
    See: Radiation and Radiology

Safety
Sanitation
Seventh-Day Adventists
Sexuality
    See: Human Sexuality
Smoking
Social Service
Sophrology
    See: Stress
Space and Undersea Medicine
Speech Correction
    See: Deafness and Speech
        Corrections
Sports Medicine
Statistics
    See: Health Records and
        Statistics

Sterilization
Stress
Stuttering
Suicide
Surgery

Tay-Sachs Disease
Thoracic Surgery
    See: Surgery
Toxicology
    See: Poisoning
Trachoma
    See: Ophthalmology
Trade Organizations
    See: Manufacturing and Trade
        Organizations
Transplants
    See: Post Mortem and Organ
        Donations; Surgery
Tropical Diseases
Tuberculosis

Undersea Medicine
    See: Space and Undersea
        Medicine
United Church of Christ
United Methodist Church
Urology

Vascular Diseases
    See: Angiology
Venereal Diseases
Veterans
Veterinary Medicine

Weight Reduction
    See: Bariatrics
Women in Medicine

X-Ray
    See: Radiation and Radiology

ACCREDITATION AND CERTIFICATION (Continued)

Liaison Committee on Medical Education   1116
Medical Council of Canada   1130
National Accreditation Association and the American Examining Board of Psychoanalysis   1161
National Accreditation Council for Agencies Serving the Blind and Visually Handicapped   1162
National Accrediting Agency for Clinical Laboratory Sciences   1163
National Association for Practical Nurse Education and Service, Inc.   1171
National Association of Boards of Pharmacy   1175
National Association of Human Services Technologists   1182
National Board for Respiratory Therapy   1205
National Board of Examiners for Osteopathic Physicians and Surgeons, Inc.   1206
National Board of Medical Examiners   1207
National Dental Examining Board of Canada   1224
National Hearing Aid Society   1244
National Herbalist Association   1247
National Registry in Clinical Chemistry   1272
Professional Examination Service   1364

ACUPUNCTURE

Acupuncture Foundation of Canada   15
British Acupuncture Association and Register, Ltd.   595
International College of Acupuncture and Electro-Therapeutics   959
International Society of Acupuncture   1045

ADMINISTRATION
See: HEALTH ADMINISTRATION

AGING

American Aging Association   79
American Association of Homes for the Aging   133
American Association of Senior Physicians   163
American Baptist Homes and Hospitals Association   174
American Conference of Therapeutic Selfhelp/Self-health Social Action Clubs   268
American Geriatrics Society   300
American Society for Geriatric Dentistry   410
Blue Card, Inc.   585
Center for the Study of Aging and Human Development   682
Citizens for Better Care, Inc.   702
Committee for an Extended Lifespan   714

Gerontological Society of America   851
Institute of Gerontology   901
International Federation on Ageing   1008
International Health Foundation   1012
National Association of Jewish Homes for the Aged   1183
National Council of Senior Citizens   1216
National Council on the Aging, Inc.   1220
National Geriatrics Society, Inc.   1240

AID, MEDICAL
See: EMERGENCY HEALTH SERVICES;
      FOUNDATIONS AND GRANT-MAKING
      ORGANIZATIONS

ALCOHOLISM

Al-Anon Family Group Headquarters, Inc.   23
Alcohol and Drug Problems Association of North America   24
Alcohol Education for Youth, Inc.   25
Alcoholics Anonymous, Inc.   26
Alcoholism and Drug Addiction Research Foundation   27
American Medical Society on Alcoholism   334
Christopher D. Smithers Foundation, Inc.   701
Do It Now Foundation   778
DOC (Doctors Ought to Care)   779
International Christian Federation for the Prevention of Alcoholism and Drug Addiction   956
International Commission for the Prevention of Alcoholism   964
International Committee on Alcohol, Drugs and Traffic Safety   974
International Council on Alcohol and Addictions   981
International Doctors in Alcoholics Anonymous   986
International Federation of the Temperance Blue Cross Societies   1006
International Temperance Association   1071
International Temperance Blue Cross Union   1072
Menninger Foundation   1138
National Clearinghouse for Alcohol Information   1214
National Council on Alcoholism, Inc.   1217
National Institute on Alcohol Abuse and Alcoholism   1254
National Save-A-Life League   1280
Rutgers Center of Alcohol Studies   1393

ALLERGY
See also: IMMUNOLOGY

Allergy Information Association   30

ALLERGY (Continued)

American Academy of Allergy   36
American Allergy Association   80
American Association for Clinical Immunology and
    Allergy   90
American Board of Allergy and Immunology   178
American College of Allergists, Inc.   225
American Dermatologic Society for Allergy and
    Immunology   282
American Society of Ophthalmologic and Otolaryn-
    gologic Allergy   457
Association of Allergists for Mycological Investiga-
    tions   519
Asthma and Allergy Foundation of America   565
International Correspondence Society of Allergists
    977
International Organization of Allergology and Clinical
    Immunology   1028

AMPUTATION
    See: HANDICAPPED;   ORTHOPEDICS

ANALGESIA
    See: ANESTHESIOLOGY

ANATOMY
    See also: BIOLOGY

American Association of Anatomists   109
American Association of Veterinary Anatomists   165
Canadian Association of Anatomists   606

ANEMIA
    See: BLOOD

ANESTHESIOLOGY

American Association of Nurse Anesthetists   145
American Board of Anesthesiology, Inc.   179
American College of Anesthesiologists   226
American Dental Society of Anesthesiology   278
American Society for the Advancement of Anesthesia
    in Dentistry   429
American Society of Anesthesiologists   432
Association of University Anesthetists   559
International Anesthesia Research Society   919
International Association of French Speaking
    Anaesthetist-Reanimators   936

Scandinavian Society of Anesthesiologists   1406
Society of Air Force Anesthesiologists   1434

ANGIOLOGY
    See also: BLOOD

International Union of Angiology   1077

ANIMAL HEALTH
    See: VETERINARY MEDICINE

ANOREXIA NERVOSA

American Anorexia Nervosa Association, Inc.   84
National Association of Anorexia Nervosa and
    Associated Disorders, Inc.   1174

APHASIA
    See: DEAFNESS AND SPEECH CORRECTIONS

ARTHRITIS

Arthritis Foundation   488
Canadian Rheumatism Association   657
European League Against Rheumatism   808
International League Against Rheumatism   1016

ASSISTANCE, MEDICAL
    See: MEDICAL ASSISTANCE

ASTHMA
    See also: ALLERGY

Asthma and Allergy Foundation of America   565
National Foundation for Asthma, Inc.   1232
National Jewish Hospital/National Asthma Center
    1256

AVIATION MEDICINE
    See: SPACE AND UNDERSEA MEDICINE

Subject Index

Subject Index

Subject Index

DENTISTRY (Continued)

Scandinavian Society of Forensic Odontology   1407
Southern Society of Orthodontists   1457
Xi Psi Phi   1513

DERMATOLOGY

Acne Health Care Centers International, Inc.   14
American Academy of Dermatology   44
American Academy of Veterinary Dermatology   78
American Board of Dermatology, Inc.   185
American Dermatologic Society for Allergy and
    Immunology   282
American Osteopathic College of Dermatology   360
Canadian Dermatological Association   627
Dermatology Board of the American College of
    Veterinary Internal Medicine   772
Dermatology Foundation   773
Dystrophic Epidermolysis Bullosa Research Association
    of America, Inc.   785
Ibero Latin-American College of Dermatology   889
International League of Dermatological Societies
    1017
International Society of Tropical Dermatology   1068
North American Clinical Dermatologic Society   1301
Pacific Dermatologic Association   1327
Psoriasis Research Association, Inc.   1370
Society for Investigative Dermatology   1418

DIABETES

American Association of Diabetes Educators   123
British Diabetic Association   596
Canadian Diabetes Association   628
City of Hope National Medical Center   703
European Association for the Study of Diabetes   798
French Language Association for Research on Diabetes
    and Metabolic Diseases   846
International Diabetes Federation   985

DIALYSIS
    See: KIDNEY DISEASES

DIETETICS
    See: NUTRITION

DIGESTIVE DISEASES
    See: GASTROENTEROLOGY

DISABILITIES
    See: HANDICAPPED

DOWN'S SYNDROME
    See: MENTAL RETARDATION

DRUGS
    See: NARCOTICS; PHARMACY

EAR DISEASES
    See: DEAFNESS AND SPEECH CORRECTIONS;
        OTOLARYNGOLOGY; OTOLOGY;
        OTORHINOLARYNGOLOGY

ELECTRODIAGNOSIS

American Association of Electromyography and
    Electrodiagnosis   124
American Electrolysis Association   287

ELECTROENCEPHALOGRAPHY

American Encephalographic Society   286
American Medical Electroencephalographic
    Association   330
American Society of Electroencephalographic
    Technologists   443
Canadian Association of Electroencephalograph
    Technologists, Inc.   607
Canadian Board of Registration of Electroencephalo-
    graph Technologists   615
Canadian Society of Electroencephalographers,
    Electromygraphers and Clinical Neurophysiologists
    664
Central Association of Electroencephalographers   684
International Federation of Societies for Electro-
    encephalography and Clinical Neurophysiology
    1002

ELECTROMYOGRAPHY

American Association of Electromyography and
    Electrodiagnosis   124
Canadian Society of Electroencephalographers,
    Electromyographers and Clinical Neurophysiolo-
    gists   664

EMERGENCY HEALTH SERVICES

Africare, Inc.   19
Aid for International Medicine, Inc.   20
American Ambulance Association   82
American Association of Critical Care Nurses   119
American Bureau for Medical Advancement in China   214
American Burn Association   215
American College of Emergency Physicians   232
American Dentists for Foreign Service   281
American Physicians Fellowship for Medicine in Israel   374
American Red Cross   392
American Surgical Trade Association   474
American Women's Hospitals Service   483
Brother's Brother Foundation   598
Canadian Medic Alert Foundation, Inc.   639
Canadian Red Cross Society   656
Catholic Medical Mission Board   679
Dental Health International   770
Direct Relief Foundation   776
ECRI (Emergency Care Research Institute)   787
Emergency Department Nurses Association   790
Interchurch Medical Assistance, Inc.   912
International Association for Life Saving and First Aid to the Injured   925
International Committee for Life Assurance Medicine   969
International Committee of the Red Cross   972
International Rescue and Emergency Care Association   1034
International Society for Burn Injuries   1038
International Society for Ski Traumatology and Medicine of Winter Sports   1044
League of Red Cross Societies   1114
Map International   1124
Medic Alert Foundation International   1129
Medical Group Missions of the Christian Medical Society   1133
National Association for Search and Rescue   1172
Option, Inc.   1318
OXFAM   1325
Priory of Canada of the Most Venerable Order of the Hospital of St. John of Jerusalem (St. John Ambulance)   1363
Society of Critical Care Medicine   1436
University Association for Emergency Medicine   1480
World Medical Relief, Inc.   1509

ENDOCRINOLOGY

Barren Foundation   570
Committee for the Promotion of Medical Research   715

Endocrine Society   793
International Society of Endocrinology   1056
Pan American Federation of Endocrine Societies   1330

ENDODONTICS
See: DENTISTRY

ENVIRONMENTAL HEALTH

Air Pollution Control Association   21
American Academy of Environmental Engineers   45
American Industrial Hygiene Association   313
Coalition for the Environment   708
European Committee for the Protection of the Population Against the Hazard of Chronic Toxicity   806
Inhalation Toxicology Research Institute – Lovelace Biomedical and Environmental Research Institute, Inc.   893
Institute of Environmental Sciences   900
Institute of Occupational and Environmental Health   905
Interamerican Association of Sanitary Engineering and Environment   909
International Association of Agricultural Medicine and Rural Health   929
International Association on Water Pollution Research   946
National Environmental Health Association   1226
Natural Food Associates, Inc.   1291
Water Pollution Control Federation   1488

EPIDEMIOLOGY

American Epidemiological Society   289
International Epidemiological Association   987

EPILEPSY

American Epilepsy Society   290
Epilepsy Foundation of America   794

EPISCOPAL ORGANIZATIONS

Assembly of Episcopal Hospitals and Chaplains   490
Episcopal Conference of the Deaf   795
Episcopal Guild for the Blind   796

Subject Index

Subject Index

Subject Index

HANDICAPPED (Continued)

World Federation of Occupational Therapists 1504
Young Adult Institute and Workshops 1514

HAY FEVER
See: ALLERGY

HEADACHE
See: NEUROLOGY

HEALTH ADMINISTRATION

Academy of Health Care Consultants 5
Accrediting Commission on Education for Health Services 13
American Academy of Dental Practice Administration 42
American Academy of Medical Administrators 53
American Academy of Medical Directors 54
American Academy of Podiatry Administration 75
American Association for Laboratory Animal Science 94
American Association of Hospital Consultants 134
American Association of Psychiatric Administrators 157
American College of Hospital Administrators 238
American College of Medical Group Administrators 242
American College of Nursing Home Administrators 248
American College of Osteopathic Hospital Administrators 250
American Conference of Governmental Industrial Hygienists 267
American Health Planning Association 305
American Medical Record Association 333
American Professional Practice Association 380
American Society for Hospital Central Service Personnel 413
American Society for Hospital Food Service Administrators 415
American Society for Hospital Personnel Administration 416
American Society for Hospital Public Relations 417
American Society for Hospital Purchasing and Materials Management 418
American Society for Hospital Risk Management 419
American Society for Nursing Service Administrators 422
American Society for Public Administration 427
Association of Medical Rehabilitation Directors and Coordinators 534

Association of Medical School Pediatric Department Chairmen 535
Association of Mental Health Administrators 536
Association of Orthopaedic Chairmen 542
Association of Pathology Chairmen, Inc. 543
Association of State and Territorial Dental Directors 552
Association of State and Territorial Health Officials 553
Association of State and Territorial Maternal and Child Health and Crippled Children's Directors 554
Association of State and Territorial Public Health Nutrition Directors 550
Association of University Programs in Health Administration 560
Center for Health Administration Studies 680
Commission on Professional and Hospital Activities 713
Conference of Educational Administrators Serving the Deaf, Inc. 721
Conference of Public Health Laboratory Directors 722
Conference of State and Territorial Directors of Public Health Education 724
Council of State Administrators of Vocational Rehabilitation 746
ECRI (Emergency Care Research Institute) 787
European Association of Programmes in Health Service Studies 801
Forum for Medical Affairs 842
Health and Education Resources, Inc. 864
Hospital Financial Management Association 879
Hospital Food Directors Association, Inc. 880
Hospital Information Systems Sharing Group 881
Hospital Management Systems Society 883
Hospital Research and Educational Trust 884
International Association of Hospital Central Service Management 938
International Association of Industrial Accident Boards and Commissions 941
Medical Group Management Association 1132
National Association for Hospital Development 1167
National Association of State Mental Health Program Directors 1198
National Council on Health Centers 1218
National Executive Housekeepers Association, Inc. 1227
National Rehabilitation Administration Association 1273
National Safety Management Society 1278
Occupational Medical Administrators' Association 1310
Radiation Therapy Oncology Group 1377
Society for Advanced Medical Systems 1414
United States Conference of City Health Officers 1476
Upper Midwest Hospital Conference 1481

HEALTH CARE PLANS

HEALTH INSURANCE

HEALTH JOURNALISM

HEALTH RECORDS AND STATISTICS

HEARING DEFECTS

HEART DISEASES

HEMATOLOGY

HEMOPHILIA

HEPATOLOGY

HEREDITY

Subject Index

HISTOCHEMISTRY
    See: CYTOLOGY

HISTOLOGY
    See: CYTOLOGY

HOMEOPATHY
    See: NATURAL HEALING AND LIVING

HOMOSEXUALITY
    See: HUMAN SEXUALITY

HOSPITAL ADMINISTRATION
    See: HEALTH ADMINISTRATION

HOSPITAL INSURANCE
    See: HEALTH CARE PLANS

HOSPITALS

Academy of Health Care Consultants   5
American Association for Hospital Planning   93
American Association of Hospital Consultants   134
American Association of Hospital Dentists   135
American Association of Hospital Podiatrists, Inc.
    136
American Baptist Homes and Hospitals Association
    174
American College of Hospital Administrators   238
American College of Osteopathic Hospital
    Administrators   250
American Hospital Association   311
American Osteopathic Hospital Association   364
American Protestant Hospital Association   382
American Society for Hospital Central Service
    Personnel   413
American Society for Hospital Engineering   414
American Society for Hospital Food Service
    Administrators   415
American Society for Hospital Personnel Administration
    416
American Society for Hospital Public Relations   417
American Society for Hospital Purchasing and Materials
    Management   418

American Society for Hospital Risk Management   419
American Society of Hospital Attorneys   447
American Society of Hospital Pharmacists   448
American Women's Hospitals Service   483
Assembly of Episcopal Hospitals and Chaplains   490
Assembly of Hospital Schools of Nursing   491
Association for Hospital Medical Education   502
Association of Western Hospitals   563
Brethren's Home   594
Canadian Council on Hospital Accreditation   622
Canadian Hospital Association   636
Canadian Society of Hospital Pharmacists   665
Commission on Professional and Hospital Activities
    713
Council of Teaching Hospitals   747
ECRI (Emergency Care Research Institute)   787
Federation of American Hospitals   824
Hospital Bureau, Inc.   878
Hospital Financial Management Association   879
Hospital Food Directors Association, Inc.   880
Hospital Information Systems Sharing Group   881
Hospital, Institution and Educational Food Service
    Society   882
Hospital Management Systems Society   883
Hospital Research and Educational Trust   884
International Association of Hospital Central
    Service Management   938
International Hospital Federation   1014
Joint Commission on Accreditation of Hospitals
    1096
Lutheran Hospital Association of America   1122
Lutheran Hospitals and Homes Society of America
    1123
Middle Atlantic Health Congress   1148
Mid-West Health Congress   1149
National Association for Hospital Development   1167
National Association of Private Psychiatric Hospitals
    1189
National Jewish Hospital-National Asthma Center
    1256
New England Hospital Assembly   1296
Psychiatric Services Section of the American
    Hospital Association   1373
Upper Midwest Hospital Conference   1481
Veterans Hospital Radio and Television Guild   1482

HUMAN SEXUALITY

Bay Area Physicians for Human Rights   571
C.S. Mott Center for Human Growth and
    Development   600
Compliment Club, Inc.   720
Institute for Sex Research   898
Janus Information Facility   1090
Sex Information and Education Council of the United
    States   1409
Society for the Scientific Study of Sex, Inc.   1429

HUMAN SEXUALITY (Continued)

Society for the Study of Reproduction   1432

HUNTINGTON'S DISEASE

Committee to Combat Huntington's Disease, Inc. 716

HYGIENE
See: INDUSTRIAL AND OCCUPATIONAL
MEDICINE; NATURAL HEALING AND
LIVING; PUBLIC HEALTH; SANITATION

HYPNOSIS

Academy of Scientific Hypnotherapy   10
American Board of Clinical Hypnosis   182
American Board of Psychological Hypnosis   208
American Hypnotists' Association, Inc.   312
American Society of Clinical Hypnosis   435
American Society of Psychosomatic Dentistry and
Medicine   462
Association to Advance Ethical Hypnosis   564
Council of Societies in Dental Hypnosis   745
Society for Clinical and Experimental Hypnosis
1415

IMMUNOLOGY
See also: ALLERGY

American Association for Clinical Immunology and
Allergy   90
American Association for the Study of Neoplastic
Diseases   104
American Association of Immunologists   137
American Board of Allergy and Immunology   178
American Dermatologic Society for Allergy and
Immunology   282
American Type Culture Collection   479
Committee for the Promotion of Medical Research
715
Foundation for Cure   845
International Organization of Allergology and
Clinical Immunology   1028
National Jewish Hospital/National Asthma Center
1256
Transplantation Society   1468
World Association of Veterinary Microbiologists,
Immunologists and Specialists in Infectious
Diseases   1497

INDUSTRIAL AND OCCUPATIONAL MEDICINE

American Academy of Compensation Medicine   38
American Academy of Occupational Medicine   59
American Association of Industrial Veterinarians   138
American Association of Occupational Health Nurses,
Inc.   147
American Association of Railway Surgeons   161
American Board of Preventive Medicine   204
American Conference of Governmental Industrial
Hygienists   267
American Industrial Hygiene Association   313
American Occupational Medical Association   346
American Occupational Therapy Association, Inc.
347
Center for Occupational Hazards, Inc.   681
Coalition for the Environment   708
Collegium Medicorum Theatri   711
ECRI (Emergency Care Research Institute)   787
Industrial Health Foundation, Inc.   891
Institute of Occupational and Environmental Health
905
International Association of Agricultural Medicine
and Rural Health   929
National Institute of Hypertension Studies   1252
National Safety Management Society   1278
Occupational Medical Administrators' Association
1310
Permanent Commission and International Association
on Occupational Health   1343
World Federation of Occupational Therapists   1504

INFECTIOUS DISEASES
See: PUBLIC HEALTH

INFORMATION CENTERS
See: LIBRARIES AND INFORMATION CENTERS

INSANITY
See: MENTAL HEALTH; MENTAL RETARDATION;
PSYCHIATRY AND PSYCHOLOGY

INSURANCE, HEALTH
See: HEALTH CARE PLANS

INSTRUMENTATION, MEDICAL
See: MEDICAL INSTRUMENTATION

Subject Index

Subject Index

SUBJECT INDEX OF ORGANIZATIONS

MOTHERHOOD
See: OBSTETRICS AND GYNECOLOGY;
PARENTHOOD

MULTIPLE SCLEROSIS

International Federation of Multiple Sclerosis
Societies   998
Multiple Sclerosis Society of Canada   1155

MUSIC THERAPY
See: MENTAL HEALTH

MYCOLOGY

American Type Culture Collection   479
Association of Allergists for Mycological Investigations
519
International Society for Human and Animal Mycology
1042

NAPRAPATHY
See: NATURAL HEALING AND LIVING

NARCOTICS

Addiction Research and Treatment Corporation   16
Alcohol and Drug Problems Association of North
America   24
Alcoholism and Drug Addiction Research Foundation
27
Do It Now Foundation   778
DOC (Doctors Ought to Care)   779
International Christian Federation for the Prevention
of Alcoholism and Drug Addiction   956
International Committee on Alcohol, Drugs and
Traffic Safety   974
International Council on Alcohol and Addictions   981
International Narcotics Control Board   1023
International Narcotics Enforcement Officers Associa-
tion   1024
International Temperance Association   1071
International Temperance Blue Cross Union   1072
Medical Letter, Inc.   1134
Narcotics Education, Inc.   1159
National Save-A-Life League   1280
Synanon Church   1463

NATURAL HEALING AND LIVING

American Holistic Medical Association   308
American Holistic Medical Institute   309
American Massage and Therapy Association   326
American Naprapathic Association   340
American Natural Hygiene Society, Inc.   342
Council for Homeopathic Research and Education,
Inc.   739
Healing Research Trust   863
Holistic Health Havens   877
International Myomassethics Federation, Inc.   1022
International Naturist Federation   1025
International Vegetarian Union   1083
National Council on Wholistic Therapeutics and
Medicine   1220
National Herbalist Association   1247
National Institute of Medical Herbalists   1253
Natural Food Associates, Inc.   1291
North American Academy of Manipulative Medicine
1300
Research Institute for Supersensonic Healing Energies
1385
ROLF Institute   1391

NATUROPATHICS
See: NATURAL HEALING AND LIVING

NEPHROLOGY
See: KIDNEY DISEASES

NERVOUS DISEASES
See: MENTAL HEALTH; NEUROLOGY;
PSYCHIATRY AND PSYCHOLOGY

NEUROLOGY

American Academy of Neurological Surgery   57
American Academy of Neurology   58
American Association for the Study of Headache   102
American Association of Neurological Surgeons   142
American Association of Neuropathologists   143
American Association of Neurosurgical Nurses   144
American Board of Neurological Surgery   189
American Board of Psychiatry and Neurology, Inc.
207
American College of Neuropsychiatrists   244
American College of Neuropsychopharmacology   245
American Neurological Association   343

NEUROLOGY (Continued)

American Society of Neuroradiology 456

Association for Research in Nervous and Mental Disease, Inc. 506

Association for the Psychophysiological Study of Sleep 514

Brain Information Service 591

Cajal Club 601

Canadian Society of Electroencephalographers, Electromyographers and Clinical Neurophysiologists 664

Congress of Neurological Surgeons 726

Dysautonomia Foundation, Inc. 784

European Brain and Behaviour Society 803

International Brain Research Organization 947

International Federation of Multiple Sclerosis Societies 998

International Federation of Societies for Electroencephalography and Clinical Neurophysiology 1002

International Society for Pediatric Neurosurgery 1043

International Society of Neuropathology 1060

Mario Negri Institute for Pharmacological Research 1126

Migraine Foundation 1151

Montreal Neurological Institute 1153

National Migraine Foundation 1263

Neurosurgical Society of America 1293

Scandinavian Neurosurgical Society 1402

Society for Neuroscience 1419

Society of Biological Psychiatry 1435

Society of French-Speaking Neurosurgeons 1438

Society of Neurological Surgeons 1442

World Federation of Neurology 1502

World Federation of Neurosurgical Societies 1503

NOSE DISEASES
See: OTORHINOLARYNGOLOGY; RHINOLOGY

NURSING

American Association of Critical-Care Nurses 119

American Association of Nephrology Nurses and Technicians 141

American Association of Neurosurgical Nurses 144

American Association of Nurse Anesthetists 145

American Association of Occupational Health Nurses, Inc. 147

American College of Nurse-Midwives 247

American Journal of Nursing Company 320

American Nurses' Association, Inc. 344

American Nurses' Foundation, Inc. 345

American Society for Nursing Service Administrators 422

Assembly of Hospital Schools of Nursing 491

Association of Operating Room Nurses 541

Association of Pediatric Oncology Nurses 544

Association of Rehabilitation Nurses 549

Canadian Nurses' Association 642

Emergency Department Nurses Association 790

International Committee of Catholic Nurses 970

International Confederation of Midwives 976

International Council of Nurses 978

National Association for Practical Nurse Education and Service, Inc. 1171

National Association of Physicians' Nurses 1188

National Federation of Licensed Practical Nurses, Inc. 1229

National League for Nursing 1258

National Student Nurses' Association, Inc. 1286

Nurses Association of the American College of Obstetricians and Gynecologists 1303

Nurses Christian Fellowship International 1304

Nurses Christian Fellowship (United States) 1305

Nurses' Educational Funds, Inc. 1306

Psychiatric Nurses Association of Canada 1372

Victorian Order of Nurses of Canada 1483

NURSING HOMES

American Association of Homes for the Aging 133

American Baptist Homes and Hospitals Association 174

American College of Nursing Home Administrators 248

American Health Care Association 303

Brethren's Home 594

Citizens for Better Care, Inc. 702

Lutheran Hospitals and Homes Society of America 1123

National Association of Jewish Homes for the Aged 1183

NUTRITION
See also: GASTROENTEROLOGY; NATURAL HEALING AND LIVING

Adrenal Metabolic Research Society of the Hypoglycemia Foundation, Inc. 17

American Anorexia Nervos Association, Inc. 84

American Dietetic Association 283

American Digestive Disease Society 284

American Holistic Medical Association 308

American Holistic Medical Institute 309

American Institute of Nutrition 316

American Natural Hygiene Society, Inc. 342

American Society for Clinical Nutrition 407

American Society for Hospital Food Service Administrators 415

American Society for Parenteral and Enteral Nutrition, Inc. 423

NUTRITION (Continued)

OBESITY
See: BARIATRICS

OBSTETRICS AND GYNECOLOGY

OCCUPATIONAL MEDICINE
See: INDUSTRIAL AND OCCUPATIONAL
   MEDICINE

ONCOLOGY
See: CANCER

OPHTHALMOLOGY

Subject Index

Subject Index

Subject Index

Subject Index

Subject Index

Subject Index

Subject Index

Subject Index

Subject Index

Subject Index

SUBJECT INDEX OF ORGANIZATIONS

Subject Index

VETERINARY MEDICINE (Continued)

National Association of Federal Veterinarians   1179
National Association of State Public Health
    Veterinarians   1200
World Association for Buiatrics   1493
World Association for the Advancement of Veterinary
    Parasitology   1494
World Association of Veterinary Food Hygienists
    1496
World Association of Veterinary Microbiologists,
    Immunologists and Specialists in Infectious
    Diseases   1497
World Association of Veterinary Pathologists   1498
World Veterinary Association   1511
World Veterinary Poultry Association   1512

WEIGHT REDUCTION
    See: BARIATRICS

WOMEN IN MEDICINE

American Association of Women Dentists   169
American Medical Women's Association, Inc.   337
American Women's Hospitals Service   483
Association for Women Veterinarians   516
Delta Omega National Sorority   764
Federation of Medical Women of Canada   827
Kappa Epsilon Fraternity   1102
Lambda Kappa Sigma - International Pharmacy
    Fraternity   1107
Pan American Medical Women's Alliance   1333

X-RAY
    See: RADIATION AND RADIOLOGY

Subject Index